NEW JERSEY

Introduction by John T. Cunningham

*Pictorial Research by Charles F. Cummings
and Catharine M. Fogarty*

Contributions by David Fleming

"Partners in Progress" by David Fleming

*Produced in Cooperation with the
New Jersey State Chamber of Commerce*

*Windsor Publications, Inc.
Northridge, California*

NEW JERSEY

HISTORY OF INGENUITY AND INDUSTRY

JAMES P. JOHNSON

Windsor Publications, Inc.—History Book Division
Vice President, Publishing: Hal Silverman
Editorial Director: Teri Davis Greenberg
Design Director: Alexander D'Anca

Staff for *New Jersey: History of Ingenuity and Industry*
Editors: Lane Powell, Lynn Kronzek
Proofreader: Susan J. Muhler
Director, Corporate Biographies: Karen Story
Assistant Director, Corporate Biographies: Phyllis Gray
Editors, Corporate Biographies: Judith L. Hunter, Rita Johnson
Production Editor: Una FitzSimons
Editorial Assistants: Brenda Berryhill, Kathy M. Brown, Susan Kanga,
 Pat Pittman
Sales Representatives: Steve Hung, Rob Ottenheimer
Layout Artist, Corporate Biographies: Mari Catherine Preimesberger

Design and Layout: Christina McKibbin

Library of Congress Cataloging-in-Publication Data:
Johnson, James P., 1937-
  New Jersey: history of ingenuity and industry.

Bibliography: p.614
Includes index.
1. New Jersey—Economic conditions.   2. New Jersey—
Industries—History.   I. Title.
HC107.N5J64   1987   338.09749   87-8247
ISBN 0-89781-206-9

Previous page: Twin lighthouses at Atlantic Highlands overlook the Navesink River in this early engraving by Granville Perkins. Erected in 1806 to guide shipping in New York harbor, the towers were replaced in 1862 by the present massive brownstone structure. Designated a national landmark in 1965, the lighthouse is now a museum. Courtesy, Newark Public Library

Contents

This European view of New Jersey and neighboring states is from an atlas probably published in Nuremberg in 1759 by Homann Heirs, successors to the firm established by John Baptist Homann (1664-1724). The Homann family, prolific cartographers, dominated German map-making for over 100 years. Courtesy, New Jersey Room, Fairleigh Dickinson University

Acknowledgments

I would like to thank the librarians of the New Jersey Room of the Rutgers University Library; the Plainfield Public Library, particularly Mrs. Dottie Tutweiler and Mrs. Cathy Harper; the Summit Public Library; the Westfield Public Library, particularly Mrs. Pam Ferguson; and the Newark Public Library for their assistance.

John T. Cunningham gave the manuscript a critical reading and made many useful suggestions which improved the book. My colleagues Donald Gerardi and Ari Hoogenboom offered thoughtful ideas about particular sections. Michelle Felix worked hard as a research assistant, and Joan Lowell Smith did some excellent editing on the early chapters.

Thanks also go to the following individuals, who sent me materials about individual firms and organizations: Charles J. Smith, director, News and Information, RCA; Mr. Ellis L. Marples, captain, New Jersey Wing, Civil Air Patrol; Mary A. Tomenko, director of communications, Midlantic National Bank; Katherine Ingrassia, Public Relations, Hoffmann-La Roche; Dorothy A. Voss, editor, *Tel-news*, New Jersey Bell; Gary D. Plummer, media relations manager, GPU Service Corporation; Richard A. Cross, general manager, Public Service Electric and Gas Company; Robert G. Lewis, division manager, Public Relations, AT&T; James M. Langan, marketing, Combustion Engineering; Roni C. Velmer, manager, Divisional Public Relations, Englehard Corporation; Peter Harrigan, director of public relations, Lockheed Electronics Company, Inc.

I also appreciated having the historical materials sent to me by D. C. Vaillancourt, vice president, corporate communications and consumer affairs, The Grand Union Company; Henry C. Patterson III, assistant vice president, public relations, Elizabethtown Water Company; Lorraine Kelley of the Bates Manufacturing Company; Hilda Costanzo, vice president and secretary of the Howard Savings Bank; Richard F. Blanchard, president, William Blanchard Co.; Allan P. Kapkowski, Public Affairs Department, Exxon; Karen Gregory, public relations manager, First Jersey National Corporation; and Margaret Griffin, Public Relations Department, First Fidelity Bancorporation.

Fred Westphal and Arthur Cox of the State Chamber of Commerce helped me contact many of the above individuals, which was very helpful. Deep thanks go to the State Chamber of Commerce, which is celebrating its seventy-fifth birthday this year and which sponsored this volume. As usual, an author's largest debt is to his spouse, and in this instance my wife Carolyn helped with this project more than she knows by taking on extra responsibilities so that I could meet deadlines. Without her assistance, I could not have written this book.

Introduction

New Jersey was founded as a business in 1664 and has never lost the image. When the Duke of York gave New Jersey to two court friends, George Carteret and John Berkeley, on June 24, 1664, he bestowed power both to govern and to sell real estate. That magnificent real estate encouragement eventually became the East New Jersey and West New Jersey Boards of Proprietors (still in existence and among the oldest corporations in America). The 1664 gift defined the area and gave it the name New Jersey. Unknown at the time, the most vital parts of the area were the deep, wide rivers (Hudson and Delaware) that formed major east and west boundaries.

Any region between two natural harbors had to be a region of business, industry, and ingenuity. New York and Philadelphia rose beside those rivers. They would provide markets, capital, and transportation vitality. Ironworks were established as early as 1685, and in 1739 the first successful glassworks in America was founded in Salem County. A vast iron empire headed by the self-styled "Baron" Hasenclever rose in the northern New Jersey mountains before the American Revolution. During the Revolution, the presence of iron mines and saltworks helped prompt George Washington to spend more time here than in any other state.

New Jersey became a magnet for ingenuity. Seth Boyden came from Massachusetts to Newark in 1813 to produce America's first patent leather and first malleable iron. Massachusetts-reared Thomas Rogers chose Paterson, founding in 1835 a company that by the Civil War was the largest locomotive-building plant in the United States. John Stevens (New Jersey-born) sent out the first ocean-going steamboat at Hoboken in 1809 and in 1825 built the first steam locomotive in America. He was following the lead of Trenton gunsmith John Fitch, who in 1786 sailed America's first steamboat between Burlington and Philadelphia.

The list of New Jersey's nineteenth-century innovative geniuses is almost endless. A sampling (to show the diversity) would include James Birch, a Burlington carriagemaker who by 1900 also made most of the world's jinrikishas; Peter Ballantine, a Scot who made this nation's first ale in Newark, a city of German beer drinkers; John Ryle, who founded America's first silk mill in Paterson; John Roebling of Trenton, maker of America's first suspension bridges, including the Brooklyn and Golden Gate bridges; and Joseph Campbell, first in the nation to pack tomatoes in cans for commercial sale.

Obviously, no eighteenth-century innovator topped Thomas A. Edison, another "outsider" who saw the commercial benefits of New Jersey between New York and Philadelphia. He came from Ohio, by way of Boston, settled in Newark in 1870 and never left the state. He established the world's first research laboratory at Menlo Park in 1876, astride the mainline railroad.

Edison's contributions at Menlo Park (and, after 1887, at West Orange) are almost beyond comprehension. The electric lamp, a system of electrical power distribution, the phonograph, movies, storage batteries, and literally a thousand more inventions remain as Edison's legacy.

By the end of the nineteenth century, New Jersey products rolled off the lines—pottery at Trenton; rubber at Trenton and Butler; leather and jewelry at Newark; ships, pen points, and condensed soup at Camden; antiseptic bandages at New Brunswick; textiles at Passaic and Paterson; cast iron pipe from Weymouth in the southern New Jersey Pine Barrens; saltwater taffy from Atlantic City; and giant ships at Camden.

The state's industrial genius served the state well during both world wars. During World War II, New Jersey ranked fifth in production of war materiel, including battleships, medicines, airplane engines, electronic equipment, explosives, and chemicals.

Many of the huge manufacturing plants of the World War II era have vanished, made obsolete by efficient manufactories in other nations. New Jersey still leads the nation in the production of chemicals and medicines, is close to the top in electronic gear, and maintains a reputation for thousands of smaller plants that turn out a myriad of arcane parts used in assembling larger items.

Ingenuity now sprouts in hundreds of huge, carefully landscaped research installations; New Jersey is a national leader in research. The once-rural landscape is witnessing the rise of office buildings surrounded by acres of parking lots. Business has gone to the country.

New Jersey will not lose its competitive edge. New York and Philadelphia will not disappear, and even the most chauvinistic of Jerseyans would agree that those cities have a dominant effect on the state's economy. But the harbors will remain. Genius will stay in place. Astride the main transportation corridor in the nation, New Jersey is still the place to be.

Dr. John T. Cunningham

European Settlement and Development

Perspective

Europe's search for economic gain gave birth to New Jersey. On April 6, 1609, English sailor Henry Hudson and his ship, the *Half Moon*, sailed from Texel, Holland, for the Dutch East India Company in search of the "Northwest Passage" to the profitable trade with the Orient. Instead, Hudson found New Jersey.

His discovery of the region encouraged the Dutch, the Swedes, and the English to settle and exploit the riches of this peninsula between the Atlantic Ocean and the Delaware River. Down to 1702 settlers from various nations and of differing religious persuasions created outposts in New Jersey's wilderness. The Dutch settled in the Jersey City area. The Swedes came to the Delaware Valley. The Dutch conquered the Swedes only to be overpowered by the English, who bequeathed the land to proprietors in order to encourage other Englishmen from New England and Long Island to settle there.

Under arrangements made by proprietors who granted freedoms of

Little is known about Henry Hudson other than during the brief span of time between 1607 and 1611, when he made four exploratory voyages seeking a passage to the East. On his third trip he explored Delaware Bay, Sandy Hook, the Navesink Highlands, and the Hudson River as far as Troy. On Hudson's fourth and fatal voyage, a mutiny left him, his son, and seven others adrift to die an unrecorded death. From Memorial History of the City of New York *and the Hudson River Valley, 1892*

Above: The seal of the Province of East New Jersey was adopted in 1682, the year the Duke of York confirmed the purchase of the province by William Penn and eleven other proprietors. The original seal may have been destroyed when the government of East New Jersey was transferred to the British Crown. From East Jersey Under the Proprietary Governments, *1846*

Right: The Long Ferry Tavern in Perth Amboy, an early important commercial building in the province of East New Jersey, served as that community's first public house, accommodating travelers on the ferry that Deputy-Governor Lawrie established across the Raritan in 1684. Little is known about its proprietors, but in 1761 the tavern was owned by St. Peter's Church, whose vestry voted to construct the first of two wharves adjacent to the site. This 1832 sketch shows the original building with the two dormer windows. From Contributions to the Early History of Perth Amboy and Adjoining Country, *1856*

worship and government, Puritans, Baptists, and Quakers migrated into the region. By 1702, when England reasserted royal control over New Jersey, the first New Jerseyans had established outposts in the wilderness and had begun to develop a frontier economy.

Between 1609 and 1702, the colonists developed the region in ways that paralleled the economic growth of the United States itself. The early settlers farmed, dug iron mines and exported pig iron, built lumber- and gristmills, and tanned leather. They also worked at the traditional household industries. Under the English Navigation Acts, the English Crown encouraged settlers to export raw materials that the mother country could turn into finished goods to be sold. During the eighteenth century, the colony of New Jersey became a breadbasket for neighboring Philadelphia and Manhattan. In the 1770s New Jersey served, in Leonard London's phrase, as the "cockpit of the American Revolution," a strategic center for General George Washington's campaigns.

Although the American Revolution halted the economic development of the state, New Jerseyans soon launched their own industrial revolution, particularly in Newark, Trenton, and Paterson. New Jerseyans played key roles in developing the American railroad and the young iron and steel industries. For a new, early-nineteenth-century nation, industrious laborers made rubber, iron, porcelain, pottery, bricks, paper, textiles, jewelry, hats, leather, steam engines, and glass.

After the economy recovered from the Civil War, a host of ingenious late-nineteenth-century entrepreneurs, including Thomas Edison, Guglielmo

Marconi, Alfred Vail, Edward Weston, and John Wesley Hyatt, helped shape the modern economy. During the First World War, New Jerseyans refined oil and built explosives, ships, chemicals, and airplanes. The Great Depression began the weakening of New Jersey's manufacturing sector and even destroyed many industries in New Jersey's cities. During the Second World War, New Jerseyans revitalized the state's economy and developed the road and port systems which encouraged businesses to locate in New Jersey after the war.

As foreign competition after the war hurt American manufacturing industries, New Jerseyans again helped shape a new economic era: the postindustrial age of service and high-technology industries. Colonial New Jersey had been described as "a beer keg tapped at both ends, with all the live beer flowing into Philadelphia and New York." Postindustrial New Jersey became known as the "headquarters state," or the "research state," where researchers living within an easy drive of a campus-style headquarters of an international corporation developed new technologies. In the 1980s New Jersey's container ports, a growing international airport, research centers, and central location in the great Eastern market positioned the state on the cutting edge of change.

What follows is the story of the ingenious and industrious New Jerseyans who worked to shape commercial New Jersey from the time Hudson's *Half Moon* landed until the CYBER 205, the new supercomputer at Princeton, went on-line.

Explorers and Proprietors Set the Patterns

The development of postindustrial New Jersey might not have amazed Hudson, who was a visionary of his own time. He landed at the mouth of the Delaware, probably near present Jersey City, in late August 1609. Hudson began the economic development of New Jersey. He would have gone upriver, but he ran aground in the shallows of the mouth, and no doubt the outward flow of the current convinced him that the Northwest Passage lay elsewhere. "The Sunne arose," *Half Moon* first mate Robert Juet wrote, "and we steered away North againe."

On September 4 Hudson and his crew dropped anchor in Sandy Hook Bay. "This is a very good Land to fall with, and a pleasant Land to see," wrote Juet. They encountered North American Indians. "This day," wrote Hudson's mate, "the people of the Country came aboard of us, seemingly very glad of our coming and brought greene Tobacco, and gave us of it for Knives and Beads."

Struck by the land "pleasant with Grasses and Flowers, and goodly Trees," a small party from the *Half Moon* crew set out from the ship to circumnavigate Staten Island. Two large Indian canoes set upon them and mortally wounded John Coleman. Hudson and the crew buried the body on Sandy Hook.

Hudson went up the river named for him as far as the site of present

VREELAND'S
TRADIN' POST - 1678
THE FIRST BUILDING IN PASSAIC.

Above: Lenni-Lenape women cooked their food in pottery vessels formed from wet clay, dried in the shade, and baked over open fires. The pots shown here were decorated in geometric patterns using cords pressed into the wet clay. The larger vessel is twenty-seven inches high and holds twenty gallons. Courtesy, Dr. Herbert C. Kraft

Left: Johan Bjorsson Printz, whose arms appear here, served as governor of New Sweden from 1643 until 1653. To protect Swedish interests along the Delaware River, Printz built Fort Elfsborg on Varkens Kill (now Salem Creek) and other fortifications in New Jersey and Pennsylvania. However, Dutch control of the approaches to New Sweden, and the skirmish that followed on September 26, 1655, marked the end of Swedish rule in New Jersey and North America. Courtesy, Newark Public Library

Facing page, top: Lenni-Lenape Indians hunted game with spears tipped with points of stone. In this drawing, the hunter is using an atlatl, or spear-thrower, devised to increase the accuracy and force of the weapon. Drawing by John T. Kraft. Courtesy, Dr. Herbert C. Kraft

Facing page, bottom: An artist's conception of the Indian trading post that Hartman Michaelsen established in 1678 on the island in the Passaic River that is now part of the mainland in Pulaski Park, Passaic. Michaelsen, one of the first settlers at Acquackanonk, was the son of a Communipaw fur trader whose family adopted the name Vreeland for reasons that are not clear. Courtesy, Herbert A. Fisher Collection, Julius Forstmann Library

Lenni-Lenape Indian chiefs Tishcohan and Lapowinsa in portraits attributed to Gustavus Hesselius, a Swedish portrait artist who moved to the Philadelphia area circa 1740. Unlike Tishcohan, whose name in the Delaware language translates as "he who never blackens himself," Lapowinsa was well decorated with bird and snake tattoos on his forehead, and lines on his face and neck. Both wear tobacco pouches on their chests. The portraits are believed to have been painted at the request of John or Thomas Penn. Courtesy, Newark Public Library

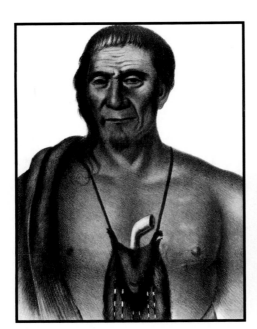

Albany. Again having failed to find the nonexistent Northwest Passage, Hudson returned to Holland something of a failure.

But Juet's journal told European readers of "good furres," "skins of divers sorts," and commented on the New Jersey natives' copper ornaments. Juet thought that there might be a "Copper or Silver Myne" on the Jersey side of the Hudson.

Hudson's voyage thus excited the Dutch about the economic advantages of colonization. In 1610 an expedition from Holland set out to exploit the fur-trading opportunities. Europeans developed joint-stock companies that began to settle New Jersey. In 1614 the Dutch formed the United New Netherland Company and sent Captain Cornelius Jacobsen Mey on a voyage to the New World. He ascended the Delaware beyond the Schuykill River and returned three years later to establish Fort Nassau, on the New Jersey side, just north of the mouth of the Schuykill near what is now Gloucester County's Red Bank. In 1618 the Dutch established a trading station at Bergen. In 1621 the Dutch States-General chartered the Dutch West India Company and empowered it to colonize in the New World and in Africa.

The new Dutch company spent more money on its West Indian ventures than on the one eventually developed by Peter Minuit on Man-a-hat-ta, or "heavenly land." But to promote farm settlement, the company announced in 1629 a patroon system to grant large tracts of land in exchange for colonization. Under this system, Michael Pauw got a large tract of land near Jersey City in 1630. He never left Holland, however, and he failed to get the fifty people for his feudal grant. But in 1633 settlers built the first two homes in New Jersey at Pavonia.

Unfortunately, New Amsterdam Governor William Kieft's brutality toward the Tappan Indians provoked a savage Indian war throughout the region. "Not a white person was safe," says one account, "except those who sought and found refuge within the palisades of Fort Amsterdam." The

The New Netherland, *of the West India Company, transported 100 Walloons from Holland to the New World three years after the company's charter in 1621. Their arrival marked the first permanent colonization of New Netherland, formerly inhabited by transient fur traders and West India Company employees. From* Genealogical History of Bergen and Hudson Counties, *1900*

Indians destroyed Pavonia. After a 1655 war with the Indians, the first New Jersey settlers deserted the area and fled to Manhattan.

By 1658 Peter Stuyvesant got new settlers to concentrate their dwellings inside a stockade and in 1660 founded the Town of Bergen (Jersey City). Bergen got a court and local government in 1661—the beginning of a political system of New Jersey. Because settlers from New Netherland included Norwegians, Danes, Germans, Scots, and Irish as well as Hollanders, we may never know the ethnic background of some of the "Dutch" settlers, but some hardy souls from New Netherland resettled Pavonia into a stockaded city after the Indian wars, built a road between the two towns, and opened a ferry to New Amsterdam.

These earliest New Jerseyans were already pursuing the American dream, and looking for the main chance. Some adventurous ones from the Dutch towns pushed west and found copper on the western side of the Kittatinny Mountains, near modern Pahaquarry. For some five years they mined copper from these hills and transported it on the 100-mile-long Old Mine Road to Esopus (Kingston, New York), and from there to Holland. In one location these settlers dug a tunnel some 100 feet into the side of the mountain and then dug tunnels off this shaft to bring out copper—all by hand.

The first European to see New Jersey was probably Florentine navigator Giovanni da Verrazano, who is believed to have stopped at Sandy Hook in 1524 and explored Upper New York Bay as far as the New Jersey Shore. In 1609, nearly a century later, arrived Henry Hudson, whose explorations took him on tour of New Jersey's entire coastline and beyond.

Henry Hudson's ship, the *Half Moon*, touched New Jersey's coast at the mouth of the Delaware River—not the river just farther north which would later be named after him. The English explorer, sailing for the Dutch East India Company in search of the fabled Northwest Passage to India, tried to sail up the Delaware but ran aground. And so he sailed up the coast of what is now New Jersey.

Henry Hudson's voyage at the helm of the *Half Moon* in 1609 is recounted in a small journal kept by ship's officer Robert Juet during the voyage. Thanks to Juet's journal, Dutch interest in America soared, and Henry Hudson's name became famous through subsequent centuries. Since Hudson was abandoned at sea by a mutinous crew in 1611, he may never have become renowned without this journal.

According to Juet's journal, between May 5 and May 19 of 1609, Hudson's already-disgruntled crew forced him to change course from the northwest to the south and west. The ship sailed as far south as present-day Virginia but returned northward along the Atlantic Coast.

Juet wrote that he first saw what is now New Jersey on the "eight and twentieth" of August 1609, while Captain Hudson tried unsuccessfully to sail the ship into "a great bay"—now known as Delaware Bay. The ship ran aground, and so Hudson went back out to sea and continued north along the coast. The following day, Juet wrote in his journal: "Wee weighed at the breake of day, and stood toward the Norther Land, which we found to bee all Ilands to our sight." This was undoubtedly the long sandy stretch of islands between what are now Wildwood (near Cape May) and Atlantic City.

Just inland along the coastline, Juet wrote that he saw a "great fire" on September 2, evidence that someone—namely the Lenni-Lenape Indians—lived there. Late that same day, the *Half Moon* came within sight of "high Hills," which were either the Navesink Highlands (just inland of Sandy Hook) or Staten Island, according to historians. Juet concluded his day by writing: "This is a very good Land to fall with, and a pleasant Land to see."

On September 4, 1609, the *Half Moon* ran aground in Sandy Hook Bay. Henry Hudson and his crew then met up with the Lenni-Lenape Indians of the region. Robert Juet described in his journal a visit of the Indians to the boat: "This day the people of the country came aboard of us, seeming very glad of our coming, and brought green tobacco and gave us of it for knives and beads. They go in deer skins loose, well dressed. They have yellow copper. They desire clothes and are very civil."

Meanwhile, Captain Hudson had dispatched a smaller boat to explore Newark Bay. It returned several days later, carrying John Coleman, who had been killed by an arrow in the throat. The *Half Moon's* crew buried him on Sandy Hook. Coleman was the first recorded victim of the Indian wars, and after his death, the relationship with the Lenni-Lenape Indians became increasingly tense. There would be much more bloodshed to come: later during this voyage, seven or eight Indians were felled by gunfire from the *Half Moon*.

It was during this trip that Henry Hudson navigated the *Half Moon* all the way up to near what is today Albany, only to find that this narrowing river was not the passage to India. Meanwhile, Juet described the river valley's lush lands and Indian natives. Henry Hudson sailed back down the river that would one day be named for him. When they arrived at the mouth of the river in early October, Captain Hudson and his mutinous, disappointed crew—who were angered at not finding the Northwest Passage to India and the riches that it would have brought—sailed for Holland.

These doings described in Juet's journal greatly excited the shareholders of the Dutch East India Company, sponsors of Hudson's voyage. Company officials waxed enthusiastic about reports of "good furres," "skins of divers sorts," and descriptions of copper ornaments worn by natives. Juet enticed them with a description of a "White green" cliff on the New Jersey side that held either "a Copper or Silver Myne."

Several other explorers followed Hudson's trip around New Jersey. In 1610 Lord Samuel Argall of England sailed into the bay and river at the south of present-day New Jersey and named both for Lord De La Warr, governor of Virginia. In 1616, Cornelius Hendrickson, who was part of the first Dutch settlement on Manhattan Island, sailed his thirty-eight-foot ship, the *Onrust*, high up the De La Warr River, or De Zuydt River (South River) as the Dutch called it, reaching "the place of the tall pines" near modern Philadelphia.

With voyages between 1616 and 1621, Cornelius Jacobsen Mey extended Dutch claims throughout New Jersey—despite the increasing friction with British colonists. Captain Mey navigated his ship close along New Jersey's Atlantic Coast and sailed up the Delaware river to establish Fort Nassau, near present-day Gloucester. Today Cape May (the name was since anglicized) is named for Captain Mey.

—David Fleming

Swedes Settle the Delaware Valley

In addition to the Dutch, the Swedes made an effort to develop outposts along the Delaware River. William Usselinx, founder of the Dutch West India Company, had become disenchanted with the States-General of the Netherlands. He turned to Sweden's King Gustavus Adolphus and convinced him to "establish a General Trading Company for Asia, Africa, America." Unfortunately, Adolphus died in 1632, the funds for the trading company were undersubscribed, and defeat in Germany killed the trading company.

Peter Minuit, another expert on the New World who had become disenchanted with his role in the Dutch West India Company, in 1635 revived Swedish plans to send trading expeditions to the New World under the name New Sweden. More profits, Minuit thought, would come from permanent settlement than from trading alone.

In 1638 Minuit established Fort Christina near present Wilmington. Unfortunately, Minuit's tragic death in a hurricane that June on his return trip to Sweden weakened Sweden's presence in the New World. In 1643 the Swedes built Fort Nya Elfsborg on the mosquito-infested Jersey shore of the Delaware River below Salem Creek. Swedish soldiers soon dubbed the fort "Myggenborg," or "Mosquito castle." One eyewitness reported that the mosquitoes "almost ate the people up there . . . they sucked the blood from our people so they became very weary and sick of it."

Building forts and blockhouses, the Swedes pushed as far upriver as Trenton. In 1651 after the wily, one-legged Stuyvesant sent 120 men to strengthen Fort Nassau (near Gloucester) and made a deal with Indian chiefs for land below Fort Christina, the outflanked Swedes withdrew from Fort Nya Elfsborg. Later Jerseyans, of course, have debated whether it was the Dutch or the mosquitoes that drove the Swedes out.

After the Swedes captured the Dutch Fort Casimir on the Delaware, Stuyvesant retaliated with a force of 317 soldiers and some sailors, two battleships, and other vessels in August 1655, and forced the Swedes to relinquish their nation's claims to the Delaware Valley.

These Scandinavian woodsmen of South Jersey who had settled under Swedish protection never numbered more than 400 people. Mostly Finns, recruited for New World settlement because they had penetrated Sweden's forests and earned the name "forest destroyers," or "forest burners," they gave America the log cabin.

In 1697 Jaspar Danckerts visited one of these houses near "Borling-ton" and noted in his journal that it was a "block-house, being nothing else than entire trees, split through the middle, or squared out of the rough, and placed in the form of a square, one upon the other, as high as they wish to have the house. . . .

"The whole structure is thus made, without a nail or spike. . . .The doors are wide enough, but very low, so that you have to stoop in entering.

These houses are quite tight and warm; but the chimney is placed in a corner."

The log cabins of these Swedes and Finns have disappeared, but the names of their settlements—Finns Point, Elsinboro, Mullica Hill, and Swedesboro, New Jersey—are still with us. Because the Swedes could not convince enough of their countrymen to leave home, and because their leaders were more concerned with European than American matters, they played only a minor part in shaping southern New Jersey. But the conflict between the Dutch and the Swedes showed that Europeans were willing to fight for control of the potential riches of New Jersey.

The English Conquer in 1664

New Jersey would be neither the province of the Swedes nor the Dutch, however, but of the English, who claimed the New Jersey area following the voyages of the Cabots of 1497. The English would give New Jersey its basic economic and political institutions. Although New Jerseyans would chafe under the mercantile policies of England in the eighteenth century, in the seventeenth century English mercantile policies shaped the economic development of the colony. The English had no respect at all for the Dutch settlements, and they believed that by trading in tobacco, the Dutch were violating England's Navigation Acts.

In 1632 Charles I (1625-1649) gave Sir Edmund Plowden of Ireland a huge grant that included New Jersey, Delaware, Maryland, and Pennsylvania. In 1634 Captain Thomas Yong sailed from England for Plowden. Yong pushed up the Delaware and found some Dutchmen trading with the Indians at Trenton. He informed them that the country belonged to the King of England and that they must cease trading and leave within two days.

"After much discourse to and fro," wrote Yong in his *Relation of Captain Thomas Yong*, published in 1634, "they have publikely declared, that if the king of England please to owne this River, they will obey, and they humbly desire that he will declare to them their limits in these parts of America, which they will also observe." The Dutch then returned to New Netherland.

To these early explorers, New Jersey seemed dazzling. Yong wrote of his amazement at the quantity of fish and fowl in New Jersey. "For my part," he concluded, "I am confident that this River is the most heathfull, fruitfull and commodious River in the North of America."

But even such glowing reports did not attract enough English settlers to please Earl Plowden, who in 1642 set out to explore his own empire. Marooned by mutineers on an island in Delaware Bay, Plowden eventually returned to England and made another effort in 1650, but he never could gather the 150 colonists he needed to settle his "New Albion." Plowden's claim to his private empire in the New World ended with his death.

Some English settlers from New Haven came down and founded the town of Salem in 1642. At the request of the Swedes, they left, but would not relinquish their claims. A fertile and rich land lay in wait for the

Left: Sir George Carteret and his wife, Lady Elizabeth Carteret, were court favorites and prominent in the English Restoration. With John, Lord Berkeley, Sir George was granted rights of proprietorship over the colony of New Jersey as a reward for his support of King Charles and James, Duke of York, whom he sheltered during the English Puritan Revolution. While some authorities dispute the fact, it is generally believed that Elizabeth, N.J., was named for Lady Elizabeth. Courtesy, Elizabeth Public Library

industrious settlers who could see ways to exploit New Jersey's resources.

When the Royalists restored Charles II to the English throne in 1660 after the Puritan Commonwealth, Charles needed a way to repay supporters. One obvious recipient would be his brother James, Duke of York, Lord High Admiral, who had promoted the Royal African Company to compete with the Dutch in the slave trade.

On March 12, 1664, therefore, Charles II encouraged the Duke of York's interests in blocking the Dutch in the New World. He gave the duke a royal patent for all the land between the Connecticut and Delaware rivers. The obstinate, revengeful, and covetous James then dispatched Colonel Robert Nicolls with four ships and several hundred troops to drive out the Dutch.

Nicolls left England in May 1664. When his forces confronted the Dutch settlement at New Amsterdam in mid-August, the Dutch settlers begged the grumpy old warhorse Stuyvesant to surrender. Without a shot, the Dutch flag fell on August 27. New Amsterdam became New York. The English could now encourage development of New Jersey under their mercantile policies, which aimed at getting Englishmen to settle in New Jersey.

The Proprietorship Begins, 1664-1702

The king gave the Duke of York such an immense grant of land that the duke was willing to give some of it away to reward two friends for past services. On June 23, 1664, the duke bequeathed the area between the Hudson and the Delaware rivers, including some of the area Nicolls had just captured, to two friends, Sir George Carteret and John, Lord Berkeley. George Carteret had defended his native island of Jersey for the Royalists in the English Civil War, and so the region was called Nova Caesaria, or New Jersey. Lord Berkeley had also served Charles II during the period he

Below: James II, as Duke of York and Albany in 1664, received a royal patent for lands in America, which included New Jersey. The towns of New Amsterdam and Fort Orange were renamed New York and Albany in his honor when the British seized New Netherland in 1664. Courtesy, Newark Public Library

This is the official seal used by Philip Carteret as governor of the Province of New Jersey. From East Jersey Under the Proprietary Governments, *1846*

was in exile. Two courtiers who essentially wanted to profit from investments here, Carteret and Berkeley mistakenly thought that they also had powers of government. Understandably, the lease would complicate politics in the New World immensely.

Unaware of these developments, Governor Nicolls, to whom the duke had given wide powers to administer the region, based himself in Manhattan and sent Sir Robert Carr to take the New Jersey area, which Carr did with unnecessary force.

After firing two broadsides into the Dutchmen's "Dellawarr Fort," Sir Robert recalled that his soldiers "neaver stopped untill they stormed ye fort, and soe consequently to plundering: the seamen, noe less given to that sporte, were quickly within & have gotten good store of booty." Several weeks later, brutality in the English seizure of Albany, and in some settlements on the Delaware, led to English victory over the Dutch. The Treaty of Breda confirmed English supremacy in the region in 1667.

But first, New Englanders and Long Islanders pressed Nicolls to allow them to move into the New Jersey area. A month before he learned of the duke's lease to the proprietors, Nicolls granted a Long Island group of "associates" permission to move into the area. On October 28, 1664, the associates purchased from the Indians territory between the Raritan and the Passaic rivers that extended thirty miles into the wilderness. In honor of Sir George Carteret's wife, they named this first permanent English settlement Elizabethtown.

On April 8, 1665, Nicolls also confirmed with a group of Baptists from Rhode Island and some Quakers from Gravesend, Long Island, title to the Monmouth Grant, extending west from Sandy Hook along Raritan Bay. Both groups had been harshly treated by New England Puritans. Granted liberty of conscience and the right to have their own assembly by Nicolls, the Baptists developed Middletown and the Quakers settled at Shrewsbury.

Understandably, Governor Nicolls was dismayed when he learned of the duke's grant to Berkeley and Carteret. Nicolls wrote the Duke of York that the duke had given away "all the improveable part" of the holding west of the Hudson, which, he noted, "could receive twenty times more people than Long Island" and offered "the fair hope of Rich mines."

But Berkeley and Carteret wanted to attract settlers, and they were willing to give those who had settled in the area religious freedoms and a popular assembly. To make this offer and to govern the area, they empowered Sir George's twenty-six year-old cousin, Philip Carteret, as governor, and authorized him to grant the "Concessions and Agreements" of February 20, 1665, which granted jury trial, religious freedom, local governmental power—including the right of self-taxation—for everyone who would settle in the New World. All the settlers needed was "a good musket" and their agreement to swear allegiance to Charles II and to pay the proprietors a quitrent—set in 1670 at a half-penny an acre. The Quakers would not like the oath to the king, and no one already settled would like the quitrent.

The agreement also offered a headright for every slave imported into the colony.

In 1665 some 200 people under the Dutch leadership had settled in Hoboken, Bergen, and Weehawken. The Baptists and Quakers had made their homes in Middletown and Shrewsbury. But when Philip Carteret in 1665 brought his entourage and prepared to govern Elizabethtown in the name of the proprietors, he found just four families living there. Undoubtedly disturbed that Nicolls had alienated two tracts of the proprietors' lands, Carteret set out to encourage settlement in New Jersey in accordance with the proprietors' goals.

Philip Carteret became a shareholder in the Elizabethtown group. In 1666 he also encouraged a group of "Godly" men and women who were disgusted with the religious moderation then evident in their New Haven Colony to settle in the area which would become Newark. To these Puritan settlers led by Robert Treat, Carteret granted a tract bounded by Newark Bay, the Passaic River, and the Watchung Mountains and gave them the same political and religious freedoms that the earlier settlers had.

In 1666 these Connecticut Puritans established a Congregationalist theocracy in Newark, which they named in honor of their spiritual leader, the Reverend Abraham Pierson of Newark-on-Trent, England. In an early representation of the opposites which would blend to become New Jersey, Monmouth became home to Quakers and Baptists fleeing Puritan repression, and Newark was settled by the hard-line Puritan types who had driven the Baptists and Quakers to Monmouth.

Carteret also granted to two other New England Puritan groups lands in Woodbridge and Piscataway in 1666 as part of the Elizabethtown tract. In September 1668 he granted a charter to the Dutch village of Bergen. Thus, in the 1660s, under Berkeley and Carteret and their agents Nicolls and Philip Carteret, the towns of Newark, Bergen, Middletown, and

This twentieth-century mural in the Essex County Court House shows the landing of Captain Philip Carteret, cousin of Sir George Carteret and first English governor at Elizabethtown in 1665. The previous year the Duke of York had created New Jersey and granted the lands between the Delaware and Hudson rivers to his two favorites, John, Lord Berkeley, and Sir George Carteret. Upon his arrival, Governor Philip Carteret was confronted by four families already settled in Elizabethtown upon lands previously granted by New York's Deputy Governor Nicolls. Disputed land titles continued to cause dissension in East New Jersey during the entire colonial period. Courtesy, Newark Public Library

Above: Although William Penn is popularly associated with the settlement of Pennsylvania, his plans for a refuge for members of the Society of Friends in the New World originally included New Jersey as well. Penn held proprietorships in both East and West New Jersey. He signed the Quintipartite deed which divided the province in 1676, and is credited with having contributed to the democratic and liberal principles of the "Concessions and Agreements" of 1677—West Jersey's model constitution. Courtesy, Special Collections, Alexander Library, Rutgers University

Right: Acting upon authority conferred by the Concessions and Agreements of 1665, Governor Carteret summoned delegates from Bergen, Newark, Elizabethtown, Woodbridge, Shrewsbury, Middletown, and Piscataway to represent East New Jersey for the first meeting of the East New Jersey General Assembly on May 26, 1668, in Elizabethtown—the beginning of representative government in New Jersey. Artist Harry Devlin re-created the event for New Jersey Bell Tel-News magazine on the 300th anniversary of the event in 1968. Courtesy, New Jersey Bell

Shrewsbury were launched. New Jersey was finally attracting needed settlers.

Philip Carteret got along with the Dutch in the Bergen area, and under the Concessions and Agreements the first Assembly convened on May 26, 1668, in Elizabethtown for five days. They set annual meetings on the first Tuesday in November, levied a tax of £30—apportioned among the six towns—to pay for the government, and established a criminal code that applied the death penalty for kidnapping, murder, arson, witchcraft, certain kinds of burglary, and even for the cursing of parents by children. Those who took the Lord's name in vain paid a shilling fine, of which the informer got half.

But because Nicolls's grants to the Monmouth residents seemed to be in jeopardy with Carteret's grants, the Monmouth settlers would not swear loyalty or pay quitrents to the proprietors. On these issues and others, the second session of the assembly collapsed.

In the "Revolution of 1672," the disaffected group declared that it was the "assembly," met in Elizabethtown, and overthrew Philip Carteret. The Dutch made another attempt at regaining the area and held New York for about a year in 1673, but when the English again assumed control in 1674, they reinstalled Philip Carteret as governor.

Lord Berkeley Sells his Shares

In 1674 for £1,000, Lord Berkeley sold his interest in New Jersey to fellow Quaker John Fenwick, who was acting for Edward Byllynge, a Quaker and Lord Berkeley's close friend. In debt, he thereafter turned over his interest to William Penn and two other trustees. In the famous Quintipartite Deed of July 1, 1676, Penn drew a line from Little Egg Harbor in the east to the northwest corner of the province and created East Jersey (modern "North Jersey") which was held by Carteret, and West Jersey (modern "South Jersey") which was held by the group of Quaker proprietors.

Because the Duke of York had not given governmental powers to Carteret and Berkeley, the governmental arrangements in East and West

Jersey were not strictly legal. The duke, in fact, challenged the usurpation of his rights and sent over Sir Edmund Andros to govern both New York and the Jerseys. Philip Carteret attempted to resist Andros's authority and got the duke to repudiate Andros. To end the controversy temporarily, the duke and the East New Jersey proprietors agreed to an arbitration, which went in favor of the proprietors. In 1680 the Duke of York relinquished all claims to political authority in both Jerseys.

Quakers Purchase Carteret's East Jersey

When George Carteret died in 1681, William Penn and eleven other Quakers bought East Jersey at auction for £3,400. They shortly thereafter brought in an additional twelve proprietors, half of whom were Scotsmen. In March 1683 King Charles II recognized the rights of these "Twenty-Four Proprietors" to both soil and government. East Jersey promptly became a haven for Scottish Presbyterians who were being persecuted by their king. In the next two years some 500 Scots arrived in Middlesex, Monmouth, and Somerset counties. They added another variety to an already diverse population.

Although proprietary leadership brought settlers to New Jersey, the system was doomed from the beginning. There were some honest disputes concerning clear land titles because of the grants made by Nicolls, George Carteret, and Lord Berkeley. But it should have been clear to all that the Duke of York could not have transmitted to any other parties the governing powers that King Charles II had given him.

When the Duke of York came to power in England in 1685 as James II, he moved to reassert royal governing authority. To many in England, the proprietors seemed to have lost control of the Jerseys. Smugglers could evade the Navigation Acts and the proprietors could not effectively collect quitrents from the people. By taking advantage of complaints by the collector of customs in New York that the East Jersey shippers were refusing to pay duties, the king said they were defying royal power. King James transferred to Governor Sir Edmund Andros, then governing New England, political authority over the Jerseys. New Jersey thus became part of the Dominion of New England.

After Parliament deposed James II in the "Glorious Revolution" of 1688-1689, the Board of Trade in England stripped the proprietors of their shaky claim to political rights. On April 15, 1702, the two sets of proprietors "surrendered" their political powers to Queen Anne, who "graciously accepted." New Jersey became a royal colony. The proprietors kept the title to the land, however, and the Council of Proprietors of the Western Division of New Jersey still has offices in Burlington.

The Economy of West Jersey Develops

The division of New Jersey into East and West Jersey ensured that the early economic development proceeded somewhat differently in the two regions.

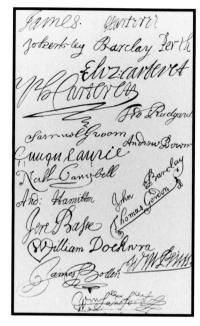

Led by the imperial "James" (James II, formerly Duke of York), this collection includes a number of signatures of the original twenty-four proprietors of East New Jersey, a group described in Wynne's British Empire *as "high prerogative men . . . dissenters, papists and Quakers." The facsimiles include three Carterets as well as others prominent in the settlement and government of the new province. The last, and most ornate, signature on the page is that of William Sandford, one of the first settlers of what is now Bergen County. From* East Jersey Under the Proprietary Governments, *1846*

The Quaker proprietors divided the lands in West Jersey into 100 shares, which they sold to prospective Quaker colonists. For assisting Byllynge, John Fenwick got 10 of the original 100 shares and in 1675 established the first English colony on the Delaware at Salem.

In 1677 Yorkshire and London Quakers used their shares to establish the main Quaker settlement at Burlington. In the next years some 1,500 Quakers followed. Quaker Mahlon Stacy pushed upriver to Trenton at "ye falls of ye de la Warr." There in 1679 he built his house and gristmill. William Emley, one of the settlers who joined Stacy, wrote on leaving Burlington: "We are now going to settle a Town at the Falls, at a place

reported . . . to be without compare to any other yet known: none equal for pleasant helthful air; Lovely Situation; second to none for Fertility." In 1681 a group from Dublin, Ireland, settled Gloucester County. But Quaker activity centered in Burlington, the capital. The Quakers created courts there and at Salem.

Intent on giving power to the settlers, the Quaker proprietors in 1677 put forth "The Concessions and Agreement of the Proprietors, Freeholders and Inhabitants of West New Jersey in America." Drafted largely by William Penn, this document gave extraordinary political and religious freedom to

An Hiftorical and Geographical Account

OF THE

PROVINCE and COUNTRY

OF

PENSILVANIA;

AND OF

Weſt-New-Jerſey

IN

AMERICA.

The Richneſs of the Soil, the Sweetneſs of the Situation the Wholeſomneſs of the Air, the Navigable Rivers, and others, the prodigious Encreaſe of Corn, the flouriſhing Condition of the City of *Philadelphia*, with the ſtately Buildings, and other Improvements there. The ſtrange Creatures, as *Birds, Beaſts, Fiſhes*, and *Fowls*, with the ſeveral ſorts of *Minerals, Purging Waters*, and *Stones*, lately diſcovered. The *Natives, Aborogmes*, their *Language, Religion, Laws*, and *Cuſtoms*; The firſt Planters, the *Dutch, Sweeds*, and *Engliſh*, with the number of its Inhabitants; As alſo a Touch upon *George Keith's New Religion*, in his ſecond Change ſince he left the *QUAKERS*.

With a Map of both Countries.

By GABRIEL THOMAS,

Who reſided there about Fifteen Years.

London, Printed for, and Sold by *A. Baldwin*, at the *Oxon Arms* in *Warwick-Lane*, 1698.

Left: Gabriel Thomas included a glowing description of West Jersey in this promotional pamphlet intended to encourage settlement in the New World. Thomas, a birthright Quaker, described West Jersey as a land of plenty occupied by busy tradesmen, prosperous fur traders, whalers, lumbermen, and farmers, whose crops included rice and cranberries. From An Historical and Geographical Account of the Province of Pensilvania and of West-New Jersey

Facing page: Conceived and originally settled by Quakers, West Jersey owed much of its social cohesion to the Society of Friends. Farmers, craftsmen, and tradesmen, they dedicated themselves to living together in simplicity and peace. Their stubborn allegiance to responsible individual freedoms was reflected in New Jersey's early charter—their heritage to the state. The Burlington Monthly Meeting, the second in West Jersey, met in members' homes until the hexagonal Meeting House, pictured here, was completed in 1693. With the addition of a wing in 1691, the building was used for nearly 100 years. Courtesy, Newark Public Library

the settlers and encouraged settlement in West Jersey.

With their community center and their monthly meetings and their economic and political center in Burlington, the Quakers lived orderly lives in West Jersey. Although under the shadow of the more powerful Quaker province of Pennsylvania, the Jersey Quakers expanded southeastward from their main settlement in Burlington in a wide strip down toward the Delaware Bay.

West Jersey settlers built larger farms farther from each other than did East Jerseyans. Because they shunned idleness and vice, West Jersey Quakers made successful farmers, whether or not they had been farmers in the Old World. They gave the menial work to indentured whites or black slaves.

In Burlington some craftsmen, bakers, and tavern keepers opened for

The Revell House, probably the second oldest in Burlington, was built by George Hutchinson, a wealthy Quaker, in 1685, and was used as an office by Thomas Revell who served as the registrar of the Proprietors of West New Jersey and clerk of the New Jersey General Assembly. In recent years the house was moved from Pearl Street to its present location on Wood Street. The venerable building also served as the headquarters of the Annis Stockton Chapter of the Daughters of the American Revolution. Sketch By T. Korneff. Courtesy, Burlington City Historian

business. Gabriel Thomas, who surveyed the Burlington scene in 1698, found it a "fine Market-Town," well supplied with "Bread, Beer, Beef, and Pork; as also Butter and Cheese, of which they freight several vessels, and send them to Barbadoes, and other Islands." Burlington was also full of "most sorts of Tradesmen, *viz.* Cloath-Workers, who make very good Serges, Druggets, Crapes, Camblets (part camel's hair, part silk) and good Plushes." Isaac Pearson made clocks in Burlington.

Successful Quakers built houses of brick on Burlington's streets. Following Mahlon Stacy's example, shippers exported beef, port, grain, and flour from Burlington and Salem to Philadelphia. Sometime near 1685, Dr. Daniel Coxe, a chief proprietor in West Jersey who never visited America, attempted to open a "white and chiney ware" pottery operation in Burlington, but it soon failed. Richard Bassnett opened a brewery next to his brick home sometime before 1690.

The Quakers did enough business to attract crowds to Burlington's fairs. A law of 1681 authorized two yearly fairs in Market Street "for all sorts of cattle and all manner of merchandise." Salem fairs may have been more raucous. A 1683 law authorizing fairs there gave six days' freedom from arrest unless the reveller acted against the king or queen or the "peace of our Lord."

"Here," Ester Huckens wrote from an English settlement on the Delaware in 1676, "is no want of any thing but good people to Inhabit; here is liberty for the honest-hearted that truly desire to fear the Lord; here is Liberty from the Cares and Bondage of this World, and after one year or two, you may live very well with very little labour; here is great store of Fish and Fowl, and plenty of Corn, and Cows, Hoggs, Horses, Oxen, Sheep, Venison,

Nuts[,] Strawberries, Grapes; and here is good English wheat ripe in three months."

In 1680 Mahlon Stacy wrote to his brother in England that West Jersey was "a country that produces all things for the sustenance of man in a plentiful manner. . . . It is my judgment that fruit trees in this country destroy themselves by the very weight of their fruit." He wrote of driving herring into a Delaware River pinfold with birch branches: "We drove thousands before us, and as many got into our trap as it would hold. Then we began to throw them on shore as fast as three or four of us could by two or three at a time. After this manner in half an hour we could have filled a three bushel sack with as fine herring as ever I saw."

"I wonder," he concluded, "at our Yorkshire people in England—that they had rather live in servitude, work hard all the year and not be three pence the better at the years' end, than to stir out of the chimney-corner and transport themselves to a place where, with like pains, in two or three

In contrast to the Quaker proprietors who envisioned West Jersey primarily as a haven from persecution, Dr. Daniel Coxe and his son, Daniel (pictured here), regarded their proprietorships as an opportunity to establish a feudal empire in the New World. In addition to 600,000 acres in West Jersey, Dr. Coxe had extensive holdings in other areas of North America. The family's ambitious plans included whale fishing, salt works, forestry, and ship building, as well as viticulture, centered upon Coxe Hall, a manor in Cape May County; and a pottery and iron forge in the Burlington area. Courtesy, Special Collections, Alexander Library, Rutgers University

years they might know better things. I live as well to my content and in as great plenty as every I did, and in far more likely way to get an estate."

West Jerseymen traded furs, fished, and harvested great quantities of oysters and clams in the seaside communities. In 1669 Governor Carteret gave John Ogden and twenty others the whaling rights from Barnegat Bay to Sandy Hook. In 1690 some whalers from Long Island or New England came to Cape May County and built thirteen houses at Town Bank, overlooking Delaware Bay. An eyewitness noted that their voyages produced vast quantities of "Oyl and Whale-Bone." The West Jersey legislature soon provided that any nonresident whalers who "bring to shore any whale or whales . . . shall pay one full and entire tenth of all the oyl and bone made out of the said whale or whales unto the present Governor of this Province for the time being."

South Jerseymen discovered bog ore in a swamp near the Little Egg Harbor River and in the beds of streams in Gloucester and Burlington counties. Eventually New Jersey would rival Pennsylvania as a producer of pig iron. The forests in West Jersey provided lumber for a nascent shipbuilding industry and yielded tar and turpentine for export. Brickmakers were numerous enough in 1683 for the West Jersey Assembly to pass an act regulating the size and quality of bricks. Inspectors broke faulty bricks and fined the makers.

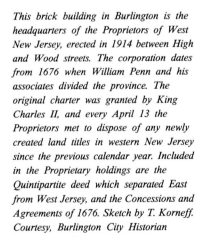

This brick building in Burlington is the headquarters of the Proprietors of West New Jersey, erected in 1914 between High and Wood streets. The corporation dates from 1676 when William Penn and his associates divided the province. The original charter was granted by King Charles II, and every April 13 the Proprietors met to dispose of any newly created land titles in western New Jersey since the previous calendar year. Included in the Proprietary holdings are the Quintipartite deed which separated East from West Jersey, and the Concessions and Agreements of 1676. Sketch by T. Korneff. Courtesy, Burlington City Historian

Early farm life in New Jersey was, first and foremost, extremely varied. Though the area of New Jersey is relatively small, it has a wide variety of surfaces and soils, and its first farmers reflected that variety in their farming activities. Dutchmen, New Englanders, Swedes, Scots, Germans, and English and Irish Quakers all brought their own seeds, animals, tools, and knowledge to eventually cultivate a wide variety of agricultural products.

New Jersey's first European farmers were the Dutch and Walloons in New Netherland on the western bank of Hudson River, and the Swedes and Finns in the part of New Sweden east of the Delaware River and Delaware Bay. These early farming centers were primarily in the Bergen-Newark-Elizabethtown-Perth Amboy area in the north, and the Salem-Burlington-Trenton area in the south.

In 1630 Michiel Reyniersz Pauw, a Dutch merchant-nobleman, was granted a large tract of land on the peninsula that is today lower Hudson County. The area was called Pavonia, after its proprietor, and it was excellent farmland. Pauw's first tenant on the land was Cornelius van Vorst: he was, by all reliable accounts, New Jersey's first farmer. Van Vorst established his "bouwerie"—the Dutch word for plantation—within the boundaries of present-day Jersey City, and he called it Ahismus.

In the 1630s there were not many dutchmen with the pioneer spirit of Cornelius van Vorst. It was difficult to coax many Dutchmen to settle in such a frightening place as the wilderness across the river from New Amsterdam. Thus, Pauw re-sold his land to the Dutch West India Company, which continued renting to the van Vorst family. Under the supervision of the company, some new bouweries were granted, but most of the new farming was practiced by people who commuted across the Hudson by boat.

In 1638, a change in company policy in 1638 stated that people who lived on the New Jersey side of the Hudson would be to trade furs as well as farm. This prospect lured several entrepreneur-farmers to Pavonia. Across the Hudson to settle came Aert Teunnison, founder of Hoboken, who brought with him small herds of cattle, hogs, sheep, and goats. David de Vries, a noted shipowner, who was known for getting along with the Indians, also launched a farm at Vriesendale—later named Old Tappan—where he would grow tobacco and brew beer. The bouwerie of Achter Col (now Ridgefield Park) had also become a well-established farm by the end of 1643.

All this farming progress was suddenly interrupted by the Indian war of 1643. In that conflict, all the bouweries west of the Hudson were destroyed, except for Ahismus, the original bouwerie of Cornelius van Vorst. A promising start at agriculture in New Jersey received a stunning setback.

With the arrival of Governor Peter Stuyvesant in 1647, more farm tracts were established on the west side of the Hudson, and the old bouweries at Ahismus and Hoboken continued to be held by their original families. About one dozen new settlements were made at places like Communipaw and Paulus Hook, which became two of the leading bouweries.

In 1655, the Indians struck again and burned every bouwerie west of the Hudson except Communipaw, killing all the adults they could find and capturing children for ransom. Except for the proprietors of Ahismus, who had survived two Indian wars, no settlers were subsequently allowed to return west of the Hudson until a treaty was reached with the Indians in 1658.

In 1660 the Dutch established a major new farming settlement—with fifty-nine lots all carefully laid out for protection against the Indians—around the village of Bergen, which became the major settlement of the area.

Meanwhile, in the Delaware Valley, the Dutch, Swedes, and Finns were busy settling the area's earliest farms. After British rule was firmly established in 1665, several immigrant groups came down from New England to settle New Jersey farmland, taking land being granted south of Raritan Bay and the Raritan River. In all, New England farmers did much to help New Jersey's early farming development: they established themselves in other areas in New Jersey that would later grow to become towns like Elizabethtown, Woodbridge, and Piscataway.

These early farmers concentrated primarily on growing corn and raising cattle. They soon began alternating corn with such crops as wheat, rye, oats, barley, and peas, and, as time went on, farmers began to prolifically cultivate vegetables such as lettuce, cabbages, parsnips, turnips, carrots, beets, radishes, spinach, endive, onions, parsley, leeks, garden peas, and many herbs.

Most of these early New Jersey farmers received help from Europe and/or kept close ties with their earlier American homes. Much of their livestock was brought over from New England and the Netherlands, including draft and riding horses, sheep, hogs, and cattle.

Tools for clearing forests were simple but adequate, and the local blacksmith became an important partner for the new farmer. Most early farmhouses were frame houses, and Swedish and Finnish immigrants introduced their wooden plank houses, which would be modified by the English to become the renowned log cabins. In the early farming days, there were problems of rampaging goats, cows, and horses trampling crops, but this situation was soon rectified when strict fencing laws were implemented.

—David Fleming

East Jersey Grows

Despite the fact that they also were predominantly yeoman farmers, East Jerseymen presented a somewhat different picture. The people in the region were more diverse, and the farms were smaller. The New Englanders laid out the seven towns of East Jersey—Elizabethtown, Middletown, Shrewsbury, Woodbridge, Piscataway, Bergen, and Newark—around a central common, New England-style.

New Jersey was healthful, wrote Richard Hartshorne in 1675. "In Middletown, where I live, in 6 years and upwards, there have dyed but one Woman about 80 years old, one Man about 60, a Boy about five years old, and one little Infant or 2."

"We make our Soap & Candles & all such things ourselves," wrote Hartshorne, "in the Winter we make good fires, and eat good meat; and our Women & Children are healthy; Sugar is cheap, Venison, Geese, Turkies, Pidgeons, Fowle, & Fish plenty; and one great happiness we enjoy, which is, we are very quiet."

Hartshorne also told of how land purchases from the Indians might seem different to the bargaining parties. He had bought land from some Indians, but they kept coming back on the land to hunt and fish—and to gather the wild beach plums that grew there. Since the Indians' concept of "sale" did not preclude them from using the land, Hartshorne had to buy the land a second time—this time he bought the exclusive rights to everything, including the beach plums.

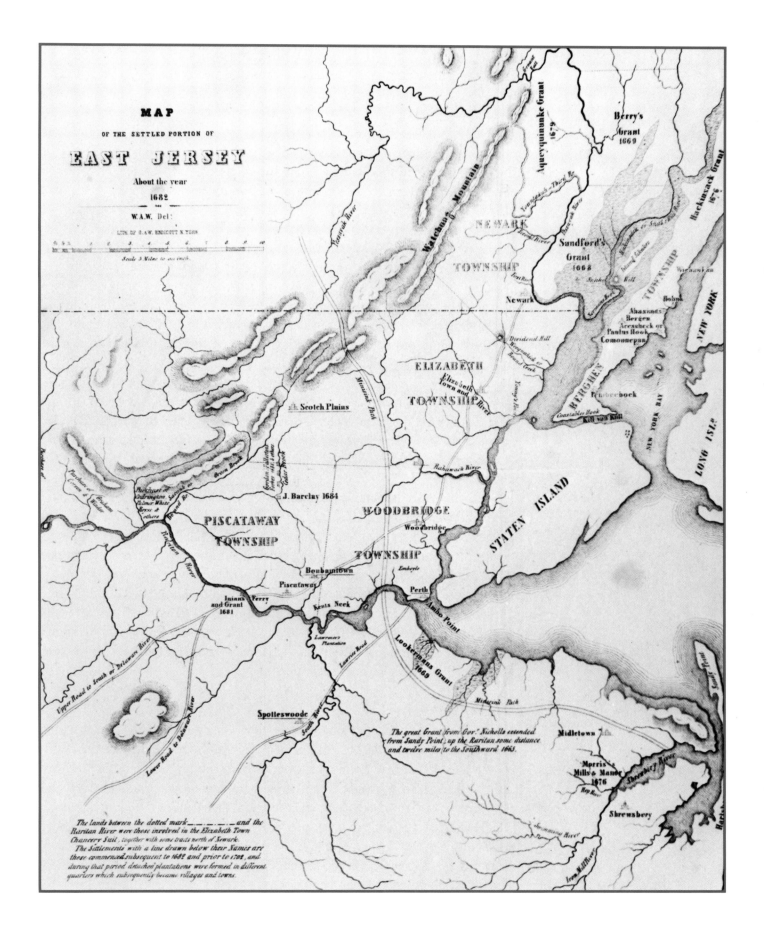

MAP

OF THE SETTLED PORTION OF

EAST JERSEY

About the year

1682

W.A.W. Del.

LITH. OF G.&W. ENDICOTT N.YORK

Scale 3 Miles to an inch.

John Ogden introduced tanning in Elizabethtown sometime after 1664. By 1674 the general assembly prohibited tanners from making or selling leather that was not inspected and approved by a "Sealer's hand and Approbation."

Numerous water-powered mills sprang up on streams for grinding flour and cutting lumber. Woodbridge had a sawmill run by Jonathan Bishop in the 1680s. In Newark, Robert Treat and Richard Harrison agreed with the town in the 1670s to erect and maintain "a sufficient corn mill . . . to grind all town grist into good meal." For this they received some foodstuffs in advance and one-twelfth of the Indian corn and one-sixteenth of the other grains they ground. New Jerseyans also erected windmills, but many fewer than New Englanders or those on the Long Island colonial outposts.

One early gristmill made a powerful impression on an observer. "One's nostrils," he wrote, "were tickled by the floating particles in the floury atmosphere; the building trembled with the rumbling of turning shafts and swiftly running gears. . . . The burring sound of the millstones was pleasant to the ears."

In 1674 in Tinton Manor—now Tinton Falls, Monmouth County— James Grover built an iron plantation, which he then sold to Lewis Morris. East Jerseymen dug magnetite and hematite in Morris, Bergen, and Sussex counties. In 1674 at a Shrewsbury ironworks, sixty black slaves smelted ore. A century later this works produced munitions for George Washington's army.

Brewing also became an important industry in both Jerseys. Hoboken had a brewery in 1642, and Burlington was brewing in the late seventeenth century. Newarkers marketed their cider and applejack widely.

In 1685 the East New Jersey proprietors hired George Scott to encourage settlement. He echoed the theme that crowned heads and proprietors had announced since Hudson's voyage: come to the New World. Scott particularly summoned craftsmen. "All Sorts of Tradesmen," wrote Scott, "may make a brave Lively-hood there, such as Carpenters, Shipwrights, Rope-makers, Smith, Brickmakers, Taylors, Tanners, Cowpers, Mill-wright, Joyners, Shoe makers and such like."

New Jersey in 1702

Under the English Crown since 1664, New Jersey needed to attract people. Letters home and statements like that of George Scott pointed to the reality of the young colony. Economic opportunities abounded, but the colony needed settlers to exploit them. Those who had come into either of the provinces of New Jersey kept encouraging their fellows to join them.

Because it was still undeveloped, the area was relatively poor compared with New York or Pennsylvania. But a colonial economy had begun. Among New Jerseyans could be found farmers, blacksmiths, brickmakers, carpenters, weavers, tailors, merchants, shoemakers, coopers, tanners, miners, and butchers. Many farmers were jacks-of-all-trades. They brewed beer, shod

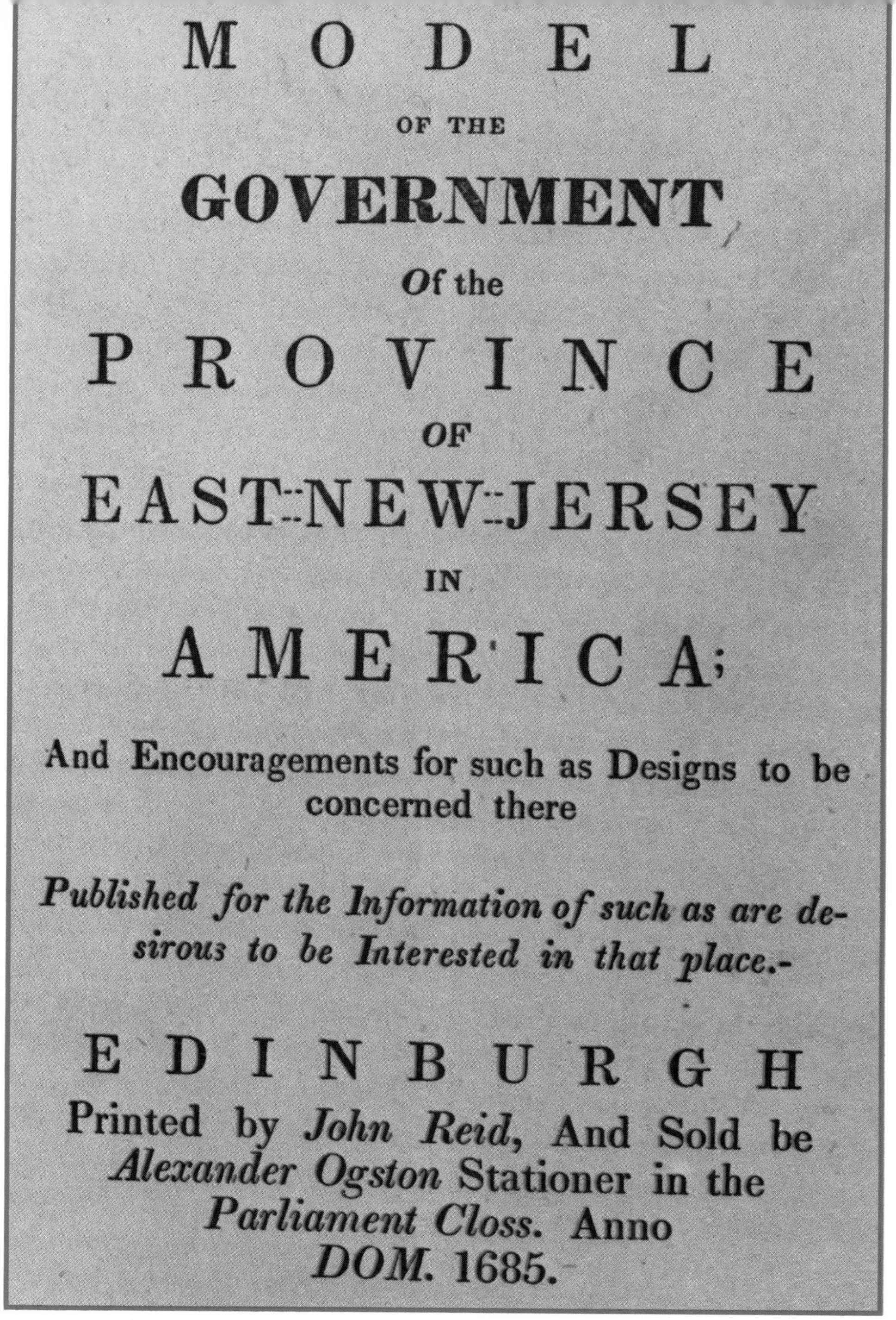

MODEL

OF THE

GOVERNMENT,

Of the

PROVINCE

OF

EAST-NEW-JERSEY

IN

AMERICA;

And Encouragements for such as Designs to be concerned there

Published for the Information of such as are desirous to be Interested in that place.

EDINBURGH

Printed by *John Reid,* And Sold be *Alexander Ogston* Stationer in the *Parliament Closs.* Anno DOM. 1685.

The tract shown here was commissioned by the Scotch proprietors of East Jersey in an effort to induce more of their countrymen to emigrate to that province. Written by George Scot, who received 500 acres in the new land for his efforts, the pamphlet also includes letters from early settlers to friends and relatives back home. From East Jersey Under the Proprietary Governments, *1875*

horses, tanned leather, and built structures. Taverns abounded. Scattered about the state, doctors, lawyers, goldsmiths, schoolmasters, servants, surveyors, and peddlers served their clients.

The colony lay under the economic shadow of both New York and Philadelphia, whose harbors and locations would lead them to dominate New Jersey, but proprietary government had laid a foundation for New Jersey's economic development. Berkeley and Carteret's Concessions and Agreements of 1665—issued, ironically, under the reign of Charles II, who had illegally confiscated privately owned lands when he granted them to Berkeley and Carteret—gave Jerseymen a sense of rights, economic freedom, religious toleration, and popular government. Under the proprietors, town and county government took form, the boundaries of the state were determined, and the industrious New Jerseyans of the seventeenth century began the trades and enterprises that gave the colony its economic base. Under direct royal control, however, mercantile restraints would fuel a revolution.

Chapter Two

A Rebellion Against Mercantilism

Born in Philadelphia, Francis Hopkinson settled in Bordentown in 1774, six years after his marriage to Ann Borden of Bordentown. As a delegate to the First Continental Congress, he signed the Declaration of Independance. A prolific writer and poet, he ridiculed the British with satire. A man of many talents, Hopkinson designed the Great Seal of New Jersey and is credited by some for designing the final form of the American flag. Courtesy, Special Collectons, Alexander Library, Rutgers University

After 1692 the royal colony of New Jersey fell more directly under the control of the Crown and thus under the rigorous rules of mercantilism that regulated New Jersey's economic development. During the first two-thirds of the eighteenth century, New Jerseyans developed their farms and exported grains and flour. They erected sawmills, mined iron and copper, developed a glass industry, and began tanneries. But the ineptness of some of the governors the Crown appointed, the inevitable conflicts between the landholders and the landless squatters, and a shortage of currency led to conflicts between governors and the governed.

These conflicts heightened after 1763, when the British drove the French out of the area beyond the Appalachian Mountains, and Parliament began to reassert its mercantile rights over a colony that it had neglected during the earlier part of the eighteenth century. Many New Jerseyans resented this reassertion of authority as a violation of their rights and, rather than submit, followed the leads of Massachusetts and Virginia in rebelling against the Crown.

Anne, Queen of Great Britain and Ireland, was monarch at the time the proprietors surrendered their right of government to the British Crown. Described by historians as a good queen, her appointment of Edward Hyde, Lord Cornbury, as royal governor of New York and New Jersey, provoked dissension in the colony throughout his term. Courtesy, Newark Public Library

Mercantilism Hampers Growth

English mercantilists sought to use the colonies, or "plantations," as sources of raw materials and markets for finished goods. They also attempted to sell to foreign nations but buy little from them, and to increase home production of commodities by means of bounties and special privileges. Essentially, the mercantilists wanted a favorable balance of trade to increase England's gold supply for war.

Between 1650 and 1767, to regulate and control foreign trade and to subordinate the colonial interest to the interest of the mother country, Parliament enacted a series of Acts of Trade and Navigation. Aimed primarily at the Dutch traders, the early English laws prohibited importation of goods into England except from the place of production and required that the goods be carried in English ships or in ships of the country of origin. Parliament prohibited foreign ships from trading in the colonies without special license. Parliament also enumerated certain products manufactured in the English plantations and required that they be shipped directly to England.

In the Act of 1696 Parliament required that all colonial trade be carried in English-built ships, gave provincial customs officers the same powers as those in England, required that bonds be posted on enumerated commodities even where duties were paid, enhanced the colonial naval officers' duties, and voided all colonial laws that were contrary to the Navigation Acts. Under this system, England achieved a favorable balance of trade at the expense of the colonies, which from 1701 to 1773 had an unfavorable trade balance with the mother country of £20 million.

Unfortunately, the mercantile system was not the only straitjacket on the eighteenth-century New Jersey economy. The colony also struggled with the issues that traditionally face underdeveloped nations. New Jersey lacked labor, capital (both money and credit), an efficient transportation system, and access to markets. Pirates and privateering during the international wars of the century also hampered New Jersey's colonial trade.

Lacking transportation and capital, New Jersey settlers developed household industries. They spun flax and coarse wool into homespun cloth. They tanned leather, made shoes, soap, tallow, farm implements, applejack, peach brandy, and furniture. Up and down the American coast, household industries supplied the colonists with three-quarters of all their cloth—particularly the coarser variety.

Both economic and mercantile laws determined that New Jerseyans concentrate on primary, or first-stage, manufacture: bread, flour, lumber, some naval stores, some bricks, and pig iron for the markets of Philadelphia and New York. Secondary manufacturing—the production of paper, hats, furniture, steel, and iron implements—was to be left to the mother country.

New Jersey's role in the mercantile system was similar to that of other colonies. Before the American Revolution, even the more developed colonies of the South and New England had little industry except lumbering, shipbuilding, naval stores, fishing, whaling, workshop crafts, putting out homespun, flour milling, and simple iron manufacture. Only after the war would secondary industry and the wealth it spawned appear.

The Colony Supplies Food

Restricted by mercantilism and its own lack of capital, credit, labor and transportation systems, the eighteenth-century New Jersey economy developed slowly along primarily agricultural lines. Land was plentiful, so labor was scarce. For most settlers, farming provided a greater opportunity than industry.

Colonial New Jersey farmers fertilized with fish but otherwise used planting, harvesting, and threshing techniques as old as the Bible. Despite these crude methods, New Jersey became—along with Long Island and the Hudson and Mohawk valleys—one of the chief wheat-producing sections in America thanks to the soils and growing season.

The Swedes and Finns along the Delaware in Salem and Gloucester counties initially farmed rye, but at the end of the seventeenth century they shifted to wheat, which had been the choice of the other settlers. The New Jersey Scots, who settled in Middlesex and Monmouth counties, raised barley for feed and for human consumption. The Dutch farmers of Somerset and Bergen counties accumulated holdings of several hundred acres where they raised cattle with slave labor and applied more modern farming techniques than did their Yankee neighbors.

New England Yankees farmed Morris County. According to one observer who was comparing them with the Dutch, the Puritans "affect more gentility, are more apt to run in Debt, to scheme and speculate, are litigious, and have more Genius and Learning, fond of Arms, Liberty and Democracy." The Puritans farmed by ancient techniques and also compared unfavorably with the Hunterdon and Sussex County Germans, who discovered and used limestone soils, practiced crop rotations, planted cover crops, and fertilized with manure.

Informed observers criticized those colonial farmers, who did not employ soil-conservation techniques. As intensive farming depleted the soil, wheat production gradually shifted west.

But until soils declined, New Jerseyans worked agricultural marvels. Carrots, parsnips, peas, turnips, squash, cabbage, and melons ripened in New Jersey gardens. Even Swede Peter Kalm, who criticized the farming techniques followed throughout the colony, was forced to note that peaches, which were scarce in Sweden, were so plentiful on one New Jersey farm that "we could scarcely walk in the orchard without treading upon the peaches that had fallen off."

New Jerseyans supplied foodstuffs, particularly grain, to New York and Philadelphia. In his 1765 *History of the Colony of Nova Caesaria or New Jersey* Samuel Smith remarked on the 500-600 bushels of grain being rafted down the Delaware River from Burlington to Philadelphia. Smith also saw

This black side chair with elaborately carved crest was doubtless copied by a Colonial craftsman from an English style brought to America circa 1690. One of a pair that have been in the Gill family for eight generations, the chair's original owner is thought to be John Gill I, an early Haddonfield settler who arrived at the beginning of the eighteenth century. Courtesy, Collection of the Newark Museum

large quantities of Raritan Valley wheat going down the Raritan River for shipment to New York. Before the revolution, boats took New Jersey fruits and vegetables to Philadelphia and New York City. In these cities New Jerseyans traded flour, beef, bacon, lumber, and shingles for West Indian rum and sugar, Spanish wines and olive oil, and manufactured goods from England. New Jersey was, according to an eighteenth-century quip attributed to both James Madison and Ben Franklin, a "barrel, tapped at both ends, with all the live beer running into New York and Philadelphia."

In the eighteenth century the New Jersey farmer followed the Connecticut yeoman in using wooden plows drawn by horses to cultivate corn. Peter Kalm saw New Jersey corn that was "usually eight feet high, more or less."

In East Jersey, cattle—either branded or distinguished with marks on their ears—roamed the common in the center of each town. To house stray

In 1835 Thomas and Samuel Whitney purchased a glassworks that had undergone multiple ownership since the Stanger family had sold it in 1783 to the Whitneys' grandfather, Colonel Thomas Heston, the "fighting Quaker" of the Revolution. Under the Whitney management, the firm became the largest industry in Glassboro. The site was later occupied by the firm of Owens-Illinois. Courtesy, Special Collections, Alexander Library, Rutgers University

cows Newarkers built a pen in the middle of town. Elsewhere cows grazed in the woods and fields. In 1675 Richard Hartshorne wrote from Middletown that, with his thirty to forty head of cattle and seven or eight riding horses, he felt economically privileged. Horses, he said, commonly ran wild and required no feed. New Jerseyans advertised horses for stud. In 1704 Newarkers hired a shepherd. By 1750 farmers began stall-feeding cattle for Philadelphia and New York export markets.

Eighteenth-century New Jerseyans lived a hard life in a developing farm economy. But the land was rich and the growing season long. Throughout the state, social life revolved around farming at numerous harvests, butcherings, cattle drives, "bees," and "frolics." As Governor Belcher noted in 1748: "Take this Province in the lump, it is the best country I have seen for men of middling fortunes, and for people who have to live by the sweat of their brows."

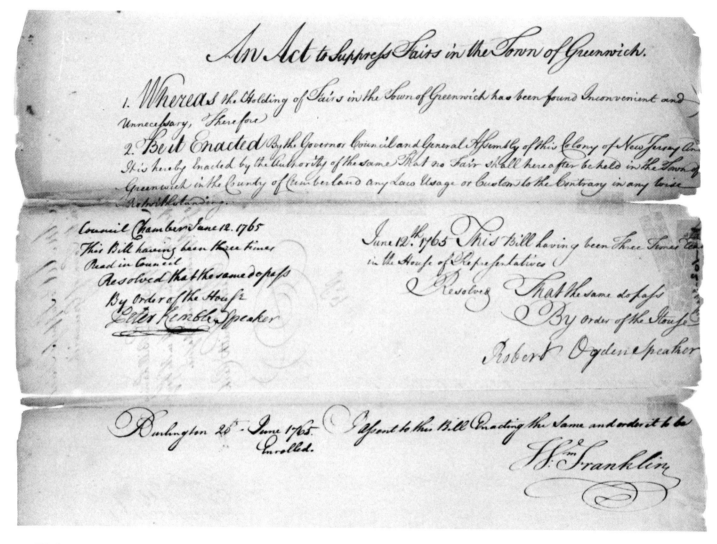

Eighteenth-century New Jersey attracted a much-needed, heterogeneous, and rapidly growing population. From 1702 to 1775, the population doubled each generation and grew from 15,000 to 100,000. Slightly less than half of eighteenth-century New Jerseyans came from England. One-sixth came from Wales, Scotland, or Ireland. One-sixth were Dutch, one-tenth were German, and a smaller number were either Swedish or French. Many immigrants came to New Jersey as bond servants, agreeing to work for a period of time, usually four years, in exchange for a parcel of land, and the standard servant's contract terms of "ten bushels of corn, necessary apparel, two hoes and an ax" when they completed servitude.

During the eighteenth century black slaves made up one-twelfth of the New Jersey population. A tiny fraction of New Jerseyans were Indian slaves, acquired after the French and Indian War. All together these two groups of slaves numbered about 14,000 in 1790. Whites used them to work the iron forges, in farming, as servants, coachmen, boatmen, coopers, and millers.

Known as "pagans" in New Jersey, the African and Indian slaves were considered property by their owners, including Colonel Lewis Morris, who

From 1695 to 1765, fairs in Greenwich were held annually in April and October. The passage of "An Act to Suppress Fairs in the town of Greenwich" was allegedly the work of Greenwich Quaker Ebenezer Miller, a member of the Assembly representing Greenwich merchants who resented the competition of the fairs. Greenwich was at that time the business center of Cumberland County. Courtesy, New Jersey Room, Fairleigh Dickinson University

had been a planter in Barbados. They were also feared. In 1734 near Somerville, one slave was hanged, the ears were cut off several others, and a group was whipped because the owners thought they were planning an insurrection. Laws condemned the slaves to special courts and harsher punishment than non-slaves, including burning at the stake if guilty of murder, rape, or robbery of money valued over £5.

By 1745 half of New Jersey's slaves lived in Bergen, Middlesex, and Monmouth counties, where they farmed and labored in the ironworks. Slavers sold slaves at public auction at the Perth Amboy slave mart. Despite Quaker qualms about slavery, Hunterdon and Burlington County New Jerseyans also held slaves, although many fewer did so than in West Jersey.

Pressures against the slave trade grew during the eighteenth century, particularly from the Quaker population, but not until 1767 did the governor and council tax the importation of slaves. And not until after the American Revolution would the legislature provide for gradual abolition by making the children of slave mothers free. As late as 1826 the Supreme Court of New Jersey held that all black men "should be regarded as slaves until proven to be free." The legacy of slavery stained New Jersey into the twentieth century.

By 1750 white New Jerseyans had incorporated five towns: Elizabethtown, Perth Amboy, New Brunswick, Trenton, and Burlington. In addition, settlements of fifty to one hundred houses stood in Newark,

The oldest of Trenton's landmarks, the William Trent House, was built in 1719 by the person for whom Trenton is named. After Trent's death, the house passed through a succession of owners, including Loyalist sympathizer Dr. William Bryant, and John Cox, an iron manufacturer at Batsto. The house is now on the National Register of Historic Sites. Courtesy, Newark Public Library

The Proprietary House and the old Jail are two important buildings in the ancient capital of Perth Amboy. The Proprietary House, built between 1768 and 1770, was the residence of Governor William Franklin, New Jersey's last royal governor. The building later became a private home, a hotel, a residence for retired ministers, and finally a boardinghouse. The old Jail, authorized by Act of the Assembly on June 28, 1766, was finished the following year at the cost of £200. From Contributions to the Early History of Perth Amboy and Adjoining Country, *1856*

A workman prepares to cut shingles from a half-buried cedar log, as this drawing from the 1856 New Jersey Geological Survey Annual Report, *illustrates. Cedar swamps were common in the counties south of Monmouth, and by 1805 "mining" or logging operations became a local occupation. Workmen used iron rods to locate buried trunks, and skilled workers were able to judge their direction, size, and length.*

Princeton, Bordentown, Salem, Bridgeton, Freehold, Bergen, Hackensack, and Morristown.

Although early settlers had erected only crude dwellings, many of the homes in Elizabeth by the eighteenth century were surrounded by orchards and gardens. Two churches, Anglican and Presbyterian, dominated the Elizabeth landscape. The spired town hall, a stone barracks, and various mansions graced this center of eastern New Jersey culture. Here lived the Daytons, the Ogdens, the Boudinots, and the Jouets—the first families of New Jersey.

Set between the Passaic River and the Orange Mountains and close in size to Elizabeth, Newark had its long Broad Street, two churches, some tanneries, and an academy. Apple orchards surrounded the town.

Guarding the mouth of the Raritan River, Perth Amboy had only 700 residents. But the town was nicely structured on a rectangular grid around a central brick market. Chartered in 1731, Anglican New Brunswick, with its courthouse, barracks, grammar school, market house, and college, stood farther up the Raritan River and was the market town for the Raritan Valley. In 1766 New Brunswick became the seat of Queen's College (now Rutgers).

Nassau Hall and some lovely homes, including Richard Stockton's, gave Princeton its flavor. The College of New Jersey also gave Princeton special cultural status. At the falls of the Delaware River, 100 families resided at Trenton. "Trent's Town" had, of course, been named for William Trent, a wealthy Philadelphia merchant who developed Mahlon Stacy's settlement at the falls. He rebuilt Stacy's mills in stone and constructed a brick home for himself.

The town also boasted a tavern, a store that facilitated travel and movement of goods to Philadelphia, a Quaker Meeting House, St. Michael's Anglican Church, and the native-stone Presbyterian church, built in 1726. Already large estates had begun to cap the northern hills of the town. Burlington had St. Mary's Church plus its rows of neat, brick Quaker homes and the summer residences of some Philadelphians. Without towns the size of New York or Philadelphia, eighteenth-century New Jersey had few large merchants. But as one governor of New Jersey wrote sometime around 1740, New Jerseyans were "the most Easie and happy people of any colony in North America."

William Alexander, who claimed the title of Earl of Stirling, was born in New York City in 1726. In New Jersey he became prominent in public life and served with distinction in the American Revolution. His business interests included the Hibernia furnace and forge in Rockaway Township, Morris County, which he owned with Colonel Jacob Ford, Jr., of Morristown. Courtesy, Special Collections, Alexander Library, Rutgers University

A Frontier Economy is Established

Colonists erected sawmills on the many rivers of the colony. From the lumber mills came the barrel staves for West Indian hogsheads and—from ancient white cedars that were found in the swamps of South Jersey—the popular cedar shakes used for shingles. Shippers used the Delaware, the Raritan, and the Passaic rivers to transport lumber products.

Very early in the eighteenth century, Trenton had a mill economy. Lumber, wheat, and other grains moved by wagon into Trenton, where Trentonians processed lumber and grains, produced paper, tanned leather, and packed and pickled sturgeon. They then loaded these products into Durham boats and sent them to Philadelphia. A leading miller, William Trent, had also built an ironworks, but its dam had been damaged by a flood in 1733. Isaac Smith advertised in the *New Jersey Gazette* that he made cowbells, smoothing irons, and other metal products in his Trenton steelworks. Trenton soon surpassed Burlington economically.

Ironworks sprang up at Shrewsbury in Monmouth County, at Mine Hill in Morris County, and in the Western Highlands to exploit New Jersey's main mineral resource. New Jerseyans had forests which yielded charcoal for smelting, limestone for flux in forges, and water power to operate the bellows for their ironworks. New Jersey forges operated on the banks of the Whippany and Rockaway rivers, on the South Branch of the Raritan River at High Bridge, and at Oxford. Ironmongers shipped pig iron and bars on horseback to Newark or New York. New Jersey slitting mills made nails,

Right: The Andover Iron Mine was located on a tract in Sussex County, surveyed for William Penn in 1714. Worked before the Revolution by the English Company, the mine was commandeered during the war to supply iron for munitions for the Continental Army. At the time of this 1856 sketch, the mine was owned by the Trenton Iron Company. From Second Annual Report of the Geological Survey of the State of New Jersey for the Year 1855, *1856*

Below: The Dickerson Mine at Succasunna, Morris County, was purchased from the proprietors of West Jersey in 1713, but was not successfully worked until the next century when it came under the management of Mahlon Dickerson, governor of New Jersey (1815-1817). This view shows the exterior works of the Dickerson Succasunna Mining Company incorporated after Dickerson's death in 1853. From Second Annual Report of the Geological Survey of the State of New Jersey for the Year 1855, *1856*

and steel furnaces produced steel plate.

In 1750 Parliament banned additional colonial slitting mills, rolling mills, and steel furnaces but admitted pig and bar iron to Britain without duty. In 1751 Burlington politician, entrepreneur, and land speculator Charles Read found bog iron in some Burlington County cedar swamplands, and launched the South Jersey bog-iron industry. Bog iron came from vegetable matter which seeped into deposits of iron salts and marl; by heating it until impurities came to the surface, the South Jersey entrepreneurs could produce pig iron. Batsto became the center of iron gathering and Atsion the center of bar-iron production.

To turn either bog ores or hard iron ores into useful metal, New Jerseyans constructed twenty-foot-high, four-sided furnaces lined with firebrick and sometimes built into the hillside. They built arches which extended into the core on the sides and allowed air to be forced in, iron ore and flux to be added, and molten iron to be drawn off. The operators would fire these furnaces with charcoal for weeks at a time, adding ore and flux and blowing air into the molten mass to agitate it. They could then allow the mass to

This 1860 sketch of a mine in the Hibernia tract illustrates miners engaged in "stope mining"—extracting ore from successive terraces or steps. Timbers reinforced the walls of the shaft from which the ore has already been extracted. From Harper's New Monthly Magazine, *April 1860*

Left: This stove and kettle were made from bog iron at Batsto Furnace, built circa 1766 by Charles Read on the Batsto River in the Pine Barrens of Burlington County. During the Revolutionary War, the furnace produced shot, camp kettles, and other iron products for the Continental Army. In 1784, William Richards purchased the Batsto works and it continued to be productive in that family until 1854. Courtesy, Newark Public Library

Right: This iron grave marker was made at Weymouth Furnace, which was built in Hamilton Township on Great Egg Harbor River. Similar markers in the old cemetery at Weymouth, although exposed to the weather for over a hundred years, have remained remarkably rust-free, a characteristic claimed by early iron workers to be typical of bog iron. Courtesy, Camden County Historical Society

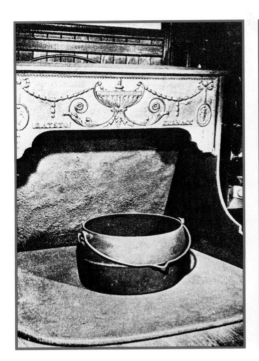

separate into slag on the top and molten iron on the bottom, both of which could be drawn off.

In 1763 "Baron" Peter Hasenclever launched the major New Jersey iron project in the Ramapo Valley. At Charlotteburg, Ringwood, and Long Pond, Hasenclever spent liberally of the funds of a group of English investors in a vain attempt to create a major ironworks in the valley. The investors removed the spendthrift "baron" in 1769. In a 1768 report, Governor William Franklin noted that the colony held eight blast furnaces and forty-two forges. New Jerseyans had also begun a slitting mill, a steel furnace, and one plating mill; but, Franklin noted, "I am told that none of the three latter are carried on with vigor, and that scarce anything has been done at the Steel Furnace for several Years last." Begun in 1770, the Franklin iron industry proved to be one of the most durable in the state.

Legend says that early in the eighteenth century a slave turned over a greenish stone on Philip Schuyler's estate in North Arlington near Newark. All the slave got for the find, according to legend, was what he asked: to be allowed to stay with Schuyler for the rest of his life, to have all the tobacco he could smoke, and to own a dressing gown with brass buttons, like Schuyler's. Pressed by Schuyler for another suggestion, the slave decided that he would like some more tobacco. By 1721 Schuyler shipped 110 casks of high-grade copper ore to Holland, and he shipped many more tons to England in the next decade. On average, the mine produced 100 tons annually.

Colonists also mined copper at New Brunswick, Rocky Hill, near Mt. Vernon, and in sites in the Watchung Mountains. From his Burlington farm, Benjamin Franklin wrote in 1750 that Schuyler's copper mine was the only one he knew of in America, and that it "has turned out vast wealth to the owners." To improve the Arlington mines, Schuyler's son imported a machine destined to revolutionize the Western world—a steam engine to pump out the mine's flooded shafts. The impact of the steam engine would not be felt, of course, until the early nineteenth century.

Until then, it was not machines but craftsmen who built New Jersey industry. In the craft of glassmaking, New Jerseyans took a lead that would become the basis for a prosperous industry into the twentieth century. Palatinate German Casper Wistar, who settled in Philadelphia and made buttons for a time, in 1738 founded a glass-blowing establishment in a tiny Salem County community that soon became known as Wistarburg. He found vast quantities of pure sand, extensive woodlands for fuel for furnaces, and potash for the alkali which was used in forming the molten mass that became glass. Most important, he had a market for the product in the Philadelphia aristocracy. With four Rotterdam experts he lured to the New World by a guarantee of one-third of the profits, he turned Wistarburg into the cradle of American glass making.

They advertised in the *Pennsylvania Gazette* that they produced "most sort of bottles . . . cafe bottles, snuff bottles, and mustard bottles." As the Wistar works grew, Wistar imported more German workmen and made a much wider variety of articles, including scent and drug bottles, lamp glasses, and glass balls for stoppers. The Wistars became famous for their turquoise-blue and amber pieces. Their trademarks included layering the article with a second covering for decoration or wrapping a glass thread or cord around the neck of each bottle, pitcher, or mug.

The enterprise at Wistarburg also provided the nation with a lineage of glassmakers that included Jacob Stanger and his brothers, who created a

Under the Richards' family tenure, Batsto was practically a self-contained operation, complete with workers' housing, village store, blacksmith shop, and mills. This photograph shows the sawmill erected in 1882 as it appeared before Batsto was declared a State Historic Site. Courtesy, Camden County Historical Society

The first steam engine manufactured in the United States was produced on the site of the Hendricks Copper Mill in Belleville, shown here as it appeared in 1939. The early works were named Soho by Nicholas Roosevelt, a partner in the enterprise with Philip A. Schuyler, Josiah Hornblower, and others. In 1824 the plant was sold to the Hendricks family and remained in their hands until 1928. From Reminiscences of 75 Years of Belleville, Franklin, and Newark, *1890*

glassworks in what became Glassboro. Stanger sold out at the end of the Revolutionary War to Thomas Heston and Thomas Carpenter. John Landis Mason, a Vinelander who moved to New York, invented the Mason jar, which was patented in 1858 and produced in Samuel Crowley's glassworks near Batsto.

Brickmaking boomed near Burlington—enough to force the West Jersey Assembly to regulate the industry. But not until after the American Revolution would the New Jersey ceramic industry take shape around Trenton.

Newark and Elizabethtown took the lead in tanning leather. Called the "Mother of Tanners," Elizabethtown began exporting tanned leather at the end of the seventeenth century and served to train a host of tanners for the Middle Atlantic economy. One Elizabethtown tanner, William Edwards, moved on to Northampton, Massachusetts, where he revolutionized tanning by using chemicals. He also developed the hide mill and the beating and rolling mill.

By the "watering place" at Market Street, a group of Newark leather-workers tanned the hides of local cattle in vats filled with oak bark. Slowly during the eighteenth century, Newark surpassed Elizabethtown's output.

Stonecutters cut building materials near Branch Brook in Newark early in the century.

The last of the colonies to have a newspaper, New Jersey got its first printing presses in the 1720s and 1730s to print the certificates of the loan offices. James Parker was printing in Woodbridge in 1751. In 1757 Parker started *The New American Magazine* which lasted three years.

With no permanent newspapers, travelers or settlers got their news in the local taverns from the single-page newspapers from New York or Philadelphia. Simple clapboard or log buildings, most eighteenth-century taverns had only two small rooms—one in which the innkeeper and perhaps his wife lived, the other room in which the guests ate and drank. At night the common room became the bedroom for whomever might be staying the night. Often a lean-to at the back of the building served as both kitchen and woodshed.

By the Revolution there would be nearly 500 taverns in the colony. Even in the seventeenth century there were enough taverns to generate a 1664 regulation by the Duke of York which required that a tavern keeper have a "Certificate of his good behavior from the Constable and two Overseers at least of the parish wherein he dwelt and a Lycence first obtained under the hand of two Justices of the peace in the Sessions upon pain of forfeiting five pounds for every such offence, or Imprisonment at the discretion of the Court."

Tavern keepers often served as justices of the peace or held other office or position in the militia. Men played handball and other games against the tavern walls. At Cross Keys Tavern in 1750 horsemen held races that offered a grand prize of twenty pistols. Families came to see entertainment and traveling shows.

Quaker John Woolman noted in his journal that he was at the Three Tun Tavern in Mount Holly during a show. He "Laboured to convince them [the others waiting for the show] that this Assembling to see those Tricks or Slights of hand, & bestowing their money to support men who in that capacity were of no use in the world, was Contrary to the Nature of Christian Religion."

Owners built taverns near the churches or meeting houses, and the worshippers stopped in at the heated taverns before attending meetings in the heatless churches. Because this practice led some to become too drunk to get to the meetings, the legislature prohibited the sale of spirits during the hours of church services. "The townsmen," said one observer, "were frozen out of the taverns to be frozen in the meeting-houses."

The precautions against gambling in taverns did not inhibit the bettors. The General Assembly in 1739 found "to the great Grief and Concern of all sober and well disposed Persons, that many of the Inhabitants of the Province, of mean and low Fortunes do make it their constant Practice to frequent Taverns [where they gamble and drink] to the Great Damage, Affliction and Distress of their poor Families, and Destruction of themselves."

Government and the Economy to 1756

Once New Jersey became a royal colony, the bureaucracy of the English colonial system replaced the proprietors. Power now shifted to the appointed governor, and the economic and political wars between proprietors and settlers now reshaped themselves into struggles between the everyday settlers and the governors, who invariably sided with the wealthier classes.

Since the governor represented the Crown, the confrontations between governor and settlers played a role in causing New Jerseyans to consider breaking with the mother country. Until 1738 the governors of New Jersey were also governors of New York, causing the New Jersey Assembly to feel that "the heart burnings amongst the Inhabitants [of New Jersey], and the Grievances of the Country are not known and understood, or at least never regarded."

Worse, Lord Cornbury, the first governor of the united Jerseys, was an unqualified disaster. To govern the Jerseys, Queen Anne selected Edward,

Left: Edward Hyde, Viscount Cornbury, was appointed royal governor of New York and later first royal governor of New Jersey by his counsin, Queen Anne. His administration was generally considered a disaster. Lewis Morris and Samuel Jennings complained to the Assembly that Cornbury " . . . forfeited respect publicly appearing in woman's attire." A long series of administrative blunders and misdeeds resulted in the Assembly's condemnation of him in 1708. Courtesy, Special Collections, Alexander Library, Rutgers University

Right: Nephew and ward of Colonel Lewis Morris, owner of Tinton Manor in Monmouth County, Governor Lewis Morris was active in the provincial affairs of New York and New Jersey, working assiduously for the appointment of a separate governor for the latter. In 1738, he became New Jersey's first royal governor. From Memorial Cyclopedia Of New Jersey, *1915*

Lord Cornbury, her black-sheep cousin. Lord Cornbury had dissipated his fortune and was trying to recoup by using his political connections to profit in the New World. Cornbury already had secured the governorship of New York for himself when he was appointed governor of New Jersey.

Cornbury ruled with advice from an appointed council of men of wealth and influence who had administrative, judicial, and legislative powers. "The people" elected the assembly. But only those with 100 acres could vote for the assembly, and only those with 1,000 acres of land could sit in it. Since the assembly alone could tax, it could coerce the governor. Cornbury, however, could prorogue and dissolve the assembly and call for new elections to get assemblies that suited his purposes.

Little interested in the rights of the settlers, Cornbury alienated almost

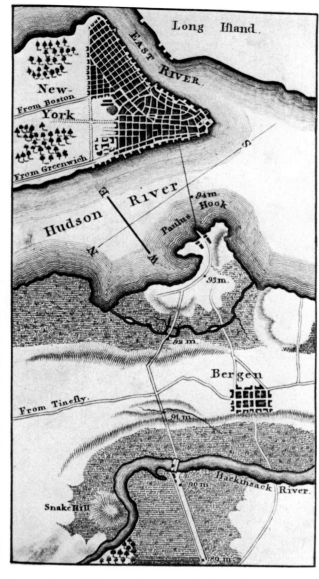

everyone in New Jersey. He took a bribe to fix an election, formed a "ring" to sell more than a half-million acres of New Jersey land, and throughout his term he battled the assembly over money. He persuaded the assembly to pass a Militia Act which angered the Quakers, and—in what some said was an attempt to resemble Queen Anne—he persisted in wearing women's clothes in public.

Under the leadership of Lewis Morris, Cornbury's opponents in the assembly fired off a detailed complaint about him to the secretary of state in England. Among other things, Morris attacked Cornbury for "dressing publickly in women's clothes every day and putting a stop to all Publique business while he is pleasing himself with yt (sic.) peculiar but detestable magot." Queen Anne thereupon removed her fortune-hunting cousin. The assembly thanked the Queen for "putting an end to the worst administration New Jersey ever knew." Following the short-lived governorships of John, Lord Lovelace, and Richard Ingoldsby, Robert Hunter became governor in 1710. He soothed political feelings in New Jersey, replaced the Cornbury hacks with more able councilmen, and introduced a variety of healing reforms. Called "the most nearly ideal governor colonial New Jersey ever had" by historian Donald L. Kemmerer, Hunter is remembered today by the county that bears his name.

William Burnet, another governor with a good sense of the political tides

This painting shows the Campbell brothers producing wampum strings and shell ornaments in their factory in what is now Park Ridge in Bergen County. The business was established in 1775 as a cottage industry by John Campbell, and counted among its customers John Jacob Astor, who used wampum in trading for furs. Courtesy, Newark Public Library

in New Jersey, followed Hunter and was succeeded by James Montgomerie and then by William Cosby. Under Montgomerie and Cosby, the assembly moved to center stage. When Cosby died in 1736, the Crown wisely determined that New Jersey should have its own governor.

In 1738 the Queen appointed Lewis Morris as New Jersey's first governor independent of New York. Morris was the man who had led the attack on Cornbury. By Morris's time, people began to settle the regions outside the Delaware and Raritan valleys. New Jerseyans established Newton, Westfield, Bordentown, Plainfield, Mt. Holly, Morristown, Dover, and Freehold. Inhabitants widened many of the ruts that called themselves New Jersey's roads and improved them to the point that freight carriers could advertise the shipment of goods "once every week" between Burlington and Perth Amboy.

Formerly the "people's champion," Morris became self-centered and fought with both council and assembly. Something of a common scold, Morris repeatedly sided with the proprietors against the townsmen and squatters in the traditional squabbles about land and quitrents. The assembly cut his pay. He scalded them with vituperation.

In 1745 officials arrested one Essex County squatter named Samuel Baldwin and two others and threw them into the Newark jail for "making great havock with his saw mill of the best timber" on a proprietor's land. Popular sentiment in the town ran strongly with Baldwin and against the proprietary upper classes. A mob assembled outside the Broad Street jail in Newark. "Armed with Cudgels [they] rescued the Prisoners in a very violent Manner." Morris denounced the riots as "high treason." Such outbreaks, he said, were all "too likely to end in Rebellion and throwing off His Majesty's Authority." Morris died shortly thereafter, but in 1776 his prophecy proved accurate.

Paper Money Becomes Scarce

If the problems of squatters were one harbinger of the American Revolution, scarce money was another. Because New Jersey imported more than she exported, capital flowed out of the colony to England. Capital investment from England, Scotland, Sweden, and Holland had, of course, financed the settlements in New Jersey. But when the trade balance tipped slightly in the colony's favor in the eighteenth century, shipping costs and other services demanded by English merchants soon offset the flow of capital from Europe.

Since settlers bartered, they did not need much money. They could pay taxes, for example, in beaver skins. To expand the available hard currency, mostly silver Spanish dollars, the colonists began to cut them into quarters (two bits), eighths, and sixteenths. But the shortage of paper money in a developing economy repeatedly disrupted Crown-colony relations, and the Crown was insensitive to the problem until it was too late.

To buy land from the Indians, the New Jersey settlers used wampum. Settlers of Bergen paid eighty fathoms of wampum for their lands. Newark cost 850 fathoms of wampum. To no one's surprise, the settlers began to produce wampum in such quantity that it lost its value. Franklin Township

Commissioners of the Monmouth County loan office granted William Lawrie of Freehold £47.17.4 in bills of credit secured by the mortgage recorded here. Lawrie was required to pay 5 percent interest and to repay a portion of the principal annually. Courtesy, New Jersey Room, Fairleigh Dickinson University

in Bergen County was one counterfeiting center. William Campbell made so much wampum that his home was known as "The Mint."

Old World tokens such as "Newbie coppers" or "Patrick pence," copper coins brought to the New World by Mark Newbie from Ireland, circulated as money in the Gloucester County area. The West Jersey Assembly endorsed such uses, with the following caveat: "said Mark, give sufficient security to the Speaker of This House for use of the General Assembly from time to time being, that he the said Mark, his executors and administrators, shall and will change the said half-pence and pay equivalent upon demand; and provided also that no Person or Persons be here obliged to take more than five shillings in one payment."

To expand the supply of money, the Assembly in 1723 created an office to loan £40,000 in amounts averaging £35 for a period of twelve years. The precursors of our modern banks, the loan offices issued denominations from one shilling to 3, carrying 5 percent interest. Counties received quotas to loan, and the system was repeated in 1733. As the bills neared their retirement dates, however, they deflated. After 1740 Parliament disallowed them.

The assembly in 1709 also issued, in small amounts, bills of credit with no backing. Tax collectors accepted these at face value. Tried again in the French and Indian War, the colony raised some £342,500 with bills of credit. Parliament disallowed this issuance of paper in 1764, but it reversed itself and allowed another £100,000 issue in 1774. Unfortunately, this reversal came after the Boston Tea Party, when sentiment against the mother country was already running high.

The Colonists Rebel

The Tea Crisis itself emerged from the settlements of the French and Indian War of 1756-1763, a war which set in motion forces that would bring revolution. England battled France for colonial supremacy, William Pitt and the British navy destroyed French commerce, choking off French sugar trade with the Caribbean, and crushed the French in India.

To British appeals for money the New Jersey Assembly responded that the colony was simply too poor to raise funds—unless, of course, the Crown would allow a new loan office bill for £70,000. Only after the French and Indians defeated General Edward Braddock and Lieutenant Colonel George Washington on the Monongahela River, and some braves penetrated Sussex County, did New Jersey even fortify her western areas.

In 1757 the Crown relented and allowed the assembly to pass two loan-office bills. The assembly then built some barracks for British troops in New Brunswick, Perth Amboy, Trenton, Burlington, and Elizabethtown. New Jersey also sent militiamen under Colonel Peter Schuyler of Newark to fight in New York State, but they were overcome by Montcalm's forces at Oswego.

The British victory over the French and the 1763 Treaty of Paris weakened French power in North America. But it also ended a period of benign neglect of the colonies by Parliament. To raise money to pay off the debt incurred in fighting the war and to improve, systematize, and tighten the mercantile system to deal with smugglers, Parliament passed a series of laws between 1763 and 1765 that brought forth the protests that would ultimately separate the colonies from the mother country.

Parliament blundered first in the Proclamation of 1763, which blocked settlement beyond the Appalachian Mountains and angered land speculators and Westerners. The Sugar Act of 1764 lowered the six-pence-per-gallon tax on molasses imported from non-British sources to three pence per gallon but stipulated that violators would be tried in vice-admiralty courts. The act also provided for odious writs of assistance and further tax increases on a variety of non-British imports.

To protect creditors in England, to whom New Jersey settlers owed nearly £350,000, Parliament then banned issuance of currency in the American colonies in the Currency Act of 1764. To house the 10,000 troops being sent to defend the colony, Parliament demanded the erection of more barracks under the Quartering Act of 1764.

The Stamp Act of 1765 turned the tide of public sentiment. This tax on newspapers, almanacs, pamphlets, broadsides, legal documents, insurance policies, ship's papers, licenses, and playing cards could be used to pay the New Jersey governor's salary, thus depriving the New Jersey Assembly of a main check on Governor William Franklin. Moreover, this first direct tax fell on groups able to marshal public opinion. New Jersey lawyers met in Perth Amboy and resolved not to transact business requiring stamps. Elizabethtown crowds gathered to hear spokesmen label the Stamp Act the "overthrow of long-enjoyed, boasted and invaluable liberties." According to the *New York Gazette*, the Elizabethtown residents were united in their hostility against any "Stamp pimp, informer, favourer and encourager of the execution of said act."

Up and down the American coast, the Sons of Liberty forced the stamp collectors to resign. Massachusetts called for the assembling of a Stamp Act

New Jersey's last royal governor, William Franklin, son of Benjamin Franklin, received his royal appointment in 1763. Interested in practical reforms, Franklin's tenure was relatively harmonious until the outbreak of the Revolutionary War. For his outspoken loyalty to the Crown, Franklin was sent to a Connecticut prison in 1776 by order of the Provincial Congress. In 1779 the King granted him a pension. Franklin died in England in 1813. From Contributions to the Early History of Perth Amboy and Adjoining Country, *1856*

Left: Richard Stockton, first of the New Jersey delegation to sign the Declaration of Independence, was a graduate of the College of New Jersey (now Princeton). He was appointed to Governor Franklin's Provincial Council in 1768, and he served as a delegate to the Continental Congress in 1776-1777. During the Revolutionary War his capture was actively sought by the British. Courtesy, Special Collections, Alexander Library, Rutgers University

Right: John Hart, nicknamed "Honest John Hart," was another of New Jersey's political leaders who suffered great personal losses in the Revolutionary War. With only a modest education, Hart owned a large farm in Hopewell, operated two mills, and held political office under both the colonial and state governments. When British forces invaded New Jersey, Hart fled his home, but later returned to Trenton and was elected speaker of the Assembly. He died in 1779, his health broken by the privations he suffered while eluding the British. Courtesy, Special Collections, Alexander Library, Rutgers University

Congress in New York. After some delay, New Jersey Assembly Speaker Robert Ogden, Hendrick Fisher, and Joseph Borden attended for the colony. Although Ogden disapproved of John Dickenson's famous "Declaration of Rights and Grievances," which the Congress adopted, the New Jersey Legislature approved it and agreed to the boycott on English goods.

"The only representatives of the people of this colony," said the unanimously endorsed resolutions of the New Jersey Assembly in November 1765, "are people chosen by themselves, and . . . no taxes . . . can be imposed on them . . . but by their own legislature."

The boycott worked. English exports to the colonies fell. Parliament repealed the Stamp Act. But in the Declaratory Act of March 1766, she asserted her authority to make laws binding on the American colonies "in all cases whatsoever." Parliament then compounded this blunder by refusing to approve a new loan-office bill and by endorsing the Townshend Acts of 1767, which taxed glass, lead, paints, paper, and tea.

Parliament then attempted to rescue the near-bankrupt East India Company by giving it a virtual monopoly on tea sales in the American colonies. This last assertion of the mercantile minds of London, the 1773 Tea Act, pushed the American colonists into open rebellion. Bostonians dumped the tea into the Charles River and New Jerseyans burned a shipload of the tea at Greenwich on the Cohansey River.

An outraged Parliament retaliated with the Coercive (or "Intolerable") Acts of 1774, closing the port of Boston and annulling the Massachusetts Charter, among other things. Members of the New Jersey Committee of Correspondence met in New Brunswick on July 21, 1774, to condemn Parliament's taxes, to agree not to consume or import English goods, and

Right: The only clergyman to sign the Declaration of Independence, John Witherspoon came from Scotland in 1768 to become president of the College of New Jersey, now Princeton University. An outspoken patriot, he was a member of the First Provincial Congress in 1775, and the following year, a delegate to the Continental Congress where he served for seven years. Courtesy, Special Collections, Alexander Library, Rutgers University

Left: Abraham Clark was born in 1726 on his father's farm in what is now Roselle. At the outbreak of the Revolution he served in the first New Jersey Provincial Congress and the Committee of Safety. In 1776 he was sent to Congress where he signed the Declaration of Independence and served throughout the war, always championing the rights of the common man. Courtesy, Newark Public Library

to approve the convening of an intercolonial congress. New Jersey and eleven other colonies shortly afterward sent delegates to the Continental Congress in Philadelphia's Carpenters Hall.

The First Continental Congress restated colonial objections to Parliament's actions and organized resistance to importing from and exporting to England. On April 19, 1775, British troops fought New Englanders on Lexington Green.

Four days later, Newark residents cheered the dispatch rider who brought the news of the fighting in Lexington and Concord. On May 23, 1776, New Jersey's first Provincial Congress, a revolutionary government, met in Trenton, created a militia system, and provided for annual elections of the members of a permanent new government. The new, more democratic New Jersey Constitution provided the vote for every male whose property of any kind was worth £50.

That July the Second Continental Congress adopted the Declaration of Independence, which New Jersey delegates Richard Stockton of Princeton, John Hart, farmer from Hopewell, Bordentown's Francis Hopkinson, Abraham Clark of Elizabethtown, and Dr. John Witherspoon, president of the College of New Jersey, signed.

Governor William Franklin, who had stayed loyal to the Crown throughout his term, had found himself unable to halt the tide of revolution. The Provincial Congress declared Franklin to be in contempt of the Continental Congress and arrested him. The revolutionaries then took him "as delicately as may be" to Connecticut, where Governor Jonathan Trumbull, ardent revolutionary, could keep him under house arrest.

In 1782 Franklin went to England, where he remained until his death in 1813. A new General Assembly elected in 1776 selected William Livingston as the first governor of the new State of New Jersey. It remained to be seen, now that New Jersey was about to break free from mercantilism, whether its economy would blossom or wither in wartime.

Chapter Three

Economic Growth as a New State

Flags bedeck Robert L. Stevens' innovatively designed side-wheeler, the Trenton, built at Hoboken in 1825. This Delaware River steamboat ran from Philadelphia to Bordentown, and, after 1834, to Burlington, where passengers boarded cars of the Camden and Amboy Railroad, visible in the background. At Amboy they continued their journey by steamer to New York. Courtesy, Camden County Historical Society

Unfortunately, as the bridge between two key Northern port cities, New Jersey became the "cockpit" of the American Revolution. The war disrupted New Jersey's business and economic life perhaps more than any other colony's. After the war, New Jersey struggled through economic depression, a currency shortage, and tariff wars. New Jersey then played a significant role in the creation of the United States Constitution, which helped stabilize intercolonial trade. The outbreak of the French Revolution shortly afterward brought war orders and helped to revive the economy. During these first fifty years as a state, New Jerseyans developed some banking and insurance institutions; built roads and bridges; designed, built, and ran steamboats; built an experimental industrial city in Paterson; and launched the leather, jewelry, and carriage industries in Newark. In short, like people in a modern emerging nation, New Jerseyans between 1776 and 1826 fought their war of independence and then struggled to develop their new state.

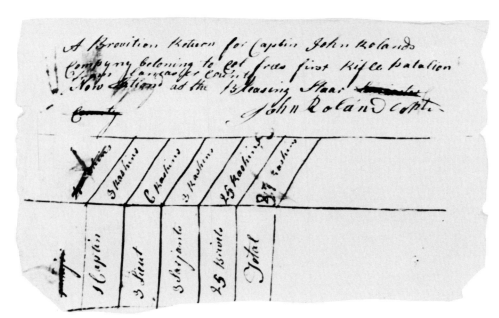

The American Revolution Jolts the Economy

The American Revolution proved a great economic and political trial for New Jersey. General Washington took refuge in New Jersey throughout the war. Armies of both sides crossed the state at various times and plundered or seized goods and property.

Washington's retreat from New York City in 1776 took him from Fort Lee to Trenton. Newark's Tories waved handkerchiefs to the entering British army that November. Because Lord Cornwallis lingered in Newark from November 28 to October 2, Washington was able to escape. As the two armies tramped across the state, they were so close at times that they could hear each other's music. Since they both lived off the land, they ravaged New Jersey's economy.

Bordentown resident Thomas Paine traveled with Washington on that retreat and on the head of a drum in a New Jersey camp wrote *The Crisis*. "These are," Paine wrote, "the times that try men's souls. The summer soldier and the sunshine patriot will, in this crisis shrink from the service of the country."

Washington retreated into Pennsylvania. On December 26 he staged the masterful dawn attack on Colonel Jonathan Rall's Hessians at Trenton. Days later Washington again outmaneuvered Cornwallis at Princeton and went into winter quarters in the Morristown hills.

After the horrible suffering and death during that winter of 1777-1778 at Valley Forge, Washington struck out in the spring and pursued General Clinton across New Jersey. On June 28, 1778, he engaged Clinton's forces near Monmouth Court House. Mrs. Mary Ludwig Hays had followed cannoneer husband John to the battle of Monmouth, where she carried a pitcher of water for the soldiers. "Molly Pitcher" also replaced him at his cannon when he was wounded.

The American forces beat back repeated attacks by the redcoats, who withdrew during the night to Sandy Hook and boarded transports for New York City. The Battle of Monmouth ended the struggle for New Jersey. The British turned their attention from the New Jersey war zone to the South.

Savannah fell in 1778 and Charleston, South Carolina, collapsed in 1780. During this phase of the war, New Jersey privateers moved out of southern New Jersey harbors to pester British shipping. Washington's winter at Morristown in 1779-1780 proved "a period of far worse suffering," according to expert Douglas Southall Freeman, "than the corresponding months of 1777-1778 at Valley Forge." Economic conditions for the state and the young nation grew dismal. In Morristown Connecticut regiments, unpaid for five months, mutinied, only to be halted by Pennsylvania troops.

That spring Continental Colonel Elias Dayton and General William Maxwell's New Jersey Brigade repulsed two attempts by Hessian General William von Knyphausen to advance to Morristown through Elizabethtown. Then, fearing that General Clinton, who had returned from the South, might move on West Point, Washington shifted some of his Morristown forces in 1781 to New Windsor, New York.

But the young government could not pay its soldiers. When the Pennsylvania Line veterans in Morristown mutinied in January 1781 and marched toward Philadelphia, it took the intervention in Princeton of the president of Pennsylvania's Executive Council to persuade them back to camp. Over half of them left the service. A similar mutiny in Pompton, New Jersey, that winter forced Washington to execute two of the mutineers.

In August of that year, Washington and the French forces from New York again marched across the state to pin Lord Cornwallis down on the Virginia shore at Yorktown. With the French fleet of Baron De Grasse in

This photograph shows the Old Barracks in Trenton after the building was restored by the Old Barracks Association. Built by the British in 1758 and 1759 during the French and Indian War, it housed troops until 1765. British and Hessian troops as well as Loyalist refugees were quartered here until the Battle of Trenton, after which the facility was used by American and French forces. Courtesy, Newark Public Library

command of the sea, Cornwallis surrendered to the rebels. Eight thousand British laid down their arms to concede the American Revolution to the Continental forces.

The *New Jersey Gazette*, New Jersey's only paper, proclaimed the news seven weeks later. In Trenton, Governor William Livingston and the legislature gave thanks at the Presbyterian Church. At Princeton a member of the faculty gave an "address suited to the institution of the day," and at New Brunswick, celebrants gathered in "festivity and gladness" at the local tavern.

The problems of finance, however, still plagued the Congress created in 1781 under the Articles of Confederation. When Pennsylvania troops marched on Philadelphia to demand their back pay, Elias Boudinot reassembled the Congress in his hometown of Princeton. Thus it was that Washington formally accepted the thanks of his government in Nassau Hall. In Princeton on November 1, 1783, the Congress received the news of the conclusion of the definitive treaty between Great Britain and the United States.

This William Faden map, published in 1784, shows the position of General Knyphausen's forces after they had withdrawn to Elizabeth Town Point following the battle of Connecticut Farms in June 1780. John Hills, who prepared the map, was a surveyor and engineer and military mapper for British General Sir Henry Clinton. Courtesy, New Jersey State Museum Collection, Trenton

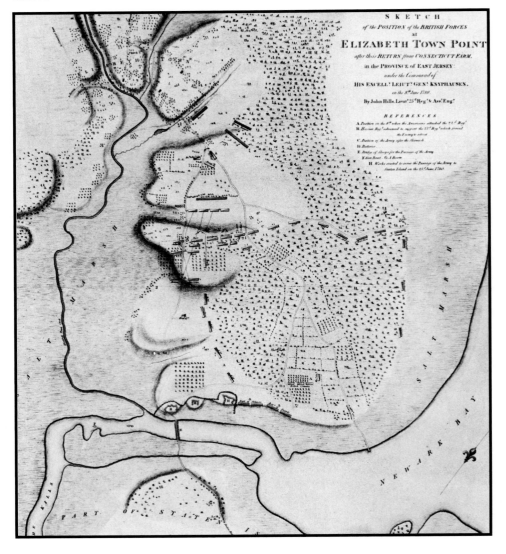

NEW-JERSEY GAZETTE.

WEDNESDAY, MAY 3, 1780.

Primarily conceived as a vehicle to combat Loyalist propaganda and to rally support for the Revolutionary cause, the New-Jersey Gazette *was published by Isaac Collins from 1777 until 1778 in Burlington, and later in Trenton. In addition to its coverage of the war, the paper carried international news, classified advertisements, and public notices. Courtesy, New Jersey Room, Fairleigh Dickinson University*

Stagecoach Travel

New Jersey was the birthplace of the American stagecoach. The state's earliest indigenous vehicles were the Jersey Wagons, which emerged in the 1730s. Used to transport goods, the wagons were enormous, with huge wheels and cloth-covered tops, and teams of four to six horses were needed to pull them. When New Jersey got into the business of transporting people, the Jersey Wagon was slightly cut down in size, and it became the first American stagecoach.

Colonial New Jersey was primed for such major developments in transportation because of its pivotal position between America's two most important cities of the time, New York and Philadelphia. Bringing products of the farming and iron industries to these markets made development of a road system imperative. By the early 1700s a transportation system for goods had already emerged with the Jersey Wagon, and a stagecoach system for people was on the way.

As early as 1773 an advertisement in a Philadelphia newspaper proclaimed that Solomon Smith and James Moon were running two "stage wagons" between Burlington and Perth Amboy. Their schedule was once a week— "or off'ter if . . . business presents." This venture constituted the first regular public transportation service in American history.

Rival stagecoach drivers soon appeared, some trying alternate routes to speed the journey. By 1738, new stage wagons were running a route between Trenton and Brunswick. In 1740 a third route was running from South Amboy to Bordentown on the Delaware River. Competition was intense, causing operators to improve their service with changes of horses, stronger wagons, and more direct routes. They filled the newspapers with advertisements accusing one another of cheating their customers. The public, however, was getting its first taste of a fare war, profitting from lower rates and quicker travel due to competition.

SEA BATHING.

Philadelphia and Absecombe Accommodation Line of
STAGES.

THE Subscribers respectfully inform their friends and the public generally that they have established a new and superior line of Stages, which commenced on Monday, the 3d of August, inst. and run in the following order, to wit :

Leave Reeve's Ferry, Market street, Philadelphia, every Monday, Wednesday and Friday morning, at 4 1-2 o'clock, and Toy's ferry, Camden, at 5—and passing through Mount Ephraim, Chew's Landing, Blackwoodtown, Cross Keys, Squankum, Freewill and New Brooklyn Glassworks, Blue Anchor, Winslow Glassworks, Pennypot, Weymouth Ironworks, May's Landing, Catawba, and Somer's Point, arriving at Absecombe early in the afternoon. Returning, leave Absecomb on Tuesday, Thursday and Saturday morning, by the same route and arrive at Toy's ferry in season to reach the city the same afternoon.

Fare as heretofore.

Six sets of excellent horses and good stages, have been provided, which together with careful drivers, and strict attention to the comfort and accommodation of passengers, it is hoped will ensure a liberal share of public patronage. It may be remarked, that Somer's Point and Absecomb, possess superior advantages for bathing, fishing, fowling, &c. and the accommodations at both places are excellent.

☞ For seats apply at May's Landing, to Capt. John Pennington, and Abraham Izzard—at Somer's Point to Mr. Somers.

WM. NORCROSS & CO.

Blackwood, Aug. 19, 1835—3m

In 1752 Joseph Borden, inaugurating a new stage line out of Bordentown, advertised a trip from New York to Philadelphia in "only" thirty to forty hours. This estimate only included the actual driving time: stopovers, delays, and breakdowns would make the trip about seventy-two hours. Nonetheless, this was a major improvement over the previous five-day journey. Today, trains cover the distance in one hour and thirty-five minutes.

As many as eight horses were needed to haul these wagons over the "roads" that were often dreadful dust heaps and mud bogs. Though stagecoaches were often brightly and attractively painted, they did not provide much comfort: a strip of leather nailed across the back of a seat was considered first-class travel. Washouts on the roads

In 1834 two or three stagecoaches left Camden daily for South Jersey. The stage line advertised here left Camden at 5:00 a.m. and arrived at "Absecome" (Atlantic City) "early in the afternoon." In addition to those interested in sea bathing, the stage would carry passengers bound for the iron and glass works along the route. Courtesy, Camden County Historical Society

were frequent, and passengers faced the constant danger of falling from the wagons. The only comfort on the trip was provided by roadside inns or "stage boats," which advertised "fine commodious cabins, fitted with tea tables and sundry other articles of convenience to add to the comfort of the ladies." At the end of the stagecoach journey at the water's edge of either the Delaware or the Hudson, boats brought the traveler to his destination in New York or Philadelphia.

In 1764 a new stage company speeded the trip by starting a wagon in Philadelphia and sending it over the ferry at Trenton. The same year Sovereign Sybrandt came near to establishing an all-land route between New York and Philadelphia by running his stage overland from New Brunswick to Elizabethtown, then to Paulus Hook (Jersey City) by post road. Though he avoided the bays, his journey still required five ferryings. In 1771 the time of the trip was cut to two days by Joseph Mercereau's "Flying Machine" stagecoach, and within a few years heavy coaches greatly reduced the dangers of the journey.

The proliferation of stagecoaches convinced the New Jersey legislature to improve New Jersey's roads. During the 1790s, the state commissioned construction of bridges over the Passaic and Hackensack rivers (and later, the Raritan), and stagecoach travel improved. By the early 1800s the state was chartering turnpikes to replace the mud and log roads.

During the 1790s, a new toll road built from Newark's Passaic River bridge to the Hoboken ferry created a new and still-thriving species: the New Jersey commuter. Three stagecoaches per day carried people who "lived in Newark and had their business in New York" to Manhattan at six o'clock each morning, returning in the early evening after work.

One might suppose that the dangers of hurtling on high-speed thoroughfares are unique to the modern era, but that is not so: such dangers existed even in 1790. On their sometimes frenzied journeys, stagecoaches often flipped over, went out of control going down steep hills, and ran over pedestrians. The basic rules of traffic and safety were often ignored—much as some would say they are today.

Between 1801 and 1829, the legislature gave charters to fifty-one turnpike companies, and about half of them managed to build toll roads totaling some 550 miles. The Morris Turnpike, chartered in 1801, connected the upper Delaware Valley with Newark Bay and soon had four stagecoach companies competing for its travel routes. Another turnpike connected New Brunswick and Trenton, and the Middlesex Turnpike connected New Brunswick, Elizabethtown, and Newark. All these turnpikes further improved stage travel, and they also formed the basis for some of the best roads in the state today.

—David Fleming

Economic Problems Persist in Peace

Victory in war brought insecurity in peace. Economic problems beset New Jersey: shortage of money, loss of the skills and fortunes of the loyalists, inability to export due to the high tariffs of the bordering states, and the plunge of Continental currency. Marauding British troops had wreaked havoc. The counties of Bergen, Essex, Middlesex, Somerset, and Burlington together calculated some 2,000 instances of wartime destruction, each instance involving more than £100. In Middlesex alone the properties of 655 individuals had been either destroyed or seriously damaged by the war.

Loyalists had fled their estates and their debts. One Tory named John Edison went to Nova Scotia after the war. His descendants later moved to Ohio, where in 1847 a boy, Thomas Alva, was born. Fortunately for New Jersey, this loyalist descendant returned to Newark in 1871.

During the last two years of the war, Tories doing business with the British brought goods and hard money into the state, but after 1781 hard money became scarce. Without Congress's war orders, the state's iron industry declined.

The collapse of the Continental currency severely damaged the New Jersey economy. To replace the depreciated currency of $7 million, the state issued $291,000 "emission money," which—like the earlier issues of the loan office—was to be withdrawn as it depreciated. By 1784 the emission money had lost two-thirds of its face value. Another New Jersey issue offered to the public in 1786 plummeted by one-third before the Constitution forbade state issuance of paper money.

General depression gripped the state. The southern New Jersey glassworks halted production. England flooded New York and Philadelphia markets with cheap goods which attracted New Jersey cash. "A Plain Farmer" complained in the *New Jersey Gazette* of July 1782 that Americans were squandering their money on "British geegaws." He estimated that forty or fifty thousand pounds had flowed out of New Jersey. "We can deal with an open enemy," he continued, "but now, like worms, they are eating through the bottom of the vessel, and we go down without seeing our destruction." Governor William Livingston exhorted New Jerseymen to "have the patriotism to disappoint both Gaul and Albion in their arts to drain your every copper for their trifles and baubles!"

High tariffs in New York and Pennsylvania also hurt trade. To protest these tariffs, New Jersey repeatedly refused to pay its allotment of taxes until the central government was empowered to set uniform, national tariffs on imports. In 1786 state officials rebuffed a delegation of three which had come to plead for New Jersey's payment.

New York charged that goods entering tariff-free New Jersey were later smuggled into New York. But when New York attempted to end the illegal trade, New Jersey responded by taxing the lighthouse New York had placed at Sandy Hook. To attract international trade, the state government made Perth Amboy and Burlington free ports for twenty-five years. But sea trade in and out of these two cities never materialized. The commerce from Burlington, Salem, and Trenton also failed to develop. By pointing up the inadequacies in the central government's ability to tax imports, however, New Jersey's refusal to pay taxes prodded others to call for a constitutional convention.

With its own western expansion blocked by the new state of Pennsylvania, New Jersey also tried to ensure that western territories would be "national" rather than claimed by individual states. Under pressure from New Jersey and other states, Congress passed the 1787 Northwest Ordinance, which set the rules for the creation of new states in the West. Jerseymen

No. 110 Commiſſioner's Office.
June 10 1799

RECEIVED of *James Ewing*, Commiſſioner of Loans in the State of New-Jerſey, on Stock in the Funds of the United States, to the 31 Day of March 1799 the following Sums, viz.

For Intereſt and Principal on 6 per Cent. Stock, 9.73
Intereſt on 3 per Cent. Stock, 2.16

11.89

amounting to eleven
Dollars and eighty nine Cents, for which I have ſigned Duplicate Receipts.

Jos. Lewis

Henry Southard

11 89/100 Dollars.

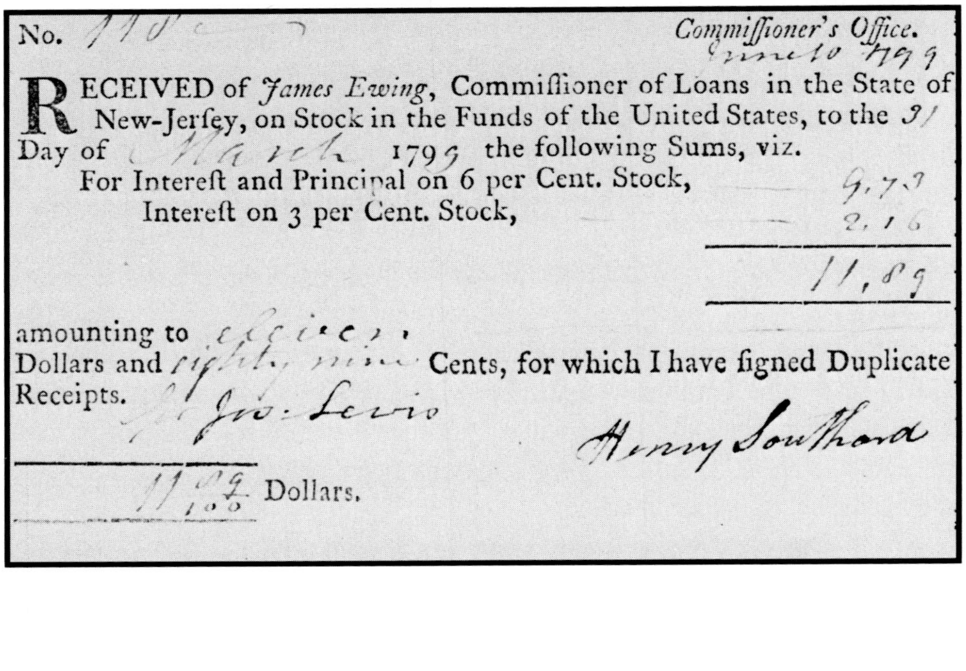

In response to a 1790 federal law to fund payment of national and state debts incurred during the Revolution, creditors holding certificates of the Debt of the State of New Jersey could exchange these for stock in the United States Treasury. The lower interest rate on Henry Southard's receipt pictured here was paid on his continental securities. Courtesy, New Jersey Room, Fairleigh Dickinson University

lounging about the streets, and leaning against door-posts, with quids of tobacco in their mouths, or segars stuck between their lips, and with dirty hands and faces.

Already, visionaries like Colonel John Stevens of Hoboken realized that road travel could be dramatically altered by the use of steam power. In 1783 Stevens had invented and patented a multitubular steam-engine boiler, but despite his advanced thinking about land railroads, steam power first altered the New Jerseyans' travel on water.

Entrepreneurs Launch Commerce On The Rivers

In 1786 steamboat inventor John Fitch persuaded the New Jersey Legislature to grant him a fourteen-year charter for exclusive steamboat rights on the Delaware River. During the late eighteenth century, the spindly, hollow-chested inventor had experimented with a variety of boats. Eventually he attached paddles to a drum and produced the side-wheel steamboat. His craft steamed between Philadelphia and Burlington on a regular basis, once covering the twenty miles in a record three hours and ten minutes. In the

Facing page, left: Jacob Bonnell, clock-maker of Chatham, made this tall case clock which bears his name in the lunette on the dial. Son of Captain Nathaniel Bonnell and grandson of Nathaniel, an early settler in the Passaic Valley, Jacob was born in 1767 and died in 1841. The inventory made of his possessions after his death listed six unfinished clocks, one "musick clock," and clockmaking tools. Courtesy, Collection of the Newark Museum

Facing page, right: Travel by stage decreased as railroads crossed the state. Like other stage lines, the Newark and Elizabeth Town stage attempted to compete by offering passengers door-to-door service. Courtesy, Newark Public Library

1790s he averaged eight miles an hour on runs between Philadelphia and Trenton.

But Fitch failed to move swiftly enough to get into the Hudson River traffic ahead of his competitor, Robert Fulton. In fact, when Fulton secretly gained access to his plans and drawings, Fitch grew despondent and abandoned the Delaware for Kentucky, where he committed suicide.

Fulton in 1808 secured a monopoly from the New York Legislature for steam navigation in the waters of the state of New York. Simultaneous with Fulton's acquisition of the rights on the Hudson, Colonel John Stevens of Hoboken, who had been improving steam boilers, completed his 100-foot ship *Phoenix*, which averaged over 5.5 miles an hour.

But no New Jerseyan could break the monopoly granted Fulton on the Hudson River. Stevens took his *Phoenix* out in the Atlantic and down to

Above: John Fitch launched this craft on the Delaware River in 1787, one year after he received exclusive rights in New Jersey to construct and operate steamboats. The Perservance was propelled by twelve steam-driven paddles, six on each side. From The Original Steam-boat Supported; or a Reply to Mr. James Rumsey's Pamphlet, 1788

In a reversal of roles, ferrymen transport horses across the Delaware River in this early view of the Market Street ferry in Camden. Although some ferries at the time sported sail, the rowboat had no need to depend on a favorable breeze. Steamboats did not make an appearance until 1810. Courtesy, Camden County Historical Society

the Delaware River, making it the first steamboat to travel the open seas. Thomas Gibbons of Elizabeth defied Fulton's Hudson River monopoly. His *Bellona* steamboat sailed the Hudson from the Jersey side carrying the banner "New Jersey Must Be Free!"

It fell to Thomas Gibbons, who had a federal steamboat license, to take Aaron Ogden, the successor to the Fulton monopoly, to court over the rights to steam navigation between New York and New Jersey. Chief Justice John Marshall in 1824 broadly construed the commerce clause in the famous *Gibbons* v. *Ogden* decision. Marshall argued that Congressional power to regulate interstate and foreign commerce did "not stop at the jurisdictional lines of the several states." Although too late to aid Fitch, the decision freed interstate transportation from state control.

James Silk Buckingham, a member of the British Parliament who lectured and toured America in the 1830s, wrote in *America, Historical, Statistical and Descriptive* that between New York, Jersey City, and Hoboken

there are steam ferry-boats going every hour of the day and these are as comfortable as bridges, for persons in carriages need not alight but may drive onto the boat, and remain there undisturbed to the end of the passage and then drive on shore again; while passengers not riding or driving are accommodated with pleasant cabins and warm and comfortable fires.

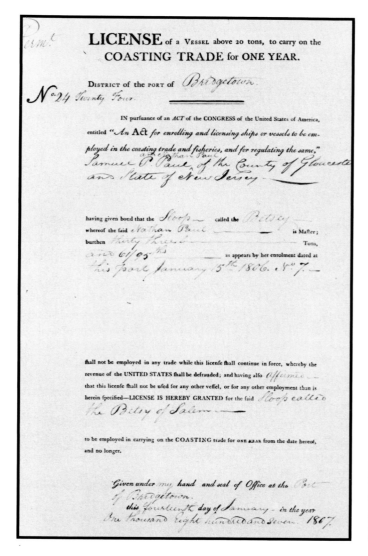

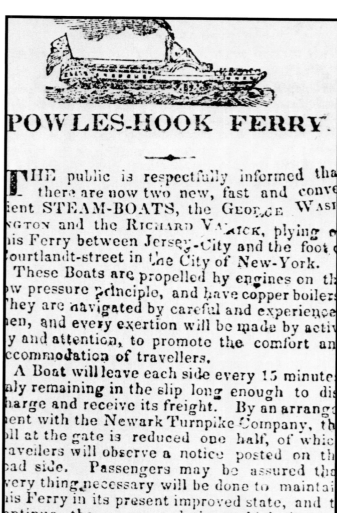

Jersey City at this time, Buckingham noted, was "chiefly occupied with trade and is a busy and thriving city."

Miss Anne Royall, a Southerner who toured the United States between 1824 and 1829, recalled the thrills of steamboats racing across the Hudson:

No sooner were we in the boats . . . than the steam was liberally plied to the wheels, and a race between the "Legislator" and the "Olive Branch," commenced from New York. The former was our heroine, and a stately boat she was; but although she drew up alongside somewhat boldly, and sometimes had the presumption to run ahead, which her ability to sail in shoal water enabled her to do; often, however, she lagged behind. It was quite an interesting sight to see such vast machines, in all their majesty, flying as it were, their decks covered with well-dressed people face to face, so near to each other as to be able to converse. It is well calculated to amuse the traveller, were it not for a lurking fear that we might burst the boilers. I confess for one, I would rather lose the race than win it, (which we did,) under such circumstances.

Above, right: Ferry rights at Powles Hook were acquired by a corporation named Associates of the Jersey Company, incorporated in 1804. Steamboats advertised here replaced a more primitive type built for the company by Robert Fulton. As the advertisement states, the ferries ran every fifteen minutes between Jersey City and New York, with special discounts for Newark travelers. Courtesy, Newark Public Library

Above, left: The Port of Bridgeton controlled all marine traffic in Southern New Jersey below Camden. Located at the head of navigation on the Cohansey River, Bridgeton was an important harbor for the coasting trade. Small vessels like the Betsey of Salem moved passengers and freight along the coast far more rapidly than was possible by inland transportation. Courtesy, New Jersey Room, Fairleigh Dickinson University

The Steamboat in New Jersey

In the late eighteenth century, a rare few men dreamed of revolutionizing water travel by applying the principle of James Watt's stationary steam engine to sailing vessels.

Two of these men were John Fitch, an impoverished clock repairer from Connecticut who resided for a time in Trenton, and Colonel John Stevens, a wealthy engineer from Hoboken. They would pioneer efforts to bring the steamboat to New Jersey waters.

Early in 1786 New Jersey's legislature granted John Fitch exclusive rights to operate steam-propelled craft on New Jersey waters. That summer, Fitch took his first run on the Delaware River with a bizarre-looking craft decked out with a row of paddles on each side. This was America's first steamboat. This trial run was not especially well-received, but it was successful enough to justify construction of two more boats, which were completed in 1787 and 1788.

But John Fitch's masterpiece was his commercial steamboat of 1790. Following a regular schedule, it carried both freight and passengers to various points along the Schuylkill and the Delaware and made regular runs between Philadelphia and Trenton. However, "Poor John" Fitch, as he was known, lived up to his nickname on this project: despite its proven safety and seaworthiness, this steamboat received so little business that it was forced to shut down.

Although most people laughed at John Fitch's Delaware River steamboat follies, John Stevens saw the potential. In 1791 he obtained a patent for a new paddleboat engine with increased steam power and an improved boiler.

Seven years later, Stevens completed his steamboat at the Soho Works in Second River (now Belleville), and he tested this new craft on a trial voyage down the Passaic River. Six years after that, in 1804, he built another craft, the first steamboat in history to use twin propellers: the *Little Juliana*.

But it was not until 1808 that Stevens designed and constructed the *Phoenix*, his best boat, a steam ferry which ran between Hoboken and New York. The *Phoenix* was 100 feet long and 16 feet wide and traveled at over 5.5 miles per hour. This ship was a great success, but its promising career was cut short by the Hudson River monopoly that Robert Fulton and his financial backer Robert Livingston had obtained after Fulton sailed his steamboat *Clermont* up the river a year earlier, in 1807.

The Fulton-Livingston monopoly kept Stevens from using the *Phoenix* for the Hoboken-New York ferry route, so the daring colonel in June 1809 sailed the *Phoenix* out into the Atlantic Ocean and around Cape May to Philadelphia. The *Phoenix* thus became the first steamboat ever to sail on the open sea, and it headed up the Delaware for service there.

Stevens continued to fight the Fulton-Livingston domination of the Hudson. His ferry boat *Juliana* carried as many as 1,500 passengers daily between Hoboken and New York until 1813. But then the *Juliana* fled through Long Island Sound to Connecticut as six of Fulton's steamboats tried to catch her, but could not. Though Stevens had won that battle, Fulton and Livingston had essentially won the war.

Eventually, to fight Fulton's monopolistic hold on the Hudson River, Stevens and others used a clever new invention: the "teamboat" ferry. The boat's paddle wheels were driven by teams of horses which walked in circles on the boat deck to revolve the drive shaft. This craft actually operated successfully for some time, but by then Stevens had become more interested in steam power for railroads, an area in which he would achieve greater fame.

Later, the issue of Fulton-Livingston monopoly spawned some wild battles over New York Harbor. Though the power of interstate monopolies was rampant in the nineteenth century, there were many newcomers fighting fiercely, both in the courts and out on the water.

Particularly memorable were the efforts of a young steamboat captain from Staten Island named Cornelius Vanderbilt, who would later win much greater notoriety in the railroad business. Vanderbilt was the commercial ship captain of Elizabeth entrepreneur Thomas Gibbons. The bold young captain would ply the monopoly waters of Fulton and Livingston in his steamboat *Bellona*, craftily evading the enforcers of the Hudson River monopoly. His ship flew a flag from its bridge with the words, "New Jersey Must Be Free!" Vanderbilt's exploits were widely publicized and made him something of a folk hero on the New York waterfront.

But the real battle of the Hudson River monopoly—or actually, state monopolies in general—still had to be settled in the courts. The bitter dispute eventually reached the U.S. Supreme Court, which, through Chief Justice John Marshall, declared in 1824 that the monopoly could not rule interstate waters. Only Congress could regulate interstate commerce, Marshall wrote.

The monopoly had been defeated, thanks to the battling spirit of Cornelius Vanderbilt and Thomas Gibbons and the wisdom of Chief Justice Marshall. New York thus became a free port, and steamboat traffic, liberated from state monopolies, surged rapidly into the future.

—David Fleming

Banking and Insurance Appear

As commercial enterprise continued to grow in the market regions around Newark and Trenton, banking began. In May 1804 some Newarkers gathered at Archer Gifford's Tavern on Broad and Market streets to seek a charter for New Jersey's first bank, the Newark Banking and Insurance Company. Later known as "Old Bank," it issued its own notes, which pictured Israel Crane's quarry and Luther Goble's shoe factory. Trenton also chartered the Trenton Banking Company in 1804, and New Brunswick organized the Bank of New Brunswick in 1807.

The state legislature inserted in each of the four early charters a clause reserving a certain amount of stock to the state if the state legislature wanted to subscribe. If the state exercised its option, it could appoint directors and participate in profits. But rather than subscribe to the bank's stock, the legislature sold its rights, except in the case of the Trenton Banking Company.

The United States Treasury Department apparently deemed New Jersey economically insubstantial. The state did not qualify for a branch of the First Bank of the United States, founded by Alexander Hamilton, secretary of the treasury. When the charter of the Bank of the United States ran out in 1811, New Jersey's banks increased their own note issues, but at discounts up to 20 percent. In 1812 the state passed a law chartering six banks, among them the State Bank of Newark, which was born at a meeting of city leaders

Colonel John Stevens' "'76 House" lay on the slope above his ferry landing to offer refreshment to New Yorkers seeking rest amid the rural delights of Hoboken. Periaguas are docked at the landing and New York City appears in the background. From Hopoghan Hacking, *1895*

Above: One of the first banks to be chartered in the state, the Newark Banking and Insurance Company was incorporated in 1804. The bank's first president was Elisha Boudinot, a New Jersey Supreme Court justice, member of the Colonial Congress, and personal friend of George Washington. The bank was organized in Archer Gifford's tavern, and in 1805 completed the building shown here on Broad Street. The bank is now part of the Midlantic Bank system. Courtesy, Newark Public Library

This John Collins sketch of the Mechanics Bank in Burlington was doubtless executed shortly after the building's erection in 1845. In previous years, the West Jersey Proprietors of the London and Yorkshire Tenths met every April 10 under the willow tree at the right in the picture. From Views of the City of Burlington, N.J., *1847*

at Roff's Tavern. Cashiers, armed with swords and pistols, served also as night watchmen in those days and lived in the building to guard the money and notes, then kept in heavy, wooden, metal-bound boxes. Once or twice a week messengers on horseback would gallop into Newark with out-of-town notes for clearance.

In 1816 Congress chartered the Second Bank of the United States. Of the nineteen branches opened, again none was in New Jersey. Perhaps because of the state's lack of important commercial centers, the availability of banking facilities in New York and Philadelphia and their commercial dominance over New Jersey, the conservative New Jersey Legislature, or the agricultural dominance of the state, New Jerseyans developed banking haltingly.

New Jersey banks in the nineteenth century issued their own paper money, which they were required to back with gold or silver coins. This bank note from the Mechanics Bank, incorporated in 1831, emphasizes the city's debt to commerce and industry with engravings of land and water transportation, and a blacksmith at work. Courtesy, Newark Public Library

The state chartered only forty-two banks between 1804 and 1837, although Massachusetts chartered seventy-two between 1830 and 1836. The legislature also gave banking privileges in the state to various corporations. It chartered the Salem Steam Mill and Banking Company in 1822, the New Jersey Manufacturing Company in 1823, and the Morris Canal and Banking Company in 1824. Not until 1847, after the legislature passed a law to encourage the establishment of "mutual savings associations," did New Jersey get its first savings and loan association.

Between 1804 and 1832, fourteen New Jersey banks went bankrupt. The Second Bank of the United States ended in February 1836 as a result of President Andrew Jackson's opposition and the policies of the bank under Nicholas Biddle. Then following runaway Western land speculation, Andrew Jackson issued his "Specie Circular" requiring that hard money be paid for public lands. This decision curbed land speculation, but it launched the nationwide deflation and the Panic of 1837. New Jersey banks collapsed. The New Jersey Legislature suspended payments in hard cash. The state suffered through the depressed economy of the late 1830s.

Although the Newark Banking and Insurance company issued insurance, the insurance industry in the state began in earnest after an 1807 fire consumed a Market Street stable in Newark. The building had been insured, as had some others in New Jersey, through New York or London companies. Prompt payment of the claim by the insurer convinced a group to meet at an "early candle lighting" in the Court House. There the group formed the Newark Mutual Fire Assurance Company and named Joseph C. Hornblower, a young lawyer, as secretary. Hornblower later became chief justice of the Supreme Court of New Jersey.

The success of the Newark Mutual Fire Assurance Company promoted the development of mutual companies. Camden Fire Insurance Association began in 1841, New Brunswick Fire Insurance Company launched its

Above: Alexander Hamilton, who conceived the plan for the Society for Useful Manufactures, proposed to build a model for industrial production in the United States. He was the corporation's attorney and was also active in the planning, promotion, and financing of the new enterprise. Courtesy, Newark Public Library

Right: This is the seal of the Society for Useful Manufactures, the first business incorporated by the state of New Jersey. Incorporated in 1791, the SUM was responsible for the founding and development of the City of Paterson. Courtesy, Paterson Museum Archives

business in 1826, and Fireman's Mutual Insurance Company of Newark began in 1855. These mutual companies often took extra deposits which could be used to pay for losses and expenses after premiums had been exhausted. If these monies, which were credited by giving the depositor scrip, were not used, they were repaid to the depositor. Often later reorganized as stock companies, the mutual companies allowed the owners of the scrip to turn it in for stock certificates.

Even with its banks and insurance companies, the state still lagged behind others economically. Throughout the colonies during the years after the Revolution, Americans depended upon Great Britain for their manufactured products and shipped the British raw materials. The Americans relied upon English financiers for much of the investment capital in a developing economy. The industrial revolution which would revolutionize the United States and transform New Jersey was yet to come.

Experimental Paterson Struggles

A group of gentlemen led by Alexander Hamilton sought to develop American industry. In 1791 Hamilton issued a report on the necessity of establishing American manufacturing on a sound basis. He proposed that a Society for Useful Manufactures (SUM), a million-dollar corporation, be created to build an industrial city—a kind of American Manchester—to manufacture paper, sailcloth, linen, cotton cloth, shoes, thread, stockings, pottery, ribbons, carpets, brass, and ironware. "There are reasons," Hamilton wrote in the prospectus, "which strongly recommend the State of New Jersey. . . . It is thickly populated—provisions are there abundant and cheap. The State having scarcely any external commerce and no waste lands to be peopled can feel the impulse of no supposed interest hostile to the advancement of manufactures. Its situation seems to insure a constant friendly disposition."

After receiving other enthusiastic reports about the location on the Great Falls of the Passaic River, the SUM began the enterprise in Paterson in 1792. The SUM purchased 700 acres for something more than $8,000 and hired Pierre Charles L'Enfant to design the town and supervise its construction, including a system of raceways to bring waterpower to the mills. The SUM imported skilled mechanics from England and Scotland. The magnificent falls,

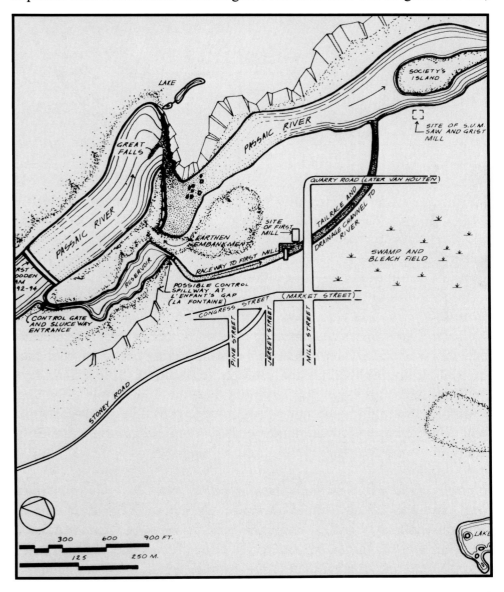

This plan shows the raceways designed for the SUM by Pierre L'Enfant, the French engineer who had previously drawn the plans for Washington, D.C. The SUM's first mill, located on this plan, was a stone cotton mill first operated by waterpower in 1794. Courtesy, Paterson Museum Archives

Above: The lottery tickets shown here were issued by the Society for Useful Manufactures under a provision of their charter that empowered them to raise $100,000 in this manner for protection against losses that the new corporation might incur in the opening stages of operation. Courtesy, Special Collections, Alexander Library, Rutgers University

Right: This "Shoemaker Map" was drawn in 1806 by Charles Basham, and is one of the earliest documents illustrating the industrial development of Newark—a community founded as an agricultural settlement. By 1806, one-third of Newark's inhabitants were employed in manufacturing, and the city was producing carriages, coach lace, leather shoes, and works of stone and marble. Courtesy, Newark Public Library

some thought, would eventually supply the power. Chartered by the New Jersey Legislature, named for Governor William Paterson, who signed the charter giving the six-square-mile area tax exemption, Paterson was launched under the leadership of Superintendent General Peter Colt from Connecticut. By 1794 Colt had developed a factory powered by the Passaic River. Between 1792 and 1797, the city grew from 50 to 500 inhabitants.

Unfortunately the SUM suffered from the collapse of the stock market in 1792, and from the crooked machinations of one of its principals. The million dollars was not raised (Hamilton had not invested any of his own money), the plans for the city were frequently altered, and the Society could not bring enough artisans to Paterson. Concentrating on cotton manufacture proved to be a mistake.

In 1795 the SUM abandoned the industrial empire, and Paterson struggled for decades. The Colt family purchased most of the shares and tried to lease shares of the power of the falls. President Jefferson's embargo

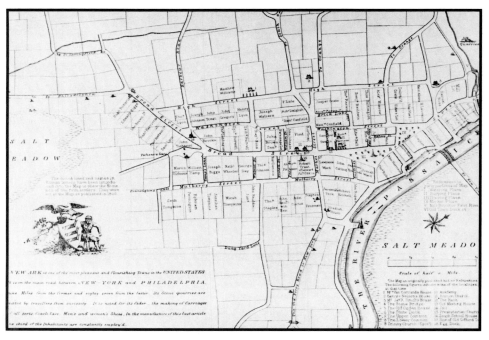

and the War of 1812 hurt Paterson's economy along with that of the rest of New Jersey. Colt's son John made cotton sailcloth for the U.S. navy. Paterson began manufacturing locomotives in the 1830s.

In the 1830s, after new entrepreneurs tried to revive the spinning factories, one Captain Frederick Marryat came away from Paterson to write in his Diary in America:

in such a beauteous spot you commune with Nature alone. But turn round with your back to the Fall—look below, and all is changed: art in full activity—millions of reels whirling in their sockets—the bright polished cylinders incessantly turning, and never tiring. What formerly was the occupation of thousands of industrious females, who sat with their distaff at

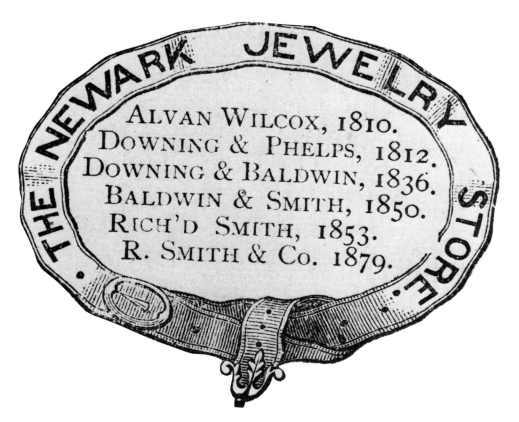

Operating variously from three Broad Street addresses, the Newark Jewelry Store provided a market for the city's silversmiths from 1810 to 1889. The store's cartouche, illustrated here, lists early Newark silversmiths and the dates from which the wares of each were carried by the store. Courtesy, Collection of the Newark Museum

the cottage door, is now effected in a hundredth part of the time. . . . But machinery cannot perform everything, and notwithstanding this reduction of labour, the romantic falls of the Passaic find employment for the industry of thousands.

Newark Develops

Newark grew slowly. Its enterprise centered on its shoemakers, headed by Moses Combs. Combs developed a business which Englishman John Davis said was "probably the largest cobblers' stall in the United States of America." The Duke de la Rochefaucault of France visited it in 1795. Combs employed, the duke estimated, "between three hundred and four hundred workmen."

Combs successfully developed an export market for his shoes in the South, and during Washington's second term he convinced the legislature to build a road from Newark Court House to Paulus Hook with drawbridges across the Passaic and Hackensack rivers. This gave Newark access to the ferries for New York and stimulated commerce in the city. During the early days of the nation, Newark was home to seven shoe manufacturers. Many shoemakers organized farmers to make shoes during the winter months on a putting-out basis. Organizers, or masters, gave the farmers the materials, did the selling, and paid by the piece. Eventually Newarkers opened small shops or factories. By 1826 a third of Newark's workers made shoes.

Newarkers also made carriages, saddles, harnesses, and jewelry. In the

1820s Newark employed some 200 carriage makers. In 1821 Smith and Wright moved their saddle and harness factory from Connecticut to Newark, where it eventually became the largest in the nation. Jewelry design and manufacture began in 1792, when Benjamin Cleveland traded gold and silver in the city. But Epaphras Hinsdale pioneered in jewelry. His 1801 firm eventually took in John Taylor, who, when Hinsdale died in 1811, joined with Colonel Isaac Baldwin to create the firm of Taylor & Baldwin, which then developed the manufacture of quality jewelry.

As Newark expanded, Orange broke away in 1806, and Bloomfield separated in 1813. But Newark had become a center for a variety of businesses. Newark's promoters put out a map which proclaimed:

Newark is one of the most pleasant and flourishing towns in the United States. It is on the main road between NEW YORK AND PHILADELPHIA, nine miles from the former and eighty seven from the latter. Its stone quarries are visited by travelers from curiosity. It is noted for its cider, the making of carriages of all sorts, coach lace, men's and women's shoes. In the manufacture of this last article one third of the inhabitants are constantly employed.

In the 1820s Newark had developed its central business district to the point that the town fathers decided to move the cemetery out of town. By 1826 assessor Isaac Nicholls noted that the population totaled 8,017—ten times that of 1776. Nicholls noted as well that there were seventeen factories, three distilleries, two breweries, and two gristmills. Newark had recently built a looking-glass plant and a tobacco factory. One scholar has concluded that more than three-fourths of Newark's labor force worked in manufacturing. The workers, however, still saw themselves as "mechanics" with artisan skills.

Above: This monogrammed silver ladle was made by Benjamin Horton Cleveland, clockmaker and silversmith, who came to Newark from Southold, Long Island, circa 1790. In June 1792 he advertised in Wood's Newark Gazette *that in addition to his wares in silver and gold, "he carefully repairs and cleans clocks [and] watches, for which he will receive country produce as the market price." Courtesy, New Jersey State Museum Collection, Trenton*

Facing page, right: This silver creampot was made by Nathaniel Coleman, a silversmith active in Burlington from 1787 until 1830. A Quaker and minister in the Society of Friends, Nathaniel, and his brother Samuel, were prolific silversmiths, filling orders from Burlington County and adjoining areas. Courtesy, New Jersey State Museum Collection, Trenton

Facing page, left: The beaker and goblets were from Baldwin and Co., an early firm of Newark jewelers and silversmiths. Isaac Baldwin, who lived at 399 Broad Street, was mayor of Newark in 1845. After his death in 1853, the firm continued until 1869. Newark Museum purchased these three pieces in South Carolina, which suggests that silverware was among the goods in the trade between Newark and the South before the Civil War. Courtesy, Collection of the Newark Museum

A true and perfect Inventory of all the personal
property including Ballances due on Book
Accounts of the Estate of Eph'l Hinsdale Dec'd
taken the 25 Day of Nov'r 1811 taken by the admin
istrators and appraised by Isaac Nichols &
Stephen Hays Sen'r ___

wearing apparel of the Deceased	35 ~
one watch	20 ~
one side Board Glass &c ~	40 ~
One Bureau Book Case & books	50 ~
One Marble time piece	45 ~
One Carpet & window Curtains	25 ~
Three Mahogany Tables & one Stand	10 ~
One Looking glass & Eleven pictures	10 ~
One pair hand Iron Shovel & tongs }	
& 5 Candlesticks Snuffers & Stands }	8 ~
10 Chairs & three window blinds	7 ~
2 trays & China	4 ~
1 Silver Tea pot Soup ladle 10 Table }	
Spoons 22 Tea Spoons	40 ~
	294 ~

THE RURAL VISITER.

" Homo sum ; humani nihil a me alienum puto."

VOL. I.   BURLINGTON, SEVENTH MONTH 30th, 1810.   No. 1.

☞ *Postmasters and others to whom this Number of the Rural Visiter is directed, will please to give the design such publicity as is immediately convenient; and forward to the Editor the names of such persons as may incline to patronize it, with the advance money, deducting commissions.*

PLAN OF THE RURAL VISITER.

THE conductor of this publication intends to make a fair trial, which may determine if a Gazette can succeed in these times, independent of the passions or the patronage of a party. It is not for him to censure the motives or scruple the prudence of other editors, who, taking political sides, derive from thence either profit or popularity.

It would seem indeed from the universality of this course, that a deviation might be regarded as hazardous, and a paper professing to belong to no political sect, for that reason be liable to incur the dislike of all. Notwithstanding the temper of the times, and the habit of the press in this particular, the editor cannot but hope a more flattering result from his attempt to cultivate *another* taste, by making "THE RURAL VISITER" a vehicle of useful and agreeable information to country people; information unmingled with bitterness and falsehood, designed to promote the felicities of a rational existence, and to gratify the desires of a laudable curiosity.

As centinels upon government, and the advocates of constitutional liberty, political journals might and ought to have, if united in their object and honestly conducted, a most salutary influence : but a degeneracy, baleful as it is universal, has fallen upon the high office of the press ; it has ceased to be the friend of man and the candid expositor of his rights and duties ; it no longer, even in profession, embraces the commonwealth of citizens seeking to express their feelings or sentiments : through its perversion, one half of the community is set against the other, a systematic proscription and opposition is on all sides maintained, and truth, utility, and true patriotism have lost their way and their influence amidst the conflicts of party, and the assumptions of ignorance and selfishness.

The public mind, always indeed aiming to be informed, is perplexed, and even confounded : subjects which it concerns a free and virtuous people to comprehend, and judge upon with a cool understanding, are obscured and distorted through the agency of party

newspapers : violent, if not sometimes venal, editors present to their respective subscribers, exaggerated and contradictory statements : confidence in the wisdom and virtue of our best men is thereby impaired, and this great Republic, (if the language and representations of these gazettes are true), would seem in its first stage of manhood to be sinking beneath corruption and imbecility : and it is to be feared, indeed, if they proceed in this career; the time is not far distant when these calamities will be realized upon a deceived and divided country.

On this troubled sea the editor intends not to adventure his little bark : he has not the resolution, even were he inclined, to engage in the conflict of such angry elements : if others take the care of our public liberties, and assume to direct the government, be theirs the honor and the reward : the publisher of a small sheet for the country, will be excused for choosing to follow an humbler path; he is content to leave the commonwealth to real statesmen and politicians, and if the gazetteers will not agree to this, then he submits its direction to *printers* for a party, and to parties who put their faith upon a printer. The time is not yet come when *truth*, even as it respects political transactions, is deemed worthy of common solicitude and common support. It is to be hoped the period will arrive when names shall not stand for principles, nor professions for conduct ; and when patriotism or love of country, undisguised with violence and calumny, shall shine out in its native dignity, breathing forbearance, charity, and public spirit, and animating all to deeds worthy of men and of christians.

It must suffice for the editor of this paper, to limit his views and his labors to the circle of social and common life : if he shall in any degree add to its *enjoyments* by the diffusion of useful knowledge, refine its manners by the instilment of just sentiments, or by incentives to industry and virtuous exertion, assist to mend the civil and moral condition of his fellow men—his utmost wishes, and more than his hopes, will be attained.

The propagation of peculiar and personal opinions and creeds, whether relating to politics, or other subjects, on which parties and sects seem resolved to differ, will be sedulously avoided in the columns of the Visiter. The editor declares an impartial neutrality, and old fashioned as it may appear, all his powers will be directed to make his weekly repository welcome, or at least inoffensive to *every* one : This he hopes for by its devotion to innocence, to truth and utility, and, in the admirable language of Lord Bacon, by making it subservient " to whatsoever comes home to the business and bosoms of men."—

With these preliminary remarks, he submits to the public his Plan, and the objects of the Rural Visiter.

A publication of this kind naturally divides itself into *Miscellany*, or various reading, *Advertisements*, and *News*.

As to the *Miscellany* it will be a favourite and comprehensive part of our weekly fare. It will contain,

1. A summary of private and domestic occurrences, whether abroad or at home ; such as marriages, deaths, and whatever of a singular or local kind seems to be interesting, avoiding, however, the relation of incidents shocking to humanity, or recitals of romantic extravagance, as unfit to answer any purpose of the Visiter.

2. The Miscellany will contain particular notices, views and facts, connected with husbandry, domestic manufactures, and the various mechanic arts and handy craft occupations : not merely general and scientific speculations, and elementary essays upon these subjects ; but information and elucidations level to common apprehension, and reducible to practical uses by men in the ordinary and common pursuits of business and industry : such, for instance, as to give plain accounts of new inventions and discoveries in philosophy, medicine, and the useful arts ; discoveries tending to the preservation of life and health, to save or assist labor, produce cheapness, comfort and economy in living, and effect beneficial results of various kinds to the agriculturist, manufacturer, architect, mechanic and labourer. We purpose to make this a very amusing as well as profitable part of our repository : It will occasionally branch itself into almost every department of human occupation : under the head of *husbandry*, for instance, we shall exhibit many essays, advices and hints in regard to *improvements* in the method of rearing horses, cattle and sheep—in the culture of hemp, grasses, grains, and fruit—in the formation and uses of manures—in the construction of farming implements, and in clearing, draining and enclosing of land : indeed our attention will be closely drawn to whatever stands connected with the great interests of the land owner and tenant, firmly believing as we do, that the real wealth and strength and even the duration of a republic, depends upon the happy and independent condition of the cultivators of its soil.

We need scarcely to dwell upon this part of our plan, so novel, yet so obviously important : we dare to promise our readers, those who have been in the habit of poring over the rant of politics, a grateful relief in turning now and then to our humble Visiter ; and if perchance they should find there but a

Burlington, the venerable capital of West Jersey, was also a market town where farmers gathered to exchange goods and gossip. The market shown here was built in 1794 at the intersection of High and East Union streets, and functioned until it was replaced in 1852. The upper room in the two-story building served as City Hall. The jail, called the dungeon, was in the basement. Courtesy, Special Collections, Alexander Library, Rutgers University

In Newark stood one true genius—Seth Boyden. In 1815 Boyden came to Newark from Massachusetts with two of his inventions: a slitting machine for separating leather, which helped leather makers get more useful pieces from each hide, and some machines to make brads and files. At fifteen he had been repairing watches; then he learned to engrave labels on steel plates. He also invented an air rifle.

He gave up a successful harness business to develop a technique for silver-plating buckles and then turned to attempting to improve leather. Boyden developed a technique to varnish leather to turn it into "patent leather." But Boyden was so unconcerned with protecting his system that he got no patent.

New Jersey, Young at Fifty

Although ingenious and industrious New Jerseyans had labored hard developing trades during the fifty years since the Declaration of Independence, they, like most Americans, worked mostly in the fields as farmers. Wagon trains of westward settlers passed through New Jersey. Soil depletion in Cumberland and Salem counties in the years 1800 to 1820 pushed farmers westward. People from Salem County went to Salem, Indiana, Salem, Iowa, and then founded Salem, Oregon. New Jersey had been a "cockpit" during

the revolution, but it was not the center of American economic developments during the Early National Period. "While other states grew," historian John Cunningham has written, "New Jersey stagnated."

The young republic, however, still gloried in its revolution. On the fiftieth anniversary, July 4, 1826, Newark held a fine parade featuring the few remaining heroes of the war. They and a new generation marched up the long Broad Street. William Halsey, lawyer and later mayor, addressed the celebrants and praised both the Revolutionary War heroes and those who had built the nation's economy. Revelers partied in Newark taverns past midnight.

As the marchers paraded that day, Seth Boyden, New Jersey's non-commercial inventor, slaved over a project he had been working on for months. But that day he realized success. He discovered that by baking pig iron for nine days at high temperatures, he could produce malleable iron. His discovery, patented in 1831, freed Americans from having to import malleable castings and thus aided New Jerseyans in the industrial development of the state, a development that began with a revolution in transportation.

Chapter Four

A Revolution in Transportation

John A. Roebling is reported to have moved his wire-rope factory to Trenton because that city offered a superior transportation combination of railroad and canal. This view of the John A. Roebling's Sons Company at the turn of the century was taken from across the Delaware and Raritan Canal and prophetically includes the railroad, which would shortly effect the canal's demise. Courtesy, Trenton Public Library

Let us then bind the nation together," South Carolina Senator John C. Calhoun told the Congress, "with a perfect system of roads and canals."

President James Madison disagreed, and thought that internal improvements should be left to the individual states.

Madison's veto stuck, and New Jersey and other states set out on their own to build roads, railroads, and canals to broaden markets, move goods, and generally improve transportation in the young nation. New Jerseyans developed two major canals and spearheaded the development of American railroading. These innovations, like others throughout the nation, buoyed the economy and helped generate an industrial revolution.

By 1860 the railroad had become the backbone of the American transportation system. Profits from the railroad and the canals generated other enterprises, brought a generation of immigrant laborers to New Jersey, and extended the markets for New Jersey pottery, cloth, iron, steel, and glass. Cities mushroomed. On the eve of the Civil War, the state was ready to flex its industrial muscle.

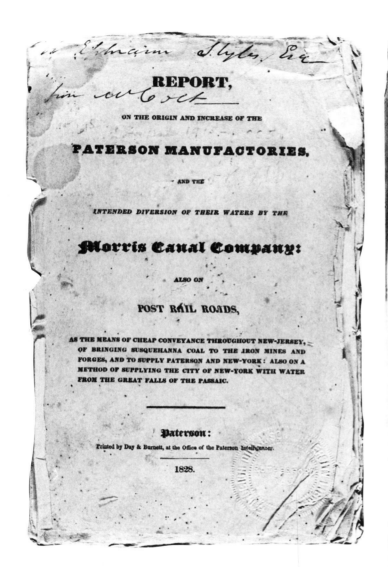

REPORT,

ON THE ORIGIN AND INCREASE OF THE

PATERSON MANUFACTORIES,

AND THE

INTENDED DIVERSION OF THEIR WATERS BY THE

Morris Canal Company:

ALSO ON

POST RAIL ROADS,

AS THE MEANS OF CHEAP CONVEYANCE THROUGHOUT NEW-JERSEY,
OF BRINGING SUSQUEHANNA COAL TO THE IRON MINES AND
FORGES, AND TO SUPPLY PATERSON AND NEW-YORK: ALSO ON A
METHOD OF SUPPLYING THE CITY OF NEW-YORK WITH WATER
FROM THE GREAT FALLS OF THE PASSAIC.

Paterson:

Printed by Day & Burnett, at the Office of the Paterson Intelligencer.

1828.

REPORT

OF THE

COMMISSIONERS

Appointed by the Legislature of the State of

New-Jersey,

FOR THE PURPOSE OF EXPLORING THE ROUTE OF

A CANAL

TO UNITE THE RIVER DELAWARE, NEAR EASTON,

WITH THE PASSAIC, NEAR NEWARK,

WITH

ACCOMPANYING

DOCUMENTS.

Morris-Town:

PRINTED BY JACOB MANN.

1823.

Above: This pamphlet contains the report of the SUM engineer relative to the injunction obtained in 1830 by that corporation against the Morris Canal. This case was the first to establish the riparian rights of the SUM to water in the Passaic River and its tributaries above the Great Falls. From Report on the Origin & Increase of the Paterson Manufactories, 1828

Right: To no one's surprise, the Legislative Commission on the Morris Canal, appointed in 1822 and led by George P. McCulloch, reported favorably in support of the enterprise. Accompanying documents included engineering reports, a mineralogical survey, and estimates of costs and revenues. From Report of the Commissioners . . . [on] a Canal to Unite the Delaware . . . with the Passaic, 1823

Canal Mania Sweeps Across the State

Early-nineteenth-century Americans knew that transportation connections between the inland areas and the sea coast could spur America's economic development. With New Jersey's thin waist, Secretary of the Treasury Albert Gallatin in 1808, for example, realized that sea vessels "drawing eight feet of water" might cross New Jersey from the Raritan to the Delaware rivers.

He submitted a report arguing this point, among others, to the United States Senate that year. The War of 1812 delayed implementation. But the British blockade of the Eastern Seaboard strangled coastal commerce and pointed to the need for a system of internal improvements in transportation.

But when James Madison's veto killed Calhoun's proposal, New York began to build the Erie Canal to link the Hudson River with Lake Erie.

Opened in 1825, it proved an instant success. It reduced the cost of transportation between Buffalo and Albany to 10 percent of what it had been.

"Canal mania" began. As the Erie Canal was being completed, Henry Clay of Kentucky sponsored "The American System," whereby a tariff would produce revenues for road and canals that would link the sections of America. Support from the West for internal improvements led to passage in 1824 of a General Survey Bill which empowered the president to initiate surveys and estimates of roads and canals. Eastern industry needed raw materials and ways to send goods west. "Canal fever" swept the East. Between 1815 and 1860 laborers dug 4,254 miles of canal, 2,188 miles of which were

A workman is loading a Morris Canal maintenance scow with barrels of tar from the shed at left in this photograph of the inclined plane at Montville. Cradles went up or down the planes, attached to cables regulated by the water-powered mechanism in the powerhouse at the top of the picture. Courtesy, Newark Public Library

completed between 1815 and 1834.

New York built 800 miles of canals by 1850. To secure trade from the Midwest for Philadelphia, between 1826 and 1834 Pennsylvanians built the 395-mile-long Main Line Canal from Philadelphia to Pittsburgh. The state eventually built 950 miles of canals. Ohio built 792 miles of canals to connect the Ohio River with Lake Erie.

The Morris Canal Connects East and West New Jersey

Caught up in this canal fever, Morristown engineer and teacher George P. MacCulloch realized it might be possible to dam Great Pond, as Lake Hopatcong was then known, to deepen it, and then connect it with canals along the Musconetcong River in the west and the Rockaway River Valley and the Passaic River Valley in the east.

This canal, he argued, could bring Lehigh Valley anthracite to Morris County's declining ironworks and move the iron to Newark. It might revive the declining agricultural production of Morris County by importing fertilizer and exporting produce. According to the November 1823 report of the canal commissioners who surveyed the terrain, it would even contribute to the "good morals of the community." A canal system, they explained, would allow the apples and cider of Morris County to be exported rather than be "converted into ardent spirits."

Commissioner James Renwick, professor of natural and experimental philosophy at Columbia University, showed the legislature how the difficult terrain could be overcome with a combination of inclined planes and traditional canal locks. Using inclined planes was startlingly innovative, and the Morris Canal became an engineering marvel.

Among the states building canals at the time, New Jersey remained unique in putting only private capital to work by offering transportation monopolies to corporations. When the legislature chartered the Morris Canal and Banking Company on December 29, 1824, investors fought to get the $100 shares.

On October 15, 1825, at Lake Hopatcong cannons boomed as the first spadeful of dirt was turned. Cadwallader D. Colden, the president of the Morris Canal and Banking Company and the former mayor of New York, led the celebrants in a toast to "American Commerce and Transportation—may they prove rich as the lifeblood in the veins of our fair Republic."

The managers hired 1,000 immigrant Irish workingmen at one dollar a day. Without labor-saving devices or machinery, save for some wheelbarrows and 100 mules, they worked from sunrise to sunset to construct twelve inclined planes and sixteen locks from Great Pond to Jersey City, which, rather than Newark, became the eastern terminus. On the western section between the lake and the Delaware River, the men built eleven inclined planes and seven locks.

To go up the inclined planes, canallers had to maneuver the boats

Left: The Old Point House in the Woodside section of Newark along the Passaic River was built in the 1750s and has served a variety of purposes. Until the 1820s it was used as a residence and a tavern. Later it became a stopping place for fishing parties; a print and dye factory for silk handkerchiefs; and in 1855, it was a fireworks factory. Later in the nineteenth century it served as a headquarters for the scull races so popular on the Passaic River. Courtesy, Newark Public Library

Below: By this deed dated April 1683, Samuel Bacon bought land along the Cohansey Creek from two Indians. In addition to the usual purchase goods, he paid one guilder of wampum for land he called "Bacon's Adventure." Bacon came to Cumberland County by way of Woodbridge, where he had been granted a patent in 1670. Courtesy, Collection of the Newark Museum

Above: Colonel John Stevens built America's first steam locomotive to demonstrate his confidence in the railroad as a superior means of transportation. Visitors to the circular track at Castle Point in Hoboken rode on the sixteen-foot "Steam-Waggon" at the breath-taking pace of six miles per hour. Courtesy, Newark Public Library

Right: The Van Nuis Carriage Factory was established in New Brunswick in 1810. After the War of 1812, the business steadily prospered, expanding into the South and to the West Indies. During the Civil War the firm suffered heavy losses from which it never completely recovered. Courtesy, New Jersey Historical Society

Above: In the engraving on this bank note issued by the State Bank at Newark in 1862, the bank appears at the left, next to its neighbor on Broad Street, Old First Church. Courtesy, Collection of the Newark Museum

Left: New Jersey copper cents called "Horse Heads" were struck at mints in Rahway and Morristown under contract from the state in 1786. The Latin term for New Jersey appears over the horse head and plow of the state seal. Courtesy, Collection of the Newark Museum

Right: As with smaller fairs, Newark's Waverly Fair was financed principally by horse racing. Held annually after the Civil War by the New Jersey State Agricultural Society, the fair's revenues declined after New Jersey's constitutional amendment prohibiting gambling was passed in 1892. Seven years later, the Essex County Park Commission purchased the fairground to establish Weequahic Park. Courtesy, Newark Public Library

Facing page: A listing for Robert C. Stoutenberg, merchant, appears in the first city directory of Newark, published in 1836. These trade cards were issued by the firm during its long tenure as a Newark clothier. The political card was one of a series featuring United States presidents and vice-presidents; the card printed in German on both sides was targeted to Newark's large German population. Courtesy, Special Collections, Alexander Library, Rutgers University

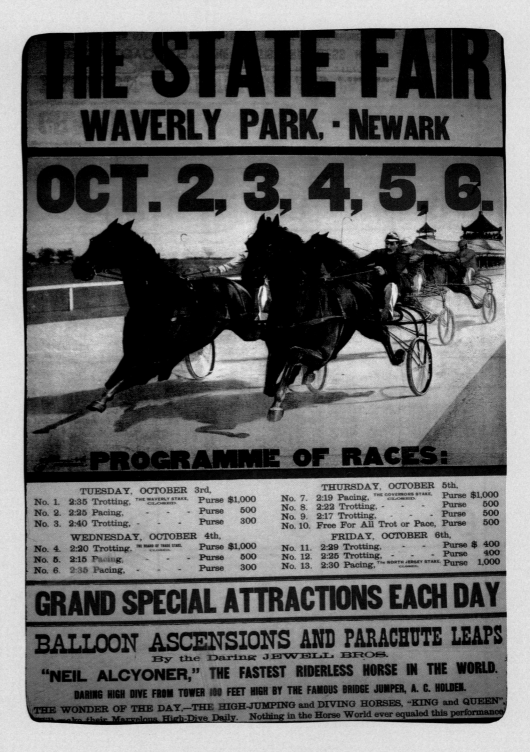

STOUTENBURGH & CO.
Newarker Kleiderhändler,
803 und 805 Broad Strasse.

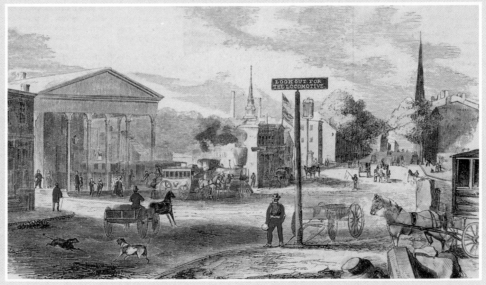

Above: Picturesque Weehawken, with its cliffs and bays, provided a summer haven for prosperous New York City business-men, whose mansions provided unparal-leled views of the Hudson River. A contemporary account expressed regret that Weehawken had come to be considered a vulgar resort by the "fashionable," because it was being frequented by the "poorer classes of society." 1839 illustration by William H. Bartlett. Courtesy, Newark Public Library

Right: A flagman stops traffic for a New Jersey Rail Road train leaving Newark's Market Street Depot circa 1840. After the station was built in 1838, new streets were laid out in the area and property values rose. The New Jersey Rail Road and Transportation Company had been char-tered in 1832 to build a railroad from Newark to Jersey City, and by the end of the decade had extended its line to the banks of the Raritan opposite New Brunswick. Courtesy, Newark Public Library

Above: When Charles Magnus sketched New Brunswick in 1842, the city was a century old and incorporated for half that time. Located at the head of navigation on the Raritan River, and accessible by train, steamboat, and canal, New Brunswick's strategic location between New York and Philadelphia assured the city's growth as a trading and manufacturing center. Courtesy, Special Collections, Alexander Library, Rutgers University

Left: Phoenix Mill, built circa 1823, appears in the background of this bucolic view of the Whippany River. The paper mill was operated successfully by Vail, Trench and Company until it was sold for $10,000 in 1844, to be rebuilt and renamed Eden Mill. Between 1860 and 1870 Eden Mill produced between eight and ten tons of white paper per week for Frank Leslie's Illustrated Newspaper *and other journals. Courtesy, Newark Public Library*

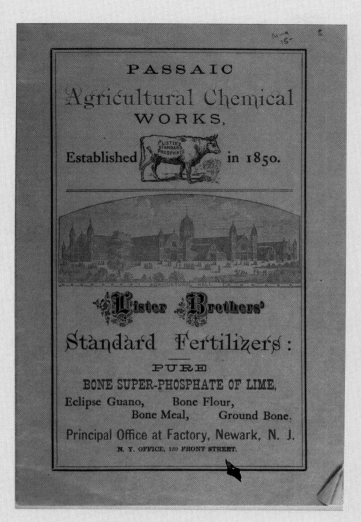

NEW JERSEY STATE FAIR,
AT WAVERLEY, NEAR NEWARK, N. J.
Sept. 17, 18, 19, 20, 21, 1888.

Facing page, top: W.H. Baker chose the alchemist to decorate his 1875 trade card. On the verso he advertised medicinal whiskeys guaranteed by the Board of Health of Washington, D.C., to be "full proof, fine flavor and free of all impurities." Courtesy, Special Collections, Alexander Library, Rutgers University

Facing page, bottom: Prior to 1886 Prudential Insurance Company insured only industrial workers whose small premiums were collected weekly by Prudential agents. The agent in this trade card issued in 1883 appears to be paying a death claim to a widow with small children. Courtesy, Special Collections, Alexander Library, Rutgers University

Above: One of a series of amusing trade cards that personified vegetables and flowers, which was exhibited at the Waverly Fair in Newark in the late-nineteenth century. Courtesy, Special Collections, Alexander Library, Rutgers University

Above, left: At the time this brochure was published, Newark's Passaic Agricultural Works on the Passaic River had been supplying New Jersey farmers with Lister Brothers' fertilizer for over a quarter-century. Note the engraving of Agricultural Hall, a farmer's mecca at the Philadelphia Centennial Exposition of 1876. Courtesy, New Jersey Room, Fairleigh Dickinson University

Above: During the 1880s Lakewood
became a popular resort frequented by the
wealthy and famous, some of whom, like
the Goulds and the Rockefellers, enjoyed
spacious estates in the area. The Laurel
House, pictured on this early postcard, once
entertained Rudyard Kipling. Courtesy,
Newark Public Library

Right: Jersey City's railroad depot was the
terminus of all the important railroads, and
its ferries provided an important commercial gateway to New York City.
Passenger traffic through the busy yards
included commuters as well as newly
arrived immigrants, many bound for the
West. Courtesy, Newark Public Library

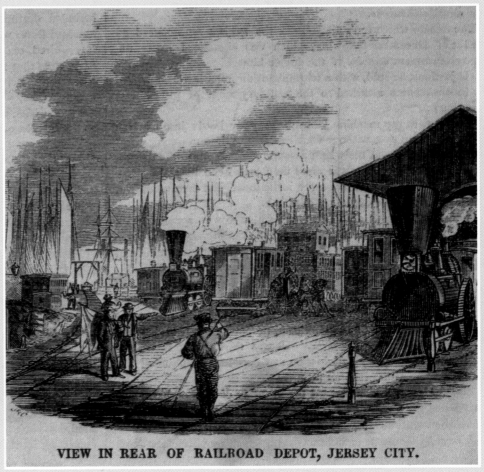

VIEW IN REAR OF RAILROAD DEPOT, JERSEY CITY.

110

The site for the Chalfonte House at Cape May City was purchased by Colonel H.W. Sawyer in 1876, and the structure was completed two years later on the former salt marsh. A contemporary advertisement described its flower garden as "intersected with trees and a variety of shrubbery." The building was "supplied with gas, water, drainage, and other comforts equal to a city hotel, showing a remarkable spirit of enterprise." Courtesy, New Jersey Historical Society

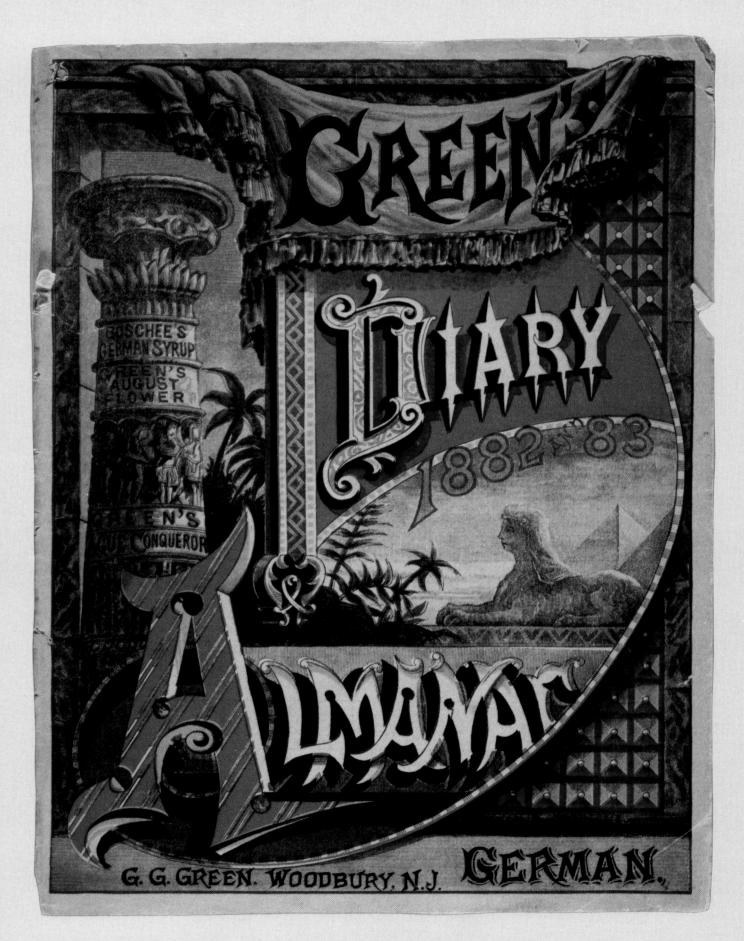

GREEN'S DIARY 1882 & '83 ALMANAC

BOSCHEE'S GERMAN SYRUP
GREEN'S AUGUST FLOWER
GREEN'S CONQUEROR

G. G. GREEN. WOODBURY, N.J. GERMAN.

into cradles, which were winched up by chains. To cross the Passaic and the Pompton rivers, the workmen built aqueducts. They also dug a tunnel so the canal could pass beneath Newark's Center Market near Mulberry Street. After four years of hard labor, water flowed in the canal. The company opened the canal in 1831.

Soon inland port cities—Port Murray, Port Colden, Rockport, and Port Morris—sprang up along the route. Boats with names like *Socrates, Bridge Smasher, Wild Irishman,* and *Lager Bier* plied the canal. During the early years as many as 100 boats a week made the trip, pulled by mules and hauling mostly coal.

French visitor Mrs. Frances Trollop toured the Morris Canal in 1832. "There is no point in the national character of the Americans which commands so much respect as the boldness and energy with which public works are undertaken and carried through," she wrote in her *Domestic Manners of the Americans:*

Nothing stops them if a profitable result can be fairly hoped for.

We spent a delightful day in New Jersey, in visiting, with a most agreeable party, the inclined planes, which are used instead of locks on the Morris canal.

This is a very interesting work; it is one among a thousand which prove the people of America to be the most enterprising in the world.

Above: At Little Falls, the Morris Canal crossed the Passaic River on an aqueduct of local brownstone sixty feet above the river. Courtesy, Newark Public Library

Facing page: An early advocate of advertising, G.G. Green, Jr., distributed free almanacs printed in English, German, French, and Spanish, wherever his patent medicines were sold. Green's laboratory, established in Woodbury in 1872, produced "August Flower," a vegetable compound to treat "liver complaint, dyspepsia or any disease arising from a deranged stomach"; "German Syrup," recommended for consumption and lung disease; and "Ague Conqueror," for chills and fever. Courtesy, New Jersey Room, Fairleigh Dickinson University

. . . The planes average about sixty feet of perpendicular lift each, and are to support about forty tons. The time consumed in passing them is twelve minutes for one hundred feet of perpendicular rise. The expense is less than a third of what locks would be for surmounting the same rise.

But the Morris Canal was more of an engineering success than an economic one. Soon after Trollop's visit, the Panic of 1837 forced the shares in the company to seven dollars. In 1844 the corporation reorganized. In its day, however, the canal revitalized the iron industry in the western part of the state and industrially transformed Rockaway, Boonton, Little Falls, Newark, and Dover by attracting industries and people. Canal boats transported the hides and tanbark from the west to the Newark leather-goods industry. Canallers hauled scrap iron ore, pig iron, zinc, sand, clay, lime, lumber, and farm products along the Morris Canal. But canallers carried more coal than anything else.

The canal also evoked a romantic response. New Jerseyans longed to

Behind Thomas Monaghan is the house in which he was born sixty-seven years previously when his father tended the Morris Canal's Lock 15 East at Bloomfield, a job he held for thirty years. Thomas himself tended Plane No. 11, a little over a mile away. When this picture was taken in 1924, Monaghan still lived along the canal, in a house forty feet from his birthplace. Courtesy, Newark Public Library

know about the canallers whose families lived on canal boats. Those on the route grew accustomed to the shrill sound of the boatmen's conch-shell horns signaling to the lock tenders. Popular songs about the canal made their way into folklore:

Construction of the Morris Canal was contracted out in sections, which were used locally as each one was finished. After an enlargement program was completed in 1860, the canal could accommodate barges with greater tonnage capacity. Dredges, such as the one shown here in 1896, were constantly engaged in removing silt that accumulated in the channel, which was maintained at a depth of five feet. Courtesy, Newark Public Library

Old Canal Song

*Old Bill Miller
Ridin' on the tiller
Steering round the Browertown Bend;
Old Davy Ross
With a ten dollar hoss
Comin' up the Pompton Plane*

But the canal disappointed its planners. Freight never rose over one million tons annually and declined after the Civil War. The canal lost out to the swifter and more direct railroads, and in 1871 the Lehigh Valley Railroad leased the waterway for ninety-nine years. Four years later the Eastern and Amboy Railroad crossed central New Jersey and bypassed the canal.

By 1902 the canal carried only 27,392 tons of goods. In 1922 the state took over all properties of the defunct company except those in Phillipsburg and Jersey City. The state drained the canal in the spring of 1924. Newarkers first built a trolley line in the old canal bed, then they converted it into a subway. When you drive on Raymond Boulevard in Newark, you are following the bed of the old Morris and Essex Canal. When you enjoy Lake Hopatcong State Park, think of the old canal that once reached east and west from this beautiful spot.

The Rise and Fall of Canals

During the nineteenth century New Jersey built two major canals that became renowned, only to be doomed by the advent of the railroad. Today the Morris Canal (which ran over the high hills of North Jersey) and the Delaware & Raritan Canal (which cut across the state's midsection) represent a vanished era in New Jersey's transportation history.

These canals were built to speed transportation and increase trade with Pennsylvania. The Morris Canal, chartered in 1824, passed through an iron-mining and industrial corridor running from Jersey City to Phillipsburg. The canal linked the Delaware and Lehigh rivers with the Passaic River and the ocean at Newark Bay. Completed in 1831, the Morris Canal would become a white elephant, never achieving the stature envisioned by those who planned it.

The Morris Canal was nonetheless one of the engineering wonders of its time. Conceived in 1822 by Morristown engineer George P. MacCulloch, it was, to say the least, an ambitious plan. Firstly, the water level of Lake Hopatcong in northwest New Jersey would be raised. With Lake Hopatcong as its epicenter, the canal would travel off in two opposite directons: westward down the Musconetcong River Valley to reach Pennsylvania's coal centers, and eastward down the Rockaway River Valley to Morris County's ironworks, and beyond to Newark.

Work began in late 1825, and within one year workmen had dug the canal's base through the high hills. In 1827 came construction of a dam to raise Lake Hopatcong's water level by five feet. The first boats passed from Phillipsburg to Newark in November 1831.

From Newark Bay to its peak height at Lake Hopatcong, the waterway had to actually *climb* some 914 feet. Then it dropped to 760 feet on the way to the Delaware River opposite Easton, Pennsylvania—a total rise and fall of 1,674 feet in 90 miles. How to make the water

climb? Engineer James Renwick designed twenty-three inclined planes on which the water could negotiate the grades. With the aid of ropes and cables, canal boats moved up these watery inclines on "cradles" drawn by water power.

But other problems were not so elegantly solved. The canal was only thirty-one feet wide at the surface, twenty feet wide at the bottom, and four feet deep: it could carry boats of up to only twenty-five tons, a relatively small capacity. Thus, further improvements were needed: the canal was enlarged to handle boats carrying up to seventy tons of coal from Pennsylvania, and in 1836 it was extended to New York Bay with a twelve-mile extension built across Bayonne Neck to Jersey City.

These improvements, along with an industrial boom before the Civil War, saw the Morris Canal through to a period of prosperity. During the 1860s the wateray showed substantial profits and carried massive amounts of Pennsylvania coal to places like Boonton and Dover, where many forges were located.

But the canal's future was doomed, its fleeting prosperity about to be shattered by the railroads: when the Lehigh Valley Railroad entered the coal business in the late 1860s, its trains could carry coal shipments to Jersey City in five to eight hours. On the Morris Canal, those same shipments took three days.

In 1871 the Lehigh Valley Railroad itself leased the Morris Canal, and the waterway gradually fell into decline. In 1903 the legislature took over the canal, and in 1924 it was destroyed by the state: its stone aqueduct across the gorge at Passaic was blown up with dynamite.

The Morris Canal never quite achieved its original goals, and it is often recalled as something of a misadventure. Nevertheless, the fact remains that George MacCulloch's canal brought the Morris County hills an economic prosperity which endured for decades.

The Delaware & Raritan Canal had a somewhat happier history. The forty-three-mile-long waterway, chartered in

By improving access to raw materials and facilitating movement of manufactured goods, the Delaware and Raritan Canal ensured the development of Trenton as an industrial city. The canal is shown here on its route through Trenton in 1948. Trenton's famous Battle Monument, visible in the background, commemorates the spot where American troops opened fire in 1776 during the Battle of Trenton. Courtesy, Newark Public Library

1830 and completed in 1833, provided an alternative to the long ocean route between New York and Philadelphia. Serving Bordentown, Trenton, and New Brunswick, the canal primarily transported coal from the Schuylkill River Valley to those areas.

Though doomed by the railroads, the D&R had a very long and distinguished career. Massive amounts of coal—by far its major cargo—floated down the waterway during the nineteenth century. In some years, the canal's tonnage exceeded even that of the Erie Canal.

Though the advent of the railroads would slowly devastate the D&R, the waterway did not go down without a fight: in the early 1890s, it was still carrying more than one million tons of freight annually, and it was still being used even up to the early 1920s.

The Delaware & Raritan Canal was abandoned in 1933 and acquired by the state in 1934. Part of the canal bed was used for highways during the 1950s. Today the D&R's section from Trenton to New Brunswick is used to supply water for residential and industrial use, and in 1974 much of the area surrounding the old canal was designated a state park.

—David Fleming

CIRCULAR.

TO ALL WHOM IT MAY CONCERN.

This certifies that the bearer, Mr. THOMAS ELING, is well known by the Christian people of New Brunswick, N. J., of which he is a resident, as an earnest and devoted Christian man. He is also well known as a laborious and successful Canal Missionary, employed by the Philadelphia Sabbath Association, and laboring among boatmen on the Delaware and Raritan and Morris Canals.

We, the undersigned, recommend him to the sympathy of all Christian friends on the line of our canals:

SILAS E. WEIR,
City Missionary.

D. C. ENGLISH,
President Y. M. C. A.

G. S. WEBB.

WM. P. DAVIS,
Pastor 1st M. E. Church.

J. E. PRICE,
Pastor St. James' M. E. Church.

THOMAS C. EASTON,
Pastor 1st Reformed Church.

W. H. H. MARSH,
Pastor Remsen Avenue Baptist Church.

WM. H. CAMPBELL.

W. J. McKNIGHT,
Pastor 1st Presbyterian Church.

Left: In this circular, Thomas Eling reported on his missionary work among canallers from May 1 to November 27, 1881. During that time the missionary visited 967 boats, held over 100 meetings, and distributed an impressive number of tracts and other religious papers. He reported 101 "hopeful conversions," one in poignant detail. Courtesy, New Jersey Room, Fairleigh Dickinson University

Below: The canal boats photographed here in 1902 were waiting at Phillipsburg at the Morris Canal's western terminus. Here coal barges returning from the tidewater ports of Newark and Jersey City could proceed across the Delaware River assisted by a cable, to enter the Lehigh or Delaware canals. Courtesy, Newark Public Library

This is a view of the Morris Canal's Lock 17 East in Newark in 1894. The canal boat shown here had passed under Broad Street and Center Market and is now on its way to Jersey City. Courtesy, Newark Public Library

The Delaware and Raritan Canal Brings Trade

Like the sponsors of the Morris Canal, the sponsors of the Delaware and Raritan Canal aimed to transport anthracite from Pennsylvania to the port of New York. In 1816 Governor Mahlon Dickinson envisioned a canal along the Delaware River and up the Raritan River which, he said, "would form an important link in that vast chain of internal navigation which our country admits of, and which will, at some future time afford us security in war, and abundant source of wealth in peace."

Dickinson saw a canal shaped as a gigantic "Y." The left branch, beginning on the Delaware River at Raven Rock and extending to Trenton, would serve as a "feeder canal" to bring water to the right branch, which

Veteran lock tenders John H. Lackey, John Voorhees, and John J. McFaul (l-r) at Kingston on the Delaware and Raritan Canal pose in 1928 behind the balance beam used to open and close the lock gates to control the water level in the lock. Courtesy, Newark Public Library

extended from Trenton to New Brunswick, following the Millstone and Raritan rivers. The stem of the "Y" ran from Trenton to Bordentown.

But from the very beginning, the organizers of the Delaware and Raritan Canal faced competition from railroad enthusiasts. As planners were discussing the canal during the 1820s, those who sought to build a railroad along the same route, led by Robert and John C. Stevens, maneuvered to get the state monopoly ahead of Robert F. Stockton and James Neilson, who headed the canal group. During the 1829 Trenton Christmas season, legend has it that hotheads from the two sides took to carrying pistols on the street for self-defense.

At a New York meeting the two sides finally reached a compromise. The legislature would issue two monopoly charters simultaneously, one to the Camden and Amboy Railroad, the other to the Delaware and Raritan Canal, then being organized by John Stevens. The railroad charter specifically noted "That it shall not be lawful, at any time during the said rail road charter, to construct any other rail road or rail roads in this state, without

The southern terminus of the Delaware and Raritan Canal was photographed a century after it had been completed in 1834. Barges loaded with coal from the Pennsylvania anthracite fields entered the canal here to cross the narrow waist of New Jersey to New Brunswick, where coal, lumber, and other cargoes were transshipped to ports along the Hudson River. Courtesy, Newark Public Library

the consent of the said companies, which shall be intended or used for the transportation of passengers or merchandise between the cities of New York and Philadelphia, or to compete in business with the rail road authorized by the act to which this supplement is relative."

On February 4, 1830, the rivals offered their stock to the public. The railroad stock sold within minutes. But the Stockton faction could not sell the canal stock. Even after a year, the funds were not fully subscribed. Fortunately for the Delaware and Raritan Canal, Stockton's father-in-law, John Potter, advanced Stockton nearly $500,000 to get "Stockton's Folly" into the ground.

On February 15, 1831, to ensure that both the canal and the railroad would be completed, the legislature "married" the railroad and the canal into the Joint Companies. The law allowed the Camden and Amboy Railroad

In the years after the Civil War, competition from railroads slowly doomed the Delaware and Raritan Canal, shown here where the waterway divides Millstone and East Millstone. This photograph was taken in 1924, only a few years before the canal was abandoned. Courtesy, Newark Public Library

and the Delaware and Raritan Canal to consolidate, thus extending the canal's corporate life by twenty years. A Princeton paper wrote, "Married: At Trenton, by the Honorable the Legislature of New Jersey, Mr. Magnus Fluvius Canal to Miss Agilis Rail Road."

In return for the monopoly, the Joint Companies were to pay the state 10 cents per passenger and 15 cents for each ton of goods carried, and they gave the state 1,000 shares of non-voting stock. But, because tariff rates were set high, the taxes really came from the pockets of the users. The companies thus guaranteed the state an annual income of $30,000, which the companies paid throughout the nineteenth century. Not until 1875, long after many states had acted, would New Jerseyans amend their constitution to forbid special incorporation laws.

As had been true for the Morris and Essex Canal, immigrant Irish labor dug the Delaware and Raritan Canal with hand tools. In the summer of 1832, cholera struck the workers. Blacks, whom whites assumed to be immune, carried the sick workingmen to a makeshift hospital at the Princeton town hall. Because many of the Irish laborers had no relatives in this land, survivors buried the many dead in unmarked graves along the canal. Some fifty of these graves lie at Bull's Island.

But the epidemic subsided, and the Irish finally dug the forty-three miles of canal to connect Bordentown and New Brunswick. At the formal New Brunswick opening of the canal on June 25, 1834, a brass band and a twenty-four-gun salute greeted Governor Peter Vroom. Lacking boats for the opening, the Delaware and Raritan Canal Company had to borrow some from the Chesapeake and Delaware Canal Company.

In 1840 the barges that came down Pennsylvania's Delaware Division Canal could leave that system at New Hope through outlet locks and, hooked onto a huge cable, cross the Delaware to Lambertville, where they entered the Delaware and Raritan Canal system. Sometimes lumber entered the feeder at Raven Rock.

In the 1850s a steam tug, the *Robert F. Stockton*, opened the era of mechanically propelled barges on American canals. To protect the sides of the canal from the wash of the tug, workmen constructed a stone "rip rap" to a depth of 3.5 feet. Gunboats used the canal during the Civil War.

The canal moved an immense amount of Pennsylvania coal into New Brunswick for transshipment to New York. The canal influenced the choice of Trenton for Peter Cooper's ironworks and John A. Roebling's wireworks—choices which established Trenton industrially. After the Civil War the company built a new lock at New Brunswick to speed up the trip, and in 1871 canallers moved nearly three million tons of goods, most of it coal.

That year, however, the Pennsylvania Railroad leased the properties to secure a rail connection to New York City and thereafter paid less attention to the canal than the railroad. Then in 1876 the Reading Railroad connected the coal fields directly with New York. The railroad was faster and, since it ran all year, more reliable than the canal. When the Pennsylvania Railroad went to four tracks across the state in 1893, the canal began to lose money.

Barges serving Johnson & Johnson and Standard Oil Company of New Jersey continued to use the waterway during the 1920s, and private groups of that era partied up and down the canals in yachts, but in 1932 the Pennsylvania Railroad began negotiations with the state to sell the property. The state took over the canal in 1934. When you drive the Trenton Freeway, realize that you are riding on what once was a major American canal. The sections along the Millstone and the Raritan rivers still make excellent hiking trails.

Imagine, if you will, as you visit these sites, the old ninety-foot-long barges known as "Chunkers" passing down from the mines at Mauch Chunk near

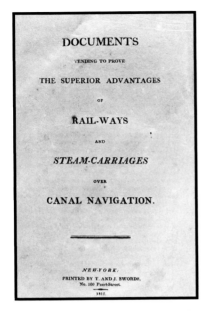

DOCUMENTS
TENDING TO PROVE
THE SUPERIOR ADVANTAGES
OF
RAIL-WAYS
AND
STEAM-CARRIAGES
OVER
CANAL NAVIGATION.

NEW-YORK:
PRINTED BY T. AND J. SWORDS,
No. 160 Pearl-Street.
1812.

Twenty years before the term "railroad" became a household word, Colonel John Stevens foresaw the dramatic impact of this new form of transportation upon the growing economy of the country. His arguments in this pamphlet were a vain attempt to convince the canal-oriented New Jersey Legislature to pursue an alternate course. Courtesy, New Jersey Room, Fairleigh Dickinson University

Allentown, or the "Skukers" from the Schuylkill Navigation Canal, piloted by characters like "Smokestack Gallagher," who smoked a cigar, wore a top hat, and treated the people in the inns along the canal to champagne.

Can't you imagine the site where one owner backing on the canal chained a pet monkey to his fence? The canallers peppered the monkey with enough coal for the owner's winter heat, as the story went, and even gave him enough to sell to his neighbors.

After the demise of the canal, an unknown poet waxed nostalgic in the *New Brunswick Sunday Times* of September 12, 1937:

The Century Old Canal

My heart goes out to the old canal
A relic of days gone by,
With its soggy banks
And its rushes and danks;
The haunts of the dragon fly.
We love you for all that you used to be
In the days that our fathers knew,
When they toiled with their load
Over the Amwell Road
With struggle, and cry, and hue.

The canals of New Jersey lowered transportation rates, opened new areas for settlement, and improved prosperity of communities along routes. They applied what economists call the multiplier-accelerator effect, which raised economic development at both ends of routes. But railroads proved faster and more dependable, and they drove the canals out of business and then worked their own economic effects on New Jersey.

The "Neigh of the Iron Horse" Awakens the Countryside

Hoboken steamboat magnate John Stevens, one of the men responsible for the U.S. Patent Law of 1790, had learned enough about steamboating to realize that some kind of rail connection between the Delaware River ports and those on the Raritan River would pay handsome dividends. In 1811 while George Stephenson, the inventor of the steam railroad engine, was still attempting to put the steam engine on wheels in England, John Stevens, whose own steam boiler had been patented in 1791, sought a railroad charter for such a connection from the New Jersey Legislature.

Stevens foresaw how railroads could cut transportation costs. A veteran of the steamboat wars between states and companies, he advocated that the federal government promote and control the railroad system he envisioned. This "father of American railroading" particularly believed that a railway would be a better way than a canal, then under discussion, to link the Hudson River and the Great Lakes. In 1812 he published "Documents Tending to

Prove the Superior Advantages of Railway and Steam Carriages Over Canal Navigation."

"I can see nothing to hinder a steam-engine from moving with a velocity of 100 miles per hour," wrote Stevens. "In practice it may not be advisable to exceed 20 to 30 miles per hour," he said, "but I should not be surprised at seeing carriages propelled at 40 or 50."

Too quixotic and impractical, said the legislature. The War of 1812 stopped Stevens momentarily. But in 1814 Stevens hiked the territory between New Brunswick and Trenton to see for himself how easy it would be to construct a rail line. Armed with the survey he made, he finally won in 1815. The New Jersey Legislature granted him America's first railroad charter. The charter did not mention steam power, and Stevens could have used horses on the tracks.

But Stevens could not find enough financial supporters for either a horse- or a steam-railroad. So in 1825 to demonstrate the possibilities of steam power, he laid out a 630-foot circular track near his villa in Hoboken, on

which he ran the first American railroad locomotive. His "Steam Waggon" had a one-cylinder engine and a twenty-tube boiler. It used a spur wheel to grip a rack rail between the tracks and drive itself forward.

Despite the tight circle it ran on, this "Steam Waggon" attained speeds of twelve miles per hour and lumbered up the thirty-inch slope Stevens built into the track to show nay-sayers that the engine could climb hills. The publicity that came from the *New York Evening Post* story about his locomotive helped Stevens raise money to build the Camden and Amboy Railroad. But the engine really was not much more than a toy. It had little influence on the design of future locomotives, which followed the much more advanced models imported from England. Stevens also planned the first low-pressure engine constructed on the American continent and installed it in a boat on the Hudson three years before Robert Fulton launched his *Clermont*.

John Stevens turned the railroading enterprise over to his son Robert, who worked with Robert F. Stockton to get the Camden and Amboy

The coaches of the English-built locomotive, the John Bull, resemble carriages in tandem. The original locomotive with cow-catcher and 1836-style coaches was restored and exhibited at the World's Columbian Exposition at Chicago in 1893. Currently the train may be seen at the Smithsonian Institution in Washington, D.C. Courtesy, Camden County Historical Society

Although the timetable pictured here advertised "N. York," the end of the line for the Paterson and Hudson River Railroad was Jersey City and its ferries. By 1836 the "fleet and gentle horses" that drew double-decked carriages when the line opened in 1832 had been replaced by steam engines imported from England. Courtesy, Paterson Museum Archives

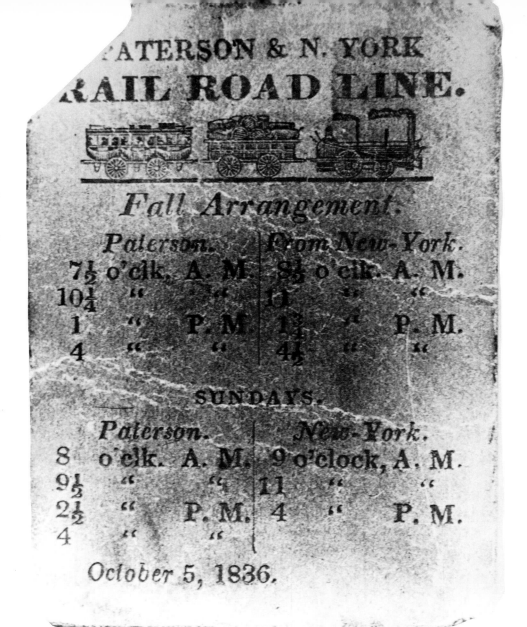

Railroad charter from the state legislature in 1830 as part of the joint railroad-canal monopoly. At this time the senior Stevens was eighty. This charter, which authorized a line from South Amboy to Bordentown, would provide traffic movement over this territory when the steamboats might be mired in ice.

By 1831 Robert Stevens built the first part of the line near Bordentown. He also sailed to England to import a ten-ton locomotive, the John Bull, built by George Stephenson. Mechanic Isaac Dripps assembled the locomotive in Bordentown. A flatcar behind the engine held a whiskey barrel for water, which was brought to the engine by a leather hose made by a Bordentown shoemaker.

The Camden and Amboy Railroad finished laying its track from South Amboy to Bordentown in 1833 and began service with horses. The *American Railroad Journal* of May 1883 recounted the early horse-drawn railroad experience:

We have recently journeyed between Philadelphia and New York by the railroad line. Yesterday we left New York in the beautiful and spacious boat the New Philadelphia, at about a quarter past six o'clock, A. M., and arrived

*at Chestnut Street wharf before three P. M. The New Philadelphia reached
South Amboy in two hours and a quarter. The fine and commodious cars
on the railroad were drawn to Bordentown eleven miles the hour, without
undue fatigue of the horses, or any circumstance that could lessen the sense
of security and comfort with which every passenger seems to set out.*

*This conveyance is truly admirable for the ease and order which attend
it for all parties. Each car is divided into three compartments, and contains
twenty-four persons. Two horses are attached to it tandem; they pursue the
track, under the guidance of skillful drivers, with the nicest exactness. We
could not perceive, by the motion of the vehicle, the slightest deviation from
the grooves; and the route is of more than 30 miles. One track is complete:
great activity prevails in the work necessary for the accomplishment of the
whole design. The average duration of the journey between the two great
cities, by this railroad line, is not eight or eight and a half hours. It
will be less, considerably, when a locomotive engine shall be employed.*

The first trial run of a locomotive, the John Bull, on November 12, 1831,
was graced by Napoleon Bonaparte's niece, Mme. Caroline Murat of
Bordentown, who was determined to be the first woman to ride on the
revolutionary steam-powered train. The John Bull made the trip across the
state in the fall of 1833. Stevens extended the line from Bordentown to South
Amboy through Hightstown and Jamesburg and then south to Camden from
Bordentown in 1834. In the two years following the Panic of 1837 Stevens
built it piece by piece to New Brunswick, where it connected in 1839
with a line from Jersey City.

Robert Stevens, the developer of the Camden and Amboy Railroad,
made many significant contributions to railroading in America. He designed
the model for the "T-rail" to replace the wooden ones which had iron strips
nailed to them. These iron strips often curled up at the ends into dangerous
"snake heads," which could derail trains. The "T-rails" were hard to roll,
and their use did not spread rapidly, but they were cheaper than the others,
and by the 1840s Trenton mills were rolling them. Stevens also developed
the modern spike and the "iron tongues" or "fishplates" which bolted
one rail to another.

Inmates of New York's Sing Sing prison cut the stones on which the
Camden and Amboy Railroad's first rails were fastened. When production
slowed too much for Stevens, he ordered some of the track from Amboy
to Bordentown constructed over logs which workmen set into packed, broken
rock. Thus Stevens originated the modern American roadbed which was
cheaper and easier to lay than the stone-block system of the English.

Because American terrain was more difficult and required tight turns
which were hard for English locomotives to negotiate, Stevens also developed
the "pilot" oak frame, which was attached to the locomotive's front axle,
to assist it in taking sharp curves. A variant of the device was later known

as the "cowcatcher."

Service by horse cost more than by steam. In these early railroad days the railroads were considered public property, and anyone with "similar" carriages could use the tracks on payment of three cents per ton of freight or single passenger per mile.

This situation led to accidents, and because there was only one track, locomotives often wrecked head-on. When oncoming trains met, the train that had passed a certain post was supposed to yield and back onto a turnout. But the system did not always work. Passengers commonly helped push cars and locomotives back on the track after derailments.

On one trip the John Bull hit and decapitated a hog and so unnerved a passenger that he turned a somersault out of a window. On a 1833 trip in which the crew was speeding to recover lost time, the train derailed when an axle snapped. Former President John Quincy Adams escaped injury, but fellow passenger Cornelius Vanderbilt's chest was crushed in the rubble. After a rash of head-on collisions, the Camden and Amboy Railroad developed a schedule.

The canal owners, turnpike companies, stagecoach and steamboat operators, tavern keepers, and wagon freighters united against the iron horse. One stage operator took out a newspaper advertisement, warning passengers of "the great danger and inconvenience which they are subject to in traveling on crooked railroads, so often experienced in consequence of the cars getting off the tracks at the curves and turnouts, and thereby liable to upset." Experts claimed that passengers traveling over fifteen miles an hour would find blood spouting from mouth, nose, and ears.

Fearless J. S. Buckingham took the trip from Bordentown to Amboy in 1838. "The weather," he wrote in his *America, Historical, Statistical and Descriptive*, published in 1838,

was delightful, as a fresh breeze greatly tempered the head of the atmosphere; but from some defect in the construction of the engines which requires reform, the ashes thrown up with the smoke of the chimney fell in such quantities on the passengers in the cars as to be extremely disagreeable, besides burning the dresses of such of the ladies as were nearest the engines, the sparks fall on their persons before the fire in them was completely extinguished, so that innumerable small holes were burned through the parts of their garments on which they fell.

Commuters took to wearing "dusters," which were supposed to keep clothes clean from both the sparks and the tallow from the candles that illuminated some cars. Travel on the Camden and Amboy Railroad was costly, irregular, and dangerous. But the taxes, dividends, and duties from its chartered operation flowed into the state's coffers and provided 69 percent of the state's expenditures between 1834 and 1850.

Protected by its monopoly, the Camden and Amboy piled profit on profit.

Between 1830 and 1860, it never paid less than a 6-percent dividend, and sometimes paid as much as 30 percent. Its investment was worth $30.5 million in 1869. The railroad moved a huge amount of traffic, but it charged high fares, nearly twice the national average. Unwilling to disturb the monies flowing into the state's coffers, legislators looked the other way. Many critics have alleged that the Joint Companies paid off individuals to protect its monopoly. The U.S. Congress debated which committee might investigate the Camden and Amboy monopoly, and then sent the issue to the Post Office Committee, where it was never heard from again.

Other Lines Develop

On March 7, 1832, the legislature chartered the New Jersey Railroad Company to go from Jersey City to New Brunswick to link with the Camden and Amboy Railroad. The embankments of cedar trees and dirt built over the marshes took a year to settle, but by 1835 service began to Elizabeth. In 1836 the New Jersey Railroad completed a bridge over the Raritan River, and in 1839 the company did indeed connect with the Camden and Amboy. In 1867 the stock of the New Jersey Railroad was consolidated with that of the Camden and Amboy to create the United Companies (United Canal and Railroad Companies of New Jersey). Then in the 1870s the Pennsylvania Railroad, which sought to get rights into New York Harbor, leased the United Companies for 999 years.

Other railroad lines spread across the state. Launched in 1831, the Elizabethtown and Somerville Railroad in its early days lost a race to a team of horses between Elizabethtown and Westfield and then, along with other New Jersey enterprises, suffered through the bad years after the Panic of 1837. When the road finally reached to Somerville in 1841, the *Somerville Messenger* noted: "To see a Locomotive puffing through Somerville sets the natives agog, and the children crazy." John T. Johnston took over the Elizabethtown and Somerville Railroad in 1848, merged the line with the Somerville-to-Easton line, and changed the name to Central Rail Road Company in 1849.

Johnston put his trainmen into uniform and hooked on a special car for unescorted women. In 1852 the Central Rail Road Company connected Phillipsburg with Elizabethport. A writer quoted by John T. Cunningham in *Rail Roading in New Jersey* described the day:

Eight splendid cars, drawn by the gigantic Pennsylvania, and accompanied by Dodsworth's Band, sped through the glorious landscapes of Hunterdon and Warren to the wonder of thousands of delighted inhabitants who thronged to stations and greeted the party with the firing of guns and the waving of handkerchiefs and banners. From this day that undeveloped iron country began to yield up its wealth . . . the country sang with the ring of the tilt hammer, and log cabins were exchanged for beautiful dwellings.

The Brooklyn Bridge

The Brooklyn Bridge was the world's first steel-wire suspension bridge. It was built between 1869 and 1883 over the East River, linking the New York City boroughs of Manhattan and Brooklyn. Designed by John A. Roebling and his son, Washington A. Roebling, it was the world's longest suspension bridge at the time of its completion. Today the Brooklyn Bridge is considered by many to be the world's most beautiful bridge. It was certainly a triumph of engineering: in 1883 only New York's Trinity Church was higher, and the view from the bridge's pedestrian promenade is still spectacular today.

John Augustus Roebling (1809-1869), an immigrant from Prussia in 1831, began his life in America as a farmer. Soon he began working on canal systems, and he developed the wire rope, or cable, that would make him world famous. After demonstrating the practical uses of this steel cable from his small steel mill in western Pennsylvania, in 1848 Roebling moved this wire-rope factory to Trenton. Trenton became a renowned steel city during the mid-nineteenth century, with steel companies like John A. Roebling & Sons and the Trenton Iron Company, which was run by Peter Cooper and Abram S. Hewitt and was the nation's largest iron company for a time. The erection of the Brooklyn Bridge a generation later would make both Roebling and Trenton world-famous.

While John Roebling became a steel magnate, he also became a pioneer in the building of suspension bridges. Beginning in 1844, he designed suspension bridges of increasing size at Pittsburgh; Niagara Falls; Wheeling, West Virginia; and Cincinnati. His Niagara Falls railroad suspension bridge, completed in 1854, attracted national attention. Business boomed at the Trenton factory.

In 1869 John Roebling started designing and surveying his most ambitious undertaking: the Brooklyn Bridge. His plans for an East River bridge included towers with pointed openings, iron trusses to stiffen the roadway, and a web of iron stays running diagonally from the towers, which would give the completed bridge its rare beauty. Those stays, according to Roebling, also made the bridge so stable that the structure would not fall even if all the main cables snapped.

Only a week after these plans gained final approval, a boat docking at Brooklyn's Fulton Ferry landing crushed the toes of John Roebling's right foot. Tragically, he died of tetanus three weeks later, before construction had even begun. His son, Washington Augustus Roebling (1837-1926), took over supervision of the work and also took charge of the family's Trenton steel plant.

The project proceeded slowly, hampered by blowouts of the compressed air in the caissons, fire, the dangers of "caisson disease" (the bends, whose cause was not yet understood), fraud, a taxpayer's suit against the bridge, and lack of funds. Construction would last fourteen years. During the last ten years of the project, Washington Roebling, stricken by the bends, was confined to a wheelchair. His wife Emily became the liaison between her husband and the bridge workers, while Roebling himself oversaw the project from his apartment window with a telescope.

On May 24, 1883, the Brooklyn Bridge finally opened, amidst many jubilant ceremonies and celebrations. It had been built at a cost of about fifteen million dollars and soon came to be described as the "eighth wonder of the world," the longest suspension bridge of its time.

Throughout its long history, the bridge has inspired painters such as watercolor artist John Marin and abstractionist Joseph Stella, as well as writers including Walt Whitman, Hart Crane, and Thomas Wolfe. A sense of romance and mystery surrounds the bridge, beginning with the tragedies in the Roebling family and the death of twenty workers during its construction. The week after it opened, twelve pedestrians died, crushed by a panic-stricken mob who thought the bridge was collapsing. In 1884 P.T. Barnum took twenty-one elephants over it and said thereafter that he was convinced it was totally safe. In 1885 Robert Odlum, a swimming instructor, died after jumping from the bridge in a bright red swimming costume. In 1886 Steven Brodie, an unemployed Irishman, claimed to have jumped off the bridge and survived. In the bridge's abutment on the Manhattan side there are underground vaults, used for many years to store wine but sealed during Prohibition.

The length of the Brooklyn Bridge's river span is 1,595.5 feet, and its total length is 5,989 feet. The bridge floor's width is 85 feet, and it is supported by four cables each 15.75 inches in diameter and 3,578.5 feet long. Each cable contains 5,434 wires, making a total wire length of 3,515 miles per cable.

The Brooklyn foundations of the Brooklyn Bridge reach a depth of 44.5 feet below the high-water level. The Manhattan foundations are 78.5 feet below the high-water level. The bridge's beautiful towers are 276.5 feet above high-water, and the roadway is 119 feet above the water at the towers. The total weight of this massive and remarkable bridge is 14,680 tons.

The Trenton steel firm of John A. Roebling & Sons, rendered world famous by the Brooklyn Bridge, went on to supply cables for two other of America's most renowned spans: the George Washington Bridge and the Golden Gate Bridge.

—David Fleming

Hyperbole, perhaps, but the line moved much Pennsylvania coal, and when a bridge spanned Newark Bay during the Civil War, the Central Jersey ran on into Jersey City, where steamers took passengers and freight to New York City.

Chartered in 1835, the Morris and Essex Railroad climbed over the Orange Mountains. In 1837 Seth Boyden built the six-ton Orange locomotive which he personally drove up the hills to Orange and back six weeks later. Unfortunately, just before the end of the trial of the Orange, two men were killed in a derailment.

The Morris and Essex Railroad reached Morristown on January 1, 1838. By 1838 the first commuters were taking the three-hour ride to New York City on the early-morning eastbound and returning on the late-evening westbound. The line reached Dover in 1848, got to Hackettstown in 1854, and made the Phillipsburg coal connection in 1865. Three years later the Delaware, Lackawanna, and Western Railroad bought out the Morris and Essex Railroad.

The Railroad Creates Atlantic City

Southern New Jersey saw little railroad development until the 1850s, when Richard B. Osborne and some associates built a railroad line from

The Mount Vernon Hotel in Cape May was considered suitably elegant to command mention in the Illustrated London News. *Rooms that rented for $2.50 per day were lighted by gas and accompanied by private baths with hot and cold running water. The Mount Vernon undoubtedly accommodated many of the Southern planters who vacationed along the New Jersey shore before the Civil War. From* Illustrated London News, *1853*

Philadelphia to Absecon Island and turned the island into a "bathing village" and the "lungs of Philadelphia." Dr. Jonathan Pitney and the twenty-one eligible voters there boasted that people could get healthy at Atlantic City. In 1854 some 600 dignitaries and the press traveled to the United States Hotel—itself still being built—for the grand opening.

In fifteen years the population quadrupled. Then hotel owners Alexander Boardman and Jacob Keim built the Boardwalk as a way of keeping sand off their furniture and rugs. The original Boardwalk, only ten feet wide, was so popular that people bumped each other off when it was crowded. The population of Atlantic City again went up by tenfold in the ensuing twenty years. By the 1890s Atlantic City claimed to be "the nation's prime summer resort." In 1896 the Phoenix Bridge Company built the final, permanent Boardwalk. Several feet above the beach, the new structure was forty feet wide and extended four miles.

Other railroad builders developed new routes between existing cities. The United Companies built subsidiary lines which were later consolidated under the Pennsylvania Railroad. A narrow-gauge line ran from Camden to Atlantic City through Hammonton and Pleasantville. In the 1850s the Raritan and Delaware Bay Railroad stretched itself from Port Monmouth to Eatontown, Long Branch, and Lakehurst. After the Civil War, the line went bankrupt and then was reorganized and developed to Vineland and Bridgeton. In 1879 the Jersey Central acquired its lease.

Large and small craft dot Jersey City's busy harbor, sketched after 1847 when it became home to the steamships of the Cunard Line. With the advent of the New Jersey Rail Road in 1834 and the subsequent addition of other railroad terminals, Jersey City became the area's gateway to the West. Courtesy, Newark Public Library

In an attempt to capitalize on the tide of immigration, railroads offered reduced fares, special cars, and on occasion, separate trains for immigrants to encourage settlement of the western land served by their lines. In this broadside of 1876, the New Jersey Southern Railroad had adopted a similar policy, with discount fares for newly arrived travelers on their way to Camden and Philadelphia. Courtesy, New Jersey Room, Fairleigh Dickinson University

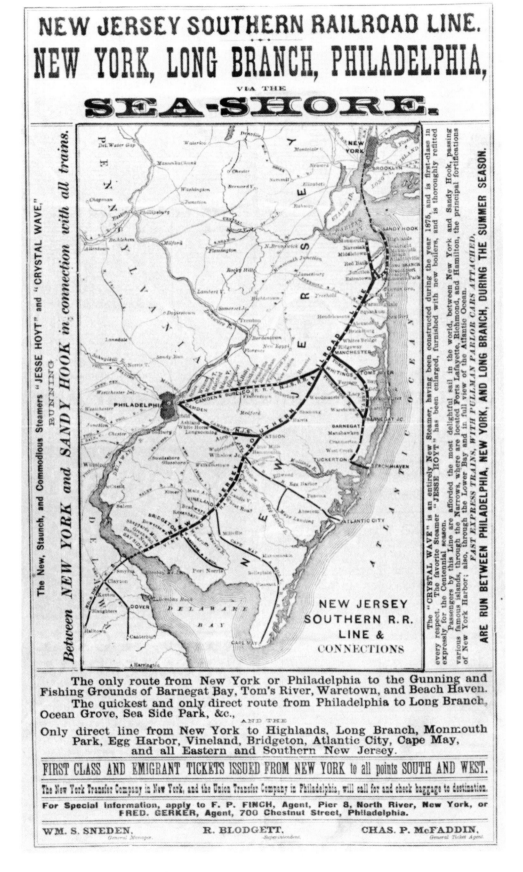

NEW JERSEY SOUTHERN RAILROAD LINE.
NEW YORK, LONG BRANCH, PHILADELPHIA,
VIA THE
SEA-SHORE.

The New, Staunch, and Commodious Steamers "JESSE HOYT" and "CRYSTAL WAVE,"
RUNNING
Between NEW YORK and SANDY HOOK in connection with all trains.

The "CRYSTAL WAVE" is an entirely New Steamer, having been constructed during the year 1875, and is first-class in every respect. The favorite Steamer "JESSE HOYT" has been enlarged, furnished with new boilers, and is thoroughly refitted expressly for the Centennial season.

Passengers by this Line are afforded the most delightful sail in the world, between New York and Sandy Hook, passing various famous islands, through the Narrows, where are located Forts Lafayette, Richmond, and Hamilton, the principal fortifications of New York Harbor; also, through the Lower Bay and in full view of the Atlantic Ocean.

FAST EXPRESS TRAINS, WITH PULLMAN PARLOR CARS ATTACHED, ARE RUN BETWEEN PHILADELPHIA, NEW YORK, AND LONG BRANCH, DURING THE SUMMER SEASON.

NEW JERSEY SOUTHERN R. R. LINE & CONNECTIONS

The only route from New York or Philadelphia to the Gunning and Fishing Grounds of Barnegat Bay, Tom's River, Waretown, and Beach Haven.
The quickest and only direct route from Philadelphia to Long Branch, Ocean Grove, Sea Side Park, &c., AND THE
Only direct line from New York to Highlands, Long Branch, Monmouth Park, Egg Harbor, Vineland, Bridgeton, Atlantic City, Cape May, and all Eastern and Southern New Jersey.

FIRST CLASS AND EMIGRANT TICKETS ISSUED FROM NEW YORK to all points SOUTH AND WEST.

The New York Transfer Company in New York, and the Union Transfer Company in Philadelphia, will call for and check baggage to destination.

For Special information, apply to F. P. FINCH, Agent, Pier 8, North River, New York, or FRED. GERKER, Agent, 700 Chestnut Street, Philadelphia.

| WM. S. SNEDEN, | R. BLODGETT, | CHAS. P. McFADDIN, |
| General Manager. | Superintendent. | General Ticket Agent. |

The railroads hurt the canal trade. Because the railroads expanded industrial markets and made shipment easier, they also hurt the South Jersey bog-iron works, which could not compete with the Middle Western iron producers. In a similar way the roads hurt the big flour producers, ruined the beef and wool producers, and hurt the glassmakers.

But the railroads generally aided the state's economy. The railroads moved raw materials and opened markets, allowed more specialization in agriculture, and made New Jersey farming more commercial. The Camden and Atlantic Railroad and the Raritan and Delaware Bay Railroad developed the recreation industry on the Shore.

According to H. Jerome Cranmer, a Drew University economist, in *New Jersey in the Automobile Age*, by the Civil War the railroad had broken down the local markets and produced a greater and greater concentration of industry, which, although it killed the iron industry of the western part of the state, turned Paterson into a locomotive-manufacturing center. New Jersey shifted from primary metals to metalworking. And although the railroad took away some local markets for farm goods, it then replaced them with other markets for milk, for instance, which could be transported long distances in the refrigerated tank cars which the railroads developed.

The railroads, which had major termini in New York and Philadelphia, also helped to make those cities the major Eastern ports. Water transportation continued to be cheaper, but railroading was much faster and more certain. With consolidation of the national lines during the 1850s and the tripling of the trackage during that decade, the railroads revolutionized transportation. By 1860 the railroad was the single most important method of transportation in the United States.

Together the railroad and the canals provided capital for other business ventures, encouraged immigration, and gave employment to thousands of Irish and German laborers. With its major cities linked by rail or water, New Jersey was on its way to becoming an urban state.

As a railroad terminus, Jersey City grew into an industrial center for the iron, glass, and weaving industries. Camden, terminus of the Camden and Amboy, grew into a shipbuilding center. Newark's tanning, leather-working, jewelry, and carriage- and harness-making businesses shipped by rail. Trentonians developed their pottery, iron, and steel industries after the canal and railroad connected the city with markets and raw materials. Because of the railroad and the canal, the cities became the centers of opportunity and began to grow.

The railroad brought many changes to New Jersey, and much of the development of the iron horse came in New Jersey. "The whole country along the line of the roads," said the *National Standard and Salem County Advertiser* of December 26, 1860, "is undergoing a peaceful revolution. . . . The residents . . . seem to have been awakened from their Rip Van Winkle sleep by the neigh of the iron horse."

Chapter Five

Industrial Expansion to 1860

In this engraving, mid-nineteenth century visitors view the Great Falls at Paterson in full flood, a spectacle not always possible when the mills were in full operation. Water from above the falls was diverted into mill raceways and returned to the Passaic River in the basin below. A natural phenomena described as early as 1680, the Passaic River and its Great Falls were critical to the industrial development of Paterson. Courtesy, Newark Public Library

Spurred by the railroads, American industry moved into a "takeoff period" from the 1830s until the Civil War. The Panic of 1837 retarded growth, but in the decade prior to the war, prices and wages held firm, and investment in American manufacturing increased and drove industrial output up 85 percent. Between 1830 and the war, the steam engine made factories more efficient. Railroads and canals generated a transportation revolution. Interchangeable parts gave birth to the assembly line. These dramatic growth triggers, together with the expansion of the limited-liability corporation, all drove industry forward. Concurrently the domestic market for goods expanded, distribution improved, and both imports and exports grew. These years set the stage for the explosive post-Civil War economy.

New Jerseyans developed their key industries: iron, locomotives, and textiles—particularly men's hats and clothing—as well as leather, jewelry, and rubber. Between 1836 and 1860, New Jersey's population doubled—from 320,779 to 672,035. Because the state's economic

It was possible to move this "portable" steam engine from one location to another to substitute for manual labor in "pumping, hoisting, grinding . . . printing" whenever the need for power arose. In 1853 the Speedwell Iron Works were managed by Stephen Vail's son, George Vail, and grandson, Isaac A. Canfield. Courtesy, Special Collections, Alexander Library, Rutgers University

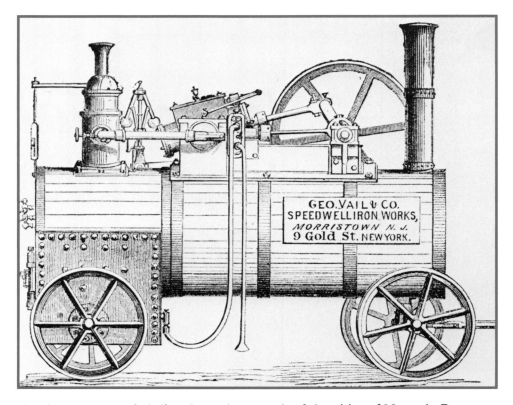

development was tied directly to the growth of the cities of Newark, Paterson, Jersey City, Trenton, and Camden, it is through the industrial development of these cities that the story of this era is best told.

Newark and Environs Grow

In *The Story of New Jersey*, William Starr Myers noted that although the "state's record as a whole was not impressive until mid-century, Newark was clearly on its way toward its unique record of diversified productivity" before the war. Double the size of any other city in the state, Newark grew from 8,017 in 1826 to 71,941 in 1860. Between 1836 and 1850 nearly 3,000 new houses, factories, and business buildings altered the skyline of the city. By 1860, according to historian Susan Hirsch, Newark had become "America's major industrial city."

One resident who had returned to Newark in 1834 after an extended absence noted with amazement, "The numerous streets, spires and wharves, proclaim that the population and commerce have spread further and wider, and the hum of business declares that the march of improvements has not yet ceased."

So much had happened, he wrote, that "I cannot realize as my home. The time was when I could call every inhabitant of the town by name. Now I can walk half a mile in the principal street and every face I meet is a stranger's." Many of the strangers, no doubt, were the Irish and German immigrants who had swelled Newark's population.

In the 1830s Newarkers manufactured shoes, hats, carriages, saddles, harnesses, and clothing. In 1836 Newarkers produced shoes valued at

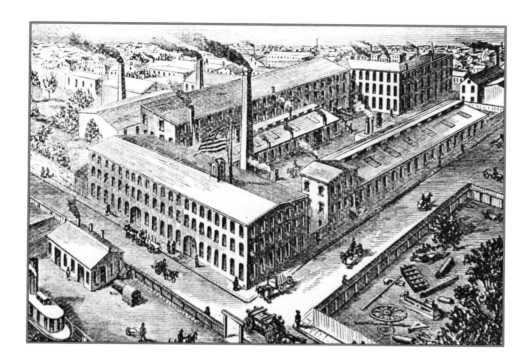

J.L. Hewes and J.M. Phillips were former apprentices of Seth Boyden. Hewes and Phillips steam engines gained wide renown, and the company's dock on the Passaic River in Newark was often loaded with their products awaiting shipments. However, by 1875 the rival company of Watts Campbell had become a major competitor, and in 1920 took over the Hewes and Phillips operations. Courtesy, Newark Public Library

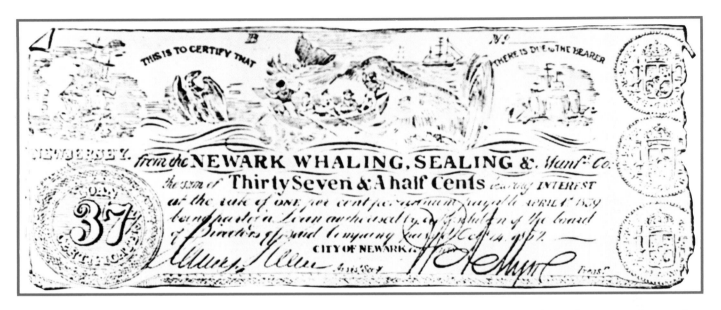

The Newark Whaling, Sealing and Manufacturing Company's whaling expedition was financed partly by the scrip shown here. One of the two ships that sailed from Newark in 1837 foundered on an iceberg in the Arctic Ocean, but the other returned bearing 8,000 barrels of oil and much whalebone. Courtesy, Newark Public Library

$1.5 million, hats worth one million dollars and carriages worth another million dollars. The average firm numbered some twenty workers.

Shoemakers Shipman, Crane & Company were large enough to sell nearly $500,000 worth of shoes to the Southern market. Between the 1830s and the Civil War, new industries in iron, zinc, and brewing burst forth, while those who built steam engines increased Newark's industrial diversity.

Named an official port of entry in 1836, Newark received foreign ships and cleared American ships for foreign destinations. The Irish built the docks, as they had the canals. Port Collector Archer Gifford noted in 1835 that some eighty-two ships had used the ports but only nine had been destined for foreign waters. Several whaling ships, including the *John Wells* and the *Columbus*, rounded Cape Horn in search of the mighty whale. Eventually the owner of the *John Wells* sold his ship to some New Bedford whalers.

Although the port stimulated commerce, domestic manufacturing provided Newark's economic base. Seth Boyden had failed to get a patent for patent leather, but that did not stop Newarkers from making the city the patent-leather capital of the United States. In 1840, after Samuel Halsey bought out David Crockett's patent-leather firm, Halsey and his brother Joseph dominated their rivals, T. P. Howell Company, James A. Banister Company, and William J. Dudley Company. On the eve of the Civil War, Noah F. Blanchard founded a patent-leather firm which flourished into the twentieth century.

Newark craftsmen became renowned for the fine shoes they made, particularly the better women's shoes made from the morocco leather tanned in Newark. By the 1850s Newark's shoemakers produced two million shoes annually. The revenues for the endowment of The Peddie School in Hightstown came from Thomas B. Peddie's successful leather business. Camden also developed a fine shoe industry rivaling Newark's.

The irrepressible Boyden, of course, diversified dramatically. Besides manufacturing malleable iron in his Newark foundry, Boyden also made fruit

Austrian Rochus Heinisch began manufacturing scissors in Newark in the 1820s. In 1848 a Swiss named Jacob Wiss, on his way to Texas with two large dogs and a treadmill, stopped in Newark. Wiss worked for Heinisch for a time, then struck out on his own. The two competed in high-quality shear production until Jacob's son acquired the Heinisch enterprise in 1914.

John N. Cumming launched a brewery in Newark in 1805, which Thomas Morton took over in 1831. After the Panic of 1837 hurt the business, Peter Ballantine, a malt seller from Scotland, joined with Erastus Paterson to buy out Morton in 1840. Moving the plant to the Passaic River bank, Ballantine produced a rich and heavy workingman's ale. When he took in his three sons in 1857, P. Ballantine & Sons was born. According to legend, the famous three-ring trademark came from Peter's practice of tasting his beer three times. Since he set his glass down three times, it left the three rings. Another tradition holds that the rings stood for the three sons.

In this twentieth-century advertising promotion, Krueger drivers reenact the delivery of the firm's nineteenth-century product. Courtesy, Newark Public Library

Germans flooded into Newark in the 1840s, and they demanded good beer. Not satisfied to be merely consumers, several Germans joined the industry alongside Peter Ballantine, who sold them malt. John Laible, Joseph Hensler, Peter Hauch, the Schalk brothers, and Gottfried Krueger expanded Newark's breweries before the Civil War. With Gottlieb Hill, Krueger founded the famous Krueger enterprise and then bought out Laible. After the Civil War, brewmaster Christian Feigenspan worked for Laible and then launched his own brewery in 1875.

Germans so dominated the brewing business in Newark that the meetings of the national Brewers' Association were transacted in German until 1872, when the association began using English in alternate years.

The Newark area's economic success before the war in beer, tanning, shoes, jewelry, men's clothing, zinc, hatting, and paint led business-directory compiler Pierson to write in 1849: "People appear to be flocking from every direction to share with us in the luxury of living in so pleasant and beautiful a city as Newark, where anyone who is willing to work can earn enough to make both ends meet, and have something left over at the end of the year, if economy is exercised."

By 1860 Newark was becoming a satellite of New York City. Capital from New York financed Newark's industry, and the larger city also provided both a market and a labor pool. Jewelry in particular depended on New York buyers. Newark, in turn, attracted manufacturers who sought lower rents. By 1860 Newark's labor force found itself working in larger, more industrial factories. Nearly one-fourth of all shoe workers were working in factories of 100 or more employees. The same was true for 60 percent of saddle workers, 44 percent of jewelry workers, two-thirds of leather workers, and 57 percent of hatters. By the Civil War, Newarkers had built an industrial city.

Paterson Revives

Although the Society for Useful Manufactures abandoned its Paterson experiment in the eighteenth century, the city continued to be a textiles center. John Colt developed the manufacture of sail duck in Paterson in 1822 and also manufactured domestic Sea Island cotton and flax products. By 1834 only Lowell, Massachusetts, equaled Paterson's forty-five cotton mills. Output from Colt's Duck Mill peaked in the 1840s, as did that of the other cotton manufacturers. The Paterson cotton industry fed the need for calico bleaching and printing in Paterson, Belleville, and Rahway.

In the late 1830s, however, silk captured the minds of Patersonians. Learning of the secrets of the silkworm, Paterson residents began planting mulberry trees in a speculative frenzy. Eventually the town boasted some

Learning of the secrets of the silkworm, Paterson residents began planting mulberry trees in a speculative frenzy. Eventually the town boasted some 200 mulberry trees. Between 1836 and 1838 eight Paterson companies sprang up to turn the silk into cloth, making Paterson a silk center. Patersonians made America's first silk flag, first skein of sewing silk, and first wound-silk on a spool.

But the the speculators went wild. The state secretary of agriculture noted later that the "craze for mulberry trees became so great that seedlings were priced far above the value of the silk they could produce—providing they were sufficiently cultivated to thrive at all. In the frenzy of buying, planting, selling or speculating in trees, the silkworms were neglected entirely." The "silkworm rage" soon died down and the market in trees collapsed.

Silk production went forward intermittently. Christopher Colt brought silk-manufacturing equipment from Hartford into Paterson and established a silk business at the end of the craze. When Colt's silk company failed in New Jersey, John Ryle, an immigrant silkworker from England, bought Colt's crude machines for George Murray, who financed a new silk-spinning plant. Soon Murray and Ryle were producing sewing silk. By 1860 others had joined the silk enterprise, bringing Paterson's silk producers to six.

Samuel Colt in 1836 invented the Colt revolver and founded the

Above: An early engraving of the Rogers, Ketchum & Grosvenor locomotive and machine works established by William Rogers in 1832 with the backing of New York capitalists Morris Ketchum and Jasper Grosvenor. A description of the Rogers works in 1867 describes it as "filled with machinery of the most ingenious construction, much of it the invention of Mr. Thomas Rogers, . . ." [above] Courtesy, Paterson

The Sandusky, the first locomotive made in Paterson, was manufactured at Rogers, Ketchum & Grosvenor. Completed in 1837 after sixteen months during which Rogers and William Swinburne, his chief mechanic, experimented, designed tools, and trained mechanics, the locomotive was delivered to the Mad River and Lake Erie Railroad in Ohio. Courtesy, Paterson Museum Archives

turning out wheels and axles for the South Carolina Railroad and ironwork for the Passaic and Hackensack bridges then under construction. Then Rogers, Ketchum & Grosvenor assembled the locomotive *McNeill*, which had been imported from England. These shrewd New Jerseyans copied what they assembled and produced the Sandusky from the design. On October 3, 1837, the Sandusky, the first locomotive constructed in America, made its first run.

Ohio railroadmen placed orders. Rogers's reputation for flexibility and his firm's veteran workers expanded its list of customers. Ohioans set their gauge by the Sandusky's, and by 1850 Rogers, Ketchum & Grosvenor were manufacturing 100 locomotives a year, colorful ones, glorious in their yellows, reds, and blues, their brass bells and whistles.

An observer wrote to the *American Railroad Journal and Mechanic's Magazine* about the Rogers, Ketchum & Grosvenor locomotives in 1839:

Owing to some circumstances, of which I am not informed, it became necessary for a locomotive on the way from Jersey City to New Brunswick, to take, in addition to its own load, the cars attached to another engine, which made the number equal to 25 loaded four-wheeled cars, and with as much apparent ease as could be desired, notwithstanding the grade for four miles is equal to 26 ft. per mile, stopping on the grade to take in passengers, and starting again with the greatest ease.

The average speed on the grade was 24 and 1/2 miles per hour. This may not be in your estimation anything extraordinary, yet, I consider it a performance worth recording, by way of contrast with the greatest and most extraordinary performance of a locomotive ever heard of in those days, which occurred on the Liverpool and Manchester Railroad in 1829, only ten years ago.

Twenty tons on a level road at the rate of ten miles per hour, was then considered wonderful! Astonishing! even in a country famed for its extraordinary discoveries; yet here, only ten years after we see an engine built in this country too, taking a load probably equal, cars and tender included, to 120 or 180 tons at the rate of 24 and 1/2 half miles per hour, up a grade of 25 ft. per mile.

This engine was built, I understand at Paterson, New Jersey, by Messrs. Rogers, Ketchum & Grosvenor, a concern not yet so well known to this railroad community of manufacturers of locomotives as they ought to be, or as they soon will be, if they continue to turn out such machines as the one above alluded to.

If such have been the improvements in the past, what may then not be, permit me to ask, in the next ten years?

The taller of the top-hatted gentlemen to the left resembles Edwin Prall, who in 1852 lured John Cooke, superintendent of Rogers, Ketchum & Grosvenor, to begin the manufacture of locomotives in Charles Danforth's cotton and cotton machinery factory. As railroad transportation expanded, the firm of Danforth and Cooke prospered, with customers throughout the United States, Mexico, and Central America. Courtesy, Paterson Museum Archives

Others emulated the Rogers, Ketchum & Grosvenor success. Two renegades broke away from Rogers, Ketchum & Grosvenor in 1845 to establish Swinburne, Smith & Co., which became the New Jersey Locomotive Company in 1852 and the Grant Locomotive Works after the Civil War. In 1852 Charles "Big Indian" Danforth formed the locomotive firm of Danforth, Cooke & Co.

By the Civil War the Paterson locomotive plants were making products valued at $1.5 million. An observant essayist wrote: "The advantages which Paterson possesses for a manufacturing town are obvious. An abundant and steady supply of water; a healthy, pleasant, and fruitful country, supplying its markets fully with excellent meats and vegetables; its proximity to New York, where it obtains the raw materials, and sale for manufactured goods; and with which it is connected by the sloop navigation of the Passaic, by the Morris Canal, by a turnpike, and by a railroad—tender it one of the most desirable sites in the Union."

Rogers eventually built his famous building at the corner of Spruce and Market streets, where his locomotives were assembled at the rate of one every other day. Workers there could assemble twelve locomotives at one time. When the building was finished in 1871, Rogers had grown into the busiest locomotive manufacturer in the United States.

By 1867 Swinburne, Smith & Co. had a five-acre plant. In 1867 they built the America, which was called a "poem in steel and silver" and which won the Grand Prize at the Paris Exposition of 1867. In the 1880s many railroadmen agreed that the Rogers works was unsurpassed in the world, but in 1885 Grant moved to Philadelphia, and Rogers closed its doors in 1904. The boom ended.

Between 1840 and the outbreak of the war, Paterson had grown from 7,596 to approximately 20,000 residents, and produced $6 million in goods annually. Some 3,500 men and 1,600 women worked in the factories and mills, making locomotives, cotton goods, some sewing silk, steam engines, and other machinery.

New Jerseyans Produce Paper and Newspapers

In 1807 Patersonian Charles Kinsey had patented a technique for making paper into a continuous roll. Nearly a century earlier William Bradford had erected the first paper mill in New Jersey at Elizabethtown, where he made rag paper. But Kinsey's invention, plus the large number of New Jersey streams, led residents to develop the New Jersey paper business. In Springfield alone there were some ten paper mills on the West Branch of the Rahway River.

New York and Philadelphia newspapers turned to New Jersey for paper. New York City buyers bought from Millburn's Condit Mill and Whippany's Eden Mill, which made eight to ten tons weekly for *Frank Leslie's Illustrated Newspaper*. By 1850 New Jersey was the fifth leading paper-producing state in the nation.

Colgate and the Colgate Clock

When William Colgate moved his soap factory from New York City to Jersey City's old Paulus Hook in 1847, skeptics dubbed the new plant "Colgate's Folly."

But this expansive new Jersey City plant became a modern industrial marvel of its day, its factory floors producing huge quantities of soap—as much as 45,000 pounds of soap bubbling at one time in a single vat. "Colgate's Folly" has proved the skeptics wrong, and its employment ranks soon numbered hundreds of people.

Today, although the Colgate-Palmolive Company has expanded to many other plants across the country and around the world, a huge piece of its history and its heart remains in Jersey City.

The Colgate-Palmolive Company office and factory complex off the Jersey City waterfront is a familiar landmark to all area residents on both sides of the Hudson. Especially familiar is its big clock on the roof at 105 Hudson Street, still advertising soap and perfumes.

And in 1908 the first Colgate Clock, its face measuring 37.5 feet in diameter and covering an area of 1,104 square feet, was installed on the roof of the Jersey City factory buildings. Later, this clock was moved to a new company factory at Jeffersonville, Indiana. But a brand new clock—the one known so well today—was installed on the Jersey City building in 1924.

And since noon, December 1, 1924, this octagon-shaped clock overlooking the Hudson River and Manhattan has attracted nearly as much attention in New York Harbor as the Statue of Liberty. The clock, measuring fifty feet in diameter, sits atop an eight-story building at the Colgate-Palmolive plant in Jersey City, visible to the thousands of commuters from New Jersey, Staten Island, and the Bronx. In fact, the clock, which is also brightly illuminated at night, can be seen from as far away as twenty miles.

The clock was designed by the late Warren Davy, a Colgate engineer, and the Seth Thomas Clock Company. Its octagonal shape derives from the trademark of Octagon Soap, a Colgate product which first began selling in 1887.

The total surface area of the Colgate Clock is 1,963.5 square feet—larger than most city lots. The framework of the clock is made of structural steel, and the face is made of stainless steel slats about four inches wide, spaced two inches apart.

The giant hands of the Colgate Clock were originally made of seven-ply wood reinforced with steel forgings from hub to tip. The minute hand is twenty-five feet, ten inches long and the hour hand is twenty feet long. Together, they weigh just under a ton apiece. Nonetheless, they are so delicately balanced that they can be adjusted with just a touch of the finger.

The tip of the minute hand travels 31 inches per minute or 155 feet per hour (one mile every 34 hours and 4 minutes). This giant timepiece usually stays within one minute of the correct time. If it exceeds this margin, an alarm bell automatically sounds to alert maintenance personnel. This is in stark contrast to the many public clocks which, keeping incorrect time, have lost the confidence of the public.

The movement of the Colgate Clock is controlled by a small master clock located in the Colgate-Palmolive plant's reception office. Finished in gold leaf and placed in a glass case, the master clock is connected with a nationwide wire-service system that provides the precise time as reported by the U.S. Naval Observatory in Washington D.C., the nation's official time-keeping agency.

The clock operates on the principle of a giant cuckoo clock. Weighted chains geared to the mechanism descend and are rewound by motors. When the rewinding cycle is completed, a limit switch stops the motors and the weights are ready for another descent. The rewinding cycle for the weight that controls the "seconds timer" occurs every seven minutes for a duration of ten seconds. The weight that

The Colgate Company, founded by William Colgate in New York in 1806, moved to Jersey City in 1847. In the buildings, which cover seven city blocks, the firm manufactures soap, glycerines, perfumes, and toothpaste, along with other products. Their landmark clock will be keenly missed after the firm's proposed departure in 1987 or 1988. Courtesy, The Star Ledger

advances the hands of the clock is rewound every eleven minutes.

Power for these motors is supplied by twenty-eight large-volt batteries which are automatically recharged. In case of an electric power shutdown, the clock will run at least forty-eight hours before the batteries are exhausted. A regular inspection of the batteries, electrical circuits, and clock mechanism is made weekly. The first battery, installed when the Colgate Clock was erected, gave twenty-four years of continuous service before it was replaced.

The sign next to the clock bears the legend "COLGATE'S" and beneath that "SOAPS—PERFUMES" in slightly smaller letters. The sign has remained the same, even though the company is now named Colgate-Palmolive and no longer sells perfumes. And as for the Colgate Clock itself, it remains as a sentimental landmark to the millions who have viewed it and relied upon it during the day, and admired its illuminated face by night.

—David Fleming

Right: John R. Watson's clay bank south of Mutton Hollow Brook supplied his brickworks, established in 1836 in Perth Amboy. As his broadside advertises, he also sold kaolin, the fine white clay used to make porcelain. Courtesy, Special Collections, Alexander Library, Rutgers University

Below: Salamander Works in Woodbridge was in operation from 1825 until it was destroyed by fire in 1896. At one time the largest clay products plant in the state, Salamander Works produced fire-brick, sewer and water pipes, ovens, furnaces, retorts, and crucibles. This molded stoneware pitcher with its lively firefighting scene came in five sizes according to an 1837 handbill. Courtesy, New Jersey State Museum Collection, Trenton

Watson's Fire Brick Manufactory,

ESTABLISHED 1836.

JOHN R. WATSON,

PERTH AMBOY, NEW JERSEY,

Manufacturer of Fire Brick

For Rolling Mills, Blast Furnaces, Foundries, Gas Works, Lime Kilns, Tanneries, Boiler and Grate Setting. Glass Works, &c.

FIRE CLAYS, FIRE SAND AND KAOLIN

FOR SALE.

Trenton Industrializes

Although it lacked good clay nearby, Trenton also became a pottery center. There was enough clay to encourage John Smith to establish a brickyard in 1817. Morgan Beakes also made bricks there in the 1820s and 1830s—upwards of 300,000 annually. Others, such as James Rhodes and John Morton, made coarse red earthenware "in Pot-Works" and "Earthen-Ware Manufactories" outside Trenton. Jacob Haster & Sons produced what they called "Earthenware of the best quality" in 1817. Joseph McCully and his nephew of the same name produced red earthenware during the first half of the nineteenth century, and others in the family kept the business going through the Civil War.

A more specialized product, salt-glazed stoneware, required special stoneware clays that were costly to obtain in Trenton. But Bernard Hanlon claimed in an advertisement in the *New Jersey Gazette* of 1780 that he made "a good assortment of Stone Ware: Potts, Jugs, Mugs, and Pans of different sizes." It may have been the success of these potters that lured William Taylor—the first person to fire his kiln with anthracite—and Henry Speeler back from East Liverpool, Ohio, in 1852. They began to produce Rockingham ware, named for its origins in Rockingham, England, and yellow ware. Rockingham ware supplanted redware in popularity during the third decade of the nineteenth century.

In the early nineteenth century, Trenton was thus known for its pottery, its flour mills, sawmills, ironworks, and its cotton mills. Trenton supplied both New York and Philadelphia with grain. In 1831 Trentonians completed the Trenton Water Power Canal, which produced power for a growing number of mills along its banks and gave a boost to the Delaware mill town.

The completion of the Delaware and Raritan Canal in 1838 spurred Trenton's economy even more. Coal from the Lehigh Valley came down the canal to be used and shipped by the Philadelphia and Trenton Railroad and the Camden and Amboy Railroad. Something of a sleepy river town before the 1830s, the city began to grow. By the 1840s, Trenton had fifty retail stores, four academies, a lyceum, eleven churches, and two banks. From 1840 to 1860 her population shot up from 4,035 to 17,228.

Trenton's pre-Civil War fame, of course, lay in iron and steel and in the careers of three men: Peter Cooper, Abraham S. Hewitt, and John Roebling. In 1845 Peter Cooper founded the South Trenton Iron Company to roll steel. In 1847, partnered with the stocky, bearded Abraham S. Hewitt, Cooper incorporated as the Trenton Iron Works. Railroad "T-Rails" began to flow from their mills. With the high-grade ore from the Andover furnace, Cooper and Hewitt produced a superior product and soon had orders from the Camden and Amboy Railroad for $180,000 in rails. Hewitt bought out the Ringwood ironworks revitalized by Peter Hasenclever in the eighteenth century. Cooper and Hewitt built blast furnaces at Phillipsburg and drove out the bog-iron competition.

By 1850 Cooper and Hewitt had built fifty-eight furnaces and six rolling mills, and the Trenton Iron Company had established itself as the "nation's foremost iron establishment," causing historian Allan Nevins to declare that Hewitt and Cooper had "the best-rounded iron works in the land."

In 1854 Cooper and Hewitt made the nation's first structural iron beams. Trenton's iron workers produced the structural beams for America's most important buildings and thus transformed American architecture. Trenton beams restored Princeton's Nassau Hall when it was gutted by fire. Trenton beams supported the new dome on the Capitol in Washington, which replaced the old cupola. Trenton's pre-Civil War fame led other states to order Trenton structural iron for public buildings. Peter Cooper used Trenton's iron beams to make the famous Cooper Union Building in New York City fireproof.

Cooper and Hewitt also tested the important Bessemer process in Phillipsburg long before anyone else in America. By injecting a cold blast of air into molten pig iron they hoped to drive out the carbon, silicon, and sulphur and convert the rest to steel. But they lacked the proper ores, and the process did not work. After the Civil War, however, Cooper and Hewitt would use the Siemens-Martin system to turn out their first "open hearth" steel.

In 1859 John A. Roebling moved his wire-rope factory from western

The Trenton Iron Company was incorporated by Peter and Edward Cooper, James Hall, and Abraham S. Hewitt. The firm obtained a contract for $180,000 for iron rails for the Camden and Amboy Railroad. Firsts for the company included the first American experiment with the Bessemer process, the use of the Siemens-Martin open-hearth methods, and the manufacture of rolled I beams which made possible the construction of multiple-storied buildings. Courtesy, Newark Public Library

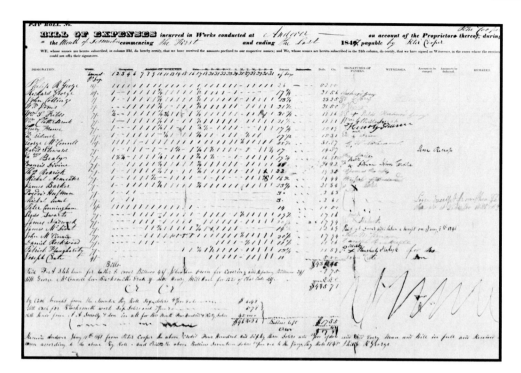

Workmen at the Andover Mine signed for their pay in December 1847, the year in which the Trenton Iron Works bought the mine to supply iron ore for their two new blast furnaces at Phillipsburg. Courtesy, New Jersey Room, Fairleigh Dickinson University

Pennsylvania to Trenton. There he planned the Brooklyn Bridge. John A. Roebling Company gave employment to scores of Italian and Slavic immigrants who made the cable for the Brooklyn Bridge. Because John A. Roebling died in 1869, he never saw his son, Colonel Washington A. Roebling, complete America's most famous nineteenth-century bridge. The Roeblings eventually built an entire town on the Delaware that bore their name.

Trenton's iron-manufacturing industry grew up with the city and the country. By 1860 twenty-three iron businesses had opened—a number which nearly doubled by the 1890s. Even by the Civil War Trenton's ironworks had supplanted the predominance of the grain and cotton mills.

Other sections of New Jersey participated in the development of the state's pre-Civil War iron industry. East Jersey Iron Manufacturing Company invested $283,000 in blast furnaces in Boonton. After the Morris Canal was opened, East Jersey Iron's 200 employees and 4 forges made pig iron, hoops, band iron, and locomotive tires. They also built the passenger cars for the Camden and Amboy Railroad.

Forges and foundries covered Morris County. Hanover township had five forges. Rockaway boasted two ironworks, and iron workers toiled at

The art of wire drawing—making strong cables from twisted wires—originated in Saxony, which was, by coincidence, the birthplace of John A. Roebling. Roebling began the process in Trenton in the mid-nineteenth century in this modest building, which was later expanded to become one of the foremost wire-rope manufactories in the world. Courtesy, Trenton Public Library

VENDUE.

THE Subscriber will offer for sale at Public Vendue, at his Store in Rockaway, Morris County, N. J., on

WEDNESDAY, August 11th,

At 12 o'clock, noon, of that day, all his REAL ESTATE in the county of Morris, consisting of the following described property, to wit: his

IRON WORKS,

Consisting of

TWO ROLLING MILLS, AND A FORGE WITH TWO FIRES,

With the tract of Land adjoining, containing about *Forty-Five Acres of Land*, through which the Morris and Essex Railroad passes within an eighth of a mile, and on which are three good DWELLING HOUSES, with a number of lots fronting on the R. R. Depot. The Mills and Forge are in good order, and the Rolls and Tools will be sold with the Mills and Forge.

Also, a Lot of Land on the Morris Canal, within an eighth of a mile of the Rolling Mills, on which is a

STEEL FURNACE,

A good DWELLING HOUSE, and a large and commodious BASIN and DOCK, all in good repair.

Also, a valuable **MINE** of Iron Ore, known as the " Mine," within three miles of the Works, with the Lot on which it is opened containing *One Hundred and Eighty-Seven Acres;* the length of vein on the lot is about thirty chains.

Also, a **Wood Lot** adjoining the above Mine Lot, containing *Two Hundred and Seven Acres.*

Also, a lot of **Farm Land** in the village of Rockaway, and fronting on the Rail Road and Public Highway, containing about *Forty Acres.*

Also, several

HOUSES AND LOTS

in the village of Rockaway.

Also, a lot of *Farm and Wood Land* near the village, containing about Ninety Acres. Likewise, about

Two Hundred Acres of Wood Land

In one parcel, near the village of Rockaway, and another of Seventy Acres, and a third of Fourteen Acres.

An unusually favorable opportunity will be presented for a safe and profitable investment of Capital. The conditions of sale, which will be very liberal and accommodating, will be made known on the day of sale, and previously on application by letter to the subscriber, if desired. The attention of Capitalists and Mechanics is solicited.

JOSEPH JACKSON.

Rockaway, Morris Co., N. J., July 13, 1852.

S. F. HULL, P'R. MORRISTOWN.

158

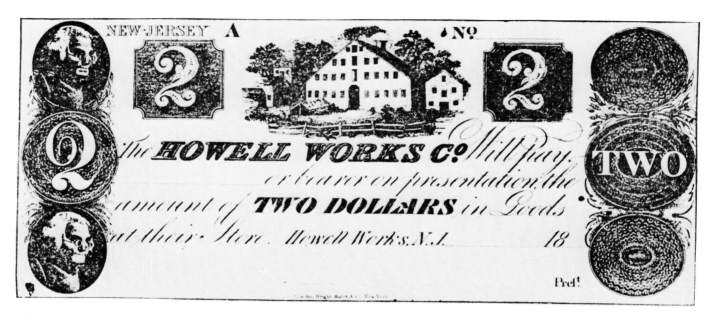

Millville, Weymouth, Bridgeton, and Morristown's Speedwell Iron Works. In 1834 William Henry developed the hot blast furnace at Oxford. This technique, which both increased production and reduced fuel consumption substantially, was a turning point in American iron production. Stanhope ironmongers built the first anthracite furnace outside Pennsylvania. The Morris County area soon teemed with them. To move the iron to the canals and railroads, special "iron mine railroads" were constructed throughout the iron region. By 1860 New Jersey's output of iron—her most valuable product at this time—placed her third in the United States, behind Pennsylvania and Ohio.

Trenton made iron. But it also became a rubber-producing center before the Civil War. In 1839, in New Brunswick, Horace Day had been producing rubber shoes, which some said "smelled to high heaven in the Summer and became hard as bricks in the Winter." Day probably cared little, for they sold well.

The stubborn Day refused to admit that he was infringing on Charles Goodyear's patented vulcanization process and retorted that Goodyear was violating *his* process. Daniel Webster took Goodyear's side in the legal case which followed. In his last major court appearance, the leonine, barrel-chested Webster outdid himself in playing to the courtroom crowd. Of course, everyone in the case was cowed by his towering reputation and his rhythmic oratory. Day's lawyers were crushed and Goodyear vindicated.

Christopher Meyer, who worked for Day but had broken away to launch his own rubber plant in Milltown, took Goodyear's side in the case and later became the major rubber producer in New Jersey. By 1852 his Milltown factories were turning out 1.8 million pairs of shoes annually. Charles V. Mead, one of Goodyear's investigators, closed the Trenton rubber plant of Hiram Dunbar and Garett Schenck, only to open it later himself and then expand it to five rubber plants in Trenton to make Trenton the state's rubber center.

This scrip was issued by James P. Allaire's Howell Works, the former Monmouth Furnace and Forge ten miles from Freehold, New Jersey. Allaire enlarged the works and added buildings to accommodate the increased operations and his numerous employees. After Allaire's death in 1858, his once-prosperous village fell into disrepair. The "Deserted Village" has now been restored as Allaire State Park. Courtesy, Newark Public Library

Facing page: Joseph Jackson of Rockaway was eighty-two when he advertised the sale of his ironworks. A grandson, son, and brother of Morris County iron masters, he had been associated with his father, Stephen, in mining and manufacturing since 1793. In 1820 he and his brother William built the rolling mills advertised here and the venture prospered through profitable U.S. government contracts. In 1852 the forge and rolling mills were conveyed to Freeman Wood for the manufacture of steel. Courtesy, Joint Free Public Library of Morristown and Morris Township

Left: At Speedwell Iron Works in Morristown, Stephen Vail and his sons produced iron machinery and tools, steam engines, and, with Samuel Morse, the electromagnetic telegraph. Vail's inventive genius contributed in no small way to the developments of the Industrial Revolution in America. Vail's factory, which survived a disastrous fire in 1908, is now one of the core buildings of "Speedwell Village," designated a National Historic Landmark in 1975. Courtesy, Joint Free Public Library of Morristown and Morris

Below: Although Alfred Vail was later associated with the invention of the telegraph, his contributions were at the time largely overlooked. Vail declined to put forth a claim, and Samuel Morse never acknowledged his associate's part in the instrument's invention. At Speedwell in Morristown, Vail provided the capital and worked with Morse to perfect the machine. The horizontal lever or key mechanism was devised by Vail. Courtesy, Special Collections, Alexander Library, Rutgers University

Facing page: In the eighteenth century, the Mount Hope mines were worked by Jacob Ford, and supplied ore for John Jacob Faesch's furnace and forges. The company whose scrip is illustrated here was incorporated in 1831, and in an 1882 history of Morris County, was termed "one of the most extensive and productive mineral properties in the state." Courtesy, Joint Free Public Library of Morristown and Morris Township

Sir Joseph Lister, the renowned nineteenth-century British surgeon, was the first physician to identify airborne germs as a source of infection in the operating room. In his theory of antisepsis, Lister presciently called these germs the "invisible assassins." Though other doctors were recognizing the need for greater care in protecting the wound area, Lister's concept of myriad living organisms, unseen and deadly, was beyond the grasp of many nineteenth-century surgeons, who were doubtful or even contemptuous of Lister's work.

One man who did not question Lister's theory of antisepsis was Robert Wood Johnson, who heard Lister speak in 1876. For years afterward, Robert Wood Johnson nurtured a plan for practical application of Lister's teachings. He envisioned a new type of surgical dressing, ready-made, sterile, wrapped and sealed in individual packages, and suitable for instant use without the risk of contamination.

Prior to Lister's discoveries, the postoperative mortality rate was as high as 90 percent in some hospitals. Surgeons could not imagine that they were contaminating their own patients by operating with unsterile instruments and without gloves.

Lister's methods required complex and bulky equipment suited only to the largest hospitals, of which there were few. A solution or spray of carbolic acid bathed the operating room and the patient in a foggy mist. This was nonetheless a major advance over standard procedures: unclean cotton, collected from floor sweepings of textile mills, was used for surgical dressing; surgeons operated in street clothes and wore their same blood-spattered frock coat many times over.

Robert Wood Johnson determined that there ought to be a better way. Mr. Johnson teamed up with his two brothers, James Wood Johnson and Edward Mead Johnson, who had already formed a partnership. In 1886 the three brothers launched their new venture in New Brunswick with just fourteen employees, on the fourth floor of a small building that was once a wallpaper factory. In 1887 the company was incorporated as Johnson & Johnson.

With few hospitals in the United States in 1887 large enough to use Lister's methods, Johnson & Johnson entered the surgical dressings industry. Its first products were improved medicinal plasters containing medical compounds mixed in an adhesive. Then the company designed a revolutionary new product: a soft, absorbent, cotton-and-gauze surgical dressing that could be mass-produced and shipped in quantity to hospitals, as well as to every local physician and druggist.

Meanwhile, Johnson & Johnson widely promoted antiseptic surgical procedures and in 1888 published a book, *Modern Methods of Antiseptic Wound Treatment*. For many years, this pioneering book was the standard text on antiseptic practices.

By 1890 Johnson & Johnson was treating cotton and gauze dressings by dry heat, trying to produce not only an antiseptic product but a sterile one. Early in 1892 the firm did indeed develop a sterile product, using a continuous method of handling dressings, which during production were kept under aseptic conditions and repeatedly sterilized. These new sterilization processes were done first by dry heat and later by steam and pressure. In 1897 the company developed another major contribution to surgery, an improved sterilizing technique for catgut sutures.

An important figure behind these developments was Fred B. Kilmer, Johnson & Johnson's scientific director, who served in that post for forty-five years beginning in 1888 and who was also the father of poet Joyce Kilmer. A highly respected writer on scientific and medical subjects, Kilmer influenced the profession's attitude through articles in Johnson & Johnson magazines such as *Red Cross Notes* and *The Red Cross Messenger*.

Cooperating with several top American surgeons, Johnson & Johnson in 1899 developed the zinc oxide-type of adhesive plaster. Its greater strength and quick sticking quality made this plaster an important new surgical tool. It also prevented irritation to delicate skin, bringing relief to many a patient.

In 1910 Johnson & Johnson's first president, Robert Wood Johnson, passed away. Under his leadership the company had firmly established itself as a health-care leader. James W. Johnson succeeded his brother, serving as president until 1932.

The company's international growth, begun in 1919 with the opening of an affiliate in Canada, was launched in earnest in 1923 after a worldwide tour by Robert Wood Johnson's two sons —namesake Robert Wood Johnson and J. Seward Johnson. The two brothers returned convinced that the company must establish an international presence. In the following year, 1924, Johnson & Johnson created its first overseas affiliate, Johnson & Johnson Ltd., in Great Britain.

During this period the company increased its diversity, introducing in 1921 what would become one of the best-known and most widely used of all Johnson & Johnson products—Bandaid Brand Adhesive Bandages—and many other new products, including Johnson's Baby Cream.

The rest, as they say, is history. The company's growth, diversification, and internationalization from the 1920s onward has been staggering. Today Johnson & Johnson is a worldwide group of 165 companies marketing health-care products in 153 countries. It has over 70,000 employees making products for a wide array of medical needs, ranging from baby care, first-aid and hospital products to ethical pharmaceuticals, diagnostics, and products relating to family planning, dental care, dermatology, and feminine hygiene.

—David Fleming

Glassmakers Become Farmers

Pioneered by Casper Wistar and John Stanger, glassmaking had developed during and after the American Revolution in the area around Glassboro and Millville, where there was plenty of good New Jersey sand. The Stangers worked out of Glassboro. James Lee, who had started a glassworks in Port Elizabeth in 1799, opened an enterprise in Millville in Cumberland County near the Williamstown and Millville sand beds. Under a protective tariff during the early days of the New Republic, glassmaking prospered in New Jersey.

In Jersey City, P. C. Dummer founded Jersey Glass in 1824. There he developed a glass-pressing mold, which he patented in October 1827.
In Glassboro in 1840, Captain Eben Whitney absorbed the Stangers into his Whitney Glass Works, which was thereupon swallowed in the twentieth century by the Owens Company (named for Michael Owens of Toledo, Ohio, who invented the Owens Bottle Making Machine).

Captain Whitney also added to American political lore long before the "Glassboro Summit" between Lyndon Johnson and Aleksei N. Kosygin. In the presidential election of 1840 one of William Henry Harrison's detractors chided that Harrison should be given "a barrel of hard cider" so he could sit in a log cabin and "study moral philosophy." Harrison's forces quickly turned the sneer into a slogan. And Whitney got the bid to develop the log-cabin souvenir bottles. Labeled "E. B. Booz's Old Cabinet Whiskey," they became collector's items in the election in which log-cabin candidate Harrison ("Tippecanoe and Tyler too") bested Martin Van Buren.

During the nineteenth century, New Jersey glassblowers became famous. Millville glassblowers created extraordinary items from sand that contained an almost pure silicon dioxide, which tinted the glassware a distinctive aquamarine.

Above: With this token a Whitney Glass Works employee could buy one cent's worth of merchandise at the company store. Courtesy, Camden County Historical Society

Top: Pressed-glass salt dishes from George Dummer's Jersey Glass Works bear the address of the Jersey City firm's New York sales office. Begun in 1824 at Communipaw Cove south of the Morris Canal, the firm specialized in cut glass, for which it won numerous prizes. Dummer ceased operation during the Civil War, probably in 1862. Courtesy, New Jersey State Museum Collection, Trenton

The DeWitt Wire Cloth factory in Belleville began as a copper wire and rolling mill operated by William Stephens, son-in-law of Josiah Hornblower's eldest son James. Among other products, this firm manufactured the telegraph wire that ran from Washington to Baltimore in 1844 in the third and most widely publicized demonstration of this significant invention. From Reminiscences of 75 years of Belleville, Franklin and Newark, *1890*

DeWITT WIRE CLOTH CO.

MANUFACTURERS OF ALL GRADES

Brass, Copper, Iron & Steel Wire Cloth.

Wire Ropes Wire Sash Cords. Copper Lightning Rods

Wire Window Screens and Guards.

Galvanized Wire Poultry Netting and Wire Fencing.

Brass, Copper and German Silver Wire.

Paper Makers' Materials.

Fourdrinier Wires. Cylinder and Washer Wires, Dandy

Rolls and Dryer Felts.

32 Reade Street.

NEW YORK.

Recent research concerning the buildings of the Passaic Steam Laundry, located in North Arlington, indicates that they originally housed the Stephens Brass and Lamp factory, operated in 1831 by William Stephens and John Dodd. Stephens later moved to Belleville to establish the firm later known as the DeWitt Wire Cloth Company. From Reminiscences of 75 years of Belleville, Franklin and Newark, *1890*

Producing some 200 bottles per day, the blowers often did their most creative work after hours, when they gave reign to their artistic natures. George and Helen McKearin have described the glassblowers' work in *American Glass*:

Since the blowers, whether in the late eighteenth or nineteenth century glasshouses, were under no compulsion to meet a current fashion in glassware, they formed their pieces as fancy or taste dictated. . . . But no matter how delicate or graceful in shape and decorative treatment, the pieces created by these blowers were invested with a quality of sturdiness rather than the feeling of fragility which characterizes more sophisticated ware. It is for these reasons that the glass in the South Jersey tradition has the intangible but distinctive characteristics of individuality and of the naivete and peasant quality associated with folk art. In fact, it has often been called American folk art in glass.

But, of course, as the glass industry adopted Owens' machines, the glassblowers of South Jersey died out.

A Jamesburg gardener working as assistant steward and chief gardener at Lafayette College in Easton, Pennsylvania, also made minor industrial

John Jelliff, Newark's leading nineteenth-century furniture maker, was born in Connecticut in 1813 and made his name in Newark producing handmade furniture at a time when machine-made furniture had become the vogue. This view of Jelliff's Broad Street warehouse was well known to local patrons who bought his Empire, Gothic, French-style, and Renaissance chairs and cabinets. Courtesy, Newark Public Library

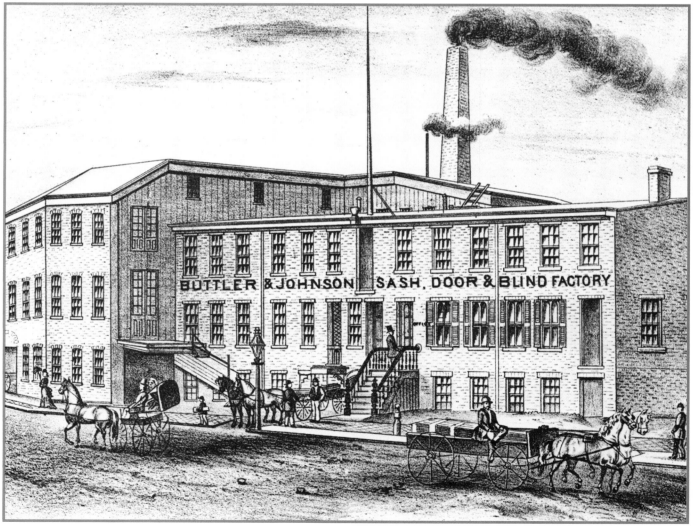

MARBLE CUTTERS.
CHARLES GRANT,
107 Market street opposite Harrision.
Manufacturer of Marble Mantels,
Tablets, Monuments, Tomb and Grave stones,
of the best Egyptian, Italian and American Marbles,
Executed in the best modern style. Also stone work for
Buildings, Made to order, of Connecticut or
Newark Stone.

Left: Quarrying and stonecutting was one of Newark's earliest industries. There were four stone quarries in Newark in the 1880s. In 1881, $120,000 worth of stone products were shipped to New York, New Haven, and Princeton. Charles Grant's "Marble Cutters" advertisement appeared in a mid-nineteenth-century Newark City Directory. Courtesy, Newark Public Library

Facing page, top: This 1873 view shows the Singer sewing machine plant, one of the state's and nation's most important industrial complexes in Elizabeth, New Jersey. Isaac Singer applied for an improvement patent on the sewing machine in 1851. Five years later he was producing the "iron needle woman" for $125. To make the expensive machines affordable, Singer and his partner Samuel Clark developed the concept of payment on the installment plan. Courtesy, Newark Public Library

Facing page, bottom: In 1859, partners Butler and Johnson became the new owners of the sash and blind shop located at the foot of Morris Street in New Brunswick. Fifteen years later operations had expanded into three-story brick buildings heated by the steam that also provided power for the factory's saws, planers, and moulding mills. The company's fancy woodwork no doubt included the "gingerbread" ornamentation so popular in Victorian architecture. Courtesy, Special Collections, Alexander Library, Rutgers University

history. Harrison Woodhull Crosby cooked tomatoes in seashore pails with lids and then soldered the lids to the cans. He found that this process allowed the tomatoes to be stored for a long time and thus developed the principle of canning. A shrewd publicist, he sent samples around to newspapers and even to Queen Victoria and President James K. Polk. Crosby later managed the N. H. Dudley Cannery at New Brunswick. After the Civil War, Joseph Campbell built a canning factory in Camden that would become Campbell Soup.

By the 1850s New Jersey was beginning to mature industrially. The state had grown particularly strong in iron, food and drink, men's clothing, textiles, and leather goods. Headed by the Trenton Iron Works, the largest single ironworks in the nation, the state produced iron goods worth $10.8 million, placing New Jersey among the four leading states in iron production on the eve of the Civil War. But the center of the industry was shifting westward, and by World War II New Jersey made only one percent of American iron. By the Civil War Newark produced 85 percent of all the patent leather made

Above: This worktable made by A.E. Noe is the only surviving labeled piece from the cabinetmaker who worked in Newark and Rahway. In 1845, the table, probably designed for a bedroom, sold for a surprisingly expensive twenty-one dollars.

Right: Newark's famous furniture maker John Jelliff made this chair for his daughter Mary Jelliff Peshine from designs she submitted circa 1850. This rosewood reception chair in the Gothic style was intended to introduce an intriguing element into a conventional Victorian parlor. Courtesy, Collection of the Newark Museum

in the country. The Delaware and Raritan Canal had helped bring Trenton to life as an iron and rubber center. By 1860 there were 56,000 factory workers in the state. Of these some 8,000 produced textiles; 11,000 sewed clothing, mostly men's; 8,000 worked in the iron industry; and 6,500 made leather goods.

New Jersey produced foodstuffs and beverages valued at $10 million, of which Newark's beer industry was an important part, but the bulk was still grains and bread products. New Jerseyans produced apparel valued at nine million dollars, mostly men's clothing and hats (23 percent of the national total of men's hats), and millinery. By 1860, 5.2 percent of men's clothing produced in the United States was manufactured in New Jersey. Much of the output of men's clothing, along with many other items, New Jerseyans sold to Southerners. Textile production, mainly cotton, but also some wool and some silk, totaled $8.7 million. Leather output was valued at $8.16 million.

New Jerseyans also produced carriages, ships, nonferrous metals, jewelry, stone, clay, glass, chemicals, paints, dyes, and drugs (the latter would become New Jersey's main product in the twentieth century). Strong in 1850, lumber and timber would decline after 1865. Elizabeth and Camden kept their carriage factories humming before the Civil War. New Brunswick created wallpaper and rubber factories and established the first nickel works in America.

But in 1860 a nation torn apart over the issue of slavery in the territories had to pick a new president. The state's electorate would have to vote in the most significant election of the nineteenth century. The two-party system shattered. Abraham Lincoln swept the electoral college but got only 40 percent of the popular vote. Radicals in the South determined that they would rather secede than remain loyal to a man and a party that won a minority of the popular vote. The nation began the catastrophic Civil War, which would transform the American and the New Jersey economies.

The brothers William R. and Henry L. Janeway started their wallpaper company in New Brunswick in 1848. By 1873 their Water Street factory (seen here in 1920) employed 150 people and produced two million rolls of paper hangings, borders, and window shades per year. A contemporary account notes that "this factory's work stands high in the market for excellence . . . for elegance of design and artistic finish, and it occupied a very important place among the industries of the city." Courtesy, Special Collections, Alexander Library, Rutgers University

Industrialism Ascendant

In August 1872, Newark industralists and businessmen mounted the first exhibition devoted exclusively to Newark manufacturers, and designed to prove that Newark, far from being a mere suburb of New York City, could lay claim to being New Jersey's premier manufacturing city. This sketch shows the various booths in the "Rink" on Washington Street, originally built for skating. Between August and September 1872, the exhibition attracted 130,000 visitors. Courtesy, Newark Public Library

The Civil War split New Jersey. Economically tied to Southern markets, New Jersey divided its electoral votes in the 1860 presidential election and gave candidate Lincoln four and Stephen A. Douglas three. Lincoln tried to make amends by visiting the state on his way from Springfield, Illinois, to his inauguration. Four years later, in the 1864 election, George McClellan, who lived in West Orange, carried New Jersey against Lincoln—one of the three states McClellan won.

The only state in the North to have slaves within its borders in 1860, New Jersey was also partially below the Mason-Dixon line. Editorial writer Edward N. Fuller of the *Newark Journal* supported secession. Bergen and Essex County Democrats opposed the war. After the Union forces had been routed in the Battle of Bull Run, Bergen County residents held peace rallies.

New Jerseyans denounced the Emancipation Proclamation as "unjust," "fanatical," and "unconstitutional." Both houses of the New Jersey Legislature passed antiwar resolutions and protested Lincoln's conduct of the war. Trenton Judge David Naar noted cynically of the war, "We are cutting each other's throats for the sake of a few worthless Negroes."

Slow to ratify the Thirteenth, Fourteenth, and Fifteenth amendments, not

George Brinton McClellan, New Jersey's choice for president in 1864, was a controversial figure in both his military and political careers. Relieved of his post as general-in-chief of the federal armies, and soundly defeated in the Electoral College, he retired from the national scene. He served as governor of New Jersey from 1878 to 1881. Courtesy, Newark Public Library

until 1875 would New Jerseyans strike the word "white" from the requirements for voting in their constitution.

But New Jersey officially did her duty to the nation during the Civil War. The state met her quotas for troops as fast as did other Union states. Thomas Nast, the famous Morristown cartoonist, used his trenchant drawings to became a fervent champion of the Union cause. Nast, said Lincoln, "is our best recruiting sergeant." Over 6,000 New Jerseyans gave their lives in the war. As New Jersey supplied food, arms, flags, and uniforms to the Union armies, the leading New Jersey industries—iron, food and drink, apparel and millinery, textiles, and leather and leather goods—all expanded.

For a state so ambivalent about the Union cause in the Civil War, New Jersey fared very well economically during the conflict. Indeed, contracts flooded the state. New Jersey workers made turret rings for the *Monitor* and turned out rifles for the Union troops. Hewes & Phillips's Newark factory converted 50,000 muskets from flintlock to percussion for the Union armies. The Rogers Locomotive Works in Paterson turned out nineteen locomotives for the government of the United States, and in 1863 the Trenton Arms Company made 3,000 rifles for the war.

Not surprisingly for a state with a schizophrenic approach to the Civil War, two Paterson-built locomotives made history in April 1862, one for the Union forces, one for the Confederate forces. Union forces in the Rogers-built General were destroying railroad tracks in Georgia as they moved toward the key railroad city of Chattanooga, when the Texas, another Paterson locomotive constructed by the Danforth-Cooke Works for the

Confederacy, began to pursue the General. After a sixty-five-mile race, the Texas caught the General and took its operators prisoner.

Postwar Growth

On May 17, 1866, a year after the end of the Civil War, Newark celebrated its two hundredth birthday with a parade. To get a bird's-eye view of what 200 years had done for Newark, a writer for the *Northern Monthly* climbed to the top of the Fagin & Company flour mill near the Passaic River.

From there, wrote the author, the view was grand, "as every hive of industry is grand from such an outlook, beautiful as few cities are—and surrounded by reaches of hill and dale, of grove and broad-spreading plain.

"The city is almost embowered with green. It is said that there is not a street in all Newark that is not adorned with shade trees. They cluster about the very factory doors; they line the busiest thoroughfares; the Broadway of the town is thick with them from end to end. The smokes of forges and engine-fires float up from amid the foliage, and the drayman's wheels mingle their rattle with the musical rustling of the leaves."

But in taking stock and in looking back, the Newarkers of those days, like many New Jerseyans, were hardly aware of what startling industrial changes lay ahead.

After the Civil War, a nation that had only begun to industrialize became

Above: Originally opposed to the Civil War, New Jersey's Governor Joel Parker played a major role in securing that state's ultimate support of the Union cause. Through Parker's diplomatic maneuvers in Washington, New Jersey was allowed to fill Union Army quotes through volunteers alone. Consequently, the federal draft was not exercised in the state. Courtesy, Special Collections, Alexander Library, Rutgers University

Above, left: Thomas Dunn English, educated as a physician, was a poet, novelist, and journalist as well. A member of the New Jersey General Assembly from Bergen County, English was an active member of the Peace Party in the state legislature and was a prominent speaker at peace meetings, where he denounced the Civil War as a "useless and wicked war." Courtesy, Newark Public Library

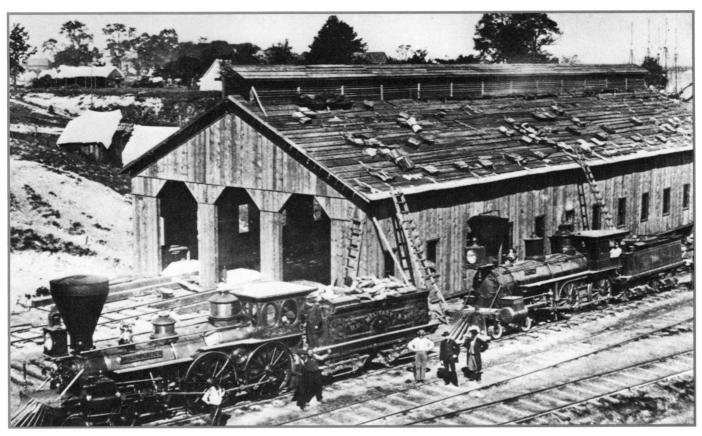

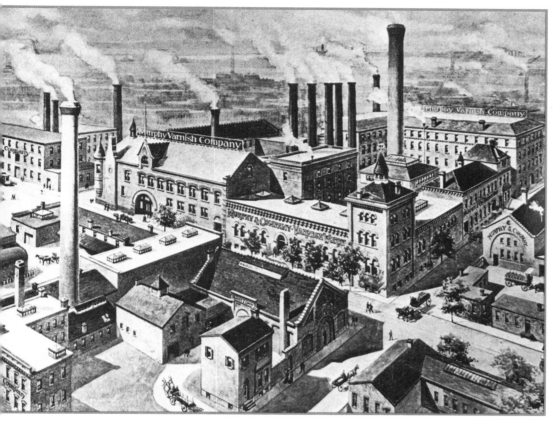

Left: Murphy Varnish Company in Newark, founded in 1865, was one of the state's best-known companies. The factory complex at Chestnut and McWhorter streets occupied two full city blocks in buildings that included an eclectic assortment of architectural styles—Italianate, Victorian, and Renaissance. Varnish made there was considered the nation's finest. Courtesy, Newark Public Library

Facing page, top: The General Grant, a Rogers-built locomotive, was photographed on a siding of the U.S. Military Rail Road at City Point, Virginia. During the Civil War, Paterson's locomotive works produced an average of one locomotive per day. Courtesy, Paterson Museum Archives

Facing page, bottom: Since the Rogers locomotive works had no direct railroad connection, the finished locomotive shown here circa 1860 would be carted across town to the tracks of the Paterson and Hudson River Rail Road, where it could proceed under its own steam. Aptly enough, the weathervane on the building smokestack is a locomotive. Courtesy, Paterson Museum Archives

a colossus among world manufacturers. The synergism of inventions and technological breakthroughs, exploitation of new raw materials, an expanding transportation system, the development of capital, and an influx of immigrant workers pushed the American gross national product from $1.8 billion in 1859 to over $13 billion in 1899.

New Jersey's iron industry, discussed in Chapter 5, which ranked third in the nation at the outbreak of the Civil War, continued to be a central force in the postwar American economy. Although the national industry shifted to the sources of ore and coal in the Pittsburgh region, Dover, Wharton, Rockaway, Stanhope, Paterson, Phillipsburg, Trenton, and Bridgeton all made and rolled iron after the war. In fact, Morris and Sussex County iron mines hit their record 932,762 tons in 1882.

Railroads and Trolleys Unite the State

As discussed in Chapter 4, the railroads also continued to generate economic growth. The development and consolidation of the trunk lines of the New York Central, the Erie, the Pennsylvania, and the Baltimore and Ohio railroads moved goods and helped lower prices. The expanding railroad lines stimulated the economy by encouraging technological breakthroughs like the telegraph, the improvement of steel, and the invention of the air brake. The railroads moved masses of workers to new regions and new jobs.

As the corridor for the Pennsylvania Railroad's connection to New York City, New Jersey developed economically along its railroad lines from

This portrait of Daniel F. Beatty may very well have been a reproduction of the "life-size likeness" painted in oil, which hung in Beatty's office at the time of a reporter's visit to Beatty's organ and piano factory in Washington, Morris County, during the 1880s. Beatty, born in the Musconetcong Valley, developed a business that became the chief industry in the town of Washington. Courtesy, Newark Public Library

The Birch "Madagascar" Pousse-Pousse, No. 7 With hood

"Jinrikishas," or man-power wagons, were manufactured by J.H. Birch Carriage Company in Burlington, from the 1870s until the plant closed in 1918. The conveyance was the idea of the Reverend Jonathan Goble, a Baptist minister in Yokohama who needed a way to transport his ill wife. It soon spread to most of the Orient, including Japan, China, India, Burma, and the Philippines. Courtesy, Newark Public Library

Below: The American Star bicycle was manufactured by H.B. Smith Machine Company in Smithville, a model industrial community planned by Hezekiah B. Smith. As designed by George Pressey, the bike's smaller front wheel provided greater stability for the high wheelers popular in the 1880s. Courtesy, Special Collections, Alexander Library, Rutgers University

New York to Philadelphia, and the stretch between New Brunswick and Trenton became, according to historian John T. Cunningham, the "most intensely traveled stretch of land on the continent." The proximity of the railroad and the connections between New York and Philadelphia brought Thomas Edison to New Jersey.

In 1862 the Jersey Central got a charter for a bridge across Newark Bay. During the war, for safety and to speed movement of goods and people, the corridor between Trenton and New Brunswick went to double track. The Camden and Amboy's Ashbel Welch in 1863 developed the "all clear ahead" signal system. He later designed the first interlocking switch system, which cut accidents. When on June 30, 1871, the Pennsylvania Railroad leased all rights-of-way owned by the United Canal and Railroad Companies for 999 years, the Pennsylvania, with its new access to New York

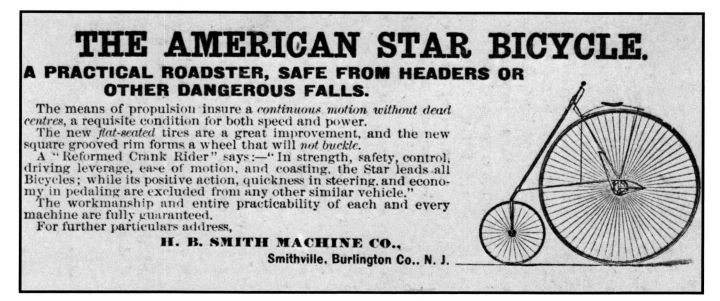

THE AMERICAN STAR BICYCLE.

A PRACTICAL ROADSTER, SAFE FROM HEADERS OR OTHER DANGEROUS FALLS.

The means of propulsion insure a *continuous motion without dead centres*, a requisite condition for both speed and power.

The new *flat-seated* tires are a great improvement, and the new square grooved rim forms a wheel that will *not buckle*.

A "Reformed Crank Rider" says:—"In strength, safety, control, driving leverage, ease of motion, and coasting, the Star leads all Bicycles; while its positive action, quickness in steering, and economy in pedaling are excluded from any other similar vehicle."

The workmanship and entire practicability of each and every machine are fully guaranteed.

For further particulars address,

H. B. SMITH MACHINE CO.,
Smithville, Burlington Co., N. J.

NARRAGANSETT STEAMSHIP CO.

NEW JERSEY SOUTHERN RAILROAD LINE

—— FOR ——

LONG BRANCH,

PORT MONMOUTH, FARMINGDALE,   And Intermediate Points.   MANCHESTER, TOMS RIVER.

On and after MONDAY, JUNE 20th, 1870,

THE MAGNIFICENT SALOON STEAMERS

Plymouth Rock,

Commander L. V. TILTON, and

JESSE HOYT,

Commander JAS. SEELEY, Will leave from

PIER 28, North River, foot of MURRAY ST., DAILY, Sundays excepted, as follows: PLYMOUTH ROCK at 6.45 A. M., 4.30 P. M.; JESSE HOYT at 9.45 A. M., 3.30 & 11 P. M., connecting at Sandy Hook with the New Jersey Southern Railroad for Long Branch. By this Route Passengers enjoy a delightful excursion down the Bay to Sandy Hook, from thence, twenty minutes railway travel on the ocean shore to Long Branch. A GRAND

Promenade Concert on the Plymouth Rock

DAILY, BY THE Celebrated Brass, Reed and String Band of the Ninth Regiment, N. G. S. N. Y.

RETURNING as follows: JESSE HOYT leaves Port Monmouth pier, via Sandy Hook, 6.50 A. M., leaves Sandy Hook at 7.28 A. M., connecting with the Trains from Long Branch. PLYMOUTH ROCK leaves Sandy Hook 8.15 A. M., 7.26 P. M.

For Freight, 9 P. M., or on arrival of Trains from the above-named points. Freight received up to 9.00 o'clock P. M.

JAMES FISK, JR.,

PRESIDENT.

JUNE 1870.

M. R. SIMONS, Managing Director.
CHAS. B. KIMBALL, Gen. Pass. Agent.
H. H. MANGAM, Freight Agent.

Above: Travelers arriving at the Long Branch depot of the New Jersey Southern Railroad found themselves loudly solicited by hack drivers for the various hotels. The coach loading passengers at left is bound for the Ocean Hotel, a popular hostelry in the center of town. From Frank Leslie's Illustrated Newspaper, *July 26, 1873*

Left: The Philadelphia and Reading Railroad, successor to the Philadelphia and Atlantic, was double-tracked in 1889. The gentlemen pictured here could look forward to a trip of fifty-four miles lasting seventy or eighty minutes. He might also ride in an "elaborately furnished parlor car in charge of attentive porters." Courtesy, Atlantic City Public Library

Facing page: After a pleasant trip across New York Bay, passengers on the New Jersey Southern Railroad's Steamer Division could board a train at Sandy Hook bound for the horseraces at Long Branch or for other delights of the New Jersey shore. Courtesy, New Jersey Room, Fairleigh Dickinson University

179

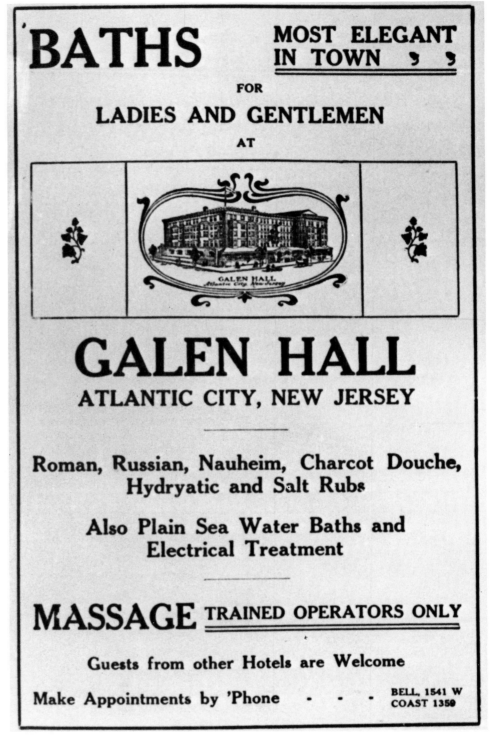

harbor, became a major railroad influence in the state.

Three railroad "wars" riveted the public's attention during the 1870s. When the Jersey Central attempted to dump garbage from New York City in Jersey City to create landfill for a station, the "garbage war" was on. In 1870, when the Erie Railroad Company sought to block the Lackawanna from using a tunnel through Bergen Hill, their workers placed a locomotive across the tracks, initiating the "tunnel war."

In 1873 the state legislature passed a law enabling any railroad to lay track where it wanted without special state charter. Small New Jersey towns celebrated. Between 1870 and 1880, trackage in the state jumped almost 50 percent. Encouraged by this law, the Delaware & Bound Brook Railroad Company began laying track from Jenkintown, Pennsylvania, to Bound

FRANK LESLIE'S
ILLUSTRATED
NEWSPAPER

Entered according to the Act of Congress, in the year 1873, by Frank Leslie, in the office of the Librarian of Congress, at Washington.

934—Vol. XXXVI.] NEW YORK, AUGUST 23, 1873. [Price, 10 Cents.

Brook, where the line would cross part of the Pennsylvania line near Hopewell. The Pennsylvania Railroad Company opposed their placing a "frog" crossover where the tracks met. The "frog war" was on. The courts finally decided in favor of the Delaware & Bound Brook.

As the late-nineteenth-century railroad system developed, New Jersey commerce expanded and businessmen began commuting to New York City and elsewhere. In the 1880s the roads added refrigerated cars, which expanded New Jersey produce markets.

Although the Pennsylvania became a major railroad power in the state, many observers understood that the Camden and Amboy Railroad dominated the New Jersey Legislature. William Sackett wrote of the Camden and Amboy Railroad, "So absolute was its control of all departments of the State government that the state itself came to be known derisively among the people of other states as the 'State of Camden and Amboy.' There never was a more complete master anywhere of the destinies of a state than was

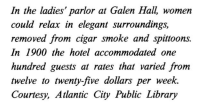

In the ladies' parlor at Galen Hall, women could relax in elegant surroundings, removed from cigar smoke and spittoons. In 1900 the hotel accommodated one hundred guests at rates that varied from twelve to twenty-five dollars per week. Courtesy, Atlantic City Public Library

this master monopoly of the affairs of New Jersey."

In 1854 Richard B. Osborne and his friends had launched their "Bathing Village" of Atlantic City by building a railroad line to take guests there. Thirty-five years later, Atlantic City entrepreneurs built a cousin of the railroad, New Jersey's first trolley, to take vacationers up and down Atlantic Avenue. Many townspeople feared the trolley, which they thought was "run by lightning."

"Boys welcomed the cars as a source of sport," another observer noted, "and irritated the conductor by stealing rides. Some of the more daring stretched full length on the tracks, jumping up as the motorman ground on his brakes and the crowd gasped. A casualty is threatened unless a restraining influence is brought to bear."

There is no saltwater in Atlantic City's famous saltwater taffy. However, Fralinger's in the 1920s claimed sea air and sunshine as ingredients in their award-winning candy. Established in 1885 by Joseph Fralinger, the firm's original molasses-flavored taffy cost five cents for six individually wrapped pieces. Courtesy, Atlantic City Public Library

But horse wagons were on the way out. The Irvington Street Railway Company abandoned its cable-car system in 1888 when the grip on the cable failed to open and sent the car lurching forward. By 1890 Passaic, Garfield, and Clifton had linked their three towns with the new electric trains. Introduction of the air brake in the early 1900s reassured some about safety.

The Public Service Corporation, chartered in 1903, developed a thorough system of street railways in Jersey City, Newark, and the rest of northern New Jersey. They even ran lines to Trenton and Camden from northern New Jersey, but these were not financially successful. By 1911 Public Service had bought or built nearly 1,000 trolleys. The corporation constructed its terminal and office building in Newark in 1916, a year that nearly half a million passengers used Public Service trolleys. The Public Service Corporation's gas division supplied gas and electric service to the general public as well as providing the company's streetcars with electricity. The Morris County Traction Company ran its line from Elizabeth through Morristown to Lake Hopatcong.

Within a decade only Phillipsburg among major New Jersey towns still employed horses alone to haul trolleys. The interurban lines proved less financially successful than the local lines, but both were having difficulties in the 1920s, as the gas jitneys appeared. In 1924 the Public Service Transportation Corporation developed bus lines that, because they were more efficient, dispatched the trolleys into history. Only Newark's City Subway stands as a reminder of the days of the New Jersey trolley.

The horse cars shown here at the corner of West Broadway and Broadway in Paterson belonged to the Paterson Railway Company, a consolidation of all former horse railroad companies in the city. The company, which introduced electric trolleys in 1891, was headed by Garret A. Hobart, vice-president of the United States under William McKinley in 1897-1899. Courtesy, Paterson Museum Archives.

Broad Street in Newark in 1890. On the left is City Hall, on the right is the tower of Old First Church, and in the background can be seen the large Romanesque-style Prudential Insurance Company of America building. Horse-drawn streetcars began service in June 1860, and by the 1890s the first electric trolley cars began to appear on city streets. Courtesy, Newark Public Library

As the state's population increased and suburbs proliferated, trolley cars met the need for local transportation. Horse cars were supplanted by electric trolleys in the 1890s, an event that gave some communities cause for celebration. The first electric trolley in New Brunswick was bedecked with flowers and flags in 1894 as the Brunswick Traction Company celebrated the first anniversary of its horseless car. Courtesy, Special Collections, Alexander Library, Rutgers University

Above: A horse car and an electric trolley await Philadelphia passengers at the Market Street Terminal of the West Jersey Rail Road Company in Camden. This view was taken circa 1895 from the hotel built by the West Jersey Ferry Company in 1849. Courtesy, Camden County Historical Society

Left: In Milltown on the first anniversary of electric trolley service in 1896, citizens were treated to a nostalgic ride on the Middlesex and Somerset Traction Line's former horse trolley. Courtesy, Newark Public Library

By the latter part of the nineteenth century, New Jersey had its share of wealth, industry, and powerful corporate home offices, but when Standard Oil came to New Jersey at that time, it was nonetheless quite an addition.

New Jersey's strategic strong point for commerce has always been its location between two major cities, New York and Philadelphia. In the late-nineteenth century New Jersey also boasted very liberal chartering laws, and many big businesses such as Standard Oil flocked to establish their headquarters there.

John D. Rockefeller, an ex-book-keeper from Cleveland, Ohio, and partners first established an oil refinery in 1863. In 1870 he organized the Standard Oil Company of Ohio and started building his staggering oil fortune by acquiring small Pennsylvania oil refineries one by one, amalgamating them into Standard Oil. By 1878 Standard Oil, in connection with other Rockefeller companies, controlled about 85 percent of the American oil industry.

Trust laws aside, Rockefeller also liked New Jersey for its location and its ample port facilities. From the wharves and docks of Hudson County, Standard Oil's kerosene and crude oil could be shipped to any location in the world.

And so in 1878, Standard Oil entered the New Jersey market, purchasing a small refinery in Bayonne. The company built a 400-mile pipeline connecting the Bayonne refinery with the oil fields in western Pennsylvania. The pipeline was a remarkable engineering achievement in its day, winding through the Pennsylvania and New Jersey countryside, snaking over hills, rivers, and streams.

Rockefeller was not the first oil baron to set up shop in Bayonne. The town had started to become a major refining center in 1875, when the Prentice Refining Company established a still there. Then came John D. Rockefeller, and within a decade three other companies were also refining oil in Bayonne. The establishment of Prentice in 1875 thus marked a turning point in Bayonne's history, as the town grew to be known as one of the world's major refining centers.

Standard Oil continued to expand its own facilities, producing ever more kerosene for foreign and domestic markets. Interestingly, the company could not find a use for the "gasoline" that remained after the refining of the kerosene, sealing wax, and lubricants. So this useless gasoline was simply burned away. It would still be some time before the advent of the automobile would change all that.

Meanwhile, back in Ohio, by 1881 Rockefeller had created the Standard Oil Trust to own the stock of Standard Oil's various companies across the nation. The United States Supreme Court ordered that trust dissolved in 1892 after a suit was filed by the State of Ohio.

By 1889 nearly every state in the Union began passing tough antitrust legislation, but New Jersey legislators passed a law *authorizing* "holding corporations." Standard Oil promptly took advantage of the laissez-faire New Jersey law, setting up a state-based trust to include its companies from coast to coast. The law permitted Jersey Standard—or any companies "domiciled in New Jersey"—to hold stock in any other companies, contrary to laws in nearly all other states.

Thus, Standard Oil reincorporated under the Revised Act of the State of New Jersey. In 1899 Rockefeller created the Standard Oil Company of New Jersey as the holding company for all the separate units which the Standard Oil Trust had been forced to yield up. By 1907 the new Standard Oil controlled sixty-seven companies in all phases of the oil industry.

By the turn of the nineteenth century, some 3,000 people at Bayonne were refining 40,000 barrels of crude oil per day. But in 1909, Standard Oil opened a modern new refinery at Bayway in the Arthur Kill, where oil tankers could come and go with ease. The modern Union County plant was known as "the kerosene factory," presenting further proof that kerosene was still dominant and that gasoline was not yet important. The Bayway refinery is still going strong today.

Though its major activity was in Bayonne, Standard Oil Company of New Jersey's official headquarters was located in the scenic, bucolic town of Flemington, the seat of Hunterdon County and quite distant from the shores of Bayonne. This was done to take advantage of certain complex clauses in the New Jersey tax laws and is testament to the complexities of Standard Oil's enormous operations.

In time, the Supreme Court found the new Standard Oil trust based in New Jersey to be in violation of the Sherman Anti-Trust Act and ordered it broken up in 1911. Today, Exxon Corporation is a direct descendant of the Standard Oil Company of Ohio. Three other of the world's largest oil companies are also products of the 1911 dismantling of Standard Oil: Standard Oil of California (Chevron), Mobil Oil, and Standard Oil of Indiana (American Oil).

—David Fleming

New Jerseyans Refine Oil

Although the Sherman Antitrust Act of 1890 intended to outlaw conspiracies in restraint of trade, in 1895 Supreme Court Justice Melville Fuller held in *U.S.* v. *E.C. Knight Company* (or the "Sugar Trust Case") that "commerce succeeds to manufacture, and is not part of it." Manufacturing, he wrote, affects commerce "only incidentally and indirectly." Therefore, the American Sugar Company, which manufactured over 90 percent of American sugar, was not a conspiracy in restraint of trade. Even though American Sugar's monopoly of production might "unquestionably tend to restrain" commerce, wrote Fuller, it did not do so directly.

This decision, which only Justice John Marshall Harlan opposed, opened the door to manufacturing "trusts." The state fathers had always encouraged business and had placed no limits on the capitalization or bonded indebtedness of firms in the state. The legislature kept corporation taxes low. State laws tolerated interlocking directorates and stock-watering. During the Gilded Age, corporate influence on state legislation grew. Industrialists' hostility to the collection of the data emasculated the pro-labor Bureau of Statistics of Labor and Industry of New Jersey.

In 1895 the legislature amended the corporation laws to encourage the incorporation of holding companies. New Jersey became known as the "mother of trusts." The state attracted out-of-state firms, including John D. Rockefeller's Standard Oil group, whose lawyers had invented the concept of the trust.

To take advantage of Bayonne's water supplies and the city's proximity to markets, Prentice Oil Company built a refinery in Bayonne in 1875. In 1877 Rockefeller built his refinery there. He competed not only with Prentice but also with the Tidewater Oil Company, which had built an amazing 400-mile pipeline over the Alleghenies to Bayonne and brought in western Pennsylvania crude oil. Accomplished with enormous skill by Tidewater's engineer Herman Haupt, who also kept the Rockefeller interests guessing by commissioning a series of false surveys to distract them, the pipeline compared in engineering skill with the Brooklyn Bridge and carried over one million barrels of oil during its first year.

By 1881 Rockefeller's Standard Oil group controlled about 90 percent of the petroleum industry. Despite this fact, John D. Rockefeller could not defeat the competition from Tidewater's pipeline. But he worked out a compromise arrangement regarding the pipeline that both Tidewater and Standard Oil could claim was a victory. In the 1880s another waterfront refinery, Borne & Scrymser, was sending oil all around the globe from its South Elizabeth operations.

By 1900 the two giant Bayonne companies were refining over 40,000 barrels daily and employing some 3,000 men. In 1899 New Jersey's largest four oil refineries produced 8.6 million barrels of petroleum products. In need of room, Standard Oil in 1909 began a refinery at Bayway in the Arthur

The benefit performance at the Paterson Opera House was no doubt designed to replenish the coffers of the Dyers' Union in the wake of an abortive strike on February 9, 1887. Sixteen hundred workers left their dye boxes after silk manufacturers refused to meet the demand of the Knights of Labor for a union shop. Courtesy, New Jersey Room, Fairleigh Dickinson University

OPERA HOUSE!

MONDAY EVENING, MARCH 28, 1887.

Complimentary Testimonial Benefit

—IN AID OF THE—

Dyers' Union

On which occasion, by special request the popular young author,

JOHN J. McKENNA,

will once more appear as "GERALD CLAYTON," a Confidential Clerk,
Supported by the LYNWOOD DRAMATIC COMPANY,
In his successful Romantic Drama,

SHADOWS OF CRIME!

PROGRAMME.

OVERTURE..ORCHESTRA

CAST OF CHARACTERS.

EMILY ARMSTRONG	The Banker's Daughter	MRS. J. J. McKENNA
HETTIE MARION		MISS MARY McKENNA
NORAH CASSIDY	a domestic	MR. THOS. A. MURRAY
PETE KING	a coachman	MR. J. SCANLAN
JAMES ALBERTS	a clerk	MR. J. ORR
LEVI COHN	a money lender	MR. J. F. ALLGIER
KINGSTON	a detective	MR. CHAS. KINNEY
CHAS. ARMSTRONG	a banker	MR. E. C. CRYSTAL
MICHAEL O'GRADY	"one of the finest"	MR. J. T. MURPHY
BILLY KANE	a tough	MR. F. BOTT

Policemen and toughs by the company.

Synopsis of Scenery and Incidents.

ACT I.—The banker's office. The Plot. "My God, I have been robbed!" The ticket for Canada. I'll keep those papers, they may be useful. I may have a chance to prove my innocence. TABLEAU.

ACT II.—(After three years.) SCENE 1st.—Street. "Hello Cohen!" Do you want to squeeze the hand off me? SCENE 2nd.—Gardens of the Armstrong mansion. "Oh, Lord, I'm stabbed!" Oh, Pete dere she am, brace up. The meeting after three years. Acum. What was that? Good bye. I love you. Do you wish to insult me? The story. Go. Now for Levi Cohen. Pete! Pete! Clayton home again. F fifteen thousand, just think of it. There he goes. Five hundred cases. SCENE 3rd—Street. I must see Kingston. SCENE 4th.—Broadway at night. The happy apple woman. Helle, Aunty? The finest police. Move on or I'll ate ye. The fatal letter. The struggle and the murder. Dead. I have been stabbed. I swear. The knife. Police! police! police! What is the meaning of this? That man. The arrest. Pete, stop here. I, Emily, I saw him do it. You lie. I wish I was home. Take full charge of her. I will keep the promise to her father. TABLEAU.

ACT III.—Reception room in the Armstrong mansion. The dream and the vision. It was he, James Alberts. You are nervous. He coming here, thank God. I will tell the Miss. The detective. The story to save him. Take charge of her. The prayer. Trust in him. I don't like to see her. Ma has gone to Connecticut. I am all persperation. I hear it. I'll convict you. Emily. Gerald. My prayer has been answered. The knife. Nearly drives me mad. Not until I have brought James Alberts to justice. FIRST TABLEAU—An old account. My God, the dead shall rest. Thanks. Complete my mission. SECOND TABLEAU.

ACT IV.—Cemetery in snow, and by moonlight. Cohen let me in. The gang. There is the fire, go in. I must go to the city. They are going. The arrest. Clayton. The first of the gang. The crazy Jew. $15,000. The moon is up. She coming here? Abduct her. I'll fix his room. Clayton. The struggle for life. Open the door. Take things cool, Gerald Clayton. FIRST TABLEAU. —Have no fear, Miss. Thank God. Trust in him. Blow twice. The arrest. What am I arrested for? The murder of my father. SECOND TABLEAU.

ACT V.—Front and back parlors in Armstrong mansion. The happy Irish woman. Hettie. The comic love scene. Your promise to the dead. By battering his brains out against the bars of his cell. He has cheated the justice on this earth, but he can't cheat justice there. TABLEAU.

THEO. M. HOLLAND,

Paterson's Favorite Magician, justly surnamed the Prince of Magicians, in his Feats of Ledgerdemain.

Next to apppear will be

DREXLER & FITZPATRICK,

In their Jigs and Reels.

Now comes the King of Clubs

MR. M. G. DURKIN,

In his Artistic Manipulations of the Indian Clubs.

NOTE.—This gentleman stands second to none for grace, style and execution.

PROF. ANDY JOHNS,

The Premier Ventriloquist of the world, in his pleasing parlor entertainment introducing his Phamily of Phunny Pholks.

The performance to conclude with Dr. Alex. Davis, optical illusion,

FLORA, THE GODDESS OF FLOWERS

ORCHESTRA UNDER THE DIRECTION OF PROFESSOR RIPPEY.

Mr. E. C. Crystal	Stage Manager
Mr. John Murphy	Manager
Mr. J. W. McCarty	Master of Properties

Costumes by Lorrinne of Brooklyn.

"Call" Steam Print.

Kill which became the outstanding operation of its kind. Bayway and Bayonne grew to be significant centers of the American oil industry in the late nineteenth century. The most extensive on the East Coast, Bayway became one of the nation's largest petroleum refining facilities.

Labor Unions Surge

Between 1870 and 1890 the national work force mushroomed from 885,000 to 3.2 million—an increase of 370 percent. Industrialization brought a national economy and with it booms and recessions. Women entered the work force. The standard of living rose, but unskilled workers generally did not maintain a decent living standard. The harshness of late-nineteenth-century American industrialism spawned the union movement in which New Jerseyans played significant roles.

Even though real living standards rose with the gross national product, which skyrocketed 44 percent between 1874 and 1889, unskilled workers grew discontented with their long hours, the disparity between their lot and that of the rich, who were piling up great fortunes, and the impersonality of the new, mechanized society, which robbed them of their dignity.

In New Jersey in the 1880s, workers flocked into labor organizations. Under the leadership of Isaac J. Neall, the molders built locals in Paterson, Newark, Jersey City, and Elizabethport during the Civil War. But the depression of 1866-1867 decimated the molders' locals. Cigar makers, pottery workers, brewers, electrical workers, typographers (whose Newark Typographical Local 103 is the oldest continuously functioning union in the state), metalworkers, clothing salesmen, bakers, builders, and printing pressmen all joined New Jersey unions.

In the 1860s Neall and others also attempted to form the National Labor Union to make workers a political force. Described by historian Norman Ware as "a typical American politico-reform organization led by labor leaders without organizations, politicians without parties, women without husbands and cranks, visionaries, and agitators without jobs," the National Labor Union lacked broad appeal and collapsed in 1872, when its presidential candidate, Judge David Davis of Illinois, withdrew.

New Jerseyan Uriah Stephens launched America's second attempt at forming a national labor organization. Born in Cape May, and a onetime candidate for the ministry, Stephens taught school and then went into the needle trades. He organized the Knights of Labor in Philadelphia in 1869. His ideological organization attempted to unite all American workers into a brotherhood. Later led by Terrence Powderly, who wrote the famous autobiography *The Path I Trod*, the Knights developed more than 80 locals by the end of 1873. They built a New Jersey stronghold in Trenton.

In 1879 the Knights founded the New Jersey State Labor Congress (NJSLC). Before 1883 in New Jersey, there was no legal protection for collective bargaining. But that year the legislature passed what labor called its Magna Charta, a law protecting the right to organize and "to enter into

A sketch in the New York Daily Graphic, *July 29, 1885, recorded Newark's Labor Day parade passing along Broad Street in front of the former City Hall, almost ten years before Congress declared Labor Day a national holiday.*

any combination for organizing, leaving or entering into the employment of other persons."

By 1886 the Knights dwarfed the nascent American Federation of Labor (AFL), which cigar makers Adolph Strasser and Samuel Gompers organized that year. The Knights founded the group that became the leading county association of unions in New Jersey, the Essex County Trades Assembly. In 1886 the Knights added 64 assemblies in New Jersey, giving them a total of 122 membership units and over 40,000 New Jersey members. But the Knights, a secret, interracial organization which reached out to every class of workers, including women in factories, were too visionary for the 1880s.

The future in the New Jersey and national union movement lay with the craft workers, who in 1886 were organized into 22 regular trade-union locals, with about 18,000 members statewide. New Jersey locals were particularly strong in the apparel and building trades.

In the late 1870s and early 1880s, strikes disrupted the New Jersey economy. Pottery workers in Trenton struck in 1877-1878 and then in 1883-1884. Management held firm and forced the workers to take an 8-percent salary cut to go back to work. The pottery strikes drove some of the owners to Ohio. In 1886 a Newark brewery strike engulfed Elizabeth, Paterson, and New Brunswick. The brewers won the ten-hour day, a 30-50 percent wage increase, and the ending of Sunday work. Strikes in company towns in South Jersey's glassworks in 1886, 1893, and 1899 all failed to end company stores there.

The labor agitation of the 1880s reached a peak in 1886. There were twice as many strikes that year than any previous year. The Haymarket bombing of 1886 in Chicago, in which seven police died when an anarchist threw a bomb into a crowd protesting the death of a striker at the McCormick Harvesting Machine Company, crystallized public opinion. The public incorrectly believed that the Knights were somehow tied to the bombing and stigmatized them as violent radicals.

In New Jersey and across the nation, led by the Cigarmakers Union, the AFL gradually outstripped the Knights. More practical, organized around the "bread-and-butter" concept of collective bargaining to improve working conditions and contracts, the crafts unions were simply better suited to the capitalist marketplace. "Our organization does not consist of idealists," said Strasser. "We do not control the production of the world. That is controlled by the employers. . . . I look to cigars."

Using this business-unionism philosophy, the AFL built itself into the dominant labor federation in the state in the 1890s and into the twentieth century. The NJSLC became the New Jersey State Federation of Labor, AFL, in 1888, and then became the State AFL-CIO in 1961.

In this interior view of Benjamin F. Boyer's Mill in Camden circa 1900, employees prepare worsted yarn. The Boyer Mill was one of a number of woolen and worsted mills, which made Camden the seventh-leading woolen producer in 1890. Courtesy, Camden County Historical Society

Textiles Expand

The depression of the mid-1870s shut down some of the cotton mills, but textiles—particularly silk—remained a strong element in the New Jersey economy after the Civil War. A high-priced fashion item, silk fared better than cotton during the mid-1870s decline. New Jersey maintained its lead in American silk output in the 1870s, and Paterson remained the center of the textile industry. By 1900 some 175 companies there employed over 20,000 silk workers. Silk cascaded from the mills: ribbons, yard goods for dresses, upholstery and drapery goods, linings, braids, and other items. The Millville textile development, begun by Richard D. Wood in 1856, grew after the war, as did the Washington Mills of Gloucester City, which had begun operation in 1844. Northeastern Pennsylvania also developed as a silk producer at the end of the century.

But Paterson would be the national silk center until the strike of 1913, which attracted worldwide attention and was backed by the romantic and radical International Workers of the World (IWW) and their colorful leaders "Big Bill" Haywood, Carlo Tresca, and Elizabeth Gurley Flynn. In 1913 the owners had a large inventory, and by maintaining control of the local police and by shifting production to their Pennsylvania divisions, the owners stuck together and won the strike, which lasted 149 days, saw 5 die, 2,000 blacklisted, and cost $9.5 million in wages and profits.

After the Civil War, George A. Clark, a Scot with both industrial experience and financial resources, began the Clark Thread Company on Newark's Fulton Street. By 1881 Clark, who came from a family that had been producing cotton sewing thread in Paisley since the Napoleonic Wars, employed over 2,000 workers. He branched out into Kearny, Harrison, and East Newark. The initials O.N.T.— "Our New Thread"—eventually became one of New Jersey's most famous advertising slogans.

In the 1870s immigrant workers in Newark, Jersey City, and Paterson made clothing on Isaac M. Singer's sewing machines. Singer consolidated his sewing-machine-manufacturing operations in 1873 in a $3 million Elizabethport plant which employed 3,000 workers. He later built the largest sewing-machine factory in the world at Elizabeth, and New Jersey led the world in producing sewing machines.

After the Civil War, Passaic developed cotton, woolen, and cashmere mills. Passaic led the rest of the nation in the manufacture of linens and linen thread. By the 1880s and 1890s, New Jerseyans manufactured suits, overcoats, shirts, ties, underwear, and nightshirts. In fact, the state became a needle-trades center. By 1900 over 130 custom tailors worked in Newark.

In 1889 Eduard Stoehr hired some German workers and established the Botany Mills in Passaic. Botany combined finishing, spinning, and weaving together in one location and prospered even during the depression of the mid-1890s. Other Europeans joined the Passaic concentration of mills at the turn of the century: Christian Bohnsen came from Denmark to

At the turn of the century, silk dyeing was an exclusively male occupation. Here Paterson workers prepare skeins of silk for the dyeing vats. One worker, in a necktie, proceeding up the aisle, appears to be quite young. Courtesy, American Labor Museum

Above: The prosperous Clark Thread complex on the Passaic River at Kearny was begun by brothers George and William Clark in 1864. The brothers developed a thread suitable for machine and hand sewing, which they labeled O.N.T.—Our New Thread. In 1888 the great chimney of the Clark Mill "Possessed the distinction of being the tallest chimney in America, and the fourth tallest in the world." Courtesy, Newark Public Library

found Gera Mills, and Julius G. Forstmann developed a textile enterprise in Passaic. In Freehold, Armenians Arshaug and Miran Karagheusian imported rugs; then in 1904, they began a mill. In the 1920s, they built a spinning plant in Roselle Park.

New Banking Laws Affect the State

During the Civil War, currency grew scarce. Boston, New York, and Philadelphia banks suspended hard-cash payments. New Jersey followed. Bankers soon realized that the national government, with its wartime capital requirements of one million dollars a day, needed an expanded, uniform, better-controlled currency, and a new banking system.

In 1863 Congress established the National Banking System, amended in 1864, which provided a market for government bonds, made possible speedier transactions among financial centers, stabilized the currency, and generated capital formation. The act levied a 10-percent tax against state bank notes and drove them from circulation.

The new law required national banks to have one-third of their capital invested in U.S. securities. With this investment, they were allowed to issue notes up to 90 percent of the U.S. bond holdings. Many New Jersey state banks thus were forced into becoming national banks. Under the plan New York City became the national banking center. The federal government had thus finally devised a method of selling national bonds and providing a more flexible and adequate control of the nation's banking. The system lasted without major change until the Federal Reserve Act of 1913.

In 1865 another federal statute placed a prohibitory tax on state bank notes and forced even more banks into the national system. This law also created the national currency system. After the Civil War, bankers created trust banks, until by 1900 there were twenty-nine of them, with assets of $57.5 million. By 1917 there were 207 trust companies with assets of $1.3 billion. Savings banks held firm at between twenty-eight and forty from 1875 into the 1920s. In 1927 the national banks were allowed to create savings departments.

Although the Civil War banking acts created a national banking system to replace or supplement local systems and to provide a paper currency, they did not provide enough flexibility and elasticity in the monetary system, as a succession of panics in 1873, 1883, and 1893 showed. The Panic of 1907 finally provoked the Congress to create the Federal Reserve System, which all of New Jersey's national banks immediately joined.

Aproned employees in the Clark Thread Mill are shown here circa 1880 placing skeins of cotton upon wooden frames, from which the thread will be wound onto bobbins arrayed along the top of the machines. Courtesy, Newark Public Library

The shore town of Long Branch, located just south of Sandy Hook and the Highlands, was once the playground of U.S. presidents and America's wealthy. Today only a few rambling Victorian houses linger from those glory days, but if these houses could speak, they would recount a forgotten chapter of American history.

At the start of the 1800s Long Branch became known as a health spa. By 1830 it had begun to take on a holiday atmosphere, offering bowling, billiards, dancing, card playing, and other resort activities. By 1860 Long Branch's hotels and boardinghouses were plentiful enough to host more than 4,000 people.

Soon Long Branch was being visited by wealthy Americans like George F. Baker, Jay Gould, and George W. Childs, publisher of the Philadelphia *Public Ledger*. In the summer of 1869, George W. Childs invited newly elected President Ulysses S. Grant to Long Branch. He convinced Grant that the Jersey Shore was the ideal alternative to Washington's sweltering summer and the hordes of office-seekers besieging the new president.

President Grant and his family created an instant sensation at Long Branch. Thousands of people poured into town just to catch a glimpse of this famous war hero and national leader. Almost overnight, celebrities and society leaders were booking every hotel room in Long Branch.

Grant loved this shore town and told Childs he wanted to make it the site of his summer White House. Encouraged by the prestige and increased real-estate values this would bring, Childs, George Pullman, and New York financier Moses Taylor purchased a cottage at 991 Ocean Avenue and presented it to Grant as a gift. In those days, before the scrutiny that accompanies such matters, President Grant accepted the house.

Soon, Grant's Long Branch house was being billed as "the summer capital." Two and a half stories high, it had an octagonal porch and a design that one reporter called "a mixture of English villa and Swiss chalet." During his carefree summer vacation days, Grant would sit on his porch in white hat and linen duster, smoking a cigar and swapping stories with his police guards and friends. Or the president could be seen parading down the street in his horse and buggy, dressed in smart summer attire.

Grant's favorite recreation was galloping on horseback along the shore and around Long Branch's two picturesque bays, Egypt and Cincinnati. The president was an excellent horseman with a passionate interest in anything equestrian. Thus, in 1870, when several entrepreneurs opened Monmouth Park Race Track, Grant purchased a box and seldom missed a race. The Monmouth Park track sent Long Branch's popularity to new heights.

President Grant returned to Long Branch every summer for the two terms of his presidency, and except for a few summers spent traveling abroad, continued to vacation there every year until the end of his life.

Grant's Republican successors followed in his footsteps and spent at least part of every summer at Long Branch. Rutherford B. Hayes and his wife vacationed there, though they carefully avoided the resort's more excessive activities: by the time they arrived in 1876, little old Long Branch had become the Las Vegas of its day. On the corner of Brighton and Ocean avenues, the opulent Pennsylvania Club featured roulette, rouge et noir, birdcage, and many other games in fabulously decorated rooms. Other entrepreneurs were countering with equally lavish gaming houses.

President James Garfield sustained Long Branch's predominance as a presidential playground. Garfield arrived early in the summer of 1881 to settle his family, and then returned to Washington briefly to finish up some paperwork. On July 2, Lucretia Garfield received the horrifying news that her husband had been shot by a crazed, disappointed office-seeker in Washington's Union Station.

The badly wounded president was transferred to Long Branch at his own insistence. But the sea air was not enough to help Garfield, and he died on Sunday, September 18. Vice president Chester A. Arthur, who had already rented a house in Long Branch, assumed the presidency and returned to enjoy the "presidential playground" each summer for the rest of his term.

By this time, many of Long Branch's millionaires had begun to move on to places such as Saratoga and Newport. When Democrat Grover Cleveland won the presidency in 1884, he assiduously avoided Long Branch—despite the fact that he was a native New Jerseyan—in order not to emulate his Republican predecessors.

Although Republican Benjamin Harrison spent some time at Long Branch during his single term (1888-1892), the resort's star had begun to fade. During the 1890s puritanical reforms swept much of America, including New Jersey, and Long Branch's gaming houses and racetrack were closed. Although William McKinley paid Long Branch a visit during his presidency, his stopover was considered a largely ceremonial political gesture. By this time, the nation's attention was being captured by another New Jersey resort town: Atlantic City.

—David Fleming

Insurance Centers in New Jersey

New Jersey's insurance development is, of course, rooted in the success story of the Prudential Insurance Company, which would become, by a large margin, the largest in the state. In 1873 John F. Dryden founded it as an offshoot of the England-based Prudential Company, which had begun to issue weekly premium policies in 1854. Dryden's Widows' and Orphans' Friendly Society entered a very competitive field of some twenty-six companies, which had 17,318 policies in force at the time. But the Prudential forged ahead with weekly premiums of three cents, five cents or multiples thereof.

Dryden made gains in the 1870s—times when economic catastrophe following the Panic of 1873 had brought many insurance companies into bankruptcy. In 1877 his company became the Prudential Insurance Company of America. By 1878 the Prudential had annual receipts of four million dollars. In 1892 it moved to its "castle" on Newark's Broad Street. Over its first 20 years it distributed benefits of $630 million. The Mutual Benefit

Above: John Fairfield Dryden was founder and early president of the Prudential Insurance Company, a name adopted by the firm in 1877. Patterned after a British firm with a similar name, the company originally provided little more than burial payments to families of workingmen who had contributed small weekly premiums. Courtesy, Newark Public Library

Left: Women employees of Prudential Insurance Company (circa 1896) were provided with steel pens and individual inkwells for their clerical duties at the firm's Newark office. Courtesy, Newark Public Library

Insurance Company was founded in 1845, and the Colonial Life Insurance Company was launched in 1897 in Jersey City, but neither has matched the resiliency and success of the Prudential.

Agriculture Rebounds

The Civil War dramatized New Jersey's agricultural prowess. New Jersey served as a source of food for the Union armies and broadened the state's reputation as a garden state. Since its earliest days, of course, New Jersey had been a breadbasket colony. New Jersey had been referred to as the "Garden of the World" in Scotland in 1684, and after the Civil War, Newark still had the largest flour mill in the nation, capable of producing 2,000 barrels of flour every day. Farming declined, however, as people burned out the soil and moved west in the early nineteenth century.

Agriculture rebounded in the 1830s with the discovery in the Pine Barrens of marl, a potash-rich soil. When spread on the soil, marl

Right: Mutual Benefit Life Insurance Company, the oldest life insurance firm in New Jersey, was founded in Newark in 1845 by Robert Livingston Patterson, a New York City merchant born in 1776. The firm moved their offices to this imposing building on Broadway in 1927. Thirty years later the building was sold to the Catholic Diocese of Newark to house Essex Catholic Regional High School. Today it serves as a health care center. Courtesy, Newark Public Library

Below: New Jersey farmers dug marl out of N. Stratton's marl pit near Mullica Hill on Racoon Creek in Gloucester County in the mid-nineteenth century. Marl, already in use by English farmers, was popular in New Jersey as a fertilizer from 1845 through 1860. Monmouth, Burlington, Camden, Salem, and Gloucester counties were the sources for New Jersey's well-known greensand marl. Courtesy, Newark Public Library

increased output as much as 400 percent. In the 1850s farmers also began to use lime to improve the soil.

During the war, the extraordinary work in soil science of Dr. George H. Cook, a Rutgers chemistry professor, brought Rutgers a grant under the Morrill Act of 1862. Named New Jersey state geologist in 1864, Cook turned a worthless ninety-eight-acre farm Rutgers bought into a productive one and made it the New Jersey State Experimental Station. He helped convince Congress to pass the Hatch Act of 1887, committing the federal government to establishing agricultural stations. As first director of the Agricultural Experimental Station at Rutgers, he made Rutgers a force for agricultural development in the state and developed research in botany, biology, and entomology. The Experimental Station developed artificial insemination for cattle, created the first collegiate department of environmental science in 1921, and pioneered research on the impact of fiber in diet to control hardening of the arteries. By 1980 the Experimental Station was conducting 250 separate research projects.

Edward B. Voorhees, the second director of the Experimental Station, created the Department of Soil Chemistry in 1907—the first of its kind in the nation. Jacob B. Lipman succeeded Voorhees and became the first dean of Rutgers Agricultural College in 1915. Under his leadership the college added a host of new departments, including agronomy, farm management, and plant physiology.

After the Civil War, milk cows gradually replaced beef cattle in the state. Sussex, Warren, and Hunterdon County farmers raised white holsteins particularly. In Cresskill farmers began incubating chickens, and by the 1880s were hatching 10,000 white leghorns a week. The New Jersey Poultry Association exhibited its poultry in Newark in 1879.

In 1869 Joseph Campbell, a fruit merchant, and Abraham Anderson, an icebox manufacturer, began canning beefsteak tomatoes, vegetables, jellies, condiments, and mincemeat on a large scale in Camden, where they operated

When the introduction of refrigerator cars in the 1880s brought western beef to the east, New Jersey cattle raisers turned from beef to dairy cattle. The most popular purebred herds were Ayshire, Guernsey, and Jersey. Courtesy, Thirty-fifth Annual Fair of the Burlington County Agricultural Society, 1881

JERSEY CATTLE

OF ILLUSTRIOUS FAMILIES,

BUTTER QUALITIES & FANCY POINTS.

PATTIE MC. 2D (5034.

FOUR OF THE HIGHEST PRIZE MEDALS

—AWARDED AT THE—

CENTENNIAL EXHIBITION

—TO THE—

ELMS STOCK FARM,

—ALSO—

NEW JERSEY STATE FAIR, 1874—1876.

SPECIAL HERD PRIZE, STATE PRIZE, BEST JERSEY COW; SOCIETY PRIZE BEST JERSEY COW, EACH YEAR, AND

FIRST PRIZE AT BURLINGTON COUNTY FAIR THREE SUCCESSIVE YEARS.

WILLIAM S. TAYLOR,

Burlington, N. J.

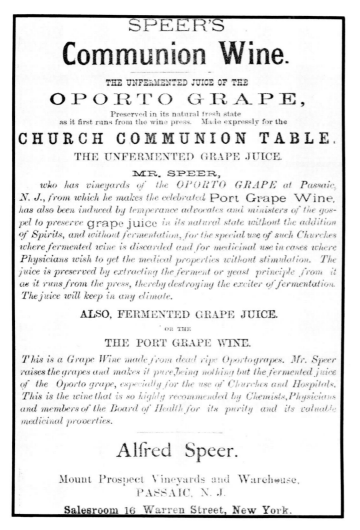

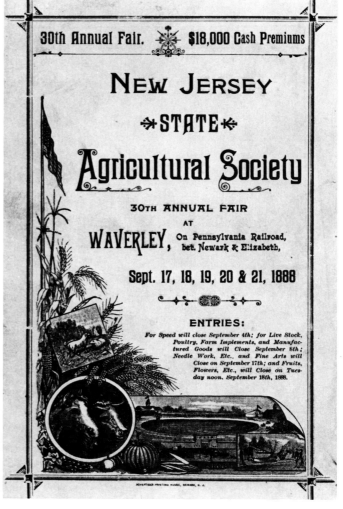

their first plant. Anderson developed a fine reputation for the "Celebrated Beef Steak Tomato."

In 1876 Anderson and Campbell won a medal at the New Jersey Centennial Celebration. In 1876 Campbell bought out Anderson but lost control of the company to Arthur Dorrance in 1889, ending the connection of the Campbell family to the company. Arthur's nephew, Jack Dorrance, developed the Campbell Soup line, with its red-and-white label, derived from the colors of the Cornell College football uniforms.

In 1869 Thomas B. Welch, a Vineland Methodist of sincere religious persuasion, came up with the idea of using grape juice rather than wine for communion. Originally produced for friends and given away, Welch's Grape Juice developed into a national beverage. Other canneries, bottlers, and packers developed throughout Atlantic, Burlington, Cumberland, Gloucester, Hunterdon, Monmouth, and Salem counties and stimulated farming in these regions.

Sweet potatoes became Gloucester County's specialty. Farmers there produced two million bushels in 1899. Under the leadership of T. J. Slaughter, Madison became the "Rose City." By 1900, in Madison, Chatham,

Above: New Jersey State Agricultural Society fairs in Waverly attracted northern New Jersey farmers for over thirty years, until financial problems forced the sale of the eighty-acre tract. In 1899 the Essex County Parks Commission purchased the land, now known as Weequahic Park. Courtesy, New Jersey Room, Fairleigh Dickinson University

Above, left: Alfred Speer experimented with European grapes until he arrived at a strain that thrived in his Mount Prospect vineyards in Passaic. During the late-nineteenth century, Speer's vineyards and wine vaults were the most extensive in the eastern states. As the advertising bill suggests, he also produced unfermented grape juice for communion wine. Courtesy, Special Collections, Alexander Library, Rutgers University

and Summit, rose gardeners had developed masses of rose ranges clustered together. "Nowhere," said E. B. Ellwanger in his 1898 book, *The Rose*, are roses as perfect as "in the neighborhood of Summit and Madison."

With railroad connections to the West, the port cities of Newark and Jersey City became stockyard centers after the Civil War. In 1866 Central Stockyard & Transit began slaughtering cattle, and by 1880 over 1.5 million animals had become sides of beef there. With the coming of refrigerated cars, however, the giant Chicago packers either outsold Newark and Jersey City or bought out most of the New Jersey packing houses.

The Patent Medicine Fad

One New Jerseyan tapped a rich vein in nineteenth-century America: the belief in elixirs as cure-alls. Suffering from "liver complaints"? Try Boschee's German Syrup developed and made by Woodbury's Colonel George G. Green. Your ailment will vanish "like magic."

Colonel Green produced patent medicines in Woodbury during the last quarter of the nineteenth century and made himself into the town's first multimillionaire. His wares sold all across America. His German Syrup, August Flower, and Ague Conqueror were supposed to cure a multitude of illnesses, from "sick headaches" to liver disease and stomach problems.

Employing women from Woodbury to fill the bottles with the "health-giving" liquids from an 800-gallon tank, Green dispatched orders throughout the world. His almanacs, posters, and placards were printed in Spanish, French, German, and English.

With the profits from his elixirs, he built the Woodbury Glass Works, the Standard Window Glass Works, the Woodbury Castor Works, and Green's Steam Planing Mill. He built a vacation home at Lake Hopatcong, a hotel in California, and, like the other tycoons of the Victorian era, had his specially built railroad car and three yachts. Patent medicines died out with the coming of the Great War, but this Civil War veteran put Woodbury on the map and himself into the Victorian good life.

A Ceramics Industry Grows Up

The first clay mined in the United States came from New Jersey, and clay, which lay beneath most of central New Jersey, became one of New Jersey's most abundant natural resources. After the Civil War, brick works sprang up around the sources of good clay in the Hackensack and Raritan River valleys. The eight firms that succeeded near the Raritan River were making fifty-four million bricks a year by 1878. Formed in 1850 by Newarker James R. Sayre and New Yorker Peter Fisher, the firm of Sayre & Fisher steadily bought up the prime clay land. By the First World War, Sayre & Fisher was turning out 178 million bricks annually, and by the centennial of the firm it had baked 6.25 billion bricks.

In Perth Amboy, Henry Maurer, who ran the Excelsior firebrick works, turned out a hollow yellow brick similar to those he had seen in Europe.

It was easier to transport, strong, and good as an insulator. By 1881 Maurer was baking some 500,000 a year. Three years earlier, the first scientific article in English about clay appeared. Written by George H. Cook and entitled "The Clays of New Jersey," it examined the resources which had made so many ceramic industries successful.

In the 1870s, in the Hackensack and Little Ferry area in Bergen County, six firms were producing 9.5 million bricks annually. Merhoff's brickyard in Little Ferry baked over 100,000 bricks a day in 1880 and topped 100 million annually in 1895.

Thomas Maddock, who came from Longport, England, to New York in 1847 and then settled in Trenton, pioneered the manufacture of sanitary ware for Millington & Ashbury in Trenton in the 1870s. To break into the English-dominated market, he ingeniously labeled his bowls and water closets the "Best Staffordshire earthenware made for the American market." Through this technique and aggressive personal marketing in New York and Brooklyn, Maddock cracked the English hold on the sanitary ware field. He prided himself on never wearing an overcoat or carrying an umbrella and lugged his own wares, tied up in muslin. He won a patent for the first satisfactory connection of a toilet with a flushing-water supply. His only Trenton competitor was the Enterprise Pottery Company, founded in 1879. By the 1880s nearly all of the United States' bathroom fixtures were made in Trenton. Maddock's firm eventually became American Standard Inc., the

Here are the Hacksensack River clay pits as they appeared in the late-nineteenth century, at which time they had provided raw materials for Bergen County potters and brick makers for over 100 years. The clay pits illustrated here may have belonged to Merhoff Brothers in Little Ferry, successful brick makers whose business, begun after the Civil War, continued well into the twentieth century. Courtesy, Newark Public Library

world's largest producer of plumbing fixtures.

James Taylor, a Staffordshireman who came to America in 1829 and eventually settled in Trenton in 1852, made Trenton pottery with Henry Speeler, an Englishman from East Liverpool. Nineteenth-century Trenton, the "Staffordshire of America," also attracted two professional craftsmen, Thomas Ott and John Hart Brewer, who introduced the manufacture of porcelain to the state during the Civil War. Their firm, Etruria Pottery, produced a popular line of busts—featuring Ulysses S. Grant, the Virgin Mary, and Cleopatra (modeled by a Mrs. Thompson of Trenton) for the 1876 Centennial. These famous pieces were the work of Isaac Broome, who sculpted the Baseball Vase, one of the nineteenth century's porcelain masterpieces.

Ott and Brewer enticed William Bromley to move to Trenton from Belleek, Ireland. With Bromley's expertise, Etruria reproduced the Belleek porcelain, a thin, translucent material with a pearly glaze. Brewer also organized the United States Potters' Association and the Trenton Potters' Association. Another Trentonian, Walter Scott Lenox, served an apprenticeship with Isaac Davis in Trenton, and then worked for Ott and Brewer. At thirty, Lenox joined with Jonathan Coxon and produced fine china in Trenton at the Ceramic Art Company which they began in 1889. Lenox struggled to make Lenox china competitive with the finest china in the world and in 1918 finally succeeded in getting fellow New Jerseyan, President Woodrow Wilson, to use it as the replacement for the traditional Wedgwood in the White House. By 1919, when Lenox had finally made his firm solvent, he had also gone blind. He died two years later. His pottery has been exhibited at the Sevres Museum in France, where only the finest ceramics are displayed. Later in the twentieth century, Polish craftsman Boleslaw Cybis made his distinctive figurines for the world market, and Edward Marshall Boehm, Inc., founded in 1950, produced artful birds, animals, and flowers in porcelain.

Copper Refining Begins in Middlesex County

Edward Balbach had refined gold and silver sweepings from the floors of jewelry houses in Newark before the Civil War. In the 1870s his son, Edward Balbach, Jr., realized that copper wire would carry the current Thomas Edison was harnessing for light, and he built in Newark the nation's first commercial electrolytic copper refinery.

At the turn of the century, Balbach's success led three copper refiners—the Guggenheim group, the New England Electrolytic Copper Company, and the Raritan Copper Works—to build operations in Middlesex County near the waters of the Raritan Bay and the Arthur Kill. Ore came into these refiners by sea, and coal by railroad. The refiners sent their copper to New York. Soon the Middlesex refiners were producing over half the nation's copper, and this corner of Middlesex County became the world's most important copper-refining area.

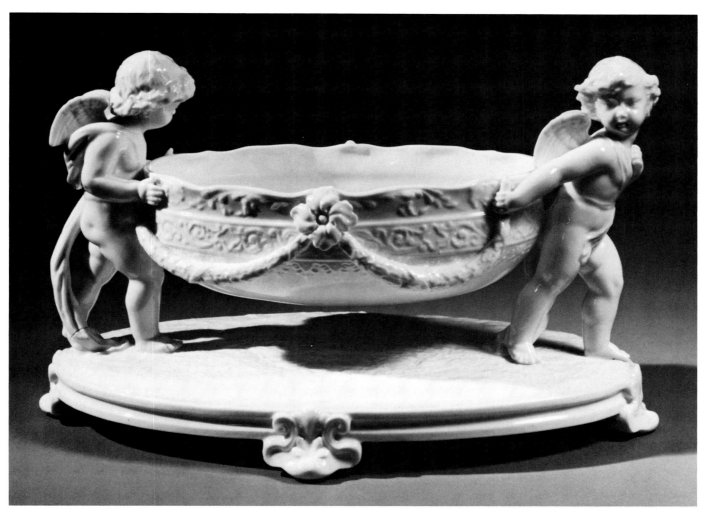

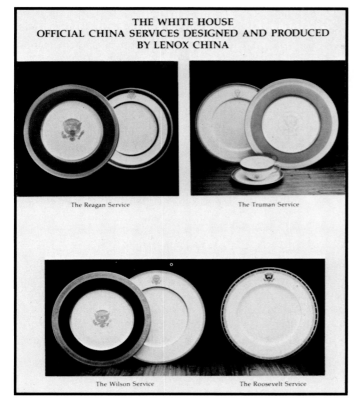

THE WHITE HOUSE
OFFICIAL CHINA SERVICES DESIGNED AND PRODUCED
BY LENOX CHINA

The Reagan Service

The Truman Service

The Wilson Service

The Roosevelt Service

COMPLIMENTS OF
BRAND'S CREDIT PALACE
COMPLETE OUTFITTERS & HOUSEFURNISH
124-126-128 N. Broad St.,
TRENTON, N.J.

In 1869 Joseph Campbell, a fruit merchant, and Abram Anderson, an icebox manufacturer, established a canning and preserving business in Camden, New Jersey. This new facility, which canned tomatoes, vegetables, jellies, condiments, and mincemeat, would become one of the world's greatest industrial canning plants.

Under the Anderson and Campbell label, the new venture established a strong reputation from the start, primarily from the "Celebrated Beef Steak Tomato . . . so large that only one was packed to a can," but also from its peas, corn, jams, jellies, and other items. Various soups were also made during these early days.

By 1876, after seven years of success, Joseph Campbell wanted to expand this business. But Abram Anderson opposed the idea and thus left the partnership. Campbell purchased Anderson's interest and ran the canning plant himself, under the new name Joseph Campbell Company.

Business continued to grow over the next several years, along with the need for new equipment and larger quarters. Campbell then hired his son-in-law, Arthur S. Spackman, into the firm. Spackman in turn suggested another member, close personal friend Arthur Dorrance of Bristol, Pennsylvania, who had sizable amounts of money to invest. In 1882 a partnership was formed with Arthur Dorrance, Walter S. Spackman, and Joseph S. Campbell, under the name Joseph Campbell Preserving Company. In 1894 Arthur Dorrance succeeded Joseph Campbell as president, as Mr. Campbell retired from handling the day-to-day activities of the business.

In 1897 Dr. J.T. Dorrance, nephew of Arthur, joined the company, bringing with him a formal education in chemical engineering and a desire to achieve. It was J.T. Dorrance who, shortly thereafter, originated the concept of canned condensed soup. This product, more than any other, made the Campbell name world famous.

In 1898 the Campbell's Soup red-and-white label was first introduced, the colors having derived from Cornell College football uniforms. And the familiar medallion began gracing the labels of "Campbell's" condensed soups after it was awarded to the company at the Paris International Exposition of 1900.

Joseph Campbell died in 1900, at age eighty-three, ending the long association of the Campbell family with the company, and ending one of the most important careers in the history of the American food business.

Under the direction of Arthur Dorrance, the company continued to expand and diversify. By 1904 Campbell's had introduced Campell's Pork & Beans. That same year, Philadelphia artist Grace Gebbie Drayton created the "Campbell Kid" characters, the cartoon children that became world famous as a Campbell's trademark. The "Campbell Kids" thus launched a "career" that made them among the most well-known and lovable characters in the history of American advertising.

When Campbell's Soups entered the California market in 1911, the company had achieved its goal of gaining a national distribution network. And in 1914, the Campbell's condensed soup creator J.T. Dorrance assumed the presidency of the company.

The following year, Campbell's added the products of Franco-American Food Company of New Jersey, a maker of gourmet foods and soups. The Franco-American brand was also continued by Campbell for spaghetti and other pasta products.

In 1929 Campbell's opened its second major soup plant in Chicago. The following year, J.T. Dorrance died and was succeeded as president by his brother, Arthur C. Dorrance.

Meanwhile, Campbell's began to acquire an international presence that would increase by leaps and bounds in subsequent decades. The company's first foreign subsidiary, Campbell Soup Company Ltd., began operations in Canada in 1930.

Over the next decade, Campbell's continued to become more diversified and more international, introducing Campbell's Tomato Juice in 1932, organizing a British Company—Campbell's Soups, Limited—in 1933, and introducing Chicken Noodle and Cream of Mushroom soups in 1934. In 1936 Campbell began to manufacture its own cans: today, it is the third-largest sanitary (food) can producer in the world, although it manufactures only for its own needs.

This strong and steady growth period during the 1920s and 1930s began to be translated into smashing results on the bottom line: in 1942 the company's sales topped the $100 million mark for the first time.

Continuing to diversify and expand both at home and abroad, Campbell's prospered. In 1954 the company made a public offering, with one class of common stock, and was admitted to trading on the New York Stock Exchange. In 1957 Campbell's opened its new General Office Building in Camden and also established an International Division. This staggering growth and internationalization saw sales exceed $500 million by 1958.

By 1971, after the addition of brand names like Pepperidge Farm and the addition of other products such as new soups, frozen foods, as well as expanded research activities and new plants throughout Europe, Latin America, and Canada, company sales had topped one billion dollars. And by 1979, with more acquisitions and diversification, sales grew to over two billion dollars. Today the company has not slowed down one bit, still growing and still prospering. The Campbell Soup Company remains one of the most dynamic—and historically important—food companies in America.

—David Fleming

Campbell Soup Company began in Camden in 1869 as Anderson and Campbell, a canning factory for fruits and vegetables. Joseph Campbell bought out his partner, and his name continued to appear on Campbell Soup labels long after his association with the firm ended in 1889. The famous "beef steak" tomato was allegedly so large that only one would fit in a can. Courtesy, Camden County Historical Society

The Riverside Rubber Company of Belleville, manufacturer of a variety of rubber products, was founded in 1878 and later became known as Hardman Tire and Rubber Company. The industry flourished until 1910, when it burned and was sold. Courtesy, Newark Public Library

RIVERSIDE RUBBER COMPANY,

James Hardman Jr., Pres't.   John C. Hardman, Treas.

MANUFACTURERS OF

Rubber & Metal Specialties and Druggists' & Stationers

Supplies.

FACTORY AND PRINCIPAL OFFICE **Belleville, N. J.**

Edison's Menlo Park Research Lab

In 1876 Edison advertised for men with "light fingers" to staff an "invention factory" at Menlo Park. On the basis of his interviews and tests, Edison hired John Ott, his assistant; Charles Batchelor, an English machinist from the Clark Thread Works; Sigmund Bergmann, a German; and John Kruesi, a Swiss clockmaker. At Menlo Park he installed excellent scientific instruments along with steam engines, dynamos, furnaces, and chemicals.

Not a theorist, Edison used trial and error to get his results. He worked for days with only naps as rest. He paid no attention to his dress or personal habits, leading some to call him "dungyard." Blunt, cranky, and deaf, he shouted (and often in obscenities) when dealing with his workers. Not surprisingly, he had very few close friends.

But he founded the modern research laboratory—and set New Jersey on the path of becoming the research home for many major corporations. In fact, despite his many individual inventions, Edison's creation of the modern research laboratory may be his most important contribution to science. Edison deliberately, even compulsively, had to invent more and more. He set out to get patents in an organized way with his team of model makers, scientists, mathematicians, mechanics, chemists, and engineers. Between 1876 and 1882 he amassed 300 patents. By the end of his life, he had 1,300 patents.

He defensively poked fun at the scientific community: "I can always hire mathematicians," he said, "but they can't hire me." They retorted that he was anti-intellectual and sneeringly called his trial-and-error system "Edisonian." One prominent member of the scientific community announced that Edison had "the most airy ignorance of the fundamental principles both of electricity and dynamics."

Edison defied the theoreticians of his day and claimed that he was only an "empirical inventor" after the "silver dollar." But he did understand the main principles of the science of his time.

At Menlo Park he set out in 1877 to record telegraph messages automatically on a paper disk revolving on a plate. First he developed the diaphragm, then attached it to a device that caused a toy figure to saw wood when someone spoke into the funnel containing the diaphragm. He quickly realized that he could record sound waves.

He made a sketch and handed it to John Kruesi. "Make this," said Edison. Kruesi built a machine according to the design for eighteen dollars. Asked what his device was for, Edison said casually, "This machine is going to talk."

Edison wrapped a piece of tinfoil around a cylinder and spoke "Mary had a little lamb" into the mouthpiece of the machine. When it spoke back, Kruesi blanched. Others were thunderstruck. Edison had invented the phonograph. It remained his favorite accomplishment. He particularly liked to play the "Battle Hymn of the Republic" on recordings which were later developed.

Above: Before the phonograph became commonplace in the family parlor, Edison dealers found it profitable to promote "phonograph entertainments" during which they presented selections from an extensive list of Edison records. A 1906 catalog also recommends the entertainments for fund raisers for church and charitable groups as well as enterprising small boys. Courtesy, Special Collections, Alexander Library, Rutgers University

Right: Technicians from Edison's Menlo Park laboratory were passengers on the trial run of his first electric locomotive. Perched on a beer crate, Charles Turner Hughes, an Edison associate, guided the train along the track, which ran nearly two-and-a-half miles around the laboratory. Courtesy, Newark Public Library

Backed by Western Union and one of the Morgan partners, Edison then put aside the phonograph for work on developing a small light that could substitute for gas lamps in homes and businesses. As had others before him, Edison found that most filaments quickly burned out. He hired Francis Upton, a Princeton graduate, as chief scientific assistant and mathematician. Upton calculated the resistance requirements for the filament and helped Edison select materials. After trying a host of various filaments to conduct the electric current inside the bulb—including a hair from the beard of one of his staff—Edison finally found what he was seeking.

He discovered that carbonized cotton sewing thread (thread burned to an ash) would produce light. On October 19, 1879, Edison got it to glow. The light lasted through two nights and one day—some forty hours. To impress the visitors who flocked to Menlo Park to see the discovery, he and his men quickly organized incandescent lamps to light the streets and the laboratory, office, and library. Observers marveled at the "bright, beautiful

Heavy beams and girders were installed to support the weight of the dynamos and steam engines of the Edison Electric Illuminating Company of New York, located in a four-story building on Pearl Street in the financial district. To compete with gas lighting, the company supplied their customers with free light bulbs. Courtesy, Newark Public Library

225

light, like the mellow sunset of an Italian autumn." At the pinnacle of his career, Edison assured his admirers that he would be able to illuminate even the greatest cities. A year earlier, Edison and some major financial figures had formed the Edison Electric Light Company to manufacture this bulb.

In 1882 Edison built the Pearl Street Generating Station in New York City which brought electricity to eighty-five customers. His 330-volt dynamo in Roselle, New Jersey, made that town the first in the world to be lighted electrically. To produce his bulbs, he built a large lamp factory in Harrison. He also made improvements in the telephone that ended the need to shout. By the end of the 1880s, Edison's bulb factories were turning out nearly a million bulbs a year.

Edison's most important purely scientific discovery came to him somewhat accidentally, and he may not have thoroughly understood it. It was the "Edison effect," the result of his need to control the outmigration of carbon atoms in his light bulb. By introducing a third wire into the bulb, Edison reduced the outmigration of atoms. His discovery was later used by Heinrich Hertz, Guglielmo Marconi, and Lee De Forest, who built the Audion radio tube.

Unfortunately, the man who lighted the world was convinced that direct current was better than the alternating current of George Westinghouse, who formed Westinghouse Electric Company in 1886. Alternating current, however, could be boosted to high voltages and sent over much longer distances than low-voltage direct current.

Edison had other stubborn prejudices as well. He slept in his clothes because he believed that taking them off or changing them brought insomnia. Rats ran freely in his laboratories. He nearly starved to death because he believed that food would poison his intestines.

Edison Develops a Movie Studio at West Orange

In 1887 Edison built an enlarged and improved workshop in West Orange, New Jersey. There he developed and improved his earlier inventions and organized companies to make and sell his devices. With Englishman William Laurie Dickson, Edison worked out the reproduction of pictures on a cylinder and improved the camera developed by George Eastman and others.
His device, the Edison Kinetoscope, eventually led to the motion-picture camera in 1889. One of the earliest films made on this camera has become known as "The Dickson Violin," and shows Edison playing a violin into a recorder while two of his workers dance.

New Jersey became a film center. In West Orange, Edison constructed the first movie studio, the "Black Maria," a black tar paper shack that swung on a pivot to allow direct sunlight into the stage. It brought the movie industry to New Jersey. Alexander Victor converted a Newark store into a movie theater in 1897. Edwin S. Porter made *The Great Train Robbery* in West Orange and "on location" near Paterson. Mary Pickford, D. W. Griffith, Norma Talmadge, Theda Bara, Irene Castle, Warner Oland,

The "Black Maria" was constructed in 1893 at Edison's West Orange laboratory for $638 to accommodate his kinetograph camera, which recorded sixteen-second film sequences for kinetoscopes (viewing machines designed for one-person use). The center section of this rudimentary studio was two stories high with a section that could be opened as a skylight. Courtesy, Newark Public Library

Fatty Arbuckle, and Mack Sennet, among others, made pictures in New Jersey's film capital. After the movies themselves came the grand movie houses of the state: Jacob Fabian's 2,500-seat playhouse in Paterson, Newark's Branford and Mosque theaters, and Fabian's 5,000-seat Stanley Theater in Jersey City.

In 1914 Edison combined the phonograph and camera to make talking pictures, but he left it to others to improve and perfect the equipment. In his late years he developed the cement mixer, the dictaphone, the storage battery, and the duplicating machine. He also teamed with Harvey Firestone and Henry Ford to find a way to get rubber from domestic goldenrod plants, but the results did not come until after he died.

In 1928 Congress gave him a gold medal for "development and application of inventions that have revolutionized civilization in the last

From the apparatus pictured here, workmen poured concrete into a distributing tank, from which it flowed to fill the molds to form a concrete house like those to the left and right. Although Edison demonstrated the practicality of a durable waterproof and fireproof dwelling with the 1906 construction of the Blenheim Hotel in Atlantic City, his vision of mass-producing houses cheaply for the workingman was never realized. Courtesy, Newark Public Library

century." People believed him to be the "most useful American." He envisioned helicopters and hovercraft. In his last years he said he was working on a device that would "pick up" the evidence of life after death. He told a writer for Scientific American:

Our personalities pass on to another existence or sphere. I don't claim anything because I don't know anything. . . . But I do claim that it is possible to construct an apparatus . . . so delicate that if there are personalities in another existence or sphere who wish to get in touch with us . . . this apparatus will at least give them a better opportunity to express themselves

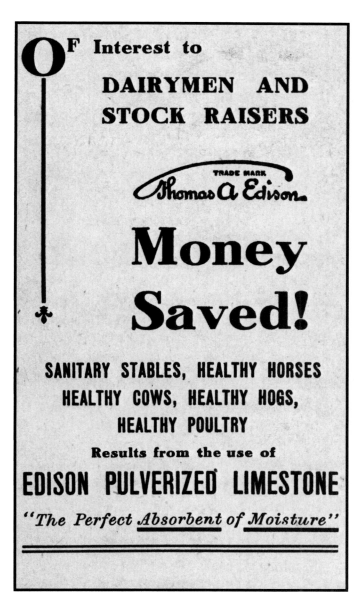

The marketing of pulverized limestone, a by-product of the Edison Portland Cement Company, was targeted to New Jersey's farmers. These brochures recommended uses of pulverized limestone for poultry farms, dairy and horse stables, and for the improvement of soils. The plant started operation in 1902 on a large tract of limestone-bearing land in Stewartsville, New Jersey, but after a series of closures and bankruptcies, the plant was closed in the mid-thirties after Edison's death. Courtesy, New Jersey Room, Fairleigh Dickinson University

English-born Edward Weston arrived in Newark in 1877 to apply his inventive genius to the evolving applications of electrical power and light. Probably his most significant contribution was the invention and manufacture of instruments to measure and control electrical energy. With the replacement of steam power by electricity in manufacturing, the products of the Weston Electrical Instrument Company gained widespread use. Courtesy, Newark Public Library

than the tilting tables and ouija boards and mediums and the other crude methods now purported to be the only means of communication.

An assistant had died while working on the project and Edison believed that "he ought to be the first man to contact us if he is able to do so." No one ever developed such a machine or model to do it. Edison died at 84 in West Orange on October 18, 1931. Edison was a transitional figure, a link between the somewhat crude system of mechanical invention and the modern technique of experiment and research, particularly the "team approach." Throughout his career after Menlo Park, he had relied on the mechanical skills of Charles Batchelor, John Ott, and John Kruesi, as well as the college-trained scientists he kidded, but used. When Herbert Hoover planned to have the nation's dynamos stop to honor the "Wizard of Menlo Park," he found that the electrical power unleashed by the world's first research director could not be halted even for three minutes.

Edward Weston Devises a Dynamo

English-born Edward Weston came to New York City in 1870 with a degree in medicine but no interest in practicing. He married Wilhelmina Seidel a year later. Work as a chemist and in electroplating companies led him to devise a dynamo to replace the batteries then used in electroplating. Once he had developed his dynamos, he came to Newark to manufacture them. By 1877 Weston had gotten the financial backing to create the Weston Dynamo Electric Machine Company.

Like Edison and others of the day, Weston wanted to improve outdoor lighting. He improved the carbon arc lamps of the day by adding metal salts to the carbon to produce a more pleasing light. Weston changed the name of his firm to the Weston Electric Light Company and began making arc lamps. His installation of lights in Newark's Military Park in 1878 developed 7,000 candlepower and attracted every bug within miles.

The light impressed the city fathers enough to award Weston a contract to light the municipality electrically. In 1881 Weston and others founded the Newark College of Engineering. A year later his company was absorbed by the United States Electric Lighting Company, where he became chief engineer.

At United States Electric, Weston developed the squirted filament, the "getter" (a technique which helped maintain a vacuum), and the flashing process. Weston installed the eighty arc lights on the mighty Brooklyn Bridge that impressed some observers more than the fireworks did when the bridge opened in 1883.

In 1886 Weston retired from U.S. Electric to research and invent on his own. In 1888 he formed the Weston Electrical Instrument Company and developed and manufactured portable and accurate electric meters that became widely recognized for their precision and dependability. The same year he was elected president of the American Institute of Electrical Engineers, where he was a charter member. Weston also developed the Normal Cell, creating the first reliable way to measure the volt, although this achievement was not recognized by some in the scientific community until 1908. In 1924 the Franklin Institute gave Weston the Franklin Medal.

Illustrated here is the machinery Edward Weston developed to maintain a vacuum in the manufacture of electric light bulbs. Courtesy, Newark Public Library

Morristown: City of Millionaires

For Morristown is the city of millionaires, and there is not another community like it in the United States—possibly not in the world. Here are gathered together in one little circle, within a radius of three miles, more men of millions than can be found elsewhere in many times the country area over.

With these words, a writer for *World Magazine* in 1905 described the spectacular wealth in the Morristown area at the turn of the century. While Morristown is remembered for being the winter headquarters of George Washington during the American Revolution, it is often forgotten for its place in history as a "millionaire's mecca" equal to Fifth Avenue and Newport.

In its early-nineteenth-century days, Morristown had grown as an industrial center for the iron industry. But later that industry largely shifted west, leaving Morristown to develop as a residential and shopping town. And it became the home of many rich and famous Americans of the time.

In the latter part of the nineteenth century, Morristown's millionaire populace made up a community that seemed straight out of the English nobility in the countryside. The super rich were, of course, lovers of horses and fox hunts, and it was not uncommon on a Sunday morning to hear the blast of the hunting horn and see the charge of a brightly colored fox-hunting party on horseback.

Wall Street financiers, railroad magnates, and other wealthy Americans moved to this elegant spot in the late nineteenth century. Many started out as summertime residents but became so enamored of the place that they would come out for long stays the whole year round. The train which these wealthy men would take to New York City was called the "Millionaire's Express." When

it pulled into Morristown in the late afternoon, lines of limousines with servants at the ready would be there to meet their charges and escort them home to their mansions.

By 1890, many millionaires' mansions were nestled in the mountains surrounding Morristown. Some of these estates were thirty-room "cottages," while the largest ones were giant stone castles, modeled on European originals. It is important to remember that many of these millionaires' estates were second or third homes, added to equally fancy dwellings on Fifth Avenue and in Newport.

During this period approximately 100 very wealthy families had mansions within the Morristown area. According to reliable sources of the day, the area had some ninety-two homeowners worth at least one million dollars. Forty-nine of these ninety-two families were worth only one million dollars, but fourteen of them were worth two million dollars each and another fourteen had assets of over ten million dollars each. The combined wealth of these millionaires reached over $400 million, an unthinkable sum of money in those days.

Famous were the annual parties given by the late Otto Kahn for his staff of servants and caretakers—who numbered upwards of 100—on his forested estate in the Normandy Park section. Today the estate is the proud headquarters of one of New Jersey's largest and most successful companies, Allied Chemical.

But perhaps the wealthiest of these Morristown millionaires were Mr. and Mrs. Hamilton McK. Twombly, whose combined assets totaled at least seventy million dollars. Mrs. Florence Twombly was the granddaughter of Commodore Vanderbilt: her inherited wealth and Twombly's millions from sulphur mines

made them a very rich couple indeed.

The Twomblys became famous for their grandiose parties in this heyday of the Morristown aristocracy. For one of their "modest" country dances in 1891, they spent $6,000 just for electric lights. The couple called their 900-acre estate "Florham" for "Florence and Hamilton" and convinced the little New Jersey village of Afton—where their estate was located—to change its name to Florham Park, still its name today.

The Twomblys were a fairly typical example of Morristown wealth in those days. They had a mansion on Fifth Avenue and a giant villa in Newport. But closest to their heart was the "unpretentious" 100-room country house of theirs in Morris County. Modeled after Hampton Court Palace in England, the estate cost about two million dollars at the time.

Aside from Otto Kahn and the Twomblys, other famous millionaire names in the Morristown area—and in Somerset hills to the southwest—included Dr. D. Leslie Ward, Luther Kountze, Robert H. McCurdy, John F. Dryden, James Cox Brady, Charles Scribner, John I. Waterbury, Robert Dumont Foote, Gustav E. Kissel, Frederic P. Olcott, C. Ledyard Blair, Percy R. Pyne, Walter G. Ladd, and others. This part of New Jersey, stretching from Morristown to Far Hills, contained a virtual compendium of the wealthiest American families of the day.

Morristown's heyday of millionaires was brought to an end following the advent of World War I, as well as factors which caused some migration of the rich to other areas. Today the area retains much of its aristocratic past and appearance, and Morristown's downtown center is garnering an increasing amount of corporate office space.

—David Fleming

Chapter Eight

The War And The New Era

The Grace Line's Santa Rosa *was launched down the ways of the Federal Shipbuilding and Dry Dock Company in Kearny in March 1932. A subsidiary of U.S. Steel, Federal began operations in response to an emergency shipbuilding program during World War I, and continued in business throughout World War II, during which it contributed 298 vessels to the war effort. In 1948, the yard was taken over by the U.S. Navy. Courtesy, Newark Pubic Library*

World War I significantly changed the political economy of the United States and with it that of New Jersey. Even before America became a belligerent in 1917, American factories supplying the Allies pulled the nation out of the recession of 1913. Once the U.S. went to war, President Woodrow Wilson placed the state and national economy under the control of a War Industries Board, which allocated materials; a Railroad Administration, which took over the rail lines; a Food Administration, which encouraged the saving of food and tried to improve the movement of food to the European fronts; and a Fuel Administration, which sought to spur the output of the nation's coal mines.

Some of the bureaucracy, however, failed. The Emergency Fleet Corporation did not complete enough ships. The Railroad Administration's inability to unsnarl the rail congestion during a terrible cold snap in January 1918 led to a general industrial shutdown. The troops did not receive adequate clothing and shelter.

New Jersey Produces for War
But once again the great economic demand of war brought business to New

Jersey. Despite the Emergency Fleet Corporation's failures, shipbuilding in New Jersey surged. Wilson's government gave New Jersey shipbuilders orders for thirty destroyers, seven battleships, and sixteen transports. The Bethlehem Steel Corporation refurbished Elizabethport to build cargo ships, tankers, and oceangoing tugs. Camden's New York Shipbuilding Company built the cruiser *Washington* ten days ahead of schedule. The Submarine Boat Company of Port Newark built fabricated ships. Federal Shipbuilding Company in Kearny produced thirty steel freighters. Although many ships were not finished in time, New Jersey boatyards produced more freighter tonnage than did the Philadelphia yards.

The New Jersey aircraft story compared to the ship tale. Mismanagement at the top meant that the Aircraft Production Board produced only 1,200 of its projected 22,000 airplanes. But war orders for Keyport Aeromarine Plane & Motor Corporation started them building hydroplane trainers and the "flying boat" for the navy. Standard Aero Company, of Plainfield and Linden, made seventeen kinds of aircraft in the old Stevenson Car Works. Wright-Martin Aircraft Corporation merged with Simplex Automobile Company of New Brunswick to make eight-cylinder engines, and Wright Aeronautical Corporation of Paterson built the 200-horsepower Whirlwind and 525-horsepower, air-cooled Wright Cyclone.

When the British blockade cut off the importation of German chemical dies, New Jersey chemical plants produced American dies to take their place. Munitions flowed from New Jersey explosive plants. Middlesex County produced half of the nation's refined copper during the war. The Singer Sewing Machine Company in Elizabeth made cannon-recoil mechanisms for the French. Passaic County textile factories produced woolens for Allied blankets and uniforms. Oil flowed from the great Bayonne and Bayway

Facing page: Overhead cranes at Camden's New York Shipbuilding Corporation lift into place the steel plates of the tanker Nora's *bulkhead, under construction in 1920. A revolutionary concept pioneered by New York Ship, the prefabrication of structural steel from templates has since become standard practice in the shipbuilding industry. Courtesy, National Archives*

Below: This Teterboro factory housed the Atlantic Aircraft Company circa 1924, which was founded by Anthony Fokker, the Dutch aircraft designer responsible for the famous German fighter planes of World War I. The Fokker planes manufactured here were fitted with engines from the Wright Aeronautical Corporation in Paterson. Courtesy, Newark Public Library

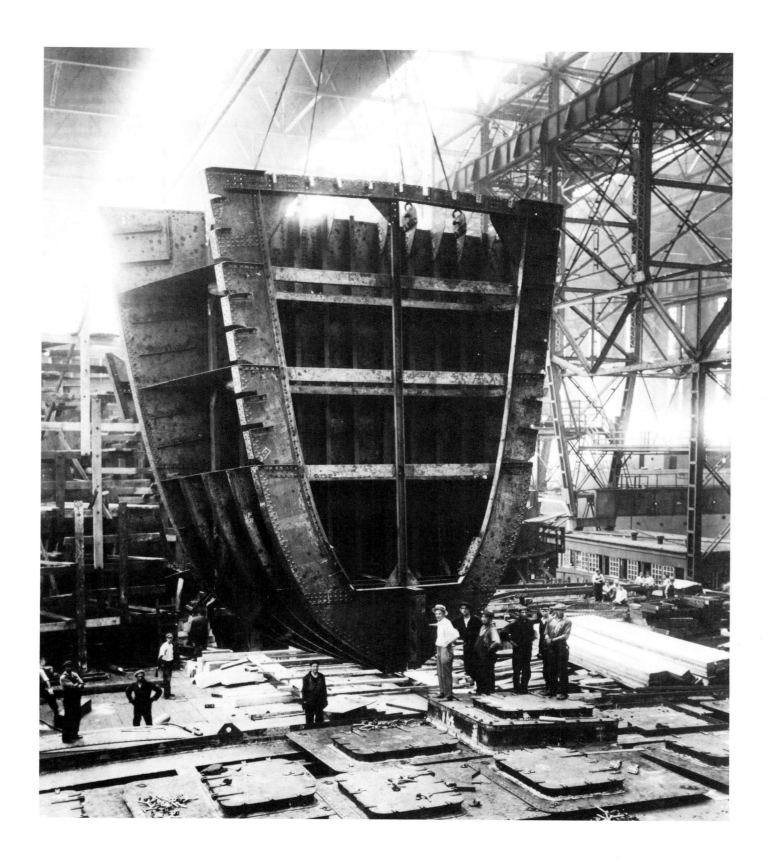

The aircraft carrier Saratoga was photographed entering the Delaware River
following its conversion from a battle
cruiser in 1925. This view of the New York
Shipbuilding Corporation shows the covered ways (inclined launching platforms),
an innovation in shipbuilding when the
yard was constructed in Camden in 1900.
Courtesy, Camden County Historical
Society

Inspectors in 1940 check cylinders for "Cyclone" engines in the plant built in Paterson in 1928 by Wright Aeronautical Corporation. The new factory was seven times larger than the area previously occupied when the firm moved to Paterson in 1921. In 1929 the aircraft engine company merged with Curtiss Aeroplane & Motor Company to become Curtiss-Wright. Courtesy, Newark Public Library

refineries. The Allies bought large numbers of New Jersey horses and mules. New Jersey became, in John Cunningham's words, "a vast arsenal of war, a training ground, a shipping point."

The great demand for goods from New Jersey's industries during the war attracted thousands to its industrial cities. Newark added some 50,000 residents, Camden grew by 19,000, and downtown areas in the state's major cities would send up skyscrapers during the 1920s. Even rural areas expanded industrially. In Mays Landing, Atlantic County, Bethlehem Steel Company built a shell-loading plant and sent the town's population from approximately 2,000 to something over 20,000, including Belcoville, a nearby settlement that mushroomed to handle the workers' families. Du Pont's smokeless power plant in Salem County sent the population of Penns Grove from 2,000 to 10,000 overnight and brought with it soaring crime rates and congestion.

Despite the imposition of economic controls by Wilson's administration, which did a good job of holding down war profiteering, the economy of the state and nation skyrocketed. Production, national income, per-capita income, and employment all gained during the war. Average wages grew some 78 percent, while prices jumped 62 percent between 1916 and 1919.

One process in silk manufacture was recorded in this view of a Paterson mill. Silk thread moved from the bobbins at left to the large revolving warping frame, from which it would be rewound on a large "beam," hidden here by the frame. The warp will then be ready for the loom. Courtesy, Paterson Museum Archives

Since the operation of some machines required manual dexterity rather than strength, women operators always predominated in certain procedures of silk manufacture. This group of silk employees was photographed during a meal in a Paterson mill's lunchroom. Courtesy, Paterson Museum Archives

During the war the index of manufacturing production was two and a half times what it had been at the turn of the century. The war laid the basis, after the postwar stagflation, for a growth economy during the 1920s.

For some New Jersey workers, the war meant their first Sunday silk shirt from Paterson's mills. For others it meant moving from agricultural work into Du Pont's explosives factories. For many it meant a new life in a city. For nearly 200,000 young men, it meant military service; for 3,836, it meant death.

Young New Jersey men poured into the 106 local draft boards created under the Selective Service Act of May 18, 1917. That month construction began on Fort Dix Military Reservation. Eventually some 1,600 buildings were constructed on the 6,800-acre forest near Wrightstown. The army trained some 70,000 men there for the fighting in Europe. So many businessmen flooded into the hitherto sparsely inhabited region that the state Department of Health had to enforce rigid sanitation rules.

The American Expeditionary Forces disembarked from Hoboken, and 600,000 passed through Creeskill's Camp Merritt on their way to Hoboken docks and embarkation. On some days as many as 40,000 spent their last hours in America there. The young heroes preferred to think in the terms of the camp slogan, "Hoboken, here we come." But after Hoboken, the destination was "over there."

War Inflames New Jersey Passions

As they had during the Civil War, dissenters opposed Wilson's "war to make the world safe for democracy." On July 30, 1916, German saboteurs were said to have caused the devastating munitions explosion on Black Tom Island that killed three, resulted in $22 million in property losses, and sent shrapnel onto the Statue of Liberty and along the lower Hudson County shoreline. German dock workers in Hoboken sabotaged the seized German liners that U.S. officials hoped to use in transporting troops to the front. Saboteurs caused the Lyndhurst Canadian Car and Foundry explosion of January 11, 1917, where 500,000 shells exploded over a 12-hour period and did $16,750,000 damage. Spies in Tuckerton were discovered transmitting radio messages to the enemy from a station with an 840-foot tower.

Wilson's Committee on Public Information, which propagandized the war extraordinarily effectively, whipped New Jerseyans into a frenzy. Films extolling the war effort played in theaters across the state: The *Kaiser, Beast of Berlin* (shot in Fort Lee), *Wolves of Kultur*, and *Hounds of Hunland*. The sweepstakes for the classic propaganda story of the time was won by *From Base Ball to Boche*. Nourished on such fare, superpatriotic groups attacked everything they could find that smacked of being "hun."

Hoboken examined the "huns entrenched in City Hall," Newark's Hamburg Place became Wilson Avenue, Hunterdon's Germantown became Oldwick. Westfield banned the sale of German-language periodicals in town. The Free Public Library there cancelled its subscription to the *New Republic*, then including Walter Lippmann on its editorial board, because it was of "the slacker variety."

Silk manufacturers sought public sympathy for their intransigent stance by attacking the strike organizers—the International Workers of the World—as radical socialist revolutionaries attempting to undermine the fabric of American capitalism. IWW strike leaders photographed in 1913 include, from left, Patrick Quinlan, Carlo Tresca, Elizabeth Gurley Flynn, Adolph Lessig, and William D. Haywood. Lessig was a silk weaver and leader of IWW Local 152. Courtesy, American Labor Museum

New Jerseyans Produce Explosives

Ever since New Jerseyans developed iron in the state before the American Revolution, New Jersey had been a leader in explosives. Morristown's Jacob Ford built the first powder mill in 1776. Ford supplied powder to the Continental Congress to fight for American independence.

Sweden's Alfred Nobel discovered how to manufacture dynamite in 1866. That year the United States Blasting Oil Company built a factory in Little Ferry. Shortly afterward San Francisco's Giant Powder Company opened an explosives plant in McCainesville (present Kenvil), which grew into the Hercules Powder Company. Lammont Du Pont in 1879 constructed a plant in Gloucester County on the Delaware River, and in 1883 American Forcite Power Company produced gelatin dynamite in Morris County at the southern end of Lake Hopatcong.

John Wesley Hyatt's experiments to produce celluloid helped make nitrocellulose safer to handle. Hudson Maxim developed and made "stabilite," a smokeless powder, and Maximite. The E. I. Du Pont de Nemours Company opened smokeless-powder plants in Salem County's Carney's Point and in Pompton Lakes. They also began one of the nation's earliest industrial research laboratories at Gibbstown, where they developed a low-freezing dynamite. The U.S. Army had established the Picatinny Arsenal in 1879 and in 1907 began the army's first powder factory at Picatinny, a site favored because the valley and surrounding ridges would protect other towns from explosion.

E. I.'s great-grandson, Thomas Coleman Du Pont, had pressed his company forward in explosives research at the turn of the century. They perfected trinitrotoluene, or TNT, in 1909. Du Pont began to acquire other explosive plants. He eliminated sixty-five of his competitors, and through his New Jersey holding company, E. I. Du Pont de Nemours Co. of New Jersey, he dominated U.S. military powder production and made over two-thirds of all American explosives.

A Justice Department attack under the Sherman Act had forced Du Pont in 1912 to fragment into three branches with operations in New Jersey: Hercules Powder, E. I. Du Pont de Nemours Powder Company, and Atlas Powder Company. When America entered World War I in 1917, these New Jersey firms became the major suppliers of military explosives.

In addition, New Jersey handled 76 percent of the shell-loading operations for the nation during the war. Most of these plants were located in Middlesex County near the Raritan Arsenal. Hercules Powder Company produced the first United States "cordite" during the first World War and would in World War II produce the bazooka rocket.

During the war itself, on October 5, 1918, an explosion at the T.A. Gillespie Loading Company at Morgan killed approximately 100 people, filled the streets of Perth Amboy and South Amboy with shards of glass, caused some $25 million in property damage, and rocked all of Central and North Jersey.

Facing page, top: Woolen mill workers left Botany Mills in Passaic on March 26, 1912, in a strike called by the Industrial Workers of the World, who were attempting to organize the firm's 8,000 workers. The strike followed by three days a similar job action at Forstmann and Huffman, another prominent Passaic mill, which 1,200 employees left in orderly fashion following a teenager bearing a red flag. Courtesy, National Archives

Facing page, bottom: Seventy-five deputies were sworn in by Hudson County Sheriff Eugene F. Kincaid to keep the peace in Bayonne during the Standard Oil strike in the summer of 1915. It was largely through the efforts of Sheriff Kincaid that workers and management were finally reconciled. The strikers, who were never unionized throughout the struggle, returned to work when Standard Oil offered them a 10 percent wage increase. Courtesy, Newark Public Library

New Jersey's Newark Airport is the oldest major airport in the New York metropolitan area. Both Kennedy and La Guardia airports were developed during World War II, though La Guardia Airport had been a private flying field since 1929.

But it was in 1927 that the City of Newark allotted some sixty-eight acres of land for the first major metropolitan airport in the tristate area. In January of 1928 trucks dumped massive amounts of fill to cover the bogs and dumps of the swampy airport site. Workers then laid a 1,600-foot asphalt runway—the first hard-surface runway ever on a commercial airport—and constructed a hangar sheltering twenty-five acres.

Newark Airport—later to become Newark International Airport—was born.

Newark Airport became the East Coast terminus of the national air-mail system in 1929. That same year it also became the starting point for scheduled passenger service by four airlines. In 1929, these commercial airlines made some 4,000 passenger flights from this busy new airfield.

In October 1930, passenger service from Newark was reaching to the West Coast, and by 1931 that trip was being flown in "only" thirty-six hours, thanks to new 110-mile-an-hour, three-engine planes. By the end of that same year, Newark Airport was handling some 120 flights per day and was able to lay claim to the title of "busiest airport in the world."

At this point, each of the four commercial airlines at Newark Airport had its own terminal. In 1934 a new administration building was erected for the mail-carrying army pilots. When the military stopped handling the mail flights, this building was renovated for commercial use and became the airport's central terminal.

Through the 1930s, the commercial air-transportation industry began to grow, contributing major amounts of revenue to the New Jersey economy. And the aviation sector was busy making history.

The historic achievements of air pioneers at Newark Airport are numerous. In 1934, Captain Eddie Rickenbacker landed at Newark Airport from Los Angeles to set a new coast-to-coast passenger flight record of thirteen hours, two minutes. A Los Angeles-Newark air-mail flight record was set by Jack Frye, who made the trip in eleven hours, thirty-one minutes. In 1935, Amelia Earhart flew nonstop from Mexico City to Newark in fourteen hours, nineteen minutes. The following year, Howard Hughes landed at Newark nine hours, twenty-six minutes after leaving Burbank, California, setting a new coast-to-coast record. In 1937, Hughes broke his own record by two hours. Along with these record-breaking flights came the introduction of the DC-2 and the DC-3, which marked the dawn of modern aerial transportation.

With all these accomplishments, it is easy to see that Newark was an important spot in the history of commercial aviation. And its place in aviation would continue to grow.

Newark Airport was operated by the U.S. Air Corps during World War II, but since 1948 the Port Authority has operated Newark International Airport under a lease agreement with the City of Newark. The airport has since greatly expanded, and today Newark International Airport has some 1,100 flight operations per day, serving nearly 30 million customers a year.

New Jersey also boasts a second important airfield. Teterboro Airport covers some 787 acres and is used by personal and corporate aircraft. The airfield is owned by the Port Authority of New York and New Jersey, which purchased it in 1949.

The property was originally acquired in 1917 by Walter C. Teter, and during World War I was the site of a North American Aviation manufacturing plant. After World War I, Teterboro became the base of operations for Anthony Fokker, the Dutch aircraft designer whose name lives on in the Fokker's world-famous aviation company.

During World War II Teterboro was used by the U.S. Army Air Force and in 1949 was purchased by the Port Authority for just over three million dollars. Today this modern airport has two runways and state-of-the-art flight-control equipment.

New Jersey, of course, also has many local airports. Interstate commercial airlines have flights to and from Newark, Trenton, and Atlantic City. Mercer County Airport, on 1,000 acres near Interstate 295 north of Trenton, serves scheduled airplanes and is used heavily by state officials traveling to and from New Jersey's capital. This airport has regular commercial flights as well as private corporate flights.

Other important New Jersey airports include Princeton, Morristown, Red Bank, Hanover, Lincoln Park, Caldwell-Wright, Colts Neck, Preston, Asbury Park, Towaco, Linden Greenwood Lake, Manville-Krupper, Somerset, and Somerset Hills.

—David Fleming

Building the Newark airport involved draining the marsh and pumping fill in from Newark Bay. The airport's top layers were made with tons of cinders and gravel covered with oil. Opened in 1928, the sixty-acre site was the first commercial airport with a paved runway, and the first to install a traffic control system. Courtesy, Newark Public Library

The Great Surge in Petro-Chemicals

With its rivers, streams, bays, and its proximity to the markets of New York, New Jersey was a logical location for chemical firms. The loss of German chemical expertise and materials hurt New Jersey during the war. The Passaic County textile industry depended on German dies, and the TNT manufacturers at Du Pont and Hercules nearly shut down because of an inability to get toluene.

The industry had developed steadily up to the war. William Colgate and Company made chemically produced soap products in Jersey City from the 1840s. George Rose manufactured phosphorus for the match industry of the 1870s, and the Newark paint companies had grown during the nineteenth century. Oil refining at Bayonne and then at Bayway increased the need for sulphuric acid, which was eventually met in part by the Grasselli Chemical Company's heavy-chemicals plant at Tremley Point in Union County.

At the turn of the century Perth Amboy Chemical Company had made formaldehyde. General Bakelite Company nearby produced Belgian-born Leo H. Baekeland's patented resin, Bakelite, which differed from Hyatt's celluloid. During the Great Depression, Union Carbide would make General Bakelite its Plastics Division. Because of New Jersey's harbors, General Chemical Company built plants at Bayonne, Passaic, Edgewater, and Camden. By 1914 New Jersey had 5,046 chemical workers.

When the war severed the sources of German chemicals, some twenty-three New Jersey firms jumped in to fill the void. In the Somerville-Bound Brook area, Calco (Cott-a-lapp Chemical Company) chemists taught themselves how to make the coal-tar chemicals they could no longer get from Germany. In 1925 Bakelite Company, later to be taken over by Union Carbide & Carbon Corporation, opened plants and research laboratories in the Somerville-Bound Brook area.

Du Pont invested $43 million into operations at Deepwater in Salem

Benjamin Moore & Co., a well-known Newark paint manufacturer, built this plant in Carteret, New Jersey, in 1912 to manufacture Muresco, an early wall finish that was sold as a dry powder and then mixed with water at the job site. The process combined Irish Moss, a fungus growth of the sea, with finely ground clay. Courtesy, Benjamin Moore & Co.

In the 1920s, Du Pont workers in the firm's Parlin plant wore goggles to protect their vision from the ultraviolet rays used in the process that measured the impact of climatological conditions upon Duco Paint. A paint that carried color easily, flowed smoothly, and most importantly, dried quickly, Duco was almost immediately adopted by the automobile industry. Courtesy, Newark Public Library

County to make dyes. Although it took ten years to produce profits at the operation, the Du Pont Deepwater facility grew into one of the largest chemical plants anywhere. In the 1920s it produced the antiknock compound, tetraethyl, and during World War II it made the synthetic rubber, neoprene, along with synthetic camphor.

Although divested of its monopoly in explosives in 1912, Du Pont bought an Arlington pyroxylin manufacturer just prior to the American entry into the war. There Du Pont chemists produced the tough lacquer known as Duco, which coated washing machines, gasoline pumps, furniture, golf clubs, and automobiles during the 1920s. Du Pont also acquired a section of the Grasselli Chemical Company in 1928 and the entirety of Roessler & Hasslacher Chemical Company in Perth Amboy in 1930 to become New Jersey's largest chemical manufacturer.

By 1925 chemicals were the fifth-largest income producer in the state. Begun in Linden before the war as a fertilizer producer, American Cyanamid Company bought Calco Chemical Company in 1929. It expanded its Bound Brook operation to some 4,000 employees, making American Cyanamid second only to Du Pont in the state. By placing a sheet of clear pyraline plastic between two sheets of glass, the Arlington Company, a division of Du Pont, developed auto safety glass. American Cyanamid developed beetle ware and Melmac, a heat-resistant plastic. In Newark the Sherwin Williams Company and Benjamin Moore & Company, who also had a plant in Carteret, and Pittsburgh Plate Glass Company produced paint during the 1920s.

New Jersey scientists made major advances in oil-cracking technology. At the Standard Oil Development Company at Bayway, E. Murphree and other researchers developed a fluid catalytic cracking process in 1919 and a "double coil" process in 1920. These techniques, plus the fractional distillation process developed during the 1920s, made available various grades of petroleum. During the 1920s, Standard's Engineering Consultant Warren Lewis designed the fractionating tower, which used the different weights of the vapors to separate them. Standard Oil truly began the petrochemical industry in 1919 when scientists at Bayway developed a process to convert propylene into isopropyl alcohol in commercial quantities.

In 1919-1921 cancelled war orders threw many out of work, and industrial output in New Jersey dropped by over a billion dollars. But by then the nation had turned its back on the moralistic President Wilson from New Jersey and elected Warren G. Harding, who summoned Americans to "return to normalcy."

During the 1920s the American economy expanded. Gross national product, personal income, capital formation, industrial productivity, labor efficiency, and mass distribution all advanced. New consumer goods, particularly automobiles, gave the era a sense of dynamic expansion. The general prosperity, however, obscured high unemployment and weakness in the farm economy.

The Automobile Comes of Age

Between 1913 and 1929 automobile registration in America jumped from 1.2 million to 26.5 million. Passenger-car production shot up from 1.5 million annually in 1921 to 4.7 million in 1929. In 1918 New Jerseyans registered 163,419 automobiles, and by 1929 the number jumped to more than 800,000. The State Highway Department judged in 1930 that the average driver annually put nearly 9,000 miles on the family car.

Trucking surged as well during the postwar period. In 1918 there were 26,134 trucks in the state, but by 1927 there were 125,886. Only six states had more truck registrations.

New Jersey also became a major automobile-assembly state. General Motors had incorporated in New Jersey in 1908 to take advantage of the liberal incorporation laws, and Alfred P. Sloan, who would later head GM, originally sold Hyatt roller bearings from his Harrison factory to Oldsmobile, Cadillac, Buick, and Ford. In 1916 GM made Hyatt Roller Bearing

This 1915 photograph shows the yard of the nationally known wheelwright, Phineas Jones and Company. Founded in Massachusetts, the company moved to Newark in 1860 and began making wheels for a variety of vehicles. A 1915 Newark City Directory described the "celebrated Jones Wheels, with or without rubber tires, for automobiles and horse drawn vehicles." The Jones Company manufactured the first tires for Henry Ford's automobiles as well as the heavy wheels to transport Ringling Brothers Circus wagons. Courtesy, Newark Public Library

Corporation a division.

Ford built a huge assembly plant in Kearny during the war and employed some 8,000 men who assembled 700 cars a day there after the conflict. W. C. Durant purchased a Willys-Overland factory in Elizabeth in 1922 to assemble the Star automobile. Although the enterprise collapsed at the end of the decade, during 1927 Durant had 1,000 people assembling automobiles. That year New Jerseyans produced $154 million of automobiles and parts. General Motors exported Chevrolets during the 1920s from a Bloomfield plant.

As New Jerseyans took to the highways, they demanded road improvements. During the war, voters endorsed a seven-million-dollar bond issue to build the state highway system. When the funds ran out during 1917, the legislature passed additional taxes. Unfortunately, State Engineer George W. Goethals was called into the war.

But this was the automobile age, and the State Chamber of Commerce was campaigning for a state highway system and a state police force. In 1922 voters endorsed $40 million to build the state highway system. Originally to include 525 miles of roads, the state enlarged the highway system to 1,800 miles by 1927. Camden built America's first traffic circle. Crews widened roads to three lanes. Drivers began to pay a gasoline tax of two cents per gallon to maintain the road system that was becoming recognized as one of the best in the nation.

The end of the war meant resumption of world trade, and that revived

The origin of the term "turnpike" is illustrated by this photograph of a tollgate still operating circa 1915. Upon receiving the toll, the gatekeeper would open the gate (turn the pike) to allow the traveler to pass. This tollgate was in South Woodbury, on the way to Mantua. Courtesy, Newark Public Library

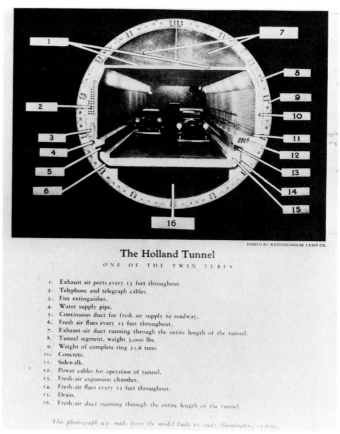

The Holland Tunnel
ONE OF THE TWIN TUBES

1. Exhaust air ports every 15 feet throughout.
2. Telephone and telegraph cables.
3. Fire extinguisher.
4. Water supply pipe.
5. Continuous duct for fresh air supply to roadway.
6. Fresh air flues every 15 feet throughout.
7. Exhaust-air duct running through the entire length of the tunnel.
8. Tunnel segment, weight 3,000 lbs.
9. Weight of complete ring 21.6 tons.
10. Concrete.
11. Sidewalk.
12. Power cables for operation of tunnel.
13. Fresh-air expansion chamber.
14. Fresh-air flues every 15 feet throughout.
15. Drain.
16. Fresh-air duct running through the entire length of the tunnel.

This photograph was made from the model built to study illumination systems.

another transportation problem that had been plaguing New Jersey and New York for years: how to ensure coherence in goods movement throughout the New York-New Jersey port area, a port that handled over half of the foreign commerce of the United States.

Created in 1921 by New Jersey and New York, and assented to by Congress, the Port Authority of New York and New Jersey sought to ease the movement of freight to and from any section of the port. Some 1,500 miles of territory—25 miles in any direction from the Statue of Liberty—fell under the jurisdiction of the new authority.

Railroad trunk lines terminating in New Jersey needed to have easy access to New York City. New England trains wanted connections to New Jersey. To meet these needs, the authority had to construct new highways between terminals, piers, and industrial establishments that did not have their own railroad sidings. The new highways had to connect with existing or projected bridges, tunnels, and ferries.

Port Authority designers planned four new bridges: the George Washington, the Bayonne, the Goethals, and the Outerbridge. Unfortunately, the Port Authority found that it could not bring the involved railroads under its administration.

But in 1927 the New York State Bridge and Tunnel Commission and the New Jersey Interstate Bridge and Tunnel Commission finished the Holland Tunnel at a cost of $50 million. Made of cast-iron tubes covered

Above: This cross section of a model of the Holland Tunnel was prepared by Westinghouse Lamp Company during planning of the tunnel lighting. A joint project of the states of New Jersey and New York, completed in 1927, the tunnel's twin tubes connect lower Manhattan and Jersey City under the Hudson River. Courtesy, Newark Public Library

Left: When George Washington Goethals was hired as consulting engineer for the bridge later named in his honor, he had already distinguished himself in a long career of military engineering. One of his last Army duties involved the completion of the Panama Canal, a difficult task for which he received a Congressional Medal of Honor. Goethals died in January 1928, three months before the dedication of the Goethals Bridge. Courtesy, Newark Public Library

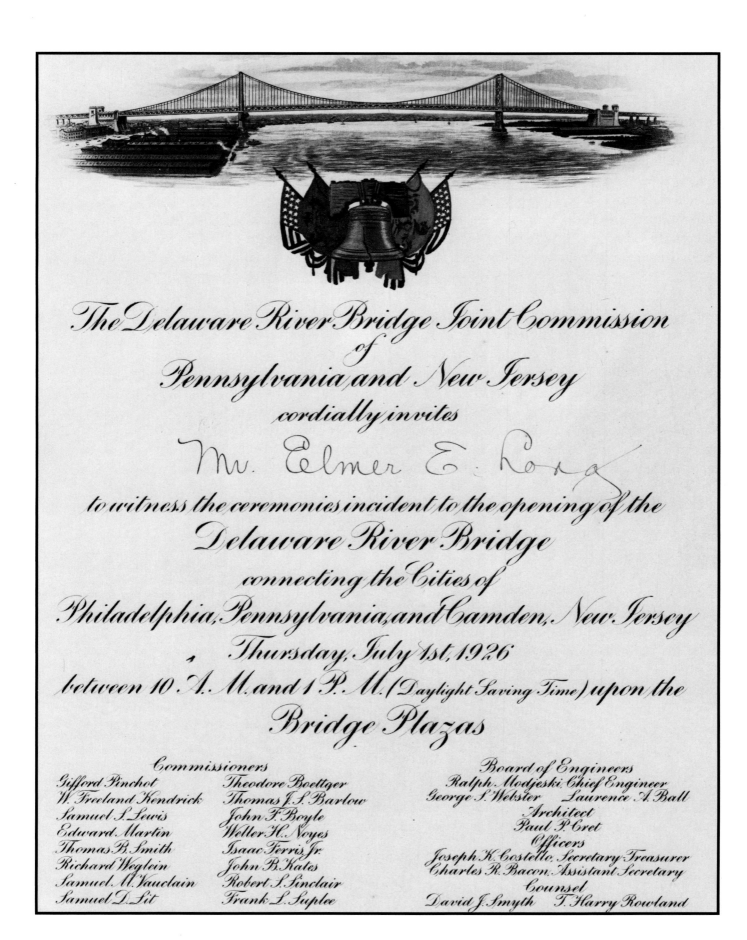

The Delaware River Bridge Joint Commission
of
Pennsylvania and New Jersey
cordially invites

Mr. Elmer E. Long

to witness the ceremonies incident to the opening of the

Delaware River Bridge

connecting the Cities of

Philadelphia, Pennsylvania, and Camden, New Jersey

Thursday, July 1st, 1926

between 10 A.M. and 1 P.M. (Daylight Saving Time) upon the

Bridge Plazas

Commissioners		Board of Engineers
Gifford Pinchot	Theodore Boettger	Ralph Modjeski, Chief Engineer
W. Freeland Kendrick	Thomas J. S. Barlow	George S. Webster Laurence A. Ball
Samuel S. Lewis	John F. Boyle	Architect
Edward Martin	Weller H. Noyes	Paul P. Cret
Thomas B. Smith	Isaac Ferris, Jr.	Officers
Richard Weglein	John B. Kates	Joseph K. Costello, Secretary-Treasurer
Samuel M. Vauclain	Robert S. Sinclair	Charles R. Bacon, Assistant Secretary
Samuel D. Lit	Frank L. Suplee	Counsel
		David J. Smyth T. Harry Rowland

with concrete, 29.5 feet in diameter and 9,250 feet long, the tunnel saw 51,000 cars move through on opening day with no accidents. Nearly nine million vehicles passed through the Holland Tunnel in its first year. In 1931 the Port of New York Authority acquired the tunnel and the revenue it produced—then $6 million annually.

A year before the Holland Tunnel was built, a thirty-six-million-dollar bridge joined Camden and Philadelphia, and touched off a brief boom in Atlantic City real estate. After the Holland Tunnel was built, the Port Authority of New York completed the Goethals Bridge in Elizabeth and Outerbridge Crossing at Perth Amboy, which linked New Jersey and Staten Island. The authority collected its first tolls on the Bayonne Bridge over the Kill van Kull to Staten Island in 1931, and Perth Amboy's Victory Bridge over the Raritan River helped sun worshippers get to the shore easily. To speed motorists over the Passaic and Hackensack rivers, the Pulaski Skyway rose some 145 feet in the air and cut driving time between Newark and Jersey City from nearly thirty minutes to five minutes by avoiding the drawbridges and the traffic lights. Newark Airport was thus more accessible for New York City travelers.

These bridges and roadways aided the motorist, but the George Washington Bridge also captured the imagination. An engineering marvel when finished in 1931, ahead of schedule and under budget, its 3,400-foot length made it twice as long as any other bridge. Its curving cables held 90,000 tons in the suspended span, which permitted six lanes of traffic to flow.

As railroads had altered the nineteenth century economy, so the automobiles and trucks rushing over the new bridges would shape the twentieth century's. By 1937, despite the Great Depression, checkers tabulated some 15 million new annual crossings of the Hudson, in addition to the 11.6 vehicles which continued to cross the river that year on the ferries.

Road-building and other transportation improvements in the state made New Jersey, for its size, the leading state in the nation in transportation and communication facilities, with 6,211 track miles of steam railroads, 1,291 miles of electric railroads, plus extensive railroad yards and its new roads and bridges.

In 1928 the Newark city fathers began to fill the swamplands to the east with garbage and create the ground for Newark Airport, which was completed by 1929. Its 100 acres of firm, level surface, its paved runways, and its lights for night landing made it one of the best-equipped airports in the world at the time. Within two years, the airport claimed to be the busiest in the world.

The National Air Transport, which operated the U.S. Post Office's air mail route between New Brunswick and Chicago, handled all of the air mail coming from New York City. National became the largest in the United States and the second largest in the world during the early 1920s. It switched its base of operations to the Newark Airport at the end of the decade.

Facing page: This invitation to the dedication of the Delaware River Bridge is the culmination of an effort, begun in 1919 with the creation of the Delaware River Bridge Joint Commission, to connect Philadelphia with Camden by what was, at that time, the longest suspension bridge in the world. In 1956, the bridge was renamed the Benjamin Franklin Bridge on the occasion of the 250th anniversary of this eminent American. Courtesy, Camden County Historical Society

Above: Steel and cables frame a lone workman on the George Washington Bridge. Opened October 24, 1931, the bridge was designed by Cass Gilbert and constructed under the supervision of Othmar Anmann. Courtesy, Newark Public Library

Left: The Hope Mill (seen here circa 1920) began as a cotton factory on Mill Street near Ellison in Paterson as early as 1822. In 1879, the firm of Hopper and Scott used the mill to manufacture silk thread. As the delivery trucks in the foreground indicate, the mill continued as a silk mill into the 1920s. Courtesy, Paterson Museum Archives

The Naval Air Station at Lakehurst housed all the lighter-than-air craft of the navy. In a hangar that had doors fifteen stories high, the navy housed the mighty Graf Zeppelin in 1928.

Manufacturers Lead the State's Economy

The road network helped industries grow. The state continued to lead in textiles (particularly silk), chemicals, machinery (particularly electrical), iron and steel, and food. Despite its small size, in 1925 New Jersey ranked sixth among the states in the value added in general manufacturing. Some 87,000 establishments added $1.5 billion to over $2 billion in raw materials. Four hundred thousand workers were employed at equipment generating some 1.25 million horsepower. New Jersey led other states in precious-metals refining, photographic printing, leather, linen goods, asbestos, blacking, stains,

and polishes.

Textile factories, which employed some 20 percent of the state's wage workers, continued to be a key element of the state's manufacturing economy. Centered in Passaic, Paterson, Newark, Garfield, Trenton, and Millville, the state's textile firms made approximately one-third of the nation's linen goods and asbestos textiles, one-fifth of the dyeing and finishing textiles, and approximately 10 percent of its worsted goods, corsets, fur-felt hats, and jute goods.

Paterson's silk industry suffered two blows. First, eastern Pennsylvania surged past it in production. Then Paterson's firms failed to get on the rayon bandwagon, and when rayon captured the public imagination, Paterson missed out. Aided by the soft water of the Passaic River, however, Paterson's silk dye works continued to thrive. But when World War II ended the importation of raw silk, and New Jersey turned its mulberry acreage into food production, Paterson's role as the "silk city" came to an end. New Jersey textiles also suffered during the 1920s as industrialists began the process of moving the textile industry to the American South.

By dollar value of product, petroleum refining led all industries in the state during the 1920s. Although the return of European competition after the war hurt New Jersey refining briefly in 1923, technology pushed the industry forward. In 1925 some 13,000 people worked in the state's eight refineries to handle one-tenth of America's petroleum. New Jersey ranked fourth in output behind only California, Texas, and Oklahoma.

In the 1920s new cracking techniques which refined oil at high pressure

Christian Syrian immigrants, among the last textile workers to join Paterson's ethnic mix, arrived in Paterson in the early twentieth century. Syrian children, seen here in 1928, are costumed for a play sponsored by St. Ann's Arabic School. Skilled textile workers from many European countries emigrated to Paterson as technological and political changes in their homelands threatened their livelihoods, and, in some cases, their lives. Courtesy, American Labor Museum

When the whistle blew in Paterson's Abby Mill (left) on Water Street, workers who lived in the company houses (right) did not have far to go. George Abby, a prosperous blacksmith and machinist, acquired a number of properties in Paterson between his arrival from England in 1850 and his death in 1902. In 1930, the mill specialized in the manufacture of silk. Courtesy, Paterson Museum Archives

and under extreme heat brought a better quality of gasoline, then in demand for aviation and automobile use. In May 1927 "Lucky" Charles A. Lindbergh powered his *Spirit of St. Louis* with a then-new seventy-five-octane fuel.

In the 1920s New Jersey's electrical-machinery industry produced only half as much total dollar value as the oil industry, but it was the second-largest employer in the state. Largely because of Edison's efforts in the 1880s and 1890s, the state became home to a mighty industry of electrical machinery, street lighting, battery and light-bulb production, and the manufacture of hoists, fans, and elevator motors, among other products.

In the 1890s Frank Sprague, one of Edison's associates, made motor hoists, electric fans, and other motors in Bloomfield, a short distance from Edison's laboratories. General Electric later bought Sprague's Bloomfield operations, expanded it during the war, and developed integrated oil burners there during the 1920s.

The same time Sprague came to Bloomfield, Francis Crocker and Schuyler Wheeler brought their electric-motor factory from New York to Crescent, near Bloomfield. They appropriately renamed the place Ampere, in honor of Andre Marie Ampere, the French physicist and mathematician who had helped develop the field of electricity. There Crocker-Wheeler produced dynamos to replace batteries in telegraph offices and then electrified the steel industry with electric motors. Over the years, Crocker-Wheeler electrified government offices in Washington, D.C., the Philadelphia Mint, and New York's Rockefeller Center.

In 1891 George Westinghouse bought out U.S. Lighting in Newark. Then

Workers of the H.W. Merriam Shoe Company were photographed in the shop in 1920. The company's four-story building was constructed in Newton in 1872, in time to join other Sussex County industries that flourished in the wake of the Sussex County Railroad, later the Delaware, Lackawanna, & Western. Courtesy, Newark Public Library

in 1906 this rival of Edison shifted his lamp works from Brooklyn to Bloomfield. Although Westinghouse Electric went bankrupt during the Panic of 1906, largely because Westinghouse was more of an inventor than he was a businessman, the firm revived under new management, and opened a lamp works in Trenton during the war. They also opened a lamp-base manufacturing plant in Belleville during the decade, and by the end of the 1920s, the Bloomfield plant needed a million feet of floor space.

These facilities, plus Edward Weston's operations in Newark, General Electric's plant in Harrison, John A. Roebling & Sons Company in Trenton, the Edison Lamp Works in Harrison, and Cooper-Hewitt Electric Co. in Hoboken, among others, placed the state fifth among American states in production of electrical equipment and supplies.

New Jersey's iron-and-steel industry continued to be important in the Roaring Twenties, but sometimes under different corporate names. U.S. Steel, formed in 1901 by J. P. Morgan as the world's first billion-dollar corporation, bought out Cooper & Hewitt's works in Trenton at the turn of the century. Other out-of-state giants made similar purchases of New Jersey's iron mines and steel firms, and the national industry continued to shift to the Midwest. But despite changed ownerships and losses to other regions, the iron-and-steel group in New Jersey still employed some 30,000 workers and ranked fourth behind only textiles, chemicals, and machinery in as far as the percentage of total value added by manufacture in 1923.

Ceramics makers continued to exploit the state's unexcelled clays. Trenton remained the center of the pottery business, Sayreville led in brick, and Perth Amboy continued its primacy in terra cotta. During the 1920s, the Scammel brothers took over the Lamberton pottery works and made Lamberton a name equal in hotel pottery to Lenox in family dinnerware. American Standard expanded its sanitary ware business by purchasing the Maddock business in Trenton in 1929 to maintain Trenton's preeminence in sanitary ware.

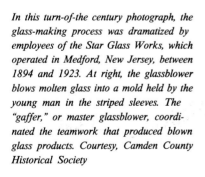

In this turn-of-the century photograph, the glass-making process was dramatized by employees of the Star Glass Works, which operated in Medford, New Jersey, between 1894 and 1923. At right, the glassblower blows molten glass into a mold held by the young man in the striped sleeves. The "gaffer," or master glassblower, coordinated the teamwork that produced blown glass products. Courtesy, Camden County Historical Society

Above: Glass workers with their apprentices and helpers gathered for their photograph at the Clayton Glass Works in 1904. Organized as the Fislerville Glass Works in 1850, the firm was purchased by John M. Moore before the Civil War. Known alternately as Moore Brothers or the Clayton Glass Works, the annual value of their products reached one-half million dollars in 1880. Courtesy, Camden County Historical Society

Left: American District Telegraph employees at the company's central station in Camden display the state of the art in security monitoring systems in 1923. ADT now maintains central offices throughout New Jersey, and has recently moved their corporate headquarters to Morris Corporate Center in Parsippany. Courtesy, American District Telegraph Co.

Blueberries and cranberries are two of New Jersey's oldest and most famous exports. They are grown in the bogs of southeastern Burlington county, where soil and water conditions are among the best in the country for such cultivation.

During the nineteenth century, the blueberry was simply a wild bush that grew haphazardly on the outer edges of cranberry bogs, and efforts to domesticate this wild berry had failed. But it was a New Jersey native, Elizabeth C. White, who succeeded in "taming" the blueberry, when in 1911 she began reading about U.S. Department of Agriculture experiments with blueberries.

Elizabeth White was one of four daughters of a leading Burlington County cranberry grower. In her readings of the Agriculture Department's blueberry experiments, she came across the writings of a Dr. Frederick Coville, who described his efforts at crossing various strains of wild blueberry to produce superior offspring. Miss White's imagination was captivated by the possibilities of this effort, and she invited Dr. Coville to use "Whitesbog," her family's property, to conduct his experiments. Thus, on her Burlington County land, she began to devote her efforts to domesticating the blueberry crop.

Working with Dr. Coville, Miss White distributed small boards with various-sized holes in them to local residents whom she had hired to pick the wild blueberries. She paid for the blueberry bushes according to the size of the largest hole that the berries would not go through on this board, and she also offered prizes for the largest blueberries.

The Department of Agriculture was becoming very interested indeed in Miss White's efforts. Soon, with Dr. Coville, she began crossbreeding the prize-winning blueberries. Taking the largest pickings, she and Dr. Coville made hybrid cuttings. Eventually they weeded out all but a few of them until they had the optimum plant. They had thus developed the modern cultivated blueberry.

The first commercial shipments from these experiments began in 1916. White's efforts led to increased blueberry cultivation. Whitesbog at New Lisbon was being used increasingly for Department of Agriculture field trials. Several successful varieties were developed during these days at Whitesbog, nearly all from the prize-winning blueberries found by local pickers.

Decades of cultivation and experimentation at Whitesbog and other places eventually led to nearly complete domestication and hybridization of the blueberry: it had gone from being a wild bush to being a field crop.

This Burlington County area of the Pine Barrens where Miss White worked had long been suited for the growth of the blueberry. The soil of around this area has a sandy base but is black in color and retentive of moisture. When wetted by the rain, these soils are ideal for cultivating cranberries and blueberries.

By 1940 there were 650 acres of blueberry crops in New Jersey and by 1946 some 2,000 acres. By the time of White's death in 1954, the acreage had hit the 5,000 mark, with 2,800 acres in Burlington County and 1,600 in Atlantic County. The state harvest of that year was 1.6 million trays of 12 pints each. Elizabeth White had truly brought the blueberry a long way out of the bushes.

Ten years later, in 1964, New Jersey had 8,300 acres and was by far the most important state for blueberry culture. The value of the crop in that year was $5.5 million. Blueberry acreage was essentially evenly split between Burlington and Atlantic counties, but in terms of harvest return Atlantic County became New Jersey's center of blueberry production. In 1969 there were slightly less than 500 commercial blueberry producers in the state. Today, much of human labor has been replaced by mechanical pickers.

New Jersey is also a major producer of cranberries. Found in New Jersey's temperate boglands, they became a New Jersey specialty, partially domesticated over the years through experiments similar to those of Miss White and the Department of Agriculture, which increased yield through fertilizing and spraying for insect pests.

Since the boggy area in which cranberries thrive is limited, the growers were also able to control prices due to lesser demand, which made the crop very profitable. Rubber-booted pickers would wade into the bogs to pick these berries, harvesting some 9,000 acres in 1909 alone. Well over half of that total was in Burlington County. Atlantic County, with 1,200 acres, was still developing new bogs at that time.

Eventually, harvesters developed a rake-like device to "scoop" the berries from the vines. Later, in the 1960s, New Jersey's cranberry crop began for the most part to be "water harvested" —knocked from the plant into the water and scooped up with rakes or conveyor belts. The berries were trucked immediately to drying sheds before being sorted and put into containers to be shipped to market.

—David Fleming

The American blueberry industry owes its origins to Elizabeth Coleman White, a self-taught scientist who, with Frederick V. Coville of the U.S. Dept. of Agriculture, domesticated and perfected the wild blueberry. At Whites Bog in Browns Mills in Burlington County, in 1916, they produced the first commercially grown crop for market. Miss White died in 1954 at age eighty-three, still working on improving her favorite fruit. Courtesy, Newark Public Library

In addition to classical and oriental shapes, in glazes of yellow or green, Clifton Art Pottery produced an unglazed line of "Indian Ware," shown here, inspired by prehistoric Indian pottery. The firm was founded by Fred Tschirner and William Long, and was active in Newark from 1905 to 1911. Courtesy, Collection of the Newark Museum

Agriculture Diversifies

The automobile and truck altered the farm economy of New Jersey. Truck farming continued to grow during the decade. Only about 4 percent of the state's population worked on farms during the 1920s, and by 1925 total farm acreage declined some 25 percent from 1910. But the state still produced farm products worth $100 million. Although still far and away the major crops, corn and grain, worth approximately $10 million annually, gave way to the marketing of truck crops, particularly tomatoes (for both canning and the market), sweet corn, strawberries, string beans, asparagus, and peppers. New Jerseyans produced one million dollars' worth of each crop annually in the 1920s. Campbell Soup Company farms 1 and 2 developed new tomatoes with improved color, shape, size and content, for canning. Cumberland County's tomatoes became famous for quality and taste. During the 1920s New Jersey ranked among the top states in the country in commercial production of strawberries, cucumbers, lettuce, onions, spinach, peas, sweet potatoes, and tomatoes.

Sussex farmers still produced valuable dairy products, although the total number of cattle in the state was falling. Yet even with fewer milk cows, because of better breeds, milk production in the state rose. New Jersey breeders of jersey and Ayrshire cows were among the best in the world. Indeed the state was among the leading states in overall cow testing and herd improvement. Thus New Jersey dairymen were able to increase the output of milk per cow from 532 to 651 gallons annually between 1919 and 1924.

Poultry-raising developed during the 1920s. In the late nineteenth century in the area around Frenchtown and Stockton, poultrymen developed the day-old-chick industry. In the 1920s huge New Jersey hatcheries worth

Left: In this interior view of a Campbell Soup factory in the early 1900s, endless chains of cans are filled, sealed, and labeled by machine. The firm became the nation's largest soup producer after Dr. John T. Dorrance developed a cost-saving procedure in 1897 for preparing condensed or concentrated soup. Courtesy, Camden County Historical Society

Below: Since the 1880s, New Jersey has been a leader in the production of chickens and eggs. To increase their yield, farmers learned to keep hens in kerosene-heated incubators. When Joseph Wilson discovered that baby chicks could be shipped by freight train, his cousin Richard Kerr opened the Kerr Hatcheries in Frenchtown. By 1923, when this photo was made, Kerr was shipping hundreds of chicks to New York, Chicago, and other cities. Today, Hunterdon County is still a major supplier of this popular food. Courtesy, Newark Public Library

Following page: This float was sponsored by the New Jersey State Chamber of Commerce in the parade that celebrated the dedication of Ocean City's new boardwalk on July 4, 1928, after the former promenade and its stores were destroyed by fire in October 1927. Courtesy, New Jersey State Chamber of Commerce

C. H. DAVIS, | **797 Broad St.,**
Clothier, | Newark, N. J.

Left: In the late 1800s, Charles H. Davis's "elegant" suits ranged in price from $4 to $25. His trade card capitalized on the fad for the oriental, then current in home decoration. The hookah-smoking child was designed to emphasize the Victorian "Turkish corner." Courtesy, Special Collections, Alexander Library, Rutgers University

Facing page: In addition to his product "Rough on Rats," also effective against "roaches, bed-bugs, chipmunks, gophers," Ephraim S. Wells of Jersey City prepared patent medicines, including Wells' Health Renewer, guaranteed to stimulate the appetite. Frenzied activity in the one 1880 handbill reflects the stereotype of the Irish immigrant depicted after the Civil War. Courtesy, Special Collections, Alexander Library, Rutgers University

Succulent Jersey corn decorated the tag that admitted one guest to the grandstand of the Great Inter-State Fair of 1893. Classic figures representing Liberty and Prosperity grace the state seal of New Jersey, drawn with artistic license for the cover of the 1896 fair brochure. The contents include premium lists and rules and regulations for eleven departments of exhibitors, from livestock and produce entries to farm machinery and floral funeral designs. Tag photo courtesy, Special Collections, Alexander Library, Rutgers University. Brochure photo courtesy, New Jersey Room, Fairleigh Dickinson University

276

The Peter Breidt City Brewery on 600-610 Pearl Street, Elizabeth, was incorporated in 1885. The company employed thirty workmen, who annually produced twenty-five thousand barrels of beer, ale, and porter. Courtesy, New Jersey Historical Society

Right: This is one of a series of trade cards that featured colorfully costumed foreigners operating Singer sewing machines. A brief description of the country appeared on the verso of each card. The complete set was offered by the Singer Sewing Machine Company as a souvenir of the World's Columbian Exposition in Chicago in 1893. Courtesy, Special Collections, Alexander Library, Rutgers University

Facing page, top: On this Eatmor Cranberries label, an attractive woman identifies the firm's Jersey Belle brand. The cranberry, a native plant, was domesticated in New Jersey toward the end of the nineteenth century through the efforts of the New Jersey Agricultural Experiment Station and other private experimenters. Courtesy, Special Collections, Alexander Library, Rutgers University

Facing page, bottom: Anderson Preserving Company, a competitor of Campbell soups, advertised its products on a blotter. Incorporated in Camden in 1885, during the canning season the cannery increased its staff from thirty to more than 300 employees. Courtesy, Special Collections, Alexander Library, Rutgers University

CHINA.

COPYRIGHT 1892 BY THE SINGER MANUFACTURING CO.

OVER

Eatmor Cranberries

JERSEY BELLE BRAND

of NEW JERSEY

JERSEY BELLE BRAND

ONE FOURTH U.S.

STANDARD BARREL

PACKED FOR THE

AMERICAN CRANBERRY EXCHANGE

| PACKER'S NUMBER | | PRODUCT OF THE U.S. OF AMERICA | NEW YORK CHICAGO |

ANDERSON'S Concentrated SOUPS

EACH CAN MAKES 6 PLATES

12 VARIETIES

TOMATO	CREAM OF CELERY
MOCK TURTLE	CREAM OF ASPARAGUS
CHICKEN	CREAM OF POTATO
CONSOMME	PUREE OF PEA
OX TAIL	PUREE OF BEAN
VEGETABLE	PUREE OF LENTIL

ANDERSON PRESERVING CO.
CAMDEN, N.J. U.S.A.

EDISON
Diamond Disc
PHONO-
GRAPHS

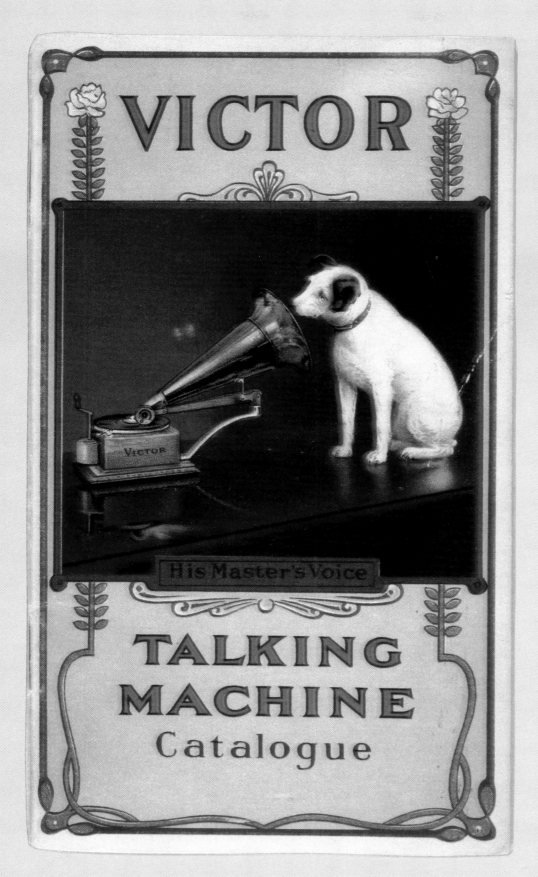

Left: The painting of Nipper, the pet of English artist Francis Barrand, was originally designed for Columbia Graphaphone, one of Victor's competitors. Victor's catalog listed recordings available, by singers like Enrico Caruso. Courtesy, New Jersey Room, Fairleigh Dickinson University

Facing page: The records for the phonograph Edison invented in 1877 were cylinders of wax. Thirty-five years later Edison marketed a phonograph capable of playing the disc records popularized by the rival Victor Talking Machine. Edison's ten-inch records played for five minutes. Courtesy, New Jersey Room, Fairleigh Dickinson University

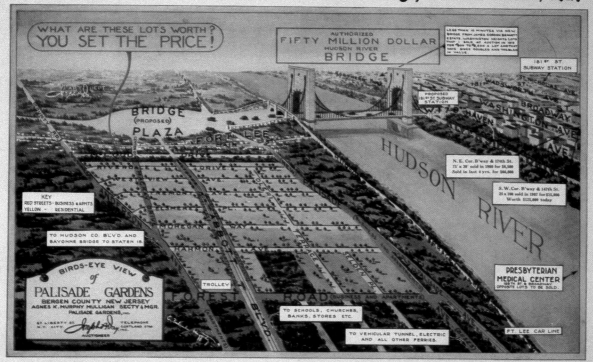

Facing page: William Howard Taft no doubt entertained himself and his guests with the Victrola in the White House Music Room. The Victor Talking Machine Company first enclosed the phonograph in a wooden cabinet in 1906, and the first model cost $200. Courtesy, New Jersey Room, Fairleigh Dickinson University

Above: Plans for the George Washington Bridge stimulated real estate speculation in many areas of Bergen County. Palisades Gardens, a 130-acre tract in Fort Lee, was developed by Agnes K. Murphy Mulligan, a real estate broker from the Bronx who had moved to Fort Lee in 1917. Courtesy, New Jersey Room, Fairleigh Dickinson University

Jersey City, N. J.   Pennsylvania Ferries

This is what Robert likes to ride on! Papa. Oct. 26, 1906.

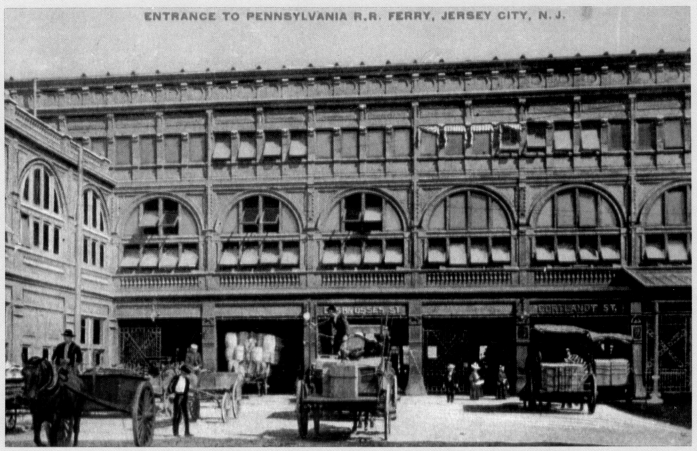

ENTRANCE TO PENNSYLVANIA R.R. FERRY, JERSEY CITY, N.J.

ALONG THE MORRIS CANAL.

JERSEY CITY, N. J.

Facing page: In the early 1900s, when these postcards were published, there were eight ferry lines connecting Jersey City with New York. Pennsylvania Rail Road ferries traveled from the Exchange Place Station to three destinations in New York City—Cortlandt, Debrosses, and West 23rd streets. Courtesy, New Jersey Room, Fairleigh Dickinson University

Above: The Morris Canal in parts of Jersey City changed from busy artery to bucolic scene circa 1900. After the 1870s, the old freight boats gradually disappeared, defeated by competition from the cheaper, faster railroads. Courtesy, New Jersey Room, Fairleigh Dickinson University

Squibb Institute microbiologists use the
pilot scale fermentor to help identify and
characterize bacteria and to find the
optimum environment for growing a new
antibiotic. Courtesy, Squibb Corporation

Human serum proteins are purified in this
electrophoresis apparatus at the Squibb
Institute for Medical Research. Courtesy,
Squibb Corporation

Above: A laboratory technician in Squibb's Parenteral Building in New Brunswick checks some of the 40 million vials of injectable medicine produced yearly in a sterile microprocessor-controlled environment. Courtesy, Squibb Corporation

Left: A McGraw-Hill worker assembles an order at the firm's Book Distribution Center at Hightstown, which ships fifteen million titles each year. More than four billion books have passed through this facility, the largest of three operated by McGraw-Hill in the United States. Courtesy, McGraw-Hill, Inc.

An ocean of chocolate treats pours from this Nabisco Brands food assembly line in New Hanover, New Jersey, on the 75th anniversary of the Oreo cookie. Created in 1911 with the Mother Goose biscuits and Veronese biscuit, the Oreo survived and remains today one of the world's most popular treats. More than twenty billion have been consumed in the last three quarters of a century. Courtesy, Nabisco Brands, Inc.

millions of dollars were sending thousands of baby chicks out across the country each spring. Electric lights courtesy of Mr. Edison helped Vineland and Toms River poultrymen to intensify egg production. New Jersey leghorn poultry farms there and elsewhere supplied the fresh white-shelled eggs for the New York markets. The commercial poultry industry moved out of relative obscurity to become one of the state's major agricultural industries.

The Garden State kept its reputation as a producer of vegetables and added to it with development of a large flower and ornamental-tree industry. A profusion of flowers sprang up each spring across New Jersey, and with an investment of some $6 million in ornamental horticulture, New Jersey ranked sixth among U.S. states. In addition, the state after the war was a significant producer of winesap apples, Oregon Evergreen blackberries, peaches, strawberries, and other fruits.

Operating out of the Agricultural College of the University of New Jersey (Rutgers), the extension service of the Department of Agriculture had county agents in 19 of the 21 counties who helped some 11,000 farmers annually

In 1927, Prudential Insurance Company employed more than 9,000 people. The company's Newark contingent stopped traffic on Broad Street in 1925 to have their pictures taken. Men and women alike wore hats to work. Courtesy, Newark Public Library

Above: There were more people on the beach than on the boardwalk in this composite Atlantic City advertisement circa 1920. Rose O'Neill's Kewpie doll dispensed homely philosophy in verse in women's magazines for two decades, beginning in 1910. The Hudson automobile on the billboard sold for $1,500 in 1915. Courtesy, Atlantic City Public Library

Left: Louis Bamberger, Felix Fuld, and Louis M. Frank established the state's largest department store, L. Bamberger and Company, in Newark in 1892. The store pursued an aggressive policy of customer-oriented merchandising and promotion that was so successful that in 1928 Bamberger's total sales ranked fourth among department stores in the nation. The photograph shows some of Bamberger's three dozen delivery trucks, one third of them motorized, parked outside the store's Halsey Street location in 1913. Courtesy, Newark Public Library

The contented family pictured here was tuned in to radio station WOR in Newark, created in 1922 by Bamberger's to promote the store's first radio receiver. WOR Radio, which actively promoted Bamberger's merchandise, was the sixth commercial radio station established in the United States. Courtesy, Bamberger's

with information about agriculture. Under its guidance and assistance, New Jersey agriculture moved from a general farm state into becoming an intensive and specialized agricultural state.

Although New Jersey continued to be the Garden State, the postwar years were the years of the city. In 1920, save for Paterson, New Jersey's great cities of Newark, Jersey City, Camden, Trenton, and Elizabeth all reached their highest population levels before 1960. Business developed in downtown areas. Jersey City rebuilt Journal Square and reconstructed Hudson Boulevard. New Jersey's industries continued to thrive in the cities. Fort Lee kept producing movies for the theaters. West Orange's Edison Electric, Linden's General Motors, New Brunswick's pharmaceuticals, Camden's Radio Corporation of America, and Campbell's Soup all grew during the prosperity decade.

Newark nearly became a metropolis. Prudential Life Insurance Company, other insurance companies, banks, and department stores, including the famous Bamberger's, made Newark a lively managerial and clerical city.

During the automobile age, however, hosts of people began the drive to the suburbs. The population of old suburbs skyrocketed during the 1920s by as much as 150 to 230 percent. Bergen County added 154,000 residents. Essex added some 181,000 people. Union and Passaic counties grew by 22 and 48 percent, respectively. Between 1920 and 1930, 64 new municipalities sprang up, giving the state a total of some 543 municipalities. By 1925 the Public Service Corporation of New Jersey, organized to acquire and regularize the transit systems of local communities, grew into the largest in New Jersey and supplied streetcar service to 147 communities.

New Jersey and the nation seemed to be maturing industrially during the 1920s. The war laid the basis, after the postwar decline, for a surging economy during the decade. Truck farmers supplied canners and markets with food. New Jerseyans built automobiles, roads, bridges, petrochemicals, iron and steel, electrical machinery, textiles. In Washington conservative business-oriented leaders encouraged capitalism.

Long thought to be a time of "normalcy," the twenties were years of change and development in New Jersey. The war had altered the American economy irrevocably. Unfortunately for the state and the nation, the general economy of the "Roaring Twenties" was nowhere near as sound as it seemed to the rabid speculators who pushed the bull market of 1928 to unprecedented heights in the fall of 1929.

In 1889 the Camden Horse Railroad Company was authorized to string trolley wires, illustrated here, above Federal Street in Camden. This photograph dates to 1915 when Public Service Corporation owned all of the city's trolley routes. Courtesy, North Jersey Chapter, National Railway Historical Society

Chapter Nine

The Great Depression and the War

Between March and November 1928, Radio Corporation of America stock symbolized the wild optimism of the bull market as it soared 400 percent. But on October 29, 1929, in the largest selling day in the history of the New York Stock Exchange, stock prices plummeted. In two months the market lost 40 percent of its value. The 1929 stock-market crash revealed the weaknesses in the American economy and triggered a cycle of bank failures and layoffs that radically challenged the American free-enterprise philosophy. By spring 1930 business indicators began to reveal a serious industrial slowdown.

The worst realized itself in a repetitive pattern. By 1933 the gross national product had declined by 25 percent; farm income had fallen by more than half; and industrial production dropped 50 percent from 1920s levels.

New Jersey Hurt Severely

The Great Depression rocked New Jersey. Because maldistribution of income was the underlying problem with the U.S. economy, the hardest-hit industries

For the wage earner in New Jersey, as in the rest of the nation, the Depression was a traumatic experience. Families of the unemployed were often hungry, cold, and sometimes homeless. This photograph gives a cross section of the unemployed men in Newark seeking federal jobs at a Newark armory at the height of the Depression in 1933. Courtesy, Newark Public Library

In Passaic, unadorned baskets of Christmas dinners were prepared for the victims of the Depression in 1937. Courtesy, Julius Forstmann Library

in America were those that manufactured consumer durables that the public could no longer afford. As a leading manufacturer of consumer durables, New Jersey suffered. Six hundred Newark factories shut down. In 1929 Newark had manufactured products worth $502 million. By 1935 the figure shrank to $328 million. Similar figures for Jersey City showed a slump from $312 million to $206 million. Banks across the state collapsed.

Industrial decline led to layoffs. The Camden shipyards laid off workers, as did the Middlesex copper refineries. On average, New Jersey personal income sank from $839 per year in 1929 to $479 in 1932 and then to $433 in 1933. In November 1930 Bergen County became the first county to hire the unemployed for public work; for seven hours' work on the roads, Bergen County paid them three dollars. Newark, Trenton, and Bayonne created similar programs.

In the fall of 1929 Herbert Hoover held conferences with businessmen to urge them not to cut wages or lay off workers. He appointed Arthur Woods to head an Emergency Committee for Employment that tried to encourage businessmen in New Jersey and elsewhere to reemploy workers.

Believing that the crisis might not turn out as badly as it did, the Hoover administration kept issuing hopeful statements: "All evidence indicates that the worst effects of the crash upon unemployment will have passed during the next 60 days." "We have now passed the worst," said the administration, "and with continued unity of effort we shall rapidly recover."

But Hoover also swung behind tax cuts to increase consuming power, for public works to create jobs and stimulate production, for cutting interest rates to stimulate borrowing, and for federal loans to banks and corporations to keep them afloat.

Hoover's Emergency Relief Administration (ERA) loaned money to the state to put some 30,000 New Jerseyans on the public payroll. In the

These travelers were photographed in a Newark Airport passenger lounge in 1933. The following year air travel to the West Coast was introduced. Passengers paid $200 to travel 118 miles per hour on a Ford tri-motor. Passengers would break the twenty-six-hour trip with an overnight stay in a Kansas City hotel ($3.50 extra). In the 1930s Newark was the busiest airport in the United States. Courtesy, Newark Public Library

industrial counties, unskilled labor got twenty dollars and skilled labor got twenty-seven dollars a week. Those in rural counties received eighteen dollars and twenty-three dollars a week for unskilled and skilled work. Unemployed college faculty were paid fourteen dollars a week to teach community college evening students in high-school buildings. The Reconstruction Finance Corporation (RFC) lent some two million dollars to New Jersey corporations and institutions.

But the reluctance of the administration to borrow and spend the sums necessary to revive the economy meant that even these programs were only palliatives. New Jerseyans developed no statewide program or agency for

Three inter-city trolleys were outward-bound from Trenton Terminal on Hanover Street in April 1934. At left, car 22 of the Trenton-Princeton Traction Company was bound for Princeton. At center and right, Pennsylvania-New Jersey Railway trolleys were headed for Yardley and Trenton. Courtesy, North Jersey Chapter, National Railway Historical Society

industrial relief. Municipalities found that they could not raise the funds to provide for the needy.

Frightened by the radicals among a group of World War I veterans who marched on Washington to demand early payment of their bonuses, Hoover called out the army to evict them from their makeshift shacks. After this fiasco, which blackened the reputation of an otherwise outstanding public servant, Hoover and his aides were unable to wage much of a reelection drive.

Vaudevillians quipped that Hoover once asked Secretary of the Treasury Mellon for a nickel to "call a friend."

"Here's a dime," Mellon was reported to reply. "Call all your friends."

At the Robert Treat Hotel in Newark, Franklin D. Roosevelt addressed a meeting of the National Emergency Council, which coordinated federal relief agencies operating throughout the Depression. The room was lined with exhibits of the work of various agencies, and their directors presented ten-minute reports. Pictured here at the January 18, 1936, meeting with President Roosevelt is Charles Edison, state director of the council. Courtesy, Newark Public Library

In the presidential election of 1932, New Jersey voted with the winner, giving 900,000 votes to Franklin D. Roosevelt and 770,000 to Herbert Hoover. As the administration packed up its bags and prepared to depart, the general economic indexes reached their nadirs. Stock exchanges closed down or operated on reduced hours. Banks shut their doors. Commercial exchanges operated under state restrictions.

The New Deal Comes to New Jersey

Franklin D. Roosevelt took office at the very bottom of the Great Depression and launched a wide-ranging and sometimes-contradictory series of legislative acts designed to stimulate the economy, relieve the unemployment problem, and reform abuses in the economic system.

First, to stem the hemorrhage in the banking system the administration closed the banks by declaring a "holiday" and reopened them with licenses from the Treasury Department when they could show they were solvent. In Westfield during the holiday, William Beard, president of the Westfield Trust Company, stood outside the closed bank doors to reassure his depositors. The Newark Clearing House Association, among others, printed scrip to use if the bank holiday, which lasted eight days, was prolonged.

Roosevelt went on radio to give the first of his avuncular "fireside chats" to the nation about the new administration's actions. With aid from the Reconstruction Finance Corporation, which loaned money to them based on their assets, many New Jersey banks reopened following the holiday. New

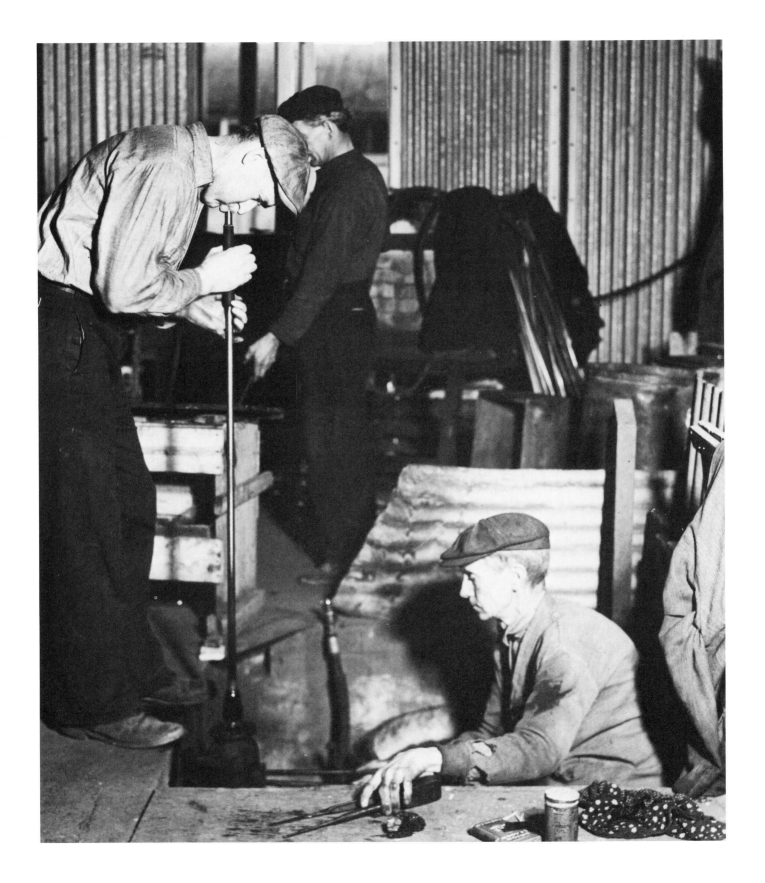

Jerseyans seemed convinced that the banks were now safe. Thousands of New Jersey depositors had been lining up to withdraw funds from the banks before the holiday. Now they flocked back to return their money.

The New Dealers reformed the banking system with four laws: the Emergency Banking Act of March 9, 1933, which endorsed Roosevelt's emergency closing; the Banking Act of June 16, 1933, which separated commercial and investment banks; the Federal Deposit Insurance Act of June 16, 1934, which protected individual accounts up to $5,000; and the 1935 Banking Act, which strengthened the Federal Reserve Board and its control over the reserve requirements and the money supply.

Many New Jersey banks closed their doors during these dark days, but many also reopened with RFC assistance and renewed public confidence. The mortgage crisis eased somewhat after the Home Owners Loan Corporation helped homeowners refinance their mortgages and helped banks free themselves from the risks of some of their bad mortgages.

A host of federal actions followed the banking bill—a total of sixteen legislative acts in 100 days. Some, like the Economy Act, which cut federal spending, were wrongheaded. Others, like the National Recovery Act, which originally came from the ideas of Walter C. Teagle of Standard Oil of New Jersey and attempted to get all New Jersey businesses to join codes of fair competition, were overly ambitious. A few, like the Tennessee Valley

Above: Trolleys of the Englewood Line in Bergen County carried passengers from Tenafly to the Edgewater ferries. The design of the Tenafly railroad station pictured here in 1934 has been attributed to architect J. Cleveland Cady, and it appears on the National List of Historic Places. Courtesy, North Jersey Chapter, National Railway Historical Society

Facing page: Glassworkers at work in 1937 at T.C. Wheaton Company (founded in 1888 in Millville) which became the largest family-owned glassworks in the world. The glassblower at left is forcing air into a "glob" of molten glass in a mold tended by the seated "mold boy." Although the firm has left New Jersey, the Wheaton Village and Museum presents the history of glassmaking in the state. Courtesy, Library of Congress

Seabrook Farms children were photographed in a staged plea supporting their
parents' wage demand for 30 cents per
hour at the South Jersey food processing
plant. A bitter strike organized by the
Agricultural and Cannery Workers
Industrial Union in the summer of 1934
culminated in a riot in which strikers
battled police. The strike was finally settled
through federal arbitration. Courtesy,
Newark Public Library

*Women employees in Seabrook Farms'
processing plant near Bridgeton are shown
here packaging green beans to be quick
frozen in the process Charles Seabrook
and Clarence Birdseye developed in the
early 1930s. Seabrook Farms became the
largest farm-freezing operation in the
world, receiving produce from 12,500 acres
before 1950. Courtesy, Library of Congress*

A resettled tailor is shown here working in the cooperative garment factory at Jersey Homesteads outside Hightstown, a project of the Federal Subsistence Homesteads Program, instituted during the Depression. The plan called for a colony of two hundred families of garment workers to become self-sufficient by combining cooperative farming with seasonal garment work. After Franklin D. Roosevelt's death in 1945, the town was renamed in his honor. Courtesy, Library of Congress

Authority, were landmarks.

But whatever the benefit of the legislation, the first weeks of the administration of Franklin D. Roosevelt restored public confidence. In West Orange, Charles Edison posted a notice on the wall of Thomas A. Edison, Inc.:

President Roosevelt has done his part: now you do something.
Buy something—buy anything, anywhere; paint your kitchen, send a telegram, give a party, get a car, pay a bill, rent a flat, fix your roof, get a haircut, see a show, build a house, take a trip, sing a song, get married.
It does not matter what you do—but get going and keep going.
This old world is starting to move.

For a state steeped in a tradition of local government, the tide was shifting. The federal government gained power during the New Deal, oversaw businesses under the NRA, encouraged labor union growth, regulated the securities markets, and hired unemployed workers.

The Emergency Relief Act of the "Hundred Days" scarcely went beyond what the previous administration had done. But during the winter of 1933-1934, the Civil Works Administration began the practice of hiring the unemployed. Fearing the creation of a class of dependent workers, Roosevelt ended the program that spring. But it was revised in 1935 in expanded form as the Works Progress Administration (WPA).

Criticized for producing only "boondoggles," the WPA hired writers to produce the marvelous *New Jersey: Guide to its Present and Past,* which has since been revised. The WPA also financed a large part of the expansion of Newark Airport from 100 acres to 420 acres. New runways and hangars improved the facility so much that by 1938 it was handling 300,000 passengers a year. Unfortunately for New Jerseyans, the completion in 1939 of the airport named for New York's Mayor Fiorello LaGuardia deprived the Garden State of its dominance in air transportation. In *New Jersey: America's Main Road* John T. Cunningham has written of the WPA:

Here are some of the evidences that those on WPA gangs went to work with a vim:

They demolished the old Newark post office; turned thirty-one acres of

After a dry spell lasting more than a decade, Newark breweries resumed operations with the repeal of the Eighteenth Amendment. Four husky Krueger employees express their pleasure on April 7, 1933, as they load the first barrrels of beer produced by the brewery after the demise of Prohibition. Courtesy, Newark Public Library

swampland at Haddon Heights into a park; reconstructed the old Bradley Beach boardwalk and converted the Delaware & Raritan Canal bed in Trenton into the base for a highway through town. They built Roosevelt Stadium in Jersey City; constructed the Bacharach Home for infantile paralysis victims at Atlantic City, built a Greek amphitheater at Montclair State College, and constructed an old-age colony in Cumberland County. They repaired Atlantic City's water mains and restored the Grover Cleveland House in Caldwell and built Speedwell Park in Morristown.

They improved county parks, built scores of post offices, dug mosquito ditches in swamplands throughout the state, installed sewer systems in many towns, constructed public schools, and provided sewing rooms where unemployed women made garments for the needy. In seven years the WPA in this state also built more than 6,000 miles of streets and highways, constructed 326 new bridges and repaired 324 others, and built or improved more than 4,000 culverts under highways.

The NRA generated a brief economic boomlet in 1933, which occurred because buyers stocked up before the NRA higher prices went into effect. Businessmen in New Jersey balked at the regulatory aspects of the NRA and cheered when the Supreme Court struck it down as unconstitutional in 1935. The Public Works Administration loaned the Port Authority of New York and New Jersey thirty-seven million dollars to build the Lincoln Tunnel and constructed some of its first housing projects in New Jersey. The Federal Housing Administration helped homeowners with mortgages. But despite its success in combatting unemployment with work programs, the New Deal could not produce economic revival in New Jersey, nor in the nation.

Facing page: Burlington County WPA workers wait in wheelbarrows during a 1936 strike. Between 800 and 1,000 men in Burlington and Mercer counties protested a wage cut from fifty to forty-five cents per hour. The strike began on August 24 and continued through early September. Courtesy, Newark Public Library

For seventy-five cents in the summer, one could buy a round trip to Ocean City on the open cars of the Atlantic City and Shore Rail Road, called the Shore Fast Line. This car, bound for the Inlet, was photographed in July 1935 at the Longport terminal. Open cars were discontinued four years later. Courtesy, North Jersey Chapter, National Railway Historical Society

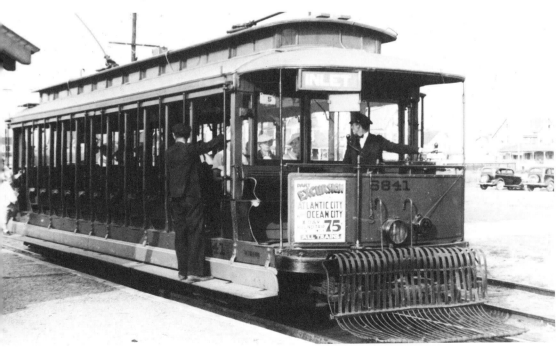

It was May 1937 at Lakehurst, New Jersey. The German zeppelin *Hindenburg* had been delayed ten hours by storms over the Atlantic, but its flight from Frankfurt, Germany, to Lakehurst had basically been routine.

Most passengers and observers were not worried about a thing. After all, Germany's zeppelins had logged over 100,000 flight miles and carried more than 32,000 passengers without a single accident.

At the U.S. Naval Air Station at Lakehurst, rain, winds, and lightning further delayed the landing, and the giant *Hindenburg* cruised overhead for several hours until the weather changed. Finally, at 7:10 p.m., the majestic airship prepared for landing, hovering just 200 feet above its mooring. Passengers had collected their hand luggage and were preparing to disembark.

The mooring lines of the big silver aircraft were lowered. On the ground, 92 navy men and 139 civilians were grabbing those lines, guiding the *Hindenburg* to its mooring mast. The giant airship moved in for its docking.

There were plenty of newsmen on hand to witness the landing of Germany's technological marvel of air travel. Camera shutters clicked, and radio announcers recorded their descriptions of the event. At 7:25 the mooring was just minutes from being completed.

Suddenly, a puff of smoke appeared at the zeppelin's stern, followed by a second, larger one. The *Hindenburg* had somehow caught fire! Next, there came a violent explosion of hydrogen gas. Within seconds, the beautiful, majestic airship had become a deadly ball of fire.

Herb Morrison of the radio station WLS was reporting the scene as the zeppelin suddenly burst into an incredible tragedy. Morrison's voice became an indelible part of history as he shouted into his microphone: "It's burst into

flames! Oh my . . . it's burning, bursting into flames . . . Oh the humanity and all the passengers."

The *Hindenburg* explosion claimed the lives of fifteen passengers, twenty crewmen, and one line handler. Of the ninety-seven people on board, many more were badly injured. The entire sequence of events had taken just thirty-four seconds. The first signs of trouble had caused panic aboard the airship: passengers smashed the windows of the ship's gondola, only to leap more than 100 feet to their deaths. Then came the loud, second explosion that sent the proud German airship to the ground, reducing it to burning rubble.

The cause of the *Hindenburg* disaster remains unclear to this very day. In their investigations, neither the U.S. nor the German authorities seemed to consider the possibility of sabotage, perhaps out of fear of creating an international incident. Officials attributed the cause of the explosion to "St. Elmo's fire"—a visible electric discharge emanating from a protrusion on the airship—though there is no other recorded case in which St. Elmo's fire actually caused an explosion.

Thus, rumors have always persisted that sabotage was at least a possibility in the *Hindenburg* disaster. Before the zeppelin's departure from Frankfurt, German authorities had allegedly suspected that there was a bomb aboard the *Hindenburg*, and searched the ship and its passengers prior to departure. No bomb was found, but two German military officers were placed on board ship as a precautionary measure. Despite this conjecture, there has never been any solid evidence to show what exactly did cause the disaster.

One tragic irony: the *Hindenburg* was actually designed to use non-explosive helium, but was filled with hydrogen gas. At the time, the United States was the only source for helium.

The more than seven million cubic feet of helium needed to float the zeppelin would have cost the Germans approximately $600,000—making it virtually prohibitive. Moreover, the Deutsch Zeppelin-Reederei Company, operators of the Graf Zeppelin passenger lines which ran the *Hindenburg,* felt the expense was unnecessary. Hydrogen was safe when handled by experts, and the Germans, with their vast experience in zeppelin flying, certainly qualified as such.

The *Hindenburg* (also known as the Z-129) was commissioned in March 1936 and had made ten round trips between Germany and the United States. Exceeding 800 feet in length, it was the largest zeppelin in the world. It had 16 gas bags containing a total of 7.2 million cubic feet of explosive hydrogen gas. Its four V-16 diesel engines with 20-foot 4-bladed props could provide 5,000 horsepower, driving the ship in silence and without vibrations at a speed of 80 knots.

The *Hindenburg* had sleeping compartments with baths for fifty passengers and a crew of thirty, as well as luxury dining rooms. Within the ship's framework, catwalks stretched across an area of sixteen ten-story-high structural rings and thirty-six longitudinal girders. With 25 tanks carrying 137,500 pounds of fuel, the *Hindenburg* had a range of 10,000 miles. Built at a cost of nearly five million dollars, it was truly the last of the great zeppelins.

The tragedy of the *Hindenburg* marked the end of the era of zeppelin travel. By 1937 the speedier airplane was emerging, even though planes carried fewer passengers and less freight. Nonetheless, a page of history was turned that tragic day in Lakehurst, New Jersey, and a new chapter—that of the airplanes—was begun.

—David Fleming

A Bright Note: Pharmaceuticals and Vitamins

Although the general state economy stayed depressed until government spending for war stimulated it, New Jersey pharmaceutical houses did important research during the Depression era, and the investment laid the basis for New Jersey's later preeminence in the field of pharmaceuticals.

Whether in over-the-counter medicines or in prescription drugs, New Jersey had been a major drug producer since World War I. Following on the work of Polish scientist Casimir Funk, who first isolated a "vitamin" from rice bran, synthetic drug development began in the World War I era. In 1910 Robert R. Williams treated Filipino children dying of beri-beri with rice-bran extract. In the 1920s he went on working on rice-bran extract in his spare time in Roselle. In 1936, with help from Merck Laboratory scientists, he synthesized vitamin B1. Founded in the 1890s by George Merck, scion of one of the leaders of the European chemical firm, Merck Laboratory produced the B1 vitamin under the name of thiamine. Merck also became a leader in producing reference works, including the *Merck Manual of Therapeutics and Materia Medica*, the *Merck Index*, and the *Merck Report*.

Another pioneering firm in vitamin research, Hoffmann-La Roche, Inc., incorporated in New Jersey in 1928 and began operations in Nutley in several buildings, a boiler house and small garage. To control myasthenia gravis, in 1933 Hoffmann-La Roche brought out Prostigmin, which was found to have multiple therapeutic benefits. As the Depression worsened, the company launched an employee fringe-benefit program that included pensions and life insurance plans.

Hoffmann-La Roche also manufactured synthetic vitamin B1 and B2 (riboflavin), which it synthesized for the first time, and a synthetic vitamin C. After the Second World War, Hoffmann-La Roche began to produce Vitamin B6. In the 1950s the firm began to make a synthetic vitamin A.

During the Great Depression, American Cyanamid of Bound Brook, formed out of the Calco Company, also produced vitamins, as did Harrison's National Oil Products Company, once a gigantic importer of cod-liver oil. During the Great Depression, New Jersey became the national leader in bulk production of vitamins.

Chemists at American Cyanamid Company in Bound Brook manu-factured the United States' first commercial sulfa drug, called sulfanilimide. Squibb, Merck, and Maltbie Chemical Company of Newark helped improve the drug. Following the pioneering work in Germany and France, Merck Laboratory scientist J. M. Sprague first synthesized the sulfapyrimidines in 1939. In 1940 the New Jersey drug houses introduced sulfathiazole powder. During the Second World War, the government sent sulfathiazole powder in huge quantities to the troops in Europe. Squibb produced blood plasma for the war effort, and Merck turned out a synthetic anti-malaria drug, atabrine. The effectiveness of the sulfa drugs sent U.S. production from 378,875 pounds in 1938 to nearly 10 million pounds in 1943.

Above: Public Service's Pavonia Line trolley has just negotiated the trestle over the main tracks of the Erie Rail Road on its way to the Jersey City terminal in 1935. Courtesy, North Jersey Chapter, National Railway Historical Society

Right: The CIBA company in Summit, N.J., is one of the forty world-wide companies of the Society of the Chemical Industry of Basel located in Basel, Switzerland. The firm produces sedatives, antihistamines, hormones, anesthetics, and a variety of drugs for cardiovascular conditions. This building was opened in 1937. Courtesy, Fairchild Aerial Surveys

A Squibb laboratory technician packages penicillin, which was eagerly awaited in military hospitals at the close of World War II. Squibb Institute for Medical Research was one of the several United States laboratories that accomplished the seemingly impossible task of manufacturing the "wonder drug" on a large scale during its initial use. Courtesy, Squibb Corporation

A bacteriology professor discovered penicillin accidentally in 1928 when he saw how the pencil-shaped spores ate up his staphylococcus cultures. But manufacturers could not find ways to produce the drug in bulk. Research on penicillin progressed in the 1930s at some sixteen laboratories, including the Merck Laboratories in Rahway and the Squibb Institute for Medical Research in New Brunswick. In 1941 Merck produced penicillin in fermentation tanks. At Squibb, George Brown, Robert Bierwirth, and Cyril Hayler produced penicillin with a radio-frequency heating technique. In 1944 in New Brunswick Squibb opened the largest penicillin production plant in the world.

Russian emigrant Selman A. Waksman came to Rutgers College in 1911 and studied bacteria and fungi in the soil. After earning his Ph.D. at the University of California, Waksman returned to Rutgers to concentrate on macrobiology.

He and aide Dr. Albert Schatz worked on tiny organisms called actinomycetes, intermediate between bacteria and imperfect fungi. Waksman and Schatz labored through the Great Depression and by World War II had finally isolated streptomycin. Rutgers joined with the Merck Laboratories in Rahway to develop and manufacture the drug. At a new Elkton, Virginia, plant, Merck eventually produced nearly all the streptomycin in the nation.

Waksman's collaboration with the scientists at Merck brought out chloromycetin, and terramycin, broad-spectrum drugs which attacked a number of bacteria. Waksman called the program, which isolated and manufactured streptomycin, "one of the most fruitful connections ever entered into between a university and an industrial organization." At the Esso Research Laboratories in Linden, petroleum research led to compounds that Rutgers scientists studied and from which came Captan, a fungicide which saved millions of dollars in crops each year.

After laboratories proved that streptomycin was effective against tuberculosis, Waksman received the Nobel Prize. Royalties from the sale of streptomycin helped build Rutgers University's famed Institute of Microbiology, the world center of research on micro-organisms.

Electronics and Communications Are Revolutionized

As the home state of Edison's many improvements in communications and electronics, and the state where the telegraph was demonstrated publicly for the first time, New Jersey continued to be a leader in electronics during the Great Depression. But during the war, when radio communications helped defeat the Axis, New Jerseyans' work in electronics became crucial to winning the war.

To understand the developments in the 1930s and 1940s, the story must go back to the turn of the century. In 1900 Reginald A. Fessenden, a physicist and onetime assistant at Edison's laboratory in West Orange, demonstrated the first radio-voice transmission. Also at the beginning of the century, Lee De Forest, a Chicagoan who came east in the early years of the century to transmit wireless reports of the America's Cup races from Sandy Hook, built a small radio and electronics laboratory and factory in Jersey City, where he perfected the audion tube.

De Forest put a metal plate around the negative filament in the vacuum tube to provide a rectifier and a modulator. He also added a zig-zag piece of platinum wire. Patented in 1907, the audion tube generated radio waves, increased the radio signal, revolutionized radio broadcasting, and opened the age of electronics.

Guglielmo Marconi, who had developed the wireless telegraph, built wireless stations at New Brunswick and Belmar in 1913 and organized the American Marconi Company in Union County to make wireless equipment. The flat New Jersey coast proved a good location for radio transmission. In 1915 American Telephone and Telegraph conducted voice tests in New Jersey of overseas transmission between Arlington, Virginia, Paris, Honolulu, and the Canal Zone.

After the war, Radio Corporation of America (RCA) took over the assets of the Marconi operation and worked out some cross-licensing arrangements with General Electric for patents which RCA acquired from Marconi. New Jersey continued to be a headquarters for electronic-equipment manufacturers. Radio boomed during the 1920s. In 1920 Walter Friis, a scientist with Western Electric, began working on a shortwave radio at Elberon, where he studied ship radio transmissions.

Before the Great Depression, New Jerseyans developed units of what would become the state's largest employer, American Telephone and Telegraph: a field station in Whippany and the building in Holmdel, where Bell Laboratories would test shortwave communications. Western Electric

The houses in the foreground of this early 1900s photograph subsequently disappeared as Victor Talking Machine Company expanded its plant on Cooper Street in Camden. Incorporated in 1901 by Eldridge R. Johnson, the phonograph firm was instantly successful, expanding their initial receipts of $500 in 1901 to twelve million dollars in 1905. Courtesy, Camden County Historical Society

This 1915 view of the factory interior shows the automatic machines that manufactured the tungsten needles produced by the Victor Talking Machine Company. The firm became part of the Radio Corporation of America in 1929. Courtesy, Newark Public Library

Manufacturing Company came to Kearny in 1923 and in 1929 expanded dramatically there and in Jersey City, Elizabeth, and Hillside. Western Electric succeeded even during the dark Depression days, and in one year after the war, the Kearny operations made enough wire to circle the globe (1.3 million times).

Radio broadcasters began in America with station KDKA in Pittsburgh, over which in 1920 they transmitted the results of the Harding-Cox presidential election. When RCA acquired Marconi, it got a radio station in New Brunswick. In 1921 RCA broadcast the Dempsey-Carpentier fight from a temporary station at Hoboken and soon after opened WDY in Roselle Park. Station WJZ Newark broadcast the first World Series in 1921 and Newark broadcasters made the world's first international radio broadcast in 1922. RCA soon went into the marketing of radio receivers, including Westinghouse's "Aeriola Senior," a one-tube model which the consumers loved.

Born in 1901, the Victor Talking Machine Company of Camden

For car 410 of the Morris County Traction Company, photographed near Landing in 1935, this was truly the end of the line. The car became The Last Round-Up diner after its transportation days had ended. Courtesy, North Jersey Chapter, National Railway Historical Society

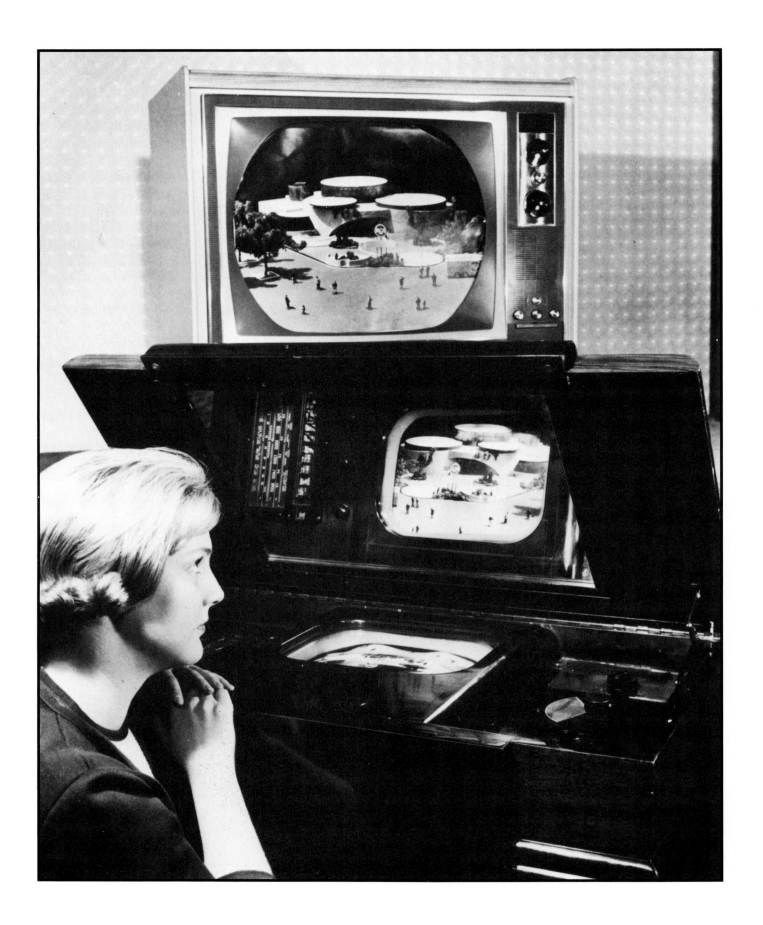

struggled to sell phonographs in competition with radio sets. In 1929 RCA purchased Victor and its famous trademark. RCA also bought the Edison Lamp Works in Harrison and a Westinghouse factory at Indianapolis and created RCA Victor. RCA Victor had thus gone from being a broadcasting enterprise which sold radio equipment that others manufactured to being a manufacturer itself and was soon turning out forty million radio tubes a year. On the eve of American involvement in World War II, they had become a major American radio manufacturer.

During the Great Depression, Americans became enthralled by the radio, which was an inexpensive form of entertainment. They could stay at home and listen to Eddie Cantor, Burns and Allen, Ed Wynn, Amos 'n' Andy, the music of Tommy Dorsey, Glenn Miller, Wayne King, and Benny Goodman. President Roosevelt took full advantage of the new medium and established his presidential leadership through his skilled use of radio. Some analysts, in fact, are convinced that he succeeded in handling the banking crisis primarily because of his ability to communicate over the airwaves. At Haddonfield, Major Edwin H. Armstrong perfected the principle of frequency modulation, or FM broadcasting. In Alpine in 1937 he built the first FM broadcasting station in America.

New Jerseyans also helped advance television, which began in the nineteenth century with William Crookes' invention of the cathode-ray tube. During the 1920s Vladimir Zworykin developed and patented the electron camera tube. In May of 1928 WGY of Schenectady, New York, began regularly scheduled telecasts. In 1929 Zworykin developed and demonstrated the kinescope, or all-electronic television receiver. That year the Bell Telephone Laboratories in Whippany transmitted a television program without wires to New York City.

Then in 1930 Zworykin, a true pioneer of the industry, joined RCA's research section in Camden. The National Broadcasting Company began television broadcasts that year, and the Columbia Broadcasting System launched experimental television broadcasts from the Empire State Building in 1931.

Another New Jerseyan, Allen Du Mont, who had worked in the Westinghouse Lamp Company in Bloomfield and with Lee De Forest, began in 1931 to work on improving the cathode-ray tube in the basement laboratory of his home in Upper Montclair. After initial failures to improve the tube's life and its size, Du Mont made the first practical and affordable home television.

He began manufacturing them in a Passaic factory. He and RCA both exhibited their television receivers at the 1939 New York World's Fair, when the first regularly scheduled television broadcasts were begun from New York City. By the coming of World War II, most of the 7,000 television sets in use in America had come either from Du Mont's Passaic operation or RCA's Camden factory. The coming of the war ended the manufacture of television sets for the duration, but sales mushroomed after the war.

Opposite page: Twenty-five years of television is portrayed by these receivers tuned to RCA's American Pavilion at the New York World's Fair of 1964-1965. The earlier set, a TRK 12, the first television set sold to the American public, was introduced by RCA at the 1939 World's Fair. Its twenty-inch picture tube was viewed indirectly through a mirror. Courtesy, Camden County Historical Society

The Love Apple

The tomato is one of New Jersey's most famous agricultural products, but it was not always so. In America's early days, the "love apple" was widely believed to be a deadly poison. But in 1830, a daring act by Colonel Robert Gibbon Johnson of Salem, New Jersey, changed the tomato's image forever—and Johnson became the man who catapulted the "Jersey Tomato" into eventual prominence.

Europeans had already been enjoying the savory sauces of this *Licopersicon esculentum* since their first return voyages from the New World, but in America it remained a forbidden fruit. Some early Americans probably had been poisoned by the tomato's foliage, which belongs to the nightshade family and does indeed contain certain dangerous alkaloids.

After a voyage overseas in 1808, Colonel Johnson introduced the tomato to Salem's farmers and began offering an annual prize for the largest locally grown "love apple." But the myth of the poisonous tomato persisted, and it was used only as an ornamental plant. The steadfast colonel knew otherwise: he foresaw its future as a major agricultural product.

And so, on September 26, 1830, (the date varies in different accounts) Colonel Johnson announced that he would appear on the courthouse steps of Salem and eat an entire basket of these supposedly deadly "wolf peaches."

The Salem townspeople reacted with alarm to Johnson's folly. The colonel's physician, Dr. James van Meeter, proclaimed: "The foolish colonel will foam and froth at the mouth and double over with appendicitis. All that oxalic acid! One dose and you're dead. . . . If the Wolf Peach is too ripe and warmed by the sun, he'll be exposing himself to brain fever. Should he survive, by some unlikely chance, I must remind that the skin of the Solanum Lycopersicum will stick to the lining of his stomach and cause cancer."

Van Meeter arrived, doctor's bag in hand, along with some 2,000 other curiosity seekers from far and wide, to watch Colonel Johnson commit suicide on the Salem courthouse steps. The colonel, a towering figure dressed in a black suit and tricorner hat, mounted the courthouse steps at high noon as the local marching band played a somber tune.

Taking a tomato from his basket, Colonel Johnson held it aloft and began his oration:
The time will come when this luscious, scarlet apple, rich in nourishment, a delight to the eye, a joy to the palate . . . will form the foundation of a great garden industry, and will be recognized, eaten, and enjoyed as an edible food. . . . And to help speed that enlightened day, to help dispel the tall tales, the fantastic fables that you have been hearing about the thing, to show you that it is not poisonous, that it will not strike you dead, I am going to eat one right now!

The colonel's first bite could be heard through the stunned crowd's silence. He bit again and again, and soon spectators began screaming and fainting with each bite. But Johnson continued to wolf down tomato after tomato, and the astonished crowd saw him still standing, hale and hearty as ever. Thus, he was

able to convince onlookers that the tomato was a safe and civilized food. As the final tomato was consumed, the band struck up a victory march and the crowd began to roar.

Colonel Johnson's heroic "bites heard 'round the nation" turned the tomato's fortunes, and it began appearing regularly in America's food markets by 1835. The story of Colonel Johnson's daring demonstration is considered apocryphal by some historians, but it certainly jibes with his renowned fiery character, and it is indeed Colonel Johnson who introduced commercial production of tomatoes into his area. In the period following his demonstration, the tomato was widely promoted in farm periodicals and was rapidly introduced throughout New Jersey as a garden vegetable.

By the 1860s, agricultural author Edmund Morris was calling the tomato "a vegetable for whose production of the soil of New Jersey is perhaps without rival." He also noted that commercial canning was growing rapidly. Morris commented that tomatoes, once shunned, by then had a "prominent place on every table" and that "few vegetables have gained so rapid and widespread a popularity as this." New Jersey was growing tomatoes for the New York and Philadelphia markets on its way to earning the name "The Garden State" for its plentiful produce supplies.

By the 1870s the differentiation among New Jersey growers between "garden tomatoes" and "field tomatoes" reflected the commercial importance of this relatively new vegetable. Field-grown tomatoes were transported by rail to the Philadelphia and New York markets in tremendous quantities, and were canned by the millions at dozens of local canneries. The tomato was by 1910 one of New Jersey's most important crops, but its most remarkable period of development was still to come, after World War I.

There were no statistics for tomatoes alone until 1919, when 37,000 acres were reported under cultivation. But tomato production in most years for over half a century had nearly as large a dollar value as that of all other New Jersey vegetables combined. By 1929, some 8,000 farmers were growing tomatoes on 42,000 acres, and the crop was worth nearly $6 million, about equal to that of the corn crop, which was grown on four times that acreage. It is no wonder that the tomato aroused a strong enthusiasm. The "love apple" had certainly come a long way.

Demand for canned tomatoes during World War II brought acreage in New Jersey to 55,000 by 1945, and the crop that year was valued at $10 million, twice the valuation of all vegetables, including tomatoes, in 1900. New Jersey's total vegetable production has traditionally been spectacular, and by the 1970s vegetable sales were providing about one-fourth of the cash receipts for New Jersey's farmers. On the tomato front, tomato harvesters were introduced by 1971, and more modern machinery has been added. During these postwar years, New Jersey's tomato growing has seen a great increase in crop yield per acre, though due in part to a sharp drop in planting acreage.

—David Fleming

As the spread of urban population raised land values in the metropolitan areas and created an increased demand for fresh vegetables, truck farms increased in New Jersey's southern counties. The Cohansey tomato boat seen here circa 1925 may have been bound for big-city markets along the Delaware River, or for the canneries in the South Jersey area. Courtesy, Special Collections, Alexander Library, Rutgers University

The War Revives New Jersey's Economy

Although the New Dealers had outspent the Hooverites, Roosevelt feared the impact of repeated government deficits. In 1937 Roosevelt cut government spending just as taxes for social security were levied on employers and employees. He succeeded in getting the Federal Reserve Board to tighten credit. The resultant economic recession of 1937-1938 may have eventually convinced him of the validity of Keynesian spending, but the foreign crisis of 1939 never gave Roosevelt a chance to test Keynes's ideas. Still, the government did begin to spend. As the "arsenal of democracy" the U.S. began to manufacture the implements of war until, by the end of 1941, the United States was producing more combat munitions than any other nation.

Then the wave of Japanese bombers which hit the United States Naval Base at Pearl Harbor at 7:55 a.m. Sunday, December 7, 1941, plunged the nation into war and total mobilization. As Yogi Berra would later say, it was "deja vu all over again." Once again the government began coordinating the nation's activities for war. But this time government deficits reached a then-unheard-of size of over $200 billion. Government spending not only revived the economy, it transformed it. New Jersey got 9 percent of the early war contracts, behind only California and New York.

Labor shortages replaced unemployment lines. One man who had been unemployed during the Great Depression refused thirteen wartime jobs. Why? "It made me feel so good," he said, "to tell them to 'go to Hell.'"

Entry-level jobs went unfilled. A sign appeared in a diner: "Waitress Wanted, Will Marry if Necessary."

With oil tankers harassed in the Atlantic by Hitler's U-boats, the federal government built the Big Inch and the Little Big Inch pipelines to bring petroleum from the oil fields of the West to Linden. To protect the refineries and the rest of the East Coast from the Nazis' submarine threat, New Jerseyans pioneered the Civil Air Patrol. Gill Robb Wilson, a New Jersey aviation writer, came home from a 1938 visit to Germany convinced of the might of the Nazi state. With gubernatorial approval, Wilson organized the New Jersey Civil Air Defense Services. Similar organizations sprang up in other states and became a Civil Air Guard, which flew missions over the Atlantic and dropped depth charges on sighted German submarines. One German U-boat commander blamed "those damned little red and yellow planes" with disrupting Hitler's attack on the sea lanes. The organization later became the Civil Air Patrol. Westfielder H. Emerson Thomas helped the War Production Board develop a system to facilitate priority shipment of high- and low-pressure gas.

Once again the Du Pont power plants stepped up output. Du Pont experts fanned out across America helping to set up government ordnance plants. Workers flocked into the explosives factories at the southern end of Lake Hopatcong. Rebuilt in the 1930s by the WPA after a 1926 explosion,

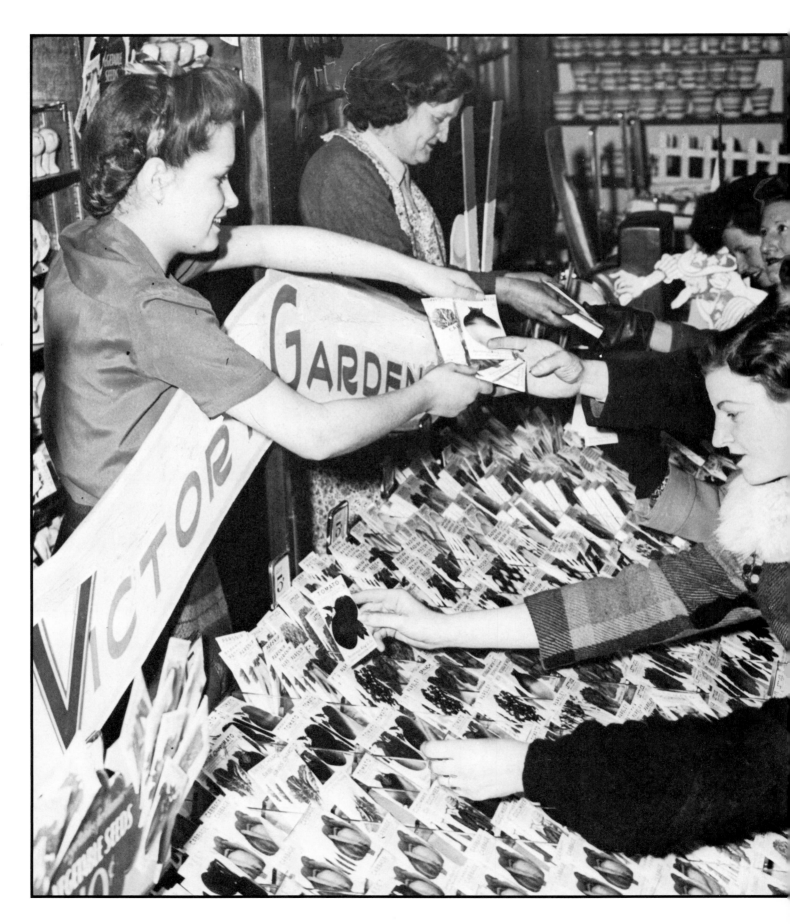

Above: During World War II, De Laval Steam Turbine Company devoted 45 percent of its facilities to supplying the Navy and the Merchant Marine. The company was established in Trenton in 1901 to manufacture machinery developed by the Swedish engineer and inventor Dr. Carl Gustav Patrik De La Val. The firm today produces giant steam turbines (pictured), pumps, compressors, gears, and other machinery. Courtesy, Trenton Public Library

Left: During World War II, civilians rallied to support the war effort. At home, Victory Gardens were found everywhere. Gardeners rushed to buy seeds at a local store in 1943, and later in the year the benefits were reaped in gardens and fields across the state. Courtesy, Newark Public Library

Above: The buildings of Curtiss-Wright's aircraft engine factory appear in the foreground of this 1953 aerial view. Erected in 1942 on a Wood-Ridge farm, the firm produced more engines during World War II than any other American manufacturer. At the time of this photograph, Curtiss-Wright was engaged in the research and production of airplane engines for commercial use. Courtesy, Newark Public Library

Facing page: Four young ladies receive the first contribution for the USO in Newark during World War II from the general chairman of the Newark United Service Organization, and from a vice-president of Bamberger's Department Store. Courtesy, Newark Public Library

Picatinny Arsenal began supplying large shells to the army and navy. Trainers there taught ordnance expertise to some 18,000 individuals. An explosion at Hercules Powder Company at Kenvil in 1940 killed fifty-two but employees had the line working eight days later. Hercules eventually produced a total of 1.8 billion pounds of explosives. Trenton's General Motors plant, opened in 1937, closed and then reopened as the Eastern Aircraft Division. It made Grumman TBF Avenger torpedo bombers for aircraft carriers. Philco in Trenton made precision electrical parts. Contracts for army clothing poured into Newark's factories. In May 1941, the Breeze Corporation announced a two-million-dollar contract for aircraft instruments.

Federal Telephone & Radio in Newark, a supplier to International Telephone & Telegraph, jumped from being one factory employing a few employees to becoming a network of forty-four plants employing 11,500 men and women. In 1943 Federal Telephone & Radio began a major plant on the border of Clifton and Nutley.

New Jersey's radio expertise proved crucial to the war effort. The U.S. Army Signal Corps Research and Development Laboratories at Fort Monmouth did much of the work that led to the development of radar (radio

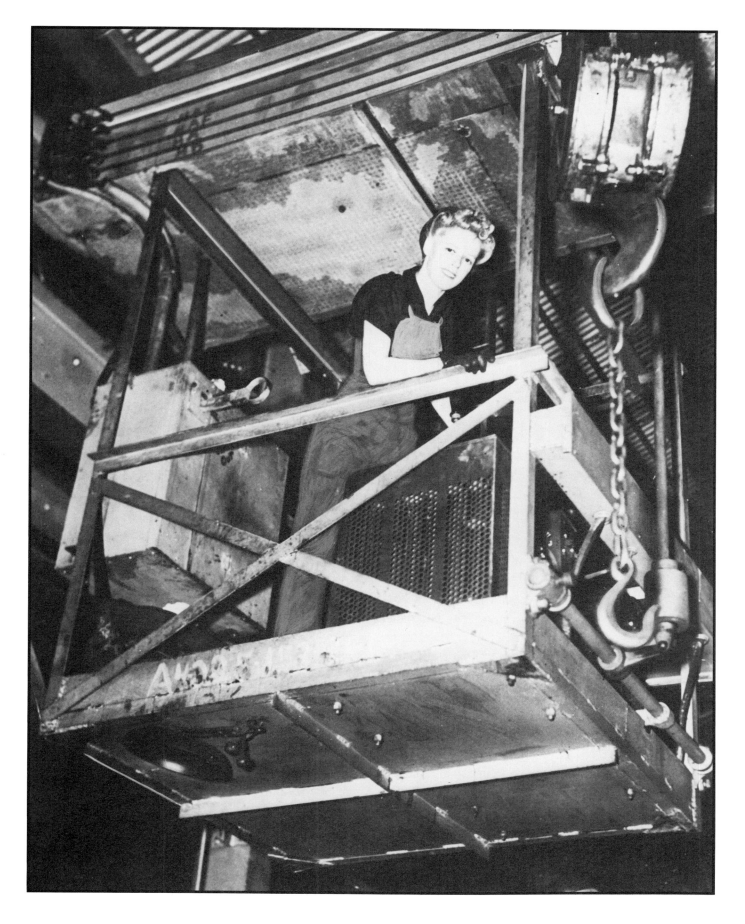

bomber, which ushered in the atomic age over Hiroshima on August 6, 1945, was also driven by New Jersey-made Curtiss-Wright engines.

Newark's Overseas Air Technical Command took over Newark Airport and Port Newark and supplied both theaters of war with aircraft, aviation gasoline, electrical generators, trailers, gliders, and other equipment for a total of over 620,000 different items of war.

New Jerseyans worked for Civilian Defense agencies, searching the night skies for incoming enemy planes, and working on rationing and draft boards. The Prudential Insurance Company turned over its recently completed building in Newark to the Office of Dependency Benefits so they could forward allowance and allotment checks to servicemen's dependents. Some 560,000 New Jerseyans served in the armed forces; 13,172 died. Among them were Congressional Medal of Honor winner Marine Sergeant John Basilone of Raritan, the "Hero of Guadalcanal," who died at Iwo Jima, and Captain Thomas G. McGuire, Jr., who shot down thirty-eight Japanese planes. Killed when he attempted to help a fellow pilot in an air chase, McGuire also received the Congressional Medal of Honor and later had McGuire Air Force Base at Fort Dix named for him.

Four "immortal chaplains," including the Reverend John P. Washington of Newark, the Reverend George Fox of Vermont, the Reverend Clark V. Poling of Schenectady, and Rabbi Alexander Goode of Washington, D.C., gave their lifebelts to soldiers as the troopship *Dorchester* sank in 1943.

New Jersey Helps Develop Atomic Energy

Driven from his native Germany by Nazi anti-Semitism, the "father of the atomic bomb," physicist Albert Einstein, took over as director of the School of Mathematics of the Institute for Advanced Study in Princeton in 1933. In 1905 he had suggested that mass and energy can be converted into each other. Building on the work of Ernest Rutherford, Niels Bohr, Ernest O. Lawrence, Enrico Fermi, and Harold C. Urey, Nazi scientists Otto Hahn and Fritz Strassmann of Germany split the uranium atom in 1938.

In the summer of 1939, Einstein warned President Roosevelt of the possibility that Germany might achieve a new weapon of overwhelming power. Roosevelt launched the Uranium Project to study the feasibility of releasing the power of a chain reaction.

Once the nation was at war, the U.S. government created the Manhattan Project, which poured two billion dollars into developing the atomic bomb. On December 2, 1942, American physicists, led by Enrico Fermi (who, while teaching at Columbia University lived in Leonia), produced a controlled chain reaction in an atomic pile at the University of Chicago. Pure uranium for the project came from work done by scientists at Westinghouse Lamp Division in Bloomfield, New Jersey, who had discovered how to produce pure uranium in pellet form.

Professor Hugh S. Taylor and his associates at Princeton produced the "heavy" water needed for the bomb. On July 16, 1945, the Manhattan

Project scientists watched the detonation of the first atomic bomb in the desert near Los Alamos, New Mexico. There they saw a light brighter than any ever seen before and a huge mushrooming cloud. Director J. Robert Oppenheimer, who would later come to New Jersey to lead the Institute for Advanced Study, thought back to the Hindu scripture: "Now I am become death, the destroyer of worlds."

On August 6, 1945, Captain Robert A. Lewis of Ridgefield Park copiloted the *Enola Gay* on its mission over Hiroshima. Three days later a second atomic bomb dropped on Nagasaki forced Japan to sue for peace.

Dr. Albert Einstein (photographed in 1939) settled in Princeton in 1933, vowing never to return to Germany while Hitler remained in power. He worked at the Institute for Advanced Study in Princeton, organized just three years before by a gift from Newark department store owner Louis Bamberger and his sister Mrs. Felix Fuld. Courtesy, Newark Public Library

Chapter Ten

The Affluent Postwar Society

To the surprise of many Americans, when the war ended the Great Depression did not resume. The war stimulated the New Jersey economy during 1941-1943. Then the war economy sagged in late 1943, and some New Jerseyans feared the nation might sink back into depression. But most residents, including those who had been unemployed for years, were happy just to be working during the war. One laborer averred in 1944 that he was doing so well that he would not mind if the war "went on for another five years."

At the war's end those fearing a relapse shuddered as the government cancelled thirty-five billion dollars in war contracts. But a six billion tax cut pumped money into the postwar New Jersey economy. As consumers began to spend their wartime savings, the nation did not return to the deflation of the Great Depression, but faced a new evil, inflation. In 1945 wages jumped 50 percent over those of 1939. Prices rose 14 percent during 1945-1946.

Franklin Roosevelt's death in 1945, of course, deprived the world and the nation of a powerful leader. Harry Truman, the "accidental President," could not fill Roosevelt's shoes. In the early months, Truman

Postwar population growth in New Jersey occurred at twice the rate of the rest of the nation, encouraging a "consumer culture" and a suburban sprawl unprecedented in the state's history. To handle the crush of commuters, the New Jersey Turnpike and Garden State Parkway were constructed; the interchange at Woodbridge is an important (and sometimes frustrating) one for travelers from north Jersey bound for the Jersey shore. Courtesy, the Star-Ledger

Left: Helen Boehm stands surrounded by porcelain sculptures of the Edward Marshall Boehm Studio in Trenton. Mrs. Boehm became head of the studio in 1969. Boehm porcelains have been chosen by United States presidents as gifts for heads of state, and they also have made their way into private collections, museum collections, and studios around the country. Courtesy, The Star-Ledger

Facing page: Two months before the attack on Pearl Harbor, Eugene Mori, a Vineland businessman, received a state permit to build the Garden State Race Track in Cherry Hill. The track was completed the following year despite the shortages of labor and building materials occasioned by World War II. In 1942 there were forty-nine racing days at the Garden State Race Track, attended by over 400,000 people. In April 1977, the track was demolished by fire. Courtesy, Camden County Historical Society

could not seem to get a handle on his awesome responsibilities. He suffered through a wave of "catch-up" strikes during the immediate postwar period.

Along with inflation, strikes, and Truman's inexperience, "reconversion" brought shortages of all sorts. During 1946 and 1947 New Jerseyans tried in vain to buy automobiles, nylons, appliances, sugar, meat, and various other commodities. The shortages ended by mid-1947. But by then the Republicans had captured both houses of Congress in the off-year elections. J. William Fulbright suggested that since Truman had no vice president, he should appoint a Republican secretary of state and resign so that the nation could have a new president who represented the will of the people as expressed in the 1946 election. As the 1948 elections approached, Democrats sported buttons that announced, "We're just mild about Harry."

Reconversion brought many troubles, but they ended by 1949. The Second World War had actually laid the basis for a surprising postwar prosperity. The postwar years became "the good years," the years of economic growth, stability, optimism and confidence for America and New Jersey. The U.S. economy outperformed even the prosperous 1920s.

Even with the difficulties of reconversion, the gross national product shot

Arrested in graceful, sinuous motion, a student monk from China's T'ang Dynasty is interpreted in porcelain as he executes the snake movement of the martial art of Kung-Fu. A limited edition of this sculpture, The Student, *was issued by Cybis Studios in 1986. Courtesy, Cybis Studio, Trenton*

up some 150 percent between 1945 and 1960, from $200 billion to $500 billion. Unemployment shrank to 5 percent. Military spending on Korea and technological improvements, including the new electronic computers that became available in the 1950s, improved corporate productivity. "Research" and "development" became industrial watchwords.

Incomes rose steadily after the war. In 1947 only 5.7 million American families earned enough to provide themselves with a life that included luxuries like travel and entertainment. By the early 1960s, the robust economy had produced some twelve million families with such middle-class incomes.

The passage of the GI Bill enabled veterans to buy suburban homes on reasonable terms. As servicemen and their wives resumed normal lives, they gave birth to a new generation of children known as the "baby boomers." Population jumped by 20 percent in the 1950s. The postwar generation had to provide schools and a host of other items for the "boomers." Postwar New Jerseyans bought automobiles and appliances. A consumer culture developed. Automobiles got more and more ostentatious and even sprouted tail fins. New products—dishwashers, garbage disposals,

The sensual curves of Leda and the Swan *dramatize the mythological account of an enamored Zeus who visited the Spartan Queen Leda in the guise of a swan. This limited edition of bisque-white porcelain is nine inches tall and was issued in 1986. Founder Boleslaw Cybis, prevented from returning to Warsaw by the outbreak of World War II, established a studio in an old carriage shop in Trenton in 1942. Despite his death in 1957, the creations of Cybis Studios, now in a new location, continue to add lustre to Trenton's reputation as the porcelain capital of the United States. Courtesy, Cybis Studio, Trenton*

television and hi-fi sets—walked out of the stores.

To finance the war the government increased its tax rates and introduced withholding, but it also borrowed $220 billion. New Jersey and other banks purchased approximately $100 billion of this debt, set against deposits credited to the United States Government. The spending of this borrowed money stimulated the economy. To deal with the inflationary aspects of this huge borrowing, the Open Market Committee of the Federal Reserve System after the war "pegged" the price of U.S. obligations at par and loaned money to banks who were willing to buy U.S. obligations.

Beginning in 1951 under the leadership of William McChesney Martin, who became chairman of the Federal Reserve Board of Governors, U.S.

The Hackensack River reflects the lights of the Bergen Generating Station, built in Ridgefield by Public Service Electric & Gas Company in 1959. At the time the station began operations, it was the second largest of the five steam-electric generating stations built by PSE & G after World War II. Courtesy, Newark Public Library

bonds were "unpegged" and allowed to find their normal levels. This practice boosted interest rates and caused many New Jersey banks to take losses on the sale of government securities, which formed about 20 percent of New Jersey bank investments.

Suburbia Sprawls Across the State

As the national population rose by 20 percent in the 1950s, suburban population shot up some 47 percent. Between 1950 and 1960 New Jersey grew twice as fast as the nation and added 1,232,000 new individuals.

Above: In a process little changed in one hundred years, a female employee tends a winding machine at a Spruce Street mill in Paterson in 1978. Skeins of silk or rayon are wound on bobbins from which the thread will be transferred to the warping frame. Courtesy, Paterson Museum Archives

Left: This aerial view shows Willingboro Township in Burlington County in 1965. The housing development was opened in 1958 and called Levittown by Levitt and Sons, builders of similar suburban communities in Pennsylvania and on Long Island. After a referendum in November 1963, the township's name of Willingboro was restored. Courtesy, Newark Public Library

The use of glass blocks to provide extra interior light was an innovative architectural technique in 1937 when Andrew J. Thomas designed this fireproof building for builder Robert L. Hecht in Plainfield. Named Prospect Park Apartments, the five-story building housed twenty-two apartments, including two penthouse duplexes with wood-burning fireplaces and outdoor terraces. Courtesy, Newark Public Library

Although the baby boom played a role, half of the New Jersey increase came from people moving into the state. Between 1940 and 1970 the state's population jumped by 3 million and stood in 1970 at 7,168,164.

Bergen County doubled in the 1950s. Madison Township in Middlesex County jumped up 209 percent, and East Brunswick rose by more than 250 percent. Older counties grew more slowly than the newer ones, which were farther from New York and Philadelphia. In the 1950s Burlington grew by 65 percent, Middlesex by 64 percent, Ocean by 91 percent, and Morris by 59 percent.

New Jerseyans developed new suburbs in Edison, Wayne, Paramus, Parsippany, Livingston, Clark, and Oakland. These areas generally had fewer high-priced homes, and lower average valuations per house than the older suburbs of Montclair, Westfield, Englewood, Ridgewood, Maplewood, Red Bank, and Chatham. The "new" suburbs had three times the number of skilled laborers.

The suburbs developed a kind of similarity. Homes throughout the state tended to look more and more like each other. Life-styles in suburbia became increasingly homogenized. The media, particularly television, which replaced newspapers as the main source of information for most people, projected this homogenized image of a white, middle-class, and suburban America.

As the suburbs gained residents and ratables, the inner cities lost both. Many inner-city people moved out to the suburbs, and others from the nearby cities flocked into suburban New Jersey. Between 1950 and 1960, Newark lost 7.6 percent of its people and dropped from being the twenty-first-largest city in America to becoming the thirtieth. Jersey City lost 7.7 percent of its residents, Elizabeth 4.5 percent, and Camden 5.9 percent. The old cities during and after the war also did not maintain per-capita income on a par with the rest of the state. Their tax bases dwindled. Just as the demand for services from the inner-city poor began to rise, the older cities discovered that they were unable to continue to provide services.

By 1960 New Jersey accounted for eight of the country's twelve most densely populated places of 25,000 or more in population. In the same year nearly 9 percent of the total U.S. population lived within a fifty-mile radius of New Brunswick. In the 1960s New Jersey jumped ahead of Rhode Island to become the most densely populated state in America. In 1961 the *Life Pictorial Atlas of the World* noted that while all the states in the Northeast had "been greatly affected, nowhere has the growth of the urban belt blotted out so much of the countryside as in New Jersey." New Jersey soon became known as "the most urban state." "As life styles and the economy have become increasingly suburbanized," argued Randall Rothenberg, "New Jersey's attractiveness has been enhanced. It is the ultimate suburban state."

The immature plantings in the central court of these Woodbridge garden apartments reveal the complex's recent construction, circa 1967. Later developers would attract purchasers with swimming pools, health clubs, and other community amenities. Courtesy, Newark Public Library

The Pine Barrens

One of the biggest myths about New Jersey is that it is one massive strip of industrial parks and suburbs. It is especially hard for outsiders to comprehend the existence of New Jersey's Pine Barrens—a huge, underpopulated expanse of white, sandy soil some eighty miles long and over thirty miles wide, abounding in pitch pines, scrub oaks, white cedar swamps, and underbrush.

The Pine Barrens runs from just above Asbury Park and reaches halfway over to Freehold, continuing southwest nearly to the Delaware River. From there it stretches south almost to Delaware Bay and then crosses the low center of the state, reaching all the way to the Atlantic Ocean. Stretches of the Pine Barrens cover Monmouth, Ocean, Atlantic, Burlington, and Cumberland counties, with the heart of the region considered to be in southern Burlington County.

This huge expanse of pine forest, only a short drive from New York City and Philadelphia, is filled with unusual plant life that has flourished since pre-historic times. This seemingly infertile, sandy land is also perfectly suited for growing cranberries and blueberries. A 12,000-acre area near the center of the Pine Barrens is called the Plains, where thick growth is usually less than four feet high.

The Pine Barrens includes about 650,000 acres, an area nearly as large as Yosemite National Park, almost identical in size with Grand Canyon National Park, and much larger than most national parks in the United States.

This stretch of land got its name from the seventeenth- and eighteenth-century pioneers who settled in New Jersey. Finnish, Swedish, and Dutch and English farmers moved inland looking for new farmland to cultivate, but they found the sandy and acid soils of this area totally unsuited for their agriculture. They left the land uncleared, and began referring to the region as the "Pine Barrens." The term is still used, and today the Pine Barrens in many spots does not look very different than it did in the 1600s.

Although New Jersey has the greatest population density in the state, huge segments of the Pine Barrens have no people in them at all, and the few towns in the central forest are extremely small. Some non-populated areas are twenty- or thirty-thousand-acre stretches. In one section of the Pine Barrens, there are only 21 people populating about 100,000 acres.

Driving down the Garden State Parkway, just north of Asbury Park, one can notice the start of the Pine Barrens, punctuated by scrub trees of pine and oak in sandy soil. This scenery remains most of the way to the southern end of the Parkway. It is also like this well inland—more than halfway to Trenton and Camden.

Taking smaller roads into the Pine Barrens, such as NJ 70 through Burlington County, one enters gradually into a more wooded region. This area of the Pine Barrens is the center of New Jersey's cranberry country. Thick walls of wilderness flank the road, with scarcely any sign of human habitation for miles. Off by the roadside at certain places are narrow trails leading into the forest. It can be tempting to try to drive down these narrow trails and roads to get a better look at the area. However, these trails often present hazards, particularly that of car wheels getting buried in sand or mud. But from the main road this area is still a pretty sight to behold: there is plenty of laurel along the roadside, and its springtime bloom is a beautiful sight.

Northwest of Batsto Village in southern Burlington County, in the area between the Mullica River and its tributary, Batsto River, lies what is considered the heart of the Pine Barrens. This is in the southeastern edge of Burlington County. Its inhabitants are still called the "Pineys." These people primarily work in the cranberry region and live in secluded places far from the main highways. Some are said to be descendants of British soldiers who deserted during the Revolution and hid there. These present-day residents have small cottages and raise vegetables and keep pigs, chickens, and other livestock. Over the years, the Pineys have become better understood, and many myths about them have been dispelled thanks to increased information from researchers and journalists as well as the opening of new roads into the area.

The Pine Barrens cover 1,875 square miles, or about a fourth of the state. Today, on all sides of the Pine Barrens, development has reduced the main forest area to about 1,000 square miles. Nonetheless, a view from one of the fire towers in the center of the Pine Barrens areas would make the visitor marvel at how such a vast expanse of wilderness can exist so close to two major metropolitan centers.

—David Fleming

In a scene all too familiar to New Jersey drivers, motorists merge into single file during the widening of Route 22 outside Newark in the late 1940s. Opened in 1932, the highway became inadequate as early as 1939, a condition which has persisted, especially in the vicinity of Newark, despite efforts to improve the roadway. Courtesy, Newark Public Library

Suburbanites Take to the Highways

Suburbanites needed private transportation. Once again, the automobile revolutionized America. From some fifteen billion gallons a year during the Great Depression, gasoline consumption jumped to thirty-five billion gallons annually by 1950 and then to ninety-two billion by 1972. At war's end the highway system clogged daily as motorists drove to work. During the 1940s the state only added some eighty miles of roads to the state system, leaving routes 46, 22, and 1 particularly troublesome.

In 1956 the national administration committed itself to the building of the interstate highway system, which changed the landscape and altered the lives of many Americans who could now commute farther to work. The movement of people into the suburbs led to demand for automobiles and produced a boom in the automobile industry. The number of privately owned automobiles doubled in a decade.

In 1937 General Motors had built a Buick-Oldsmobile-Pontiac assembly plant in Linden in the corridor between New York City, Trenton, and Philadelphia, where railroad lines and U.S. Route 1 parallel each other. To meet the expanding demand for automobiles in the postwar period, Ford Motor Company constructed a huge Lincoln-Mercury assembly plant in this corridor in Metuchen. Finished in 1948, the plant turned out 456 cars every day. During the 1950s, Studebaker also assembled cars on Route 1 in New Brunswick.

The old and the new meet in Ford Motor Company's Mahwah plant, the largest automobile assembly unit in the United States when it opened in 1955. The first car off the assembly line was a replica of Henry Ford's 1908 Model T. Courtesy, Newark Public Library

Ford also constructed the massive Mahwah assembly plant that turned out over 1,000 cars and trucks daily during the late 1950s. Other firms followed the auto makers to the suburbs. American Cyanamid, which had been operating in New Jersey since 1916, and had various operations throughout the northern part of the state, in 1962 moved its world headquarters to Wayne. Industry expanded in industrial parks in Morris and Somerset counties, in the rural parts of Union, Passaic, and Bergen counties, in Sussex, Warren, and Hunterdon counties, and in the Delaware Valley and Camden areas.

As more and more commuters generated increased traffic demands, workmen finished the second tube of the Lincoln Tunnel in 1945 and completed the third in 1957. New Jersey radically altered its road system in the postwar period. Construction crews began the New Jersey Turnpike

Seabrook Farms, an important South Jersey agribusiness, by 1920 was shipping vegetables by the carload to markets along the Atlantic Seaboard. In the 1930s, Charles Seabrook and Clarence Birdseye developed the frozen foods technology that would revolutionize the food processing industry. Courtesy, Newark Public Library

Cranberries have been grown commercially in the bogs of southern New Jersey for over 100 years. Since 1963, the wooden cranberry scoop has been replaced by water harvesting, in which mechanical beaters knock the berries into water. The workers here are gathering the floating berries onto the conveyor belts after which they will be trucked to the drying shed. Courtesy, the Star-Ledger

The Research State Is Born

As farm acreage has dwindled, some New Jerseyans have considered dropping the name "Garden State." New Jersey in the postwar years, they argue, should be called the "Research State." Ever since Edison began his "invention factory" in 1876, of course, the state has been a home to organized research. In 1962, for example, American Cyanamid built the Agricultural Research Center near Princeton to study plant and animal health. Over a hundred researchers there studied drugs and other products for animals. This combination of university libraries, the Rutgers College of Agriculture, and nearby chemical firms have made this center a thriving enterprise which houses thousands of research animals and fowl.

New Jerseyans at the Agricultural Research Center developed and

improved insecticides, herbicides, fertilizers, antibiotics, fungicides, and other compounds. At the FMC Chemical Research and Development Center near Princeton, researchers worked on screening pesticides and herbicides and studied how to use them as well as other agricultural chemicals.

In technology, the many advances New Jersey researchers made during the war laid the foundation for the significant research role the state has played since. By 1970, 10 percent of all United States research dollars were being spent in New Jersey's 700 research laboratories. By the 1960s nearly one-fifth of the research scientists in the nation lived in New Jersey, and one of eight American research workers worked there.

After the war New Jerseyans made notable breakthroughs in television, drugs, semiconductors, space technology, air defense, and many other fields.

New Jerseyans Shape a New Industry: Television

In 1946 Americans owned only 17,000 television sets. By 1960 they tuned in images on forty million sets, many made in New Jersey. During the postwar years, Americans sat glued to their sets during "I Love Lucy," "The Ed Sullivan Show", and "The Honeymooners." Television helped make, and then break, Senator Joseph McCarthy. A young senator named Richard M. Nixon skillfully used television to keep his place on the Republican ticket in the 1952 election.

"TV dinners" hit the grocery stores in 1954. That year a puzzled water commissioner of Toledo finally figured out that the rise in water consumption during certain three-minute periods stemmed from people flushing the toilets during commercials. More people in 1960 got most of their news from television than from magazines, newspapers, and radio.

Researchers looked hard for a way to develop color television. Each year after World War II, RCA researchers at the Sarnoff Research Center in Princeton struggled to come up with a list of accomplishments to announce on "General" David Sarnoff's February 27 birthday. In 1948 Sarnoff told

Above: Eight hundred tons of steel were used in building the 300-foot ITT Tower, a Nutley landmark shown here in the 1940s during construction by Trenton's American Bridge Company. Called the "Laboratory in the Sky," the facility produces prototypes of electronic communications equipment for air and space defense purposes. Courtesy, Newark Public Library

Left: This aerial view of the Esso Research Center was taken when the complex was opened in 1948. The structure in the foreground housed eighty laboratories employing nearly 650 chemists, engineers, and research assistants. The storage tanks of Standard Oil's massive Bayway Refinery appear in the background. Courtesy, Newark Public Library

the scientists that the only birthday present that would satisfy him that year would be the development and manufacture of a fully electronic color-television system.

Dr. Edward Herold took charge of a crash drive to give the "General" what he wanted. Herold gave subordinates three months to come up with a system and another month to construct an operating system. Pressure showed on the workers.

The NBC studios in New York transmitted an image of a fruit bowl to Princeton.

"We can get the banana right, but then the rest of the fruit is hopelessly off-color," said the Princeton people. They later learned that a joker in New York had painted the banana blue.

But Sarnoff's challenge produced the desired result. On February 27, 1948, RCA had developed the shadow mask picture tube—the essential element in color television.

Researchers Find New Drugs

Ingenious New Jerseyans discovered a cure for the postwar American "Age of Anxiety." They pioneered the development of a series of drugs which gave the 1950s one of its buzzwords: "tranquilizer." Indeed, New Jerseyans made some of the major breakthroughs in twentieth-century drug research. Sought as a way to combat high blood pressure, New Jersey tranquilizers replaced the barbiturates and other older sedatives. After their introduction in 1950, tranquilizers accounted for 40 percent of the then-startling increase in volume of American prescriptions.

The first tranquilizer, Reserpine, had side effects and never sold well. The second tranquilizer, Atarax, did much better. Soon after the introduction of Atarax, Ciba Pharmaceutical Company in Summit brought out Serpasil. But then Carter Wallace Products laboratories in Cranbury developed one of the most famous tranquilizers of the era, Miltown. One of the firms that came to New Jersey in the 1950s, Warner-Chilcott in Morris Plains, produced the antidepressant Nardil. Schering in 1957 put out Trilafan, "a full range" tranquilizer which could be used for both "neurotic" and "psychotic" patients.

In this "Tranquilizer War" of the 1950s, Hoffmann-La Roche had directed their researchers to find a chemical tranquilizer similar to Miltown, but different enough to not invade Carter Wallace Products' patent. Determined to explore farther afield, Leo Sternbach, a research chemist at Hoffmann-La Roche's Nutley laboratories, began experimenting with benzheptoxdiazines, a chemical group hitherto unknown to have any tranquilizing properties. When he failed to develop a Miltown clone, Sternbach was taken off the research.

But among the remains of the mixtures on Sternbach's laboratory desk, associate Earl Reeder found a related compound that had tranquilizing properties. After initial animal tests showed that the compound was an

anticonvulsant, Sternbach ingested the drug and kept his own journal on the effects. On July 16, 1957, Sternbach took a dosage that left him in a pleasant, calm state. His discovery became known as Librium.

Sternbach continued his work and in 1959 found an even more effective tranquilizer, which Hoffmann-La Roche marketed as Valium, from the Latin valere, "to be healthy." Discovered by a persistent New Jersey iconoclast, Valium became the single most prescribed drug in America.

New Jerseyans Give Birth to The Transistor

Bell Laboratories scientist Russell Ohl in 1940 found that a piece of silicon could produce electrical energy when placed under light. This discovery, made practical by G. L. Pearson, D. M. Chapin, and C. S. Fuller of Bell Laboratories, has been used since in satellites and even in pocket calculators.

In the 1940s, led by William Shockley and S. O. Morgan, Bell scientists continued to probe the nature of silicon and electricity. In 1947 they discovered the "transistor effect" which is based on the presence of both negative and positive current carriers in the same semiconductor.

By adding certain electrically active impurities, they produced a few free electrons (negative, or n-type transistor) or a lack of electrons (positive, or p-type transistor). The junction between the layers is called the "p-n junction," or rectifier. By combining these p- and n-type transistors in sequence, or layers, they produced a transistor which controlled current passing through it.

The n-p-n semiconductors are negative and function as emitters, as do cathodes in vacuum tubes. Another variety, the p-n-p, is positive and works as a collector, or anode, by attracting electrons. When electricity is applied to the p-type material, it controls the flow of electrons between the n-type layers and serves much the way a vacuum tube's grid does.

But whether made from silicon or germanium, semiconductors operate with less power than vacuum tubes and produce almost no heat. They also do not have to warm up. In the 1950s William Pfann of the Bell Telephone Laboratories at Murray Hill developed the "zone refining" system of refining crystals, a technique which has reduced impurities in germanium, for example, to one part in ten million, and thus helped perfect the germanium semiconductor.

Developed largely in New Jersey, the modern transistor became the foundation for modern switches, integrated circuits, and the basic component of the digital computer. Drs. John Bardeen, William Shockley, and Walter H. Brattain won the 1956 Nobel Prize for their discovery of the transistor effect. The Bell Labs also gave birth to the laser, the solar cell, TELSTAR, the light-emitting diode, digital switching, the electrical digital computer, cellular mobile radio, the artificial larynx, and many other major contributions to the telephone network.

In 1977 Bell's Philip Anderson, who studied fundamental electron structure of magnetic materials and disordered materials, won the Nobel Prize in physics. His ideas led to the wide-scale peaceful application of physics and helped develop the electronics boom.

Scientists Shape Space Technology

In its work on synthetic rubber, the Thiokol corporation in Trenton came up with a polysulfide rubber in 1943 that was used in the rockets in the Minuteman program and in the retro-rockets in the Mercury program. The corporation also developed polysulfide rubber as a solid fuel for the propulsion of American space probes.

The Signal Corps Laboratories at Fort Monmouth developed the "talking" Score satellite, which the Atlas missile in 1958 placed in orbit. President Dwight D. Eisenhower relayed recorded Christmas greetings from this satellite to the world.

In 1959 New Jersey RCA scientists under the Signal Corps' technical leadership also created and launched weather satellites that observed the earth's cloud cover with television cameras. These satellites carried lenses that both gave a broad view of the circulation of the atmosphere and of specific cloud formations. The breakthrough aided weather forecasting.

Signal Corps scientists at Fort Monmouth also produced the Courier satellite, which in 1960 relayed teleprinter messages from one ground station to another. That same year Bell Laboratories used the National Aeronautics and Space Administration (NASA) satellite Echo and frequency modulation with feedback to transmit voice, telegraph, and facsimile messages from their Holmdel laboratory to NASA's Jet Propulsion Laboratory at Goldstone, California. This work became a foundation for the TELSTAR communications program, which Western Electric engineers in Hillside developed.

New Jerseyans triumphed with the launching of TELSTAR. "Nearly every modern electronic component involved in the TELSTAR satellite experiment," noted John R. Pierce and Arthur Tressler in *The Research State*, "was either invented or developed significantly by scientists in New Jersey laboratories." Bell scientists at Murray Hill and Whippany did thorough tests of the transistors, solar cells, and other electronic components that went into this commercial radio satellite. Launched on July 10, 1962, TELSTAR provided a new system of radio transmission and also did experiments on the radiation in outer space.

Shortly after TELSTAR's launching, RCA engineers at the Defense Electronic Products Division in Princeton produced RELAY, another active communications satellite, which NASA launched on December 13, 1962. RELAY communicated on the East Coast with ground stations at ITT's Space Communications Center in Nutley. The experts at Nutley also completed the first transmission of active communications by satellite with South America and functioned as the originating station on European transmissions.

New Jersey Labs Devise New Air Defense

Bell Laboratories at Whippany developed the Nike missile system, with Western Electric Company as prime contractor and Douglas Aircraft as the builder. They developed the Nike Ajax, then the Nike Hercules, and finally the Nike-X. Bell also produced the Titan I missile, used to launch satellites, and designed the Distant Early Warning, or DEW line, system. The DEW line, a system of stations spaced about 100 miles apart, used high antennas to create a radar net to detect winged aircraft which might approach the United States over the polar ice cap.

From this system emerged the Ballistic Missiles Early Warning System of scanning and tracking radars to detect missiles which the Soviet Union might launch over the polar cap. Designed by RCA engineers in Camden and at the Bell Laboratories in Whippany, the system utilized undersea cable, over-the-horizon radio, and a complex computer system.

New Jerseyans at ITT's Federal Laboratories in Nutley have researched air-navigation systems for the navy and air force, an airborne distance-measuring system which provided information about plane locations, a three-dimensional display for air controllers, and LORAN, the long-range navigation system which covers most of the globe.

Many of these achievements in technology were funded, of course, by a government locked in the anti-Communism of the 1950s and the Cold War. But despite fears about Communists, New Jerseyans during the Truman and Eisenhower years had emerged from a depression and a war and had played major roles in launching the consumer culture of the postwar era.

To many looking back, it seemed a much simpler time. Eisenhower oversaw a traditionalist, small-government "middle-of-the-road" administration, which believed, for example, that a federal program of inoculation against polio was "socialized medicine." To many, this era seems to be very distant, and it has provoked much nostalgia since. But by the end of the 1950s, critics were beginning to argue that America could no longer afford an administration in which the federal government played such a limited role in American economic life.

Chapter Eleven

The Last Quarter Century

The proposed River Front development, the next step in Newark's ambitious redevelopment, will rise to the north of Penn Station. In this architectural model, the Newark Legal and Communications Center stands at left. Two office towers face the Passaic River flanking the Wintergarden. A hotel and conference center complete the complex. Courtesy, The Grad Partnership

Since 1960 America has gone through political and economic upheaval. After the three recessions of the 1950s, John F. Kennedy in the 1960 election campaign called for an activist presidency and later employed Keynesian economic policies "to get the country moving again." Kennedy sought to stimulate the economy with a tax cut. Lyndon Johnson, who took the oath of office on November 22, 1963, aboard *Air Force One* after Kennedy had been assassinated, passed the tax cut and continued to extend Kennedy's economic stimulation. Under their administrations, particularly Johnson's Great Society, the federal role in American life expanded greatly and the American and New Jersey economies grew.

But the activism and economic stimulation of those years ran simultaneously with a drive to contain Communism in Vietnam which dislocated American society and began a spiral of inflation that grew to double digits during the 1970s. Government spending for Medicare and Medicaid, VISTA, the Office of Economic Opportunity, which included a cornucopia of training, education, work-study, and other programs, when added to the cost of the war in Vietnam, strained the federal budget.

But it was the international oil cartel which devastated the American

Above: From her pleased expression, this young lady appears to be enjoying the luscious fruit featured at the Strawberry Festival at the Moravian village of Hope in Warren County. Held during the straw-berry harvest, the festival afforded the visitor an experience of eighteenth-century farm life as well as an opportunity to "pick your own" strawberries. Courtesy, the Star-Ledger

Right: The world's economic problems have often caused repercussions in New Jersey. During the gas shortage in 1979, New Jersey motorists endured long lines at filling stations and accepted various restrictions on purchases. One gas station owner employed the younger generation to bring order to the long lines at his station. Courtesy, the Star-Ledger

economy in the 1970s. In 1973 the Organization of Petroleum Exporting Countries (OPEC) raised the prices of the crude oil they controlled some 400 percent and triggered worldwide economic dislocation and inflation. New Jersey motorists faced gas lines. Factory managers cut production and threw New Jersey manufacturing workers out of their jobs. The New Jersey economy of the early 1970s sank into hard times.

Only after the Federal Reserve Board under G. William Miller and Paul Volker applied the economic brakes of high interest rates and a reduced money supply did, the inflation begin to wane in the 1980s. As inflation shrank, the economy again began to expand. Many saw in the election and reelection of Republican Ronald Reagan a vote against the expansion of the federal role in the economy. During his two terms he struggled with Congress to reduce the federal bureaucracy and return federal programs to the states.

Declining oil prices and tough Federal Reserve Board policies did more to stimulate the New Jersey economy than did Reagan's attack on the size of government, but many New Jerseyans saw the 1980s boom as a "Reagan expansion." In late 1985 the stock markets roared as if in anticipation of a growth economy. Thus, in 1986, after a tumultuous quarter-century of assassinations, skyrocketing inflation, and a war in Asia, the prospects for the U.S. and the New Jersey economy appeared reasonably bright.

The story of the last quarter-century in New Jersey can best be examined by looking at both the older, traditional areas of endeavor, such as farming, manufacturing, insurance, and automobiles, and at the newer industries that will be shaping the New Jersey of the future: resurgent tourism, health products, high technology, the "New Gold Coast" along the Hudson River opposite Manhattan, New Jersey's role in the global economy, the malls, transportation, and the energy sector.

Agriculture Declines Further

Because of declining profitability and the threat to the state's farm economy from the agribusinesses in the Sunbelt and California, which have longer growing periods, farming has dramatically declined since the 1950s. In 1985 New Jersey had 8,700 farms, encompassing 950,000 acres, down from 26,900 farms, encompassing 1.7 million acres in 1950. The average farmer

Below: Some places in New Jersey have resisted the changes of time. Tranquility in Allamuchy, Warren County, was the estate of John Rutherfurd in the 1700s. Descendants of the family remained on the farm, raising valuable Holstein cattle and Dorset sheep. Courtesy, The Star-Ledger

in New Jersey worked a sixty-seven-acre farm, a size that remained constant for the 1970s. The New Jersey Farm Bureau reported that annual New Jersey farm income in 1985, after deducting basic living expenses, was between $6,000 and $10,000. Because of increasing prices for land in the state, only about 50 percent of farmers in 1985 owned the land they worked. The others leased. Many farmers have sold their land to developers for the highest per-acre average price in the nation: $3,523, with highs of $20,000 per acre in the Route 1 corridor north and south of Princeton.

So the Garden State slowly lost much of its agricultural base. New Jersey farmers have shifted from planting primarily corn, wheat, rye, and oats toward soybeans, potatoes, tomatoes, asparagus, eggplant, and green peppers. In 1985 New Jerseyans grew enough blueberries, peaches, tomatoes, and cranberries to rank among the top five producers of these crops in the nation. One Atlantic County farmer picks five million pints of blueberries annually. New Jersey, which has more horses per square mile than any other state, ranks fifth among horse-breeding states (behind only Virginia, New York,

Left: The owner of the Del Vista Vineyard tends her vines in Frenchtown. With the exception of Atlantic County's Renault Winery and Vineyard, established in 1864, wineries did not occupy an important place in New Jersey's early agricultural industries. Production of wine grapes declined throughout the Prohibition years and for thirty years thereafter. A resurgence began in the 1960s in South Jersey, and the number of wineries doubled during the first five years of the 1980s. Courtesy, the Star-Ledger

California, and Kentucky). To fight the agribusiness challenge of California and the Sunbelt in 1985, the Department of Agriculture budgeted $325,000 to $625,000 to convince Garden State residents to buy vegetables and other crops "made" in New Jersey.

Foreign markets may also help new Jersey farmers in the future. In 1984 the BITCO-Bancorps International Trading Company of Somerset helped New Jersey farmers sell $3 million in soybeans to Spain. Those with high hopes for the return of profitability to New Jersey's farm sector in the 1990s also point to its location within a day's truck drive from nearly a third of the American population. Although farming had shrunk, New Jersey in 1985 still had a $500 million direct-produce industry.

In 1985 state Secretary of Agriculture Arthur R. Brown, Jr., a farmer himself, was positive about the state's farm economy. "Agriculture," he said, "is still a very strong and viable industry." Brown noted that the state's farmers were not dependent on federal loans and subsidies, and a large percentage were diversified—not dependent on one crop—and thus economically sounder than one-crop farmers.

Energy Research Begins

At the end of World War II, the research division at Esso Oil Company (Exxon) had grown so large that the company gave it its own seventy acres in Linden. The chemists and others there developed the fluid-catalytic-cracking process during the 1940s. Mobil researchers at the Paulsboro Mobil refinery during the 1960s developed a catalyst that increased the yield of a barrel of oil by one-third. By 1986 Exxon Research and Engineering Company had also set up laboratories in Clinton.

With the energy crisis of the 1970s, New Jersey energy research accelerated. Mobil engineers produced gasoline from methanol, a coal derivative. Hydrocarbon Research Inc. in Lawrence Township, under contract from industry and government, studied ways to produce energy from shale, refinery waste, and tar sands.

Not only have the petroleum companies begun to develop synthetic fuels and liquefy coal, but other energy researchers have begun to explore solar and nuclear energy. Public Service Electric and Gas Company has experimented with fuel-cell power plants. Englehard Industries has explored the use of catalytic converters.

The Plasma Physics Laboratory at Princeton investigated a way to develop energy from nuclear fusion—a project they had been working on since the 1940s. They fused hydrogen into helium at temperatures of over eighty million degrees. When developed, fusion energy will be far safer than fission (conventional nuclear) energy. It may be a long way off—perhaps into the twenty-first century—but they were making significant progress in late 1986. Although the glut of oil in the 1980s and the weakening of the OPEC cartel has removed energy research from the headlines, many analysts anticipate that Americans will face another oil shortage in the 1990s.

Wally Amos (right), formerly employed in booking show business personalities for the William Morris Agency in Manhattan, now promotes his "Famous Amos" chocolate-chip cookies created in his Nutley "studio." He appears here with two of the forty young guests invited to his Thanksgiving bake-off on November 24, 1980. Courtesy, the Star-Ledger

Manufacturing Sags

During World War II some 50 percent of New Jersey workers made products. After 1960 New Jersey lost many heavy-machinery, steel-processing, and auto-assembly jobs. Between 1969 and 1975 some 200,000 manufacturing jobs disappeared, but in the 1970s one-third of New Jersey workers still worked in manufacturing, and they made products in 95 percent of all classifications of U.S. goods.

Once the backbone of the Elizabeth manufacturing industry, Singer abandoned the sewing-machine business under the pressures of foreign competition. The Elizabeth site was taken over in the 1980s by Slater Electric Company, which produces electrical devices; Omega Manufacturing, a handbag maker; and Merit Mailers, a printing and mailing firm. Colgate-Palmolive closed its Jersey City plant in the 1980s.

A nineteenth-century manufacturing colossus, Newark in 1983 shipped only 1.22 percent of American manufactured items. The glass industry of South Jersey suffered in the 1980s as competing metals and plastics cut its sales of glass beverage containers. In the 1980s even the largest corporations in the state, including AT&T Information Systems, RCA, and Allied Signal, reduced their manufacturing work forces.

Some felt that high-tech gains might replace manufacturing losses. In 1980, for example, Ford closed its Mahwah assembly plant. Sharp Electronics

Corporation took over sixty-five acres of the site. Sharp's marketing manager, Dan Infanti, noted in 1985 that the firm's offices and distribution center on the site employed 750 people and were "growing at the rate of 10 percent a year."

Borden Putnam, commissioner, New Jersey Department of Commerce and Economic Development, noted that the growth of the high-tech sector of the New Jersey economy had helped recapture some 50,000 manufacturing jobs in 1984-1985. He believed that three high-tech positions would support two manufacturing jobs, and pointed out that manufacturers of high-tech, touch-sensitive buttons, cable, wire, connectors, and fuses for the computer and telephone industries had prospered in the 1980s.

In his bid for the 1984 Democratic presidential nomination, Colorado Senator Gary Hart said that the shift in New Jersey from industrial manufacturing to high-tech and service industries was the "new reality of New Jersey." Unfortunately, the increases in high-tech, pharmaceutical, and electronic sectors had not offset the losses in the manufacturing area. By the mid-1980s, state efforts to set up urban enterprise zones to hold down manufacturing losses had also not proved cost-effective.

But as manufacturing declined, services, trade, and finance grew, and by 1985 accounted for over half of New Jersey's jobs. The state economy revived in part because public officials, prodded by the leading business organizations of the state, particularly the State Chamber of Commerce, reversed policies of the 1960s that had given New Jersey a negative business image. By the 1980s the administration of Thomas Kean provided a business climate that encouraged foreign corporations to open headquarters in the state and in general promoted business development. New Jersey's central location in the Boston-Washington urban corridor meant that it was in the center of the large East Coast market area. "One third of the U.S. market for anything," said Borden R. Putnam, "whether it's corn flakes or automobiles, is accessible from New Jersey with a simple overnight truck drive. That accounted for the diversity and strength of our manufacturing industry for many years."

And location is one of the reasons that New Jersey in the 1980s led the nation in pharmaceuticals, was second in chemicals, fifth in rubber and plastics, seventh in petroleum, eighth in food and paper products, ninth in electrical machinery and fabricated metal. Since 1980, in fact, the New Jersey economy has outperformed the national economy in employment, income, retail sales, new-car sales, and housing starts. Despite the losses in its manufacturing sector, the New Jersey economy of the 1980s seems strong. The movement of foreign capital into the state, discussed later in this chapter, helped revive manufacturing in television sets, microwave ovens, and telephone products.

New Jersey Enters the Global Economy

As international trade expanded in the 1960s and 1970s, New Jersey began

to play a larger and larger role in a global economy. The state's businessmen were well situated for this change, since the state occupies a strategic position between the Hudson, the Delaware River Bay, and the Atlantic Ocean, and has two port complexes: the Port Authority of New York and New Jersey and the Delaware River Port Authority of Pennsylvania and New Jersey.

The State Chamber of Commerce organized yearly training programs to stimulate imports and exports through the Port Authority of New York and New Jersey. In 1960 New Jerseyans exported goods worth $782 million. By the end of the decade, they were exporting more than one billion dollars' worth, an amount which grew during the 1970s. During that decade New Jersey, the forty-sixth state in size, ranked eighth in exports and was second in the nation in attracting foreign investment. New Jerseyans exported primarily chemicals and electric and non-electric machinery, along with transportation equipment, metal products, food, fabricated metal products, products made from petroleum and coal, instruments, and rubber and plastic products. Newark, the Paterson-Clifton-Passaic region, and the southern counties of Camden, Burlington, and Gloucester all exported to Western Europe, Taiwan, Korea, Japan, and Latin America, as the earliest seventeenth-century settlers once had to Barbados and the Old World.

As a leader in chemicals and pharmaceuticals, New Jersey also attracted a host of foreign-based multinational corporations. By 1981 more than 537 companies from 25 nations had located in New Jersey—more foreign-owned companies than located in any other state. Of those 537 companies, 130 came from Germany, 90 from England, 85 from Japan, 70 from France, and 30 from Switzerland. Four Swiss companies grew powerful in the New Jersey economy of the 1970s and 1980s: Ciba-Geigy, in Summit; Sika Chemical, in Lyndhurst; Hoffmann-La Roche, in Nutley; and Sandoz-Wander, in East Hanover. German companies doing business during this period in New Jersey included Parsippany's BASF. Organon from the Netherlands located in West Orange. Foreign investments in New Jersey helped to offset America's growing balance-of-payments deficit of the 1970s and 1980s.

Shown here at the Port Newark/Elizabeth Marine Terminal are three of the facility's twenty-three container cranes capable of lifting cargoes as heavy as seventy tons. In 1979 the terminal, which covers more than 2,000 acres, became the largest foreign trade zone in the United States, and in 1983 handled 11.3 million tons of cargo. Courtesy, Port Authority of New York and New Jersey

In 1985 New Jersey ranked twelfth in the nation in export-dollar values and fourth in national foreign investment. In the 1980s Newark International Airport handled more and more international cargo. The first container port in this region, Port Elizabeth-Newark, which included the Elizabeth marine terminal, Port Newark, and Newark International Airport, opened in 1962, and by 1971 handled more than 10.3 million tons of general cargo, most of it containerized. The largest container facility in the United States, the Newark/Port Elizabeth complexes, in 1985 handled more than three times the tonnage of Los Angeles, which was the nation's second-largest container port.

To help firms with product but no experience in exporting, the Port Authority in 1982 created XPORT—The Port Authority Trading Company.

Above: This Fulper stoneware vase was produced circa 1915 at a Flemington pottery that had been in operation for nearly a century. Abraham Fulper purchased the works upon the death of its previous owner in 1858, and after 1906 the Fulper Pottery Company specialized in artware. Courtesy, New Jersey State Museum Collection, Trenton

Left: The creamy translucence of Lenox china was inspired by the ivory-colored porcelain produced in Belleek, Ireland, and created in this country after many difficulties by Walter Scott Lenox. The company policy of selling patterns in place-settings brought the china within reach of the nation's brides. Here a Lenox worker uses twenty-four carat gold to decorate a candlestick. Courtesy, Lenox Inc.

Above: A graceful example of the wares of Tiffany and Co., this silver and copper coffee set was made circa 1880, before the well-known firm moved its silver department to Newark in 1896. Courtesy, New Jersey State Museum Collection, Trenton

Left: Cybis sculptures of animals range from a three-inch snail to this group of white-tailed deer almost nineteen inches tall. The diagonal lines of the composition reflect the urgency of this family's flight. The leaf under foot suggests the autumn hunting season. White Tailed Deer, issued in 1986, is bisque-decorated porcelain. Courtesy, Cybis Studio, Trenton

Right: Newark International Airport's busy traffic tower appears behind the wing of a People Express plane being readied for take off. The North Terminal was formerly Newark Airport's sole terminal, and the second to be operated by the facility. Courtesy, Port Authority of New York and New Jersey

Below: Boxcar-sized containers are lifted high into the air as a freighter unloads in Port Newark/Elizabeth, the leading container port of the United States. Foreign cargo passing through the port includes the greatest number of Japanese cars shipped to any U.S. port. Courtesy, Port Authority of New York and New Jersey

Facing page, top: Originally opened by the City of Newark in 1915, the Port of Newark received its first cargo shipment, a load of Philippine mahogany, the following year. A busy place during World War I, the port later languished under military supervision. In 1948 the port was leased to the New York Port Authority, which has spent millions on the completely rebuilt facility, now one of the world's most efficient ports. Courtesy, Port Authority of New York and New Jersey

Facing page, bottom: "Trenton Makes, the World Takes," read the prize-winning slogan in a 1910 contest, which captured the pride of accomplishment of this industrial city. The present bridge, built in 1926, is the third to rest on the site. The first bridge, built in 1806, replaced a ferry that was in operation from colonial days. Photo by Eugene Guerra

Right: This picture from a Charles Engelhard, Inc., laboratory shows a production-control quantometer, which measures impurities in a variety of metals. The firm began as the American Platinum Works, established in Newark by Charles Engelhard in 1875 to refine platinum. Later, it and Baker and Company became units of Charles Engelhard, Inc., also known for its automobile pollution control devices. Courtesy, Engelhard Corporation

Below: RCA Laboratories in Princeton carries out research and development in the company's core business of communications, electronics, and entertainment, although scientists and technicians engage in medical research as well. One application of robotics technology involves the experimental treament of skin disorders. Courtesy, RCA Laboratories

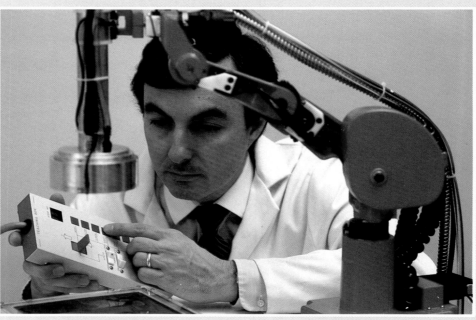

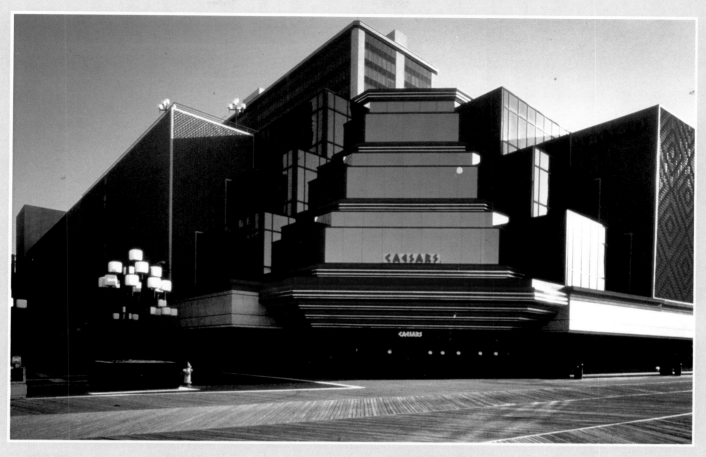

After acquiring the Howard Johnson Regency, Caesar's World erected this imposing glass-walled extension (above) behind the former motel, completing the complex along one full block of Arkansas Avenue to the Boardwalk. Known as "Caesar's Atlantic City," the hotel-casino was the second in Atlantic City, opening June 26, 1979. Players at the "slots" (left) try for the elusive jackpot. In 1983, there were 1,364 slot machines on the casino floor. Courtesy, Caesar's Atlantic City

*The Statue of Liberty presides over
"Superstars and Stripes," a revue presented
in the Atlantis Cabaret in 1986. Courtesy,
Atlantis Casino Hotel*

The beauty of the North Jersey hills and their close proximity to the New York financial and shipping centers have made them an ideal location for headquarters of many large corporations. At Montvale on the Garden State Parkway in northern Bergen County, sleepy farms have given way to the 20th century palaces of several national companies, and even a few foreign ones. One of the latter is the Bavarian Motors Works (BMW), which established its American headquarters in Montvale in the 1970s. Courtesy, the Star-Ledger

in the *Fortune* 500; Johnson & Johnson; CPC International; Campbell Soup; American Cyanamid; Merck; Warner Lambert; Ingersoll-Rand; Kidde Inc.; and Englehard. Others who might go unmentioned because they were parts of larger organizations included Nabisco Brands; Prentice-Hall; RCA; and then, of course, the health-care giants: Hoffmann-La Roche; Ciba-Geigy; Shering-Plough; Squibb; Sandoz; and Becton Dickinson.

The campus-like office complex became popular in the state with architects and CEO's, whom, it was rumored, often decided on office building locations primarily to make their commutes easier. Allied Chemical Corporation moved to a 151-acre office site in Morris Township. Union Camp Corporation located its striking Wayne office at the edge of a beautiful reflecting pond. Nabisco built a glass-and-concrete office in East Hanover, and AT&T located its monumental, Oriental-style terraced office complex in Basking Ridge. Other major American firms with offices in New Jersey included: Benjamin Moore & Company in Montvale, AT&T Long Lines in Bedminster, Western Union, David Sarnoff Research Center of Radio Corporation of America, the Great Atlantic and Pacific Tea Company, and Bell Telephone Laboratories.

In 1971 E. R. Squibb & Sons built a landscaped, glass-and-brick complex in Princeton. Lenox China built an extraordinarily beautiful white structure in Lawrenceville. Federal Paper Board placed its headquarters in Montvale on a sloping hillside graced with flowering trees. CPC International's headquarters in Englewood Cliffs had its own reflecting pool, next to which workers could eat. Liggett Group's Montvale headquarters included, as did others, outdoor patios and a gymnasium.

Foreign auto makers had headquarters in New Jersey, and American automakers continued to assemble vehicles in New Jersey. The state's four

The proposed Prudential Life office center (above) at Short Hills combines office space with a hotel and conference center. The view at right is an architect's rendering of the center's spacious atrium. The shift in the state's economy toward service industries created a need for increased office space, which many companies resolved by locating their corporate headquarters in suburban locations like Short Hills. Courtesy, The Grad Partnership

Garden State Plaza, pictured here just beyond the junction of Route 4 and 17, opened on May 1, 1957. A subsidiary of R.H. Macy & Co., the plaza has since been renovated and enclosed for climate-controlled shopping. Courtesy, Newark Public Library

automobile-assembly plants of the 1980s produced at a rate of 500,000 cars a year and provided a market for some 80 other automobile-supply industries, and hundreds more in automobile-related fields. In the 1980s four million automobiles were registered in New Jersey to get New Jerseyans to jobs, the beach, and, of course, that New Jersey institution that seems particularly suited to a state on wheels, the mall.

Malls Spring Up

The Garden State saw its first mall at the end of the 1950s, in Paramus, when the Garden State Plaza opened. A development that revolutionized merchandising, malls soon spread across the land. The Cherry Hill Mall became the state's first enclosed mall and started a trend. Its developer, the Rouse Company of Maryland, led by James W. Rouse, went from success to success, building the Echelon Mall, the Paramus Park Mall, and then Willowbrook and Woodbridge malls. By 1978 the state boasted some twenty-six malls. In Paramus Park, Rouse built a two-story waterfall.

Thomas Swick has compared the New Jersey mall with the cathedrals of the thirteenth century. The mall, he wrote in *New Jersey: Unexpected Pleasures*, "dominates and serves the suburb just as the cathedral did the town. It is peopled by its own parishioners and occasioned by pilgrims, trekking mostly for the great feast days (Thanksgiving weekend, pre-Christmas, White Sales, Summer Clearance) and the personal celebrations (Graduation, Mother's and Father's Days)."

Swick saw an "unmistakable similarity" in design, with the major department store serving as the great cathedral, "and a passage connecting numerous small specialized, boutique-like side chambers for more personal oblations." He noted that the wide halls were places "where you stroll curiously, meeting fellow pilgrims and eyeing agreeably the suburbanites as they sit or wander, interspersing consumer litanies with local gossip. And as you walk, you peer into the alluring shops, each with its own peculiar incense and icons. There is a continuous flow, from morning to night when at last the great doors close and you enter out into the world again, if not richer in spirit, at least poorer in purse. . . . Something within you has been fulfilled." Cathedrals or not, New Jersey's malls have been a central part of its economic vitality during the post-1960s rise of suburbia.

Tourism Mushrooms

In the 1980s New Jersey tourism grew from a $6.6-billion industry to one that earned $8.5 billion, which made it the state's second-largest industry, behind petrochemicals. In 1986 tourism provided work for some 350,000 New Jerseyans. New Jersey offered variety, from the ski areas of Great Gorge and Vernon Valley in the northwest to the beaches of Cape May in the southeast. Cape May instituted an October "Victorian Week," which drew large crowds, and a successful Christmas program. From Washington Crossing State Park, Swedesboro, and the cranberry bogs of the Pine Barrens to the Meadowlands Sports Complex, New Jersey attracted tourists.

Atlantic City, of course, drew more powerfully than any other tourist attraction: twenty-eight million people visited there in 1985. Although the Boardwalk has lured crowds since the Gay Nineties, the legalization of casino gambling in 1976 revived the dreams of Dr. Jonathan Pitney, who built

Atlantic City is America's No. 1 bus destination, with about 1,000 busloads of visitors arriving every day. From New York City and many locations in New Jersey and Pennsylvania, bus companies, and the casinos themselves, offer day or weekend trips to the resort. Courtesy, the Star-Ledger

The cranes shown here are hoisting steel beams during construction of the New Jersey Sports Complex arena in 1979. The building, which was designed by the Grad Partnership of Newark, has 20,000 seats, each with an unobstructed view of the action on the floor. The arena was later named for the New Jersey governor in whose term it was constructed. Courtesy, The Grad Partnership

the railroad connection to Atlantic City in 1854.

Atlantic City again became a major resort. Up and down the beach the construction of palatial gambling casinos remade the shoreline. Beginning with Resorts International, the casinos lined the sand. Since the first casino opened in 1978, some ten more have been constructed. The revenues from these enterprises approached $2 billion annually. The revival created some 40,000 new jobs in the region.

Skeptics have questioned how much the casinos have actually helped the parts of the city that are not on the Boardwalk, and Atlantic City in the 1980s had its scruffy neighborhoods. The economic development has perhaps spurred more growth in the suburban areas surrounding Atlantic City than in the non-Boardwalk parts of the city itself. "Gaming has generated more economic development than anyone ever projected," according to Steven Batzer, chief executive officer of Bayly, Martin & Far Inc., an Atlantic City insurance firm, and chairman of the Atlantic County Economic Development Council. By 1986 the casinos had invested more than $3 billion in the state, and construction plans had been fixed for the Atlantic Metroplex, the first new office building to be constructed in the area in half a century.

Out of the Hackensack swamps, New Jerseyans constructed one of the East Coast's most successful entertainment complexes. To many Easterners, "the Meadowlands" means either sports or concerts, and the Meadowlands Sports Complex became the single most-visited location of the early 1980s and drew approximately ten million spectators a year. But the Sports Complex forms only part of the revitalization of what was once a regional garbage dump and 20,000-acre saltwater marsh drained by the Hackensack River.

In 1969 the state set up the Hackensack Meadowlands Development

Commission to plan the development of this thirty-two-square-mile area. The name came from the earlier, failed ventures to dam the waters and develop "meadowlands" for dairying. Because of the unique ecological nature of the area, 130 acres have been set aside as a natural environment, and the other 1,360 acres have been turned into educational, recreational, and cultural facilities.

The New Jersey Sports and Exposition Authority built the Sports Complex, which included the Meadowlands Race Track, home of the Hambletonian, the Kentucky Derby of harness racing. Judged on the size of purses, attendance, and the quality of horses, the track became the greatest harness track in the world. The revenues from the track financed Giants Stadium, built especially for football. In 1979 Giants Stadium held fifty-two separate events. In 1985-1986 it was home to both the Giants, who removed the "NY" from their helmets, and the Jets, who abandoned Shea Stadium. The Nets and the Devils played basketball and hockey in Byrne Arena.

But "the Meadowlands" of the 1980s also included the 700-acre commercial and industrial development of Leonard Stern, chairman of Hartz Mountain Industries. The project encompassed the townhouses of Harmon Cove I and II, a marina, and a ten-story office building. Bellemeade Development Corporation constructed a "Wall Street West" at their Meadowlands Corporation Center, where nearly 100 companies had headquarters.

By channeling refuse through the Resource Recovery Plant, which processes solid waste into clean landfill, and by cleaning the toxic chemicals from the waters, the managers allowed the marsh to restore itself ecologically.

During the late 1970s and early 1980s, Great Adventure developed into the largest seasonal amusement park in the state and the third largest in the nation, behind only Disney World and Disneyland. In addition to these recently constructed tourist attractions, the historic past offered a rich selection of places with tourist appeal. The "cockpit of the American Revolution" and a major player in the Industrial Revolution in America, New Jersey boasted more historical sites than any other state, according to the Division of Travel and Tourism of the Department of Commerce and Economic Development. One hundred twenty-seven miles of beaches lured millions of sunbathers, fishermen, sailors, and surfers each summer. For those who believe that "life's a beach," New Jersey makes a dream come true.

To get this message to the nation during the early 1980s, the administration of Governor Thomas Kean launched an aggressive public-relations drive to attract tourists. In 1983 the Division of Travel and Tourism sent out over fifteen million pieces of literature with the slogan, "New Jersey & You. Perfect Together." By the middle of the decade, the state ranked fifth in tourism revenues, behind only New York, Florida, California, and Texas. Given the riches the state offered—from the beaches and natural and historical sites, to the glitz of the gaming tables, the racetracks, and the spectator sports—it is remarkable that New Jersey did not rank even higher.

The Garden State

New Jersey is one of the smallest states in the Union, larger than only Rhode Island, Delaware, Connecticut, and Hawaii. It also has the highest population density in the country. One would thus surmise that there would be no room for the great outdoors, but exactly the opposite is true. New Jersey abounds with recreation spots: state forests, state parks, wildlife and recreation areas, and, of course, the state's fabulous 120 miles of Atlantic Ocean shoreline.

For years, the long stretches of sandy beaches on New Jersey's coast have been one of the East's major vacation centers—and a major source of state revenue. During the summer months, New Jerseyans and visitors from out of state flock to New Jersey's shoreline on the Garden State Parkway, the Atlantic City Expressway, and other smaller roads. These tourists pour nearly two billion dollars into the more than forty resort towns along the coastline.

New Jersey's lake country is situated primarily up in Morris, Sussex, and Passaic counties. Just like the shoreline, the state's lakes attract huge crowds of recreational enthusiasts during the summer months, and visitors also make these lake towns prosper. Motorboat and fishing enthusiasts abound, and cottages along the lakes are rented to the luckier vacationers.

But there is no need for even the most penurious vacationer to feel left out in New Jersey, thanks to a wealth of federal and state outdoor resources providing visitors with many recreational and educational activities.

New Jersey has a total of ten state forests, which vary in size. The 14,000-acre Stokes Forest, on the Kittatinny Ridge in Sussex County, boasts Sunrise Mountain and Tillman Ravine. Its larger counterparts include the 27,000-acre Lebanon Forest in the pine belt of southern New Jersey, and the scenic Wharton Forest in parts of Atlantic, Burlington, and Camden counties. Hiking, fishing, hunting, picnicking, swimming, camping, and following scenic walking trails are all part of the activities in New Jersey's vast forest lands.

New Jersey's State Parks offer added recreational facilities, though sometimes accompanied by more stringent environmental regulations. There is plenty of fishing in these parks, although hunting is prohibited. Instead, New Jersey's wildlife is protected and is there for the hiker and nature lover to behold. New Jersey has some forty such state parks, each with its own special natural or historic significance, and all of them very different from one another.

Scenic Fort Mott Park on the Delaware River, for example, recalls Revolutionary raids in Salem County. Barnegat Lighthouse Park along the shoreline marks one of the most famous landmarks on America's entire Atlantic Coast. Edison Park in Middlesex County is dedicated to America's—and probably the world's—most prolific inventor. Island Beach Park in Ocean County has sand and surf galore, punctuated by beautiful, expressive sand dunes, white sandy beaches, and sparkling water.

And there is much more. High Point Park sits on 12,000 acres and offers a climb to the highest point in the entire state, and Shepherd Lake rings the Ramapo Mountains. On the outskirts of Trenton is Washington Crossing Park, its various statues and memorials dedicated to the memory of that winter night when Washington crossed the Delaware to rout the British.

In addition to its state forests and state parks, New Jersey also has created a number of designated recreation areas: Round Valley, a 4,000-acre tract of which more than half is water and waterfront, considered second only to Lake Hopatcong in beauty; Bull's Island, an eighty-acre area in Hunterdon County; Spruce Run, a reservoir in Hunterdon County for fishing and boating; Palisades Interstate Park, which preserves the marvelous Palisades on the Hudson in conjunction with New York State; and Morristown Historical Park, maintained by the federal government and including Washington's headquarters, the Ford Mansion and Museum, Fort Nonsense, and Jockey Hollow. New Jersey also offers many designated "natural areas," utilized primarily for scientific observation.

New Jersey's many historic sites offer the traveler a chance to make special trips to view famous houses; Colonial architecture; sites of famous Revolutionary War battles; remains of early industry such as iron furnaces and glassworks; the laboratory and home of Thomas Edison in West Orange; Walt Whitman's last home in Camden; and other intriguing places.

New Jersey also offers vacationers more than 100 campgrounds operated by private owners, and there are also approximately fifty Fish and Wildlife Management Areas in New Jersey, including lakes, rivers, creeks, pines, bogs, coastal wetlands, a refuge, a game farm, and a quail farm.

—David Fleming

A New Era In Health Products

The campaign for national health insurance begun by Harry Truman climaxed in 1965 when President Johnson won passage of Medicare, which covered private doctors' charges for the elderly. In 1966 Congress enacted Medicaid, which extended coverage to people on welfare.

In 1968 New Jersey made and sold one billion dollars' worth of health products. In the next twenty years federal money poured into the health-products economy of the nation. With its health-products manufacturing industry, including pharmaceuticals, New Jersey became the "nation's medicine chest."

In 1984, 25 percent of American health-products employees worked in New Jersey to make and ship $6.7 billion worth of health products, about one-fourth of the U.S. total. A growth industry, in 1984 health-products companies in New Jersey made nearly one-fourth of the total investment in plant and equipment in the state. In 1985, according to Hal P. Eastman, professor of management at the Graduate School of Management at Rutgers University, "If the state's size were proportional to its role nationally in the health products industry, New Jersey would cover virtually all of the U.S. east of the Mississippi River."

New Jersey's lead came from its historic and continuing emphasis on research and development. In 1985 New Jersey health firms spent some 14.9 percent of their sales dollars on "R&D," as compared to a nationwide ratio of only 2.8 percent for manufacturing firms. Research in pharmaceutical products in New Jersey in 1984 accounted for 30 percent of the national R&D expenditure.

From this expenditure has come new drugs for the treatment of high blood pressure, for patients undergoing organ transplants, and a new oral drug to treat severe acne. New Jersey scientists using recombinant-DNA technology have developed and produced pure interferon for testing against a number of cancers. The world waits as tests prove more and more conclusive. Recombinant-DNA technology has also been used to produce interleukin-2, which may help in curing acquired-immune-deficiency-syndrome (AIDS) and other diseases characterized by a suppressed immune system.

Pioneers in biotechnology, New Jersey health-products companies have also been key forces in the battle to even the trade balance. Since World War II, R&D-intensive industries have fared better in foreign markets than non-R&D-intensive industries. Since 1964 medicinal and pharmaceutical preparations have steadily developed foreign markets, and in 1984 exports of these products exceeded imports by one billion.

New Jersey Turns To High Technology

By the mid-1980s the growth of the high-technology segment of the New Jersey economy had begun to draw comments. "This sector is small, but

very fast growing—the dynamic aspect of the economy," according to Joseph J. Seneca, a Rutgers University economist and chairman of the Economic Policy Council of the state in 1985. "New Jersey," said Governor Thomas H. Kean in remarks that same year, "is on its way to achieving a national reputation as being on the cutting edge of a high-technology economy.

"We have," Kean noted, "in the past few years launched an aggressive campaign to attract high-tech programs into our state colleges and prepare our state for the economic demands of the years ahead." These efforts have begun to pay off.

Employment in the communications, engineering, computer-programming and data-programming industries and related fields skyrocketed 47.2 percent between 1977 and 1982—from 70,023 to 103,427 people. These New Jersey jobs represent 4.3 percent of the nation's total employment in these areas. New Jersey now ranks fourth in the number of high-tech firms. In 1985 about 10 percent of the work force held high-tech or related positions.

In the early 1980s New Jerseyans constructed a high-tech corridor in the Princeton area along a twenty-five-mile section of Route 1. A second

An RCA astro-electronics engineer, Robert J. Cenker, became a NASA payload specialist during the January 1986 Space Shuttle mission. One of his tasks at NASA was to support the deployment of the RCA communications satellite, which Cenker is viewing here as it was assembled at the firm's East Windsor facility. Courtesy, RCA/Aerospace and Defense/Astro-Electronics Division

These photographs offer views of the Star-Ledger's *newsroom. New Jersey's largest newspaper, and one of the leading papers in the Newhouse chain, the* Star-Ledger *has expanded its circulation in the Newark metropolitan area to include Morris, Middlesex, Somerset, and Monmouth counties. Courtesy, the* Star-Ledger

telecommunications corridor sprang up along I-287 and I-78, as the Bell Laboratories attracted smaller telecommunications companies. In 1985 the National Science Foundation put New Jersey on the scientific map when it established one of its three National Advanced Scientific Computer centers at Princeton's Forrestal Greens. The John von Neumann Center for Scientific Computing houses CYBER 205, a supercomputer, capable of from 100 million to 400 million operations per second. Those close to the subject noted that the supercomputer will potentially create a "new kind of science." "What has changed," said Cornell University astrophysicist Kenneth Wilson, "is the complexity of problems people are willing to tackle. . . . You can doodle with a pencil and paper when you're thinking about the Earth going around the Sun, but you cannot doodle when you're trying to follow 10,000 rocks going around Saturn."

Under the direction of Edward Cohen, the state Commission on Science and Technology has organized eight science-and-technology research centers for the state. In 1984 the voters approved a "Jobs, Science, and Technology" bond issue to fund these centers.

The breakup of the Bell System in 1984 threw the telecommunications market into a turmoil. Divestiture left New Jersey as home to AT&T, a firm which manufactured telephones, computers, and communications systems and conducted a long-distance communications network, as well as the Bell Atlantic, a telephone operating company and equipment marketer.

International Telephone and Telegraph (ITT), which manufactured and sold telecommunications equipment, operated out of New Jersey, as did Radio Corporation of America (RCA), which was in the business of telecommunications equipment and service as well as satellite communications. Adding together the technological expertise in these companies, the resources of their laboratories, the CYBER 205, and the new high-tech corridors in the state, makes understandable the claims of those who say that New Jersey may soon rival the output of California's Silicon Valley and Boston's Highway 128.

The New Gold Coast On the Hudson River Shore

Along eighteen miles of Hudson River waterfront, an area that Henry Hudson visited in 1609, New Jerseyans in the 1980s began construction of what has been called "collectively the biggest waterfront investment in the United States, totaling over $5 billion." Private developers, the Port Authority of New York and New Jersey, the City of Jersey City, and the State of New Jersey have combined to develop 2,300 acres between the George Washington Bridge and Bayonne.

The area was, according to John Maddocks, general manager of area development for Public Service Electric & Gas Company, "probably the most valuable real estate in the United States today." Since it will include 14.6 million square feet of office space, the "New Gold Coast" would be, according to the Port Authority of New York and New Jersey's Chief Economist Rosemary Scanlon, "equal to one-and-a-half World Trade Centers."

The project included a Romulus Development in West New York and Weehawken, a mixed-use development of 367 acres; Lincoln Harbor in Weehawken, a development of 61 acres to include residences, retail outlets, hotels, and a heliport; Hoboken Piers in Hoboken; Newport City, in Jersey City, one of the largest entirely new cities in the world, which will include some 1,200 hotel rooms, office space, and major department stores in addition to 9,000 housing units for 40,000 residents; Harismus Cove in Jersey City; and Harborside Financial Center, also in Jersey City, which will accommodate Merrill Lynch and other financial giants.

The Jersey City development will also house Caven Point-Port Liberte, Evertrust, Liberty Harbor North, Droyers Point, Exchange Place, and Greenville Yards. Jersey City's Liberty State Park will be the home of a New Jersey Science and Technology Center, with exhibits, a domed movie theater, a science library, computer stations, and workshops.

To meet an ever-increasing demand for electrical energy, Public Service Electric & Gas began construction of nuclear generating plants in Salem County. Salem 1, on Artificial Island in Lower Alloways Creek Township, began operation in 1977. This photograph shows the control room of the second unit, Salem 2, which was started up in 1981. Courtesy, the Star-Ledger

In 1850, the small shore town of Absecon was a forlorn strip of sand, far from the reaches of civilization. But Dr. Jonathan Pitney believed that Absecon would some day be the most famous resort spot on the East Coast. He and a group of associates invested in the Camden and Atlantic Railroad's project to build tracks linking the town with major population centers. In 1850 these men re-christened Absecon with a lavish new name: Atlantic City.

At that time, this so-called city had only twenty-one eligible voters and was nothing but a broad expanse of sand dunes and seashore. But Dr. Pitney saw the town as the perfect health spa and resort. As the rail link was being established, construction began on the first of many hotels. On July 1, 1854, the first Camden-Atlantic City train carried 600 dignitaries and the press to a gala party in the still-unfinished United States Hotel at Atlantic City.

By 1877, the Philadelphia & Atlantic City Narrow Gauge Railway began running trains to Atlantic City, carrying crowded carloads of people from the City of Brotherly Love. By 1890, Atlantic City had more than 500 hotels, and an expansive boardwalk with fifty-seven commercial bathhouses, ten amusement ride centers, and eighteen saltwater-taffy retailers. Myriad newspaper stories, pamphlets, and press releases portrayed Atlantic City as the national resort. And Atlantic City became the first place offering vacation enjoyment on a mass scale—not just for the elite. Dr. Pitney's vision had become a reality: the railroads had made Atlantic City the nation's primary summer resort.

As Atlantic City boomed through the turn of the century, railroad officials sold their waterfront land, purchased for as little as $17.50 per acre back in the early 1850s, at huge profits as the resort's growth surpassed their wildest dreams. By this time, Atlantic City had three railroad links to Philadelphia.

And it must be remembered that Atlantic City was the birthplace of the boardwalk, which was later imitated in hundreds of other resort towns around the world. Atlantic City's very first boardwalk was constructed in 1870. It was a wooden platform eight feet wide and a mile long, and one foot above the sand. At season's end it was folded away and stored. Storms destroyed a second boardwalk in 1883, and nearly demolished a third one in 1889.

One little-known fact about Atlantic City is that it sits at the end of an odd curve in the coastline which shields it from many of the worst storms on the New Jersey coast. In addition, the Gulf Stream comes near enough Atlantic City to temper its winter climate, making it a less frosty place than other locations on the same latitude.

Few people realize that Atlantic City is actually an island. The immense marshes traversed by highways, over which every visitor first sees the Atlantic City skyline, hide deep channels that completely cut off this densely populated strip of beach from the mainland.

During the years after World War II, Atlantic City gradually fell into decline, but legalized gambling has dramatically transformed Atlantic City's economy and lifestyle since the first casinos opened in 1978. The city's 11 casinos have been tremendously popular, achieving revenues of over $2 billion and providing some 40,000 jobs.

And the arrival of casinos continues to spur the local economy. Two more casinos opened in 1987. Plans are also being made for a new convention center to be located next to Atlantic City's railroad terminal, which will also be the terminus for a proposed high-speed rail line from Philadelphia to Atlantic City.

New Jersey's decision to legalize gambling in Atlantic City in 1976 has certainly revived the city. Casinos have invested over three billion dollars in the state and spend a billion dollars per year on goods and services. Casinos have helped spark such developments as Atlantic Metroplex, the first office building to be constructed in the area in half a century. Meanwhile, Hamilton Mall is under construction in Atlantic County, adjacent to Atlantic City Race Course in McKees City. When completed, in 1987, it will be one of the largest enclosed malls in the country.

And there is more to Atlantic City today than just gambling and sunbathing. There are some major efforts underway to make the area a high-tech zone. The Federal Aviation Administration has a major experimental and testing center in Pomona and is expected to spend two billion dollars there over the next decade as part of an eleven-billion-dollar program to upgrade the nation's air-traffic-control system. Expenditures at the FAA Technical Center are expected to attract some 200 companies involved in the project. IBM, for example, has opened a facility in Egg Harbor to support its work for the FAA, and this project will have a dramatic effect on the whole economy.

—David Fleming

Aggressively developed by the Camden and Amboy Land Company, Atlantic City's first hotels were ready to welcome 600 excursionists on the first train of the Camden and Atlantic Railroad on July 1, 1854. The railroad's tracks visible in this 1857 view were purposely run in front of the hotels so that visitors would be "landed by cars directly to their point of destination." The twin towers of the United States Hotel are visible in the background. Courtesy, Atlantic City Public Library

This nondescript building in Newark houses the New Jersey Bell Aerobics Fitness Facility next to company headquarters off Broad Street. The health and maintenance complex includes brightly colored examination rooms and exercise facilities (below), and reflects the company's concern with the health of New Jersey Bell employees. Courtesy, The Grad Partnership

Facing page: This photograph captures the dramatic entrance atrium of Gateway III. The Gateway complex was so named because Newark furnishes three gateways to world commerce through its port and airport, and New York City via PATH, Amtrak, and New Jersey Transit. Courtesy, The Grad Partnership

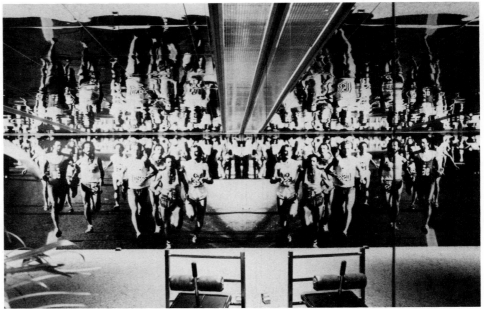

Transportation Modernizes

With its extraordinary port system, highway network, and airport, New Jersey continued to be a state that lived by transportation. During the 1980s the Port Newark/Elizabeth Seaport began improvements to handle the modern ships that can carry ten times the number of containers they used to. Planners talked of adding 145 new lane miles to the New Jersey Turnpike in the northern sections.

Workers widened the Garden State Parkway during the 1970s. Newark International Airport was handling 160,000 tons of air-freight by the early 1970s, and 347,000 overseas passengers used its facilities in 1972. Domestic and international passenger traffic soared at Newark Airport with the opening

of People Express Airlines at the old terminal. Federal deregulation stimulated competition and lowered airline fares. In the 1980s People Express took over and constructed new facilities at Terminal C. Donald Burr, the founder and chief executive of People Express, appeared on the cover of *Time* for revolutionizing the air-travel business.

Although John F. Kennedy International Airport remained the metropolitan area's most-used airport, its usage has been declining, and Newark's has been growing dramatically. According to Vincent Bonaventura, general manager of New Jersey airports for the Port Authority, Newark International, which tripled its passenger usage between 1981 and 1986 to nearly twenty-nine million, was "the fastest-growing major airport in the world."

Under the aegis of the Port of New York Authority, Newark Airport embarked upon a ten-year development program to become Newark International Airport. Satellite extension of Terminals A and B (shown here) are attached to their parent terminals by covered walkways. Newark International is rapidly overtaking La Guardia Airport as the second-busiest airfield in the metropolitan area. Courtesy, Port Authority of New York and New Jersey

Facing page, top: Public Service Electric & Gas workers pause for a look at Hope Creek Generating Station's cooling tower, the tallest structure in the state. Located just north of the twin-unit Salem 1 and 2 in Lower Alloways Creek Township, the nuclear power plant will have only one unit, scheduled to begin operation in late-1986. Courtesy, the Star-Ledger

Facing page, bottom: Professional football came to New Jersey on October 10, 1976, when Giants Stadium opened in the East Rutherford Meadows. Today, it is home to the New York Giants and hosts major college games. With 76,891 seats and parking space for 22,000 cars, it is one of America's best outdoor sports facilities. Courtesy, the Star-Ledger

The Past as Prologue

As the state moved into the 1980s, public officials created a positive business climate, and the economic picture had brightened from the dark days of the oil crisis, recession, layoffs, and inflation of the 1970s. The state's 1985 gross state product of $140 billion ranked ninth in the nation. The state's Economic Policy Council forecast the creation of 70,000 to 100,000 new jobs in 1986.

Grant Thorton's 1984 survey showed that of all the northeastern United States, New Jersey had the best business climate. In 1986 New Jersey employment hit an all-time high of 3,699,000. Although 5.5 percent of New

Jersey's work force was seeking work, unemployment had fallen to a twenty-year low.

The New Jersey Department of Commerce & Economic Development reported positive economic news. RCA began to renovate the Bibbsboro Paint Works, Subaru constructed new corporate headquarters in Cherry Hill, and the Cooper's Ferry Development Association began an office and research complex, a riverfront hotel, a public center, and a retail center along the Delaware River. Mitsubishi Motor Sales of America chose Bridgeport for its North American headquarters. This good omen, combined with the development of the 3,000 acres of Pureland Industrial Park, pointed to future growth for Gloucester County into the 1990s. Tourism continued to expand in Cape May County. Newark International Airport grew. In 1985 Borden Putnam reported that New Jersey was

second in the nation in the construction of hotels, third in the nation in the construction of airports, fourth in the nation in the construction of housings, fifth in the nation in the construction of hospitals, seventh in the nation in the construction of office buildings, ninth in the nation in the construction of factories, third in the nation in the number of corporate headquarters, and fifth in the nation in the percent of work force in high-tech.

The losses in manufacturing in the last quarter-century had been concentrated in Newark, Camden, and Elizabeth, which suffered the urban problems of the 1970s and 1980s as a result.

But optimists felt that business investment was reviving the cities. Public Service Electric & Gas and New Jersey Bell provided office space in downtown Newark. Prudential's Gateway Three complex, which included three office towers and the Hilton Hotel, gave style and economic rejuvenation to a decaying inner city. Johnson & Johnson revitalized central New Brunswick, and the Campbell Soup Company proposed a $150 million project to renovate Camden's waterfront area with a new Campbell headquarters and an aquarium. New Jersey's once-proud industrial cities began to rebuild.

Businessmen had high hopes for high-tech. High-tech innovations and the service industries created thousands of jobs. Along with the rest of the nation, New Jersey was shifting from a manufacturing base to a service and high-technology base.

New Jersey's economic history has always paralleled the nation's economic history. Discovered in 1609 by Henry Hudson, New Jersey faces the economic 1990s on the cutting edge of high technology. Bell Laboratories' microchip has replaced Trenton's smokestacks as a symbol for New Jersey industry. But whatever the means, whether with Edison's light bulb or Princeton's CYBER 205 supercomputer, ingenious and industrious New Jerseyans will continue to develop ways to shape the nation's economic development, as they have for more than three centuries.

Chapter Twelve

Partners in Progress

N ew Jerseyans launched the first steamboat, locomotive, suspension bridge, electric light, and motion picture. New Jersey's R&D laboratories produced the first transistor, the first alkaline battery, the first penicillin used on human patients, and the first antibiotics, to name just a few of this state's remarkable achievements.

New Jersey is one of America's smallest states geographically—larger than only Rhode Island, Delaware, Connecticut, and Hawaii—but throughout its history the state has been a force among its larger, sometimes chauvinistic neighbors. When New York and Pennsylvania shackled New Jersey with heavy tariffs after the Revolutionary War, New Jerseyans demanded action from Congress. And at the Constitutional Convention in 1787, New Jersey fought for equal representation of the states: Its "small state" plan established two senators from each state regardless of a state's population.

Interestingly enough, New Jersey has since become one of America's most popular states—for many good reasons. Residents have been attracted by its wealth of jobs, peaceful bedroom communities, beautiful sandy beaches, and vibrant entrepreneurial energy. Though sometimes overshadowed by the presence of New York City and Philadelphia, New Jersey's accomplishments speak for themselves.

In 1812 America's first rail charter was granted to a New Jerseyan—John Stevens of Hoboken—who built and operated America's first steam locomotive in 1825. By the mid-nineteenth century most of America's rail traffic passed through New Jersey. Thousands of Irish immigrants had come to build the railroad tracks that linked New Jersey to rail lines stretching to Chicago, St. Louis, Pittsburgh, and other major markets.

The railroads expanded industry in New Jersey's cities. Paterson, whose first textile factory opened in 1794, became a booming textile center by the mid-nineteenth century and was known first as the Cotton City and later as the Silk City. Trenton became a major national steel producer. One Trenton steel company—Roebling Steel, led by John Roebling—would become world famous for its supply of steel cable and engineering expertise for some of America's greatest suspension bridges, including the Brooklyn Bridge, the George Washington Bridge, and the Golden Gate Bridge.

The Newark refinery of Balbach and Son was located on the Passaic River within easy access of barges carrying copper ore. Originally a by-product of the Balbach's gold and silver smelting and refining operations, the production of copper assumed paramount importance in the late 1800s as the use of electricity widened. Courtesy, Newark Public Library

In the 1870s New Jersey also became a major terminal for oil and natural gas piped in from Pennsylvania and, later, from the Southwest. Bayonne became a refining center in 1875 when the Prentice Refining Company set up a still there, and Standard Oil was the next to establish itself there. Within a decade three more oil companies came to set up shop in Bayonne.

Meanwhile, Thomas Edison came from Ohio to spend his most productive years in New Jersey, establishing his first laboratory at Menlo Park in 1876. Later Edward Weston, working from his laboratory in Newark, carried on the Thomas Edison tradition. His many inventions helped establish the modern electrical utility system and helped spawn a vast electrical industry in light bulbs, phonograph records, dynamos, and power plant supplies.

And New Jersey produced many other inventors during this incredible era of innovation. In 1869 John Wesley Hyatt developed celluloid—the first commercially successful plastic—and soon began manufacturing it at factories in Newark. In 1878 Hyatt invented the injection molding machine, the major element in mass production of plastics, and in 1885 he designed his patented roller bearing, which became the major manufacturing element for General Motors, among other American giants.

There was Hannibal Goodwin of Newark, who in 1887 used celluloid to record photographic images and thus invented flexible photographic film. John Holland constructed the first workable submarine, piloting his 14-foot craft to the bottom of the Passaic River in 1878 and taking a second, larger submarine down off Staten Island in 1891. Eldridge Johnson perfected the phonograph in 1896 and founded the Victor Talking Machine Company, which made Camden one of the top recording centers of the world.

In the twentieth century New Jersey industry grew by leaps and bounds. The state's chemical industry boomed as imports from Germany stopped during World War I. New Jersey's aircraft industry was launched during that war, with Wright Aeronautical Corporation producing airplane engines in Paterson and later making the engine for Charles Lindbergh's famous *Spirit of St. Louis.*

New Jersey became one of the world's great pharmaceutical research and development centers, hosting companies like Sandoz, Squibb, Merck & Co., Hoffmann-La Roche, Ciba-Geigy, Johnson & Johnson, and many more. The state also witnessed great discoveries in the laboratories of companies like AT&T, RCA, Exxon, Lockheed, IBM, and DuPont. And despite New York's dominance as a money market, New Jersey established itself as one of the country's top financial players with its huge banks and insurance companies like Prudential, whose mammoth investments are a major part of the nation's economy.

Today New Jersey is still growing in all these areas. Banking mergers have solidified its financial prowess, and new discoveries are being made in its research labs. On the high-tech front, a "Little Silicon Valley" running up Route 1 from Trenton to New Brunswick is an expanding force in the state's economic repertoire: In the north, Newark is being steadily revitalized, and companies continue to move to New Jersey from other states and nations.

The organizations described in this chapter are New Jersey's own, and they are New Jersey's best. They have lent their support to the creation of this important literary and civic work. Each of them has contributed to the bountiful prosperity and vigor that continues to characterize New Jersey today. New Jerseyans are justifiably proud of their achievements.

NEW JERSEY STATE CHAMBER OF COMMERCE

In 1911, responding to New Jersey's tremendous economic growth, five business leaders sought to create a cooperative organization among the state's many industries. The five—Arthur S. Corbin, P.J. Hover, William Lambert, Arthur Johnson, and George B. Corsa—soon enlisted some 350 charter members, including Thomas A. Edison. And so in 1911 the New Jersey State Chamber of Commerce was born.

Today the New Jersey State Chamber of Commerce is one of the state's most powerful and respected business organizations. Through its Governmental Affairs Office in Trenton, the chamber analyzes and speaks out on legislative and regulatory proposals that affect the business sector.

Throughout its history the chamber has made some stunning legislative progress. Its studies led to the establishment of the Garden State Parkway and the New Jersey State Police. And the chamber played a major role in getting legislation passed creating actuarially sound retirement systems for public employees, teachers, and police and firefighters. During the 1960s the organization was the key player in legislative moves that abolished the local business personal property tax,

and it wrote legislation setting standards for property assessment, property reevaluations, and certification of local property tax assessors. The chamber also authored the Administrative Procedures Act, which established for the first time standards and procedures for administrative law.

The chamber continues to remain committed to business and carries on its no-nonsense approach to government issues. Recently it has been involved in a campaign to reform or eliminate unnecessary and burdensome governmental regulations that cost businesses and consumers millions of dollars annually. And in recent years the organization took the lead in arduous negotiations with labor and government that resulted in substantial reforms of the worker's and unemployment compensation systems that provide improved benefits for workers at less cost to employers.

The organization also recently

The annual New Jersey Chamber of Commerce Congressional Reception and Dinner, held in Washington, D.C., attracts 1,800 business and government leaders and is regarded as New Jersey's premier business and government event.

successfully campaigned for reforms in the Civil Service System that will permit greater efficiency in state and local government. The chamber was largely responsible for the establishment of New Jersey's Department of Commerce and Economic Development.

A frequent newsletter produced by the chamber, *Executive Eye on Trenton*, alerts members to impending legislative and regulatory action, and the chamber's 24-hour hotline provides up-to-the-minute information. The chamber traditionally sponsors live televised gubernatorial and senatorial candidates' campaign debates. The organization's annual trip via special train to Washington for a reception and dinner honoring the New Jersey Congressional Delegation, which attracts 1,800 business and government leaders, is regarded as New Jersey's premier business and government event and the largest such state-oriented annual affair in the nation's capital.

In monitoring legislation and regulatory developments in issue areas of concern to business people, the chamber has the advice of numerous standing policy advisory committees, composed of representatives of member companies who are experts in particular professional and technical fields.

The chamber also supports many social and community efforts as well as working with New Jersey's educational sector, coordinating numerous programs to encourage broader understanding and appreciation of the free-enterprise system.

Perhaps former Governor Alfred E. Driscoll best summed up the chamber's 75 years of unparalleled service to New Jersey and its people when he stated, "Over the years, the New Jersey State Chamber of Commerce has been a strong force for good government, for a sound economy, and for the development and preservation of an environment in which citizens may enjoy their constitutional rights of life, liberty, and the pursuit of happiness."

COMED INC.

A Health Maintenance Organization (HMO) provides financing and delivery of medical care to its members for a prepaid fee. Unlike traditional health plans, which reimburse such expenses, HMO programs actually furnish the services.

HMOs trace their history back to 1929, when the Ross-Loos Clinic in Los Angeles, California, offered medical services for a fixed periodic fee. The national growth of HMOs is fairly recent, linked to a 1973 federal law subsidizing the development of Health Maintenance Organizations and requiring businesses to offer HMO plans to employees as an alternative to traditional insurance programs. In 1973 the New Jersey State Legislature passed its own HMO Act, similar to the federal legislation.

That same year Frank G. White of Dover General Hospital asked Robert G. Boyd of Morristown Memorial Hospital to study the formation of such a plan with the support of the Tri-County Administrators, an informal association of the 11 general hospitals in Morris, Sussex, and Warren counties. Boyd recommended the formation of an Individual Practice Association (IPA) HMO. Under this plan, physicians and other health professionals work from their own offices and hospitals to serve both private and HMO patients.

Warren Hospital and the three Sussex County hospitals withdrew from the project, but the seven remaining institutions agreed to Boyd's proposal. The new enterprise, legally named CoMED Inc. but known as CoMED HMO, was incorporated as a not-for-profit company in June 1974.

Office space and staff assistance for the new organization were provided by Morristown Memorial until July 1976, at which time CoMED HMO obtained offices in a local New Jersey Bell facility. From 1974 through 1978 CoMED HMO applied for and was awarded several federal grants and loans. CoMED HMO became officially operational in October 1978, after being granted a $2.4-million federal government long-term loan.

CoMED HMO had 200 physicians under contract, operating in a 700-square-mile area that includes

CoMED HMO's staff and facilities in Denville, New Jersey. The Health Maintenance Organization (HMO) is available to most of the state of New Jersey through its more than 2,000 participating physicians.

all of Morris County and parts of Passaic, Somerset, Sussex, and Warren counties. By the end of 1980 its service area was expanded to about 1,000 square miles, enrollment reached 10,000, and more than 500 physicians were under contract.

In 1982 the company reached the financial break-even point for the first time. The following year it showed a profit with enrollment of 14,000 members, a figure that increased to 20,500 a year later.

By 1985 New Jersey had 12 HMOs, and CoMED carried out an expansion plan to meet the competition. It moved first into Bergen, Essex, Mercer, Middlesex, and Union counties, and the remaining sections of Passaic, Hunterdon, Somerset, Sussex, and Warren counties. In the following months the organization extended into Burlington, Camden, and Gloucester counties, and parts of Atlantic, Cumberland, Monmouth, Ocean, and Salem counties. Plans call for expansion into most other parts of the state by the summer of 1987.

By January 1, 1987, CoMED HMO had approximately 2,000 participating physicians, membership had reached more than 50,000—and CoMED HMO was still growing.

DAVID T. HOUSTON COMPANY

Founded in 1845, the David T. Houston Company is one of the oldest industrial and commercial real estate houses serving the greater New Jersey area.

The David T. Houston Company has a history of service to almost every major corporation in the state. From its offices in Bloomfield and Piscataway, the firm serves a broad area extending as far south as Princeton and Red Bank and as far north as Orange and Rockland counties in southern New York State.

The enterprise was founded in Newark by Samuel Bond as E.E. Bond & Company, and it prospered as one of the nation's earliest commercial real estate firms. David Houston began working for the firm upon his arrival from Scotland in 1912, and he soon became president. The name of the company was later changed to Houston, Bond & Company.

In 1927 the firm became the David Houston Corporation. In 1941 David T. Houston, a civil engineer from M.I.T. with a law degree as well, succeeded his father as president. He had joined the firm in 1932. Both father and son were charter members of the Society of Industrial Realtors when it was founded in 1941.

Since World War II the Houston Company has been instrumental in many of the major transactions that dramatically changed New Jersey's economic and physical landscape, such as the sale of land establishing Hartz Mountain Industries' first 750-acre development, in the Secaucus Meadowlands, and the establishment of the 2,500-acre Raritan Center industrial park in Edison.

In 1978 David T. Houston, Jr., became president of the company, and he has since continued the firm's growth-oriented direction.

The David T. Houston Company today prides itself on its vast experience in every phase of industrial and commercial real estate and its intimate knowledge of its local markets and properties. Each year the firm

David T. Houston, Jr., president of the David T. Houston Company since 1978, has followed the family tradition of company leadership established by his immigrant grandfather in 1912.

sells millions of square feet of industrial facilities, sites, and office space.

The Houston Company's business approach is based on the concept of group action: Each person in the firm contributes his or her experience and ability toward achieving the best-possible solution for the client.

This allows the Houston Company to offer clients a professional grasp of the legal, financial, economic, and geographic considerations in every transaction. It also provides a professional ability to see the long-term and immediate views, and the inventiveness to create new and profitable solutions to problems.

This group approach has three times won the David T. Houston Company the recognition of the Society of Industrial Realtors—its industry peer group—for outstanding service to the profession.

GREAT BEAR SPRING COMPANY

Cool, clear spring water has been a treasured resource in America since Indians roamed the land.

The Onondaga Indians, who originated the tale of Hiawatha, lived in the Oswego River territory, now upstate New York. According to legend, Hiawatha's father once slew an enormous bear—the "Great Bear of the Mountains." To honor the feat, the tribe blessed a prized local spring with the name Great Bear.

From that same spring has grown another story: the story of a small, family-owned company that became a modern multiproduct concern. Since its founding in 1888 Great Bear Spring Company—headquartered in Teterboro, New Jersey—has blossomed into one of the largest bottled-water producers in the nation.

The original spring named for the Great Bear, located near Fulton, New York, was used by the town's early settlers. In 1888 Frederick Emerick and three associates formed a venture to develop the spring commercially.

Three generations of Emericks would head Great Bear Spring Company over the years: Frederick Emerick passed the firm to his son Stanley, who in turn passed it to his son Alan.

Initially the enterprise sold spring water to Fulton and nearby communities. Water was poured into finely crafted bottles at a small factory in Fulton, packed in wooden crates, and delivered to homes by horse-drawn carriage.

That system contrasts sharply to today's modern methods: Water is now transported to bottling facilities by truck in stainless steel tanks, and

The Great Bear of Indian legend, symbol of the Great Bear Spring Company, greets visitors to the firm's corporate headquarters in Great Bear Plaza, Teterboro.

extensive purification methods are employed.

In 1889 Great Bear Spring Company began the first of its many expansions, opening a plant in Syracuse, New York. Spring water was shipped by railroad car from the spring in Fulton to the new facility.

Further expansion came in 1902, at which time the company established bottling branches in Albany and Buffalo. However, its headquarters remained in a small house in Fulton.

Soon after the moves to Albany and Buffalo, Great Bear began bringing water down by train to sell

In 1888 Frederick Emerick and three associates formed a venture to develop Great Bear Spring (shown here) in Fulton, New York.

in New York City. Small branch offices and distribution centers were set up in the New York-New Jersey area to tap the new market.

In 1907 the firm opened bottling plants in Brooklyn and Jersey City, marking a major move into the metropolitan area market. The Brooklyn plant was built at a cost of $80,000, a large sum of money at that time. With the opening of the new plants, the organization moved its headquarters from Fulton to Manhattan in 1908.

In the late 1930s Great Bear purchased the Sasoonan Springs near Pottstown, Pennsylvania. This move enhanced its ability to supply water to markets in Philadelphia and southern New Jersey. The march toward expansion continued.

The corporation in 1927 closed its Brooklyn and Jersey City plants and relocated its main bottling, shipping, and distribution operations to Ridgefield Park, New Jersey, where it remained for nearly 50 years. In 1976, when the company needed room to expand, it finally moved its main operations and corporate headquarters to Teterboro, New Jersey.

Teterboro—with low real estate taxes, an airport, and location near major highways—proved to be an ideal spot for expansion. The new Teterboro facility is double the size of the firm's old Ridgefield Park plant.

The firm opened bottling plants in Brooklyn (shown here) and Jersey City in 1907, marking a major move into the metropolitan market.

The corporate headquarters houses the company's main bottling facility, the main distribution and delivery center for the New York metropolitan area, fleet maintenance facilities, quality-control center, and sales offices.

Great Bear's current activities stretch far from Teterboro. The organization has three other bottling plants located in Philadelphia, Windsor (Connecticut), and Rochester (New York). Eight distribution branches serve those plants, bringing products to Northeast Coast states

The Buffalo bottling plant prior to 1917.

from New England down through New York, New Jersey, Pennsylvania, Maryland, Washington, D.C., and Virginia.

The corporation has long since left the original Great Bear Spring in Fulton, but its Pottstown spring is still going strong. For the past five years Great Bear has also used a spring in Washingtonville, New York, in the foothills of the Catskill Mountains.

Close scrutiny is paid to the choosing of a spring: The company must make sure the water is pure and that no industries are near it. "There are not many we would purchase," says Great Bear's Richard Atkinson, alluding to the firm's strict quality standards.

Great Bear's water products include spring water, salt- and chemical-free water, and purified water. Those products come in the 5-

gallon water cooler bottle, the 2.5-gallon water bottle, the one-gallon water container, and the 5-gallon "Bag in a Box" Cooler Pak.

In the 1970s Great Bear diversified into coffee-allied products—including cream and sugar, soups, cookies and crackers, and fruit juices—known as the Total Office Refreshment Systems product line. Also during that decade Great Bear began leasing office refrigerators, bottle and fountain coolers, microwave ovens, and office coffee-brewers.

The Emerick family in June 1981 sold its controlling interest in Great Bear Spring Company to the Coca-Cola Bottling Company of Los Angeles, which was part of Northwest Industries at the time. In February 1982 the Coca-Cola Bottling Company of Los Angeles was acquired by Beatrice Foods, Inc., of Chicago.

Great Bear's future now looks as exciting as its past. The entire bottled-water industry is the fastest-growing beverage category in the United States. In fact, the $800-million-a-year industry has doubled its revenue in the past five years. The sector averaged an annual growth rate of 15 percent in 1984 and 1985, and the growth rate through the rest of the decade has been projected at 20 percent per year.

The company relocated its main bottling, shipping, and distribution operations to Ridgefield Park in 1927, where they remained for 50 years.

MARCAL PAPER MILLS, INC.

Marcal Paper Mills, Inc., headquartered in Elmwood Park, New Jersey, is a fully integrated manufacturer and marketer of consumer household paper products and institutional service paper products. While Marcal's primary sales territories for its consumer products continues to be in the eastern half of the United States, its service products division supplies the entire nation with a wide spectrum of quality products. Steps are currently under way to aggressively expand its premium consumer brands, sold mainly under the Marcal brand name, into new markets throughout the southern, central, and western regions.

As this family-owned and operated business continues to grow and prosper throughout the country, its roots and current commitment to the State of New Jersey are deeply entwined with a rich and colorful history in the state, dating back over a half-decade.

The company was actually founded in 1932 by Nicholas Marcalus, an inspired inventor and entrepreneur from Italy, who created Cut Rite Wax Paper in the early 1920s. After selling off his venture in 1930, he started a new business called the Marcalus Manufacturing Company in Bloomfield, New Jersey, where the firm produced its main product, Kitchen Charm Wax Paper, a product still manufactured by the company today. In 1939, after a series of moves, Marcalus finally located his production facilities in East Paterson, New Jersey (now Elmwood Park), where the company, now named Marcal Paper Mills, Inc., continues to be headquartered today.

Possessing a shrewd business mind

Nicholas Marcalus (left), founder of Marcal Paper Mills, Inc., and Robert L. Marcalus, Sr. (right), present chairman and chief executive officer, break ground for further expansion of Marcal's Elmwood Park plant.

and a powerful motivation to succeed, Marcalus led his company to prosperity even during the Great Depression years. One of the paper industry's greatest accomplishments, producing high-grade, quality paper products from recycled paper, was

introduced and perfected by Marcalus in these early years. Since his business was located within miles of New York City, he decided to tap the vast wealth of wastepaper that was generated daily by the city's business community for his new venture. While his trucks left the plant each day filled with finished Marcal products, they returned after each trip with a fresh supply of paper that could be treated and fed into his new papermaking machines for final fabrication into the finished product. By utilizing this process of making paper from paper and not from trees the company not only saved considerably on the cost of purchasing its raw materials but also helped to preserve our nation's forests from being harmed.

As the firm's papermaking capacity grew by erecting its own papermaking machines at Elmwood Park, additional papermaking capacity was added by purchasing satellite paper mills in New Jersey, Pennsylvania, Massachusetts, and Maine. Eventually, however, all satellite operations were phased out, and all paper and pulp manufacturing was and continues to be done solely from Marcal's Elmwood Park plant.

After World War II Nicholas Marcalus' son, Robert L. Marcalus, Sr., entered the business. Bringing with him fresh entrepreneurial spirit and energy, he introduced a more sophisticated manufacturing scenario and brought Marcal even further to

Active family members in Marcal Paper Mills, Inc., include (bottom row, left to right) Robert L. Marcalus, Sr., chairman and chief executive officer, and Robert R. Marcalus, executive vice-president. Pictured in the top row (from left) are Peter Marcalus, vice-president/ new market development; Michael Mazzarino, vice-president and treasurer; and Nicholas Marcalus, president and chief operating officer.

the forefront of modern, high-speed paper manufacturing. It was in the 1960s that the father-and-son team changed the company's name to Marcal Paper Mills, Inc., to help identify it more closely with its primary trademark, Marcal.

To further solidify Marcal Paper Mills, Inc., as a strong family business, two of Robert Sr.'s sons, Nicholas R. and Robert Jr., entered the company during the 1960s. They brought new ideas in production, packaging, marketing, and sales that were implemented to ensure that Marcal continued to supply its customers with the highest-quality contemporary paper products available.

Founder Nicholas Marcalus remained active in the firm until the mid-1970s. In the early 1980s Robert L. Marcalus, Sr., became the company's chairman and chief executive officer. At the same time Nicholas R. Marcalus became president and chief operating officer, and Robert R. Marcalus, Jr., was appointed executive vice-president. Peter Marcalus, the youngest son, joined the business in the sales department and today holds the title of vice-president/new market development. Also during this period Robert Sr.'s son-in-law

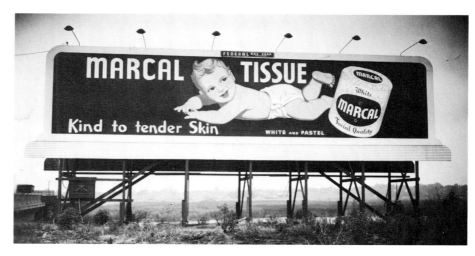

A touch of nostalgia can be seen in this vintage Marcal billboard that adorned New Jersey roadways in the 1950s.

Michael Mazzarino was appointed vice-president/finance. Today Marcal Paper Mills, Inc., remains a rarity in the paper industry in that it is still owned and managed by the founding family.

Presently at its main plant in Elmwood Park, Marcal, which employs more than 1,000 people, is a totally integrated facility, handling

Finished Marcal products roll off the line after the production process.

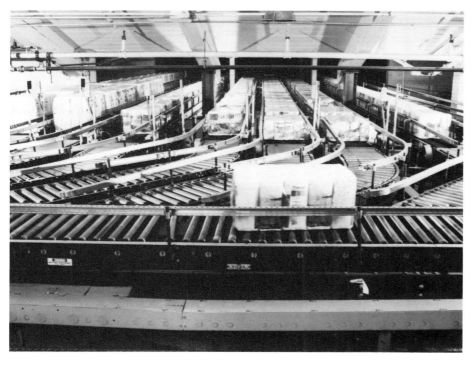

every production phase from the basic raw material to the packaged finished product. The facility's pulp mill produces high-grade pulp and makes paper on machines that turn out massive rolls of towel and tissue product. These jumbo rolls then proceed to converting or finishing operation, which produces a wide variety of products for an array of uses. The Marcal complex sits on more than 60 acres straddling both sides of Interstate 80. The facility has approximately 1.225 million square feet of space under roof for manufacturing, warehousing, and administration.

Marcal also operates three additional facilities located in Chicago, Illinois; Augusta, Georgia; and Springfield, Ohio. At these plants a wide range of paper products for both the institutional and consumer markets are produced.

The heart of Marcal's operations continues to be its Consumer Products Division, which offers a complete line of Marcal-brand household paper products, including facial tissue, bath tissue, napkins, and paper towels. Using modern and innovative procedures, the firm is able to offer consumers high-quality products at a cost far below those of most national brands. Each Marcal product is packaged with high-visual-impact packages, utilizing sophisticated, attention-getting graphics. The company prides itself on its demonstrated ability to create innovative packaging.

Marcal regularly advertises to

Marcal household paper products offer consumers the finest-quality products at reasonable prices. Each is packaged in high-visual-impact packages utilizing sophisticated, attention-getting graphics.

the consuming public with Nick Marcalus, the firm's president, having become a familiar face to millions of Americans by his appearance in Marcal's highly rated television commercials. In these commercials he advises viewers to "Marcalculate and Save." In addition, the company continually runs a heavy schedule of newspaper ads in which Marcal product coupons are circulated to give consumers further savings on Marcal products. A further dimension of Marcal's well-rounded marketing strategy is its regular advertising programs to the Hispanic community with advertising designed to reach this important segment of the consuming public. Finally, corporate and product public relations efforts are continually conducted.

In addition to the Marcal brand of consumer products, the company also enjoys a successful but much smaller private-label business that is sold to many leading retail chains.

Since adapting its product line to the needs of its customers has always been the main philosophy of Marcal, the firm has begun to market new and exciting paper-related products

in its product mix.

In 1985 Marcal purchased Augusta, Georgia-based Paper Products Incorporated and formed its M'Lady Household Products Division to market a complete line of shelf and drawer coverings. Today the division offers No-Bugs, treated with a safe, yet highly effective insecticide; Stick 'n Lift, with a semitack movable backing; Adheso, with a semipermanent adhesive finish; and White Bond, for shelf lining, book covers, and more. Sold in supermarkets, hardware, drug, and home improvement centers, the M'Lady line, which was previously available regionally, has

been launched by Marcal on a national basis.

In 1986 Marcal formed its Personal Care Division and introduced Whenever, a totally new line of feminine products. Consisting of thin maxi-pads and panty shields, each Whenever product is triple folded and neatly tucked into a pretty resealable pouch. This packaging innovation offers the utmost in confidentiality while providing the ultimate absorbant protection. Whenever products are being offered by Marcal on a national basis through supermarkets, drugstore chains, and independent retailers.

In recent years Marcal has made broad inroads into the service products and institutional sectors with a complete line of products for the food service, beauty and barber, dental, health care, and away-from-home industries. Today serving the away-from-home market with paper products is a rapidly expanding segment of the firm's sales. Marcal's Chicago facility manufactures a line of wax paper products for use in food

Marcal's president and chief operating officer, Nick Marcalus, also serves as the company's spokesman in television commercials that are shown regularly on major stations throughout its market areas.

Marcal's newest entry into the consumer marketplace is its line of Whenever feminine products including thin maxi-pads and panty shields.

service operations. In Springfield and Augusta, Marcal manufactures a complete selection of printed napkins and placemats for the food service industry.

Marcal Paper Mills, Inc., continues to display its heritage of being a good corporate citizen by supporting worthy causes as well as its surrounding communities. With more than 1,000 people employed by Marcal in New Jersey, the company also puts strong priority on doing business with local vendors, thereby contributing in a significant way to the economy of the state. Marcal is an active supporter of many important local civic and charitable causes. The firm is especially concerned about its hometown of Elmwood Park, and in many ways manifests its desire to be an outstanding corporate citizen.

On a broader national level, Marcal conducts an annual campaign called the Scenic America Plant-A-Tree program in which funds are raised through the redemption of Marcal coupons to help hundreds of communities enhance their environment through planting trees. Much of this funding has found its way back to cities and townships throughout New Jersey. In recent years the company has been honored by the National Arbor Day Foundation for its innovative and highly successful Plant-A-Tree program.

In the highly competitive paper industry, which requires unusually high capital expenditures, it is remarkable that a family-owned and -operated business such as Marcal Paper Mills, Inc., has continued to prosper for more than a half-

century. Today, under the continued leadership of the Marcalus family, Marcal Paper Mills, Inc., is moving rapidly to secure the future and to remain the strong, well-respected competitor within an industry that is increasingly dominated by publicly owned corporate giants.

The family's commitment to its heritage of innovation and its deep feeling of responsibility to the people within the company, the communities in which it operates, and its consumers are the main ingredients for Marcal's bright future as a major New Jersey-based corporation.

Marcal owns and operates its own fleet of modern tractor/trailers, which feature bold graphics for high visibility on America's highways.

THE CHILDREN'S PLACE INC.

The Children's Place made retail history from the moment it opened the doors of its first store.

The Children's Place was the brainchild of two Harvard Business School graduates, Clinton A. Clark and David Pulver, who knew they had a concept "as explosive as discounting," according to Clark. Using Clark's dining room as their first office, they developed their plans for a children's department store.

The first Children's Place store opened in February 1969 in West Hartford, Connecticut. The store was a visual delight, designed with its young customers in mind. Children used a small entrance door and tunnel leading into the store. Inside, the children came upon a play tower equipped with a slide and tunnels, as well as a small play kitchen, live gerbils, games, and cartoons—and not a "Do Not Touch" sign in sight.

Such fun and games kept the children entertained while their parents shopped in peace. (Clark and Pulver hired only personnel who were especially fond of children.) The store received rave reviews from parents and children, as well as from the local and national press.

The Children's Place was originally a department store for children, selling all varieties of children's clothing, toys, sports equipment, and shoes, plus nursery furniture and infant accessories like bottle warmers. The store also had a mothers' bookstore, a candy shop, and even a maternity shop. Later The Children's Place became a specialty apparel store, recognizing that it could not compete effectively in such a wide range of categories. Its owners decided to concentrate on a smaller area of interests and become the best in that area.

With the success of the West Hartford site, Clark and Pulver opened two stores in New Jersey: an 8,000-square-foot store in the Willowbrook Mall in Wayne, focusing on the greater New York/northern New Jersey market, and one of the same size in the Echelon Mall serving the Philadelphia/southern New Jersey market. The new stores posted weak sales in those locations and nearly bankrupted the fledgling company. Clark and Pulver went back to the drawing board.

The two principals released their experts and began doing all the buying, store design, and merchandise display themselves. By February 1973 they were ready to open a new store, in Livingston. They had halved the selling space to 4,200 square feet, and merchandise was now exclusively children's fashion sportswear and playwear. The Livingston store quickly became a phenomenal success.

The Children's Place opened another store, in East Brunswick, in October 1973. Next came the Paramus Park store in March 1974, and the company was posting sales per square foot that the partners never had dreamed possible. That year the first corporate headquarters was established in Pine Brook.

Later in 1974 a store was opened in Springfield, Pennsylvania, the first outside New Jersey except for the original West Hartford venture. In 1975 The Children's Place sold the West Hartford store.

In August 1975 two more New Jersey stores opened, in Monmouth and Deptford. The company scored yet another retail coup in October of that year by opening its first Children's Place outlet store in the Princeton Market Place. The outlet stores were an instant success for the company, featuring reduced-price fashions and manufacturers' irregulars. In 1976 came new stores, in Quakerbridge, Allentown, and Matawan, bringing the total to 12.

The Children's Place added five locations in 1977, and by the end of 1978 there were 25 stores, including a mall outlet in Philadelphia's Market East. In 1979 The Children's Place established nine more for a total of 34, including its first store in Michigan (Grand Rapids) and its first outlet in Chicago.

Ten new Children's Place stores

were added in 1980, among them its first in Texas (Sharpstown). Expansion continued at a remarkable pace in 1981 as 19 more stores opened, including the first two in Atlanta. By the end of 1981 The Children's Place had 63 stores and still was growing fast.

In 1982 The Children's Place was acquired by Federated Department Stores, Inc., of Cincinnati. Federated is a retail corporation operating more than 600 department stores, mass-merchandising stores, and other retail outlets across the United States. It is the parent company of Blooming-

dale's, Abraham & Strauss, Filene's, and many other major department stores. The Children's Place today operates as an autonomous division of Federated.

By the end of 1982 The Children's Place had 89 stores and had expanded its main warehouse to 180,000 square feet. By the close of the following year it had 114 stores throughout the nation. It continued to expand into new geographical locations and opened 44 more stores.

In January 1986 Peter M. Starrett became chairman and chief executive

The Children's Place Inc. operates 162 children's apparel stores in 27 states, all much like this one in a shopping mall in Fort Wayne, Indiana.

of the Children's Place division, and David S. Mooney was named president. They succeeded Children's Place founder Clinton A. Clark, who resigned in February 1986 as chairman and chief executive of the division. Clark's partner and co-founder, David Pulver, had left in 1983, following the acquisition by Federated.

Starrett formerly was senior vice-president and general merchandise

manager of Filene's, Federated's Boston-based retail chain, and was responsible for ready-to-wear accessories and shoes. Mooney had been executive vice-president, operations and stores, at Filene's. Before that he had been vice-president of stores for Filene's since 1978.

Today, under the leadership of Starrett and Mooney, The Children's Place Inc. operates 162 children's apparel stores in 27 states. It is the largest such store in the country, with sales reaching nearly $160 million in 1985.

INGERSOLL-RAND

In 1871 a Yankee farmer named Simon Ingersoll received a patent for a new rock drill. That drill became the cornerstone of Ingersoll-Rand, a company that grew into a multibillion-dollar corporation.

Ingersoll was an ardent inventor who patented a steam-driven wagon, a friction clutch, a gate latch, a spring scale, and many other devices; however, he was forced to sell most of his patents to support his family. He built his rock drill for John D. Minor, a New York City contractor who lamented that his machines managed only eight to 10 feet of hole per day and required three men to operate. Ingersoll's drill, mounted on a tripod, needed less manpower and was said to be considerably faster.

Pitted against New York's rocky streets, the front head of Ingersoll's new drill soon broke. He took it to the machine shop of Sergeant & Cullingworth, a partnership financed by Jose F. de Navarro. De Navarro was a legendary entrepreneur whose later ventures would include the

In 1871 a Yankee farmer named Simon Ingersoll, pictured here, received a patent for a new rock drill. That drill became the basis for Ingersoll-Rand, now a multibillion-dollar corporation.

building of New York City's first elevated rail system.

Henry Clark Sergeant examined Ingersoll's broken drill and separated the front head from the cylinder, maintaining they should be made as two pieces to resist breakage. He was right: All rock drills have been made that way ever since.

Sergeant soon persuaded de

Navarro to purchase Ingersoll's patent rights to the drill. De Navarro did so, and Simon Ingersoll's brief connection to the history of Ingersoll-Rand—a company that still bears his name—was ended. However, he continued inventing, his greatest subsequent innovation being a tripod for supporting heavy drills.

Again at Henry Sergeant's urging, de Navarro organized the Ingersoll Rock Drill Company in 1874, supplying $45,000 of the total $50,000 capital stock. When he sold his interest in 1885, he netted a return of $1,200 for each $100 of his original investment. Meanwhile, Sergeant became the firm's first president and set about improving the rock drill.

The early models were steam-powered, but it soon became clear that compressed air drills were superior and necessary when the devices were operated underground and long service lines were required. Sergeant began designing compressors, then in 1883 disposed of his New York interests and moved to Colorado—where he conceived an entire new valve for a rock drill. One year later he moved to Bridgeport, Connecticut, and formed the Sergeant Drill Company. There he manufactured his new invention: the auxiliary valve drill.

The Ingersoll and Sergeant firms soon merged to form the Ingersoll-Sergeant Drill Company, based in New York City, with Sergeant as its president. Expansion in the early 1890s led to construction of a factory in Easton, Pennsylvania. In 1902 a flood inundated the facility, and the organization sought higher ground in Phillipsburg, New Jersey, where most of its operations were transferred within two years.

Here an artist's rendering depicts an early rock drill, much like the one Simon Ingersoll invented. The drill was used for open-cut work, tunnel driving, and quarrying.

The standard machinery segment of Ingersoll-Rand provides the corporation's traditional equipment lines for construction, mining, refining, and other industries. Shown here are two Ingersoll-Rand standard machines, the pavement milling machine (left), and an air compressor (bottom left) used here for making snow.

At about the time Ingersoll's drill had appeared, Albert T. Rand of the New York-based Laflin & Rand Powder Company was seeking a new rock drill to make larger holes for his underground explosives. He asked one of his younger brothers, Addison, to develop a new drill. He did, and with his brothers, Albert and Jasper, informally organized a company that was to become Rand Drill Company, which focused on drills for the mining industry. (Ingersoll-Sergeant's area was open-cut work, tunnel driving, and quarrying.)

The enterprise developed the Little Giant tappet drill and the Rand Slugger drill, and in 1890 Rand built a plant in Tarrytown, New York. Eight years later it began making compressors at a plant in upstate Painted Post, New York. In the 1950s and 1960s that plant grew to become the world's largest individual compressor facility. Today the company's operations at Painted Post are part of the Dresser-Rand partnership described later.

Both Ingersoll-Sergeant and Rand grew steadily over the years. Because their product lines complemented each other so well, the two decided to merge to form Ingersoll-Rand in June 1905. Heir to 15 compressor designs and numerous drill patents, Ingersoll-Rand called itself "the largest builder of air power machinery in the world." The Rand branch worked out of its New York plant, while the Ingersoll branch continued production at Phillipsburg .

William Lawrence Saunders was the first president of Ingersoll-Rand, and in 1913 he became chairman of the board. A man of diverse interests, he once donned diving gear to inspect firsthand an underwater rock drilling and blasting project and then

designed a subaqueous drill rig to do the job.

In 1896 he founded *Compressed Air,* the company's industrial trade journal and oversaw the publication while handling his company responsibilities until his death in 1931. Saunders helped improve many Ingersoll-Rand products, and his inventions include the Radialaxe drill, operated by electric-air pulsator and widely used in coal mining.

Rock drills and air compressors were the foundation of the concerns that formed Ingersoll-Rand. For 30 years prior to the merger, the Rand and Ingersoll-Sergeant companies had concentrated on rock drills and compressors. After the merger came years of expansion and diversification.

Ingersoll-Rand makes such things as a wide range of pumps and waterjet cutting systems— like the one shown here, which cuts intricate shapes in glass or in other materials.

In the compressor field, the Rand-created Imperial Type 10 spawned a long line of modern machines, most of which carry an "X" in their symbols. By 1925 more than one million horsepower of the units had been sold. A new portable compressor line was introduced in 1933 and improved during the 1950s, when the first sliding-vane rotary portable unit revolutionized the compressor industry. Among heavy-duty compressors, Type HHE appeared in 1949. Today's HHE units range from 750 though 24,000 horsepower, and the largest are 30 feet long and weigh 455,100 pounds. A myriad of other compressors, large and small, were developed along the way, and some 80 percent of all Ingersoll-Rand compressors ever built are still running.

In the rock drill sector, both sides of the firm had already developed more than 70 different drills by 1892. Drill activity advanced with the 1912 acquisition of the J. George Leyner Engineering Works Company, which had commercialized a revolutionary hammer-type drill that afforded higher speed and smaller size and could be run by one man. In 1913 Ingersoll-Rand used this new technology to begin production of its famous line of jackhammers at Phillipsburg. The name soon became popular for all hand-held mechanical drills.

In 1947 the organization entered the "big drill" field with the Quarrymaster, used for quarrying, open-pit mining, excavation, and other work. The Drillmaster, a self-propelled drill jumbo, followed in 1953 and led to the introduction two years later of the Downhole drill. Acquisitions during the 1970s resulted in further expansion in equipment for blasthole, waterwell, and other types of drilling.

Ingersoll-Rand diversified into pneumatic tools in 1907 when it acquired the Imperial Pneumatic Tool Company of Athens, Pennsylvania. The plant became Ingersoll-Rand's pneumatic tool center, producing many new pneumatic, electric, and hydraulic tools over the years. The Automated Production Systems (APS) lines, widely used in auto making, was introduced there in 1952. During the 1960s and 1970s acquisitions increased the company's presence in the tools sector.

The company entered the industrial pump business in 1909 with the purchase of the A.S. Cameron Steam Pump Works of New York City. The operation was moved to Phillipsburg in 1912, and in 1913 centrifugal pumps—the workhorses in the field— were added. In 1961 the acquisition of the Aldrich Pump Company added reciprocating pumps, extending Ingersoll-Rand's capabilities for hard-to-handle fluids and slurries.

With the 1933 purchase of GE's centrifugal compressor business, Ingersoll-Rand took the lead in that sector. In 1948 it designed the first natural gas transmission centrifugal compressors, done for the Big Inch line of the Texas Eastern Transmission Corporation. Ingersoll-Rand's gas turbine/compressor packages, known as GT units, have been installed on gas lines in Europe and Mexico. Other Ingersoll-Rand centrifugal compressor products service the oil and gas and chemical processing industries.

From 1961 through 1980 the firm carried out nearly 40 acquisitions and mergers. Through those transactions it made entries into widely diversified areas. Of special importance were the 1968 acquisition of the Torrington Company, a major bearings manufacturer, and the 1975 acquisition of the Schlage Lock Company, maker of various locks, commercial and home security systems, and other door hardware. More recently, the 1985 acquisition of the Fafnir Bearing Division of Textron, Inc., made Ingersoll-Rand the largest broadline bearing maker in the United States. Fafnir is a leader in precision ball bearings for aerospace, machine tools, and other applications.

Today Ingersoll-Rand is organized into three worldwide business segments: standard machinery, engineered equipment, and bearings, locks, and tools. A glance at each segment illustrates the growth and diversification the company has undergone since its founding.

The standard machinery operation provides the corporation's traditional equipment lines for construction, mining, and other industries. It includes the construction equipment, air compressor, and mining machinery groups.

The engineered equipment division makes turbo compressors, gas engines, reciprocating process compressors, centrifugal compressors, turbines, and a wide range of pumps, pulp machinery, pellet mills, and water-jet cutting systems. On December 31, 1986, Ingersoll-Rand and Dresser Industries formed the Dresser-Rand Company, a 50/50 partnership comprising the worldwide reciprocating compressor and turbo-machinery businesses of the two companies.

The bearings, locks, and tools segment consists of the bearings and components group, the door hardware group, and the power tool and automated production systems divisions. Products include all types of bearings, automated assembly stations and lines, air-powered tools, and a wide variety of door hardware such as locks, electronic access systems, exit devices, home security systems, and other products.

Ingersoll-Rand now has 45 plants across the United States and is headquartered in Woodcliff Lake, New Jersey. The Phillipsburg plant is now dedicated to pump operations and

The bearings, locks, and tools segment consists of the bearings and components group, which manufactures such things as these large bearings (below) for heavy equipment; the door hardware group; and the power tool and automated production systems division. Included within this segment are Ingersoll-Rand's electronic access and security systems (right).

has approximately 1,500 employees. The organization has 30 international manufacturing operations, employing nearly 10,000 of its total work force of 30,000. More than one-third of its business comes from abroad, and the company serves some 125 different countries.

Were he alive today, Simon Ingersoll would doubtless be awed by such accomplishment, all of which started with his rock drill over a century ago.

FABER-CASTELL CORPORATION

The Faber name has been synonymous with pencils since 1761, when Kaspar Faber opened a small shop in Stein Bei Nuernberg, Germany. In 1784 Kaspar's son Anton Wilhelm Faber took over the business and gave the firm his own name: A.W. Faber.

The company ventured into the New World in 1843, opening an agency on Reade Street in lower Manhattan. The new American office sold A.W. Faber products in the United States.

The New York venture was the predecessor of Faber-Castell Corporation, presently headquartered in Parsippany, New Jersey. Today the German and American firms are separate entities.

The U.S. agency soon launched its own eraser-manufacturing operation. At the same time it increased its sales of quality drawing, drafting, and writing instruments imported from the German parent company. By 1894 A.W. Faber had moved into a large new factory and headquarters in Newark.

Back in Germany in 1898 a development occurred that would eventually give the company the name Faber-Castell. Count Alexander von Castell-Ruedenhausen married Baroness Ottilie Von Faber, the last family member carrying the Faber name. To keep the Faber name going, the newlyweds petitioned the

A.W. Faber's first United States establishment on Reade Street in New York City, circa 1847.

King of Bavaria to allow the Baroness' new husband, Count Alexander von Castell-Ruedenhausen, to change his name legally to Alexander von Faber Castell. The request was granted.

With the advent of World War I, the Alien Property Custodian of the

U.S. government assumed control of the German company's U.S. branch and held it from 1917 to 1919. In 1919 R.J. Metzler, a Newark industrialist, purchased the assets of A.W. Faber's U.S. branch, including its valuable trademarks, from the Alien Property Custodian. Metzler then incorporated the U.S. branch into A.W. Faber, Inc., a New Jersey corporation.

Metzler took an active role in managing A.W. Faber, Inc., until his death in 1929. In his will he left the firm to the Newark Welfare Federation.

Although the Newark Welfare Federation played a largely custodial role in the company's affairs, A.W. Faber continued to expand and improve its product line during the 1930s. Throughout the Depression A.W. Faber, Inc., remained profitable.

After World War II A.W. Faber, Inc., made a bit of history in Germany's postwar reconstruction. The firm placed "Export Order No. 1" with the German Faber-Castell Company, an order for $50,000 worth of lead refills. With this order, the German company was able to obtain raw materials to resume its manufacturing in the postwar years. The contract was negotiated with the help of the American Military Government and so became the first such order from an American to a German company after the war.

In 1947 A.W. Faber changed its name to A.W. Faber-Castell Pencil Company, Incorporated, finally adding "Castell" to the company name.

The Newark Welfare Federation sold its shares of the A.W. Faber-Castell Pencil Company in 1957 to the Wiedenmayer Group, headed by Gustave E. Wiedenmayer and comprising members of his family and other investors. At that time Gustave E. Wiedenmayer was chairman of the board of National Newark & Essex Bank, now Midlantic National Bank, in New Jersey.

Wiedenmayer had also been serving on the board of the Newark Wel-

The Faber-Castell Corporation eraser factory in Newark has been in operation since 1895.

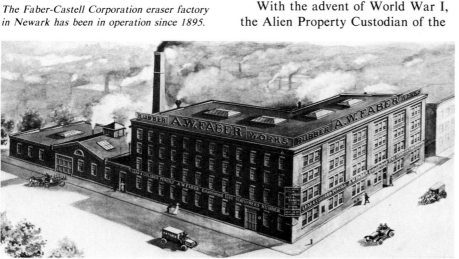

fare Federation and thus had a good knowledge of Faber-Castell's business activities. The Wiedenmayer Group controls Faber-Castell today.

In 1973 the A.W. Faber-Castell Pencil Company changed its name to Faber-Castell Corporation, its current name. The Faber-Castell product line includes numerous writing instruments and related products.

Also in 1973 the firm made a significant acquisition by purchasing Venus Esterbrook Company of Lewisburg, Tennessee. With this acquisition, Faber-Castell obtained substantial manufacturing facilities for pencils and other writing instruments. With its growing need for space, Faber-Castell moved most of its operations (customer service, accounting, data processing, and other departments) from Newark to the Lewisburg plant. The company continues to maintain its Newark plant for the manufacture of erasers and another product line, Higgins Draw-

ing Ink.

Faber-Castell's executive offices remained in Newark until 1984, when the firm moved to its more spacious, modern executive headquarters in Parsippany.

Faber-Castell has continued making important acquisitions to improve its standing in domestic and international markets. In 1969 the company acquired Carson Instruments of Toronto, which later became Faber-Castell Canada Ltd. In 1976 Faber-Castell acquired Venus Esterbrook Canada Ltd. and amalgamated that venture into Faber-Castell Canada Ltd. In 1977 the company purchased the Faber-Castell Canadian trademark rights from the German concern, an important move to aid the corporation's growth.

In 1985 a firm of Faber-Castell's

An aerial view of the Faber-Castell Corporation main plant located in Lewisburg, Tennessee.

acquired 100 percent ownership of Reliance Pen & Pencil Corp. of Lewisburg. This added substantial manufacturing space to the company's existing facilities in Lewisburg.

Faber-Castell has also formed a joint venture with the German company, a sales organization for Faber-Castell products in Hong Kong and China known as A.W. Faber-Castell Hong Kong Ltd.

Today's enterprise is vastly different than it was 30 years ago. Today Faber-Castell manufactures more than one-third of the United States consumption of pencils and is also one of the country's leading manufacturers of erasers, ball pens, and markers. Faber-Castell is both a manufacturer and importer of a wide variety of office products. In its association with partners in Europe, Asia, and South America, the Faber-Castell Group has sales in excess of $500 million in writing instruments and office products.

HIGH GRADE BEVERAGE

High Grade Beverage has grown by standing for exceptional service and superior quality through three generations.

Nicholas DeMarco and partner Harry "Butch" Levine combined forces in 1940 to operate a two-man sales operation and three delivery trucks in the heart of New Brunswick. Working out of a warehouse, they distributed Ruperts Knickerbocker Beer to taverns and retailers throughout Middlesex County and part of Somerset County.

In 1941 they became the only area distributor for Anheuser-Busch, a move that became the foundation of the company's tremendous growth in the following years. Their sales volume increased as they expanded their territory beyond Middlesex and Somerset counties to Hunterdon and Warren.

The founder's son, Joe DeMarco, became president and chief executive officer of the business in 1961; he continued High Grade's expansion by adding new businesses. In 1971 the company acquired Rutgers Distributors. As Staten Island's only Anheuser-Busch distributor, Rutgers has grown from a small operation to a distributorship requiring a 50,000-square-foot warehouse.

Although Anheuser-Busch is High Grade's main product line, the firm also distributes Heineken, Rolling Rock, Pabst, and Heileman Brewery beers as well as various wine coolers, spring water, and Eagle Snack products. In 1986 the company acquired Briars U.S.A. Birch Beer, a move that expanded its beverage-distribution business into beverage manufacturing. High Grade also operates Rutgers Empty Express, a recycling operation that uses computer scanning technology to sort and weigh recycled aluminum and glass.

An outgrowth of High Grade's distribution business was the establishing of its own interstate trucking firm, A&D Express. A&D started with three trucks and three trailers in 1951. Today the firm operates 30 trucks and 100 trailers to serve dis-

The South Brunswick headquarters of High Grade Beverage symbolizes the company's heritage—from the familiar Anheuser-Busch eagle on the wrought-iron gateway to the statue of the famous Budweiser Clydesdale named "Fantastic" standing at the entryway.

tributors and wholesalers throughout New Jersey, upstate New York, Delaware, and Pennsylvania.

In 1977 the company acquired a Volvo White Truck Sales and Service dealership in South Brunswick, and it added a Volvo White Truck business in Philadelphia in 1981.

A series of moves has paralleled the firm's continuing pattern of growth. After two expansions to larger facilities, High Grade's South Brunswick headquarters, established in 1976, had to be enlarged to keep pace with the company's tremendous growth. High Grade also operates a 100,000-square-foot distribution operation in Randolph, nearly identical to the South Brunswick facility.

The South Brunswick headquarters symbolizes the company's heritage, from the magnificent wrought-iron gateway leading to the beautifully landscaped grounds to the rich office interiors created by Elizabeth DeMarco to the warmth conveyed between the DeMarco family and their employees.

During the South Brunswick

grand opening, the firm held a dinner for employees, customers, and friends in the "Grand Ballroom." In actuality, the "Grand Ballroom" was a temporarily disconnected giant storage refrigerator that holds 7,000 kegs of beer. Although it is now used for the purpose for which it was originally intended, employees smile when they see the "Grand Ballroom" sign suspended over the refrigerator's mammoth entrance and fondly remember that evening.

The DeMarcos believe quality control and excellent service are the essentials of customer satisfaction. High Grade's computerized refrigeration system adjusts in accordance with outside temperatures to assure a proper storage environment for kegs and packaged beers. For improved climate control, the company converted to using electric forklifts that generated less heat than the conventional propane-operated type. A computerized energy-management system is employed in all of High Grade's operations. The firm designed its warehouses with a large main aisle to stage loads so incoming trucks can pick up and get on the road to customers as quickly and efficiently as possible.

High Grade's commitment to quality and professionalism is evident in its award-winning distributor

High Grade's South Brunswick headquarters was established in 1976 and has had to be enlarged since then to keep pace with the firm's tremendous growth. Joe DeMarco, current president and chief executive officer of High Grade and son of company founder Nicholas DeMarco, has helped High Grade grow and diversify while still maintaining its "first-class image." The richly landscaped grounds, complete with a man-made lake named after Joe DeMarco's wife, Elizabeth, attest to High Grade's standards of excellence and commitment to a first-class operation.

management. After winning Silver Awards for outstanding performance from Anheuser-Busch in 1981, 1982, and 1983, the Golden Ambassador Award was earned in 1984, the highest level achievable in this nationwide competition. Evaluating sales volume, inventory, management, and housekeeping, these awards recognize the achievement of meeting and exceeding the high standards expected of Anheuser-Busch Wholesalerships.

High Grade is also committed to serving the community. Joe DeMarco is a Knight of Malta and an active member of the Diocese of Metuchen. DeMarco led local efforts for the Italian-American Relief fund-raising drive to help Italian citizens affected by the country's devastating earthquake in 1983. The company also sponsors annual races at Rutgers University and is actively involved with student groups in the areas of alcohol-abuse awareness and anti-litter campaigns.

DeMarco is a dedicated man who arrives at work at 6 a.m. daily and is frequently the last to leave. After joining High Grade as a sales manager in 1956, he assumed control of the company within five years. Under DeMarco's leadership, sales have accelerated from one million to the current 10 million cases of beer annually handled by a sales force of more than 50 people and delivered to retailers by a fleet of 200-plus trucks. The company's long-term strategy of acquiring new businesses enabled him to build on the strong foundation established by his father.

High Grade Beverage is very much a family business. Hardwork-

ing and close-knit, DeMarco family members have run the firm throughout its many years. A number of employees have been with High Grade long enough to know three generations of the DeMarco family.

According to Joe DeMarco, "We're proud to be a part of the community and to project a first-class image in our service, our product, and, especially, our home. That's what High Grade is all about."

423

NABISCO BRANDS, INC.

With 240 manufacturing plants in 37 countries and annual sales of some $10 billion, Nabisco Brands is one of the largest food companies in the world.

Oreo cookies, Ritz crackers, and Planters nuts are just some of the Nabisco Brands products that are household words. Others include Shredded Wheat cereals, Life Savers candies, the Baby Ruth candy bar, Fleischmann's margarines, and Royal desserts.

Nabisco Brands, Inc., was formed through the 1981 merger of Nabisco, Inc., and Standard Brands Incorporated. Four years later it became an operating company of R.J. Reynolds Industries, Inc., now known as RJR Nabisco. That, however, is only the latest chapter in the company's storied past. Throughout America's history, a host of inventive minds have worked to develop products offered by Nabisco Brands.

During the 1890s America's bakeries were consolidating in an effort to adopt industry standards and end the problem of food contamination. Some 40 midwestern bakeries merged to become the American Biscuit & Manufacturing Company. Eight eastern bakeries formed the New York Biscuit Company, and the smaller United States Baking Company was also founded through a merger.

In 1898 those three organizations merged, and the National Biscuit Company, later to be known as Nabisco, was born.

Included in the enterprises that constituted the new Nabisco Biscuit Company were America's oldest commercial bakery, founded in Massachusetts in 1792 by John Pearson, and another Massachusetts bakery begun in 1801 by Josiah Bent, who invented a crisp, light biscuit named the "cracker."

However, the National Biscuit Company quickly looked to its future, not to its past. Led by its first chairman, Adolphus Green, it began developing products that would become famous: the Uneeda biscuit, Oreo cookies, Ritz crackers, Lorna Doones, and many others. Old-line products like Premium Saltines and Animal Crackers were marketed with renewed energy.

Standard Brands was established in 1929 through the merger of three successful food products organizations: Royal Baking Powder Company, Fleischmann Company, and Chase & Sanborn. Although born on

The Nabisco Brands, Inc., corporate headquarters in East Hanover.

the brink of the Great Depression, by 1934 Standard Brands was marketing over 100 different products and grossing more than $100 million annually, a strong showing despite enormous economic adversity. The firm's Fleischmann Division, deprived of its market for gin by Prohibition, concentrated on baker's yeast cakes; by 1937 that product was bringing in almost $20 million annually, tops among Standard Brands products.

Meanwhile, new companies and products had been created that would eventually become part of the Nabisco Brands family. Shredded Wheat had been invented in Watertown, New York, in 1892, and Cream of Wheat emerged from Grands Forks, North Dakota, just after that. Canada Dry ginger ale was being marketed by a young Irishman in Toronto by 1904, and the Planters Nut & Chocolate Co. was founded in 1906 by two Italian immigrants in Wilkes-Barre, Pennsylvania. Life Savers candies were invented in Cleveland, Ohio, in 1912.

In the 1930s both Standard Brands and the National Biscuit Company expanded internationally. By 1947 Standard Brands International had been formed, eventually expanding into more than 100 countries. The

printed customer invoices. Four models of the LCR were to sell nearly 35,000 units from its introduction through 1979.

In the early 1960s LEC began making tape recorders capable of operating unattended for long periods under extreme environmental conditions. They have since been used for missile and underwater vehicle testing, and for spacecraft. LEC tape recorders have been traveling into space since 1964, aboard earth-orbiting satellites, the space shuttle, and deep-space missions to Mercury, Venus, Mars, Jupiter, Saturn, and Uranus.

Later in the decade the firm developed what would be its largest product line: the Mk 86, the Navy's first digital fire-control system, which includes surface and air radars and a digital computer. Since production began in 1970 the company has received Navy orders for 80 Mk 86s. The system is used on guided missile cruisers, destroyers, and other surface combat ships.

In 1971 LEC entered the air traffic control sector with its ARTS-2 (Automated Radar Terminal System), which handles 250 aircraft at once and has a variety of features. During that period LEC also developed RADRU (Rapid Access Data Retrieval Unit), for telephone-system data storage and retrieval. Between 1973 and 1975 the firm was awarded contracts to supply 2,500 RADRU systems to three Bell System telephone companies.

LEC diversified into ordnance products in 1977 when it won an Army competition to produce the M732 solid-state artillery fuze. The company established its Denville Division in Denville, New Jersey, to work on the project. Subsequently, more than three million M732s were

Lockheed Electronics Company is a leader in circular-phased array antenna technology. Its AIMS IFF antenna system, which steers the radar beam electronically, is now in production for use on some of the Navy's newest ships.

An engineering drafting specialist uses a computer-assisted design and manufacturing terminal to draft plans for a subsystem for an advanced radar antenna at Lockheed Electronics Company, Watchung.

produced at the high-tech, state-of-the-art factory.

Further innovations in the late 1970s included the perfection of the circular phased-array antenna, which steers signal beams electronically—making for faster scanning and giving 360-degree coverage. The AIMS IFF (Identification Friend or Foe) system, which LEC began producing for the Navy in 1981, was the first to

An engineer uses a magnifying glass to examine a microcircuit assembled by the company as part of a research and development program.

use the new technology later widely applied by the company in other military projects.

Lockheed Electronics Company, Inc., has carried out many electronics and computer projects throughout its history. For the future it is looking to new areas of technology, such as electronic warfare, communication, and intelligence systems—all the while continuing in the areas it has developed since 1945.

MANNINGTON MILLS, INC.

Mannington Mills is a leading manufacturer of diversified floorcovering products. Recognized in the floorcovering industry for its styling and technological leadership, this growing organization is among the top 500 privately held firms in the United States. Yet it retains an intimate family atmosphere, deeply rooted in a tradition of long-term employee and customer relationships, and a commitment to product quality and innovation.

In 1913 John B. Campbell, a native of Scotland, started working for the old Salem Linoleum Works in Salem, New Jersey. Two years later he acquired control of the operation and renamed it the J.B. Campbell Manufacturing Company, producer of felt-based printed rugs. The business prospered and moved to a plant across town in 1922, but the facilities were destroyed by fire the very next year. Undaunted, Campbell built a new plant at Mannington Mills' present site in Mannington Township, near Salem City, and took its present name in 1927. Meanwhile, Campbell's two sons, Neil and Kenneth, had joined him in the business; both would later head the company.

The next several years marked a period of exciting growth and discovery in the floorcovering industry. Mannington's Rubbertex, a felt-based rug with an adhesive-tape border, met with great success in the marketplace. Elsewhere in the industry, linoleum and inlaid products were being developed during the 1920s and 1930s.

The plant had to be rebuilt in 1931 due to yet another fire, but Mannington Mills forged ahead. In 1939 the company unveiled a major new manufacturing technique: The "kiss" method of producing Thriftex rugs. Through this procedure, a sheet of felt-based rug, printed with enameled paint, was pressed against an unprinted sheet, "kissing" it to leave an impression. This resulted in two sheets instead of one, doubling production and halving overhead costs.

By 1950 Mannington's headquar-

John B. Campbell, founder of the J.B. Campbell Manufacturing Co., which was renamed Mannington Mills, Inc., in 1927.

ters employed 325 people housed in 28 buildings on 15 acres. Seven years later, with John B. Campbell II—grandson of the founder—as president, Mannington took a major technological step forward by building a 12-foot-wide rotogravure vinyling and printing complex—one of the first such plants in the world. At the 1958 Chicago Trade Market, Mannington surprised the industry with a new product: 12-foot-wide rotogravure Vinyltex. The next decade witnessed the development of vinyl with a foam inner layer, firmly establishing Mannington as a manufacturer of 12-foot rotogravure sheet vinyl floors. Vinyl had come of age, and in 1962 the firm entered the market with its Vinyl One product.

The 1960s brought major expansion for Mannington, with the acquisition of Wellco Carpet Corporation of Calhoun, Georgia, in 1968. As a Mannington subsidiary, Wellco experienced exceptional growth in the production and sale of commercial carpet. Today it is one of the country's leading manufacturers of high-

styled business carpet.

In 1973, under the leadership of president H. Arthur Williams, new facilities were built at the Salem plant to double production capacity. Mannington also expanded its sales and distribution networks across the nation and, later, the world. Advertising efforts were greatly increased to include television commercials and full-color magazine ads. Today Mannington's multimillion-dollar advertising program features celebrity spokesman Ed McMahon in an extensive national network TV and radio campaign.

In the mid-1960s, continuing its commitment to product innovation, Mannington introduced the cushioned inner layer and registered embossing, which gave rotogravure vinyls remarkable realism and depth. In 1974 a revolutionary wear layer, called JT88 Never-Wax, created a performance benefit unique to the entire industry: It was the only wear layer on the market that didn't require waxing or stripping. The JT88 product line's success has been outstanding. It remains the industry standard, and has brought Mannington unparalleled growth.

With an eye toward further penetration of the floorcovering market, Mannington acquired Mid-State Tile Co., producer of ceramic tile, with plants in Lexington and Mt. Gilead, North Carolina, in 1984. Buttressed

Mannington Mills' 75,000-square-foot corporate headquarters building was completed in 1978 and expanded in 1986. In addition to housing more than 100 employees, it is a showplace for Mannington products, which are used extensively in the interior design of the building.

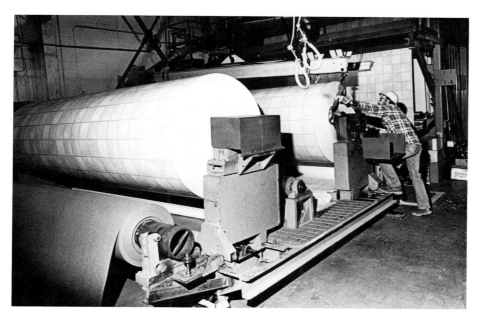

Mannington's sheet vinyl manufacturing operations in Salem include an extensive 12-foot rotogravure print complex. Here a print crew employee oversees the unwinding of a printed roll ready to receive a vinyl wear layer.

by the Mannington "muscle," Mid-State dramatically expanded its production and distribution of ceramic tile; in 1984 alone, it added 35 colors to its line.

Two years later Mannington Mills entered yet another area of flooring—hardwood plank—with the acquisition of a wood veneer producer, Linwood Manufacturing Co., Linwood, North Carolina. A new operation, Mannington Wood Floors, was developed within Linwood, and its production facilities expanded to a large plant in High Point, North Carolina. This fledgling operation is expected to become a major player in the wood industry.

Today Mannington Mills, Inc., has been restructured as the parent corporation for four floorcovering subsidiaries: Mannington Resilient Floors (Salem, New Jersey), Wellco Business Carpet (Georgia), Mid-State Tile (North Carolina), and Mannington Wood Floors (North Carolina). Mannington stands as the only producer in this country, and probably in the world, of all four major flooring products: sheet vinyl, ce-

ramic tile, carpet, and wood.

Mannington Mills' modern corporate headquarters building, completed in 1978, is testimony to the company's progress and success. Today the entire Mannington Resilient Floors complex in Salem covers 328 acres, 31 of which are occupied by 60 buildings, including a large em-

A training/hospitality center for visiting retailers and distributors of Mannington products, completed in 1986, includes a 2,270-square-foot atrium, which contains the various product displays for the Mannington floorcovering companies.

ployee cafeteria/dining room. In 1984 the H. Arthur Williams Fitness Center—named in honor of president Williams—was completed on site for the exclusive, free use of all employees, retirees, and spouses. In 1986 a wing was added to the corporate office building as a training/hospitality center for visiting distributors and retailers of Mannington products. It houses a large, airy showroom for all Mannington product displays; a 150-seat auditorium, with state-of-the-art audiovisual equipment; and formal dining areas for guests.

Johnny Campbell, who is retired from the daily administrative responsibilities of the company but remains chairman of the board, represents the third generation of Campbells in the business. Such continuity is noteworthy: Only two out of every 10 family businesses make it to their second generation; fewer than two out of 100 reach the third generation; and fewer than one out of 1,000 reach the fourth. Mannington is in its fourth generation today, with Campbell's son, Keith, as executive vice-president of Mannington Resilient Floors. The company looks forward to the fifth generation, as Johnny Campbell's grandchildren wait in the wings.

ATLANTIC ELECTRIC

On April 23, 1886, the five founders of the Electric Light Company of Atlantic City celebrated their incorporation. Eight days earlier in Bridgeton, the partners in the Bridgeton Electric Light Company had toasted their firm's founding.

The new companies faced a hard road ahead. Thomas Edison's incandescent lamp was only seven years old. His Pearl Street Station in New York, opened in 1882, still had not convinced a skeptical world. Most people thought gaslight was just fine.

The Electric Light Company of Atlantic City and the Bridgeton Electric Light Company are gone today, but they spawned an important descendant: the Atlantic City Electric Company, known as Atlantic Electric.

Atlantic Electric has been an independent power company since 1948, when it left the American Gas & Electric Company, now American Electric Power Company. Today Atlantic Electric serves a population of 1.1 million and covers 2,700 square miles, representing the southern third of the state of New Jersey.

In 1886 the founders of the Electric Light Company of Atlantic City

Atlantic Electric's Deepwater Generating Station has welcomed visitors to New Jersey since 1930. Situated at the base of the Delaware Memorial Bridge, it is one of the nation's first cogeneration facilities. Today it is one of the few plants in the nation that can burn coal, natural gas, or oil to generate electricity.

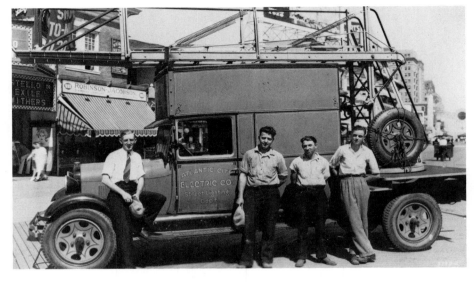

Keeping the Boardwalk of the World's Playground illuminated was a round-the-clock job for Atlantic Electric's street lighting department. Before the addition of this "modern" equipment, the men walked the entire length of the wooden way, turning each light on at dusk and off at daybreak.

(Jonas Hagan, Jonas Higbee, Thomas McGuire, George F. Currie, and Charles Lacy) built a plant on Tucker's Alley, near the corner of Baltic and Kentucky avenues in Atlantic City. The first incandescent lamplight graced the city on July 15, 1886, while many still wondered why such foolishness was needed.

By 1887, out west in Bridgeton, the Bridgeton Electric Light Company was powering a few stores and even fewer homes. In 1890 the Electric Railways Company acquired the

utility to run its streetcars. Trolley lines soon stretched to nearby Dividing Creek, bringing power to rural areas of Cumberland County. Slowly but surely, everyone began wanting electricity, and new local plants sprang up across southern New Jersey.

In Atlantic City also, the competition grew. From 1891 to 1905 three new utilities were started: the Atlantic Electric Light and Power Company, the New Jersey Hot Water Heating Company, and the Atlantic City Suburban Electric Company.

Such competition made consolidation inevitable, and in 1907 those competitors—along with the Electric Light Company of Atlantic City—merged as the Atlantic City Electric Company. The new operation was owned by the American Gas & Electric Company of Philadelphia and New York.

In 1911 Atlantic City Electric Company built a plant complete with all the latest generating technology, at Missouri Avenue in Atlantic City. In the next 16 years the utility would acquire seven new power companies, encompassing a broad area of southern New Jersey.

In those early years horse-and-wagon crews made installations and repairs. There were fights with gas companies over converting customers from gas flame, and electricity had to be sold aggressively. Company

Atlantic Electric has a long history of supporting 4-H fairs in the southern eight counties of New Jersey. In 1958 the latest in electrical appliances attracted consumers of all ages, and encouraged them to "live better electrically."

rules warned salesmen not to dress "too smooth" and not to smoke 10-cent cigars, "lest the prospect think the company is making money out of the electric game."

By 1919 a series of mergers in Cumberland and Salem counties had united the Bridgeton Electric Light Company and other, smaller utilities as the Electric Company of New Jersey.

In 1927 came a major step forward: the Atlantic City Electric Company and the Electric Company of New Jersey were merged. The combined companies stretched from the Atlantic Ocean to the Delaware River, from parts of Burlington and Ocean counties to Cape May; further acquisitions through 1930 increased that range.

The new, expansive Atlantic City Electric Company had come a long way. With the completion of a $13-million cogeneration plant next to the Du Pont Chambers Works in Deepwater, the company's generating capacity reached 57,000 kilowatts by 1930—a 780-percent increase in just 21 years.

The company kept expanding, even during the Depression; capacity hit 120,000 kilowatts in 1940. By World War II industrial sales comprised half of all electricity sold, and domestic use soared as home appliances became more common.

The firm's growth had set the stage for its next major event. Bound by the Holding Company Act, the American Gas & Electric Company in 1948 made the Atlantic City Electric Company an independent utility.

New growth came in the postwar years as industry swelled across southern New Jersey. The company aggressively sold to businesses and championed the construction of the Delaware Memorial Bridge,

the Atlantic City Expressway, and the southern reaches of the New Jersey Turnpike and Garden State Parkway.

In 1950 the Atlantic City Electric Company was listed on the New York Stock Exchange. Its power lines embraced 2,700 square miles of southern New Jersey, and the company had 121,371 users, nearly double the number in 1930. More than 200 new industries had come into the area over those years. Two new generators at Deepwater brought total capacity to 411,000 kilowatts by 1958. More power systems were added in later years, and kilowatt sales approached two billion by 1960.

Through the 1970s and 1980s Atlantic Electric has striven to stabilize its energy costs with new strategies for using the most economical fuels and power supply. In 1984 the utility set an all-time record for coal and nuclear generation, with those low-cost fuel sources providing 82 percent of total system requirements. Those cost-saving efforts continue, as Atlantic Electric works hard to power the industries and homes of southern New Jersey.

With its state-of-the-art energy management system, Atlantic Electric's systems operations department tracks the transmission and delivery of power across the company's service territory, covering 2,700 square miles in the southern one-third of New Jersey.

BENJAMIN MOORE & CO.

Benjamin Moore began his paint business in 1883 in a small building in Brooklyn. Helped by his older brother, Robert, he started with capital of only $2,000. The business started making a product called Calsom Finish, a coating for walls and ceilings. The venture posted a profit in its first year, a standard that has been met in every year since then.

In 1889 a New York corporation was formed, and shortly thereafter the present New Jersey corporation was organized with starting capital of $90,000.

In those fledgling years Benjamin Moore made a line of pure oil colors for tinting oil paints. In 1892 he completed work on a method for mixing Irish moss, a fungus growth from the sea, with finely ground clay and other substances. That product was named Muresco, a wall and ceiling finish unique at the time.

Muresco became tremendously popular, primarily because it was sold prepackaged in a full line of colors. Prior to this prepackaging method the painter had to mix his ingredients as best he could. Muresco became so successful that the name became a household word and found its way into *Webster's Collegiate Dictionary*.

Bolstered by strong sales of Muresco and other products, Benjamin Moore & Co. began expanding across the country in 1897. Over the next 10 years the firm established a subsidiary in Chicago; built a plant in Carteret, New Jersey; purchased a paint factory in Cleveland, Ohio; and started business operations in Canada.

Throughout history, paint making had always been an art rather than a science; not until the early twentieth century was science applied to paint formulation. Benjamin Moore & Co. was a pioneer in this new field of coatings science. Its first chemist, Clarence Bryce, was hired in 1904.

The company then was producing a number of new varnishes and a new interior wall paint, Sani-Flat. Sani-Flat was a decorative flat finish able to withstand frequent washings.

Prior to Sani-Flat most interior paints were made from white lead ground in linseed oil. Such paint was durable, but it contained large quantities of lead, whose dangers were recognized even then. The nonlead Sani-Flat also proved to be better than lead paints in terms of application.

Benjamin Moore died in 1917 and was succeeded by his nephew, Livingston P. Moore, who would serve as chairman and president until 1942.

Expanding its product line, Benjamin Moore & Co. had outgrown its Brooklyn plant by 1925 and had built a new factory in Newark, New Jersey. The firm's executives and sales force moved to new offices on Canal Street in New York City.

Many new products were developed during the Depression, such as Moorwhite Primer, used for exteriors, and Impervo Enamel, used for both interiors and exteriors. In 1936 the corporation expanded its operations again, acquiring the Minehart-Traylor Co. of Denver, Colorado.

Chairman Livingston P. Moore died in 1942, leaving a record of

---

Starting his paint business in Brooklyn, New York, in 1883 with capital of only $2,000, Benjamin Moore incorporated in New Jersey in 1889 with capital of $90,000 and a then-new, innovative product, Muresco—a prepackaged wall and ceiling finish that was made mainly from Irish moss and finely ground clay.

achievement. Emphasizing customer service, he had bolstered the sales program by vigorously helping distributors and retailers sell company goods. The firm's product line and its operations were expanded during his tenure, as well.

Harry A. Bonyun succeeded L.P. Moore as chairman and president. Three years later, when Bonyun died, George W. Jenkin was chosen to lead the company.

In 1952 Benjamin Moore Belcher, grandson of Benjamin Moore, became company president. Three years later he succeeded Jenkin as chairman of the board.

During the postwar period synthetic resins—particularly those that were latex based—came into their own. That development brought big changes as latex products inaugurated the do-it-yourself era. Benjamin Moore & Co. also developed expertise in industrial coatings for vehicles, appliances, cans, furniture, tools, machinery, and other products.

In the early 1960s came the purchase of industrial-coatings firms Thompson & Co. and Technical Coatings Co., expanding activity in that area. In 1967 the firm's industrial-coatings operations were reorganized under the name Technical Coatings Co.

Meanwhile, a huge demand necessitated another expansion. Between 1953 and 1966 new plants were established in Los Angeles, Jacksonville, Houston, Montreal, Quebec,

With the advent of latex-based paint products, Benjamin Moore & Co. applied their expertise to industrial coatings and expanded nation-wide. Today there are 20 Benjamin Moore & Co. factories across the United States and Canada, offering a wide variety of coatings products.

Vancouver, Pittsburgh, Boston, and Richmond.

In 1970 Belcher relinquished the company presidency to Maurice C. Workman, who had served as vice-president/finance and treasurer and is the current president.

The corporation moved its head-quarters from New York City to a modern facility in Montvale, New Jersey, in 1972. Today there are 20 Benjamin Moore & Co. factories across the United States and Canada.

In 1984, his 50th year with the company, Belcher resigned as chair-man. He was succeeded by Richard

The Chestnut Ridge Road headquarters of Benjamin Moore & Co. in Montvale, New Jersey.

Roob, former secretary and vice-chairman of the firm.

Benjamin Moore & Co. today is one of the largest of the nation's 1,200 paint manufacturers, offering a wide variety of coatings products. Its story is one of an organization that has sought international recognition, not as a widely diversified conglomerate but as a specialist maker of quality coatings. As the record shows, the company has realized its goal.

BLUE CROSS AND BLUE SHIELD OF NEW JERSEY

Blue Cross of New Jersey was the first of what became the nationwide network of Blue Cross plans. It was founded in 1932 and became operational the following year during the depths of the Depression, when health care was almost a luxury and health insurance was virtually unknown.

At that time a council of Newark-area hospitals was formed to coordinate health care "in ways which would be beneficial to patients and hospitals alike." Basing its concept on a prepayment plan used for teachers in Dallas, Texas, the council founded the Associated Hospitals of Essex County, forerunner of New Jersey Blue Cross.

The group offered prepayment coverage at the subscription rate of $10 per year, about three cents per day, and began taking subscribers in January 1933. More than 5,000 people enrolled in that first year.

The prepaid approach to health care had been used before at single hospitals, but the New Jersey Plan was the first to try it on a multihospital basis. The Plan offered subscribers a choice among the 17 participating hospitals in Essex County. The program came at a time when many hospitals were near bankruptcy. People were postponing needed care, going without it, or receiving it without being able to pay.

The Associated Hospitals of Essex County was reorganized into the Hospital Service Plan—Blue Cross of New Jersey—in 1933. The first office of Blue Cross was in Newark, in the National Newark & Essex Bank Building.

The Blue Cross Plan was the first to offer assured payment for services. In addition to giving financial stability to the voluntary hospital system, it provided a form of financial security for patients.

During the 1940s Blue Cross of New Jersey membership more than quadrupled from its initial levels. In 1947 the Plan reached a milestone with the enrollment of its one-millionth subscriber.

The Blue Cross and Blue Shield corporate office located in Newark.

The Medical-Surgical Plan of New Jersey—the Blue Shield Plan—was founded by The Medical Society of New Jersey in 1942 to offer quality health care to everyone at the lowest possible cost. The Blue Cross and Blue Shield plans merged in 1985.

In order to centralize operations and improve service, the New Jersey Blue Cross and Blue Shield headquarters building was erected in Newark in 1970. Many Plan employees and operations are housed in this modern 18-story structure, in the heart of Newark's business district and the historic James Street Commons restoration area, while others occupy space in seven buildings in the suburban office mall in Florheim Park.

Blue Cross and Blue Shield of New Jersey has been developing innovative systems of health care delivery and financing for many years. In 1973 it introduced the first Health Maintenance Organization (HMO) in New Jersey. The Medigroup

The Commercial Division of Blue Cross and Blue Shield at 12 Vreeland Road, Florham Park.

HMO program made its debut at Mercer Regional Medical Group in Trenton, offering a system of health care aimed at the prevention as well as the treatment of illness and disease.

Today "I have Blue Cross" has become a household phrase throughout America, and the Blue Cross and Blue Shield ID card is accepted in many foreign hospitals as well.

The New Jersey Blue Cross and Blue Shield Plan is a recognized leader in the health insurance field, providing health care service protection to more than 4.5 million New Jerseyans. It is the second-largest Plan in the national Blue Cross and Blue Shield network, which insures more than 85 million Americans.

Today the Plan's hospital claims-processing system is considered the best of its kind in the nation. Claims are processed within 24 hours by direct computer linkup with hospitals. Cost savings and cash flow realized by hospitals through this automated system are two reasons that, under New Jersey's hospital rate-setting law, Blue Cross and Blue Shield receives a price advantage on the amount it pays to hospitals. This helps hold down premium costs for both individual and group subscribers.

New Jersey Blue Cross and Blue Shield provides health care protection to individuals regardless of their

health. Group programs are available to as few as four employees. Medicare recipients and students can enroll in special coverage programs. Individual subscribers and groups can choose a plan to fit their needs: one covering expenses incurred from the first dollar or one with copayment and deductible features.

Blue Cross and Blue Shield also offers coverage for alternative health care delivery systems such as HMOs— both group practice and individual

The start of the Belmar Run, which is sponsored by Blue Cross and Blue Shield of New Jersey and the Belmar Kiwanis Club.

practice association (IPA) HMOs. Some innovative services offered by Blue Cross and Blue Shield include Student plans, Major Medical, Dental, Prescription, Comprehensive, and Wraparound, and major coverage for new technology services such as CT scans, dialysis, and bypass. The Plan rounds out its health care product line with Rider J and major medical to extend protection.

In 1984 Blue Cross and Blue Shield began a corporate restructuring designed to make it more customer-oriented. Now each customer segment (national accounts, large groups, small groups, and individual subscribers) has its own division. The reorganization is helping the Plan better meet the specific needs of its different groups and individual subscribers.

Blue Cross and Blue Shield phone service have been combined into one support unit. Now customers can call one phone number to have all their Blue Cross and Blue Shield questions answered. Blue Cross and Blue Shield's Special Telephone Account Representative (STAR) Unit, formed in 1984, provides direct, toll-free personal phone service for most Blue Cross and Blue Shield clients. In its first year alone STAR handled nearly 100,000 calls. In addition to STAR, the Plan's general phone service unit handles well over one million calls annually. More than 90 percent of these inquiries are resolved in the first call.

PUBLIC SERVICE ELECTRIC AND GAS COMPANY

Public Service Electric and Gas Company (PSE&G) is the largest utility in New Jersey and serves approximately 5.4 million people, nearly three-quarters of the state's population. The firm's service area, covering some 2,600 square miles, runs diagonally across the state's industrial and commercial corridor from the New York state border on the north to south of Camden. This highly diversified and heavily populated area includes the six major cities of New Jersey as well as nearly 300 suburban and rural communities.

In 1986 PSE&G, with the approval of stockholders and the New Jersey Board of Public Utilities, underwent a restructuring that resulted in the creation of a new holding company—Public Service Enterprise Group Incorporated. PSE&G is now the principal subsidiary of Enterprise and the backbone of the holding company.

Other subsidiaries of Enterprise include Community Energy Alternatives Incorporated, which invests in and develops cogeneration and small power projects, and Public Service Resources Corporation, an investment vehicle.

The organization that was to become Public Service Electric and Gas Company was founded in 1903 by a group, led by Thomas N. McCarter, which merged numerous railway, gas, and electric companies. McCarter was a lawyer and had served as attorney general of New Jersey.

At the time the large street railway systems in the state were in financial difficulty, and some plan of reorganization was necessary. The

---

Public Service Electric and Gas Company (PSE&G) is the largest utility company in New Jersey and serves nearly three-quarters of the state's population. Its headquarters, pictured here, is located in Newark.

electric companies, then the newest among the utilities, were in fair financial condition. The gas companies were sound but, for the most part, had exhausted their capacity for new capital.

The tremendous advance in the electric industry in this century has been reflected in PSE&G's growth. Electric revenues in 1985 accounted for 68 percent of PSE&G's total of $4.4 billion. Gas revenues made up the other 32 percent. PSE&G ended its participation in transportation in 1980, when Transport of New Jersey, a subsidiary, was sold to New Jersey Transit Corporation, a state agency that had been established to acquire mass transit facilities.

Today PSE&G has more than two million customers.

More than 1.7 million electric customers rely on PSE&G to provide dependable service. To help meet that demand, the company has an electric-generating capacity of some 10 million kilowatts.

PSE&G's most famous customer is the Statue of Liberty for which it has provided power since 1916. In 1986 a new, larger-capacity cable was laid to supply the statue's increased power needs as a result of restoration work and improvements.

A diversified mixture of fuels—coal, nuclear, oil, and natural gas—is used to generate electricity. Electricity is produced at 17 generating stations—from Bergen County in the north to Salem County in the south. Eleven of those stations are wholly owned by PSE&G. Ownership of three stations in New Jersey and three in Pennsylvania is shared with other utilities.

The firm's electric transmission and distribution system has more than 110,000 miles of overhead lines and 23,000 miles underground. This extensive T&D system helps assure customers of reliable service.

PSE&G is also a member of a power pool known as the Pennsylvania-New Jersey-Maryland (PJM) Interconnection. Its strong network of high-voltage connections with other

Along with coal, oil, and natural gas, nuclear power is used to generate a portion of PSE&G's electricity. The Hope Creek Nuclear Station adds 1.1 million kilowatts to the company's generating capacity.

utilities helps the company import large amounts of low-cost, coal-fueled power from other areas.

More than 1.3 million customers depend upon PSE&G for gas service. The gas is distributed through more than 12,000 miles of underground gas mains.

Natural gas from the southwest is delivered by three major interstate pipeline companies at 46 metering and regulating stations. Energy Development Corporation, PSE&G's gas exploration subsidiary, provides a significant percentage of the company's total gas supply.

PSE&G has an average daily gas capacity of about 20 million therms. That's more than enough gas to sup-

More than two million customers rely on PSE&G to provide dependable electric and gas service. To help meet that demand, the firm has an electric generating capacity of some 10 million kilowatts, and was the first utility company in the country to fully computerize its gas meter reading operations.

ply PSE&G's 1.2 million residential, 150,000 commercial, and 5,000 industrial customers.

PSE&G historically has encouraged the state's economic growth with aggressive area development and marketing activities that encourage business and industry to locate in New Jersey. The company's efforts support those of the New Jersey Department of Commerce and Economic Development, as well as other agencies.

Growth in recent years has been highlighted by the beginning of redevelopment of the Hudson River waterfront and the acceleration of construction in central New Jersey, along the Princeton-Route 1 corridor.

People are the key to a safe, continuous supply of energy to customers, and PSE&G places special emphasis on proper training. The Nuclear Training Center, one of the first of its kind in the nation, helps assure standards of performance excellence at the firm's generating stations.

PSE&G also takes a great deal of pride in its service to customers. Modern facilities and a computer-based system provide economy in operations and efficiency in service. PSE&G was one of the first utilities in the nation to use computerized, hand-held meter reading devices throughout its service territory.

A field customer service organization comprised of three divisions—northern, central, and southern—includes nine district offices and 15 customer service centers. In addition, there are two customer inquiry and accounting facilities, which handle an average of 15,000 customer calls per day, and a bill processing center.

PSE&G will continue during the rest of this century and into the next as New Jersey's major energy supplier—promoting economic growth and the well-being of the state's residents.

FIRST FIDELITY BANCORPORATION

First Fidelity's story begins in 1812, making it one of America's earliest banking companies. The story starts with the founding in Newark of its direct ancestor bank, the State Bank of Newark, and its location later that year at the southeast corner of Broad and Mechanic streets. The bank would remain there until 1967, when it moved its executive offices to 550 Broad Street, the present home of both the bank, First Fidelity Bank, N.A., New Jersey, and the parent company, First Fidelity Bancorporation. But at Broad and Mechanic streets (the latter now named Edison Place), the State Bank of Newark would rebuild its headquarters twice during the next century.

The bank's first home on the site, a home which the bank itself built in 1812, was a comfortable two-story "office," more in the exterior style of a two-story residence.

A four-story structure was built there in 1868, and a 12-story building in 1912, the centennial year. That latter building continued as the

Robert R. Ferguson, Jr., noted for his leadership roles in the affairs of New Jersey, is president and chief executive officer of First Fidelity Bancorporation.

bank's headquarters until the move in 1967 of its executive offices to a new 18-story structure at 550 Broad Street, now known as First Federal Building.

The bank's first president was William S. Pennington, a Revolutionary War captain who resigned only

eight months after the founding of the bank to campaign for governor of New Jersey. He succeeded in his quest for that office, and a son, William Pennington, followed in his famous father's footsteps, first serving as the bank's attorney (1822-1835) and later winning election as governor.

By 1814 the bank was solidly established in its small but growing community, and its future course was set. Newark was enjoying its own early growth as a center of commerce, and became a city, by incorporation, in 1836.

In 1865 the bank obtained a national charter, becoming the National State Bank of Newark. Gradual growth continued until the turn of the century, by which time assets stood at nearly $3.5 million.

The years between the Civil War and World War I saw Newark emerge as a major, diversified center of manufacturing, and the bank responded by developing its own expertise in the service of the business and industry that thrived in and near the city.

In 1911 William I. Cooper, who had started at the bank in 1876 as a clerk, became its president. Cooper's career with the institution spanned 55 years until his death in 1931. Meanwhile, National State Bank of Newark's assets rose from just under four million dollars in 1911 to more than seven million dollars in 1920.

The National State Bank of Newark rode out the storm of the Great Depression in excellent form, and during the Depression years withdrawals never were halted.

The Depression years also saw the installation of new leadership. In 1931 W. Paul Stillman, then 34 years old and a vice-president at Fidelity Union Trust Company, took over from Cooper, assuming the title

Footsteps of troops preparing for the war with the British in 1812 resounded as the first home of the State Bank of Newark was being constructed at Broad and Mechanic streets in Newark.

The 18-story First Fidelity Building, head-quarters of First Fidelity since 1967, towers over its neighbors on Broad Street.

president and chief executive officer.

He assumed the chairmanship the following year, and presided over a period of significant expansion, much of it effected through a series of post-war mergers. By 1937 the bank's resources had climbed to $24 million, and by 1940 its assets had risen to nearly $38 million.

After the war government-insured mortgages spurred home building, payment on credit became a way of life, and the migration to suburbia had begun—an accelerated growth of retail banking with it.

In 1949 came the first in a series of postwar mergers that would greatly increase the bank's strength, as Merchants and Newark Trust Company was merged into National State Bank. Their combined assets exceeded

$115 million.

The 1950s saw further mergers, reaching into the Essex County suburbs. In 1958 came another landmark merger for the bank, this one with the Federal Trust Company, located in Newark. It was New Jersey's largest bank merger up to that date, and it added assets of more than $85 million. Total assets then stood at more than $418 million.

In 1961 William H. Keith was elected president, with Stillman continuing as chairman and chief executive.

The following year, its 150th year, National State Bank of Newark's assets stood at more than a half-billion dollars, with nearly 1,000 people working at 21 branch offices. At that time the institution's board changed its name to First National State Bank of New Jersey.

Keith died in 1966 and was succeeded by Robert R. Ferguson, Jr. Ferguson had entered the organization through the Federal Trust merger, and he was to lead the bank in a new era of growth and expansion. Ferguson became president of First National State Bancorporation upon its organization in 1969 as the bank's parent company, and he crafted the program of statewide growth that followed the enactment earlier that year of New Jersey's new statewide bank holding company law. In addition, he set in motion the preparation process for the coming interstate banking era.

Ferguson succeeded Stillman as chief executive of the parent company in 1973, and continues in that role today under the title president and chief executive officer.

Having earlier established its "middle market," commercial banking foundation, First National State Bancorporation proceeded during the 1970s on a deliberate program of merger, acquisition, and internal growth aimed at assembling the large-scale, statewide retail branch system that it now operates through its seven affiliated banks, one of them a state-chartered savings bank acquired in 1986.

The early 1980s saw two very large mergers, one which brought in the former First National Bank of South Jersey, the other the former First National Bank of New Jersey, and assets rose to $6.4 billion by 1983. In August of that year, the banking community of New Jersey, and of the entire nation, heard an announcement of historic dimension—the banks of the former Fidelity Union Bancorporation would merge into the First National State Bancorporation System.

Fidelity Union traced its origins back to 1887, and in 1920 it took the name Fidelity Union Trust Company; under that name its reputation grew and flourished, producing, among other things, one of the most highly regarded trust services in America.

This merger, consummated in April 1984, was at the time the largest ever in the nation's banking history. It brought together New Jersey's largest and third-largest banking organizations, and created a $10-billion banking company.

The formal change of the parent company's name to First Fidelity, and the changes over to the First Fidelity name by all of the system's commercial banking affiliates, was accomplished over the year following the merger. Today the merged lead bank is First Fidelity Bank, N.A., New Jersey. It is headed by Edward D. Knapp, president and chief executive officer, and by Ferguson, who continues as the bank's chairman in addition to heading the parent company. That bank, with eight billion dollars in assets of its own, stands as the largest commercial bank in New Jersey.

Overall, the First Fidelity system, through its affiliates, has more than 300 branch offices throughout the state. First Fidelity Bancorporation, with about $15 billion in assets at year-end 1986, is among the 40 largest bank holding companies in America. First Fidelity also has established trust banking subsidiaries in Florida and New York. Among its other subsidiaries is a discount brokerage firm.

HELVOET PHARMA INC.

Helvoet Pharma Inc. of Pennsauken, New Jersey, and Helvoet Pharma N.V., of Alken, Belgium, subsidiaries of the Swiss Daetwyler Holding Ltd., are leading manufacturers of primary pharmaceutical packaging components, parts for medical devices, and disposable infant feeders made of rubber and/or plastics. Helvoet has been involved in this specialized field since 1939 and has contributed significantly to its progress through basic research and new developments.

Helvoet Pharma Inc. was founded in 1946 under other ownership and became a member of the Helvoet Group in 1981. The first phase of a new, state-of-the-art facility was completed in 1985 at Burlington, New Jersey.

Helvoet Pharma complies with the rules of good manufacturing practice established by the World Health Organization for the Pharmaceutical Industry. This means extensive quality control, batch-wise production, and a final quality control based on Acceptable Quality Levels (AQLs), agreed upon with customers.

Helvoet Pharma's research and development is focused on rubber formulations that are compatible with a wide range of pharmaceutical preparations. The rubber products, based on those compounds, with a very low level of extractables, allow a wide application flexibility and per-

The first phase of a new state-of-the-art facility was completed in 1985 in Burlington.

mit a reduction of handling, testing, and pretreatment before being used as part of a pharmaceutical packaging system or medical device. The use of very clean formulations, combined with advanced manufacturing processes, results in rubber products with a very low level of biological and particulate contamination, thus generally lowering the rejection rate on packaged drugs.

Helvoet Pharma's product range is divided into product groups, based on typical fields of application, each requiring special properties and product characteristics. These product groups are: pharmaceutical packaging components, parts for disposable medical devices, infant feeders, and components for biomedical devices. Parts and components are made from advanced rubber formulations with characteristics tailored to the particular requirements of each product group.

Close dimensional tolerances allow the use of Helvoet products on modern, high-speed packaging and assembling machines. Typical examples of pharmaceutical packaging components are stoppers for penicillin and insulin vials; plungers, disks, and needle covers for prefilled syringes; plungers and disks for dental anesthetic cartridges; and stoppers for large-volume intravenous solutions.

The Helvoet Pharma plant in Pennsauken was founded in 1946 under other ownership and became a member of the Helvoet Group in 1981.

Parts for disposable medical devices include stoppers for blood collection tubes, plungers for infusion pumps and for disposable hypodermic syringes, dropper bulbs, and parts for infusion administration sets.

Helvoet also manufactures a range of baby nipples made of modern rubber formulations that are in compliance with the current standards of cleanliness and chemical purity.

With more than 40 years of experience, Helvoet Pharma Inc. provides a solid record of reliability for its customers in the pharmaceutical field. Through its research and development efforts, the company continues to provide the industry with innovations, thus serving New Jersey and the world.

Helvoet Pharma Inc., a leading manufacturer of primary pharmaceutical packaging components, parts for medical devices, and disposable infant feeders made of rubber and/or plastics, has been involved in this specialized field since 1939.

THE HOWARD SAVINGS BANK

Today The Howard Savings Bank is a publicly held financial services corporation, with assets of more than four billion dollars and a statewide network of branches. From its administrative offices in a late-twentieth-century corporate park, owned and developed by the bank, it is difficult to imagine the financial world as it was on May 5, 1857, when The Howard Savings Institution opened as a mutual bank, serving individuals and families in Newark, New Jersey.

The Howard's 27 founders were civic leaders such as Moses Bigelow, varnish manufacturer and mayor of Newark, and Beach Vanderpool, a former mayor who would become the Howard's first president.

The founders admired John Howard, an eighteenth-century English philanthropist who pioneered prison reform, built schools and houses for the poor, and developed a system that helped them to raise themselves out of poverty. They named the bank for him, since their reason for establishing it was to encourage persons of small means to improve their own conditions.

From the beginning the Howard was a prestigious institution throughout northern New Jersey because of the public's respect for its founders and managers. Their conservative approach to money management guided the bank successfully through wars and "boom-or-bust" economic cycles,

The first Howard Savings Institution office was opened on May 5, 1857, on the northwest corner of Broad and Bank streets in Newark.

The site of the present-day main office of The Howard Savings Bank at 768 Broad Street in Newark, which was occupied by the bank in 1883.

so that by 1875 it was one of the state's leading savings banks.

On its 50th birthday in 1907 the Howard was the largest savings bank in New Jersey, playing a leading role in the rapid development of Newark and surrounding areas.

When the stock market crashed in 1929 many banks throughout the country were in serious difficulty. However, the Howard was able to pay all its depositors and never closed its doors during that crisis.

In the 1950s the bank's managers were among the first to recognize the importance of newly emerging, electronic data-processing technology. They installed the world's first on-line teller terminal system in 1962.

Development of a wide variety of financial services enabled the Howard to accommodate the financial needs of more and more households throughout the state, beginning its evolution into a full-service, state-wide financial corporation. In 1983 conversion from a mutual to a stock savings bank increased the supply of available capital, facilitating the rapid growth and expansion that was under way, including the formation of subsidiaries.

Howco Investment Corporation, the Howard's first subsidiary, became one of the most successful real estate development companies in New Jersey. It is regarded as a national prototype for a subsidiary operation through which banks can engage in direct development, acquisition, and management of real estate.

The year 1985 was a year of record earnings for the Howard. Total lending had reached an all-time high. The commercial loan portfolio had increased by 71 percent, representing relationships with more than 1,100 companies. Commercial real estate financing had also increased. By far the state's leading student loan provider, other consumer lines of credit, including home equity loans, were major contributors to this outstanding year.

By 1986 the Howard's employee relocation subsidiary, the Howard Relocation Group, and mortgage banking subsidiary, Mortgage Services of America, were expanding. Other subsidiaries, formed to sell insurance and to offer discount brokerage services, were also performing well.

Reporting to the third annual shareholder's meeting in April 1986, bank executives announced that The Howard Savings Bank had just completed the best first quarter in its history.

MONMOUTH COLLEGE

Monmouth College was founded in 1933 as one of six New Jersey junior colleges funded by the Federal Emergency Relief Administration.

In those bleak days of the Depression, the college offered higher education to young shore area residents who could not afford to go away to school or take time from jobs to attend classes during the day.

Initially operating from borrowed headquarters at Long Branch High School, Monmouth held classes only at night, starting at 4 when the high school students had left for the day.

The school was named Monmouth Junior College rather than Monmouth County Junior College because it admitted students from Ocean County as well, giving all area residents a chance for a college education.

Though student enthusiasm was high, Monmouth faced hard times. In 1935, in the depth of the Depression, new federal restrictions imperiled the college's very existence. Faced with losing all they had gained in their first two years, the students and faculty met with the administration to seek a way to run the college themselves, without federal help.

They then proceeded to do just that. A plan was devised whereby students would pay a "contribution" rather than tuition. A parents' group

The Great Hall of Woodrow Wilson Hall, administrative center of Monmouth College.

pledged $1,725, the County Board of Freeholders donated $500, and from Monmouth County boards of education came subsidies of various amounts. By the end of 1935 Monmouth's financial picture had cleared sufficiently for the school to survive without government aid. During that same landmark year Monmouth Junior College was accredited to award diplomas.

Dr. Edward G. Schlaefer guided the school through its early years, first as director and then as executive vice-president. He would later serve as president from 1957 to 1962.

In 1947 Monmouth had received

state authorization to confer associate degrees, and the first degrees were awarded in June 1948. In that year the college was incorporated as an independent, nonprofit private institution of higher education.

Monmouth was still operating out of borrowed facilities, and it sought to acquire its own campus. In 1955, after a long search, the college decided to purchase the Shadow Lawn estate in West Long Branch, then the home of the Highland Manor School and Junior College. Monmouth opened classes on the new campus in September 1956.

The Shadow Lawn mansion, which was President Woodrow Wilson's summer White House, was destroyed by fire in 1927. The second Shadow Lawn mansion, subsequently renamed Woodrow Wilson Hall, was built in 1931 as a private residence for F.W. Woolworth Co. president Hubert T. Parson. Now designated a National Historic Landmark, it is the centerpiece of Monmouth's campus.

The acquisition of the new campus was not the only major achievement of 1956. That same year the New Jersey State Department of Higher Education authorized Monmouth to offer baccalaureate degrees. The college thus broadened its academic base by adding the third and fourth years. That first year it offered B.A. curricula in English, history, foreign languages, and psychology. The B.S. curricula included biology, business administration, chemistry, physics, and math.

But work was still needed on the new campus. Buildings once housing cows and chickens had been converted into classrooms by the Highland Manor School, but the facilities still had to be modified for the college level. Indoor physical education facilities and library space were limited, and there were no dormitories during the first six years at Shadow Lawn. Many students lived in local motels and apartments.

Despite those problems Monmouth became firmly established in its new home. After the transitional period

The original Guggenheim Wing of the 250,000-volume Guggenheim Memorial Library at Monmouth College.

A view across the Great Lawn shows Monmouth College buildings (from left) Pollak Auditorium, the 500 Classroom Building, the Edison Science Building, and, at extreme right, Wilson Hall.

Schlaefer announced his retirement from the college's presidency, effective January 31, 1962. Dr. William G. Van Note, then president of Clarkson College of Technology, succeeded him.

During those years Monmouth College expanded its physical plant enormously. In 1961 the Murry and Leonie Guggenheim Foundation's library opened; today it houses 225,000 volumes and more than 1,700 periodicals. The Thomas A. Edison Science Building and the Alumni Memorial Gymnasium were opened in 1966. The following year the Murry and Leonie Guggenheim Carriage House was converted to the Fine Arts Building, now home of the Guggenheim Theatre, where productions are staged year round.

Also built were a new classroom building, an auditorium, and dormitories for 1,000 students. Added in 1973 was the modern College Center, the school's activity hub, housing a wide range of campus facilities.

In 1967 Monmouth College's academic base broadened again with the authorization to award master's de-

The new, main section of the Guggenheim Memorial Library.

grees.

Today Monmouth College's School of Humanities and Social Sciences offers courses in anthropology, art, criminal justice, English, foreign languages and foreign language education, history, music, philosophy and religious studies, political science, psychology, social work, sociology, and speech/communication/theater.

The School of Science and Professional Studies offers biology, chemistry, education, electronic engineering, software engineering, mathematics and computer science, medical technology, nursing, physical education, and physics.

The north entrance of the Edison Science Building.

The School of Business Administration, Monmouth's largest, focuses on accounting, computer systems for business, economics, finance, international business, management, marketing, purchasing and materials management, and military science and ROTC.

Monmouth College is today a comprehensive, coeducational institution with more than 4,000 students and a full-time faculty of 160. Its current president is Dr. Samuel H. Magill.

ELIZABETHTOWN GAS COMPANY

Elizabethtown Gas Light Company was chartered in 1855 by a special act of the legislature for the purpose of supplying gaslights to what was then known as Elizabethtown. The first meeting of stockholders was held in Shepherd's Hotel in 1855, and gas was first produced the following year.

It was shortly after this time that the name of Elizabethtown became inextricably linked with another famous New Jersey name—Kean. In 1865 John Kean—the second of his lineage to bear that name—became president of the fledgling company.

Colonel Kean, as he was known, was the son of Peter Kean, who, after a distinguished military career in the early nineteenth century, became a leader in the growing Elizabethtown community. Peter's father, the first John Kean, was a member of the Continental Congress.

When the company was formed Colonel Kean was 41 years old and

Colonel John Kean was president of the Elizabethtown Gas Light Company in the post-Civil War era.

the owner of three mills along the Elizabeth River. He was also an officer of two railroads and president of the National State Bank of Elizabethtown.

It was not surprising, then, that the new Elizabethtown Gas Light Company sought Colonel Kean's ad-

vice and experience. He led the company for the next 12 years.

At the start the firm was selling gas only for lighting purposes. Gas was far too expensive in those days of cheap wood and coal to be able to compete as a fuel. At that time gas was measured by candlepower and was made primarily from coal.

Fewer than four miles of gas mains served the consumers at the time, but the convenience of the new illuminating agent was so markedly demonstrated that growth was steady. In 1859 gas mains were extended to Elizabethport. In 1867, by legislative act, the company's territory was extended to include Union and a part of Newark.

In the period between 1878 and 1914 Elizabethtown Gas Light had the third John Kean as its president. This John Kean was better known as Senator Kean.

When he became president of the utility at age 26, the City of Elizabethtown had already shortened its name to Elizabeth and had grown in population to about 25,000. During the next 36 years the town—and the surrounding area—would vigorously expand into one of the nation's major industrial areas.

Competition arose in Elizabeth in 1889, when a rival company was organized. Gas mains were laid, and in 1890 gas was sent to various parts of the city by this new company. But two years of operation brought this concern into the hands of a receiver, and its properties were purchased by Elizabethtown Gas Light. To make this purchase, the directors of the company decided not to pay a dividend in the fall of that year. Unfortunately, the decision ruined a continuous record of dividend payments from 1855 to the present. But with this purchase the firm's geographical base for the future was being built.

While all this was happening, the third John Kean was pursuing an active political career. He was elected to the U.S. House of Representatives in 1882, was defeated two years later,

Horse-drawn wagons, such as the one pictured in this 1885 photo, made service calls to gas company customers.

The corporate headquarters and appliance showroom of Elizabethtown Gas on Broad Street, Elizabeth, in the 1930s.

and won back his seat in 1886. Kean ran unsuccessfully for governor in 1892 but was elected to the U.S. Senate in 1898.

When Senator Kean died in 1914, the new president of the Elizabethtown Gas Light Company was the senator's younger brother, Julian. A practicing attorney, he was already familiar with the company, having often handled its legal affairs.

Julian Kean had a plan. Small local gas utilities could effectively be joined together for economy of operations and for improved profits. A merger bringing in Cranford, Rahway, and Metuchen gaslight companies occurred in 1922. With considerable foresight, Kean also dropped the word "Light" from the company name as the major uses of gas changed to heating, cooking, and industrial processing.

In 1933 the presidency passed to Julian's nephew, the fourth John Kean, known as Captain John Kean because of service during World War I. Severely wounded in action, he returned to the gas company after more than a year in military hospitals.

Captain John was a man with two visions for Elizabethtown Gas. One was to continue his uncle's concept of growth by further enlarging the expanding gas company's service area. The second vision concerned the natural gas available in Louisiana and Texas.

During his presidency Elizabethtown Gas Company received nationwide acclaim by constructing what was then the world's largest all-welded gas holder, which had a capacity of 10 million cubic feet.

Captain John could see even greater growth possibilities for the company in the Perth Amboy area. Unfortunately, he did not live to witness the results of the expansion effort, but on June 1, 1950, the Perth Amboy Gas Light Company became part of the Elizabethtown system.

Captain John's second vision also was achieved posthumously. The long-awaited supplies of natural gas from the Southwest arrived in Elizabeth in 1950. Conversion of all customers to natural gas was completed in 1951. Although Elizabethtown still had facilities for making gas from oil to supplement its natural gas supply, it was now almost totally in the dis-

tribution business, gas manufacture having been greatly deemphasized.

For the next 13 years William S. Potter led the utility as its president. During this period sales and revenues increased dramatically, spurred by the postwar boom and ready availability of natural gas.

In 1963, following the retirement of Potter, Captain John's eldest son became president of the utility. He was the fifth generation of his family to carry the name John Kean and the fifth member of his family to serve in this position.

Influenced by his father's concepts of strength through growth, he sought ways to assure continuation of the company's progress. In 1965 John Kean negotiated for a group of small gas utility companies operating in the northwestern section of New Jersey. This acquisition greatly increased the service territory of Elizabethtown Gas.

In 1980 the presidency was assumed by Duncan S. Ellsworth, Jr., although John Kean remained as chairman of the board. Ellsworth retired in 1986, and Frederick W. Sullivan became president.

From its modest start more than 130 years ago, Elizabethtown Gas Company has grown and prospered. And that has to make several generations of Keans very proud.

The "Gas House Gang" kept the home fires burning during two world wars.

THOMAS & BETTS CORPORATION

Thomas & Betts Corporation is an expanding international company engaged in the design, manufacture, and marketing of electrical and electronic components and systems.

T&B's products are used for connecting, fastening, protecting, and identifying wires, components, and conduits. The corporation operates throughout North America, Western Europe, and the Far East.

Thomas & Betts was founded in 1898 by Robert McKean Thomas and Hobart D. Betts, electrical engineers who had been classmates at Princeton. Selling electrical wires and raceways—a raceway is a tube for enclosing and protecting electric wires—on a commission basis, the two men formed Thomas & Betts Company in New York City. A third partner, Adnah McMurtrie, developed products that later launched the firm's manufacturing activities.

By and large, the business was quite profitable from the start. By 1910 T&B had acquired the Standard Electric Fittings Company of Stamford, Connecticut, which had been making most of its products. T&B moved the operation to Eliza-

beth, New Jersey, built a factory, and in 1916 officially became a New Jersey company, designing, manufacturing, and selling electrical raceway accessories.

The relocated company had 125 employees and still retained an office in New York City. T&B soon built a second New Jersey plant, and in 1928 it established Thomas & Betts Ltd. of Canada.

T&B's product line continued to expand, thanks to company innovations in solderless terminations. This technique greatly improved methods of connecting and terminating wires and cables by eliminating the more expensive and less efficient soldering operation. In 1934 T&B introduced the Wedgeon®, the first solderless terminal, and the Tightbind®, a cast-copper connector that won wide approval in the industry.

During World War II T&B prod-

A vintage automobile is parked beside the dirt street that ran in front of the Thomas & Betts Company in 1918. The firm had moved to Elizabeth, New Jersey, and built this new factory two years before.

ucts were widely used in the wiring of aircraft, ships, submarines, tanks, and other armaments. Thomas & Betts received the Army/Navy "E" Award for efficiency in war production five times.

In 1959 T&B revolutionized wire tying with its TY-RAP® cable ties and straps. The TY-RAP® reduced the labor time, cut the weight of the material used, and was more reliable. TY-RAP® cable ties are still a highly profitable product line. Also in 1959 Thomas & Betts, which had been a closely held company since its birth, went public.

During the 1960s T&B went into space on the TelStar satellite and other space vehicles. T&B introduced its flat conductor cable and connectors, which also were lighter in weight, easier to install, and more reliable, making them a natural for the space program and the telecommunications industries.

In that same decade Thomas & Betts became a multinational, moving into Europe and the Far East. Today T&B has two plants in England and one each in France and Luxembourg, as well as sales compa-

of South Jersey Port Corporation's terminals.

Along with that increase in capacity has come a steady rise in annual tonnage. Total tonnage through both terminals has exceeded the million-ton mark in each year since 1974, and in 1985 traffic surpassed the two-million-ton mark for the first time ever. The year 1985 was also the first time that the Port Corporation's imports and exports both exceeded one million tons.

The Port Corporation's terminals are close to high-speed intermodal connections: direct rail service, interstate highways, and Philadelphia International Airport, which is just 15 minutes away. Shipments can reach more than half the population of the United States within 24 hours after leaving the port's gates.

South Jersey Port Corporation is well known as one of the nation's largest handlers of wood and metal products. McMillan-Bloedel, one of

Highly competitive among all ports of the world, the South Jersey Port Corporation handles more than 20 import and export categories of general and dry-bulk cargo.

the largest lumber importers and distributors in the country, has operated at the Beckett Street Terminal facilities for more than 30 years, handling in excess of 50 million board feet of lumber annually. The company's volume, along with that of other lumber importers, has made South Jersey Port Corporation the second-largest lumber terminal and distribution center on the East Coast of the United States.

Aruvil, Inc., a major importer of fencing, pipe, and pipe accessories on the East Coast, bringing in shipments from Japan, Korea, Brazil, and Europe, maintains its East Coast distribution operations on a 7.5-acre open site at the Broadway Terminal as well as 40,000 square feet of covered warehouse for product storage.

Among other companies with major facilities at the port are Able Warehousing, Tri-State Stevedores, Inc., HWR, Inc., and Stellar Technology. The southern portion of the Broadway Terminal is served by International Terminal Operating Company, which provides stevedoring and terminal facilities for numerous steamship lines. McAllister Brothers, a major East Coast-based tug and towing company, has its Delaware River tug fleet and administrative offices at Broadway Terminal.

The Port Corporation is now a major player among all ports of the world in pursuit of foreign trade. It has regularly handled more than 20 import and

The South Jersey Port Corporation has a total of nearly 300 acres of covered and open storage available to importers and exporters. In 1985 traffic surpassed the two-million-ton mark—it is no wonder then that over 1,000 jobs are provided by more than 20 tenants and shippers at the port's terminals.

export categories of general and dry-bulk cargo, and that number keeps on growing. It imports lumber from British Columbia and the Philippines; steel from Korea, Brazil, Japan, and Europe; iron ore from Sweden; titanium slage from Canada; fluorspar from Norway; zircon sand from Australia; cocoa beans from Africa and South America; petro coke from Japan and England; zinc ingots from England; rutile ore from Australia; plywood from Korea, Japan, Taiwan, Indonesia, and Malaysia; bulk and boxed manganese from Norway; pig iron from Brazil and Canada; gypsum from Newfoundland; bulk salt from Chile; and plastic raw materials from Brazil and Rumania.

South Jersey Port Corporation's affairs receive policy direction from a seven-member board of directors appointed by the governor, with the advice and consent of the state senate. The current chairman of that board is Edward J. McManimon, Jr. The Port Corporation has a seven-member board headed by an operational executive director, Robert L. Pettegrew, who has held this position since 1971 following a long career with the Port Authority of New York and New Jersey.

MIDLANTIC CORPORATION

Midlantic Corporation, headquartered in Edison, New Jersey, is a financial service company with assets exceeding $17 billion in 1987. Serving the vibrant New Jersey and Pennsylvania market with more than 400 offices, Midlantic is a premier banking organization in the mid-Atlantic region. In addition, Midlantic also operates bank-related subsidiaries in Florida, Maryland, and New York.

These operations, combined with the capabilities of Midlantic's overseas offices in London, Hong Kong, and Grand Cayman, provide individual, corporate, institutional, and governmental clients with a complete array of financial programs that include corporate, international, investment, mortgage, brokerage, trust, and personal banking services.

Chartered in 1804, Midlantic is New Jersey's oldest financial institution. Over the years Midlantic has grown with the state and the region, both contributing significantly to and benefiting from their development.

Midlantic's expansion has been particularly rapid in recent years. In 1970 Midlantic was first to take advantage of New Jersey law permitting the formation of multibank holding companies within the state. The advent of statewide banking in 1973 as well as expansion through a combination of acquisition and internal growth have further enhanced Midlantic's already strong competitive position.

In 1987 Midlantic created the framework for continued growth in the future through the establishment of Midlantic Corporation. This interstate bank holding company, formed through the affiliation of Midlantic Banks Inc. with Continental Bancorp, Inc., of Philadelphia, was the first combination of banking organizations in New Jersey and Pennsylvania.

Paralleling Midlantic's expansion

Midlantic, founded in 1804 as the state's first bank, began operations on Broad Street in Newark.

into new markets has been the development of highly attractive banking programs to serve the financial needs of major customer groups.

A significant share of Midlantic's marketing effort as a leading regional bank is directed to medium-size companies. The bank offers these companies personalized financial relationships provided by banking professionals who combine extensive credit experience with an intimate knowledge of the marketplace. Midlantic staff members have earned their reputation as the "Hungry Bankers" by developing innovative banking services that are tailored to the requirements of these companies.

Midlantic also aggressively seeks to serve the nation's major corporations, placing emphasis on firms headquartered in New Jersey and Pennsylvania and on companies nationwide that maintain facilities in these states. Midlantic's success in building multiservice relationships in this highly competitive sector results from the expertise of bank account

The headquarters of Midlantic Corporation towers above the centrally located and rapidly developing major corporate complex in Metro Park Plaza.

activities, it is in the consumer market that deregulation has caused the most sweeping changes. Midlantic's diverse banking programs serve financial needs as basic as a home mortgage or as sophisticated as an investment plan. These activities are supported by Midlantic's direct banking systems, which enable customers to perform many of their transactions by telephone and to open accounts through the mail. An extensive network of automated teller machines represents another important way to provide customers with 24-hour access to their accounts.

Midlantic has long recognized the importance of serving a growing number of individuals and families whose financial planning benefits from highly personalized banking products. Increasing levels of personal income in New Jersey are coincident with the influx of corporate executives, professionals, and entrepreneurs to the state. Midlantic draws upon the expertise of lending professionals, backed by a strong foundation of trust and investment management services, to meet the complex needs of these individuals.

A bank is regarded as one of the most essential elements of the community, and all Midlantic banks are committed to serving as responsible corporate citizens. For almost 200 years the corporation has supported the growth of New Jersey and its institutions. Midlantic provides specialized banking services and financial support to hospitals, schools, and cultural organizations. In addition, staff members volunteer many hours of their time and talent to numerous community groups throughout the state.

Midlantic Corporation is well positioned for the future and moves forward with prospects that are unmatched for providing financial services to residents and businesses in the mid-Atlantic region.

officers, the quality of lending and noncredit services, and specialized product knowledge.

With its superior port facilities and excellent trasportation systems, New Jersey is an ideal location for companies active in international trade. Capitalizing on these strengths, Midlantic facilitates and finances international trade and investment activities for regional corporations with operations overseas, local domestic affiliates of foreign companies, and area businesses engaged in international trade.

While the continuing evolution of the financial services industry has had a strong impact on all banking

ALL-STATE LEGAL SUPPLY COMPANY

In the year 1946 two penniless, young war veterans and lifelong chums put their dreams together and founded All-state Legal Supply Company. While the firm initially sold its wares only in New Jersey, its name, All-state, was prophetic. Today the company literally does market its products in all 50 states.

Operating out of Busch's basement, founders Harry Busch and Al Rubin printed, packed, and shipped by night what they sold by day. They slept on Army cots between two Ben Franklin-vintage printing presses in the basement that comprised the company's physical plant. Their dream has since evolved into the nation's largest legal supply specialty enterprise, which holds dozens of patents and trademarks for law office products, and employs more than 400 highly skilled and dedicated people.

The operation soon moved from Busch's basement to a 1,000-square-foot loft in Newark. Its product line was initially the manufacturing and sale of quality legal forms to law firms throughout New Jersey. This line gradually expanded to include printing, engraving, corporate outfits, word-processing supplies, proprietary systems developed for specialized requirements, and other law office supplies.

They launched more than a business when they started All-state Legal Supply—they launched a concept. Prior to the company's inception no one had started a business dedicated exclusively to the needs of lawyers.

All-state salespeople regularly travel to law offices to provide personalized and specialized service because they understand the legal industry better than anyone. Today many lawyers and law office administrators admiringly refer to the company as "The One-Stop Shop," since they can obtain all of their needs from a single source.

The company's legal customer base is comprised of hundreds of thousands of lawyers, practicing in huge, mega-law firms in metropolitan areas, and solo practitioners in rural and small-town America.

The company's executive force includes Harry Busch, founder, president, and chief executive officer (seated); and (from right) sons David, marketing manager; and Robert, manufacturing resource planning manager; as well as Michael Barsa, vice-president/finance and treasurer; and Edmund Taussig, vice-president/sales.

In 1949 All-state moved to new, larger quarters in Newark and began to enlarge its staff. By 1951 the firm had purchased a three-story, 4,000-square-foot building in Newark. Ten more years of growth brought another move to even larger quarters, this time a three-story, 24,000-square-foot building.

A decade later snowballing success and expansion moved All-state to a one-story, 31,000-square-foot building in Mountainside Industrial Park. A second facility on Route 22 was soon needed to house additional offices and personnel.

In 1982 the firm moved again, this time to a new 154,000-square-foot building in the Cranford Industrial Park, adjacent to the Garden State Parkway. That building today serves as corporate headquarters and houses all production and manufacturing facilities. There are satellite distribution centers in Ohio, Virginia, and California.

All-state, in Wall Street terminology, is a classic example of a true "niche company"—dominant and highly specialized in a fast-growing vertical market. Since the 1960s it has expanded its primary markets from the northeastern to the mid-

western and western United States, and today the company serves 50 percent of the lawyers in its territories.

It has 40 specially trained salespeople on the road, managed by a vice-president/sales, a national sales manager, and six district sales managers. This sales organization is supported by strong marketing and advertising departments, with more than 50 inside salespeople in telephone and direct mail sales.

All-state continues its powerful momentum and aims to capture the lion's share of the national legal specialty market. The firm acquired several specialty supply companies over the years, and in 1986 added Law Publications, Inc., Los Angeles, California, to its plan to provide complete national service.

As All-state became a success, founder Harry Busch delved into civic affairs with characteristic vigor. His community leadership credentials are impressive: chairman of the board of the Union County Chamber

An artist's rendering depicts All-state's corporate headquarters at One Commerce Drive in Cranford, where the company has operated since 1982.

From left: Aubrey A. Rogers, acting administrator, Region II, U.S. Small Business Administration, and Philip D. Kaltenbacher, chairman, Port Authority of New York and New Jersey, congratulate Harry Busch, 1986 Small Business Person of the Year.

of Commerce; sponsor of the Junior Achievement Business Program; a member of the Kean College Business Council, the national Federation of Independent Business, the New Jersey Business & Industry Association, the New Jersey Small Business Unity Council, the New Jersey State

Chamber of Commerce, and the United States Chamber of Commerce. In 1986 Busch was named New Jersey's Small Business Person of the Year by the Small Business Administration, which annually selects one outstanding business person in each state.

Busch's motivation for this extraordinary civic involvement is, as he says, "an attempt to enhance and perpetuate the wonderful American system which made my success possible and my dreams come true." And with all his business and civic activities, he still manages to sail his vessel, *Replique*, in the Marion-Bermuda and similar blue-water races.

Busch, chief executive officer and president, is on a first-name basis with all his employees. They, in turn, greet him by his first name as he tours the offices and plant—clearly an unpretentious leader.

All-state Legal Supply Company recently set a new record with the unprecedented sale and distribution of Sheffield Linen®, a patented ultra-100-percent cotton fiber paper, developed specifically to meet the requirements of laser (and other high-tech) equipment used in law firms. This historic record is coincident with the firm's 40th anniversary and sets the tenor for the next 40 years of growth.

WALDMAN GRAPHICS, INC.

Waldman Graphics, Inc., really has two stories: one of a small printing firm founded in the 1920s, and another "modern history" of a company renaissance that began in 1972.

In 1923 George Fein, who was to stay with the firm until his death in the mid-1970s, opened a letterpress printing shop with hand-set composition. By 1934 a young teenager named Raymond Waldman joined on, and 12 years later the venture was officially incorporated in Philadelphia as George Fein & Company.

As the printing industry grew, so did George Fein & Company. During the 1950s the firm had about 20 letterpress operators. But troubles came during the 1960s with the growth of offset printing and the decline of letterpress. By 1972 the company's printing business had all but disappeared; one letterpress and some minor offset equipment were all that remained.

The firm then had only six people remaining and had become a small brokerage operation, farming out most of its work to offset printers.

In 1972 came the renaissance. Having seen what the failure to keep

The latest in printing technology, a 6/c Komori sheet-fed press.

up with new technology could do, company leaders added some new talent. Harry Waldman—Ray Waldman's son—came aboard, purchasing all of Fein's interest. The company set its plans to get back into manufacturing in motion.

An offset lithography sector was launched in 1972. The next year witnessed the start of the commercial and job photocomposition division, and the installation of the first piece of bindery equipment. Computerized textbook photocomposition was inaugurated in 1975.

The following year the company was renamed Waldman Graphics, Inc., reflecting its expanding manufacturing capabilities in the graphic arts industry. By 1977 a magazine division had been started, producing *Philadelphia Magazine.*

In 1980 Waldman Graphics relocated from Philadelphia to its present site in Pennsauken, New Jersey. The move expanded manufacturing space from 8,500 to 30,000 square feet. Electronic interfacing was added, and computer-assisted make-up operations followed.

Digital color imaging was introduced in 1983, and offset lithography capacity increased. A 6,000-square-foot building addition was completed

Integrated on-line press controls for high-quality printing.

in 1984; 27,000 additional square feet are planned. Two new six-color presses have been installed, equipment with the latest in technological quality controls, to help further meet ever-increasing demands of Waldman's customers for top-quality printing.

By 1985 company employment had grown to 230, and Waldman Graphics ranked an impressive 288th among the more than 60,000 printing companies in North America.

Today Waldman Graphics, Inc., is one of the country's largest computerized phototypesetters and commercial printers, specializing in high-quality color printing and photocomposition. The company is a perennial winner of industry accolades, among them the prestigious National Graphic Arts awards.

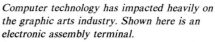

Computer technology has impacted heavily on the graphic arts industry. Shown here is an electronic assembly terminal.

HOWMET TURBINE COMPONENTS CORPORATION DOVER CASTING AND DOVER ALLOY DIVISIONS

The Dover Casting Division of Howmet and Turbine Components Corporation manufactures truly sophisticated and complicated castings, products that are used extensively but not exclusively in aircraft engines. Its products can be found in almost every type of aircraft throughout the free world: 707, 727, 747, 757, 767, DC10, F4, F111, F15, F16, virtually every vintage of helicopter, and the Space Shuttle main engines.

In contrast to its aircraft/aerospace products, the firm has applied its casting technology and skills to the manufacture of medical products. These include implants, including total knee and hip systems; bone screws and staples that are fixation devices; and medical tools such as rasps and cutting fixtures. Its diversity is further illustrated in the casting of molds used in the manufacture of ceramic cookware.

The process used to manufacture these parts is known as the Mono-Shell casting process. This is a derivative of the "lost-wax" process used by the Phoenicians to produce one-of-a-kind artifacts as long ago as 2000 B.C.

The Dover Casting Division, through the talents of its many employees, has been a pioneer in developing new technology. A history of innovation and industry leadership has produced important milestones such as the introduction of hollow castings, integral castings, complex structural castings, productionized fine-grained castings, an approved single crystal casting process, and utilization of the ultrafine-grain Microcast-X process.

When metals are melted into a liquid form, the atoms of the metals are randomly distributed throughout the liquid. When the metals are cooled, the atoms move to specific, fixed positions that they occupy in the solid metal. If the atoms establish many different sites when they group together in predictable arrays, an equiaxed casting (1) is produced. If conditions are changed so as to allow the atoms to initiate these arrays at only one end of the casting, a directionally solidified (D.S.) polycrystal casting (2) is produced. If conditions are controlled so that only one array of atoms prevails, a single crystal casting (3) is produced.

The Howmet Dover Casting Division is an outgrowth of Austenal Laboratories, Inc., a New York City-based dental lab that opened its doors in 1928. Austenal Laboratories, which became Austenal, Inc., was the first company in the world to cast supercharger buckets for B29 bombers and blades and vanes for the world's first jet engines.

Since that time the firm has gone from being privately owned to public ownership (Austenal to Howe Sound to Howmet). Through stock purchases by The Pechiney Corporation of Paris, France, the company has become a wholly owned subsidiary, rechristened Howmet Turbine Components Corporation. Austenal is now called the Dover Casting Division and has grown to approximately 240,000 square feet, providing employment opportunities for more than 1,700 people.

The casting process (from left): (1) equiax, (2) D.S. polycrystal, (3) single crystal.

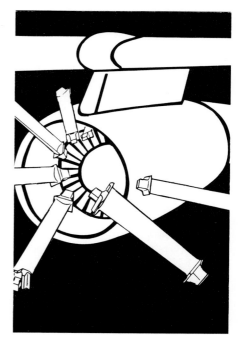

From teeth to jets.

Just across the street from the Dover Casting Division is Howmet's Dover Alloy Division, which produces complex and sophisticated super-alloys. The Alloy Division supplies these materials to Howmet's casting operations, as well as to engine makers and other outside investment casters. The medical profession uses investment cast prosthetic devices produced primarily from Howmet alloys.

Founded in 1954, Howmet's Dover Alloy Division's plant today has expanded to more than 86,000 square feet. At the heart of the alloy production process is the analytical laboratory that today contains the latest in laboratory equipment such as spark source mass spectrograph, inductively coupled plasma emission spectrograph, computerized optical emission spectrometer, and automated X-ray flourescent spectrometry.

The two Howmet divisions in Dover, along with Howmet's 18 other facilities worldwide, combine a number of diverse activities, specializing in, but not restricted to, the production of investment cast turbine components for the aircraft, power generation, and automotive industries.

THE PRUDENTIAL INSURANCE COMPANY OF AMERICA

The Prudential Insurance Company of America began as a working man's dream of providing basic life insurance for the working man. The dreamer was John F. Dryden, and the dream became industrial life insurance. It was the fundamental product that would catapult a small company into the world's largest insurer.

Dryden, who was born in Maine in 1839, was an ambitious life insurance salesman whose career had taken him to Ohio, New York, and Newark, New Jersey, by the 1860s. At the time he was selling individual insurance that had premiums geared toward upper-income people, a product similar to what is referred to as ordinary life today. Dryden, however, had heard of another type of life insurance offered in England for lower-income people. A form of low-price industrial insurance had been introduced in 1848 by The Prudential Assurance Company of Great Britain.

In 1873, while working for the Widows and Orphans Friendly Society (a charitable organization that also sold small ordinary group insurance policies), Dryden convinced the head of that small company, Allen L. Bassett, to consider a form of industrial insurance for the poorer working class. His idea was to offer factory

The Prudential's home office buildings on Broad Street, Newark, in 1916.

workers and laborers reasonably priced insurance that would cover burial expenses and perhaps could provide income for family survivors at premiums that could be as low as three cents per week.

Dryden persuaded Bassett to help

The Prudential Insurance Company began as The Prudential Friendly Society in the basement of the National State Bank on Broad Street, Newark, in 1875.

seek some investors who could provide money to launch an industrial insurance company that would produce profits while still serving the poor.

On October 13, 1875, The Prudential Friendly Society was established, with Bassett as president and Dryden as secretary. The name was inspired by England's Prudential Assurance Company, though the two were unrelated. The new company began selling weekly premium industrial life insurance.

By the end of 1875 Prudential had sold 284 policies. One year later it had more than 7,000 policies on its books. Such quick growth was only a hint of things to come.

In 1877 the company name was changed to The Prudential Insurance Company of America, and it also opened a sales office in Paterson. Additional New Jersey branches followed in the next two years, in Jersey City, Elizabeth, and Camden. The Prudential granted its first mortgage loan in 1878, starting an investment program that would one day be measured in the billions.

The Prudential established offices in New York and Philadelphia in 1879, and at that time Noah Blanchard became president. Although Dryden was Prudential's driving force, the presidency was held by someone who

risked more investment money. But when Blanchard died in 1881, Dryden was named president.

By 1885, 10-year-old Prudential's assets exceeded one million dollars. Its field force comprised about 1,500 people, and the home office in Newark had 119 employees. On May 18, 1885, the one-millionth industrial policy was issued, covering the life of John F. Dryden. It had been a phenomenal 10 years of growth.

In 1892 The Prudential, now a very big business indeed, built an opulent, 11-story building at Broad and Bank streets in Newark. In 1896 the Rock of Gibraltar trademark with the legend "The Prudential Has the Strength of Gibraltar" first appeared in advertisements.

At The Prudential's 25th anniversary in 1900, four buildings were being added in Newark. In 1909 a Toronto office opened, and Prudential agencies were in every state and territory, including Hawaii. Dryden was elected a U.S. Senator from New Jersey in 1902, and he served one term.

In 1911, when Dryden died, he was eulogized in *The New York Times* as "The father of industrial insurance." Prudential's assets then exceeded a quarter-billion dollars, built from Dryden's dream and a few thousand dollars from early investors.

Rows of cashiers work in The Prudential's main building in 1916.

Forrest F. Dryden, his son, became The Prudential's president in 1912. Although it would not become official until decades later, in 1915 The Prudential began acting as a mutual company, which meant it would be owned by its policyholders.

In 1922 Edward D. Duffield succeeded Dryden as president. The Depression came, but the company fared well. From 1930 through 1935 its life insurance policies in force rose more than $1.5 billion, and there were no employee layoffs.

Duffield died in 1938 and was succeeded by Franklin D'Olier. Under D'Olier Prudential officially became a mutual company, completing the process started in 1915.

During World War II Prudential assisted the government. D'Olier, who had a military background, served as chief of defense measures for the civilian population in New York, New Jersey, and Delaware; head of New Jersey's USO appeal; chairman of the state's war bond drive; and finally President Roosevelt's Chairman of the Strategic Bombing Survey Commission.

D'Olier retired in 1946 and was succeeded by Carroll Shanks, who was to modernize and reorganize the firm in the postwar years. D'Olier still served as chairman of the board.

By 1948 Prudential had 11,526 em-

ployees working in a seven-building complex in Newark. It opened its first regional home office, in Los Angeles, and began a major expansion and reorganization. From 1950 to 1955 there came a Canadian head office in Toronto, a southwestern home office in Houston, a north-central home office in Minneapolis, a south-central home office in Jacksonville, and a Mid-America home office in Chicago.

During the 1950s The Prudential developed its first group major medical contract and its individual sickness and accident insurance. In 1956 came its first family policy. Within four months a quarter-million fami-

The first Prudential ad to use the Rock of Gibraltar, 1896.

The founder and third president, John F. Dryden.

Assets, $15,780,000
Income,   12,500,000
Surplus,   3,300,000

A Life Insurance
Policy issued by **The Prudential**

s vastly more important to the welfare of a family than is Gibraltar to the British Empire.
The Prudential insures men, women, and children write for descriptive literature.

lies had purchased $1.5 billion worth of this new insurance, making it The Prudential's best-selling policy. Computers and data-processing equipment also arrived; the first computer was purchased in 1955.

In 1960 Prudential moved into its new, 24-story Plaza Building in Newark, which serves as its corporate headquarters today.

Through the 1960s The Prudential improved its Group Policies Department, and by 1974 group insurance boasted the best sales year in the industry's history. The Group Pension Department also became an industry leader. The Prudential's Real Estate Investment Department was a top player in its field, financing the development of the Empire State Building (which it purchased in 1961), the Merchandise Mart in Chicago, and many other major projects.

The Prudential's Bond Department and common stock investment sector expanded sharply. By the mid-1970s The Prudential's common stock portfolios were the largest in the life insurance industry, valued at more than four billion dollars.

Shanks left the presidency in 1961, having presided over an incredible postwar transformation. He was succeeded by 68-year-old Louis Menagh, who served one year until Orville Beal became president.

In 1965 The Prudential opened its northeastern home office, a 52-story building that became Boston's major modern landmark. That year The Prudential also created the eastern home office in Newark, separate from the corporate home office.

In 1967 The Prudential passed Metropolitan Life to become the largest insurance company in the world in terms of assets. And it kept on going: From 1968 through 1974, life insurance in force shot from $137.5 billion to $218.3 billion, and assets went from $26.6 billion to $35.8 billion.

Beal retired in 1969, and Donald S. MacNaughton was elected president becoming chairman and chief executive officer the following year.

Robert C. Winters, current chairman and chief executive officer.

At its centennial in 1975 Prudential had some 60,000 employees, more than any other life insurance company. In addition to being the biggest insurance company in the world, it had become one of the largest corporations of any kind, in terms of assets.

In 1978 Robert A. Beck became chairman and chief executive officer, and progress continued at The Prudential's usual astounding pace. In 1981 it acquired the Bache Group,

Inc., parent company of one of the nation's largest investment brokerage firms (Bache, Halsey, Stuart Shields Inc.), and renamed it Prudential-Bache Securities. The Prudential also began a joint venture with Sony Corporation to sell life insurance in Japan.

The Prudential restructured its individual insurance operations into four regional home offices in 1983. Group operations were reorganized into five regional group offices, separate from the regional home offices.

In 1984 the company introduced Appreciable Life Insurance, a universal life product, and it became the first company in the industry to sell Variable Appreciable Life.

Upon Beck's retirement in 1987, Robert C. Winters, a Prudential vice-chairman, was named chairman and chief executive officer.

Prudential today has assets of $134 billion, and the face value of all policies issued by Prudential still in effect stands at $638.9 billion. With nearly 78,000 employees, The Prudential Insurance Company of America continues to be an industry leader, and it is estimated that its policies protect some 60 million people.

The present corporate office, built in 1960, at 745 Broad Street in Newark.

M&M/MARS, A DIVISION OF MARS, INCORPORATED

M&M/MARS' association with New Jersey began in Newark in 1940, when Forrest E. Mars, Sr., founded M&M Limited, later to be renamed M&M Candies. It was there that "M&Ms"® Plain Chocolate Candies were introduced.

The confections were conceived as a neater, convenient way to eat chocolate. During World War II they were included in American soldiers' C Rations because they withstood extreme temperatures. In the hot tropics "M&Ms"® Plain Chocolate Candies were especially practical.

In 1954 the company introduced its peanut brand. The success of "M&M's"® Plain and Peanut Chocolate Candies soon required larger manufacturing facilities. In 1958 the firm moved from Newark to a new plant in Hackettstown, which has since been enlarged and updated several times.

The roots of M&M/MARS can be traced back to 1911, when Frank C. Mars (Forrest E. Mars' father) and his wife began making buttercream candies in the kitchen of their home in Tacoma, Washington. Soon the operations moved to Minneapolis, where in 1923 the MILKY WAY®

Bar was introduced. It was an instant success.

In 1926, the company moved to a new plant in a Chicago suburb where, during the following years, the MARS® Bar, 3 MUSKETEERS® Bar, and SNICKERS® Bar were introduced.

Today these products, along with a variety of other snacks, are produced by M&M/MARS at plants across America.

BAKER & TAYLOR

Baker & Taylor is the nation's leading supplier of books and related services to libraries and bookstores. It is also a top exporter of books of all kinds. And now, through a series of recent acquisitions, the company is also a major distributor of videocassettes, audio materials, and educational software. A division of W.R. Grace & Company, Baker & Taylor is headquartered in Bridgewater, New Jersey, operating a network of distribution and support centers nationwide.

The story of Baker & Taylor begins in a candlelit store in Hartford, Connecticut, in 1828. There David

Robinson and B.B. Barber established a bindery, published historical and subscription books, and opened a bookstore that became a distribution point for other publishers.

John Quincy Adams was America's President at the time, and Noah Webster's monumental *American Dictionary* was just being published after 20 years of preparation.

Only six years after its founding the new company had found success. In 1834 rapid growth and an expanding schoolbook business called for a

The Baker & Taylor headquarters building in Bridgewater, New Jersey.

move to more centrally located New York City.

Several combinations of partners led the firm during those years. On January 1, 1885, James S. Baker and Nelson Taylor acquired the company, and it assumed its present name. Although Baker & Taylor still published books at that time, it began focusing solely on book distribution. Baker & Taylor discontinued its publishing operations entirely in 1912 and became a full-fledged book wholesaler.

In the years after the company found its new direction, Harlan F. Stone served as its treasurer from

1912 to 1917. He went on to become Attorney General of the United States and later was appointed to the U.S. Supreme Court.

Based in New York City and with its inventory volume expanding, Baker & Taylor needed a larger plant by 1948. A site in Hillside, New Jersey, was selected, only 20 minutes from the heart of New York and with ready access to all main trucking and rail routes. Construction began, and the plant was ready by 1950.

In September of that year came one of the biggest single moves ever accomplished over one weekend: Baker & Taylor's relocation to its new headquarters. Every 20 minutes for 50 hours, working round the clock, a large truck loaded with books left the old headquarters at 55 Fifth Avenue in New York for the new plant in Hillside. On Monday morning the new book-distribution center was in operation.

In December 1958 Baker & Taylor was acquired by Parents' Magazine Enterprises Inc., publisher of *Parents' Magazine*. A major expansion program followed: After just eight years under new ownership Baker & Taylor became the largest book wholesaler in the nation.

That expansion featured a new 108,000-square-foot, air-conditioned plant in Momence, Illinois. That plant, Baker & Taylor's second major book-distribution center, firmly established the company's Midwest and Southern divisions. Momence is only 60 miles from Chicago and has good transportation links.

The growth in the 1960s continued as the firm gained a distinctly national profile. A new Western Division distribution center was built in Reno, Nevada, and a Southern Division was established in Commerce, Georgia. A new facility constructed in Somerville, New Jersey, eventually replaced the Hillside plant as the Eastern Division distribution center. Other expansions and acquisitions increased the company's national presence.

AKER AND TAYLOR: TWO LIBRARY CA

In 1984 two cats named Baker and Taylor, who live in a library in Minden, Nevada, gained fame in the library world when they appeared on a Baker & Taylor poster. Since that time they have been a regular feature in Baker & Taylor advertising and promotional materials.

Baker & Taylor has long been proud of its speedy service, and one episode serves as perhaps the most dramatic illustration of its efficiency. In 1959 officials at the American National Exhibition, then being held in Moscow, had a problem: Soviet readers had "borrowed" so many volumes from the Bookmobile (the display of American books) that the U.S. exhibit had to shut down.

A frantic search for replacement books ensued. Bookmobile officials, cooperating with the U.S. government, turned to Baker & Taylor. At 9:30 one morning the Baker & Taylor staff—on rush orders—began selecting and packing a variety of 1,800 current books. By 6:30 that night the books were at New York's Idlewild Airport, ready for airlifting to the Soviet capital. *The New York Times* called the feat "one of the fastest packing jobs in publishing annals."

In 1970 Baker & Taylor became a division of W.R. Grace & Company. Today Baker & Taylor continues to operate four strategically located re-gional warehouse distribution centers, located in New Jersey, Illinois, Nevada, and Georgia. The company also has an International Sales Division, a Professional and Technical Center, and an Electronic Data Processing Center, all in New Jersey.

In 1986 Baker & Taylor moved to its brand-new corporate headquarters in Bridgewater. Its executive offices, Professional and Technical Center, and Electronic Data Processing Center are now all housed in the Bridgewater Plant, while its Eastern Division regional distribution center is situated in Somerville.

Beyond the basic function of supplying books, Baker & Taylor offers related services designed to aid the purchasing process. Title-information computerized database systems make specific books readily identifiable and available. Specialized journals, newsletters on book selection, and many other services help make book delivery more speedy and efficient.

Carrying the largest and most diversified book inventory in the world, Baker & Taylor supplies titles from virtually every one of more than 15,000 publishers. Millions of books each year are distributed to bookstores, public libraries, academic libraries, and school libraries. The company's book inventory totals about 10 million volumes.

THE JAYDOR CORPORATION

It was a bright summer day in 1933 when Jerome Blumberg and Jerome Silverman, first cousins and good friends, took their coffee break in a Newark restaurant. Blumberg was a graduate accountant and Silverman operated several drugstores, but both young men were open to new opportunities.

As the two Jeromes sipped their coffee, a food supply salesman stopped into the restaurant on his rounds. Talk turned to Prohibition: Franklin Roosevelt had just become President, and repeal seemed likely. The salesman mentioned that his company, Austin-Nichols, would have the national agencies for several whiskey brands if repeal was passed.

The two cousins saw a chance to enter a booming, reborn industry. They expressed interest. "If you're serious, I'll see that you get the New Jersey agency for the brands we handle nationally," the salesman promised. And he did just that.

On the day Prohibition was repealed—December 6, 1933—J&J Distributing Co. made its first shipment. The firm, whose name was derived from the two cousins' first initials, became New Jersey's first liquor distributor after Prohibition.

More than 50 years later J&J has grown to become The Jaydor Corporation, a top U.S. distributor. Jaydor's annual sales today exceed $100 million, and it is the only liquor distributor with a Triple A rating from Dun & Bradstreet.

That turned out to be some coffee break back in 1933!

J&J started from a rented garage in Newark with one driver, a second-hand truck, and an office staff of one. It gained a franchise for Calvert whiskey and Christian Brothers wines and brandy, adding Seagram's and Carstairs soon afterward. Later came Scotch imports such as King's Ransom, House of Lords, Bells, and J&B. Many other products were added over the years, notably Smirnoff vodka and Harvey's Bristol Cream.

By 1939 J&J had moved into a 15,000-square-foot facility on Frelinghuysen Avenue in Newark. There now were five trucks and some 10 warehouse personnel. J&J was an established selling force.

In 1941 J&J opened a sales office in Atlantic City, run by David Geller. By 1944 that business was so strong that J&J opened a full-fledged branch there with a warehouse, sales office, and shipping department.

That same year an opportunity arose to acquire the New Jersey distribution rights for yet another prominent line of wines and spirits. For this purpose a second major division, Dorchester, was created, with offices

Executives of The Jaydor Corporation are Barry S. Silverman, president; Jerome J. Blumberg, chairman; Norman R. Silverman, chairman/executive committee, now retired; Michael D. Silverman, executive vice-president.

and warehouse in Trenton.

Years later, when the corporation's current Millburn headquarters was being planned, J&J decided to build it for both J&J and Dorchester. The current name of the parent company—The Jaydor Corporation—represents those two divisions.

By 1951 the Frelinghuysen Avenue building had been expanded to 50,000 square feet. J&J now operated 20 trucks out of Newark and six out of Atlantic City. By 1952 there were 59 salesmen, quite a jump from the original sales force of 12.

Through the rest of the 1950s and into the 1960s growth was rapid. The company was employing 305 people in 1967 and had an annual payroll exceeding $3.5 million.

In 1980 a third selling division, International Vintners, was formed to focus on the emerging wine market. Just six years later this newcomer has become a successful and vital contributor to the corporation.

Today J&J and Dorchester are two of the largest distributors in New Jersey. International Vintners is the second-largest company of its type in the state. Each has a North Jersey and a South Jersey division with its own sales and management personnel. The Southern divisions operate from Jaydor's modern Pleasantville facility, near Atlantic City.

The Northern Division and corporate headquarters are in Millburn, at 16 Bleeker Street.

The Northern Division and corporate headquarters are in Millburn.

Jaydor's total sales, administrative, distribution, supervisory, and executive personnel number about 400. Included in this number is another division, Rogers Warehouse & Transportation Co., which handles warehousing and delivery service for all three selling divisions.

Another area that receives special emphasis is data processing. In order to service its 10,000 customers and provide state-of-the-art management information, Jaydor relies on an outstanding data-processing department that has acquired a national reputation in the industry.

Over the years Jaydor developed close associations with many of the industry's outstanding suppliers. "We are proud," says Blumberg, "that our performance over time has merited the trust of our suppliers to the extent that many of them, such as Heublein, Seagram, Christian Brothers, and others, have entrusted us with their brands for as long as four or five decades."

Despite such enormous growth Jaydor is still very much a family affair. Chairman of the board and co-

The Millburn warehouse is an example of Jaydor's efficient use of modern equipment for processing customers' orders.

founder Jerome Blumberg is now 80 years old, at his desk every day, and as energetic as ever. Co-founder and president for many years Jerome Silverman died in 1974, but his brother, Norman, only recently retired after serving as president and executive committee chairman. And the younger generation has arrived: Jerome Silverman's son, Barry, is now president of the corporation. Norman Silverman's son, Michael, is

In order to service its 10,000 customers and provide state-of-the-art management information, Jaydor relies on an outstanding data processing department that has acquired a national reputation in the industry.

executive vice-president.

Community activity is part of Jaydor history. During World War II its leaders received commendations for work in the war effort and the sale of war bonds. Jerome Blumberg has been finance committee chairman of the National Conference of Christians and Jews and recently was nominated as Outstanding Wholesalers of the Year by *Time* magazine. To celebrate its 50th anniversary, Jaydor established student scholarships at Rutgers University for retail members of the wine and spirits industry of New Jersey. Also, as part of a community program, the firm periodically publishes posters of missing children and has them displayed by their thousands of customers.

It has been quite a story since the coffee break that started it all. What has been the secret of The Jaydor Corporation's success? Perhaps Jerome Silverman already knew it in 1933, when he said, "He profits most who serves best."

ELECTRICAL INSTALLATIONS, INC.

Throughout nearly four decades Electrical Installations, Inc., has put in place hundreds of millions of dollars in electrical engineering and construction in projects ranging from banks, shopping centers, and office buildings to all kinds of industrial plants, complex control systems, and high-voltage power facilities.

Electrical Installations, Inc., a unique electrical contracting and engineering firm, was founded in 1949 by Robert J. Bauer, its current president. An electrical engineering graduate from Cornell University, Bauer served in the U.S. Air Force during World War II and then worked for the Western Electric Company. He left Western Electric in 1947 to work as a supervisor and estimator for Industrial Electric, Inc., a local electrical engineering and contracting firm. From there, attracted to the possibilities of electrical contracting, Bauer set out on his own to form Electrical Installations, Inc.

Since 1949 his company's annual sales have grown from a half-million dollars to more than $20 million today. Starting with a work force of 10, Eii now employs up to 400 people for peak workload periods.

While others would choose to carve out careers solely as electrical installers, Bauer instead diversified his firm's services into electrical engineering and design, energy management, and recently into mechanical instrumentation. That diversity of skills and service has become the hallmark of Electrical Installations' uniqueness.

Eii's first office was on Van Buren Avenue in Elizabeth. Subsequently the company moved to offices in Springfield and Roselle Park, and finally to its current headquarters in Cranford.

Eii has expanded through both internal growth and acquisitions. In 1957 it acquired J.J. Tomasulo Co. of Roselle Park, a large electrical contractor working on major accounts for Exxon and many others. Two years later it purchased electrical contractor Watson-Flagg Corpo-

Robert J. Bauer (left), president, and Robert G. Guempel, vice-president of construction.

ration of Paterson, opening up the market in northern New Jersey. By the 1960s Eii had blossomed into a designing, engineering, and contracting firm active throughout central and northern New Jersey.

With its total electrical service, including installation, design, purchasing, engineering, and maintenance, Eii has aimed toward turnkey projects—performance of a total electrical project instead of just one phase of it.

Company strategy has focused on repeat business coming directly from major clients rather than through general contractors. Eii has developed a long relationship with many major companies. Its repeat clients include corporations such as Exxon, General Motors, Ford Motor Company, New Jersey Bell, AT&T, Singer, ITT, Squibb, Sea-Land, Wakefern Foods, Shop-Rite, Pathmark, and Nabisco, as well as most of the major general contractors, including Turner Construction, Gilbane Building Co., Wm. L. Crow Construction Co., Mahony-Troast, and hundreds of others.

Eii moved to computerization in 1975, before many of its competitors.

Its first computer was a large unit handling payrolls, billing, and materials and tool control. Today Eii's computer system helps with electrical designs, performs complete electrical estimates, and provides manpower loading charts and schedules.

The firm's past and present projects include many major jobs. During the 1960s it performed the electrical installation for the Fedders Corporation integrated manufacturing, design, and sales facility in Edison, and the federally sponsored Princeton nuclear laboratory. In the 1970s Eii carried out the largest electrical installation ever in Union County, a more than $6-million project for the Essex sewage-treatment plant.

One Eii specialty is powering up research laboratories, as evidenced by its recent electrical installation at Exxon's modern research laboratory in Clinton, a massive project valued at more than $500 million with Eii's portion of the electrical package in excess of $20 million. In high-tech electrification, Eii did electrical work for the Worldwide Computer Control Center for Exxon Research and Engineering at Florham Park, the largest computer operation on the East Coast.

Other high-tech accomplishments include ongoing work on a General

BACKES, WALDRON & HILL

Situated in the heart of New Jersey's capital city of Trenton, the law firm of Backes, Waldron & Hill has been a part of the state capital's history for over 100 years. The firm's history is rooted in the jurisprudential tradition of the Backes family, one of the more distinguished families in the history of New Jersey's legal profession.

In 1848 John Backes immigrated to America from Germany. Finding work as a blacksmith at Cooper, Hewitt & Co.'s rolling mill, he married Mary Hannes, from his hometown of Trier. The father of six died in 1874 from injuries sustained in an explosion at the mill.

Peter, the eldest son, who was 16 when his father died, worked for a furniture dealer, and the third son, John H., 13, became an office boy for attorney Edward H. Murphy. After reading law with Murphy, John was admitted to the bar in 1884.

Peter joined Murphy in helping develop the shore town of Point Pleasant. While John ran the law office in Trenton, his older brother worked with Murphy at the shore.

For over 100 years the law firm of Backes, Waldron & Hill has been a part of Trenton's history. Today, still vital to New Jersey's legal affairs, the firm consists of (standing, left to right) Michael J. Nizolek, William W. Backes, Jr., Robert M. Backes, Robert C. Billmeier, and (seated, left to right) Harry R. Hill, Jr., and James A. Waldron.

The law offices of Backes, Waldron & Hill at 15 West Front Street in Trenton.

Admitted to the bar in 1886, Peter joined John in the law practice.

Five of the six Backes sons went on to distinguished legal careers. John H. served the New Jersey Court of Chancery for 21 years as vice-chancellor, Theodore was assistant attorney general, William J. served as advisory master in chancery, and Albert practiced law in Newark.

Peter maintained a private practice in Trenton for 55 years. In 1913 he took his son Herbert W. as a partner, calling the firm Backes & Backes. His other son, William Wright Backes, joined the practice in 1930.

Peter Backes died in 1941, but he had already welcomed Herbert's son, Robert Maddock Backes, into the firm. A second grandson, William W. Backes, Jr., joined in 1966.

In 1954 James A. Waldron became the first non-Backes to join the firm. Four years later Harry R. Hill, Jr., became a member of the firm, and Michael J. Nizolek and Robert C. Billmeier entered the practice thereafter. With the two third-generation family members, they make up the six partners of the law firm known since 1980 as Backes, Waldron & Hill. Brenda F. Engel is associated with the firm.

The firm has served the New Jersey National Bank, New Jersey Manufacturers Insurance Company, Transamerica Delaval Inc., Roller-Bearing Company of America, Goodall Rubber, and the Trenton Savings Fund Society, and it has represented the Catholic Diocese of Trenton since 1886. Backes & Backes represented Maddock Pottery during its acquisition by American Standard in 1929 and served as counsel to John A. Roebling's Sons Company in the 1954 sale to Colorado Fuel & Iron.

From 1892 until 1925 Peter Backes' offices were in the Forst-Richey Building at State and Warren. Backes & Backes then moved into the Trenton Trust Building at 28 West State Street. In 1984 the firm relocated to 15 West Front Street.

Location in the state capital, which houses every level of New Jersey's court system, has enhanced the firm's role in New Jersey's history and legal affairs. Trenton, settled in 1679, is a city steeped in history. Backes, Waldron & Hill has been part of the city's past and will be part of its future.

GENERAL PUBLIC UTILITIES CORPORATION

The General Public Utilities Corporation (GPU) provides electricity to more than four million people in New Jersey and Pennsylvania. GPU is a holding company with three operating subsidiaries and two service companies.

GPU's New Jersey-based operating subsidiary is Jersey Central Power & Light Company (JCP&L), serving more than 815,000 New Jersey customers. Its Pennsylvania subsidiaries are Metropolitan Edison Company (Met-Ed) and Pennsylvania Electric Company (Penelec), with over 900,000 customers in Pennsylvania.

The GPU service companies are GPU Service Corporation, which serves as a "corporate staff," providing professional services to the three operating subsidiaries, and GPU Nuclear Corporation, which manages, operates, and maintains GPU's nuclear generating facilities. Like the electric-utility industry itself, General Public Utilities Corporation entered the twentieth century as a fledgling business and soon became a major enterprise.

GPU's seeds were planted in small communities stretching across the United States and extending to Canada and even to the Philippines. In those places, small local power plants began sprouting up at the turn of the twentieth century.

As the industry expanded, holding companies were formed to increase efficiency, reduce duplication, and cut costs for local electric companies. In 1906 GPU's ancestor holding company, the Associated Gas and Electric Company (AGECO), was formed by 10 electric and gas companies in New York, Ohio, and Pennsylvania, starting with total assets of $1.2 million.

In 1921 AGECO, whose assets had grown to seven million dollars, was acquired by Howard Hopson. He soon started a string of acquisitions that saw AGECO become one of America's five largest holding companies by 1929.

Under Hopson, AGECO amassed holding companies, subholding companies, electric, gas, water, ice, streetcar, bus, real estate, management, service, and investment companies under 1,800 names in 26 states, two Canadian provinces, and the Philippines.

Following the Public Utility Holding Company Act of 1935, AGECO was reorganized to become General Public Utilities in 1946. By that time the companies in the utility system had been reduced to seven major subsidiaries, operating mainly in New Jersey, Pennsylvania, and New York State.

Newly formed GPU worked to create a single, interconnected system. As electricity demand soared, GPU embarked on a massive construction program, adding new power plants and strengthening transmission and distribution capabilities. New records in load, sales, and earnings continued to be set each year during the 1950s and 1960s.

GPU's first president was Albert F. Tegen, who previously had been an SEC investigator. In 1955 Tegen had hired William G. Kuhns as corporate secretary, and when Tegen retired in 1967 Kuhns became president and in 1974 chairman, a post he will hold until his retirement in May 1987. John F. O'Leary will succeed Kuhns as chairman and chief executive officer.

In the 1960s GPU became a pioneer in commercial nuclear power. It installed a small experimental reactor in Saxton, Pennsylvania, and in 1969 it opened the Oyster Creek power plant as the nation's first large-scale commercial nuclear facility.

The 1960s also brought increasing energy demand, requiring new generation and extensive financing. Recognizing the problems of unrestrained growth, GPU reduced new-plant construction and operated facilities jointly with other utilities to cut costs. GPU was also an early leader in the conservation/load-management programs so prevalent in the industry today.

In response to the industry's new complexities, in 1971 GPU created GPU Service Corporation to increase system efficiency, centralize and coordinate rate matters and other activities, and provide administrative, financial, and technical services to GPU's operating companies.

A second operating company, GPU Nuclear, staffed with nuclear experts from around the country, was established after the March 1979 accident at GPU's Three Mile Island Unit 2 nuclear power plant in Dauphin County, Pennsylvania.

After building Three Mile Island Unit 1 in the early 1970s, GPU brought TMI Unit 2 on line in December 1978. The TMI Unit 2 accident caused major financial consequences, and threatened the GPU system with bankruptcy. The company has now returned to normal. Much was learned from the accident and cleanup, bringing new knowledge and operating effectiveness to the nu-clear industry. In 1985 TMI-1, the nuclear unit not involved in the accident, returned to service.

GPU's New Jersey subsidiary, Jersey Central Power & Light, dates back to the gaslight era in 1853, when its oldest predecessor, the Cape Island Gas Company, was founded.

In following years local utilities appeared across New Jersey, and many were small family operations. The Electric Light and Power Company of Hightstown, for example, had a founding staff in 1899 of a husband, wife, and daughter. JCP&L is in fact made up of some 100 similar forebears.

As rural and suburban areas became more heavily populated, local gas and electric plants joined forces to meet demand. In 1925, 11 utilities merged to form the Jersey Central Power & Light Company. By 1929, 13 more companies had been added, and in 1931 Eastern New Jersey Power Company, a large corporation in central Jersey, also merged into JCP&L.

In addition to its gas and electric activities, JCP&L operated water, ice, sewer, trolley, and bus companies. Those interests were disposed of over the years, and in 1952 JCP&L also sold its gas properties. JCP&L's last merger took place in 1973, when it joined with New Jersey Power & Light.

When JCP&L was organized, it had 47,000 electricity customers. The GPU subsidiary now serves about two million people in an area comprising about 43 percent of New Jersey's land mass. With about 4,000 employees, JCP&L is the largest revenue producer of the GPU companies, with average annual gross revenues of $1.35 billion in 1984, 1985, and 1986.

THE WATTS, CAMPBELL COMPANY

The Watts, Campbell Company is one of New Jersey's oldest machine shops under continuous family ownership, and the firm also owns the oldest functioning industrial facility near the Passaic River in Newark.

The Watts, Campbell Company was formed in 1851 as the Passaic Machine Works, founded by William Watts and Zachariah Belcher. In 1853, two years after launching their company, the two men moved from their factory on Washington Street to the corner of Ogden (now McCarter) and East Mill Street on the Passaic River, still the location of the firm today.

William Watts, whose father, George, had emigrated to America from Bristol, England, was born in 1825 in New York City and moved with his parents to Newark two years later. After a rudimentary education, William Watts apprenticed as a machinist in the shops of Seth Boyden, at that time a prominent maker of steam engines in Newark.

In 1850 William Watts and Zachariah Belcher established a machine shop under the name of Watts & Belcher, renamed Passaic Machine Works the following year. George Watts—William's brother—had erected a spacious shop in Newark for mechanical work, and the brothers subsequently became business partners with the move to the corner of Ogden and East Mill streets.

Belcher left Passaic Machine Works in 1855, and the company then came under ownership of William and George Watts. Ten years later Daniel Campbell became a partner, and the firm's name was changed to Watts, Campbell and Company. By then the firm was manufacturing Corliss steam engines and other machinery.

William Watts remained an active partner in the business until his death in 1883. He was remembered as a skillful mechanic who kept pace with modern mechanical science and enhanced the value of many inventions. Later in 1883 the company

By the middle of the eighteenth century steam engines had come into commercial use, but they were not used extensively in the United States until the introduction of the steam-powered locomotive, which occurred in the 1830s. This drawing of a Watts, Campbell heavy-duty, direct-connected Corliss steam engine comes from an old brochure of The Watts, Campbell Company, circa 1880.

was officially incorporated as The Watts, Campbell Company with George Watts, Daniel T. Campbell, Mary Belcher, and Charles Watts as proprietors.

The Watts, Campbell Company's main product from 1851 until about 1930 was Corliss steam engines. Steam-powered machinery was the perfect catalyst for Newark's developing industry in the middle of the nineteenth century; the Passaic River was unable to generate sufficient hydropower below the fall line, and the Morris Canal—opened to Newark in 1831—provided a transportation artery for Pennsylvania anthracite.

During the latter half of the nineteenth century and into the twentieth, Watts, Campbell and its neighbor Hewes & Phillips became the major

producers of steam engines in Newark. At the Newark Industrial Exhibition of 1872, Watts, Campbell displayed the state-of-the-art industry products of their day: vertical and horizontal steam engines.

By 1880 Watts, Campbell had 140 employees, and its steam engine products were being used extensively. Prominent Newark businesses that purchased steam engines from The Watts, Campbell Company included Clark Thread, Ballantine, The Celluloid Company, Weston Electric, T.P. Howell Leather, and Wiss Shears.

In 1884 Watts, Campbell had an annual employment of 320 workers and sales of $300,000, compared to sales of only $20,000 and just two or three employees when the firm was launched in 1851. The company's shops had expanded from an area measuring 36 by 72 feet until they covered 1.5 acres. Customers grew from just a few local purchasers to thousands in various parts of the world.

The Watts, Campbell Company steam engines were supplied to customers in Waterbury, Buffalo, Wilmington, Savannah, San Francisco, Texas, and as far away as Mexico and Cuba. Watts, Campbell was also producing machinist tools and sugar machinery, and quantities of sugar crushers and refiners went from the company plant to Cuba in the late nineteenth century. When competitor Hewes & Phillips shut down in 1913, Watts, Campbell purchased that firm's drawings and patterns.

Watts, Campbell stopped making steam engines in the 1930s, but the company still occasionally repairs old steam equipment, along with its more modern production and repair activities. Today the corporation machines large casting, weldments, and replacement parts to area chemical companies, machine shops, fabricators, and marine operations.

The firm is still at its original site at the corner of what is now McCarter and East Mill Street, though its plant has been expanded over the years. Originally it was a mansard-roofed masonry building, but in the

1950s the roof was flattened and the entire building was stuccoed. The interior, remarkably, has been unaffected and features late-nineteenth-century office equipment that is sometimes the subject of tours by history buffs.

In 1986 the Watts, Campbell building was placed on the New Jersey Register of Historic Places by the Office of New Jersey Heritage, Division of Parks and Forestry of the U.S. Department of Environmental Protection. Because of its historical

---

The interior of The Watts, Campbell Company has been unaffected by the passage of time and features many original pieces of late-nineteenth-century office equipment and machinery that are sometimes the subject of tours by such groups as the Society for Industrial Archaeology (shown here). The group is looking at a 90-inch-diameter lathe built before 1900 and a wooden boom crane capable of lifting 20,000 pounds.

value, the building is now federally protected from being encroached upon, damaged, or destroyed.

The Watts, Campbell Company today is run by Charles "Chad" H. Watts, Jr., whose great-grandfather and great-granduncle were the founders of the business. Chad joined the company in 1950 upon graduation from Rutgers University. On a tour of his plant, he can proudly point out pieces of machinery that were operating long before he joined the firm, as well as some that were built long before his father and grandfather were born.

Some of that old machinery still outperforms the competition. And it is paid for and depreciated: While a competitor might have to figure in those costs on a job bid, The Watts, Campbell Company needs to worry only about covering salaries and actual costs.

CARTERET SAVINGS BANK, FA

On May 28, 1888, nine men assembled at the Essex County Clerk's Office. Under the provisions of an April 9, 1875, act encouraging the establishment of mutual loan homestead and building associations, they formed the West End Building and Loan Association of Newark, New Jersey. Under terms of the initial charter, the association's business was to be transacted only within the city limits of Newark.

Some 50 years later the West End Building and Loan Association was reorganized, leading to the founding of the Carteret Building and Loan Association on July 10, 1939. The newly formed association was located in Newark at 866 Broad Street, still the main office. The institution's official opening came on October 10, 1939, and its name was changed to Carteret Savings and Loan Association shortly thereafter.

On January 15, 1986, the name of the savings institution was changed to its present name, Carteret Savings Bank, FA.

From the very beginning Carteret Savings forged ahead in the banking business. By 1943 its assets had reached $15 million, double the amount at the time of its founding. Five years later assets had reached $46.3 million, approximately four times the assets of 1943. By 1979 Carteret's assets were in excess of one billion dollars. Since then the bank's assets have grown immensely,

The official opening for what was then Carteret Savings and Loan Association came on October 10, 1939. Here, opened for business, the interior of the bank's first office as it looked then.

to a total of more than five billion dollars.

Carteret's rapid growth over the years was spurred by acquisitions. In 1954 the bank opened two branches, each the result of a merger. The Roseville branch, on 487 Orange Street in Newark, was acquired from the Bradford Savings and Loan Association of East Orange before being taken over by Carteret, and the other branch, on 606 Central Avenue in East Orange, was acquired from the Clarion Building and Loan Association.

In the ensuing years Carteret steadily increased its branch network. On September 30, 1982, Carteret became an interstate banking network with the acquisition of 12 branches through a merger with First Federal Savings and Loan Association of Delray Beach, Florida.

First Federal's offices on Florida's Gold Coast were augmented by the purchase of four branches in the central and Gulf Coast areas from Freedom Savings and Loan in December 1982. To date Carteret has 96 branch-offices located in New Jersey, Florida, Maryland, and Virginia.

Today Carteret Savings is ranked 40th among the *Fortune* 100 largest

An exterior view of the Carteret Savings and Loan Association's first office at 866 Broad Street in Newark shortly after it opened in 1939. In January 1986, after rapid growth and many acquisitions, Carteret changed its name to Carteret Savings Bank, FA.

diversified financial companies. The bank has its headquarters in Morristown, New Jersey, and its administrative offices in Delray Beach, Florida.

In addition to its traditional retail banking and mortgage lending, Carteret Savings Bank, FA, has diversified its activities to include commercial credit, income-property finance, consumer loans, insurance, stock brokerage, and other personal financial services. Carteret also operates subsidiaries engaging in real estate development ventures and mortgage origination and servicing.

Ernest A. Minier, Carteret's first president.

EXXON 1

On January 2, 1909, a shovelful of coal was hurled into the furnace, firing up the first shell still and starting the operation of Bayway Refinery in Linden, New Jersey.

In those days Bayway had only five batteries of stills capable of running approximately 20,000 barrels of crude oil per day. Since then it has grown into one of America's major petroleum-manufacturing facilities.

Linden was chosen as the refinery site for several reasons: The markets were nearby, the 1,500 acres of flat meadowlands made construction relatively easy, and a pumping station and nine storage tanks linked to the western oil fields already occupied part of the land.

Chemical production has also played a big part in Bayway's history. The petrochemical industry was virtually born at the plant in 1919, when Exxon Chemical Company scientists developed a process to convert propylene into isopropyl alcohol in commercial quantities.

One of five domestic refineries operated by Exxon Company U.S.A., Bayway is the largest such facility on the East Coast. Its crude oil arrives by tanker from Mexico and Alaska's North Slope. The millions of gallons of gasoline, heating oil, jet fuel, asphalt, LPG, and diesel fuel produced

The Bayway Refinery in 1911. Then it had only five batteries of stills capable of running approximately 20,000 barrels of crude oil per day. Now it has grown into one of America's major petroleum manufacturing facilities.

there are shipped to customers by barge, tank truck, pipeline, and tanker. The chemical plant produces specialty chemicals, industrial solvents, and additives that improve the quality of lubricating oils.

In 1919, the same year the chemical operation opened, Bayway Refinery formed a 26-man development department that became one of America's first industrial research laboratories. The department later became the Exxon Research and Engineering Company (ER&E), which today helps meet the parent firm's worldwide refining, marketing, and transportation needs through its research and development in petroleum products and processing, synthetic fuels processing, and engineering

systems.

The subsidiary's historical achievements include the first gasolines tailored for different seasons and climates, synthetic butyl rubber, and the fluid catalytic cracking process—which increases the amount of high-octane gasoline and aviation fuel that can be made from petroleum. It also developed the FLUID COKING and FLEXICOKING processes, which convert crude residuum into high-quality, clean-burning oils, and the FLEXSORB family of gas-treating agents, which remove contaminating hydrogen sulfide and carbon dioxide from natural gas and the gas streams of refineries and chemical plants.

The petrochemical industry was virtually born at the Bayway plant in 1911, when Exxon Chemical Company scientists developed a process to convert propylene into isopropyl alcohol in commercial quantities. Today, of the five domestic refineries operated by Exxon, Bayway is the largest such facility on the East Coast.

In 1919 the Bayway Refinery formed a 26-man development department that became one of America's first industrial research laboratories. Here a glassblower creates a special laboratory flask.

SANDOZ CORPORATION

Sandoz Corporation is the American subsidiary of Sandoz Ltd. of Basel, Switzerland, an international pharmaceutical, chemical, dyestuff, specialty food, and agrochemical company with operations in 42 countries worldwide.

Sandoz Ltd. was founded in Basel as a small dyestuff factory in 1886 by two young Swiss entrepreneurs: dyestuff chemist Alfred Kern and financier and businessman Edouard Sandoz.

In 1919 the forerunner of the Sandoz Corporation was incorporated in New York City as the Sandoz Chemical Works—a small importer of dyestuffs and chemicals from Switzerland, serving America's silk and wool manufacturers. The new company quickly found a blossoming market for its dyestuffs in the nearby New Jersey town of Paterson, then known as the Silk City. New England, at that time America's major woolen center, was another booming market, and the firm opened a branch office in Boston.

Back in Basel, the parent company was diversifying into new fields. Dr. Arthur Stoll had founded a pharmaceutical division there in 1917, conducting biochemical analyses of medicinal plants and herbs. Stoll analyzed ergot, a source of medicinal alkaloids obtained from the rye seed. Isolating ergot's main alkaloid, he called it ergotamine, a substance still used to treat conditions associated with overactivity of the sympathetic nervous system and in prevention of hemorrhage after childbirth. Ergotamine was later found to be effective in relieving pain from migraine and other forms of vascular headache.

In 1925 a pharmaceutical sales outlet was established at Sandoz in New York, and pharmaceutical manufacturing facilities were added a few years later. Activities in this sector expanded rapidly: Calcium Sandoz, developed in 1927, was the first safely injectable form of calcium (calcium gluconate) and became widely used in therapeutics. Its de-

The forerunner of the Sandoz Corporation, Sandoz Chemical Works, was incorporated in New York City in 1919.

velopment made Sandoz internationally renowned.

During those years several chemists arrived from the Swiss parent company to help launch what is now the Sandoz Pharmaceuticals Corporation. Many of them were important figures in the history of the company. Of special importance was Dr. Yves Dunant, who came from Sandoz Ltd. and was instrumental in expanding the sales force and training sales representatives, as well as making many other major efforts to advance the interests of the corporation within the pharmaceutical industry.

By the late 1940s Sandoz had outgrown its New York facilities, and it purchased 200 acres of land in East

Hanover, New Jersey, for a new corporate complex. The first building there—a pharmaceutical manufacturing plant—was opened in 1950 with fewer than 200 employees. Over the next three decades the East Hanover complex would expand to 14 buildings and more than 1,500 employees.

In mid-1986 Sandoz launched a new consumer health care group. The new unit, called Consumer Health Care Group, combines Ex-Lax Pharmaceutical Co., Inc., and Dorsey Laboratories, and is headquartered in Parsippany. In the consumer area, some of the various over-the-counter products the new division will manufacture are Ex-Lax, Gas-X, and the Triaminic line of cough and cold products.

Over the years Sandoz has produced many important ethical pharmaceuticals for mental illness, headache, endocrine disturbances, and geriatric disorders, developing more than 20 original pharmaceutical products to help relieve illness and pain. As ethical pharmaceuticals, Sandoz products are directed to the attention of the medical profession rather than the general public. They are marketed to physicians, drugstores, mental hospitals, medical schools, and nursing homes. Information on Sandoz products is provided to the medical community by highly trained service representatives. Medical professionals also receive up-to-date information from Sandoz through its medical services department, staffed by medical professionals.

In 1960 the ergotamine molecule, first studied by Dr. Stoll in 1917, was fully synthesized. Through this synthesization Sandoz developed ergoloid mesylate (Hydergine), used for treatment of depression, confusion, and dizziness in geriatric patients. Another ergot derivative is bromocriptine mesylate (Parlodel), used for treatment of Parkinson's disease. A major Sandoz product developed during the 1960s was Mellaril (thioridazine), a major tranquilizer that has played a key role in mental health advances over the past two decades.

At the Sandoz Research Institute in East Hanover, chemists, biologists, and other trained personnel are engaged in a continuing search for useful new drugs. Current efforts are concentrated on development of compounds for the treatment of heart disease, hypertension, arthritis, insomnia, and the degenerative symptoms of old age.

Recent research has focused also on the development of new compounds through alteration of molecular structures of natural parent substances. Production of original compounds has become a focal point of Sandoz research. Current efforts center on the development of compounds for prevention and treatment of diabetes, asthma, and rheumatic conditions. A new immunosuppressant, Sandimmune, has revolutionized the organ transplant field.

The Sandoz Corporation has several other divisions: the Chemicals Corporation, based in Charlotte, North Carolina; the Crop Protection Corporation, headquartered in Chicago, Illinois, and the Nutrition Corporation based in Minneapolis, Minnesota.

The Sandoz Chemicals Corpora-

An aerial photograph of the Sandoz Corporation, located on 200 acres in East Hanover.

tion makes dyes, pigments, chemicals, plastic additives, and related products. Customers include industries that produce textiles, man-made fibers, paper, metals, cosmetics, household products, coatings, and plastics. This division has also operated a plant in Fair Lawn, New Jersey, since 1948 and has other major operations in Martin, South Carolina, and Cincinnati, Ohio.

Of growing importance is the Crop Protection Corporation, developing and producing agricultural insecticides, fungicides, and herbicides. This division's operations are centered in Chicago. It has research laboratories in Palo Alto, California. Sandoz has an important niche in the field of seeds with Northrup King and Rodgers Seed.

Since the acquisition of the Wander Company by Sandoz Ltd., the U.S. subsidiary has been developing the Nutrition Corporation, with a range of quality products geared to prescription, institutional, and consumer markets.

In addition to the more than 1,500 employees that work at the Sandoz East Hanover complex, another 6,000 are employed at other Sandoz Corporation locations. The company's annual sales total nearly $1.5 billion.

ALLIED-SIGNAL INC.

In 1979 the Allied Chemical Corporation could look back at 59 successful years of activity in basic chemicals, oil and gas, and fibers. But this traditional identity of Allied Chemical would soon change dramatically, as the company undertook an unprecedented period of diversification, acquisitions, and mergers during the 1980s. Today Allied-Signal Inc. is a worldwide advanced-technology company active in aerospace, automotive components, and engineered materials.

Allied-Signal's roots go back to December 1920, when five chemical companies merged to form the Allied Chemical and Dye Corporation. During World War I shortages of dyes, pharmaceuticals, and chemicals had hampered the United States and its allies, as foreign companies, primarily German, dominated the industry.

The leaders of Allied's five founding firms saw unification as a way to strengthen America's chemical business. The five were the Barrett Com-

Here technicians are testing Bendix avionics, which are among the most widely used in the aerospace industry.

pany, supplier of coal-tar chemicals and roofing; the General Chemical Company, specializing in industrial acids; National Aniline & Chemical Company, a top dye maker; Samet-Solvay Corporation, a coke manufacturer; and Solvay Process Company, a producer of nitrogen chemicals.

Based in New York City, Allied, by 1943, had established its first corporate research lab in a rented former umbrella factory in Morristown, New Jersey. In 1948 the company built its own chemical research laboratory at the corner of Columbia Road and Park Avenue in Morris

Township, on the former estate of financier Otto Kahn.

Growing steadily through a policy of mergers and acquisitions, the firm was renamed Allied Chemical Corporation in 1958. Four years later Allied purchased the Union Texas Natural Gas Corporation, later to become Union Texas Petroleum. The acquisition proved to be an important one. John T. Connor, Secretary of Commerce under Lyndon Johnson, became Allied's chief executive officer in 1968 and served as chairman from 1969 through 1979. He transformed Union Texas from a raw-material source of Allied into a successful oil and gas business.

By 1968 Allied had started transferring its corporate headquarters from New York City to Morris Township, completing the move four years later. Edward L. Hennessy, Jr., the present chairman and chief executive officer, assumed leadership of the company in 1979, with a plan to move away from commodity chemical products, oil, and gas, and into high-tech, value-added products. Under Hennessy's leadership the firm

A view of the Allied-Signal headquarters in Morris Township where Allied-Signal today is a worldwide advanced-technology company active in aerospace, automotive components, and engineered materials.

JAMESWAY CORPORATION

In 1961 Herbert Fisher opened a store in Jamestown, New York, with virtually all his savings and just a handful of backers. Today the Jamesway discount store chain stretches through New Jersey, Pennsylvania, New York, and Virginia, as well as Delaware and Maryland, where it expanded to in 1983.

The Jamestown store generated $750,000 in sales during its first year. Today the Jamesway Corporation operates over 100 stores and had sales of $612 million in the fiscal year that ended February 1, 1987. In fact Jamesway is one of the top 20 discount department store chains in the nation.

Aside from being an acknowledged success at retailing, founder Herbert Fisher is credited with being one of the first to introduce discount retailing to many of the smaller cities and towns.

Today Jamesway offers a broad variety of name-brand hard and soft goods. Housed in modern facilities, its retail operations range in size from 30,000 to 85,000 square feet.

Merchandise departments cover a wide variety of family needs, from apparel and home furnishings to hardware, housewares, auto supplies, small appliances, health and beauty aids, and many more products. Hard goods account for about 60 percent of the sales volume with apparel and home furnishings accounting for the balance.

Arlie Lazarus, president, points out that a key element in the firm's growth has been careful site selection, involving detailed research and study. "Location is clearly one of the most important determinants of success," Fisher says. "Other criteria for success include what is inside each Jamesway store and how it's merchandised. And here you get right down to our basic retailing philosophy."

That philosophy focuses on name-brand, quality merchandise stocked in depth and offered at the best prices. Jamesway is geared to deal in large quantities so that prices are generally able to be cut, and the

Herbert Fisher, chairman and founder of Jamesway Corporation.

chain's buyers are trained to scour the market for the best buys. Minicomputers in each store implement a high-tech inventory-replenishment system and also expedite warehouse ordering, payrolls, and other work.

The company's internal structure is unique. Department managers are called group leaders: Depending on the store's size, a group leader might be in charge of as many as six departments. While department managers used to do everything themselves, group leaders delegate more work.

Jamesway involves each store and

its personnel in the life and interests of the community. Stores house community blood-donor drives and collection drives for toys and clothing for charity. Store parking lots are used on weekends for cake and merchandise sales and flea markets to raise money for worthy causes. "By being in the forefront of community activities and cosponsors of worthy local programs, the stores become closely identified with the interests of the community and its people," says Herbert Fisher.

Jamesway Corporation is a publicly owned company whose shares are listed on the New York Stock Exchange.

HOFFMANN-LA ROCHE INC.

Hoffmann-La Roche Inc. is one of the world's leading health care companies. Internationally known for its original research and development, Roche has introduced many important medical innovations.

The firm provides a wide range of health products and services, including pharmaceuticals, diagnostic test systems, clinical laboratory services, specialty chemicals, and many others. A pioneer in pure bulk synthetic vitamins, Roche supplies the food, pharmaceutical, and agricultural industries with vitamins, food additives, and animal health products.

F. Hoffmann-La Roche & Co., Ltd., was founded in 1896 by Fritz Hoffmann in Basel, Switzerland. With its headquarters still in Basel, the firm today has operations in 50 countries worldwide, employs some

46,000 people, and has annual sales of about four billion dollars.

The worldwide Roche has major research centers in Basel as well as Nutley, New Jersey; Welwyn Garden City, England; and Kamakura, Japan. Basic research is conducted at the company's Institute of Immunology in Basel and The Roche Institute of Molecular Biology in Nutley. Worldwide, Roche invests about two million dollars each working day for research and development.

In 1905 Hoffmann-La Roche Inc., also called Roche/USA, was established in New York City as the Hoffmann-La Roche Chemical Works. In 1929 the company moved to Nutley, where it is based today. The Nutley facility combines Roche/USA's administrative, research, and production headquarters.

Roche/USA has some 11,500 employees, including 1,000 researchers, with annual sales of about one billion dollars. Roche is a leader in the fields of pharmaceuticals, diagnostics, and vitamins and fine chemicals in the specific areas of human and

The Hoffmann-La Roche Inc. corporate headquarters in Nutley where the company conducts much of its internationally recognized medical research and development.

Hoffmann-La Roche's research commitment to the new biotechnologies has already led to the production of a number of valuable medicines including the first biotherapeutic or drug made from the body for treating cancer. Here a Roche researcher is setting up a DNA experiment.

Products of Roche Vitamins and Fine Chemicals Division are manufactured in Nutley and Belvidere (and elsewhere), where more than 500 distinct chemical compounds are produced. Shown here is the control room at the Belvidere manufacturing complex, which provides all the tools a skilled operator needs to ensure the uninterrupted production of 30 tons of vitamin C daily.

animal nutrition and health.

The Roche Pharmaceuticals Division is at the forefront of the prescription drug market, with new medicines and nuclear medicine diagnostic products developed from original research. Its major historic innovations include the first medicine for the nerve-muscle disease myasthenia gravis, the first effective drug for tuberculosis, revolutionary drugs for anxiety and emotional and central nervous system disorders, and many more.

Roche Diagnostics, the company's diagnostics division, is a leader in health testing. It has three components: Roche Diagnostic Systems, Roche Biomedical Laboratories, Inc., and Diagnostic Dimensions, Inc.

Roche Diagnostic Systems provides analytical systems and test-tube diagnostic kits for hospitals, laboratories, and doctors' offices. Roche Biomedical Laboratories, Inc., is a national network of clinical laboratories offering a broad spectrum of test-

tube diagnostic tests for physicians, hospitals, and other medical facilities. Diagnostic Dimensions, Inc., offers programs that address the problem of substance abuse in the work place.

Roche Vitamins and Fine Chemicals Division contributes to human and animal health with products and services that enhance nutrition and prevent and treat disease. It supplies medicines, produces safe colors and buffering agents for foods, and is America's largest manufacturer of bulk vitamins. For livestock, poultry, and other commercial and companion animals, the sector supplies vitamins and custom multivitamin premixes, drug feed additives, and other health products.

Roche, an industry leader in research and development, has some of the nation's finest scientists, including hundreds of physicians and doctoral-level scientists. Since 1980 Roche has averaged about 100 patents per year for its discoveries, and Roche scientists publish approximately 300 scientific papers annually on their research results.

The Roche Institute of Molecular Biology, based in Nutley, is the only facility devoted solely to basic research in the U.S. health care industry.

The institute was founded in 1967 for fundamental research in biochemistry, genetics, biophysics, and other areas of molecular technology. Situated on Roche's Nutley industrial campus, the institute combines the academic freedom of a university with the resources of a large corporation, and represents the company's long-term investment in pursuit of the advanced levels of scientific understanding necessary for the prevention, diagnosis, and treatment of complex diseases.

More than 90 percent of all new medicines come from companies like Roche that are investing heavily in research. Its scientists interact continually with government and academic researchers, and the firm commits millions of dollars annually

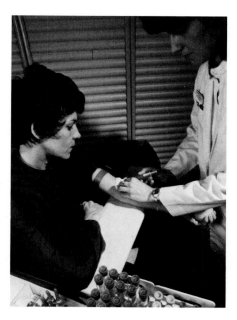

A medical technologist collects a blood sample from a patient. Roche Biomedical Laboratories, Inc., a nationwide chain of clinical laboratories, processes more than 40,000 such samples daily.

to the support of university-based research.

Roche pharmaceutical research covers infectious and inflammatory diseases, dermatological disorders, disorders of the immune system and central nervous system, cancer, cardiovascular disease, AIDS, and many others. Its diagnostic research and development concentrates on diagnostic tests and products, exploring new frontiers in disease detection.

Roche clinical laboratory research includes allergy testing, DNA probes, and rapid-detection techniques for various diseases. Human and animal nutrition and health research and development studies the use of vitamins against disease, vitamins and environmental disease, and other nutritional areas. Studies are going forward in the use of vitamins to prevent a number of animal illnesses.

Through the years Roche has developed, manufactured, and marketed medicines to fight all kinds of disease. With its renowned commitment to health care innovation, the company looks to continued progress for the benefit of mankind's health.

DENMAN & DAVIS

Denman & Davis has been a New Jersey supporter for 54 of its 99 years. The steel service company, founded in 1888 by William E. Davis and Abram Denman, has been wholly owned by the Davis family since 1904 and is now being led by the fourth generation, with Richard S. Davis, chairman, and David N. Deinzer, president.

A history of Denman & Davis could be a history of the steel distribution industry. 1888—Simple product lines that included metal bars, plates, sheets, and strips; a rudimentary processing with hacksaws and hand shears; and delivery by horse-drawn wagons. 1987—Product lines with quality traceability guaranteed; sizes, shapes, and grades unheard of 99 years ago; and processing using computer-controlled, multitorch burning units, power saws, and shears that were only dreams in 1888.

During these years of growth and change in the steel service center industry, Denman & Davis grew and moved to ever larger quarters. In 1933 the company relocated from lower Manhattan to North Bergen, and in 1956 it moved to its present corporate headquarters in Clifton. A branch was opened in Albany, New York, in 1982.

During and after World War II Denman & Davis began stocking many new steel alloys and utilized much of the new technology that was developed for processing of steel.

In 1888, when Denman & Davis was founded, there were only 38 stars in the United States flag.

This new era in steel distribution was the foundation for a new concept: "cost of possession"—meaning that it costs money to keep inventory. Space, employees, machines, insurance, and taxes make inventory a costly proposition. Cost of possession shifted the burden of carrying inven-

Denman & Davis' headquarters in Clifton, New Jersey, employing the most modern and efficient equipment, performs an integral part in cost reduction for today's metalworking industries.

tory from the customer to the steel service center. Denman & Davis thus began to assume the burden of inventory control for its customers, offering a unique additional service that became vital to its industry. Today the cost-of-possession concept has been perfected to provide innovations such as Just-In-Time, electronic data interchange, and material-requirement planning.

By the end of the 1960s the type of service provided by Denman & Davis had become a vital link between production of metals and their ultimate use. The transportation, pulp and paper, electric generation, agriculture, appliance, chemical, and aerospace industries were among those served.

In 1979 steel service centers moved ahead of the automotive industry as domestic steel's biggest customer. Today companies such as Denman & Davis supply more than 30 percent of the steel consumed in the United States annually, serving over 300,000 U.S. manufacturing plants.

Denman & Davis will be celebrating its 100th anniversary in 1988: 100 years of supplying New Jersey and the metropolitan area with quality steel and services.

HOLMAN ENTERPRISES

Holman Enterprises has been in the automobile business since 1924, when Steward C. Holman founded Rice and Holman Ford in Pennsauken. Charles M. Rice financed the venture, though he was only briefly active in the company.

The original dealership was modest at best. Two employees repaired cars in an uncovered backyard—weather permitting. But in 1925 came a move to Maple Avenue, where Rice and Holman Ford would remain for 61 years and become one of the largest Ford dealerships in the country.

Recently the firm moved to a 10-acre facility in Mount Laurel. Today Steward Holman's businesses are directed by Holman Enterprises, a corporate holding company employing 2,000 people and overseeing not only Rice and Holman Ford but also operations in more than 40 locations.

Steward C. Holman was born and raised in Lakewood, Ocean County. After graduating from Rider College and serving in the Navy during World War I, he worked briefly for Mathis Motor Co., first in Philadelphia and later in Toms River, before opening Rice and Holman Ford.

The new company had limited capital and the added burden of some nine competing Ford dealers within a 10-mile radius. Moreover, the Ford Motor Company discontinued production from 1927 to 1929, only to introduce its unsuccessful V-8 models in 1932. On top of all this, the Depression hit.

But Steward Holman persevered, and his business steadily expanded. His salesmanship had not gone unnoticed by Ford Motor Company, which in 1938 urged him to acquire the South Jersey Lincoln and Mercury distributorship. During World War II it was the only East Coast dealership exclusively selling Lincoln Mercury products to stay open. Today that dealership operates as Holman Lincoln Mercury.

Another Holman operation, Reconditioned Motors and Parts (RMP)—an authorized Ford remanufacturer

rebuilding engines and related automotive components—was launched in the late 1930s. Headquartered in Pennsauken, RMP today services Ford dealers and independent distribution channels from the Canadian border to Richmond, Virginia, and as far west as Detroit.

Holman started a Lincoln Mercury agency in Fort Lauderdale, Florida, in 1947. Today Holman Enterprises' Florida dealerships and leasing companies are located in Miami, Hollywood, and Pompano as well.

In 1948 Rice and Holman Ford organized Automotive Rentals, Inc. (ARI), which specializes in leasing fleets of automobiles and trucks to large customers. Based in Maple Shade, ARI has developed into one of the largest fleet-leasing companies in the nation.

Holman Enterprises also manages Rice and Holman Truck Center and R & H Leasing Company (Pennsauken), Holman Stratford Lincoln Mercury (Stratford), and Holman Leasing Company (Maple Shade). Recently Holman Enterprises entered the import business, opening Mitsubishi, Rolls-Royce, Hyundai, and Suzuki dealerships in South Jersey and Florida.

Under the current leadership of Joseph S. Holman, the founder's son, Holman Enterprises continues to enhance its reputation for fairness and reliability, still living by these words

Steward C. Holman (left), founder, and his son, Joseph S. Holman, the current president, with one of Ford's earliest automobiles, a Model T with a wood body and side curtains.

of Steward C. Holman: "We conscientiously try to be honest and forthright. In addition, we strongly believe in community service, and we earnestly support the professional development of our people."

After 60 years at the Maple Avenue location in Pennsauken (inset), Holman Enterprises moved to its present 10-acre Mount Laurel facility.

RCA CORPORATION

At the close of World War I the only U.S. firm able to handle commercial transatlantic radio communications was the Marconi Wireless Telegraph Company of America, an offshoot of the British Marconi Company.

General Electric Company, which owned many transmission patents at that time, and American Marconi sought to join forces. The U.S. government—and specifically Under Secretary of the Navy Franklin D. Roosevelt—encouraged negotiations, anxious to see the growing communications industry come under American ownership. A solution was reached for a new organization to be formed to acquire the largely British-owned assets of American Marconi. On October 17, 1919, the Radio Corporation of America was incorporated, and one month later it took over American Marconi's assets.

RCA was born.

GE, holding a major interest in the new enterprise, and RCA cross-licensed their radio patents and built new high-power alternator stations. In 1920 transoceanic radio service began with a major station in New Brunswick, New Jersey, transmitting to England, France, Germany, Norway, Japan, and Hawaii.

The broadcasting industry also began that year—with the world's first licensed station, KDKA of the Westinghouse Company in Pittsburgh. RCA entered broadcasting in 1921 with a one-day transmission of the Dempsey-Carpenter fight in Jersey City, New Jersey. Shortly afterward it opened station WDY at Roselle Park, New Jersey, but interference

Television history was made April 20, 1939, when David Sarnoff stood before the television cameras and dedicated RCA's pavilion at the 1939 New York World's Fair. The dedication marked the first time a news event was ever covered by television. Courtesy, RCA

from Westinghouse's WJZ of Newark shut it down. RCA then became an equal partner with Westinghouse in WJZ, and broadcasting was on its way.

From 1923 through 1925 RCA opened two broadcasting stations in New York and one in Washington, and expanded transoceanic communications in Europe and South America. In 1925, operating as a merchandiser, it began selling components to the Victor Talking Machine Company of Camden, New

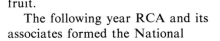

Jack Dempsey listens to a "Radio Music Box" tuned by Major J. Andrew White just before the Dempsey-Carpentier championship title fight in 1921. Courtesy, RCA

Jersey, a link that would bear further fruit.

The following year RCA and its associates formed the National Broadcasting Company. The new organization acquired a station from AT&T and operated stations owned by RCA, thereby launching the network broadcasting industry.

RCA purchased the Victor Talking Machine Company in 1929, obtaining its phonograph business, manufacturing facilities, and the Victor dog trademark. After acquiring tube manufacturing assets from GE and Westinghouse, RCA then organized the RCA-Victor Company and the RCA Radiotron Company.

By 1932 GE, Westinghouse, and AT&T had withdrawn their original interests in the firm. RCA thus became a completely self-contained organization instead of a cooperative venture with different corporate owners. It now had subsidiaries in broadcasting, communications, marine radio, manufacturing and merchandising, and the running of a radio school.

Within six years RCA began moving into electronics fields such as radar, airborne electronics, and television. At the New York World's Fair in 1939 it introduced the first public television service. The new service was only experimental, covering only the New York metropolitan area.

A family watches one of the first mass-produced, black-and-white television sets, circa 1946. Courtesy, RCA

World War II halted progress in commercial television, but activities resumed in 1946 when the first TV network linked NBC facilities in New York, Washington, Philadelphia, and Schenectady. That same year RCA introduced the famed

The superstructure of a U.S. Navy AEGIS ship seems to rise out of the corn in Moorestown, New Jersey. It actually is the Navy's Combat System Engineering Development site—a three-story building with a ship's superstructure on top—where the AEGIS Surface Ship Combat System is being tested. Courtesy, RCA

630TS television set, a reliable, economical 10-inch unit considered to be the "Model T" of the television industry. In 1949 the firm introduced its 45 RPM phonograph system, and by the following year it had developed the tri-color kinescope, which heralded the dawn of color TV.

RCA was active in military technology during World War II. During the 1950s it became a leader in the field, developing sonar, advanced radar apparatus, fire control systems, and an electronic analog computer. The Korean War increased its military electronics activities, with new projects in electronic sound, sonar, missiles, navigation, and communications.

The 1950s also saw RCA developing transistors with greater power output and higher frequency performance, and the company made advances in solid-state physics and semiconductor use as well. In 1957 RCA produced the first successful satellite radio relay equipment, which went into orbit aboard an Atlas missile and heralded a new era in global communications. By 1962 the corporation had also developed six weather satellites for NASA, and in the following year it developed the Relay communications satellite, which transmitted TV pictures between the United States and Europe and linked Latin America by radio.

RCA continued its pioneering in space through the manned space missions of the 1960s. Its cameras later flew on the Apollo missions, and in 1969 Neil Armstrong's first words on the moon were broadcast with an RCA-produced man-pack radio.

Also during that decade the organization expanded in its other traditional sectors. Color TV had emerged as a major new product, and industry retail sales of the innovation mushroomed to three billion dollars by 1966. In 1985 retail volume topped $10 billion.

In 1969 the Radio Corporation of America changed its name to the RCA Corporation, and its circular trademark with the lightning bolt

On December 12, 1975, the historic RCA Satcom I domestic communications satellite was launched from Cape Canaveral by the Delta 118 vehicle. This 1,915-pound satellite was responsible for sparking the growth of the cable television industry to the multibillion-dollar market it is today, and for ushering in the era of low-cost, long-distance telephone communications. Courtesy, RCA

was replaced by a three-letter, single-unit design. Chairman David Sarnoff, who had served in that capacity since 1947, announced his retirement in 1970. His departure signaled the end of an era for the firm.

Up through the early 1970s RCA had expanded and diversified into many areas unrelated to communications, acquiring the Random House publishing company, the Hertz Corporation, and many other operations. However, it remained essentially an electronics and communications enterprise, with about 75 percent of its activities in those areas. Throughout the late 1970s and the early 1980s the organization began divesting of those operations and concentrated more on its traditional activities.

In 1986 RCA was acquired by the General Electric Corporation—in an interesting déjà vu to its beginnings, when GE was a major shareholder.

NL CHEMICALS INC.
NL INDUSTRIES INC.

The story of NL Industries begins in 1891, with the incorporation of the National Lead Company in Jersey City. The firm produced lead, tin, and antimony but primarily transformed lead metal into basic lead carbonate—or white lead—and sold it as the major ingredient for paint.

Today NL Chemicals/NL Industries is a major international corporation, active primarily in chemicals and petroleum services. The corporation has extensive international operations, with chemical operations in Canada and Europe and petroleum service operations around the globe.

Though NL is not quite a century old, the companies that formed it dated back as far as 1772. In 1874, 24 white lead firms formed a group called The Lead Trust to establish standards and controls to deal with fierce competition. The organization disbanded in 1891 due to financial problems, and from its assets the National Lead Company was incorporated.

In those days white lead was made by the so-called Dutch process of oxidizing lead, thus originating the term "Dutch Boy" as a National Lead trademark. Newly formed NL owned lead, copper, silver, and gold smelters in western states, a string of white lead plants from St. Louis to Boston, and linseed oil crushing and

lead metal parts production facilities.

Although headquartered in New York City for many years, NL was essentially a New Jersey company and had plants throughout the state. A major NL New Jersey operation was a lead plant in Perth Amboy,

A National Lead delivery truck making its rounds, circa 1907.

National Lead's first titanium dioxide pigment plant in Niagara Falls, New York, circa 1917. National Lead invented titanium dioxide pigment, which eventually replaced white lead. Today titanium dioxide pigment is widely used in everything from cosmetics, plastics, and paints to bathroom white-wear and paper.

next to the Outerbridge Crossing, which became famous as a producer of Dutch Boy white lead in the early part of this century.

NL initially focused on lead products, but it soon moved into new metals and chemicals. Through acquisitions, joint ventures, and new operations, NL grew and diversified over the years until lead was no longer its all-important sector. Its first purchase unrelated to lead was

Magnus Metal, a railroad bearings producer, in 1907.

Major diversification came with NL's move into titanium dioxide pigments, the paint ingredient that would replace white lead. When NL purchased the Titanium Pigment Company in 1921, titanium dioxide was a little-known powder that had possibilities as a paint pigment. The venture was a tremendous success, followed by the 1927 acquisition of the Titan Company A/S of Norway, Germany, and France. That acquisition included titanium ore mines and ownership of U.S. and European titanium dioxide production patents. These resources made NL a major international force, and titanium dioxide became the company's most profitable area for many years.

Meanwhile NL garnered many operations in New Jersey. It owned the Baker Castor Oil Company in Bayonne, the oldest U.S. castor oil company, which processed more castor oil there than in any other location. NL also ran a major titanium dioxide pigments plant in Sayreville, along with several smaller operations across the state.

A key acquisition came in 1925 with the purchase of Baroid, an oil well drilling field supplier. With the growth of deep-well drilling—a Baroid specialty—and with the general spread of drilling activity, NL's oil service sector was born. NL was still predominantly a lead and metals company in the 1930s, but from the 1940s through the 1960s its principal activity became titanium dioxide pigments. By its 50th anniversary in 1941, NL sales had reached $139 million and would soar from there. Over the next 25 years NL continued to expand, carrying out some 65 purchases, joint ventures, and major new operations. Profits rose from earnings on titanium dioxide pigments and Baroid oil drilling fluids.

In 1963 NL moved its research laboratories from Brooklyn to Hightstown. Gradually the Hightstown facility was expanded to incorporate office buildings and other laborato-

ries and facilities, and today it is the administrative headquarters of NL Chemicals.

After years of growth, in the late 1960s NL's fortunes started to decline. Competitors found better ways of making titanium dioxide pigments, which NL was late in developing. Expansion had spawned organizational problems. NL had 17 divisions, 23 wholly owned subsidiaries, and 20 partially owned subsidiaries, each operating on a highly decentralized basis. The firm also faced overcapacity, tough price controls, and other problems.

In 1971 the corporate name was changed to NL Industries to reflect the fact that lead accounted for less than 20 percent of sales. That same year Ray C. Adam joined NL as executive vice-president, becoming president in 1974 and chairman and chief executive officer in 1975. Under Adam, from 1975 through 1982 NL sold about 60 operating units not related to chemicals or petroleum services. The paint business—where it all started—was sold, along with

NL Chemicals is a leading manufacturer of titanium dioxide pigments, flow control additives, and specialty resins.

the Dutch Boy trademark, company symbol since 1907. Metal and chemical units also went, along with diecasting units and many others. Meanwhile NL concentrated on petroleum services. In 1976 it acquired Rucker Petroleum Services, a drilling services company active in Canada, Norway, and Japan, and from 1972 to 1979 NL acquired 14 other oil service firms. In 1978 NL constructed its first large-scale new technology titanium dioxide pigment plant.

Today NL Industries is a successful chemicals and petroleum services firm, now actually divided into two companies: NL Chemicals Inc. and NL Industries Inc. This structure was created in 1986 prior to a successful takeover attempt by Harold Simmons.

NL Chemicals, based in Hightstown, is principally involved in two areas. One is specialty chemicals for the coating, ink, and cosmetic fields, and titanium dioxide pigments for the paint, paper, and plastics industries. NL Industries, with primary operations in Houston, is involved in petroleum services, offering services and equipment for drilling and well workover, as well as completion operations, both on land and offshore.

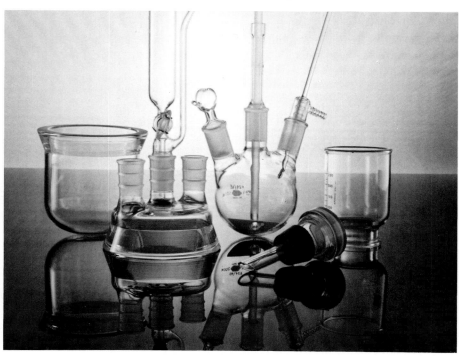

LIGHTNING ELECTRIC COMPANY

During World War I in France young Albert Richman, an electrical engineering graduate of Cooper Union in New York City, fought with the famous 78th Lightning Division. There he dreamed of forming an electric company after the war, and he decided he would name it Lightning Electric—in honor of his own Lightning Division.

Back home in Newark, Richman teamed with Ben Nadelberg, whose entrepreneurial skills complemented Richman's technical expertise. In 1920, in a small shop on Orange Street in Newark, Lightning Electric Service Company—later changed to Lightning Electric Company—was launched.

Starting with house wiring, commercial wiring, and industrial electrical work, Lightning Electric grew to cover all types of electrical installations. The company also was an electrical and radio retailer until 1942, when it decided to concentrate solely on electrical contracting.

As it grew, Lightning Electric Company moved to a new location at 481 Broad Street, Newark, and then, in 1936, to a facility at 917 Broad Street. In 1946, by then doing large industrial installations, the company went into a building on Coes Place in Newark. The move to a new plant at 40 East Willow Street in Millburn, the firm's present headquarters, was made in 1963.

Today Lightning Electric is one of New Jersey's largest electrical contractors. It has completed electrical installations for projects of all kinds, including high-rise office complexes, research labs, corporate headquarters, hotels, condominiums, industrial plants, bridges and tunnels, hospitals, schools, racetracks, shopping centers, department stores, traffic-control systems, rail power and signal work,

utility substations, sewage plants, airports, and highways.

Throughout its history Lightning Electric has never defaulted on a project or on a payment to vendors, maintaining a consistently clean financial record. The company has experience in projects with tough time constraints, rigid cost controls, and complex safety procedures. Over the years the firm has performed on major projects subject to large dollar penalties for late finish, taking pride in the fact that owners and contractors look to Lightning when scheduling is tight.

Past projects include the third tube of the Lincoln Tunnel and the second deck of the George Washington Bridge, Garden State Park Racetrack in Cherry Hill, the Beneficial management headquarters in Peapack, the People Express airport facilities in Newark, the Bell Communications Research Center in Middletown, AT&T in Middletown, Merck & Co, Inc., in Rahway, Short Hills Mall, Gardenstate Plaza, and rail electrification for the New Jersey Transit Authority.

Lightning Electric Company has literally lit New Jersey's path toward corporate achievement, helping the state grow during the past 67 years. Today the firm is still family held, led by Milton Nadelberg and Stanley Richman, sons of the founding partners.

Lightning Electric Company has been at 40 East Willow Street in Millburn since 1963.

The firm's office and shop were on Coes Place, Newark, from 1946 to 1963.

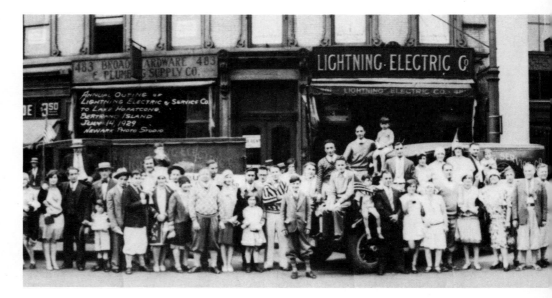

The printing on this rare old photo reads, "The annual outing of Lightning Electric & Service Co. to Lake Hopatcong, Bertrand Island, July 14, 1929." The founders, Ben Nadelberg and Albert Richman, can be seen 9th and 13th from the right, respectively.

UNITED CARTING COMPANY, INC.

United Carting Company, Inc., was founded in the late 1800s in the Greenwich Village section of New York City and was initially involved in the ash and waste removal business. The fledgling operation gradually acquired an increasing number of horse-drawn carts and began to attract some major clients, including the Waldorf-Astoria, Taft hotels, and the National Biscuit Company.

Starting with just three people, the company went on to enlarge its share of the "roll-off," or solid waste removal, business. Today United Carting, based in Fairview, offers the best in commercial, industrial, and institutional rubbish removal, serving many of New Jersey's industries and improving the environment for the state's citizens. The firm also designs and installs compaction systems for hotels, restaurants, retail stores, shopping malls, office buildings, and manufacturers. In addition, United Carting counts among its customers many of New Jersey's largest construction companies.

United became a part of New Jersey's business community as the state began its major expansion years. As northern New Jersey grew in population during the postwar period, the need for solid waste removal companies grew with it. Seizing this opportunity, United Carting, from

United Carting Company, Inc., has been a family-owned and -operated business since its inception in 1894, when Michael Mastrangelo began an ash and waste removal service in the Greenwich Village section of New York. Pictured here is Angelo Mastrangelo, who succeeded his father in the business.

Today company leader Ralph G. Mastrangelo, grandson of founder Michael Mastrangelo, operates United Carting from its headquarters in Fairview. The business has expanded to include commercial, industrial, and institutional rubbish removal.

headquarters in Fairview, became a part of northern New Jersey's growth during those years.

United Carting represents a long and fruitful family tradition. Michael Mastrangelo was the man who launched the company in 1894, and his son, Angelo, succeeded him. In 1954 Angelo's son, Ralph, became president of the company. Today there is yet another new Mastrangelo generation involved in the business: Ralph's sons, Ralph Jr. and Michael, namesake of his great-grandfather who founded the firm, currently oversees company operations and administration with his father.

Current company leader Ralph G. Mastrangelo is a key leader of his industry in the state: As a member of the National Solid Waste Management Association, he serves as president of the northern New Jersey section of that organization. United Carting Company itself is a member of the American Public Works Association and the New Jersey Motor Truck Association, in addition to playing an important role in New Jersey for the Keep America Beautiful campaign.

United Carting has had many firsts in New Jersey in its areas of expertise. For example, it was the first company in northern New Jersey to introduce the compaction systems, and recently the firm brought out new, modern stationary compactor systems and roll-off containers for faster, more efficient removal of solid waste and construction debris. Fireproof and waterproof apartment house compactors are another of the company's specialties.

United Carting's equipment is modern and dependable: Its trucks are radio dispatched and equipped with roll-off hoists to transport solid waste in open and/or closed compaction containers to be land filled. Today United Carting Company, Inc., continues to grow with the area, and it carries on its tradition of providing modern and efficient refuse collection methods for its customers.

SIX FLAGS GREAT ADVENTURE

Six Flags Great Adventure is a popular theme park and drive-through safari park. Situated in Jackson Township, New Jersey, the seasonal park is 75 miles from the center of New York City and 55 miles from Philadelphia. Today Six Flags Great Adventure is the largest seasonal theme park in the United States.

The concept of Great Adventure is to provide a larger-than-life atmosphere for the amusement of both children and adults. The park was designed by Warner LeRoy, and it was developed by Hardwicke Companies, Inc. Great Adventure had its grand opening on July 4, 1974. Initial financing had been provided by the First National Bank of Chicago.

Great Adventure was acquired at the end of 1974 by the First National Bank of Chicago.

In November 1977 the ownership of Great Adventure changed hands again. At that time the entire assets of the amusement and safari park were acquired by the Six Flags Corporation. Six Flags today is owned by the Bally Mfg. Corp., which pur-

Whiz through the 1950s and 1960s and into the 1970s and 1980s during "Evolution" featuring some of rock's greatest performers. Impersonators of Buddy Holly, Mick Jagger, Tina Turner, and the Beach Boys, to just name a few, rock at the Showcase Theatre.

The king of the beasts and his mate graze lazily in the sun at Six Flags Great Adventure's drive-through safari. There visitors can see more than 1,500 wild animals from Africa, Asia, and Australia all in their natural habitat.

chased the amusement park company, including Great Adventure, from the Penn Central Corporation in January 1982.

At the present time Six Flags Great Adventure has more than 2,000 acres in its total land parcel in Jackson Township. Of that, the

amusement park uses approximately 125 acres for its rides, shows, games, restaurants, and souvenir and gift shops.

The Six Flags Great Adventure Safari Park occupies 350 acres, and it features an extensive variety of approximately 1,500 animals. Approximately 400 acres are used for roads and support facilities, with 80 acres of guest parking, for a capacity of 8,000 cars. The remaining acreage is available for future development.

Six Flags Corporation, headquartered in Chicago, owns and operates seven major theme amusement parks across the United States. They are in Dallas/Fort Worth, Houston, Los Angeles, St. Louis, Atlanta, and Chicago, as well as in Jackson Township. In addition to the theme parks, which are entertaining visitors at a current rate of more than 13 million per year, Six Flags operates P.T. Flagg's, an indoor entertainment facility in Baltimore's Inner Harbor District, and two water parks in Hollywood, Florida, and in Houston, Texas.

On its own, New Jersey's Six Flags Great Adventure theme and safari park hosts three million visitors during its seven-month season. It is the largest private-sector employer in Ocean County and the largest sea-

sonal employer in New Jersey.

Attendance at the Six Flags Great Adventure amusement and safari park generally comprises visitors from within a 125-mile radius. According to the most recent estimates by park officials, approximately 63 percent of visitors come from the New York City and North Jersey area, 25 percent from the Philadelphia and South Jersey area, and 12 percent from other parts of the country.

Six Flags Great adventure features more than 100 rides, shows, and attractions. New in 1987 is Splashwater Falls,® a super-splashing water ride that is guaranteed to get you wet. Test your courage on other thrillers such as Ultra Twister, Freefall, Looping Starship, Lightnin' Loops, Rolling Thunder, Parachuter's Perch, and more. The Warner Brothers characters make Great Adventure their official home every season. Bugs Bunny®, Daffy Duck®, Sylvester®, Tweety Bird®, Foghorn Leg-ter®,

Bugs Bunny®, Sylvester®, and Foghorn Leghorn® celebrate the grand opening of Ultra Twister, the only ride of its kind in the world, at Six Flags Great Adventure in Jackson Township, New Jersey.

horn®, and Yosemite Sam® greet guests throughout the park and have their own show. In addition, there are 10 live shows, ranging from live birds and dolphins to a Rock and Roll Revue.

Six Flags Great Adventure has 300 full-time and 3,500 seasonal employees, estimated to be the equivalent of 1,640 full-time employees.

Great Adventure can be reached

Take off and head straight for the stars on Looping Starship. The world is turned upside down with a series of 360-degree turns before you land softly back on earth.

by car on New Jersey Secondary Road 537 in the scenic, rural northwestern portion of Ocean County. Ocean County is the second-largest county in size and the 12th largest in population in New Jersey. Its location in relatively undeveloped central New Jersey makes the park an attractive vacation spot for its visitors.

®—Indicates Trademark of Warner Brothers, copyright 1986.

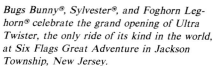

America's favorites come to life in "The Bugs Bunny® Story" featuring Daffy Duck®, Foghorn Leghorn®, Porky Pig®, and the star, Bugs Bunny. The show traces the life of that "wascally wabbit" and how these Looney Tunes® favorites became a part of his life.

NORTH AMERICAN PHILIPS LIGHTING CORPORATION

North American Philips Lighting Corporation has installed lighting systems at some of America's most famous infrastructures, from Kennedy Airport in New York City to Dodger Stadium in Los Angeles.

The firm was founded in 1935 by Jack Glassberg, Izzy Billet, and Dr. Coe, a dentist. Its first plant was on Sherman Avenue in Newark. In January 1937 the company was incorporated in Delaware and named Radiant Lamp Corporation. By the fall of 1940 two men, Leo and William Weil, had teamed up with the firm's principals.

By the spring of 1942 the Radiant Lamp Corporation had moved to 300 Jelliff Avenue in Newark. World War II had begun, and war requirements for incandescent lamps—especially aeronautical lamps—had expanded Radiant Lamp Corporation's production facilities considerably.

In February 1959 Glassberg died, and just under a year later five men with varying business experience purchased Radiant Lamp Corporation. The company's new president was David A. Foxman. By 1961 Radiant Lamp Corporation had posted annual sales of two million dollars and had a total of 200 employees.

In 1962 and 1963 Radiant Lamp Corporation installed lighting at the Pittsburgh Civic Arena and—in New York—at Kennedy International Airport (then called Idlewild), the Bronx-Whitestone and the Tri-Boro bridges, and the Tishman Building at 666 Fifth Avenue.

Nearly 400 New York City playgrounds also were using Radiant Lamp Corporation-designed R52 lamps. Other lamp installations included the Lincoln Road Mall in Miami Beach and the 1962 lighting of the new Dodger Stadium at Chavez Ravine in Los Angeles.

In the spring of 1963 a proxy fight resulted in the removal of Foxman as president and the election of Eugene R. Van Meter as president and William Cuozzi as vice-president. Leslie Ricketts, a principal, was ap-

Stephen C. Tumminello currently serves as president of North American Philips Lighting Corporation.

pointed general manager of manufacturing. Accountant Stephen C. Tumminello was named controller.

From April through July 1964 Radiant Lamp Corporation relocated from Newark to the old Hightstown Rug Company building in Hightstown. In August Ricketts became vice-president/finance, and in March 1966 Tumminello became the firm's president.

Radiant Lamp Corporation was acquired by Consolidated Electronics

Corporation in 1968. A year later the parent company name was changed to North American Philips Corporation. That development occurred through the merger of Consolidated Electronics Industries Corporation and North American Philips Company, Inc. Radiant Lamp Corporation became Radiant Lamp Division of North American Philips Lighting Corporation.

A 1969 fire in the firm's executive office area caused considerable damage. Losses were estimated at $280,000, but the company was determined to rebuild. Less than a year later a 30,600-square-foot warehouse building was completed at the Hightstown facility.

In December 1970 Radiant Lamp Division of North American Philips acquired the companies of the Lighting Products Division of Lear Siegler, Inc. The Lear Siegler companies—Verd-A-Ray, Penetray, and Par Light—were reorganized into a new Philips subsidiary named Verd-A-Ray Corporation. The Verd-A-Ray Corporation had originated in 1918 as Save Electric Corporation. Lear Siegler had acquired Verd-A-Ray in 1966.

With the Verd-A-Ray transaction, the Radiant Lamp Division of North American Philips Corporation now officially changed its name: It became North American Philips Lighting Corporation.

In December 1972 the firm completed construction of a 105,000-square-foot warehouse in South Brunswick. One year later came two major acquisitions from the International Telephone and Telegraph Corporation. These were the Large Lamp Division, located in Lynn, Massachusetts, and the Lustra Light-

ing Division, in East Rutherford, New Jersey.

The Large Lamp Division had been founded in 1900 as the Champion Lamp Company and acquired by ITT in 1967. The Lustra Lighting Division had been a sister organization to Amplex Corporation, which had been established in 1948 and also acquired in 1967 by ITT.

In 1974 North American Philips Lighting Corporation's sales reached $40 million. Four years later a new 105,000-square-foot warehouse was built at South Brunswick, adjacent to the firm's existing facilities. The following year the company posted annual sales of $105 million and its work force numbered 1,670.

With the 1980s came new expansion. In September 1980 the corporation acquired Solar Electric Corporation of Warren, Pennsylvania, which had been owned by Dutch Boy, Inc., a division of NL Industries, Inc.

The corporate headquarters of North American Philips Lighting Corporation in Somerset.

By 1981 North American Philips Lighting Corporation's sales had eclipsed the $110-million mark. In March 1982 the firm created the Fixture Division of North American Philips Lighting Corporation, a separate arm of the company concentrating on lighting fixtures. And by the end of that year the entire corporation's sales had reached $120 million.

On February 22, 1983, came the acquisition of Westinghouse Electric's Lamp Division, at that time the nation's third-largest seller of lamps. Six months later the company acquired the Danville, Kentucky, glass plant from Corning Glass Works of Corning, New York. In September 1983 the Philips Elmet Division of North American Philips Corporation—a separate manufacturing facility—was assigned to North American Philips Lighting Corporation.

Through the years the firm has had a tradition of diversification and continued expansion. Today North American Philips Lighting Corporation is one of the top companies of its kind in the United States.

DELOITTE HASKINS & SELLS

Deloitte Haskins & Sells (DH&S), one of the Big Eight accounting firms in the United States, is a worldwide organization with more than 430 offices in 73 countries. The DH&S New Jersey practice is one of the firm's largest and most dynamic.

Deloitte Haskins & Sells was founded in 1895 by Charles Waldo Haskins and Elijah Watt Sells and was originally named Haskins and Sells. In 1978 Haskins and Sells incorporated its overseas affiliate, the British accounting firm Deloitte & Company, into its corporate name in order to emphasize its worldwide activities—it in fact was the first American public accounting firm to open offices abroad. The company subsequently became known by its present name of Deloitte Haskins & Sells. Today, in the United States alone, DH&S has more than 750 partners in 100 offices throughout the nation.

Deloitte Haskins & Sells founded its first New Jersey office in Newark in 1922, the 23rd of its offices nationwide. In 1974 the firm opened additional offices in Hackensack and Morristown. Four years later most of the professionals in the Newark office moved to Hackensack to accommodate the locational shift of some of the firm's major clients. This continuing attention of the DH&S New Jersey practice to client convenience and business growth resulted in the opening of a Princeton office in 1986. Today this combined New Jersey practice serves companies and individuals throughout the entire state, with more than 300 professional employees in its three New Jersey offices.

With its present New Jersey headquarters at 111 Madison Avenue in Morristown, Deloitte Haskins & Sells offers a full range of accounting and auditing, tax, consulting, and emerging-business services. DH&S is known as one of the accounting profession's leaders in providing responsive and innovative audit services. Long recognized for its technical prowess, DH&S was the first to adopt efficient statistical audit methods, the first to develop specialized audit software, and continues to lead the profession and enhance its image of possessing the highest audit qual-

ity. The most telling measure of the firm's standing among its peers is the fact that three of the other seven of the Big Eight have chosen DH&S to conduct a peer review of their auditing operations.

Although audit services comprise the majority of the firm's activities, DH&S also provides major tax consulting services for corporate and individual tax planning, mergers and acquisitions, pensions, compensation plans, and other individual or organizational tax needs. Perhaps the fastest-growing segment of the firm's New Jersey practice is its Management Advisory Services Group, which provides professional consulting services for a variety of business needs, including financial management, electronic data processing, cost management, planning and control, and other services.

DH&S offers a number of services to small and expanding businesses, as well. The DH&S Emerging Business Group division handles accounting and reporting systems, budgets and forecasts, management consulting,

Beneficial Corporation, Peapack, New Jersey. Photo by Walter Choroszewski

and audit and tax services for tomorrow's leading businesses.

Recognizing that every client has unique needs, DH&S assembles a team of experts to meet each client's specifications. Opportunities for industry-group specialization range through a broad spectrum. In New Jersey, DH&S has resident specialists in numerous areas, including financial institutions, mergers and acquisitions, manufacturing, international operations, colleges and universities, real estate and construction, public utilities, transportation, health care organizations, not-for-profits, and many others.

Major clients of the Deloitte Haskins & Sells New Jersey practice include BASF Wyandotte Corporation, Beneficial Corporation, Benjamin Moore, Chanel, Inc., City Fed Financial Corp., Federal Paper Board Company, Inc., The Great Atlantic & Pacific Tea Company, Hacken-

Volvo North American Corporation, Rockleigh, New Jersey. Photo by Walter Choroszewski

sack Medical Center, Lea & Perrins, Inc., Merrill Lynch Bank & Trust Co., New Jersey Transit Corporation, Pennsylvania Power & Light Company, Princeton University, Public Service Electric & Gas Company, Rutgers University, Schering Plough Corporation, and Volvo North America Corporation.

The commitment to excellence and professional competence of Deloitte Haskin & Sells are the keys to its outstanding reputation in the New Jersey business community. These qualities exist in each of the professionals in the New Jersey practice of DH&S, and the firm is especially proud of its people. Its New Jersey practice has long been a nurturing ground for a large number of DH&S partners, many of whom have gone on to assume top positions within the firm. Among them are former DH&S managing partner John Queenan; Weldon Powell, the first chairman of the Accounting Principles Board of the AICPA (American Institute of Certified Public Accountants); and Oscar Gellein, an original member of the Financial Accounting Standards Board. All three of these men have been awarded the gold medal of the AICPA for distinguished service to

the profession.

The current partner-in-charge of the DH&S New Jersey practice is Victor G. Albrecht. A DH&S professional employee since 1962, Albrecht assumed his current post in 1980. During his tenure, the New Jersey practice has nearly doubled in size and has become one of the top three public accounting businesses in the state. He is a member of the AICPA, the New Jersey Society of CPAs, and the National Association of Accountants. He also serves as chairman of the board of trustees of the Summit Art Center and as a member of the board of executive advisors of Fairleigh Dickinson University, in addition to holding several other important civic positions.

Many of the firm's other distinguished employees also are involved in civic, cultural, and charitable efforts throughout the state and are leaders in their profession, actively participating in the AICPA committees, the state's Society of CPAs, and other industry and management groups in New Jersey.

Princeton University, Princeton, New Jersey. Photo by Walter Choroszewski

BROADWAY MAINTENANCE CORPORATION

Broadway Maintenance Corporation, New Jersey's largest lighting and sign maintenance service company, was founded in Newark in 1936 by I. Ralph Fox, who established the business as an extension of the firm's New York operation in electric and neon signs.

Starting from offices at 1025 Broad Street, Broadway Maintenance had only seven employees and two trucks. The company grew quickly, and in the first year the staff increased to 12 and the truck fleet grew to six. In 1941 Broadway Maintenance acquired its largest competitor, Claude Neon. The firm then moved to 353 Halsey Street, where it built the largest neon tube plant in New Jersey.

In 1942 Broadway Maintenance entered the lighting service field. The following year it purchased the Neo Light Co. and increased its volume of point-of-purchase neon signs for breweries and ice cream companies. Broadway Maintenance entered the street and highway lighting business in 1944, and during World War II it performed electrical work for the U.S. government. It purchased Rapid Neon Sign Service in 1945; by then Broadway Maintenance was employing 100 people and had a fleet of 20 trucks.

In 1954 the firm purchased 50,000 square feet of land on the new McCarter Highway and made a commitment to continue its operation in New Jersey. Building a 20,000-square-foot operation center, Broadway's management supervised many larger projects in the ensuing years as the work load rose dramatically. By the mid-1960s Broadway Maintenance was employing 200 people and had a fleet of more than 60 trucks.

In 1970 Alan J. Fox, son of I. Ralph Fox, entered the business as vice-president, and today he is the company's president. Ralph Fox subsequently retired from active involvement and became chairman. In addition to leading the firm into prominence, I. Ralph Fox was active in public affairs, serving for 25 years under five governors as Commissioner of Water Supply for the State of New Jersey. Today Alan J. Fox

The Broadway Maintenance operation center was built in 1956 in Newark and remains the company's central point for New Jersey.

guides Broadway Maintenance through its second generation of family leadership.

Over the years the company has worked on some of the state's more important electrical projects: the Meadowlands Sports Complex, Six Flags Great Adventure amusement park, Rutgers Medical School, the Newark Airport fuel distribution system, the Garden State Parkway Raritan Toll Extension, and many others.

Today Broadway Maintenance services include total lighting programs, electrical maintenance and contracting, infrared electrical fault detection, installation and maintenance of security and surveillance systems, electrical interior and exterior signage, air conditioning, energy conservation programs, architectural and environmental lighting, and lighting systems management.

In 1984 Broadway Maintenance Corporation was purchased by JWP Inc. and today is a subsidiary of that company. This added strength has allowed Broadway to expand its services while remaining autonomous and retaining the family spirit that is part of its tradition.

NEW JERSEY NATIONAL BANK

The roots of New Jersey National Bank date back to 1804. Its history and the history of this state and the United States are linked in unique ways.

New Jersey National's distinguished family tree includes two principal ancestors: the Trenton Banking Company, chartered in 1804, and the Mechanics and Manufacturers Bank, launched in 1834.

The Mechanics and Manufacturers Bank became the Mechanics National Bank under the National Banking Acts of 1863 and 1864. In 1928 it merged with the First National Bank of Trenton, becoming the First-Mechanics National Bank of Trenton. By 1930 it had dedicated its beautiful stone-and-marble office building at One West State Street, which serves as the Trenton office of New Jersey National Bank today. Constructed following the stock market crash of 1929, the building was designed to convey strength, stability, and security to a public whose faith in financial institutions had been severely tested.

The site of that building in downtown Trenton was named The Corner Historic in tribute to the many historical happenings that took place on the site. The original structure hosted sessions of the state's House of Assembly in 1780 and the Continental Congress in 1784. President-elect George Washington dined at the City Tavern en route to his inauguration in New York City in 1784, and New Jersey ratified the original Constitution of the United States in the tavern in 1787.

The Trenton Banking Company also prospered over the years. In 1958 it merged with the First-Mechanics National Bank of Trenton, forming the First Trenton National Bank and combining 278 years of banking experience.

The union of the First Trenton National Bank and Monmouth County's New Jersey National Bank and Trust Company was effected in 1970 and represented the most significant merger in the bank's history

to that date. The new bank was called New Jersey National, and it grew to become the fifth largest in the state and 121st in the nation.

One year after the formation of New Jersey National Bank, shareholders of the new institution formed New Jersey National Corporation, a registered bank holding company, which was able to organize new banks and acquire bank-related companies.

The first such move was the opening of the New Jersey National Bank of Princeton in 1973 as a corporate subsidiary. The Princeton bank was later merged into New Jersey National, the principal subsidiary.

In 1974 the holding company acquired Delaware Valley National Bank of Cherry Hill and changed its name to New Jersey National Bank-Delaware Valley. In 1976 it purchased the banking offices of First

The First-Mechanics National Bank completed construction of its new office in 1930 on The Corner Historic.

State Bank of Toms River, adding 12 branches in Ocean County to New Jersey National's growing network.

More recently, New Jersey National extended its reach into southern New Jersey with its 1984 acquisition of Citizens United Bank, N.A. Citizens added 27 offices to the New Jersey National branch network and expanded its market coverage through the 13 counties of central and southern New Jersey.

On October 30, 1986, the acquisition of New Jersey National Corporation by CoreStates Financial Corp. of Philadelphia made banking history as the first interstate banking combination to occur between New Jersey and Pennsylvania since those states' enactment of interstate banking legislation. As a member of the CoreStates family, New Jersey National is backed by the resources of a $14-billion organization.

Through more than 80 branch offices and six regional commercial centers, New Jersey National offers a complete range of corporate, consumer, and trust financial services.

HORIZON BANCORP

Horizon Bancorp, headquartered in Morristown, was formed in 1972 when American National Bank of Morristown and Princeton Bank, headquartered in Princeton, joined to form an organization that has become one of New Jersey's leading bank holding companies.

Today Horizon operates seven subsidiaries: Horizon Bank, Horizon Brokerage Services, Inc., Horizon Trust Company, Horizon Trust Company of Florida, Marine National Bank, Princeton Bank, and Princeton Bank of Pennsylvania. Throughout New Jersey, Horizon affiliates have a combined total of 123 branch banking offices—with more expansion planned—and seven trust offices. The bank holding company's assets are in excess of $3.5 billion.

In 1986 Horizon moved the headquarters of the former Bank of New Jersey, N.A., from Moorestown to downtown Philadelphia and changed the name to Princeton Bank of Pennsylvania, thus opening the first bank in Pennsylvania owned by a non-Pennsylvania bank holding company.

Though its name is relatively new, Horizon Bancorp has a rich past. Its roots in Morristown go back to 1892, when the Morristown Trust Company was established by 41 residents of Morris County. Many of the more successful families of that period had been attracted to Morristown and its environs. The area had achieved a high level of personal affluence, and the organization of the Morristown Trust Company meant to serve the needs of those people.

The bank's growth continued for the next 50 years, and its first important merger came in 1946 with the acquisition of the American Trust Company of Morristown. Continued strong growth necessitated the building of new administrative offices, and a suitable site was chosen at 225 South Street in Morristown in 1954. The facility still houses the main branch of Horizon Bank and also serves as Bancorp's headquarters.

In 1970 the Trust Company National Bank merged with the Montclair National Bank and Trust Company. The resulting new institution, retaining the Morristown headquarters, was named American National Bank & Trust.

In 1983 Northeastern Bank of Paramus, also a Horizon subsidiary, joined with American National to form the new Horizon Bank. The resulting financial institution currently operates 52 branch offices throughout northern and western New Jersey and has assets in excess of $1.5 billion.

Horizon Bancorp's second founding partner—Princeton Bank—opened its doors in Princeton, New Jersey, in October 1834.

Over the years Princeton Bank successfully rode the tide of the nation's various periods of financial uncertainty. Even in 1933, when many banks failed, the institution closed its doors only in response to the general order applicable to all U.S. banks and reopened immediately when the "holiday" was lifted.

Princeton Bank's real expansion began in 1938 with the acquisition of Princeton Savings Bank. That was followed in 1956 by the addition of Hopewell National Bank.

Princeton Bank continued to make acquisitions even after it became part of Horizon Bancorp in 1972. The Mid-Jersey National Bank was acquired in 1978, and the Fellowship

Horizon Bancorp headquarters at 225 South Street, Morristown, also houses the main branch of Horizon Bank. It is a replica of the Christopher Wren building in colonial Williamsburg, Virginia.

Bank came into the fold three years later. Today Princeton Bank, as the result of another recent merger with The Bank of New Jersey, now serves southern and central New Jersey with 50 branch offices. With assets of more than one billion dollars, Princeton Bank maintains headquarters both in Princeton and at its operations facility in Moorestown.

Marine National Bank serves Horizon customers in the southern shore area and is headquartered in Egg Harbor Township. It operates 23 branches throughout Atlantic, Cape May, Monmouth, and Ocean counties, and has total assets in excess of $440 million.

Horizon Trust Company has responsibility for more than $3.0 billion in managed assets. The company is headquartered in Morristown, with offices in Manchester, Moorestown, Princeton, Montclair, Paramus, and Westfield.

Horizon Trust Company of Florida is based in Boca Raton. It serves to extend Horizon's market area, providing trust services to many Horizon shareholders, retirees, and customers who have moved to that state. Current plans call for further expansion of trust services throughout Florida.

Horizon's stock, both common and preferred, is traded on the New York Stock Exchange. For the past several years Horizon Bancorp has consistently ranked at or near the top of the 10 largest commercial banking organizations in New Jersey and has had 11 years of uninterrupted growth in historical net operating income per share.

STEVENS INSTITUTE OF TECHNOLOGY

Stevens Institute of Technology is situated in Hoboken, where its 55-acre campus on the Castle Point promontory overlooks the Hudson River and the New York City skyline.

While Stevens has maintained its small-college environment, it has added undergraduate and graduate programs in engineering, science, and management. Stevens was also the first college in the country to require each student to own a personal computer.

The institute was born of the efforts of the Stevens family, a distinguished family in American engineering history. In 1784 Revolutionary War Colonel John Stevens purchased land that included the institute's present campus. A pioneer in the development of the steamboat, Stevens designed the first American steam locomotive in 1825.

Robert Stevens, one of Colonel Stevens' sons, invented the T-rail, the

In 1870 Stevens Institute of Technology began its academic career, offering a program for a baccalaureate degree in mechanical engineering. The curriculum was not a narrow one; it consisted of many areas of study including foreign languages and the humanities. Here, in the early 1900s, students apply their knowledge in a pattern-making workshop.

Setting a standard for the future, education at Stevens was also presented in a professional realm in addition to workshop situations. Students here study industrial engineering, circa early 1920s.

form of railroad track used today throughout the world. With his brother Edwin, Robert built and operated the first commercial railroad in the United States. Edwin also designed and built ironclad vessels for the U.S. Navy. With yet another brother, John—who was the first commodore of the New York Yacht Club—Edwin helped build and race the yacht *America*, 1851 winner of the trophy now known as the America's Cup.

Edwin Stevens, who died in 1868, bequeathed land and funds for the establishment of a college bearing his family name. In 1870 Stevens Institute of Technology opened its doors, offering a curriculum for a mechanical engineering baccalaureate degree.

Stevens' first president was Henry Morton, a noted scientist and linguist, who brought mechanical engineering education out of the workshop and into the professional realm. Using the European model of science, laboratory experiment, and research, Morton broadened the school's curriculum to include mathematics, physics, chemistry, metallurgy, me-

chanical drawing, and mechanical engineering, complemented by the humanities and foreign languages.

Under the leadership of Dr. Kenneth C. Rogers, president since 1972, Stevens' programs in engineering, science, computer science, and management retain this distinctive approach. Each program calls for study in several fields—chemistry, the humanities, management, mathematics, and physics, providing an extensive understanding of technology and the human experience.

The student body has 1,500 undergraduate and 2,000 graduate men and women. The faculty includes about 145 full-time members, 90 percent of whom hold doctoral degrees. Most are involved in research in which undergraduates have opportunities to become involved.

In its long and distinguished history, Stevens Institute of Technology has emerged as one of a select number of colleges in the country capable of tackling and solving the critical technological issues of our times.

Located on a 55-acre campus that overlooks the Hudson River and the New York City skyline, Stevens Institute of Technology today has 1,500 undergraduate and 2,000 graduate students.

McCARTER & ENGLISH

When Thomas N. McCarter and Martin Ryerson joined in the practice of law in 1844, they could not possibly have envisioned the present-day law firm of McCarter & English. Now New Jersey's oldest and largest firm, it has grown from its roots in Newton and Newark to its present national and international practice with about 150 lawyers at offices in Newark, Cherry Hill, Manhattan, and Boca Raton.

In the early nineteenth century Newton was the hub of a commerce spawned by the newly completed Morris Canal, linking the Atlantic Coast and the Delaware River. T.N. McCarter, the son of a judge of the highest state court, Errors and Appeals, began to practice in 1844 with Martin Ryerson in a thriving and growing Newton. Ryerson himself would be appointed to the Errors and Appeals Court in 1853.

In 1865 McCarter left Newton for Newark, which he correctly foresaw as the future commercial center of a

Thomas N. McCarter, Sr., the son of a judge of the highest state court, Errors and Appeals, began to practice in 1844 with Martin Ryerson in Newton.

post-Civil War New Jersey in which railroads rather than canals would be dominant.

The firm of McCarter & Keen was formed with Oscar Keen in 1868, and offices were opened at 810 Broad Street. Later the firm name became McCarter, Williamson and McCarter.

Throughout this period the firm's practice grew with McCarter's considerable fame.

McCarter's own family grew also, and his three sons were to cut a wide swath in the history of New Jersey's public and business affairs. Thomas N. McCarter, Jr., became the founder of Public Service Electric & Gas Company and a national leader of the utilities industry; Uzal McCarter was a founder of the Fidelity Bank, today the state's largest; Robert H. McCarter became attorney general, and, with Conover English, the driving force behind McCarter & English's strong growth and reputation in the early twentieth century.

In 1905 the firm became McCarter & English. Through the first half of this century the law practice flourished under McCarter and English, two of the state's outstanding lawyers. Representing business and industry as well as such clients as a West Orange tinkerer named Thomas A. Edison, a defendant in the nationally famous Hall-Mills murder case, and even a woman from the West named Annie Oakley, the firm drew strength and vigor from its increasing numbers of bright young graduates from the nation's leading law schools.

During the twentieth century the firm has been situated in Newark at the Prudential Building, the Raymond Commerce Building, and the First Fidelity Building. McCarter & English is about to move into a major new office building, Gateway IV, a joint project of the firm and Prudential Insurance Company.

The firm has experienced substantial growth in the past 40 years, catapulting it into a position of leadership among New Jersey law firms and in the region. McCarter & English is a full-service firm with specialists across the range of modern large-firm commercial practice. Today's partner travels by jet for a board meeting in London rather than by horseback for a replevin in Somerville, but the firm's basic credo remains similar to that of its professional forebears: hard work, service

Robert H. McCarter (below), son of Thomas N. McCarter, Sr., and Conover English (below right), two of the state's leading lawyers, became partners in 1905 and led the firm in the first half of this century. They represented such clients as Annie Oakley and Thomas Edison, as well as serving business and industry.

to client, and service to state.

Following in the steps of the founders, McCarter & English lawyers have given heavily of their energies to public service and charity. Among others, Judges Gerald McLoughlin of the Third Circuit, Ward J. Herbert of the Chancery Division, Merritt Lane, Jr., of the Appellate Division, and Arthur L. Nims, Jr., of the United States Tax Court have all come from the firm's ranks. Some partners have become cabinet members, others have sat on state regulatory boards. Throughout the firm's long history its partners have taken leadership positions in professional associations and learned societies as well as teaching positions at the law schools.

McCarter & English has stayed close to the state's commercial and transportation hub, with branches established elsewhere to serve the needs of clients. There are many new clients today—major corporations and individuals, and still a great variety, ranging, for example, from the Sac and Fox Indian tribes of the Midwest to the New York Giants.

It is hard to guess what Thomas McCarter and Martin Ryerson foresaw when they shook hands in Newton back in 1844. Their ideas, melded with those of the lawyers who followed in their footsteps over the next 150 years, form a vital link with what happens today when the firm's partners plan for service to clients in the twenty-first century.

McCarter & English is a very different place than it was when it first started. It surely will change still more to keep up with changing times, but in doing so it will remain true to the traditions of its distinguished historical roots.

Gateway IV, the centrally located new main office of McCarter & English. The firm plans to occupy the top six floors.

CARPENTER, BENNETT & MORRISSEY

Carpenter, Bennett & Morrissey is a law firm with a long and illustrious history. Its partners have served with distinction in the public sector on the national and statewide levels.

The history of the firm begins in 1898, when Lindley Miller Garrison (1864-1932), who later became Secretary of War under President Woodrow Wilson, formed a partnership with Francis P. McManus. The new firm opened offices on Washington Street in Jersey City.

John Mulford Enright (1876-1934) joined as a partner in 1899, and the firm's name was changed to Garrison, McManus & Enright. In 1904 Franklin Pierce McDermott (1854-1921) was admitted as a partner.

That same year Garrison left the firm to become Vice-Chancellor of the New Jersey Court of Chancery, the youngest lawyer ever appointed to that office. He served as Vice-Chancellor with distinction until March 5, 1913, when he joined President Wilson's cabinet as Secretary of War.

With a history that dates back to 1898 and includes many political distinctions, the law firm of Carpenter, Bennett & Morrissey today stands as one of the largest law firms in New Jersey.

The new Secretary became a strong advocate of national preparedness, and he argued for a strong United States military structure. During his tenure as Secretary of War, Garrison was also credited with the drafting of the bill establishing

In 1985 Carpenter, Bennett & Morrissey relocated its offices from 744 Broad Street to the Gateway Three building at 100 Mulberry Street in Newark.

the first Philippine legislature, a move that granted virtual autonomy to the Philippine people.

In 1905 the name of the law firm was changed to McDermott & Enright, and that continued until 1920, when it became McDermott, Enright & Carpenter.

James Dunton Carpenter, Jr. (1885-1972), a graduate of the University of Pennsylvania Law School, was admitted to the New Jersey Bar in 1909. He became associated with the firm in that year as "managing clerk," and in 1913 was admitted to partnership. From 1909 through 1920 Carpenter served as United

States Commissioner and Deputy Clerk in Admiralty. In that position he was responsible for enforcement of wartime statutes during World War I.

During the period leading up to the 1920s, Carpenter was also a member of the Fordham Law School faculty in New York City. In 1932 he became president of the Hudson County Bar Association, and from 1933 through 1934 he served as president of the New Jersey State Bar Association.

In 1933 Carpenter was appointed as Special Assistant Attorney General of the State of New Jersey to investigate and prosecute those responsible for widespread corruption in Passaic County. His distinguished service in that office resulted in numerous convictions, and Carpenter was named by the editors of the Associated Press newspapers in New Jersey as the outstanding news figure in the state in 1934. He was referred to as "in our time the most formidable person ever to take a hand in squelching racketeering, gambling, and jury-fixing in New Jersey," quite an impressive commendation for any lawyer serving in the public sector.

In 1942 the firm changed its name from McDermott, Enright & Carpenter to Carpenter, Gilmour & Dwyer. The firm's name became Carpenter, Bennett & Morrissey in 1958.

From 1954 to 1972 Carpenter served as a member of the House of Delegates of the American Bar Association. He had also been a member

Clients of Carpenter, Bennett & Morrissey include many multinational and national corporations, as well as New Jersey companies. Although its practice is centered in New Jersey, the firm represents clients in many states besides New Jersey, and in this respect it is a national law firm.

of its Special Committee, which successfully opposed the 1937 bill to "pack" the Supreme Court.

By the time of Carpenter's death in 1972, after a long and distinguished career, his firm had grown to become the largest in New Jersey.

Today Carpenter, Bennett & Morrissey conducts an extensive law practice on both the state and federal levels, embracing almost every field of civil law. The firm places particular emphasis on civil litigation, labor and employment law, corporate, product liability, environmental, tax,

Today Carpenter, Bennett & Morrissey has 70 attorneys, 32 of whom are partners, and embraces practically every field of civil law.

employee-benefits law, estate planning, workers' compensation, real estate, antitrust and securities regulation, bankruptcy, and creditors' rights.

Carpenter, Bennett & Morrissey's clients include many multinational and national corporations as well as New Jersey companies. Although its practice is centered in New Jersey, the firm is in many respects a national law firm. In recent years it has represented clients not only in New Jersey but also in states as far away as Illinois, Texas, and California.

Carpenter, Bennett & Morrissey today has 70 attorneys, 32 of whom are partners. The current partners are Thomas L. Morrissey, Arthur M. Lizza, Warren Lloyd Lewis, Laurence Reich, Stanley Weiss, John C. Heavey, John E. Keale, Edward F. Ryan, James J. Crowley, Jr., John P. Dwyer, David M. McCann, Michael S. Waters, Anthony C. Famulari, James G. Gardner, John F. Lynch, Jr., Francis X. O'Brien, Donald A. Romano, Robert E. Turtz, Francis X. Dee, Rudy B. Coleman, Edward F. Day, Jr., Jerome E. Sharfman, Irving L. Hurwitz, Edwin R. Alley, Rosemary J. Bruno, William A. Carpenter, Jr., Rosemary Alito, John J. Peirano, Linda B. Celauro, John D. Goldsmith, and Thomas J. Lennon.

In 1985 Carpenter, Bennett & Morrissey relocated its offices from 744 Broad Street in Newark to new quarters in the Gateway Three building at 100 Mulberry Street in Newark.

AT&T

AT&T's activities span the world, but the company is truly at home in New Jersey. It is the state's largest private-sector employer, and all of its major divisions are headquartered in New Jersey: AT&T Bell Laboratories, AT&T Communications and Information Systems, AT&T Network Systems, AT&T Technology Systems, AT&T International, and AT&T Resource Management, the corporation's real estate sector. With additional facilities in more than 100 locations throughout the state, AT&T owns or leases some 17 million square feet of space in New Jersey.

AT&T's Network Operations Center—the computerized control facility for the country's long-distance network—is also in New Jersey, and New Jersey is the starting point for some of AT&T's transatlantic cables. With its laboratories, corporate offices, and other facilities, the corporation truly is a major presence throughout the state.

AT&T's corporate heritage dates back to Alexander Graham Bell, inventor of the telephone. American Telephone and Telegraph Company was founded in 1885 as a subsidiary of the American Bell Telephone Company. It became the parent company in 1899 and established its headquarters in New York City.

The nerve center of the nation's long-distance network in Bedminster, New Jersey.

Theodore N. Vail, AT&T's first president, was a New Jerseyan. The company's first physical plant was its Western Electric facility in Kearny, a project launched in 1923. Bell Labs then opened its first New Jersey facility in Whippany in 1926. Since then AT&T has been deeply involved

The AT&T Personal Computer offers greater speed, more features, and a higher level of standard equipment than its leading competition.

in the economic growth of the state.

AT&T has been one of the world's largest international telecommunications companies for generations, and it was the world's largest private business organization until the divestiture of the Bell telephone companies at the end of 1983. Here is a look at some of the corporation's major divisions:

AT&T International coordinates the international sales of AT&T's products and services through offices in key countries and in cooperation with international companies through a variety of joint ventures.

AT&T Bell Laboratories is one of the world's premier research centers. Since its establishment in 1925 it has been granted an average of a patent a day. Its innovations over the years include computer languages and operating systems, the electrical digital computer, laser inventions, the solar battery, the transistor, cellular-mobile-phone service, Telstar communication satellites, high-fidelity and stereo sound, radio astronomy, sound motion pictures, and much more.

A total of seven AT&T Bell Laboratories scientists have received the Nobel Prize for Physics over the years: Clinton Davisson in 1937 for work in demonstrating the wave nature of matter; John Bardeen, Walter Brattain, and William Shockley in 1956 for inventing the transistor;

Phillip Anderson in 1977 for study of the electronic structure of glass and magnetic materials; and Arno Penzias and Robert Wilson in 1978 for discovering the faint background radiation remaining from the "big bang" explosion believed by many to have started the universe billions of years ago.

AT&T Bell Laboratories continues to design and develop new products, systems, and services. Recent developments include the one-megabit computer memory chip, the transmission of information by light wave at a rate of up to two billion bits a second, a semiconductor circuit operating at higher switching speeds than any known silicon circuit, and innovations in artificial intelligence and computer-aided design.

AT&T Technology Systems is a major designer, developer, and manufacturer of energy systems, customized devices, advanced integrated circuit components, and systems based on these components.

AT&T Network Systems supplies and services telecommunications systems and equipment to local telephone companies in the United States and abroad.

AT&T Communications and Information Systems provides domestic and international long-distance telecommunications for residence, business, and government customers. It also offers special voice, data, and video services.

In addition, this division manufactures, markets, installs, and maintains communications-based information systems, from "smart" telephones for the home to integrated voice and data business systems, linking tens of thousands of people and computers.

Although AT&T has earned its reputation as a technological leader, it has always concentrated on the human dimensions of science. This concern for the human spirit is also the basis for AT&T's commitment to civic and philanthropic activities throughout New Jersey. It supports major research universities such as

AT&T's high tech, 24-hour-a-day customer service support center in Iselin, New Jersey, is the "nerve center" of technical support for all AT&T voice and data communications systems used by thousands of business customers across the state of New Jersey.

Rutgers and Princeton through donations of computer equipment and visiting-professor programs. The corporation aids smaller liberal arts schools through the state's Independent College Fund. It is also a benefactor of the Governor's Teaching

Scholars Program, which provides scholarships to young people obtaining education degrees for careers in teaching.

Most of AT&T's educational support is in the area of science and technology, aimed at stimulating new talent in the high-technology area.

AT&T also has been an active donor to New Jersey's cultural, health care, and social action organizations, contributing more than five million dollars to such programs in 1986. AT&T makes such donations to strengthen the quality of life not only for its many New Jersey employees, but for the rest of the state's citizens as well, with the added dividend of helping the state's economy.

The atrium lobby of the Tower Center in East Brunswick—AT&T's newest location in Middlesex County.

RED DEVIL, INC.

Red Devil, Inc., is a company with 400 employee/partners, making specialized hand tools, chemical products, and electrical machinery.

Red Devil products are purchased by do-it-yourself home decorators, painters, glaziers and tile setters, flexible-floor and wall-covering installers, and other builders and home-improvement contractors.

Painter's tools currently make up the largest portion of Red Devil's business. Principal tool products are scraping, patching, and smoothing cutlery, and wood and paint razor scrapers. Other products in this line include ceramic tile, flooring, masonry, and glaziers' hand tools and supplies.

Chemical products account for the other important share of company sales. Caulks and sealants are this sector's principal line, made in a variety of formulations to meet particular environmental conditions. Other chemical items are spackles, fillers, cleaners, ceramic tile products, and adhesives.

Paint-conditioner machines and custom paint tinters represent the remaining part of Red Devil's business.

These products are used by paint manufacturers, distributors, retailers, and contractors to condition paint and create custom colors in paints, printing inks, dyes, and coatings.

Red Devil, Inc., is a New Jersey corporation headquartered at 2400 Vauxhall Road in Union. The firm

The first steel wheel glass cutters (above) ever made were produced in 1872 at the Landon P. Smith, Inc., plant (below) at Hill, New Hampshire. This was a predecessor of Red Devil, Inc.

is a direct successor of Smith & Hemenway Co., established in 1897, and prior to that, the New England Novelty Works, founded in 1872, among others. The enterprise was originally incorporated as Landon P. Smith, Inc., by its founder, Landon Smith, in 1926.

Half of the company's growth over the years has come through acquisitions; some 30 purchases were made during its history. In 1932 the firm acquired the wood-scraper business of Vosco Tool Co. of Philadelphia, as well as the Woodward-Hubbard Company of Hill, New Hampshire. It purchased the paint-machine business of the Roan Manufacturing Company in Racine, Wisconsin, in 1937. The following year came the purchase of Hubbard and McClary of Windsor, Vermont, maker of glaziers' points and drivers. In 1939 the company took over the floor-sanding machine business of the Rugaard Manufacturing Co., Lawrence, Massachusetts.

More acquisitions continued to increase the firm's size. In 1941 it purchased the roller-stippler and roller-painter business of the Chicago

Roller Stippler Co. The next year it bought the stock of Reddy Tee Co. of Newark, New Jersey, maker of the original wood golf tees. In 1944 the company purchased the patents and trademark of the Jak-Nife Razor Blade Holder business from the Novelty Manufacturing Co. of St. Paul, Minnesota.

On September 20, 1944, the company's name was changed from Landon P. Smith, Inc., to Red Devil Tools. In 1966 the name was changed again, to Red Devil, Inc. Twenty small businesses or product-line assets were acquired from 1944 to 1985.

Today Red Devil is a diversified company: No one customer purchases 10 percent of its output. The firm produces 1,200 products in its tool and chemical lines, along with approximately 50 machines, instruments, and other accessories. Red Devil makes 90 percent of the products it sells. It also imports complementary products for customers in North America and has exported overseas since 1880.

Red Devil also sells process technology and benefits from its copy-

Paint-conditioner machines and custom paint tinters are just some of the varied products manufactured by Red Devil, Inc., today.

right licenses and patent royalties. The company is an acknowledged leader in product innovation and creative marketing, with top management information systems and worldwide trademark recognition.

In recent years a boom in sales of Red Devil's new chemical products has outpaced tool sales. The company's custom-coloring systems are expected to become an increasingly important sector through the 1990s. It is Red Devil policy to introduce new or improved products in each of its divisions every year and to improve or eliminate obsolete or slow-moving products.

Red Devil's distribution has been strongest through independent hardware distributors, paint-related chains, and in direct sales to home centers, discount houses and department stores, and other mass-market merchants. Additional growth areas for Red Devil products are in manufacturing supplies and industrial plant maintenance.

Red Devil is proud of its special partnership with each employee and its record of minimal layoffs and business interruptions. While the company maintains an open commitment to bargain in good faith with any trade union elected by its employees, no such election or organizing drive has taken place in more than 15 years. All U.S. employees are eligible to join the Red Devil Profit Sharing Plan after one year of service.

Red Devil management has a good balance of age, education, and experience at all levels. Paid education programs, in-house training, and special projects prepare younger managers for their future. There are many family relationships and second-generation employees in the Red Devil employee group.

George L. Lee, Jr., is Red Devil's chairman of the board and chief executive officer, and Don Hall is president and chief operations officer. The company owner-managers are represented on the board of directors in rotating assignments. Two members of the Lee family's third generation and two of the fourth generation are board members. The company's vice-chairman is John L. Lee, and George L. Lee III is vice-president of planning and corporate development.

Red Devil has paid common dividends in the range of 20 to 25 percent of earnings each quarter for 34 of the past 35 years and has made timely payments of interest or amortization due to every lender for the past quarter-century. Red Devil is also decidedly a growth company: Its profits have increased in 34 of the past 40 years.

Red Devil, Inc., has manufacturing operations in Union, New Jersey, and Pryor, Oklahoma. The two facilities total 252,000 square feet.

Red Devil water motors, intended for household grinding and polishing and running a variety of small machines, were offered in Smith & Hemenway's 1931 catalog.

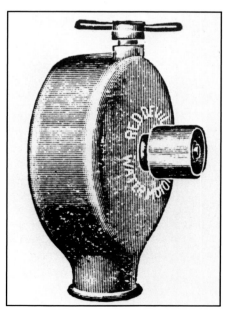

THE FIRST JERSEY NATIONAL BANK

The First Jersey National Bank was organized under the National Banking Act of 1864 and chartered on February 18 of that year as the First National Bank of Jersey City. Two months later the bank opened at One Exchange Place, the busy waterfront hub of Jersey City.

Over the next 104 years the First National Bank of Jersey City would add 11 new offices and provide quality banking service to the people and businesses of Hudson County.

In 1968 the bank's broadening base called for a change in corporate identification and a new name, The First Jersey National Bank. The following year First Jersey was reorganized into a bank holding company called First Jersey National Corporation, with the bank becoming a wholly owned subsidiary.

Statewide expansion characterized First Jersey's progress in the 1970s, starting with the acquisition of the Newark-based Bank of Commerce in 1969 and continuing with the purchase of the Belmar-Wall National Bank in Monmouth County and the establishment of various new offices. By 1979 First Jersey was operating 27 banking offices in Hudson, Essex, Bergen, Monmouth, Ocean, and Union counties.

Meanwhile, First Jersey was expanding into nonbanking service areas. It acquired Tilden Commercial Alliance, Incorporated, and Tilden Financial Corporation (industrial and automobile-leasing companies), plus Guardian Commercial Corporation, a small-loan organization.

In 1971 First Jersey became the first bank outside New York City to be approved by the New York Stock Exchange to act as a transfer agent, and it established an office in New York's financial district through its Jersey National Securities Transfer Corporation subsidiary.

That same year First Jersey's Wall Street Division, consisting of the Mutual Fund, Stock Transfer, Special Services, and Stock Bookkeeping departments, became First Jersey Financial Services Company,

an autonomous division of the bank. Using the bank's electronic data-processing equipment, staff, and files, it offered its services independently to corporations, mutual funds, and other banks, including First Jersey.

In 1976 Jersey National Securities Transfer Corporation changed its name to Exchange Place Securities Transfer Corporation, and the following year it opened a second office, in

The bank's location, close to the heart of Wall Street, prompted it to be called "The Bank of Two Cities."

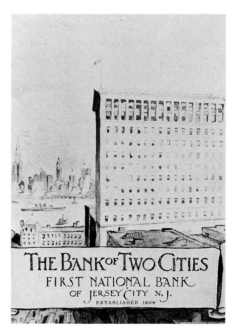

The interior of First Jersey National Bank's main office at One Exchange Place in Jersey City has changed very little in the past 86 years. The intricately worked wrought-iron tables are still used by bank customers today.

Chicago.

Entering the 1980s, First Jersey intensified its expansion. The Bank of New Jersey, N.A., was acquired in 1981, adding offices in Ocean County and precipitating the formation of a new holding company bank subsidiary, The First Jersey National Bank/South. Next came the acquisition of the Perth Amboy National Bank, with offices in Middlesex County. That led to the formation of The First Jersey National Bank/Central.

The Washington Bank in Gloucester County, acquired in 1982, became The First Jersey National Bank/Delaware Valley, which later became part of The First Jersey National Bank/South. Further acquisitions the following year brought the number of First Jersey bank offices to 51, spread throughout 11 counties, and the corporation's assets to about $1.5 billion.

In 1984 Guarantee Bank, acquired and merged into The First Jersey National Bank/South, increased the offices to 71 and assets to about two billion dollars.

Mighty cranes and bulldozers are transforming the Hudson River waterfront site that, in 1988, will support the new corporate headquarters of The First Jersey National Bank.

Midway through 1984 nine Essex County offices had been acquired—five from Fidelity Union Bank and four from First National State Bank. Later in 1984 First Jersey acquired the Bank of Beverly with five offices in Burlington County, and the Livingston National Bank with three offices in that Essex County municipality.

On April 1, 1985, the former Peoples National Bank of North Jersey was acquired and became The First Jersey National Bank/West. Headquartered in Denville, the bank operates six offices in Morris County and one in Sussex County.

In September 1985 the corporation's 100th office—and its first in Mercer County—was opened. The former office of the National State Bank at the Mercer Mall became a branch of The First Jersey National Bank/Central.

Two months later the corporation purchased the Broad Street National Bank of Trenton. This nine-office acquisition increased First Jersey's strength in Mercer County. In No-

vember the First National Bancorp in Fort Lee was purchased, and the following month the corporation announced its intention to expand into Bucks and Montgomery counties in Pennsylvania, with a new subsidiary Newmarket National Bank.

As 1986 drew to a close, First Jersey's offices in the Garden State numbered 113 in 16 counties.

Today First Jersey continues to

Thomas J. Stanton, Jr., chairman and chief executive officer of The First Jersey National Bank, studies an architectural drawing of One Exchange Place, the 30-story, glass-sheathed structure soon to rise on the waterfront of Jersey City.

play a dominant role in an increasingly competitive banking environment. First Jersey provides its retail customers with a wide range of services and a highly sophisticated electronic banking system that enables them to self-manage their money. Account information, the ability to transfer funds immediately, bill payments by telephone and a nationwide automated teller machine linkup provide customers with maximum convenience and control over their finances.

First Jersey's corporate banking area is equally responsive to the growing needs of the state's private and public sectors, and it plays a major role in supporting New Jersey's economic expansion. In the non-banking financial area, First Jersey is one of the nation's leading processors of mutual funds and provides processing, record keeping, and transfer services for the securities industry through its Financial Services Division.

In this decade First Jersey has grown to be the fourth-largest bank holding company in New Jersey. In 1980 its assets stood at about $1.2 billion, and at the end of 1986 it had nearly $4.5 billion in assets.

Ranked among New Jersey's largest banking institutions, The First Jersey National Bank has gone through enormous changes and expansion since its founding in 1864. Nonetheless, its purpose remains the same: to offer the best banking services to the people of New Jersey.

GENERAL MAGNAPLATE CORPORATION

During the early 1950s Dr. Charles Covino, a renowned chemical engineering specialist, saw that the U.S. aircraft industry was in need of better testing laboratories. With his vast scientific experience as his major asset, he established General Magnaplate Corporation in Hoboken in 1952 as a nondestructive testing (NDT) laboratory for the aircraft industry. Soon Dr. Covino expanded General Magnaplate into the metal plating or coatings field, an integral part of aircraft performance. The company's plating work gradually increased, and its testing activities became separate operations. Today General Magnaplate is headquartered in Linden, and its main business is high-technology metal coating processes.

General Magnaplate pioneered development of synergistic coatings that prevent metal wear, friction, and corrosion. The coatings improve surface hardness and give permanent lubricity to practically any metal part. These coatings are integrated with the top layers of the base metal rather than being a mere surface cover. This is why they have been termed "synergistic."

General Magnaplate developed its synergistic coatings for the NASA space program. The metals NASA used—aluminum, titanium, and high-strength steel—posed many problems: Their existing coatings did not provide long-term protection, and conventional lubricants "boiled" away in the vacuum of space. Scientists sought to bolster the performance of primary metals in outer space, and General Magnaplate had the answer. Their new coatings combined the advantages of hard-coat plating with the infusion of low-friction polymers or other dry lubricants, creating coatings that will not chip, peel, or rub off.

Although General Magnaplate's coatings were first developed for the aerospace industry, they soon came to be used in thousands of other industrial applications, including food and drug packaging, chemicals, plastics, textiles, gears, hand tools, military hardware, compressors, turbines, valves, and engines. While NASA used General Magnaplate coatings in many applications, Nabisco used a Magnaplate finish on the molds that

General Magnaplate headquarters in Linden, where its main business is high-technology metal coating processes.

make the distinctive pattern of Milk-Bone Dog Biscuits. General Magnaplate coatings are also used on the molds that make "blister packs" for many over-the-counter drugs, and scientists are finding new uses for the coatings nearly every day.

General Magnaplate has nine basic coatings, each developed to work with a specific metal or group of metals. Each of the nine coatings has many variations in type so it can be tailored to meet specific metals' performance requirements.

The nine basic coatings have unique-sounding names like Nedox, Canadize, and Tufram, but they all perform vitally important scientific functions that often touch our daily lives.

In the nondestructive testing area—the firm's original activity—General Magnaplate developed the first and only method of nondestructive testing of the thick lead structures of nuclear submarine reactors, a method that has since been used to examine every U.S. Navy atomic submarine. The company also invented testing devices for the first foolproof nuclear condenser pipe test machine, which tests even the thinnest tubing used to hold the uranium

Charles Covino, Ph.D., a renowned chemical engineering specialist, established General Magnaplate Corporation in 1952 when he observed that the U.S. aircraft industry was in need of better testing laboratories.

pellets that fuel the reactor.

Many of General Magnaplate's proprietary processes were invented and trademarked by Dr. Covino. Throughout his distinguished private-sector career, he has also served the U.S. government as a highly valued specialist. When the nuclear submarine *Thresher* sank in April 1963, Dr. Covino was immediately called to Washington by Admiral Hyman Rickover to head a task force investigating the disaster. Within 10 days Dr. Covino's report was complete. Though his top-secret analysis of problems with the sub's heater weld tubes has never been officially confirmed or denied by the Navy, it is widely believed that Dr. Covino pinpointed the problem.

Dr. Covino has also been consulted many times on U.S. space agency problems concerning metal-lurgical, material friction, coating, or lubrication matters. General Magnaplate itself has been involved in every space probe since the Mercury missions, consulting with NASA and its contractors, and Dr. Covino was the first testing specialist recognized by NASA to test and certify other testing engineers. He and other specialists became designated as "examiners" by the Navy and had four separate ratings: magnetic particle, fluorescent penetrant, utrasonic, and radiographic. Of the 25 examiners, Dr. Covino was one of only five people who were cross-rated for all four methods.

Dr. Covino remains the company's controlling influence. His daughter, Candida Aversenti, serves as vice-president of marketing, and her husband, Edmund Aversenti, is vice-president and general manager of the company's Linden Plant, where General Magnaplate's corporate headquarters is located. The company also has plants in Texas and California and employs more than 125 people nationwide.

Dr. Covino has been active in innumerable civic and charitable projects, and he has also been active in public affairs, helping alert America to its dependence on foreign countries for so much of its important exotic-metal requirements. He has spoken about the topic on radio and television and before many civic and industry groups, as well as writing extensively about it. The United States imports 22 of 27 key strategic metals—mostly from South Africa. A cutoff of these essential raw materials, for which there are no viable substitutes, would give General Magnaplate's coatings added importance. Dr. Covino is also the author of a book on quality control, published by Industrial Press, describing all aspects of developing and implementing an in-plant quality-control program. To date the book has sold more than 200,000 copies.

General Magnaplate Corporation has acquired an international reputation for its proprietary synergistic coatings and is determined to remain in the forefront of technological advance. Its growth plan includes advanced new PVD coating processes, of which Magnagold is the first of a new generation, as well as a series of interrelated industrial products that are currently being market tested.

General Magnaplate pioneered development of synergistic coatings that prevent metal wear, friction, and corrosion. The coatings improve surface hardness and give permanent lubricity to practically any metal part.

IRON HORSE FARM

Nestled in the rolling hills of historic Ringoes, New Jersey, in Hunterdon County is Iron Horse Farm, an idyllic but highly efficient breeding, boarding, and training ground for American Saddlebred horses.

Dr. Charles P. Covino, the farm's owner, is an internationally recognized metallurgical scientist and founder and board chairman of General Magnaplate Corporation, which specializes in protective coatings for metals. At Iron Horse Farm Dr. Covino has used his inventive genius to create a breeding and training complex where he and his wife, Sylvia, now live.

The Covinos have been involved with horses since their daughter Candi became a rider at the age of six. Now a mother of five and a General Magnaplate vice-president, Candi Aversenti has won national acclaim with her champion Saddlebreds. She is also proud to see her own offspring carry on the family tradition. Her oldest daughter, Ashley, has already become a national and world's champion rider, and her four other daughters, Katy, Carlin, Alex, and Danyel, are riding at the beginning stages. Though he does not ride, Candi's husband, Ed, joins in the family tradition by showing his hackney roadster pony. Dr. Covino also shows his many-time national

champion hackney show pony.

In previous years the family had to travel to southern states such as Kentucky to find quality horses and facilities, because New Jersey had few quality farms to stable such expensive horses. Correctly believing that a New Jersey farm would help rekindle this region's interest in Saddlebreds, Dr. Covino established Iron Horse Farm as a facility offering the finest in equestrian care, handling, and bloodlines. Opened in 1982, Iron Horse Farm gets its name from the old Black River & Western Railroad, which still chugs along beyond the back end of the 65-acre farm's property line.

Iron Horse Farm's facilities are both functional and beautiful. The main barn's office and lounge have large windows looking out on the indoor straightaway, permitting a perfect view of the horses being worked. A second-floor lounge also has direct viewing of the indoor arena. The main barn has a 240-foot straightaway with 50-foot by 50-foot turnabouts at each end. Horses can be worked in three areas at the same time, and the

Iron Horse Farm, located in the rolling hills of historic Ringoes in Hunterdon County, provides an idyllic setting for the breeding, boarding, and training of American Saddlebred horses.

space is protected from the weather.

The farm houses the family's own horses as well as some brought in for boarding and training. Championship horses include The Ringo Kid, Little Sport Model, Merlin's Magic, Fancy Minnikin, and breeding stallion Sir Talmage, as well as many of the nation's top show horses now used as brood mares.

The stall area features temperature-controlled automatic waterers, an automatic perfumed fly-spray system, and other high-tech equipment. The flooring has a specialized porous hard surface that allows moisture to seep through and eliminates odors and bacteria. The floor is topped by a foot of fine wood chips to ensure that the horses' hooves remain dry. Other parts of the sprawling Iron Horse Farm include a brood mare and foaling barn, an outdoor training ring, and a separate barn to house the champion hackney show ponies. The farm has six large pastures, each with its own turn-out shed and automatic waterers to house brood mares and foals.

Ringoes, New Jersey, is about 90 minutes from New York City and 45 minutes from Philadelphia. Its surrounding area, rich in Revolutionary War history, has excellent motels and restaurants, antique shops, boutiques, and handicraft shops.

NEW JERSEY INSTITUTE OF TECHNOLOGY

New Jersey Institute of Technology, founded in 1881, is the state's comprehensive technological university. Situated on a 34-acre campus in Newark's University Heights section, NJIT offers programs in engineering, architecture, management, the sciences, mathematics, and technology. About 7,400 students are enrolled in NJIT programs leading to bachelor's, master's, doctoral, or professional degrees at the main campus and at several off-campus sites throughout the state.

The institution's history spans a period in which America moved from the Industrial Revolution to the Information Age. Newark was a factory town when the tuition-free evening school known as Newark Technical School first opened its doors to 126 students. One of the institution's most ardent early supporters, the Newark Board of Trade, believed it would benefit New Jersey by increasing the state's skilled labor force.

The school's educational focus soon shifted to college-level programs, and in 1930 it became the Newark College of Engineering. By 1975, when its name was changed to the New Jersey Institute of Technology, the college was fast evolving into a technological university, educating its students for today's complex, high-tech society.

NJIT offers a broad range of un-

Researchers at NJIT are currently investigating the newest uses of robots for manufacturing procedures. This robot is housed in the university's robotics center.

The New Jersey Institute of Technology campus as seen from the library steps. Tiernan Hall can be seen in the background.

dergraduate and graduate degrees. While more than half its enrollment is in engineering, its strengths also include architecture, computer science, management, mathematics, biotechnology, and other science-oriented areas. The student body has achieved a high degree of excellence, capturing numerous national and state honors.

Nearly 25 percent of all engineers in New Jersey are NJIT graduates. Most NJIT alumni live and work in the state, an indication that educating students for high-technology jobs is good for the Garden State's future. The university believes that Newark has a bright future and is working with other academic institutions in the city to encourage economic growth.

NJIT is responding to today's educational, environmental, and social problems in many ways. The university is contributing the expertise and skills of its students and its approximately 800-member faculty and staff to a variety of educational and research projects.

Plans are under way for the construction of the NJIT Computer In-

tegrated Manufacturing Center, which will house a Factory of the Future, a state-of-the-art, computer-controlled flexible manufacturing facility.

The Industry/University Cooperative Center for Research in Hazardous and Toxic Substances opens new facilities in mid-1988. NJIT directs this nationally recognized center, an interinstitutional consortium supported by government and corporations.

The Center for Information Age Technology, a university-based outreach center, is serving the state through extension and continuing education programs.

NJIT's Computerized Conferencing and Communication Center plays a leadership role in research and development of computer-mediated conferencing.

The Center for Pre-College Programs broadens the outlook and career objectives of talented youngsters from the inner city. About 1,000 students, teachers, and counselors from New Jersey participate each year.

Biomedical engineering programs at New Jersey Institute of Technology are being carried out with New Jersey medical colleges and with pharmaceutical companies and other industries.

ENGELHARD CORPORATION

Engelhard Corporation is a world leader in developing performance products based on advanced chemical and metallurgical technologies. Working with performance minerals and precious metals, the company's scientists have invented and revolutionized processes involved in the manufacture of thousands of products critical to major industries and the quality of our daily lives—from gasoline, computers, and plastics to clothing, pharmaceuticals, and fertilizers. Engelhard products perform vital functions that enable customers to make superior products or achieve cost-efficient manufacturing.

Engelhard's product groups are organized into two major operating divisions—Specialty Chemicals and Specialty Metals. The Specialty Chemicals Division applies advanced chemical technologies in the manufacture of catalysts essential in producing gasoline, heating oil, fertilizers,

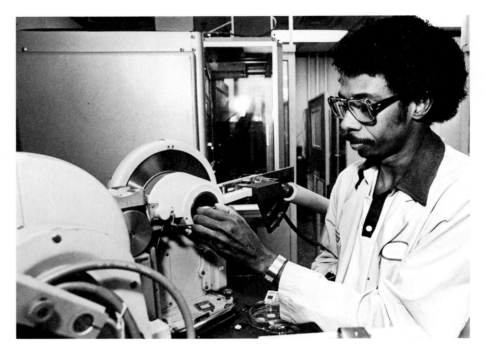

In the materials characterization lab, technician Earl Waterman loads a sample into the X-ray diffraction unit to identify its materials and minerals.

Chemist Jim Younie (left) and technician Clive Marion work Carteret's breakdown lab, where samples from the Menlo Park research labs are analyzed for precious metals content.

synthetic fibers, pharmaceuticals, and in numerous processes for creating intermediates that go into the manufacture of literally thousands of other products. Engelhard catalysts also keep the environment clean through auto and plant pollution control. In addition, the division makes performance minerals for enhancing the brightness, opacity, and printability of paper stocks and bringing critical product qualities in the manufacture of plastic, paints, and rubber. Its electronic chemicals help achieve miniaturization and reliability in making computers, space and telecommunications systems, and various entertainment products.

The Specialty Metals Division operates the only service in the world that integrates the various key steps in ensuring customers maximum efficiency in using precious metals in their manufacturing process. The division provides precious-metal-based components or processing devices and refines the expensive metal for reuse. Altogether, the firm fabricates more than 10,000 products used in manufacturing jet aircraft, ships, trucks and automobiles, machinery, and an infinite number of household goods. The corporation also manages the purchase and financing of the metal

through a worldwide network of offices.

Engelhard's origins are traced to products of three companies that eventually came together in helping structure the current organization: liquid-gold solutions for decorating ceramics, china, and glassware, brought from Europe by Charles Engelhard in the 1890s; platinum for dental and jewelry products developed by the Baker Company before the turn of the century; and use of kaolin as a performance mineral in paper production by the Edgar Brothers Company in the early 1900s.

It was during the 1920s that Engelhard began working with precious metals to speed the reaction in the catalytic process. The company has since pioneered many developments for basic processing industries, helping create catalysts for manufacturing pharmaceuticals during the 1940s, helping develop a platinum catalyst for gasoline production, and making catalysts for the chemical/petrochemical industry, which has led to modern-day mass manufacturing of numerous chemical intermediates and finished products. The firm also pioneered the catalytic converter for auto exhaust abatement.

In the 1960s Engelhard perfected the zeolitic fluid cracking catalyst, revolutionizing methods for making gasoline and distillate. The 1980s have brought many new developments, such as the ULTRASIV® fluid cracking catalyst line and now the DYNAMICS series of catalysts, which enhances production of high-octane gasolines. Engelhard has grown into being the nation's leading supplier of fluid cracking catalyst for petroleum refining. Engelhard's Asphalt Residual Treatment (ART ^{SM}) process is an exciting development. It upgrades heavier crude oils into gasoline. Eventually the world will be depending upon processing the heavier crude feedstocks.

Engelhard's Performance Minerals Group produces specialty kaolin-based coating and extender pigments for the paper, paint, and plastics industries from its facilities in McIntyre and Gordon, Georgia. The company is the world's largest supplier of specialty kaolin coating and extender pigments for papers. The technology

standard in the industry is Engelhard's ANSILEX® line of paper pigments. In 1985 the firm purchased the Freeport Kaolin Company of Gordon, Georgia, to complement its own kaolin operations and enhance its program in becoming the low-cost producer of pigments and extenders for the paper, paint, plastics, and rubber industries. Engelhard also markets high-performance attapulgite thickening agents for paint and coatings formulations.

Its ATTAGEL® thickener, designed for asphalt cutback coating systems, allowed the development of reliable, asbestos-free asphalt roof coatings and automotive underbody coatings.

Engelhard's precious metals technology is utilized in producing highly reliable, multifunctional, microelectronics components for computer, telecommunications, aerospace, military defense, and other sophisticated electronic applications. In 1985 the company acquired Millis Corporation, Millis, Massachusetts, to expand

With a printing press, lab technician Daryl Tokar can see how well inks take to paper coated with Engelhard pigments.

its capabilities in critical microcircuitry.

The firm's knowledge of precious metals as electrical conductors, heat reflectors, corrosion resistors, and temperature sensors has been used in the creation of more than 10,000 products essential in making everything from glass and steel to cars and dental fillings.

Engelhard also produces investor products such as bullion bars; silver, gold, and platinum coin blanks; and custom-minted medallions. Its customers include the U.S. and the Royal Canadian mints.

Engelhard products are marketed throughout the world. As a global company, Engelhard operates plants in Australia, Brazil, Canada, France, Italy, Japan, Korea, Mexico, New Zealand, Switzerland, the United Kingdom, the United States, Venezuela, and West Germany. In addition, sales representatives, local agents, and joint-venture sales forces are working in dozens of other countries.

As Engelhard Corporation looks to the future, its exceptional technologies will continue to expand the value its products provide major industries throughout the world.

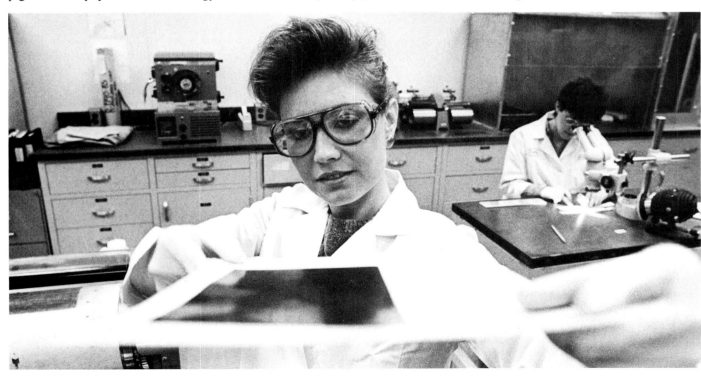

CONGOLEUM CORPORATION

When Michael Nairn converted his family's successful sailcloth business in Kirkcaldy, Scotland, into a fledgling flooring operation in the mid-1800s, local skeptics called the new enterprise "Nairn's Folly."

But people stopped laughing when Nairn's painted canvas floorcloths, a new type of product for the home, took hold. Under the direction of his son, Sir Michael, the business flourished and eventually grew into what is known today as Congoleum Corporation, the second-largest resilient flooring manufacturer and oldest in America.

For 101 years Congoleum has made New Jersey its home. As Sir Michael's business evolved from painted floorcloths to linoleum, it shared a similar growth in sales and demand. Expansion to the United States was the next natural step, and Sir Michael found the perfect site in Kearny, along the banks of the Passaic River, where he established the firm in 1886.

Even then New Jersey was seen as an excellent manufacturing and distribution site. Today, in addition to its headquarters in Kearny, Congoleum has more than 70 acres of land in Trenton, where many of its products are manufactured, and sister facilities in Pennsylvania and Maryland.

Sir Michael Nairn, founder of the Nairn Linoleum Co., which grew to become Congoleum Corporation.

It is from Congoleum's new Automated Distribution Center in Trenton that millions of rolls of floor covering are shipped annually to its national network of distributors. Inaugurated last year at a cost of $25 million, the center uses the latest computer and robotic technology to inspect, package, and ship floor covering to customers.

Developed to meet the company's service needs well into the twenty-

This turn-of-the-century illustration features the original Congoleum manufacturing plant situated along the banks of the Passaic River in Kearny.

first century, this new facility is an example of the vision and innovation that have permeated the company since its beginning.

For when Sir Michael brought his business to New Jersey, he did much more: He brought a cadre of skilled Scottish craftsmen to man the operation, and his actions had a dramatic impact on the economic and social mix of the area. Several other Scottish-based firms, including Coats & Clark Thread Mills and O&M Thread Mills, also chose Kearny as the site for their plants. More than 100 years later the Scottish influence remains remarkably evident in the townspeople, shops, and customs.

Sir Michael also established what has become a tradition of innovation and excellence in product. The "firsts" Congoleum has developed over the years have now become American standards, for the resilient flooring industry and consumers as well.

Congoleum was the first company to introduce a family of no-wax floor coverings. A great convenience to American households, no-wax flooring has forever changed the way Americans care for their homes. Time-consuming washing and stripping of wax became a thing of the past—easy maintenance, the norm.

More important, Congoleum developed a manufacturing and design process that revolutionized the look and properties of sheet-vinyl products for the world. That procedure, created and patented by Congoleum, is chemical embossing, and today more than 85 percent of the resilient flooring produced in the world is made from the Congoleum process.

In 1963 Congoleum scientists developed a process that employed chemical inhibitors in the inks used to print the flooring designs. The inhibitors controlled the level of foam throughout the product, in essence embossing or etching the design into the product.

The process gave the product dimension. Virtually any design type was possible with this new technique.

Popular Congoleum Gold Seal Art Rugs were among the most fashionable flooring products available and were heavily advertised for more than 30 years. This ad, from 1928, carries the company's Gold Seal and Satisfaction Guaranteed emblem. Congoleum reintroduced the Gold Seal in 1986 for its centennial celebration.

Delicate brush strokes of an Oriental painting could be reproduced, as well as fine wood grains, detailed florals, and realistic bricks—all combined with an unparalleled range and control of color.

This technical marvel had a tremendous impact on the sheet-vinyl business, making previous improvements pale by comparison. Congoleum product quality was inherent; the addition of chemical embossing gave consumers a seemingly limitless selection in design and color. The combination made sales history for the firm.

Much of the company's success is based on its mission to provide key decorating products for the home. Style and attention to detail are basics in every Congoleum product. From the original painted floor cloths, the advent of inlaid blocks of

color in linoleum, and the firm's nationally recognized Gold Seal Art Rugs to its most recent innovation of seamless inlaid flooring, the tradition of color and design excellence has been paramount.

While the Nairn Linoleum Co. in Kearny was flourishing, a small roofing materials firm in Erie, Pennsylvania, began manufacturing a specialty flooring product called Rug Border. This three-foot-wide simulated wood grain flooring was used to border area rugs and linoleum to finish off the look. The moderately priced product was called Congoleum, a name coined because the asphalt used in the product's felt base came from the African Belgian Congo. In 1924 the two companies merged to form Congoleum-Nairn. Its principal products were Congoleum Gold Seal Rugs and Nairn linoleum.

Over the years the firm produced a wide variety of flooring products. In the late 1930s its research scientists began working with a new material, vinyl, after its introduction at the 1936 Chicago World's Fair.

But when World War II erupted, Albert W. Hawkes, then Congoleum president, quickly transformed the company's facilities to war production. The firm maintained core linoleum production for war housing and battleships, and also produced camouflage netting, tent cloths, aerial torpedo parts and grenades, and mildew-proof sandbags. At the height of this war effort Congoleum had more than 60 acres of manufacturing facilities in Kearny and employed nearly 1,800 people.

The postwar housing boom fueled the company's growth. It acquired several smaller firms and expanded its manufacturing operation to Trenton, where it currently has more than 70 acres encompassing manufacturing, the Automated Distribution Center, Technical Operations, the Color Studio, and the Concept Studio.

The Concept Studio exemplifies

Huge printing production presses were used for manufacturing inlaid linoleum through the early 1950s.

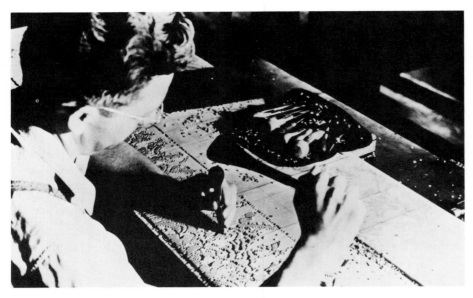

Highly trained craftsmen hand-carved the detailed designs in wood blocks for linoleum production.

Congoleum's commitment to the future. This group is expert in the fields of both technology and design. Its members devote themselves to experimenting with an unusual variety of materials generally uncommon to flooring. One result of their efforts is a patented product considered the Rolls-Royce of the floor covering business, Esteem Vinyl Flooring.

The brainchild of the Concept Studio, the Esteem product uses pearlescent vinyl chips that refract and reflect light. The effect is striking beauty and depth of color. It is one of several singular products made only by Congoleum, along with the firm's seamless inlaid vinyl flooring products and a line featuring a trio of flooring patterns designed to coordinate with each other.

The long-standing tradition of color and design expertise at Congoleum can be traced to the firm's production of Gold Seal Art Rugs in the early 1900s. The Gold Seal label, used for more than 65 years, signified beautiful flooring and guaranteed satisfaction. Symbolizing fashion, color, and styling designed to enhance the home, Gold Seal products, a Congoleum exclusive, became one of the best known brands in the

country. For its centennial celebration in 1986 Congoleum reintroduced the Gold Seal with its notation as America's First Name in Floors and created a new product line called Centennial.

The Kearny-based Styling and Design Department made a fine display of innovation and design leadership in the Centennial introduction. Using laser technology, Congoleum designers created the most outstanding rendition of Italian marble ever in resilient flooring.

The Marblesque design is an excellent example of the company's constant quest for creating unique

visuals. It is one of more than 300 colors and designs the firm offers, many of which are featured in its national advertising.

The first ad appeared in *The Saturday Evening Post* in 1911 and gave Congoleum the distinction of being the first in its industry to realize it pays to advertise. Gold Seal Art Rug ads were a staple in publications for decades afterwards, and when a brand-new medium—television—was in its infancy, Congoleum led the market to capitalize on its potential by sponsoring the "Dave Garroway Show" in 1950.

National advertising has been an integral part of the company's marketing effort for more than 75 years. Today, through a wide variety of home and decorating publications as well as television, the quality, fashion, and value of Congoleum products are known and recognized by more than 96 percent of the American public.

Stylish, innovative product has been and continues to be the driving

Congoleum Esteem, the Rolls-Royce of the flooring business, uses a patented manufacturing process of inlaid pearlescent vinyl chips that refract and reflect light. The Woodland design, featured here, is available in several colorations to meet consumer decorating needs.

force for Congoleum. It is a constantly evolving process. Modern sheet-vinyl flooring represents light years of development from the linoleum of the past. The latter, using linseed oil, flax, cork, wood flour, and pigments, took weeks to process and cure. In contrast, raw materials for Congoleum products today come out of the most sophisticated laboratories, and the manufacturing and design processes use a variety of high-tech innovations.

Yet there are parallels between then and now in the way the corporation functions. When Sir Michael started his business in Kearny, he used the services of W&J Sloane of New York to act as his sole selling agent. That firm successfully distributed the company's products for decades.

As the business grew, so did the

High fashion and high tech are successfully combined in this dramatic replica of fine Italian marble. Laser technology was used to help create this marblesque design. Two years in the making, this design is one of five featured in the Congoleum Gold Seal Centennial Collection, created in honor of the firm's 100th anniversary.

need for more quality distributors throughout the country. Congoleum now boasts a system of independent wholesale distributors that operate from nearly 125 locations throughout the United States and Canada. Its distribution family ensures that the products are delivered to a base of more than 18,000 specialty flooring outlets.

Rich in tradition, Congoleum, along with its employees, has had an impact on both New Jersey and the country. For more than 100 years it has been a major employer in New Jersey—building, growing, and contributing economically and with its leadership. Its expanded headquarters in Kearny still contains Sir Michael Nairn's original office complex.

Former president and chairman of the board Albert W. Hawkes was elected as a senator for New Jersey in 1942. Senator Hawkes also served on the New Jersey State Chamber of Commerce Executive Committee and became the president and director of the U.S. Chamber of Commerce. A former controller of the firm, Norman Ross Abrams, went on to become Assistant Postmaster General

Congoleum's headquarters has been located at 195 Belgrove Drive in Kearny since its founding in 1886. The main portion of the building was constructed in 1927 and incorporated Sir Michael Nairn's original office structure into the south wing.

of the United States during the Eisenhower Administration.

Nearly half of Congoleum's 1,500 employees are based at the firm's New Jersey locations, contributing to their local communities.

Congoleum products have beautified the kitchens, baths, foyers, and family rooms of millions of homes. Its technological innovations have helped change life-styles and become part of the American standard of living.

Continuing to earn its title as "America's First Name in Floors," Congoleum Corporation promises to maintain its leadership in product development, resilient flooring technology, color, and design for generations to come.

FAIRLEIGH DICKINSON UNIVERSITY

Fairleigh Dickinson University, serving 14,000 students, is New Jersey's largest independent university. It is a comprehensive, coeducational institution offering programs on the undergraduate, graduate, and professional levels.

Fairleigh Dickinson was founded in 1942 as a small junior college in Rutherford by Dr. Peter Sammartino and his wife, Sylvia "Sally," with an enrollment of just 153 students. In 1948 the college expanded into a four-year curriculum, and since then it has grown considerably. Today it operates five campuses, three of which are in northern New Jersey—in Madison, Teaneck/Hackensack, and Rutherford. The other two campuses are in St. Croix in the U.S. Virgin Islands and Wroxton, England.

The university offers 120 undergraduate and graduate degree programs in such areas as allied health sciences; business administration; education; engineering; hotel, restaurant, and tourism management; liberal arts; public adminstration; and sciences. Specialized curricula include a variety of M.B.A. programs, a Doctor of Dental Medicine, a Ph.D. in clinical psychology, master's degree programs in public administration and the computer sciences, programs in recreation and park administration, the Saturday College, and much more.

FDU achieved much of its major growth in the 1950s. In 1954 it expanded from its base in Rutherford to acquire a second campus in Teaneck. Formerly Bergen Junior College, it became the site of FDU's College of Dental Medicine and College of Science and Engineering. And in 1956, by action of the New Jersey State Board of Education, Fairleigh Dickinson College became Fairleigh Dickinson University. Two years later FDU established its Florham-Madison campus—its third New Jersey campus—on the former estate of Florence Vanderbilt Twombly.

It acquired its first Hackensack property in 1962, and the Teaneck

Fairleigh Dickinson University serves 14,000 students and is New Jersey's largest independent university. Here the Rutherford campus provides a rustic backdrop for students.

campus became the Teaneck-Hackensack campus. Two years later the university's Edward Williams College, a two-year institution, began classes on the Teaneck-Hackensack campus. In 1965 FDU's Wroxton College, in historic Wroxton Abbey, Oxfordshire, England, was opened for graduate and undergraduate study. Acquired from Oxford University, it became the first British-based campus owned by an American university. Dr. Sammartino retired in 1967 after 25 years of service and was designated chancellor-president emeritus. Dr. J. Osborne Fuller became FDU's second president.

FDU's School of Dentistry (now the College of Dental Medicine) moved to a new multimillion-dollar facility on the Teaneck-Hackensack campus in 1970. That same year the innovative and popular Saturday College of Edward Williams College opened, offering Friday and Saturday courses toward an associate degree. In 1972 FDU opened its second overseas campus, the West Indies Laboratory at St. Croix, for instruction and research in marine biology studies.

In 1974 Dr. Jerome M. Pollack became the third president of the university, and he served until 1983, when Walter T. Savage was appointed acting president. In September 1984 Dr. Robert H. Donaldson became the school's fourth president.

FDU's impact upon New Jersey has been widespread. About 65 percent of its 60,000 active alumni have remained in the area and work at top positions at such major New Jersey

Students on their way to and from classes at the Teaneck campus of FDU. University Hall is in the background. Photo by Junious Jones

companies as Allied-Signal, AT&T, CIBA-Geigy, Exxon, IBM, Johnson & Johnson, Merck & Co., Inc., Prudential, RCA, Schering-Plough, and Warner-Lambert. The current chairman of the board of trustees at FDU is alumnus Edward L. Hennessy, Jr., chairman of the board of Allied-Signal. The current president of FDU's Alumni Association is Harold "Cap" Hollenbeck, former U.S. congressman from Bergen County.

The Samuel J. Silberman College of Business Administration is the largest unit of the university, enrolling more than 45 percent of all FDU students. The college also has the second-largest graduate business program in the country. The College of Business Administration offers curricula at FDU's three main New Jersey campuses as well as at the Wayne Extension and the British campus. Undergraduates can choose from four majors (accounting, business management, economics and finance, and marketing) with three concentrations. The M.B.A. program—the university's oldest graduate study area, opened in 1954—includes 11 majors as well as an M.A. in economics.

Special weekend M.B.A. programs are offered for working professionals in various fields. They are designed for executives, bank managers, data-processing professionals, and other technical professionals. These programs allow students to continue their careers while enhancing their management skills. More than 80 percent of the college's graduate students take a limited number of credits each semester so that they can keep working full time.

The M.B.A. in Management (for executives), inaugurated in 1974, was among the first in the state. The two-year program provides in-depth graduate education in business administration for experienced managers. A unique aspect of the executive M.B.A. program is "the Wroxton Experience," a two-week seminar in international business at the British campus, where students are exposed to European management techniques

Students strolling and talking after class on the Rutherford campus of FDU.

through lectures from European business people and government officials, as well as through visits to local industries. The program has attracted executives from New Jersey's top corporations.

FDU offers an M.B.A. in Management for scientists, engineers, and technical managers who need the tools to run a technical organization successfully. It also has an M.B.A. in pharmaceutical/chemical studies, an M.B.A. in Aerospace Management given in conjunction with the Singer-Kearfott Corporation in Little Falls, and courses at Johnson & Johnson in New Brunswick.

Fairleigh Dickinson University's Continuing Education Department, on all three New Jersey campuses, offers certificate programs in various business areas, as well as seminars in such subjects as commerce, secretarial skills, and public administration. Music, dance, GMAT test preparation, LSAT preparation, speed read-

ing, and memory improvement are among the numerous continuing education courses.

With 120 areas of study in everything from an undergraduate degree in liberal arts to a Doctor of Dental Medicine, FDU attracts a diverse range of students, including many adults.

AUTOMATIC SWITCH COMPANY

Automatic Switch Company (ASCO) is set to celebrate its centennial year. ASCO has been headquartered in New Jersey since 1947, when it moved to Orange. Ten years later ASCO moved to its present home in Florham Park.

ASCO began in Baltimore in 1888, making elevator, compressor, and generator controls. In 1910 it became the first company to develop and manufacture an electrically operated control device called the solenoid valve. Today ASCO is the world leader in the solenoid valve field, making valves for thousands of applications.

In 1920 ASCO made another major breakthrough with the development of the first automatic transfer switch, used for the control of emergency electrical power during a utility power failure. This automatic switch can sense a power failure, and it transfers electricity from the failed power source to the emergency/standby power source. A remote-control switch specifically designed to control lighting was developed in 1930. ASCO is also the acknowledged leader in that field.

Shortly after ASCO's founding David H. Darrin joined the firm, and he soon purchased it outright. A pioneer in the field of electromagnetic

Automatic Switch Company began in Baltimore in 1888 making elevator, compressor, and generator controls. In 1910 it became the first company to develop and manufacture an electrically operated control device called the solenoid valve.

design, Darrin foresaw a big future in the field of automatic controls for all industries. The term "automation" had not yet even been coined, but Darrin knew that industrial automation would generate a tremendous

need for dependable controls.

By 1906 ASCO had moved to headquarters at 154 Grand Street in New York City. There Darrin met Wilbur F. Hurlburt, a man whose talents included those of engineer, administrator, and salesman.

When Darrin died in 1928, his wife succeeded him as ASCO's president. Following her late husband's wishes, she hired Hurlburt as a vice-president, and he later assumed the presidency. Hurlburt retired in 1951 when his son, Frank, was ready to assume the presidency.

In 1947 ASCO moved from New York City to its own new plant in Orange. Just four years later additional floors were added to meet increased demand. In 1957 ASCO moved into a new, one-story, 125,000-square-foot plant in Florham Park. That facility, which is the company's present headquarters, has since been expanded to 450,000 square feet.

Major emphasis on research and development had broadened ASCO's product lines during those years. Meanwhile, ASCO's products had become established in the United States, leading to the development of markets overseas. Today the ASCO name is a worldwide leader in many types of control equipment. The com-

pany attributes its success largely to the high quality of its products and to its research and development programs, which anticipate the changing needs of its customers.

In the mid-1970s ASCO introduced a unique line of pressure and temperature switches, designed for various industrial applications. Later ASCO added compact pressure and temperature switches, and yet smaller miniature pressure switches, for use by original equipment manufacturers.

Today ASCO sells its products across the United States and in more than 70 other countries. Applications of ASCO products are so widespread that no single customer accounts for more than 1.8 percent of ASCO sales. The firm sells many of its goods to original equipment makers and to practically every type of manufacturing and processing industry.

ASCO designs and manufactures an extensive line of control products for automation of machinery, equipment, and industrial processes, as well as for the control of emergency electric power. These ASCO products help enhance life-styles, improve public safety, aid in better health care, conserve energy, control natural resources, boost manufacturing productivity, and ease the boredom of factory labor.

Today ASCO produces more than 3,000 types of standard solenoid valves and more than 20,000 specially made varieties of those valves. Products added over the years include air-operated valves, manual reset valves, and microprocessor interface valves. These are used for the control of fluids in all types of industrial and commercial applications.

ASCO's electrical power-control products are used in the control of on-site engine generators for standby power, cogeneration, peak-load shaving, prime power, and energy management, and for lighting control and other electrical applications. Emergency power-control-system products provide continuity of power to computers, elevators, emergency lights,

lifesaving devices, and other vital equipment. These controls are used in hospitals, office buildings, manufacturing plants, communications centers, and the like.

ASCO has three subsidiaries in New Jersey. A&M Ludwig in Parsippany makes precision screw machine parts and assemblies. ASCO Electrical Products Co., also in Parsippany, manufactures electrical switchboards, distribution equipment, switchgear, enclosures, and related products. Angar Scientific Co. in Cedar Knolls makes microminiature so-

Today ASCO is the world leader in the solenoid valve field, making valves for thousands of applications. Shown here (on the right) is a modern microminiature solenoid valve, manufactured by a subsidiary company, Angar Scientific. An early solenoid valve stands on the left.

lenoid valves and controls for use in medical instrumentation, chromatography, and industrial automation.

ASCO and its New Jersey subsidiaries employ more than 2,000 people. About 20 percent of the Florham Park employees are graduate engineers, draftsmen, and laboratory personnel. Almost 40 percent of ASCO's staff has served the firm for more than 15 years, including many of the craftsmen who assemble and test ASCO's control line. Including its New Jersey operations, ASCO has more than 2,500 employees throughout the world. It is one of the 800 largest industrial companies in the United States.

Privately held until 1970, Automatic Switch Company went public in April of that year. It became a subsidiary of Emerson Electric Co. in 1985.

MAHONY-TROAST CONSTRUCTION COMPANY

Mahony-Troast Construction Company, founded in 1928 by Paul L. Troast and his brother-in-law, Arthur S. Mahony, who died in 1933, has become one of the most respected companies in the industry. During World War II the firm won major construction contracts with Wright Aeronautical and the Defense Plant Corporation as well as other projects for the U.S. Navy.

As his business continued to grow, Troast became an important figure in New Jersey's affairs. From 1949 to 1957 he served as the first chairman of the New Jersey Turnpike Authority, appointed by the governor. Under Troast's leadership the turnpike was authorized, the right-of-way was acquired, and the highway was designed and constructed in a remarkable 23 months. Troast directed that his own firm not bid on any turnpike construction.

In 1983 the company moved to the 600,000-square-foot office complex it built on Route 17 in Rutherford, near the Meadowlands Sports Complex. Today Mahony-Troast has 80 permanent employees and as many as 1,000 in the field, depending on its work load. It has been active in 17 states and has gained a

M-T has to date been the exclusive general contractor at Rockefeller Development's International Foreign Trade Zone in Mt. Olive Township, having built facilities for such notable companies as Seiko, BMW, Naarden, and Kenwood.

Paul Lyman Troast, founder.

reputation for excellence throughout its history.

During the 1950s the principals of Mahony-Troast formed Troast Enterprises, a partnership of family members that functioned as a real estate acquisition, development, and management affiliate. A wide range of facilities, from single buildings on individual sites to extensive industrial and office parks, has been developed by Troast Enterprises. These include Clifton Industrial Park and Allwood Business Center in Clifton, the Union Boulevard and Totowa Road industrial parks in Totowa, and Riverview Industrial Park in Wayne.

During the past eight years alone, more than two million square feet of

office space has been developed by Troast Enterprises. Prestigious locations include Meadows Office Complex, Rutherford; Franklin Square, Somerset; Jefferson Plaza, Hanover Township; 10 Woodbridge Center, Woodbridge; Hoes Lane, Piscataway; and Jockey Hollow, Harding Township. Most recently the firm completed Meadowlands Plaza in East Rutherford, a mixed-use complex combining a 400,000-square-foot office tower and a 450-room hotel and conference center.

Major tenants in Troast Enterprises projects include such well-known names as AT&T, Wang Laboratories, Metropolitan Life Insurance Company, Coca-Cola, and North American Philips Lighting Corporation. These developments include the finest investment-grade real estate projects, utilizing various innovative financing arrangements including joint ventures, participation mortgages, and equity placements.

Today the Troast organization has three basic operations. Mahony-Troast is a construction manager and general contractor active in competitive bids, construction management and contracting proposals, engineering, and design-and-build turnkey projects. Troast Enterprises remains the company's real estate investment division, while the Troast Group is active in site selection and acquisition, feasibility analysis, marketing, project financing, equity investments, and property management.

As construction manager, Mahony-Troast provides all professional services required. Some of the firm's long-term clients include RCA, Monsanto Chemical Company, Midlantic Bank, Xerox Corporation, United Parcel Service, Nabisco, Mobil Oil Corporation, and Sears, Roebuck and Co.

Mahony-Troast Construction Company is a pioneer in offering a design and build package, having maintained a Construction Design Department for more than 40 years. The department is staffed with architects, engineers, planners, and esti-

A wide range of facilities, from single buildings to extensive industrial and office parks, have been developed by Troast Enterprises. One of the larger developments is seen here— the Meadows Office Complex I and II. Each building is approximately 300,000 square feet with an adjacent 1,000-car parking garage.

mators attending to every detail of the project.

Among the award-winning buildings constructed by Mahony-Troast throughout New Jersey are the IBM branch office in Cranford, Ocean Spray Cranberries process and distribution facility in Bordentown, and the Hoffmann-La Roche pharmaceutical manufacturing plant in Nutley. Industrial projects range from 40,000-square-foot structures to installations such as the three-million-square-foot facility for Wright Aeronautical and the 300,00-square-foot facility for Sears in Maywood. The company has built warehouses for Georgia Pacific, Grosset & Dunlop, and others. It has also completed refinery installations for Chevron USA, Exxon, and Mobil.

Laboratories, computer rooms, quality-control areas, and other complex technical facilities are also a Mahony-Troast specialty. Clients have included large corporations such as American Cyanamid, Du Pont, Burroughs, Schering-Plough Corporation, and Allied-Signal, Incorporated.

Retail structures have been built for such companies as Bamberger's, JCPenney, and the Rouse Company. Mahony-Troast has also done institutional construction. Examples include the Jewish Community Center in Tenafly, the O'Toole Library at St. Peter's College in Jersey City, and a wing of Newark's Beth Israel Medical Center.

An innovation Mahony-Troast helped pioneer was the tilt-up construction technique that uses concrete panels poured on site. This results in lower cost and permits erection of

walls while waiting for structural steel and other long-lead items. Troast Enterprises has also utilized this technique extensively in its industrial distribution parks. Tilt-up panels can also be relocated years later, making expansion feasible. Mahony-Troast has used this method in more than 300 buildings. In addition to innovative construction, the firm uses many computer-based systems, including Critical Path Planning and Value Engineering designed to keep projects moving ahead, on time and on budget.

Today Mahony-Troast has facilities in Clifton and Rutherford, plus a Mount Laurel office that handles projects in the Washington, Delaware, and Pennsylvania areas, as well as the southern portion of New Jersey. Real estate operations are based in Rutherford.

To founder Paul Troast, excellence was a matter of family pride. His efforts to build a company dedicated to excellence have been continued, by second- and third-generation family members.

Most recently the firm completed Meadowlands Plaza in East Rutherford, a mixed-use complex combining a 400,000-square-foot office tower and a 450-room hotel and conference center.

SUBURBAN PROPANE GAS CO.

Suburban Propane's logo is seen crisply displayed on its trucks as they roll down highways and roads across New Jersey and other states. Today one of New Jersey's most important corporate citizens, Suburban Propane's beginnings are truly part of the state's business lore.

The story of the company starts at the West Orange home of Mark and Adele Anton in 1928. That year the couple had moved into their new suburban home from Newark and found that there were no gas lines in the area. Adele had learned to cook with gas and was not pleased with the idea of using electricity or kerosene, the only alternatives. Mark Anton ran a small manufacturing plant in Belleville that made luggage racks for automobiles. One day he spotted an ad in a trade journal for Rock Gas, a Pennsylvania company that sold liquefied petroleum cooking gas, known as propane. He ordered a set of equipment and a supply of gas, to Adele's delight.

In the early days of the automobile age propane was a gas that was considered useless, if not actually undesirable, because its presence in motor fuel caused gasoline to evaporate quickly. Propane, therefore, was routinely flared and wasted at the wells of the oil and gas companies.

Thinking that other suburban homemakers might share Adele's preference for cooking with gas, Mark Anton purchased additional equipment and brought propane to his neighbors in the developing suburbs. Soon his propane business overtook the luggage-rack operation. He became the first New Jersey distributor of propane through the Phillips Petroleum Company, which was building a plant in Haskell to serve the growing market.

Anton's enterprise grew and prospered, even during the bleak days of the Depression. By the end of World War II his small company had expanded to several distribution points in New Jersey and Pennsylvania. About that time people at Phillips let it be known they had not come East

Mark Anton, founder of Suburban Propane Gas Co.

to stay. He and his longtime friend, R. Gould Morehead, approached Eastman Dillon for financing. They were successful, and on December 27, 1945, Suburban Propane was launched as the first public company to devote its energies to the propane marketing business, acquiring the 13 Phillips properties in the East, as well as Mark Anton's original company.

Longtime area residents recall Suburban Propane's own "gas well"

Mark J. Anton, son of the founder and current chief executive officer.

on the roof of its Boonton office. The wooden tower, constructed to look like an old natural gas well, had a flame burning brightly on top at night, fueled by a propane tank at its base.

During the 1950s Suburban grew by expanding its markets and acquiring smaller marketers, while pioneering the use of propane for hundreds of applications. Propane gas became popular with chicken farmers in eastern Maryland and was also used as a replacement for charcoal in tobacco-curing operations in New England and the Carolinas. Although Suburban Propane's primary market was homes still out of the reach of natural gas mains, it began to service a growing number of commercial customers.

In 1951 Mark J. Anton, son of the founder and current chief executive officer, joined the firm. He became president in 1963 when his father retired to devote all his time to a host of civic and political activities. The elder Anton served as freeholder and state senator from Essex County and was involved in many civic and charitable activities.

Mark J. Anton brought Suburban Propane into the petroleum refining and marketing business, as well as oil and gas exploration and production. Some 12,000 acres were purchased in 1964 in the undeveloped natural gas field of Ozona in West Texas, and seven years later the company acquired Vangas, Inc., a large California-based propane marketer with an operation similar to Suburban's activities on the East Coast.

In 1975 Suburban added a refinery in Roosevelt, Utah, to its existing Bloomfield, New Mexico, refinery. Five years later Twin Arrow, Inc., of Rangely, Colorado, a drilling and well service firm, was added. The year 1981 saw Suburban move into the onshore deep-drilling business with the acquisition of Buzzini Drilling Company of San Antonio, Texas.

On February 17, 1983, Suburban Propane was acquired by National

Suburban Propane's first office in Belleville in the late 1920s.

Distillers and Chemical Corporation, a *Fortune* 200 company. Today National, the nation's largest polyethylene producer, through USI Chemicals Co., is also a leader in the oleochemicals business through Emery Chemicals. National had its origins in the distilled spirits business, with flagship brands such as Old Grand-Dad, Old Crow, and Old Taylor bourbons, and a host of other products. Almaden Wines completed the corporation's Spirits and Wines Division until its sale in early 1987.

Following its acquisition by National, Suburban Propane continued to expand, both internally and by acquisition. Pargas, another major propane marketer, was acquired in 1985, followed by Texgas in 1986. Signaling its leadership position as the nation's premier marketer of liquefied petroleum gas, Suburban Propane's contemporary logo went nationwide in 1986, unifying the

company's Vangas Division in the West and Pargas and Texgas operations under the Suburban banner.

Today the firm's propane marketing activities span 44 states from operations based in Whippany, New Jersey. Oil exploration and production activities, under the name SPG Exploration, operate out of San Antonio, Texas. Corporate headquarters is located at 334 Madison Avenue, Morristown, New Jersey.

The advantages of propane that led to the firm's founding—portability, versatility, and competitiveness with electricity—are just as significant today as they were years ago. Another constant factor is Suburban Propane Gas Co.'s concern for residential customers. Nationwide, approximately one million customers rely on Suburban to supply propane not only for cooking but also for such other needs as barbecuing, home heating, and hot water.

An innovative marketing tool even in 1930, Suburban Propane Gas Co.'s mobile advertisement and demonstration car provided potential customers with a chance to cook with gas using the gas range in the rear seat.

PEOPLE EXPRESS

Few companies will be remembered in history books as having had such a major impact on the country, not to mention New Jersey, as People Express. In only five years People Express grew to become one of the nation's largest airlines. Along the way it changed society's view of air travel. Moreover, it changed the economics of the country. People Express, after this rapid growth period, joined forces with another large airline company to become part of the largest transportation corporation in America.

Founded in 1980, People Express Airlines captured the country's attention with its fresh, innovative style and affordable prices, and remained the focus of attention as the fastest-growing airline in history.

As the airline that became a business legend by bringing competition to a once-regulated industry, the emergence of People Express forced the established carriers to remain in competition by reducing fares and cutting expenses. People with various backgrounds, from the traveling student to the business person, flocked to take advantage of the airline's rock bottom prices. Almost overnight People Express rose to international prominence.

The airline that started with only 250 employees and just three aircraft serving three cities had more than 3,500 employees and 79 aircraft, flying to 49 destinations in 25 states as well as London, Brussels, and Montreal in 1986. People Express became the largest single airport operation in the New York metropolitan area in 1983. The airline has carried nearly 41 million customers since it began operations in 1981.

The founder and chairman of People Express was Donald Calvin Burr. After graduating from Harvard Business School in 1965, Burr became an analyst for National Aviation Corp., a New York investment firm specializing in airline securities and venture capital. Six years later he became president of the company. At just 31 years of age Burr was becoming an

People Express Boeing 737 in flight. Low-cost, high-frequency travel for the masses finally became available in 1981, when People Express launched its first flights to Norfolk, Virginia, from its new home base at Newark International Airport.

expert in the economics of running a commercial airline.

Burr was hired away by Houston-based Texas International Airlines, a loss-ridden regional airline. Seeking to turn Texas International around, Burr introduced low-cost "peanuts fares" between selected cities.

The "peanuts" plan worked: Texas International's traffic and profits rose. In 1976 Burr became chief operating officer and in June 1979, president. Then, six months later, he resigned to make his dream of low costs, high frequency, and travel for the masses a reality. Burr was to create People Express Airlines.

Just a year before Congress had passed the Airline Deregulation Act of 1978, deregulating fares and routes and encouraging the formation of new airlines. By 1980 Burr and a team of former Texas International colleagues took offices in Houston to launch People Express. Burr sold many of his personal assets to start the company. Gerald Gitner and Melrose Dawsey, two former Texas International associates, invested smaller amounts. On April 7, 1980,

they incorporated People Express.

The fledgling firm obtained venture capital, found an airport, recruited personnel who would fit into their "one in 100" standards, and devised routes and schedules.

On October 24, 1980, the Civil Aeronautics Board granted People Express permission to operate. A few weeks later the airline received approximately $24 million from a Hambrecht & Quist public offering of People Express stock. It then purchased 17 top-quality, used Boeing 737s from Lufthansa for $4.1 million per aircraft, a cost well below the then-selling price of $16 million for a brand-new jet. Next People Express leased the abandoned North Terminal at Newark International Airport, moving its base of operation there from Houston in January 1981. The North Terminal's modest headquarters had only a few phones, desks, chairs, and portable heaters.

A cornerstone of the People Express philosophy was cross-utilization, in which employees regularly rotated jobs on a short-term basis. Pilots often handled aircraft scheduling, and customer service managers, who might spend several days in flight, could be scheduled for computer room duty.

The airline also was proud of its unique employee-relations policies. All employees were required to purchase 100 shares of company stock, at a discounted price, making each part owner of People Express. They were offered the option of financing their bought shares with minimal paycheck deductions. Employees also received profit-sharing payments that might equal 30 percent of their regular wages.

On April 30, 1981, the first of three 737s bearing the People Express logo accepted passengers bound for Norfolk, Virginia. People Express was on its way: It had opened as a regional airline flying from Newark to Columbus, Buffalo, and Norfolk.

To turn a profit on its low fares, the airline had to cut costs while not sacrificing efficiency. Coach-class seats were increased from 90 to 118 by removing the first-class and galley sections on the 737s. Innovative scheduling kept planes flying more often and more efficiently than the industry average.

And People Express itemized extra services so that customers would pay only for the services they wanted. Food and beverages were paid for in flight. Customers were offered the opportunity to save additional money by carrying on luggage that met size regulations, while checked baggage required a minimal charge.

On August 3, 1981, the Professional Air Traffic Controllers Organization went on strike, cutting People Express operations by 35 percent. With profits squeezed, People Express decided to fly planes out of Newark to Buffalo, Columbus, and Baltimore—all uncongested airports—where it picked up passengers and flew them on to Florida cities such as West Palm Beach and Sarasota. The move kept the airline flying during the strike.

One year later Morgan Stanley & Co. joined Hambrecht & Quist in a second public offering of People Express stock, and nine months later, in May 1983, the airline began flights to London.

By 1985 People Express was operating more than 400 flights daily to 49 cities, adding destinations such as

The founder and chairman of People Express Airlines, Donald Calvin Burr.

Dallas, Denver, Los Angeles, Miami, Atlanta, and New Orleans, as well as starting service to Montreal and Brussels. That same year, after forming a holding company, People Express Inc. acquired Denver-based Frontier Airlines. Shortly thereafter it agreed to buy Britt Airways, a commuter line serving 29 midwestern cities, and Provincetown-Boston Airline (PBA), a regional carrier serving Florida and cities in the Northeast. By mid-1986 People Express was flying to 133 airports and had passed the billion-dollar mark in revenues.

That same year the People Express success story peaked by flying one million passengers per month, making it the fifth-largest U.S. airline, behind United, American, Delta, and Eastern.

But later in the year People Express Inc. was heavily burdened with the failing operations of Frontier Airlines. The company was being dragged down to earth by Frontier losses averaging $10 million per month. The decision to sell all or part of People Express Inc. came hard and fast. When an offer from United Airlines for the purchase of Frontier failed, Frontier was forced into bankruptcy proceedings in August 1986, and was followed

shortly thereafter by the announcement that People Express Inc. would be sold.

An offer for the purchase of People Express, Frontier, Britt, and PBA from the Texas Air Corporation of Houston, owner of Continental Airlines, Eastern Airlines, and New York Air, was accepted before any additional operations were forced to cease. It was determined that the People Express operation would become part of the Continental Airlines systems.

With the acquisition by the Texas Air Corporation, People Express and its sister units have successfully become a part of the largest airline holding company in America.

And part of this growth is still apparent in Terminal C at Newark International Airport. Among People Express' most challenging efforts, the construction of Terminal C began in early 1985, and was to be the largest single airline facility in the world—five times the size of its original building. Upon its completion the state-of-the-art facility will service all Texas Air operations in and out of Newark.

Visitors to Terminal C will pass through its halls with wide-eyed wonder. They would do well to remember its history as the intended home of the airline that broke some rules—and rewrote them.

THE GREAT ATLANTIC & PACIFIC TEA COMPANY

Headquartered in Montvale, The Great Atlantic & Pacific Tea Company today is the nation's fourth-largest food retailer. With 81,000 employees and annual sales of nearly $9 billion, A&P operates 1,225 supermarkets in 25 states and in Canada under the trade names A&P, Super Fresh, Family Mart, Kohl's, Dominion, Food Emporium, and Waldbaums.

"New Jersey plays a major role in our overall corporate operations," says James Wood, A&P's chairman of the board. "It is the site of our corporate headquarters, and it was chosen for our recent prototype, the A&P 'Futurestore,' located in Allendale.

"New Jersey is a heavily traveled and densely populated state with tremendous ethnic diversity," Wood adds. "As such, the state offers many unique retailing opportunities for us. As supermarket operators, we must

What is known today as The Great Atlantic & Pacific Tea Company (A&P), was founded by George Gilman and George Huntington Hartford in 1859 as the Great American Tea Company. In 1869 the firm's name changed to The Great Atlantic & Pacific Tea Company to commemorate the linking of the nation's transcontinental railroad.

keep abreast of demographic and socioeconomic changes in our communities and adjust our product mix to reflect those changes."

A&P was founded in 1859 by two young entrepreneurs, George Gilman and George Huntington Hartford. Setting up shop at 31 Vesey Street in New York, the pair formed the Great American Tea Company. Gilman and Hartford's strategy was simple and innovative: buy teas at dockside and sell them directly to the customer, eliminating the middleman's commission, and pass those savings on to the customer.

During the first 10 years of their partnership, Gilman and Hartford established a solid reputation for their new operation. In 1869 they changed the corporate name to The Great Atlantic & Pacific Tea Company to commemorate the linking of the nation's transcontinental railroad.

Gilman and Hartford also began blending teas under their own private label. They introduced teas with such exotic names as "Oolong" and "Gunpowder," and added a blend of fresh bean coffee, "Eight O'Clock," named for the two most popular coffee-drinking times, 8 a.m. and 8 p.m. Eight O'Clock is still sold in supermarkets today.

By 1876 A&P had established more than 100 branch stores and was still growing. Gilman retired in 1878, handing the business over to partner Hartford. In addition to running a successful business, Hartford had also been mayor of Orange, New

Today A&P is the nation's fourth-largest food retailer with 1,225 supermarkets in 25 states and Canada. One of their latest ideas is the Futurestore Food Market.

Jersey, for 12 consecutive years.

Hartford soon brought his two sons into the business. John, known in company lore as "Mr. Outside," ran the operations end of the business. His brother George, known as "Mr. Inside," handled financial duties.

By the turn of the century, with nearly 200 stores and sales of $5.6 million, A&P began to diversify. A mail-order service was introduced, and colorful A&P horse-drawn tea wagons were enlisted to sell products over more than 5,000 established routes across America.

Through the 1920s the growing A&P introduced many retailing firsts. It became the first food chain to use refrigerated rail cars to transport produce, the first to bring fresh seafood to the Midwest, and the first to offer paid employee benefits. It also became the first food retailer to establish a standardized quality-control program for product testing, and the first to develop house-brand products and list product ingredients on the label. By 1925 A&P had 14,000 stores in its chain, including many "combination stores," selling both meat and groceries, then a rarity for a neighborhood food store.

In the 1930s supermarkets came on the scene, and by 1936 the Hartfords had converted their stores into 5,600 supermarkets while maintaining industry leadership. That same year A&P also entered the publishing field, introducing *Woman's Day* magazine for two cents a copy.

From the late 1930s through the late 1970s, A&P's industry leadership position steadily eroded. The deaths of the Hartfords, government legislation aimed at breaking up the giant corporation, and failure to take advantage of business and growth opportunities all contributed to the company's decline.

Finally, in 1979, with the company near bankruptcy, the Tengelman Group of West Germany acquired a controlling interest in A&P. With new management, A&P initiated a bold consolidation program to close its smaller, unprofitable stores and divest itself of all unprofitable manufacturing facilities. The program aimed at restructuring the company for future growth.

Returning to profitability in 1982, A&P initiated a growth-oriented program to upgrade its existing stores and acquire new ones. Those acquisitions have included Pantry Pride of Virginia, Kohl's Stores in Wisconsin, Shopwell Stores and Waldbaums in the metropolitan New York area, and Dominion Stores in Canada.

In 1982 A&P created its Super Fresh subsidiary, based in Florence, New Jersey. Formed from a cluster of 60 closed A&P stores in southern New Jersey and the Philadelphia area, Super Fresh is now one of the nation's fastest growing food chains.

Responding to changing consumer life-styles and needs, A&P recently introduced two new store prototypes—the Futurestore Food Market and the A&P Sav-A-Center.

With its black-and-white interior decor and special lighting treatments to highlight food, the Futurestore creates a distinctive shopping ambience. "Boutique" departments sell traditional, ethnic, and specialty foods. Customer conveniences, such as a "talking" electronic product locater and computer-assisted scanning checkouts, add to the store's uniqueness.

The A&P Sav-A-Center is a more promotion-oriented store. Vibrant food graphics promote both selection and value. Customers help themselves from bulk displays and dispensers or are assisted at an array of service areas including bakery, delicatessen, and fresh seafood departments.

In 1986 A&P announced the start of a three-year, $345-million capital spending program to open 106 new stores (many of which will be Futurestores and Sav-A-Centers) and

Another new store prototype is the A&P Sav-A-Center. With vibrant food graphics and bulk displays and dispensers, the A&P Sav-A-Center provides a glimpse of futuristic grocery shopping.

to upgrade its traditional stores. Since 1980 the firm has built, acquired, or reopened 337 stores and improved another 346. Today A&P is a revitalized company with its sights set on returning to its industry leadership position.

NEW JERSEY SPORTS AND EXPOSITION AUTHORITY

Giants, Jets, Generals, Nets, and Devils games create only some of the excitement at the playing areas of New Jersey's Meadowlands Sports Complex. In just over 10 years the Meadowlands has become a king-size sports and entertainment facility, thrusting the Garden State into national prominence.

In its young history the Meadowlands Sports Complex's Racetrack, Giants Stadium, and Meadowlands Arena have hosted more than 70 million visitors at more than 3,000 events.

During the 1960s the area known as the Meadowlands belied its pastoral name. Once a pristine tidal marsh, it had become a dumping ground for industrial wastes and had given way to warehouses, truck terminals, and garbage dumps. The slow destruction of the Meadowlands led to state and local efforts to rehabilitate the area.

In 1971 the state legislature created the New Jersey Sports and Exposition Authority to develop 750 acres of that swampland in East Rutherford, a community four miles west of the Lincoln Tunnel and eight miles south of the George Washington Bridge.

The authority's first chairman was Sonny Werblin, the prominent Thoroughbred horseman and former New York Jets owner who helped merge the American and National football leagues. Werblin's impressive resumé also included his tenure as chairman of the Madison Square Garden Corporation.

Granted a $5-million loan, the authority was required to sign a lease with an existing major league franchise before starting development. As events unfolded, the National Football League's New York Giants were willing to leave their home city, and the sports authority offered them a new home. The Giants' decision to relocate was the key factor in the launching of the sports complex.

Securing a major league franchise turned out to be the easy step: The authority faced 14 lawsuits from en-

Meadowlands Racetrack (left) and Giants Stadium under construction. Both facilities opened in 1976 and celebrated their 10th anniversary in the fall of 1986.

vironmental groups, the Borough of East Rutherford, and other factions. All the suits were won by the authority, including two that reached the United States Supreme Court.

The authority also faced financial hurdles. Twice underwriters withdrew sports authority bond offerings due to lack of support from banks and investors. The idea of building a football stadium supported by revenues generated by a harness and Thoroughbred racetrack met with a lukewarm response.

In 1974 the state guaranteed a planned offering of sports authority bonds, and the bonds were brought to market. Three years after its creation, the authority was finally ready to build a sports complex, and work began on the football stadium and racetrack.

On September 1, 1976, the Meadowlands Racetrack became the first facility to open at the complex, drawing an opening-night crowd of more than 42,000. One month later Giants Stadium opened, and its first football game attracted a sellout crowd of 76,000—the first of a still-

unbroken string of sellout games.

The New Jersey Sports and Exposition Authority is run by an 11-member board, appointed by the governor, whose members serve without compensation. Real estate executive Jon F. Hanson is chairman of the board, and Robert E. Mulcahy III serves as president and chief executive officer. Other current members include William F. Taggart, Peter L. Levine, Thomas C. Knowles, Robert R. Ferguson, Jr., S. Rogers Benjamin, State Treasurer Feather O'Connor, State Attorney General W. Cary Edwards, and Eleanore Nissley, representative of the Hackensack Meadow-

Giants Stadium fills to its 76,500-seat capacity when the NFL Giants and Jets play home games.

Meadowlands Racetrack is the home of night harness and Thoroughbred racing. Top trotters and pacers are featured January through August, and flats take over from September through December.

Meadowlands Racetrack is the number one harness track in America, with the highest attendance and handle in the country, plus major stakes races including the Meadowlands Pace and Hambletonian.

lands Development Commission.

In July 1981 the 20,000-seat Meadowlands Arena opened to a series of six sold-out concerts by New Jersey's own Bruce Springsteen. The new arena brought to the Meadowlands music, family shows, indoor sports, and a variety of expositions and trade shows. Heralded as one of the nation's top indoor sports and entertainment facilities, the arena has twice been named by *Performance* magazine as Arena of the Year.

With the arena established, the authority looked to obtain a professional hockey team for New Jersey. Years of planning came to fruition in May 1982, when the National Hockey League approved the New Jersey Devils franchise for the Meadowlands. In their first season the Devils drew a half-million spectators, exciting fans with their tough, spirited play.

The sports authority then landed a United States Football League franchise for Giants Stadium. The New Jersey Generals, with quarterback phenom Doug Flutie and star running back Herschel Walker, became one of the league's most successful teams.

In 1984 the New York Jets decided to cross the Hudson River to the Meadowlands, and Giants Stadium became the only football facility in the world to be the home of three professional football teams.

In the summer of that year the roar of Indy cars sounded throughout the Meadowlands as it hosted the first U.S. Grand Prix. Top drivers, including race-winner Mario Andretti, competed over the twisting road course on the internal roadways of the sports complex. Nearly 40,000 spectators turned out for the race despite pouring rain, and millions watched it live on national television.

In September 1985 the authority acquired Monmouth Park Racetrack, located in Oceanport, Monmouth County. Monmouth Park is on 500 lush acres near the Jersey shore and is one of the country's premier resort racetracks.

From January through August the Meadowlands Racetrack offers the world's finest harness racing in terms of the size of its purses and betting volume, the quality of its horses, and the extent of its fan attendance. In 1980 the track hosted horse racing's first million-dollar event, the Meadowlands Pace. The racetrack is the home of the Hambletonian, the "Kentucky Derby of harness racing."

From Labor Day through December the Meadowlands offers nighttime Thoroughbred racing, an innovation in the East that has expanded the appeal of a sport traditionally unavailable to most daytime workers. In 1985 alone the harness and Thoroughbred meets at the Meadowlands attracted nearly four million fans, who wagered over $600 million.

In addition to being the home

The multitiered grandstand at Meadowlands Racetrack is totally climate controlled, with expansive standee areas along the track surface.

Some of the best Thoroughbreds in the world compete in the fall in major Meadowlands stakes races, including the Ballentine's Scotch Classic, Meadowlands Cup, and Young America.

Olympic track and field meet; the Ringling Brothers Barnum & Bailey Circus; and concert stars such as Frank Sinatra, Barry Manilow, and U2.

The authority's approximately 3,600 employees make the Sports Complex one of the state's largest employers, with a payroll exceeding $40 million. Since 1976 the Meadowlands has provided well over $100 million in revenue for the state without requiring or spending one dollar of taxpayers' money. The approximately $450 million needed to construct the three facilities at the Meadowlands and the purchase of Monmouth Park were raised through the sale of bonds bought by New Jersey banks, financial institutions, and private investors.

Today the New Jersey Sports and Exposition Authority has statewide jurisdiction, which has enabled it to own Monmouth Park Racetrack. The authority also is planning an aquarium on the Delaware River, and a hotel-exposition center is authorized adjacent to the sports complex site.

The authority is now seeking to build a baseball stadium in New Jersey and land a major league franchise. It has guaranteed two million in attendance for each of the first five years that a major league team plays in the state.

of the Giants and Jets, Giants Stadium is the site of college football contests such as the preseason Kick-off Classic. That annual game, aired on national television, has featured Penn State against Nebraska, Miami and Auburn, Brigham Young and Boston College, and Ohio State vs. Alabama.

Giants Stadium has also seen some spectacular concerts. Stars who have filled the stadium to capacity include Willie Nelson, Diana Ross, Michael Jackson, and Bruce Springsteen.

Adding to the diversity provided by the National Hockey League's New Jersey Devils and the National Basketball Association's New Jersey Nets are professional wrestling, tennis, and boxing; NCAA college basketball and wrestling; the Vitalis/U.S.

The Meadowlands' Brendan Byrne Arena, with a seating capacity of 20,000, is the home of the NHL New Jersey Devils, NBA New Jersey Nets, family shows, concerts, expositions, college athletics, and more.

Yet another crowning event was celebrated on July 6, 1986, when the eyes of the world were on New Jersey and the Meadowlands as the closing ceremonies of the rededication of the Statue of Liberty were telecast throughout the globe from Meadowlands Arena and Giants Stadium.

In its brief history the Meadowlands Sports Complex has awakened a tremendous sense of pride in New Jersey, and surveys show that the overwhelming majority of New Jersey's citizens say its activities have raised the quality of life in the state.

BRENDAN BYRNE ARENA

NEW JERSEY BELL

Before New Jersey Bell was formed, the Delaware and Atlantic Telegraph and Telephone Company (incorporated in 1904) handled telephone service in southern New Jersey, and a subsidiary of the New York Telephone Company operated in northern New Jersey. Both were operating facilities of American Telephone and Telegraph Company (AT&T).

In September 1927 Delaware and Atlantic changed its name to New Jersey Bell Telephone Company and purchased the New Jersey properties of New York Telephone for $73.4 million. On November 1, 1927, Delaware and Atlantic was officially incorporated as New Jersey Bell.

In forming New Jersey Bell, AT&T in 1927 said, "The (telecommunications) business has now grown to such proportions in New Jersey that it merits a management devoted exclusively to its interests." AT&T added, "In the course of time, the effect of this [incorporation] will be advantageous to the service, especially as the business continues to grow."

New Jersey Bell remained an AT&T subsidiary until divestiture took place on January 1, 1984. At

These two special switchboards in the Terrance (Newark) machine switching office handled toll, long-distance, and special calls, and completed calls coming from nearby central offices to Terrance subscribers in 1923.

that time it became a wholly owned operating company of Bell Atlantic Corporation.

New Jersey Bell's first corporate headquarters was a temporary facility at 1060 Broad Street in Newark. In January 1929 the company moved to permanent headquarters at 540 Broad Street. This impressive Art Deco building still serves as New Jersey Bell's headquarters.

The bare copper wires that once were New Jersey Bell's single-channel pathways have evolved into coaxial cable, microwave and other radio links, and fiber-optic channels. Using new technology in both fiber and lasers, New Jersey Bell can send data at a rate of 1.7 billion bits per second. With today's fiber cable, the entire contents of the *Encyclopedia Britannica* can be transmitted in half a second!

In 1927 operators at New Jersey Bell's switching centers would turn a toggle switch or two to make connections. Today all-electronic, computerized switches perform this job instantly and also allow New Jersey Bell to provide new services.

One such service is called Central Office-based Local Area Network, or CO-LAN. With CO-LAN, a main

computer can be linked with satellite computers and hundreds of personal computers throughout various locations, allowing a swift and easy data-exchange link between them.

Another new service is Public Data Network, or PDN. Through packet switching, PDN can sandwich many data messages on a single pathway so that expensive data circuits need not be purchased by those who require only occasional data hookups. With lower expenses, the cost barrier to widespread home data services, such as Videotex, home banking, and electronic mail, may finally be broken.

Through its tradition of service and development of new innovations, New Jersey Bell reaches its 60th year in stride, continuing to serve the state's business and residential customers.

Directory assistance operator Cynthia Dudley quickly handles customers' information requests with New Jersey Bell's new audio response system.

In January 1929 New Jersey Bell moved to this impressive Art Deco headquarters building at 540 Broad Street, where it remains today.

FLEMINGTON CUT GLASS COMPANY, INC.

The late nineteenth century/early twentieth century was known as the Brilliant Period in America's cut crystal history, when American cut crystal was the best in the world, and the industry thrived.

During this Brilliant Period Alphonse G. Muller founded Flemington Cut Glass Company, which became a New Jersey operation on February 13, 1908, after founder A.G. Muller and partner Charles McMullen had moved to Flemington from Brooklyn. McMullen would later divest his interest in the business, leaving it under the control of the Muller family.

Today Flemington Cut Glass president George D. Muller is the proud upholder of his family's distinguished tradition in the glass-cutting business. Five generations of Mullers have been in glass cutting, and three generations have run the Flemington Cut Glass Company.

In 1870 George Muller's great-grandfather, the son of a glass cutter, emigrated from St. Louis, Alsace, to America, where he too worked in glass cutting. His son, company founder A.G. Muller, relocated from Brooklyn to Flemington to help start a cooperative named Empire Cut Glass Company. From there he went on to form Flemington Cut Glass.

Muller was attracted to Flemington also because blanks—the manufactured glass he cut—came primarily from nearby Pennsylvania. Another plus: The town was served by three rail lines.

After World War I most glass companies moved out of cut glass and into more profitable lines such as pressed glass and glass containers. Flemington Cut Glass stayed with its traditional industry, although by 1925 it had started retailing imported glassware and china.

A.G. Muller's son Ralph joined in 1928, and under his direction the firm became more retail oriented through World War II and the postwar years, leaving cut glass production as a small part of the business.

Today Flemington Cut Glass is a retailer of a vast array of glassware and has diversified into other tabletop-related items. Occupying six buildings in the heart of historic Flemington, the company carries more than 150,000 items of china, glass, and other gifts.

Flemington Cut Glass still retains glass cutters and sells its cut glass products, continuing the Muller tradition. It also makes custom cut glass items for corporations such as AT&T and Pan Am.

The Flemington Cut Glass Company was founded by Alphonse G. Muller, the son of a European glass cutter, at a time in American history when American cut crystal was the best in the world. In 1908 Muller and business partner Charles McMullen moved the company from Brooklyn to New Jersey, where it has remained a Muller family enterprise ever since.

Muller family members have always been active in the Flemington community, serving on the board of directors of the Flemington National Bank, the local chamber of commerce, and many other organizations. The family has also worked on Flemington's historic preservation projects, helping acquire buildings for restoration. Flemington is in fact a particularly scenic town, with a gracious, historic ambience.

President George Muller's mother, Claire Johnson, serves as company chairman; his sister, Barbara Hill, is secretary, and his brother Roy is treasurer. Muller's nephew, David Hill, has joined the business, representing the fourth generation to keep the art of glass cutting very much alive at Flemington Cut Glass Company.

PVC CONTAINER CORPORATION

PVC Container Corporation first made plastic bottles and containers in 1968 from polyvinyl chloride, or PVC, from which the company name derives.

In 1982 PVC began producing its own polyvinyl chloride compounds—the raw material for its bottles—thereby expanding its product line. Today PVC makes two products: bottles and bottle compounds. While using some of its compounds for its own bottle manufacturing, PVC markets most of the compounds through Novatec Plastics & Chemicals Co., Inc., its wholly owned subsidiary.

Founded in 1968, PVC is a $27-million company: $13 million of its business is in bottles, and the compound sector has jumped to $14 million from zero in 1982. Compounds now surpass the bottle business, according to John D'Avella, PVC's vice-president, sales and marketing.

PVC has grown to become an international business, active in Canada and exporting to other countries as well. The primary market for PVC's bottle business stretches from Chicago to the East Coast. The firm also makes PE (polyethylene) bottles. PVC operates two plants in Eatontown.

PVC Container Corporation started with 10 employees, and by the late 1970s it employed about 40 people. Since then, with the expansion into the compound business, the company's growth has been remarkable. Today, under the direction of president and chief executive officer Phillip Friedman, PVC has 250 employees and is the country's third-largest PVC bottle compound manufacturer.

PVC makes over 125 million plastic bottles and containers per year. Its compound-making facilities in mid-1986 had a production volume of 35 to 40 million pounds annually, with capability for 50 million pounds and long-range capacity targeted at 75 million pounds per year. PVC supplies its own bottle-manufacturing plant with a major portion of its PVC compound requirements; the

PVC Container Corporation makes two products, bottles and bottle compounds, and is the country's third-largest polyvinyl chloride bottle compound manufacturer. Shown here are some of the products of the firm's bottle compound division.

rest is sold to outside industries.

The company serves a wide range of packaging customers, from young, burgeoning businesses to established *Fortune* 500 companies. PVC bottles are used for the packaging of cosmetics, toiletries, pharmaceuticals, foods, household products, health aids, automotive and pet products, and many other packaged consumer goods.

PVC makes bottles to an exclusive design, and it also can assist customers in developing bottles specifically suited to their needs. With the focus for corporate growth on Novatec and its compound production, that subsidiary makes various PVC compounds for blow molding of bottles, film extrusion, profile extrusion, injection molding, and other applications.

PVC is unique compared to other bottle manufacturers because it is the only successful blow molder that has back-integrated into making its own PVC compounds. As both a bottle molder and a compound supplier, PVC Container Corporation therefore understands the needs of both the processor and the end user. This synergism has been an important factor in the company's rapid growth and success.

The bottle division of the PVC Container Corporation produces bottles that are used for the packaging of cosmetics, toiletries, pharmaceuticals, foods, household products, health aids, automotive and pet products, and many other packaged consumer goods.

AMERICAN WATER WORKS SYSTEM EASTERN REGION

American Water Works Company, Inc., is the largest investor-owned water utility in the nation.

The Delaware Company, with operating subsidiaries across the United States, recently chose Voorhees, New Jersey, as the location for its new corporate headquarters. The three-story, 42,500-square-foot structure will house the company's executive offices, its management and technical services subsidiaries, and an employee development center for company-sponsored training programs. Occupancy is planned for the fall of 1987.

The 27 operating subsidiaries of American Water Works provide water service to about five million people in 20 states. American Water Works is particularly strong in New Jersey. The firm's Eastern Region, with headquarters in Haddon Heights, includes five operating companies, three of them in New Jersey. New Jersey Water Company, Commonwealth Water Company, and Monmouth Consolidated Water Company serve more than a quarter-million customers in 102 communities. The other two regional subsidiaries—New York-American Water Company, Inc., and Connecticut-American Water Company—serve more than 37,000 customers in those two states.

New Jersey subsidiaries have played an important role in the state's economic and community development over the past 100 years by consistently responding to increasing customer demands for an adequate and quality water supply. The American Water Works Service Company provides the operating subsidiaries with a wide range of services, including financing, community relations, water quality control, engineering, legal counsel, human resources, risk and materials management, and rate designs.

New Jersey Water Company operates 12 water systems and two wastewater systems, many of which started nearly a century ago and were merged in 1970. The firm serves more than 129,000 water and 16,000 sewer customers. It includes five operating districts: Haddon, Shore, Lakewood, Washington, and Delaware Valley.

The Haddon District was the original New Jersey Water Company, formed in 1925 when the Stockton Water Company, which served parts of Camden City and Pennsauken Township, merged with the New Jersey Water Service Company. Some of the firm's service areas date back

The new corporate headquarters for American Water Works Company, Inc., in Voorhees. Occupancy is planned for the fall of 1987.

as far as 1886. Once a predominantly rural farming area, the service territory now is a fast-growing, sprawling suburban region near Philadelphia; it includes portions of Camden and 25 other communities in Camden and Burlington counties. The district draws water from 50 wells and provides service through 743 miles of pipeline.

The Shore District began in 1892, when Joseph Steelman and several Philadelphia partners began the Ocean City Water Company in what was then a small family resort in Cape May County. Today the district serves customers in nine municipalities in Atlantic and Cape May counties. Sanitary sewer service is provided in Ocean City, Cape May County. The district's service area is the fastest-growing American property in New Jersey, spurred by the impact of casino gambling in Atlantic City. The district draws its supply from 14 wells situated throughout the service territory.

Lakewood District's first water operation was formed in 1886 by a group of local businessmen supplying water to the popular resort community. The water supply, drawn from Lake Manetta, was used to serve the community and the area's nineteenth-century hotels and mansions. Having celebrated its 100th anniversary, the

district currently manages three separate systems in Ocean and Middlesex counties, supplying water service to Lakewood and seven other municipalities. Sanitary sewer service is also provided to Lakewood Township. The district's water supply is derived from 12 wells.

The origin of the Washington District operation can be traced back to 1881, when a group of local businessmen formed the Washington Water Company and drew its supplies from two large reservoirs on the Montana Mountain. Hunterdon County customers in Washington Boro, Washington Township, and Frenchtown now receive water supplies from the firm's four wells. Although the service area is largely rural, a great deal of residential and commercial growth is expected in the next decade.

In Western Burlington County, the Delaware Valley District began with the incorporation of the Riverton and Palmyra Water Company in 1888. Located along the Delaware River, large Victorian riverbank homes are reminiscent of the district's early beginnings. Still primarily residential, a number of commercial, light, and industrial commercial customers are located in the nine communities served by Delaware Valley. Water for the service territory is derived from 17 wells.

Commonwealth Water Company dates back to 1890, when a young engineer, Carroll Bassett, obtained the company's first franchise in Summit, and a single well and pump house provided water to 14 customers. Today Commonwealth serves customers in 24 municipalities in Essex, Morris, Somerset, Union, and Passaic counties. Water from the Passaic River and Canoe Brook are stored in three reservoirs, which comprise one-third of the firm's water supply. The remaining two-thirds is obtained from 23 wells and purchased water from the Passaic Valley Water Commission and Elizabethtown Water Company. Service is provided to more than 66,000 residential and commercial customers.

Through daily monitoring of water quality, American Water Works Company ensures its customers safe drinking water. The Canoe Brook laboratory at Commonwealth Water Company is one of three company-owned laboratories in the state of New Jersey.

Monmouth Consolidated Water Company was incorporated in 1926 following the merger of three small operations that initiated water service in the late 1800s. Located in historic Monmouth County, the firm served nine U.S. Presidents who vacationed along the New Jersey coastline. Keeping pace with the needs of the fast-growing county, Monmouth now provides service to more than 70,000

In 1986 Monmouth Consolidated Water Company, Monmouth County's largest water purveyor, began construction of a $3.5-million pipeline project to bring five million gallons of water per day from the Manasquan River to the firm's Glendola Reservoir.

customers in 23 communities and is the largest water purveyor in the county. Today more than 93 percent of the company's water supplies are derived from two reservoirs fed by the Shark River and Jumping Brook. Four wells supplement the surface supplies.

Water is an essential commodity; quality water service is equally essential. Over the years companies in the American Water Works System have provided that quality service. "Our service has spurred economic development, added to the quality of life, and provided a valuable public safety service through fire protection," says William R. Cobb, president of the operating companies in New Jersey, New York, and Connecticut. "We are proud of the contribution our companies have made to the communities we serve."

TOUCHE ROSS

Touche Ross New Jersey keeps young through innovation. Though its roots are deep in the state's history, the accounting firm is still characterized by fresh approaches and a refusal to be bound by tradition. This two-fold character is reflected in the firm's two New Jersey offices: its state headquarters in Newark's modern Gateway complex—a symbol of New Jersey's current dynamic growth—and its Trenton office, a landmark brownstone opposite the Statehouse, representing the best qualities of the past.

The story of Touche Ross and its predecessor firms reflects the extraordinary developments in the accounting field since it began as an organized profession in Scotland in the 1850s. These developments also mirror the course of economic history—the increased size of businesses, growth of government regulation, impact of science and technology, and increasing internationalization of business.

To begin at the beginning is to mention John Ballantine Niven (1871-1954), son of Alexander Thomas Niven, one of the founders of the world's first society of public accountants in Edinburgh in 1854. After training in Edinburgh, he sought the New World, and in New York on March 1, 1900, he entered into an accounting partnership with George A. Touche of London and Birmingham.

Although Touche Niven's first headquarters was at 30 Broad Street in Manhattan, Niven's involvement in New Jersey affairs is shown by his presidency of the New Jersey Society of Public Accountants in 1916 and of the New Jersey Board of Public Accountants from 1915 to 1921. He also exercised considerable influence over the formative years of the American Institute of Certified Public Accountants.

Touche Niven was one of the three firms that merged in 1947 to form a new entity—Touche, Niven, Bailey & Smart—that has evolved into the Touche Ross of today. Start-ing with a respectable list of clients and 10 offices in as many cities, Touche Ross has since risen to a commanding position in the profession, with 84 practice locations in this country. The firm serves internationally through Touche Ross International, an organization uniting 54 member firms in 90 countries.

The Touche Ross office in Trenton is a landmark brownstone that stands opposite the Statehouse.

The New Jersey practice has 33 partners and a professional staff of more than 300. Since 1964 six mergers have added to the capabilities of the New Jersey practice. The most significant of those was in 1969, with Puder & Puder, which made Touche Ross the largest accounting firm in New Jersey.

Touche Ross has always recognized the need for innovation, to provide management consulting and tax services beyond traditional accounting and auditing. "Business wants integrated services from one firm," as

one founder put it. The firm is structured into four major functions: auditing and accounting, tax consulting, management consulting, and actuarial/benefits consulting.

Touche Ross professionals may also specialize in a wide range of industries, including health care, real estate and construction, retailing, financial services, and government. They may work within a component known as the Enterprise Group, which provides across-the-board services to emerging, entrepreneurially oriented companies. Other special groups used by the practice offices are the Financial Services Center in Lower Manhattan, which draws on expertise from the financial capital of the country, and the Washington Service Center, which focuses on federal government decisions that may affect clients. Touche Ross New Jersey thus has the resources of a national firm while retaining the advantages inherent in a smaller operation.

Touche Ross New Jersey has developed special expertise in the areas

With a somewhat surreal reflection of Newark, a historic city currently being revitalized, in its windows, the Gateway complex serves as Touche Ross' modern New Jersey headquarters.

of strategic planning, feasibility studies, and mergers and acquisitions. Its feasibility study for the Meadowlands Sports Complex is just one example. As one partner described the project, "It's the most renowned entity of its type in the country. Our job was to determine in advance whether it would be economically feasible. We determined that it was." Touche Ross later helped put together financing for the project. Touche Ross' other public-sector engagements, as independent accountants and advisers, currently include The Port Authority of New York and New Jersey, by far the largest agency of its kind in the world, and the New Jersey Highway Authority. Touche Ross has served the New Jersey Highway Authority in this capacity

since the authority was formed in 1952.

New Jersey has been a leader in the field of health care, and today an important part of the Touche Ross practice involves strategic planning for health care providers such as hospitals, health maintenance organizations, and physicians' groups. The firm helps them respond to regulatory and competitive changes and adapt to increasing cost pressures by eliminating overlapping services, developing and maintaining state-of-the-art data processing systems, adopting contemporary corporate structures, and planning for future capacity.

Other Touche Ross New Jersey clients include The Prudential, the world's largest insurance and financial services corporation, and Supermarkets General Corporation (Pathmark), an accounting client ever since it consisted of three family-owned grocery stores.

For retail clients, Touche Ross helps select and develop computer systems, conducts market research, provides financial and investment training, handles strategic planning, advises on inventory control issues, and aids in site selection. Manufacturers make up a large portion of the firm's clientele. Real estate and construction have been important to the firm since the Garden State Parkway opened central New Jersey to development in the 1950s and 1960s; many of the developers were Touche Ross clients.

Touche Ross has both professional and personal involvement in the state. As one member of the firm put it, "We obtain our livelihood from our communities. We want to give something back." Firm members' leadership roles include president of the Essex and West Hudson United Way, chairman of the New Jersey Historical Society, member of the board of the New Jersey State Chamber of Commerce, council member of the Newark Museum, member of the board of trustees of NJIT, and many others.

THE GRAND UNION COMPANY

Founded in 1872 as a one-man, one-store operation in Scranton, Pennsylvania, The Grand Union Company of modern times bears little resemblance to that of its early days.

In the 1800s Cyrus Jones and his two brothers, Frank and Charles, sold coffee, tea, spices, baking powder, and flavoring extracts from their small store. As business grew they opened additional locations in eastern Pennsylvania, using The Grand Union Tea Company as their trade name. Later the Jones brothers branched out to Michigan and into New York, eventually establishing a headquarters for their thriving business in a warehouse in Brooklyn.

By its 40th year the company had grown to a network of more than 200 small stores throughout most of the nation, along with nearly 5,000 door-to-door salesmen. Most products were delivered in colorful, horse-drawn wagons bearing the distinctive Grand Union trademark.

The acquisition of several food chains, including the Progressive Grocery Stores, Union Pacific Tea Company, and Glenwood Stores, considerably increased the organization's size. In 1929 it became a public company listed on the New York Stock Exchange under the name The Grand Union Company.

Through the Depression and into World War II Grand Union continued to grow. Its byword was quality food offered by courteous people at competitive prices, a tradition upheld today.

In the 1950s Grand Union moved out of its crowded New York City headquarters and into a red brick-towered building in Elmwood Park, New Jersey, that became a local landmark. The company recently moved to new corporate headquarters in Wayne. Today Grand Union is a top New Jersey corporate citizen, its 45 New Jersey stores employing approximately 6,000 people in the state.

Growth subsided in the early 1950s as Grand Union consolidated its properties into a profitable nu-

Founded in 1872 in Scranton, Pennsylvania, Cyrus Jones and his two brothers, Frank and Charles, sold coffee, tea, spices, and flavoring extracts from their small store using The Grand Union Tea Company as their trade name.

cleus of stores and adapted its facilities to self-service, the new mode of customer shopping. But by the late 1950s and early 1960s Grand Union was once again poised for growth. Through a series of acquisitions and internal growth, the firm's operations

The gleaming, state-of-the-art Grand Union Food Market in Paramus, New Jersey, is one of the company's 368 stores along the Eastern Seaboard.

grew to more than 500 supermarkets and other facilities stretching along the Eastern Seaboard and into the U.S. Virgin Islands. Sales climbed past the billion-dollar mark in 1968.

In December 1973 Cavenham Limited, a subsidiary of Paris-based Generale Occidentale, a success story in its own right, acquired Grand Union. Cavenham's acquisition came at a time when Grand Union was struggling to cope with rapidly escalating inflation, soaring expenses, and a general downturn in the food industry. But soon Grand Union resumed its growth pattern. A number of older, obsolete supermarkets were closed, profitable stores were modernized, and new locations within ex-

isting operating areas were selected for development of ultramodern retail food operations.

In August 1978 Grand Union announced the acquisition of Colonial Stores, Inc., of Atlanta, a chain of 359 supermarkets in seven Southeastern states. Like Grand Union, Colonial was a regional chain with a tradition of good service and quality merchandise.

As Grand Union advanced in the early 1980s, it was a company that had rapidly expanded in terms of store numbers and geographic locations.

In 1979 Grand Union had begun experimenting with an entirely new concept in food retailing called the Food Market. Grand Union opened a prototype in Wyckoff, taking the core of a traditional food store and enhancing it with specialty food departments featuring gourmet foods and increased service levels.

Grand Union's experiment was so successful that in 1982 it announced plans to renovate the majority of its stores into Food Markets and Community Stores, a scaled-down version of a Food Market. In 1983 the firm announced plans to develop a third type of store, a Food Center in the 50,000-square-foot range. The first

The festive Cooks' Harvest allows customers to help themselves from old-fashioned barrels and bins of more than 300 items, including coffees, teas, dried fruits, grains, and a rainbow of nuts and candies.

Our Taste Place incorporates more than 250 domestic and imported cheeses. This department also features fresh pasta, homemade pizza, sauces, and even several varieties of quiche.

Food Center opened in Marietta, Georgia, in 1985, and others are under development.

Operating under the Grand Union and Big Star trade names, the company currently has 368 stores in 11 eastern states. It has retail outlets in numerous major markets, including Albany, New York City, Atlanta, and Raleigh.

Grand Union's stores are designed to offer the consumer convenient one-stop shopping for a wide range of groceries, meats, produce, dairy products, domestic and imported wines where allowed by law, health and beauty aids, and several merchandise items. The new Food Markets have bakeries, service delicatessens, fresh fish departments, cheese and pasta shops, natural and international food sections, specialized coffee and tea areas, and prime meat service areas.

The majority of Grand Union's more than 2,500 private-label goods are manufactured by others to rigid Grand Union specifications. The chain maintains its own quality-control laboratory and uses independent laboratories to assure maximum quality control for all products bearing any of its trade names. Grand Union's private-label items also provide food at prices below those of na-

tionally branded manufacturers. They are an important factor in today's economy, when shoppers are trying to tailor their purchasing to fight spiraling food inflation.

Grand Union has a strong commitment to its community, perhaps best exemplified by its fund-raising campaign to help restore the Statue of Liberty and Ellis Island. As one of the 20 official sponsors (and the exclusive supermarket official sponsor) for the Statue of Liberty-Ellis Island Foundation, Inc., The Grand Union Company raised $1.25 million for the project. The firm also provides funding and makes its store space available for a host of less-publicized community activities.

Big Star general manager Jim Vurnakes of the Durham, North Carolina, Food Market gives a young shopper a tasty treat from the scratch bakery.

HIP OF NEW JERSEY

HIP of New Jersey is a federally qualified health maintenance organization (HMO) affiliated with the Health Insurance Plan of Greater New York (HIP), which has been providing group practice medical care for more than 40 years.

HIP-NJ has a network of professional medical care facilities throughout the state. These multispecialty medical centers provide coordinated, quality care, offering one-stop service for virtually all of the members' medical needs. Each center includes physicians' offices, examination rooms, laboratories, X-ray and required specialty services, and are staffed by a medical group affiliated with HIP-NJ, providing full-time primary care physicians and specialists with medical/technical support personnel.

HIP-NJ's Paramus Center, for example, has an extensive medical team that includes specialists in adult medicine, obstetrics and gynecology, pediatrics, allergy, dermatology, gastroenterology, endocrinology, cardiology, orthopedics, nephrology, oncology, urology, neurology, radiology, and other areas. The staff also includes a mental health team consisting of a psychiatrist, psychiatric social worker, and counselor, as well as a nutritionist, registered nurses, and nurse practitioners. This $3.5-million, state-of-the-art medical center has the latest in diagnostic equip-

Medford Health Center, a member of HIP-NJ's statewide network of professional medical care facilities.

ment, a comprehensive laboratory, and minor-ambulatory-surgery facilities.

There are several key differences between HIP-NJ and traditional health insurance plans. Typically, the latter are generally limited to the payment of claims based on scheduled benefits, in most cases, only for medical services necessitated by illness or accident. They rarely cover physical examinations and other preventive services, and usually require deductibles and coinsurance payments.

HIP-NJ, on the other hand, not only pays for all covered services—both inpatient and outpatient—but provides the actual care. This program includes both treatment related to illness and important well-care services. Covered benefits are prepaid by a fixed premium. This prepaid system is designed to remove the financial barriers that might otherwise cause individuals to delay seeking early care and treatment. Its inherent predictability also facilitates budgeting for many members.

Each member selects a personal physician from the HIP-NJ staff—a specialist in internal medicine, obstetrics/gynecology, or pediatrics, depending on members' needs. Mem-

bers also have access to the organization's many other specialists. As noted, most members receive their care at one of HIP-NJ's convenient medical centers, but in some areas primary care is provided by participating physicians in their own offices. HIP-NJ's comprehensive program provides for access to emergency care 24 hours a day, seven days a week, and hospitalization is also fully covered.

The HIP organization—including the New Jersey, New York, and Florida operations—is one of the largest HMOs in the United States, currently serving the needs of approximately one million members. This membership is composed largely of groups of employees from employer organizations. HIP-NJ is always offered as a choice to the employer groups. Among these groups are employees of small and medium-size businesses; municipal, state, and federal government agencies; and many *Fortune* 500 companies. HIP's membership is continuing to grow at a rapid rate, and a program of further expansion is currently under way.

HIP of New Jersey also contracts with the Health Care Financing Administration to provide medical care to Medicare beneficiaries. HIP's membership is growing at a rapid rate, and further expansion will take place to allow the plan to continue serving the residents of New Jersey.

The HIP of New Jersey Paramus medical and executive offices at One Sears Drive.

STANDARD TOOL & MANUFACTURING CO.

Standard Tool & Manufacturing Co. was founded in 1910 by B.J. Keating as a small machine shop making metal parts. The first shop, powered by a five-horsepower engine, was a two-car garage in Kearny.

Today STM, headquartered in Lyndhurst, offers machine tool equipment and engineering for custom automatic production machinery. It has one of the most extensive general-purpose metalworking machinery production facilities on the Eastern Seaboard, covering more than 200,000 square feet.

In the 1920s STM started making mass production machinery for incandescent lamps, primarily for GE and Westinghouse. With the advent of radio tubes, STM used its experience to make vacuum tube equipment for the new company RCA, and other businesses soon became clients. STM also started making production machinery for glassware and allied products.

The firm established a contract engineering department in 1940 for the design and development of custom-built automatic production equipment. STM had long since left its garage and had vastly expanded its Kearny plant to nearly 45,000 square feet. During World War II the company won the Army Navy Award for Excellence in Production for its mass production machinery.

In 1947 STM designed its first proprietary item, the Index Unit, one of the basic drives for automated production equipment. Three years later it acquired a second plant in Lyndhurst, almost doubling floor space. The Lyndhurst facility has become STM's corporate headquarters, having been expanded to include increased production facilities as well as sales, engineering, and executive offices.

In 1958 STM fully diversified into proprietary equipment such as dial machines and transfer lines. The following year the company acquired the patent for the Multiple Secondary Operation machine, known by its trade name MSO. Purchasers of the

The Standard Tool & Manufacturing Co., circa 1935. Founded by B.J. Keating in 1910, the firm progressed rapidly from making metal parts to the mass production of machinery and general contract engineering.

MSO have included Honeywell, Bell & Howell, and many others.

During the 1960s STM introduced more proprietary products for metal cutting machinery in high-volume production industries, such as the automotive and appliance fields. The firm also began making complex vacuum equipment for TV tube production for RCA's color TV line.

Today STM offers a lengthy catalog of machine tool products and continues to do contract work, designing equipment to meet any customer's needs. Its business is about evenly divided between proprietary equipment and contract work.

STM continues to expand its pro-

prietary line into numerically controlled equipment and computer-programmed machine centers. In its present research and development phase STM is focusing on flexible transfer lines.

Still run by the founding family, which is now in its third generation of company leadership, Standard Tool & Manufacturing Co. has served some of the most prominent corporate clients in New Jersey and the world, including RCA, Westinghouse, Corning Glass, Nabisco, Ethicon, TRW, IBM, GE, Ingersoll-Rand, GM, Ford, Stanadyne, and Briggs & Stratton.

Today the Lyndhurst facility serves as STM's corporate headquarters. Still run by the founding family (in its third generation), Standard Tool & Manufacturing Co. offers a lengthy catalog of machine tool products and continues to do contract work.

UNION CARBIDE

Union Carbide is a worldwide corporation active in 36 countries, and New Jersey has played a major role in its growth and development. The root of what is today Union Carbide's largest business group—chemicals and plastics—began in New Jersey as early as 1910.

It was then that Dr. Leo Baekeland, a pioneer in the discovery of phenolic plastics, formed the Bakelite Company in Perth Amboy. Many industry experts equate the founding of Bakelite with the dawn of modern plastics. Bakelite became America's leading plastics manufacturing company, producing phenol-formaldehyde resins and related products. In 1931 Bakelite moved to its present location on River Road near Bound Brook, and in 1939 it was acquired by Union Carbide.

Today this Bound Brook facility is the largest of Union Carbide's New Jersey operations. Since becoming part of Union Carbide, the Bound Brook plant has grown from a small group of buildings on an 80-acre site with 270 employees to a 275-acre complex with 30 major buildings. Some 1,000 people work at Bound Brook in manufacturing, engineering, research and development, and administration. Bound Brook today is considered one of Union Carbide's major chemicals and plastics manu-

The original Bakelite Plant in Perth Amboy as it looked in the early 1930s. This was the home of the first plastic resin manufacturer in the United States.

facturing facilities worldwide, producing more than 10 million pounds of plastic resins, compounds, and chemicals monthly.

Activities at Bound Brook have spearheaded Union Carbide's surge into specialty chemicals, highly specialized thermosetting and thermoplastic resins, and other high-technology quality products. This evolution away from large-scale com-

A recent aerial photo of the Union Carbide Bound Brook manufacturing and research and development complex. Dr. Baekeland's company moved here in 1939 and the complex has continued to grow.

modity resins has helped create the "New Carbide," an evolving company moving into new product areas and stressing quality products, safety and environmental commitment, and increased customer services.

The Bound Brook plant produces hundreds of different products within several basic families of plastics. Marketed to industries as raw materials, these products comprise polyethylenes, phenolics, and phenoxies. They are used for polyethylene compounds to insulate wires and cables for electric and telecommunications networks; industrial cable compounds for schools, factories, and transit lines; phenoxy resins for videotape and industrial coating; phenolic resins for industrial paints, glues, varnishes, microchips, plastics, and molded products; and synthetic thickeners for the paint industry.

The Bound Brook facility's Technical Center, constructed in 1958, is one of Union Carbide's major research and development arms. Activity there focuses on developing new specialty chemicals and plastics, upgrading existing products, and improving production and fabrication processes. Work is done with a variety of commercial plastics, especially low-density and high-density polyethylenes, phenoxies, phenolics, and polysulfone.

Over the years research and development at Bound Brook has resulted in plastic and chemical products that have improved the quality of life and provided new jobs. Developments

have included new plastics (parylene and polysulfone), substitutes for wood and metal (rigid foams and glass fiber reinforced thermoplastics), and artificial-heart components. The Research Center has received numerous industry awards for its outstanding technical achievements.

Union Carbide's current strides in technology are making new history. Bound Brook research and development is the foremost technology center for polyethylene, coatings materials, and specialty polymers. On a continuing basis significant technology advances have been made in these areas for more than 25 years. Current work with new water-soluble polymers for personal care products, mining, and petroleum drilling, coupled with new products for purifying natural and refinery gases, along with new biocides, offer exciting possibilities for Union Carbide. In addition, catalysts as well as concepts for the new Unipol low-density polyethylene and polypropylene technology were developed at Bound Brook, making Union Carbide the world's technical leader in this area. New materials for coatings include solvents that are compatible with environmental concerns. High solids water-borne resins and new cross-

Process computer technology controls the phenoxy resin process, one of the most recent resin developments at the Union Carbide plant in Bound Brook. This resin is used for state-of-the-art electronics coatings and automotive corrosion resistancy coatings.

linking agents and radiation cross-linking resins for cured coatings are current contributions to Union Carbide's sales portfolio.

Bound Brook is by no means the only Union Carbide facility in New Jersey. Other operations include production and distribution facilities for oxygen and nitrogen gases in Keasby, and a coatings and materials plant in Somerset. One of the world's largest marine terminals, at Perth Amboy, supplies Union Carbide with raw products from plants on the Gulf Coast, Puerto Rico, and Europe. In addition, a new R&D facility and pilot plant for polyolefin specialty products was dedicated in Somerset in 1987. There are also several sales and management offices in other locations throughout the state.

Union Carbide recently streamlined its operations in order to become more customer responsive. Four major business groups have been created in the restructuring: Specialties and Services, Carbon Products, Chemicals and Plastics, and Industrial Gases. The four major business groups each have a president and worldwide responsibility for their product lines. This simplified structure has eliminated several layers of organization within the corporation.

Union Carbide has ongoing programs to safeguard New Jersey's environment. Water used at Bound Brook for processing and cooling, sanitary sewage, and normal rain runoff are discharged into the Middlesex County tank sewer for treatment and disposal. In compliance with New Jersey Department of Environmental Protection guidelines, the Bound Brook plant uses low-sulfur oil, noise suppressors, and air-pollution-control devices. Union Carbide has spent hundreds of thousands of dollars on these pollution-control measures to clean and protect the state's atmosphere and its rivers and streams.

Union Carbide and its employees play an active role in the New Jersey community, participating in civic, church, educational, and political ac-

Drs. I.J. Levine and F.J. Karol, the recipients of the 1982 Thomas A. Edison Patent Award, stand before a UNIPOL pilot plant at the Bound Brook research and development center.

tivities. The firm's New Jersey Public Affairs Committee (NJ-PAC), comprising New Jersey-based Carbide managers, evaluates legislation affecting its business, and it involves itself in community activities. Each year the PAC sends more than 10 New Jersey high school students to a weeklong seminar in Washington, D.C., where they join 125 other students sponsored by Union Carbide sites from around the nation, meeting with senators and representatives and learning firsthand how America's system of government works. The PAC also sponsors safety-awareness programs, particularly for school-age children, providing educational materials and school presentations to bring safety awareness home to thousands of youngsters.

CAESARS ATLANTIC CITY HOTEL/CASINO

Since it opened in 1979 Caesars Atlantic City Hotel/Casino has become one of the nation's premium resort entertainment centers. The luxury hotel has featured star performers such as Joan Rivers, George Burns, and the Pointer Sisters. Caesars also has hosted nationally televised comedy and variety shows and sporting events.

Caesars Atlantic City's image is rooted in the 25-year-old tradition of its sister resort in Las Vegas, Caesars Palace. In Atlantic City, Caesars was born when the company acquired the 425-room Howard Johnson's Regency Motor Hotel on the Boardwalk at Arkansas Avenue. In November 1978, exactly one year after the New Jersey voters approved casino gaming in Atlantic City, ground was broken on a $75-million project to convert the building—renamed the Boardwalk Regency—into a hotel/casino. Following a remarkably fast-paced effort by architects, engineers, construction crews, and Caesars executives, the hotel/casino was completed by May 24, 1979.

When the hotel/casino opened its doors for business in June 1979, visitors were awed by what they saw. The casino stretched out across 48,000 square feet of floor space and glimmered with reflective wallcoverings topped by a towering octagonal skylight. Patrons could play blackjack, roulette, baccarat, craps, big six wheels, and slot machines.

As the Atlantic City market dramatically expanded, so did Caesars. Ground was broken on September 23, 1983, for a three-phase multimillion-dollar expansion and renovation project. The project was completed in May 1985, at which time the facility was renamed Caesars Atlantic City. This included an additional 12,000 square feet of casino space, bringing the total casino space to 60,000 square feet. A new tower was added to the facility with 140 luxury suites, a full-service health club, the Circus Maximus 1,100-seat showroom, and three gourmet restaurants.

Today Caesars Atlantic City has

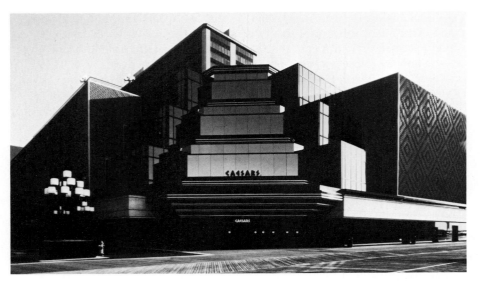

Caesars Atlantic City on the Boardwalk at Arkansas Avenue. In 1979, after casinos were legalized in Atlantic City in 1977, Caesars obtained and converted the 425-room Howard Johnson's Regency Motor Hotel into a $75-million hotel/casino.

645 guest rooms and suites as well as abundant recreational activities. On the wide expanse of beach, in front of the building, 15 cabanas face the ocean in a semicircle, linked by a mini-boardwalk. Caesars Atlantic City's third floor features an indoor swimming pool area, covered by a transparent dome. Adjacent to the health club, on the roof, are three tennis courts, an outdoor swimming pool, two paddle tennis courts, and a promenade overlooking the ocean. Children can play in a supervised recreational area—or they can enjoy the Electric Company, a spacious electronic game room on the second level.

Caesars Atlantic City has three lounges and nine restaurants. Just off the casino floor is the Arena Lounge, seating 125 and offering live, contemporary musical entertainment. The Rolling Chair Lounge, on the third level, is a popular gathering spot featuring two wide-screen televisions that broadcast sporting events. The new, romantic Forum Lounge overlooks the ocean at the gateway to Caesars' three newest restaurants and has live entertainment.

Caesars newest luxury restaurants

are LePosh, offering gourmet continental cuisine; Primavera, featuring specialties from Northern and Southern Italy; and Oriental Palace, offering Chinese food in a luxurious setting.

Six other restaurants round out Caesars array of fine dining. The Boardwalk Cafe, overlooking the ocean, is on the building's third level. On the same level is the Hyakumi, Caesars Teppan-Yaki-style Japanese restaurant. A stroll over a wooden footbridge and through a tree-lined Japanese garden leads to the Imperial Steak House, a luxury steak and seafood restaurant. The other three restaurants are Ambrosia, open

Caesars Circus Maximus at night. Since it opened in May 1985, it has become one of the nation's top resort entertainment centers, featuring such performers as Joan Rivers, George Burns, and the Pointer Sisters.

24 hours a day; Milt and Sonny's Deli; and On A Roll, a fast-service sandwich shop.

Caesars Atlantic City also houses fine men's, women's, and children's clothing shops; a jewelry shop; and Gucci.

In addition, Caesars Atlantic City can accommodate conventions, meetings, and banquets in the Emperors Ballroom, which can be divided into eight rooms, and the Marcus Aurelius Room, measuring 7,000 square feet and overlooking the ocean.

As at Caesars Palace in Las Vegas, Caesars Atlantic City has staged numerous entertainment extravaganzas that exceed normal concepts of resort entertainment. One of its biggest productions was Caesars Great Vibrations Week, which ran from July 4 to July 11, 1983. The week was highlighted by a Fourth of July concert by the Beach Boys. More than 250,000 people attended the concert, which was followed by the largest fireworks display in Atlantic City's history. Two years later Caesars hosted a performance starring opera singers Luciano Pavarotti and Dame Joan Sutherland, bringing the opera legends together for the first time. In September 1986 Caesars was the site of the World Welterweight Champi-

Caesars at night.

onship fight in which Britain's Lloyd Honeyghan defeated Texas' Donald Curry.

In addition to contributing to the arts, Caesars has played a major role in Atlantic City's community affairs. With its business, civic, and charitable activities, Caesars has revitalized Atlantic City. It has participated in many charitable and community events, and has donated major sums of money to such groups as the Atlantic City Medical Center, Atlantic County Association for Retarded

Citizens, Atlantic County Cancer Fund, and United Way.

In 1985 Caesars Atlantic City was the first casino to establish a program against drunk driving, called CADD—Caesars Against Drunk Driving. In addition, the hotel/casino assisted the New Jersey Governor's Office of Highway Safety in the S.O.B.E.R. Campaign (Stay Off the Bottle, Enjoy the Road), by providing recording stars Kool and the Gang to be the state's spokesmen.

Caesars Atlantic City is a subsidiary of Caesars World, Inc., headquartered in Los Angeles, a leading company in the gaming industry. Its luxurious Caesars Palace in Las Vegas, Nevada, is internationally famous. The company also operates hotel/casino specialized Poconos resorts and Caesars Tahoe in Stateline, Nevada.

Caesars World also is looking toward the future in Atlantic City. In 1977 the firm acquired a six-acre Boardwalk site, several blocks from Caesars Atlantic City, formerly occupied by the Traymore and Brighton hotels. Caesars has since expanded that site to 7.2 acres and plans to contruct a $300-million hotel/casino on the site.

The fast-paced casino holds 1,000 slot machines and about 100 table games, including baccarat, blackjack, along with roulette and big sixes.

CONSOLIDATED RAIL CORPORATION

In the early 1970s six of America's most important railroad companies—all serving the industrialized Northeast—were bankrupt and ready to cease operations. The region faced a loss of staggering economic proportions.

Those loss-ridden railroads were the Penn Central Transportation Company, Central Railroad of New Jersey, Lehigh Valley Railroad Company, Reading Company, Lehigh and Hudson River Railway, and Erie Lackawanna Railway. The six railroads carried half the rail freight in the Northeast, the most heavily industrialized area in the United States.

On April 1, 1976, thanks to earlier Congressional action, an economic crisis was averted when Conrail—a corporation combining most of the facilities of the six bankrupt systems—began operations. As a for-profit corporation, Conrail was directed to create a financially self-sufficient freight rail service system in the Northeast and Midwest.

Clearly that was not going to be an easy task. The new company needed a multibillion-dollar improvement of its physical plant and equipment, and that was accomplished, for the most part, from 1976 to 1980,

aided by substantial government funding. Concurrently, Conrail reported net losses of $1.5 billion for the 1976-1980 time frame.

From 1980 to 1984, however, Conrail completed an amazing turnaround, and in 1984 posted a record net income of $500 million. Progress continued the following year with a $442-million net income, which—on an apples-to-apples basis—was better than 1984, when Conrail employee wages were below industry scale wage levels for the first six months. Had Conrail paid industry scale wages for all of 1984, net income for that year would have been $435 million.

For the full year 1986, Conrail reported net income of $431 million ($15.34 per share), compared with 1985's full-year net income of $442 million ($16.02 per share). Conrail's traffic in 1986, as measured by tariff-based ton miles (the product of the

Conrail introduced double-stack container service to the East in 1984 by providing service for American President Lines to Conrail's intermodal terminal in Kearny. Since then double-stack service for Maersk Lines, K Line, and U.S. Lines has been added to Conrail's Croxton intermodal terminal in Jersey City.

weight of freight carried for hire and the distance in tariff miles between origin and destination) was 3.2 percent higher than 1985.

Conrail plays a vital role in New Jersey's economy, providing vital transportation services and serving as a major employer. Some 2,600 Conrail employees live in New Jersey, and the railroad operates about 1,100 route miles of track throughout the state.

Conrail has invested more than $160 million since 1976 to upgrade New Jersey's track system. For customers in the New York-New Jersey area, the company handled more than 700,000 rail cars and intermodal shipments of freight in 1986.

Intermodal service is an important feature of the firm's northern New Jersey freight activity. Conrail intermodal terminals serve Croxton (in Jersey City), Kearny, North Bergen, and Portside (adjacent to The Port Authority of New York-New Jersey's Port Newark-Port Elizabeth containership facility). High-speed intermodal trains carry highway trailers or ocean-shipping containers mounted on flatcars, which contain such freight as appliances and consumer electronic equipment, wines and liquors, and parcels.

Piggy Packer crane lifts a Conrail TrailVan trailer onto a railroad flatcar at Conrail's major piggyback terminal in Kearny.

In August 1983 Conrail opened a million-dollar transmodal terminal facility at Croxton Yard in Jersey City. The terminal includes Conrail's Flexi-Flo, bulk-commodity transfer system, using hydraulic pumps and vacuum suction to transfer bulk goods, such as plastic pellets, grain, powders, and liquids, between rail tank cars and trucks. A Lumber Transfer Distribution Center—which provides similar rail-truck services for wood and wood products—is located in Elizabeth, New Jersey.

The following year Conrail initiated double-stack container service in Kearny on behalf of American President Lines (APL). Shipments run between West Coast ports and Kearny: Trains move from the West Coast on the Union Pacific Railroad and are delivered to Conrail at Chicago by the Chicago and North Western. From there Conrail brings the train east to Kearny. Similar services were started at Croxton for Maersk Lines in June 1985 and for K Line and U.S. Lines, in 1986.

In early 1986 Conrail joined with other railroads in establishing special intermodal services between the New York-New Jersey area and major markets in the Southwest and South. One service, in cooperation with Union Pacific Railroad, cuts a full day off delivery time between the New York City area and Dallas. Another program, with CSX Transportation, offers truck-competitive rates between the New York-New Jersey market and Atlanta and Florida.

The Oak Island Yard in Newark is also a major Conrail facility. About 15 daily through-trains begin or end their runs at Oak Island, linking the northern New Jersey terminal area with Conrail's 13,000-route-mile system in the Northeast and Midwest.

Conrail operates an automobile terminal at Doremus Avenue near Port Newark, where imported autos and finished autos from midwestern assembly plants are transferred from multilevel rail cars to motor carriers for delivery to dealers. The firm operates a similar terminal at Little Ferry for inbound and outbound fin-

ished vehicles. Other Conrail freight car classification yards on the New Jersey side of New York Harbor and the Hudson River include Bayonne, Jersey City, North Bergen, South Amboy, Linden (serving a General Motors assembly plant), and Metuchen (serving a Ford Motor Company plant).

Conrail's Perishables Express high-priority refrigerated boxcar service from Chicago, via Selkirk, New York, offers fifth-morning delivery of West Coast produce to the East Coast, and these trains stop at New Jersey food distribution centers.

In southern New Jersey, Conrail's center of operations is Pavonia Yard in Camden, serving traffic bound for area industries. The company dispatches an average of 20 train crews daily from Pavonia and about 13,000 freight cars a month for service to the plastics and chemical, food-processing, and sand-aggregate industries. Trains from Pavonia also deliver coal to South Jersey utilities.

Under the Northeast Rail Service Act of 1981 the government solicited bids for the purchase of its 85-percent interest in Conrail. In February 1985 the U.S. Department of Transportation endorsed a takeover proposal by one of Conrail's principal competitors, Norfolk Southern Corporation (NS). However, strong opposition to the NS plan from Conrail management, labor, shippers, and many members of Congress led to NS's withdrawal of its purchase offer in August 1986. This cleared the way for enactment (in October 1986) of the Conrail Privatization Act authorizing a public offering of Conrail stock. After the Department of Transportation selected six co-lead underwriters for the offering in November 1986, Conrail filed a Registration Statement with the Securities and Exchange Commission in February 1987 (amended in March 1987 as to the initial offering price), which led to a public offering of Conrail common stock in late March 1987, culminating in Conrail's listing on the New York Stock Exchange.

PORT AUTHORITY OF NEW YORK AND NEW JERSEY

On April 30, 1921, the states of New Jersey and New York created the Port Authority to undertake port and regional improvements that private investment was unlikely to invest in or either state likely to undertake alone. That April date was also historically significant since it marked the creation of the first interstate agency empowered under the clause of the United States Constitution that permits compacts between states with congressional consent.

The creation of the agency brought to an end a quarrelsome nineteenth century between the two states, whose disputes over boundary lines through the harbor and Hudson River once led state police to exchange shots in the middle of the waterway. In addition, the coming of the railroads was a source of bitter litigation between the states as New Jersey interests saw an advantage in charging one set of freight rail rates to the New Jersey railheads and another higher set to the New York side.

Finally both sides agreed that the area around the port was, in effect, one community, and that the factionalism between states was detrimental to the port's economic potential. The states then sought a governmental forum to administer port affairs and found a role model in the Port of London, administered by what was then the only public authority in the world.

Initially given only start-up funds for administration, the Port Authority struggled through its first few years until 1930, when the states gave it control of the Holland Tunnel as a financial cornerstone. From that point on the Port Authority began to make landmark contributions to the region. Its bridges and tunnels were constructed in the late 1920s and into the 1930s. Three airports were leased from the cities of Newark and New York in 1948 and made ready for the jet age.

From its early years to the present day, the Port Authority of New York and New Jersey advanced the region's interests in unanticipated

World-famous symbols of liberty and commerce in the New York-New Jersey Harbor.

ways, finding itself involved in statewide mass transportation programs, encouraging foreign investment, building industrial parks and containerports, promoting the development of the region's 750-mile waterfront, and sharing in marketing and tourism projects.

While the airports, bridges, towers, and tunnels the Port Authority built—such as the double-decked George Washington Bridge and the World Trade Center—are among the world's engineering marvels, little known are its many inventions, innovations, and discoveries with worldwide and national application. They include developing the concept of container shipping and building the world's first containerport; designing the taxiway lighting and signing that have become the approved standard for airports throughout the world; building the exclusive bus lane, the first reversed highway lane to accommodate peak-hour bus traffic; developing the world's first teleport; pioneering the application of micro-

fiche technology to medical records; building the world's first over-water airplane runways; and isolating polyurethane foam as a source of explosive fires and starting a national campaign to make all plastic furniture fire-resistant.

Today through its facilities—the Kennedy, LaGuardia, Newark, and Teterboro airports; two heliports; the Holland and Lincoln tunnels; the George Washington Bridge and Bus Station; the Bayonne, Goethals, and Outerbridge crossings; the Bathgate, Elizabeth, and Yonkers industrial parks; the PATH rail transit system; the Port Newark-Elizabeth, Brooklyn, Red Hook, Howland Hook, and Columbia Street marine terminals; the New York City Passenger Ship Terminal; the Erie Basin Fishport; the World Trade Center and Teleport; and the Port Authority Bus Terminal, Journal Square Transportation Center, Newark Legal and Communications Center, and the New York Union Motor Truck Terminal—the Port Authority of New York and New Jersey is one of the region's most important economic generators.

LUM, HOENS, ABELES, CONANT & DANZIS

The law firm of Lum, Hoens, Abeles, Conant & Danzis, now in its 118th year, has a long and important tradition in the practice of law throughout New Jersey.

William B. Guild, Jr., of Newark, a leading trial lawyer who commenced practice in June 1854, formed a partnership, then known as Guild & Lum, with Frederick H. Lum in 1870. During his distinguished career, Guild served as Newark City Counsel, and was a member of the Newark Board of Health and the Newark Police Board. Frederick H. Lum of Chatham drafted New Jersey's first Borough Act in 1897 and later became the first mayor of the Borough of Chatham.

Another of the firm's early partners, Frank Sommer, who became a partner in 1893, was instrumental in creating the Board of Public Utility Commissioners, and in enacting the 1937 Revision of the New Jersey Statutory Law. He gained national prominence as the dean of the School of Law at New York University.

Charles Lum, Frederick's younger brother, joined the firm soon after its founding and practiced for many years, serving in numerous public service capacities. Ralph E. Lum, son of Frederick, became a partner at the turn of the century. Ralph served as president of the New Jersey State Bar Association from 1929 to 1930, and played a key role in the arrangements for the erection of the renowned Gutzon Borglum statues at the Essex County Courthouse and Military Park in Newark between 1908 and 1926. Ralph's younger brother, Ernest, also became a partner in the firm, beginning his practice in 1905. Richard Lum, nephew of founding partner Frederick Lum, and his son, William Boyce Lum, have carried the Lum tradition to the present.

Throughout its history the firm has prided itself on being a professional family, with experienced lawyers passing their acquired knowledge, judgment, and involvement on to the next generation. From its

Frederick H. Lum (above), of Chatham, and William B. Guild, Jr. (above right), of Newark, formed a partnership in 1870 under the name Guild & Lum. Today that partnership has become, through the generations, the law firm of Lum, Hoens, Abeles, Conant & Danzis.

ranks have come federal and state judges, state legislators, U.S. attorneys, a U.S. Assistant Attorney General, a counsel to the governor, a county prosecutor, mayors, and many others involved in municipal government.

Today the firm engages in the general practice of law with specialization in the area of corporate and commercial law; litigation; chancery practice; labor and employment law;

The new offices of Lum, Hoens, Abeles, Conant & Danzis at 103 Eisenhower Parkway in Roseland. The firm presently has 30 attorneys.

real estate, trusts, and estates; taxation; banking law; bankruptcy law; condemnation; fidelity and surety law; environmental law; malpractice and personal injury litigation; construction law; intellectual property matters; matrimonial law; and securities and antitrust law.

The firm takes an active part in the American, New Jersey State, and County bar associations. Various members of the firm serve as committee chairmen in the areas of fidelity and surety law, labor and employment law, litigation, intellectual properties, and probate law.

In October 1986 the firm relocated from Newark to its new offices at 103 Eisenhower Parkway in Roseland, where it presently has 30 attorneys. Lum, Hoens, Abeles, Conant & Danzis looks forward to carrying on its proud traditions to another generation.

NATIONAL STARCH AND CHEMICAL CORPORATION

Throughout its 92-year history National Starch and Chemical Corporation has used its scientific skills to become an industry leader. Starting as a small compounder of starch-based adhesives, National later developed synthetic adhesives and other products and expanded its activities around the globe.

Its story begins in 1895, when company founder Alexander Alexander purchased New York City-based National Gum Mica Company for $1,200. The firm produced glue sizings (used to prepare paper and textiles for printing), related materials such as gold gums and mica pulp, and paste for boxes.

National's destiny would be linked to its development of adhesives. The advent of package goods created a new industry, and National's adhesives business evolved with this new field. Specialized fast-drying adhesives, based on corn, potato, tapioca, and other starches, were developed. In 1920 National introduced adhesives for the paper-converting industry (boxes, envelopes, and related products) and the packaging business (labeling of bottles, cans, sealing cartons, and corrugated cases).

National's adhesives business grew quickly. Adhesives sales in 1920 were only $300,000, but within six years volume jumped to one million dollars. During the early 1930s National built a new starch refinery in Plainfield and bolstered research activities to create an expanded line of starch-based adhesives.

In 1928 National merged with two smaller adhesives companies—Glucol Manufacturing Company of Cleveland and Dextro Products Company of Buffalo. The corporate name became National Adhesives Corporation. A San Francisco plant was acquired in the merger, and National became one of the first adhesives companies on the West Coast.

With cornstarch as the basis of National's liquid adhesives, the firm sought its own cornstarch supply. In 1939, in a major strategic move, National purchased the Piel Brothers

Flexible web laminations in food packaging use waterborne adhesives technology pioneered by National to meet strict environmental regulations.

Starch Company in Indianapolis and obtained its own cornstarch plant. That same year National changed its name to National Starch Products Inc. to reflect its diversified product line.

National immediately instituted a major research effort that continues to this day. Employing both chemical and genetic modification techniques, the company became and remains

the leader in developing and marketing specialty starches for use by the food, pharmaceutical, paper, corrugated board, textile, and related industries.

With the onset of World War II the U.S. armed forces needed water- and temperature-resistant adhesives for vital shipments overseas. Going beyond starch-based adhesives, National developed polyvinyl acetate adhesives—synthetic-resin formulations that are moisture resistant and favorable to high-speed packaging. National's polyvinyl acetates served the military in varied climates around the globe, and National became the only company of its kind to win the Army/Navy "E" Award for production excellence.

Meanwhile, National was also developing other materials, such as water-based paints and coatings and bindings to give paper coatings cohesive strength. Research also led to the development of resins for hair-spray applications, as National used its skills to serve new needs.

With this expanded technology came enormous growth. Sales grew

National stands alone in the food industry in its ability to provide food prototypes with natural taste and texture. Food starches provide a creamy texture, lending a natural homemade appearance.

from $16 million in 1949 to $65 million by 1961. With the development of synthetic adhesives, chemistry had become a major part of the business, and so in 1959 the company changed its name to National Starch and Chemical Corporation.

By 1960 National had subsidiaries in Canada, England, and Mexico, with more expansion still to come. In 1967 it acquired LePage's Ltd. of Canada, a marketer of glues, furniture finishes, and home-maintenance aids, and two years later built a starch plant in Ontario. Overseas joint ventures were forged in England, France, and the Netherlands, and National acquired full ownership of International Adhesives & Resins Pty. Ltd., of Australia. Domestically, expanding from its plants in Plainfield, Chicago, and San Francisco, National, in 1963, began building several regional adhesives plants to improve distribution.

In the 1970s the firm became active in high-technology adhesives for

Hair and skin care products are formulated with specialty polymers from National. They provide wet combing, conditioning, and setting characteristics, and copolymers. They are used as bases for aerosol hairsprays in a strongly growing market for personal care products.

Coated publication mills use National's cationic starch products for increased strength and improved machine efficiency, while new lines of specialty coating binders give outstanding printability on gravure and offset grades.

the automotive, machinery, and appliance industries. In 1974 the company purchased California-based Ablestik Laboratories, maker of adhesives for the electronics industry. The next year National bought Permabond International Corporation, now a leader in cyanoacrylate and anaerobic adhesives—two high-technology adhesive types. Several food-seasonings and -flavoring companies also were acquired during the decade.

Today, with some 100 manufacturing and customer service centers around the world, National manufactures more than 2,000 products serving many industries. Its basic product categories are adhesives and sealants for packaging, publishing, disposables, furniture, construction, transportation equipment, appliances, and electronics; resins and chemicals for cosmetics and toiletries, paper, nonwovens, textiles, building products, industrial coatings, photography, water treatment, oil field services, and other specialties; industrial starches for paper, textiles, corrugating, building products, gummed products and adhesives, cosmetics and oil field services; and food products for baby foods, bakery goods and desserts, confections, sauces and dressings, beverages and soups, meat products, snack foods, frozen foods, pet foods,

and pharmaceuticals.

Bolstered by a 450-person research and development staff, National has been granted more than 1,000 worldwide patents, and many of its products are industry standards. Today more than half of the company's sales come from products developed within the past 10 years, an indication of the firm's research and development strength.

In 1973 National purchased the former Johns-Manville Research Center at Bridgewater, a 97-acre complex with 550,000 square feet of floor space, combining administrative, research, and marketing operations. National also maintains facilities in Plainfield and Bloomfield.

Today at National Starch and Chemical Corporation a close-knit atmosphere remains despite the years of enormous growth. Employees are all on a first-name basis, and some have worked there for 40 and even 65 years. Teamwork and cooperation are at the core of National's character, and that philosophy certainly seems to have proved successful.

RUTGERS, THE STATE UNIVERSITY OF NEW JERSEY

Through more than two centuries of growth and change, Rutgers, The State University of New Jersey, has been the educational nurturing ground for some of America's most distinguished achievers—people such as actor-singer Paul Robeson, economist Milton Friedman, writer Judith Viorst, U.S. Senator Clifford Case, businessman and sports entrepreneur David "Sonny" Werblin, and microbiologist Selman Waksman.

Today Rutgers has more than 48,000 students, 7,400 faculty and staff, and 25 colleges and schools on campuses in New Brunswick, Newark, and Camden. And within New Jersey's business community, Rutgers has achieved top stature for its high-technology research, joining with government and business in major new high-tech research initiatives that are benefiting the state's economy.

Rutgers is the eighth-oldest institution of higher education in the United States. It was chartered in 1766 as Queen's College in New Brunswick, a colonial college with a few students and a classical liberal arts curriculum. Colonel Henry

Rutgers, a former trustee and Revolutionary War colonel whose friends had included George Washington and the Marquis de Lafayette, was the inspiration for the college's name change in 1825.

Rutgers' first century was devoted to educating young men in the classics and liberal arts, but the college expanded its horizons in 1864 when the Rutgers Scientific School was established, offering courses in agriculture, chemistry, and engineering. That same year the state legislature designated Rutgers the land grant college of New Jersey.

But Rutgers has experienced its greatest growth in the years since World War I. In 1917 it established what is now the largest women's college in the country—Douglass College. During the 1920s and 1930s Rutgers added the School of Education (now the Graduate School of Education), the College of Pharmacy, and University College, the degree-granting adult evening school.

In 1946 Rutgers absorbed the former University of Newark, acquiring a new college of arts and sciences, a law school, a school of nursing, and a business school (now the Graduate School of Management). Today the Newark campus enrolls more than 9,600 students. In 1950 Rutgers acquired the College of

The Center for Advanced Food Technology at Rutgers conducts research aimed at improving the quality and shelf life of packaged food products, enhancing food value, developing new and better packaging systems, and perfecting the use of extrusion and emulsion technologies.

South Jersey at Camden, which was a two-year college with a law school. It became a four-year institution, the law school flourished, and a graduate school and evening college were added. The Camden campus now has 5,000 students. Rutgers had assumed university status in 1924, and in 1956 it officially became The State University of New Jersey.

Rutgers' partnership with the corporate and industrial community and the state government is fostering a new era of progress. A major development in that three-way collaboration came with the 1984 approval of New Jersey's $90-million Jobs, Science, and Technology Bond Issue.

A number of Rutgers' advanced-technology centers epitomize this new concept of business-government-university cooperation in high-technology research. The Rutgers Center for Ceramics Research is now being bolstered with a $10-million facility under construction in Piscataway, scheduled for completion by the spring of 1989. The 45,000-

A view of the Rutgers Queens Campus at the turn of the century. The buildings are (from left) Schank Observatory, the President's House (later Alumni House and now torn down), Kirkpatrick Chapel, Old Queens, Geological Hall, and Van Nest Hall.

square-foot building is financed primarily by nine million dollars from the 1984 bond issue. Operating support comes from Rutgers, the State Commission on Science and Technology, the National Science Foundation, and membership fees from 31 major industrial firms and government laboratories.

Among the center's current research projects is the perfection of a method for fabricating high-strength structural ceramics for use in spark plugs, machine tools, and automotive engines. Associated with the Center for Ceramics Research is Rutgers' Program in Fiber Optic Materials Research, which involves scientists from Rutgers, government, and private industry in advancing research in this revolutionary telecommunications field.

Under development is the New Jersey Center for Advanced Biotechnology and Medicine, operated jointly by Rutgers and the University of Medicine and Dentistry of New Jersey. This facility will be a world-class scientific research and development center. With scientists and technicians from academic institutions and private industry, the center will accelerate basic research and clinical applications of advanced biotechnology, fostering even closer links with such industries as pharmaceuti-

A student lab technician program at Rutgers' College of Engineering provides ceramic engineering majors an early start on their high-tech careers. Shown here are Jocelyn Kowalski, a 1986 Rutgers graduate, and Otto Wilson, a current student, monitoring an experiment at the control panel of a vacuum hot press, used for compressing ceramic composites under very high temperatures.

cals and health care.

Operations are also under way at the new Center for Advanced Food Technology on Rutgers' Cook College campus in New Brunswick, a cooperative venture between the university and the food industry to coordinate food science research with the needs of industry. The center will be housed in an addition planned for the existing Food Science Building at the Cook College campus, with occupancy slated for early 1989.

Another example of this university-industry-government partnership is

Rutgers' Center for Computer Aids for Industrial Productivity, created to support research in computer science and engineering and to advance industrial applications for computer technology. Research will focus on artificial intelligence, computer image processing, applied mathematics, and robotics. Partially funded through the New Jersey Commission on Science and Technology, the center is also supported by member corporations. The facility is presently housed at Rutgers' Hill Center in Piscataway, but a new building is planned on adjacent land. Rutgers is also a founding partner in the new Consortium for Scientific Computing, which provides access to a "supercomputer," equipment comprising the cutting edge of computer technology. The 13-member consortium is headquartered in the $118-million John von Neumann Center near Princeton.

There are several other new initiatives on the various Rutgers campuses in the area of plastics recycling, fisheries and aquaculture, molecular and behavioral neuroscience, and physics. New Jersey's high-technology industries benefit from higher education, and they are being helped greatly by Rutgers' research facilities and the future employees who emanate from Rutgers' halls of learning.

Students at Rutgers have erected a two-story drawing tower (at right) to produce optical fibers for use in a broad range of fields—including medicine, telecommunications, and environmental research. The students' feat represents a milestone in Rutgers' Program in Fiber Optic Materials Research, the first of its kind at a U.S. college or university.

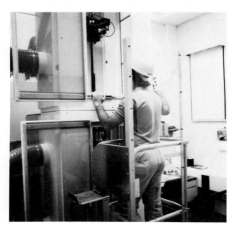

KRAFT & HUGHES

Viewing the three floors of Kraft & Hughes' expansive offices in Newark's One Gateway Center, it is hard to believe that the law firm is only 15 years old. But such is the character of Kraft & Hughes: a youthful, dynamic firm with energetic partners and associates. And in its short history Kraft & Hughes has established itself as one of New Jersey's leading law firms.

As the first bond counsel firm established in the state, Kraft & Hughes has filled a major gap in New Jersey's legal services industry. For 1985 it ranked 11th in the nation among firms doing bond counsel work, with $3.4 billion in bonds approved during that year. Kraft & Hughes served as bond counsel for the largest single bond issue in the entire nation, a $2-billion project for the New Jersey Turnpike Authority, but the firm also handles bond issues as low as $100,000 for smaller muni-

cipalities, school districts, and communities.

The driving force behind Kraft & Hughes' history is John L. Kraft. A 1964 Yale Law School graduate and a lifelong New Jersey resident, Kraft sought to involve himself in the legal affairs of his home state from the start of his legal career. Trained in the highly technical field of public finance law, Kraft served as associate counsel to the governor of New Jersey in 1970-1971.

Seeing an opportunity to establish the first New Jersey-based bond counsel firm, Kraft left his position in the governor's office in 1971 to join with Mark F. Hughes, Jr., a former Assistant U.S. Attorney in the Southern District of New York and a partner in a Newark firm, to form Kraft & Hughes. Hughes' ex-

Mark F. Hughes, Jr., and John L. Kraft, founding partners.

pertise was in the area of complex litigation, the other main area of the firm's original practice. The partners opened offices with just one secretary, who is still with the firm. Today Kraft & Hughes includes 45 attorneys and a staff in excess of 75. In addition to its main headquarters in Newark, New Jersey's largest city, the firm has added offices in midtown Manhattan and Rochester, New York.

Over the past 15 years the firm has developed high levels of expertise in other sophisticated areas of the law. When casino gambling came to Atlantic City, Kraft & Hughes was called upon to represent the lending banks in the first long-term loan transaction for a casino. Since then the firm has been involved in many major loan transactions to Atlantic City casinos. Kraft & Hughes routinely represents the major New Jersey and New York lending insti-

tutions in their transactions throughout the state. The need to service the firm's clients in multistate transactions recently prompted the firm to open offices at 245 Park Avenue in New York City.

Corporate securities work, once the province of out-of-state firms, also is an important facet of Kraft & Hughes. Whether it's winning a proxy fight, bringing a company public, finding venture capital for a new idea, or setting up mergers and acquisitions, Kraft & Hughes provides the legal strategies for its clients.

Taxation—both business and personal—also is an important part of the firm's practice. Kraft & Hughes attracted to its ranks the former head of New Jersey's Division of Taxation, Sidney I. Glaser, who is a national expert in all phases of state and local taxation. The firm's trust and estate practice is headed up by one of the state's leading experts in this sensitive and most personal field. General business and personal counseling rounds out the firm's practice.

Kraft & Hughes attributes its success to its dedication to a high

Four of the firm's senior partners (standing, left to right) are E. Kenneth Williams, Jr.; John L. Kraft; Edward J. McManimon III; and Jerome M. St. John.

standard of legal services, and to its commitment to the community and clients it serves. The firm is general counsel to the Greater Newark Chamber of Commerce and to Renaissance Newark, a volunteer group dedicated to improving the Newark business district. Members of the firm lecture at Rutgers, The State University of New Jersey, and Seton Hall Law School, and are frequent commentators on issues affecting municipal bonds. Kraft is a member of the Banking Advisory Board of the State of New Jersey. Partner Robert C. Neff is a member of the New Jersey Racing Commission, and other partners and associates devote substantial time and effort to a variety of civic and community efforts.

While many major law firms have left Newark over the past 10 years, Kraft & Hughes has stood firmly by its belief in Newark as a top business location. The firm has served as bond

counsel to the City of Newark, and represents many of the banks and companies that keep Newark the business capital of New Jersey.

All of this hard work by the attorneys and staff at Kraft & Hughes has not created a "sweat shop" atmosphere at the firm. On the contrary, in 1985 Kraft & Hughes was selected by the *Business Journal of New Jersey* as one of the 10 best places to work in New Jersey, sharing the honor with such corporate leaders as Johnson & Johnson. The camaraderie and spirit of the firm comes through loud and clear whether at a firm softball game or in meeting important deadlines in the service of its clients.

Kraft & Hughes has brought a valuable asset to the New Jersey legal community with its nationally recognized expertise as municipal bond counsel. More noteworthy, while most of the major New Jersey law firms have long histories behind their excellent reputations, Kraft & Hughes is unique in having become one of the state's top law firms at such a young age.

OHAUS SCALE CORPORATION

In 1907 young Gustav Ohaus and his father, Karl Louis Ohaus, a German-born scale mechanic, opened a scale repair shop in Newark. Shortly thereafter they began manufacturing their own scales and weights for science and industry. The company's first laboratory product was the now-famous Harvard Trip Scale. With its introduction, and others like it, Ohaus balances and scales quickly became known for their high level of precision.

Today Ohaus Scale Corporation of Florham Park is a worldwide operation with a solid reputation in its industry. Its mechanical and electronic balances and scales are a universal standard in schools, colleges, laboratories, factories, and commercial enterprises.

Ohaus outgrew its first facility in 1914 and moved to a new plant on Hobson Street in Newark. There it was incorporated as the Newark Scale Works. That same year the company received its first patent and introduced its first grain-testing scale line.

Over the next two decades Ohaus grew tremendously, both in size and reputation. Improving its product lines, the firm obtained a self-aligning bearing patent in 1928, followed by the introduction of die-casting and compression-molded plastic technology to the manufacturing process.

The firm was incorporated as Ohaus Scale Corporation in 1947, and three years later it moved again to a new plant in Union. A third Ohaus generation became active in the company in 1946 as today's chairman, Robert E. Ohaus, joined in an engineering and manufacturing role. President William G. Ohaus, his brother, came on board in 1950 in a sales, marketing, and administrative capacity.

By the mid-1960s the Union plant had quadrupled in size, and in 1968, the year Gustav Ohaus died, land was acquired for a new plant in Florham Park. The following year the firm moved its manufacturing facility

An early Ohaus mechanical scale. During the early 1900s these were used mainly in science and industry.

and corporate headquarters to its present location.

Ohaus at Florham Park—now more than twice as large as it was in 1969—comprises over 3.25 acres devoted to research and development, engineering, design, testing, and manufacturing of Ohaus precision scales and balances. The company also has facilities in England, West Germany, and Mexico, and its products are sold in 80 countries throughout the world.

The fourth Ohaus generation is now in the firm's management: Robert Ohaus' son, Jim, is executive vice-president of operations, and William Ohaus' son, Dick, is vice-president of planning and development.

Today more laboratory balances around the world carry the Ohaus name than any other. That's because people who use the scales and balances in laboratories, industry, and education have found the Ohaus brand superior in quality, value, and service.

The business philosophy that made such a reputation possible—an unswerving commitment to serving

the needs of the customer first—is sustained strongly by current Ohaus leaders. The very same pride and attention that went into Ohaus products 80 years ago goes into every balance offered today. Whether it is electronic or mechanical, an Ohaus Scale Corporation balance is well-conceived, properly designed, and then manufactured and tested under the strictest quality controls.

The Galaxy 4000D precision electronic balance—today's Ohaus product. Modern Ohaus scales, both mechanical and electronic, are used in schools, colleges, and commercial enterprises.

NEW JERSEY HOSPITAL ASSOCIATION

In 1918 a group of seven New Jersey hospital executives saw the need for an organization to promote the concerns of the health care industry and find solutions to common management problems. Meeting at Newark City Hospital, they established the New Jersey Hospital Association (NJHA).

Today, representing a $4-billion-per-year industry that employs more than 94,000, NJHA's 126 members are drawn to a trade group that provides leadership necessary to assist them in shaping policy and improving the organization and delivery of quality health care for all New Jerseyans.

The hospitals represented at the association's founding were Muhlenberg Hospital in Plainfield, Elizabeth General Hospital, Hudson Tuberculosis Hospital and Sanitarium in Secaucus, Morristown Hospital, Paterson General Hospital, Christ Hospital in Jersey City, and Newark City Hospital. Nearly seven decades later, acute-care, psychiatric, long-term care, and rehabilitative institutions make up the ranks of the association.

In its early years the association held periodic meetings to discuss hospital management and share information. By the mid-1920s the NJHA

had begun to grow and hosted two American Hospital Association annual conventions in Atlantic City.

During the Depression years NJHA led a movement to increase access to hospital care for the middle class and the poor, and through the 1940s the group was at the forefront of improving health care administration techniques.

In 1945, following an extensive study, the NJHA Welfare Committee recommended that legal responsibilities for providing good hospital care be defined more clearly, that public authorities recognize that the indigent were entitled to a high standard of care, and that payment to hospitals be commensurate with services rendered so that a hospital's financial status would not be jeopardized.

In 1948 NJHA research and input helped lead to congressional passage of the Hill-Burton Act, which gave aid to hospital construction and provided low-interest loans in exchange for pledges to absorb a percentage of charity cases. Many of the state's

The Center for Health Affairs headquarters in Princeton, home of the New Jersey Hospital Association.

hospitals benefited from this program during the 1950s and 1960s.

Most recently, the association has helped members comply with a variety of cost-containment initiatives that have provided a health care bargain for state residents. In 1984 New Jersey patients paid $338 less per hospital visit than the average acute-care patient paid nationwide. Concurrently, New Jersey ranked 48th out of 50 states and the District of Columbia in rate of increase of hospital expenses.

NJHA's president, longtime health care executive Louis P. Scibetta, leads a full-time staff of 33. Association operations are directed by its 25-member board of trustees. In turn, the board relies on seven councils to aid in identifying issues and guiding action. Today the association's mission remains that of being an advocate of New Jersey hospitals, their health care systems, and the services they provide.

With the help of affiliated corporations based at its Center for Health Affairs headquarters in Princeton, the New Jersey Hospital Association offers a variety of services—from legislative to administrative, health promotion to group purchasing—that yield more efficient use of time, cost, and personnel for New Jersey hospitals.

CONCURRENT COMPUTER CORPORATION

Concurrent Computer Corporation, based in Oceanport, is a relatively young company with a history of just over 20 years. In that short time the firm has compiled a track record of technological leadership in the minicomputer field.

Over the years the company changed its name three times, but it has never altered its most important attribute—the ability to come up with innovations in the field of computer science. The original goal of the firm, which was founded in 1966 under the name Interdata, was to produce a minicomputer with the powerful architectural advantages that had been available only in much larger mainframe computers. Concurrent Computer Corporation's very first product—the Model 3, introduced in 1967—began a series of technological breakthroughs for the firm by bringing microprogramming to the minicomputer market.

In 1974 the company introduced the first 32-bit minicomputer. Today virtually all of the industry's high-performance minicomputers employ 32-bit architectures.

Innovations by Concurrent Computer Corporation have not been limited to hardware alone. In 1979 the company introduced the first globally optimizing FORTRAN compiler. Two years later the firm devised the first minicomputer with a relational data base. In 1982 it became the first minicomputer company to fully support the now-popular UNIX operating system (UNIX is a registered trademark of AT&T).

Since 1974 Concurrent Computer Corporation had been a division of the Perkin-Elmer Corporation. But in early 1986 it was reorganized to become a publicly held company, separate from Perkin-Elmer. Today Current Computer Corporation employs 2,500 people in 16 countries, and it has sales distribution operations in an additional 17 countries. During its most recent fiscal year reported, the company had $245 million in sales.

Looking toward the turn of this century and beyond, Concurrent Computer Corporation says it will remain committed to meeting the computer market's needs for increased

Within 20 years Concurrent Computer Corporation has become a technological leader and innovator in the minicomputer field. Today the company employs 2,500 people in 16 countries and has sales distribution operations in an additional 17 countries.

computing power at lower cost, specifically by the use of parallel processing: employing two or more processors simultaneously to perform portions of the same application. This is expected to be the company's focus in the years to come.

With its vast amount of experience acquired over such a short period of time, Concurrent Computer Corporation is clearly well positioned for growth. It has an extensive line of product offerings that deliver the power, speed, flexibility, and reliability needed by an ever-expanding array of applications. The firm is ready to meet the challenges of the future as the computer becomes a continually more vital factor in the business world.

WM. BLANCHARD CO.

In 1860 Isaac Blanchard set up shop in Newark as a mason and builder specializing in the construction of bakers' ovens. As his reputation grew and the demand for new ovens increased, he expanded his activities into other parts of northern New Jersey.

With the industrial growth of the state during the 1880s, Blanchard began to construct industrial and commercial buildings and enlarged his business with the help of his son, William L. Blanchard.

By the turn of the century William L. Blanchard had assumed active management and continued to expand operations. In 1902 he built the Hahne & Co. stables in Newark, the first reinforced-concrete structures in the state.

With the death of Isaac Blanchard in 1907, the firm was incorporated as Wm. L. Blanchard Co. Under the leadership of William L. Blanchard and his son, Isaac C. Blanchard, the company constructed many of Newark's important buildings. In less than seven months in 1913 they built Newark's Shubert Theatre, described by the press as "the largest and costliest in New Jersey." In 1925 the firm completed the eight-story Goerke Department Store, so spacious that "a regular-size bungalow with six rooms and sun parlor" was placed on the fourth floor "completely furnished, as a suggestion to customers."

William F. Blanchard, the elder son of Isaac C. Blanchard, became company president in 1937 upon the death of his grandfather. With the onset of World War II and a new

An artist's rendering of the office and construction yard of Isaac Blanchard as it appeared in the 1880s.

era of industrial activity, Wm. L. Blanchard Co. earned the Army/Navy Award for Excellence in Production for conversion of automobile factories for fighter plane production. Peacetime brought reconversion and a diversity of construction, including "the largest department store warehouse in the world" for L. Bamberger & Co.

Growth in the 1950s was marked by movement of commerce and industry to the suburbs, with new department stores for Altman's and Bamberger's, and factory and office buildings for city firms needing space available in the suburbs. The 1960s brought renewed activity in urban locations, including the construction

The St. Barnabas Medical Center in Livingston was constructed by Wm. Blanchard Co. in 1961. Today it remains the largest private hospital in New Jersey.

of several office buildings for the Mutual Benefit group in Newark.

In the early 1960s Wm. Blanchard Co. embarked upon a program of hospital construction, which to this day is an important part of its work. St. Barnabas Medical Center was completed in Livingston in 1961 and remains the largest private hospital in New Jersey. Other health care facilities followed, including major projects for Middlesex General University Hospital, Pascack Valley Hospital, Riverview Medical Center, and The General Hospital Center at Passaic.

Over the years the firm has also constructed buildings for lease, and Blanchard now owns a variety of tenant-occupied properties throughout northern New Jersey.

When Wm. Blanchard Co. celebrated its 100th anniversary in 1960, its hopes were well expressed at a commemorative ceremony: "The performance of Wm. Blanchard Co. in a business noted for the short lives of its competitors suggests something of the quality of this group and their ability to meet the next hundred years."

Today Wm. Blanchard Co. continues to grow with New Jersey. The business remains a family enterprise, managed by the great-great-grandsons of the founders. Over a span of five generations, the Blanchards have constructed more than 6,000 structures and are now in their 127th year as New Jersey builders.

SUBARU OF AMERICA

Subaru of America is not a traditional automobile company—it is a publicly owned marketing company that is the exclusive importer of cars and trucks manufactured by Fuji Heavy Industries in Japan. Today Subaru of America is one of the most successful automobile importers in the United States, in recent years achieving an impressive 55.5-percent average return in equity, ranking it as one of the most profitable companies in America.

Subaru of America was cofounded by Harvey Lamm (its current chairman and chief executive officer) and Malcom Bricklin (now chairman of Bricklin Industries, Inc.), in 1968. The first Subaru, a mini-car weighing about 1,000 pounds with a 22-horsepower engine, was marketed in the United States in May of that year. At that time Subaru's stock traded on the over-the-counter market for three dollars per share. Before splitting eight to one in May 1985, that same Subaru share sold for $244.

Subaru's start was slow, however. In the late 1960s America's love affair with Japanese cars was not even a flirtation. The situation improved in 1970, when Subaru offered the first Japanese front-wheel-drive passenger car to hit America. Then, in 1975, Subaru marketed the first four-wheel-drive passenger car, which became the company's market niche and brought a major turning point in its fortunes. The next year the U.S. Ski Team designated Subaru its Official Car, a distinction that remains and has earned the company virtual dominance in ski country and rural climates.

Subaru's organization has also grown. In 1981 Thomas R. Gibson, a member of Lee Iacocca's management team at Ford and later at Chrysler, joined Subaru as senior vice-president of marketing, elevated in 1986 to president and chief operating officer under Harvey Lamm.

The company outgrew its longtime headquarters in Pennsauken, which was actually a converted parts warehouse. During the summer of 1986 the firm moved into a new $18-million, seven-story corporate headquarters on Route 70 in Cherry Hill. The sleek, concrete-and-glass structure is a testament to how far the company has come since its start in 1968. The new, 115,000-square-foot corporate office houses more than 400 employees, while another 130 people work at the Pennsauken offices, renovated to serve as a Subaru national data-processing facility.

In the meantime Subaru's model line has grown to include vehicles in seven body styles and a wide variety of engine and transmission combinations to suit each customer. The company's product development thrust is embodied in the XT, a stylish and sporty coupe vehicle available with four-wheel drive, adjustable air suspension, turbocharging, and other features that have come to symbolize Subaru value and technology. Though the XT represents hi-tech driving advancement, the firm has not abandoned its original product, economy cars. Today the Subaru Justy, a 1.2-liter mini-car that many auto writers consider the best in its class, is positioned to create yet still another profitable niche for Subaru of America.

Subaru is the nation's fifth-largest importer, achieving record sales and earnings the past 11 years. For 1986 the company earned $94 million on sales of $1.9 billion, a 22-percent increase in earnings, with a record 183,242 units for a 29-percent increase in sales. The sales volume represents about 70 percent of Fuji Heavy Industries' worldwide production: Subaru of America is, in fact, Fuji's largest customer, and the United States is Fuji's largest market.

In keeping with the desire to serve the American consumer, Fuji has announced plans to build a plant in the United States through a joint venture with Isuzu Motors. The $500-million facility, Subaru Isuzu Automotive, Inc., will be located near Lafayette, Indiana, and employ 1,400 people. When completed in late 1989, the

Harvey H. Lamm, co-founder of Subaru of America and its current chairman of the board and chief executive officer.

plant will produce cars and trucks at the rate of 120,000 units a year, with plans to double capacity by 1994.

In addition to its increased vehicle sales, expected to reach 250,000 by

Thomas R. Gibson, president and chief operating officer of Subaru of America.

the early 1990s, Lamm says growth will come from other areas as well. Subaru Financial Services, comparable to GMAC, provides dealer and consumer financing and has become a major growth business for the company. Sales of accessories and replacement parts have increased sharply with the growth in unit sales, and the firm, which owns five of the 13 Subaru distributorships nationwide, is a major beneficiary of the healthy sales and service growth of Subaru vehicles nationwide.

Even with these new projects, sales of Subaru cars and trucks are the foundation of the company's future growth, and here Subaru of America remains especially optimistic. According to a recent R.L. Polk and Co. survey, 92 percent of all Subaru cars and trucks registered since 1975 are still on the road today. According to Lamm, the firm's success is directly attributable to its commitment to putting the customer first, and independent studies back up that claim. Subaru is continually ranked in the top 10 of all automo-

---

Subaru of America's new $18-million, seven-story corporate headquarters on Route 70 in Cherry Hill.

tive nameplates in the annual J.D. Power Automobile Customer Satisfaction Index. In simplest terms, the company reports that over half of all new Subarus are sold to existing Subaru owners.

On Wall Street, Subaru of America has been one of the hottest selling glamour stocks on the OTC market. In the past five years the stock has appreciated nearly 400 percent, in the top one percent of all U.S. companies. Based on its strong foundation of earnings, management, and product quality, most analysts predict a bright future ahead for the company.

M&T CHEMICALS INC.

M&T Chemicals Inc. started as the Goldschmidt Detinning Company in Carteret, New Jersey, in 1908. In its early years the firm recycled tin makers' scrap to make products like tin tetrachloride. The silk industry used tin tetrachloride to increase the body and weight of silk fibers before the advent of nylon and other synthetic materials.

The Th. Goldschmidt Company of Essen, Germany, had been importing tin tetrachloride into the United States, and in 1908 it established the Goldschmidt Detinning Company as a New Jersey corporation. In 1918 Goldschmidt sold its interest in the firm, and a new concern, Metal & Thermit Corporation (later to be called M&T), was born.

Today M&T has $300 million in annual sales and employs 1,700 people at more than 50 plants, laboratories, and offices on five continents. Tin is an important part of M&T's heritage, and today the company makes more organotin and inorganic tin chemicals than any other producer in the world. M&T also makes chemicals based on chromium, copper, magnesium, nickel, phosphorous, zinc, and zirconium. Its product lines include electroplating systems and chemicals, plastic additives, industrial chemical intermediates, bioactive chemicals, fine chemicals, electronic chemicals, organometallics, and inorganic chemical specialties.

The "T" in M&T derives from the Thermit process, first used in Europe to produce pure metals and later modified for welding. In the early 1900s the Thermit process was used to join train rails and other large metal parts. The process was employed during World War II in shipbuilding and became a major factor in America's naval success. Innumerable other applications were found for it during the war.

By 1925 M&T had commercialized a new process called chromium plating. M&T's chromium-plated parts created sensational demand, and so the company decided to form a wholly owned subsidiary, Chro-

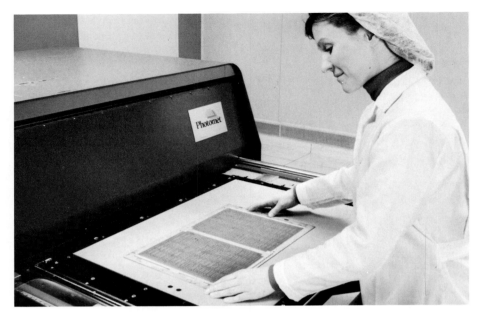

Providing technology to help electronics manufacturers produce the next generation of sophisticated circuit boards is just one example of how M&T responds to meet the needs of dynamic industries worldwide.

mium Products Company. M&T today is the worldwide leader in chromium plating, having developed more technology and patents in that area than any other corporation.

M&T had become the silk industry's leading supplier of tin tetrachloride by the early 1930s, but synthetic materials—particularly rayon—soon began competing with the silk business. When nylon was introduced in 1936, the bottom fell out of the silk industry. M&T's Carteret plant was producing millions of tons of tin tetrachloride for a market that no longer existed.

Seeking new uses for the chemi-

cal, M&T developed a method to convert tin tetrachloride to anhydrous stannous chloride. Called Stannochlor®, this chemical is still used for immersion tinning and tin plating and as a chemical intermediate. The Carteret plant was revamped for the alkaline detinning process being used at M&T plants in East Chicago, Indiana, and South San Francisco, California.

In 1943 the company developed zirconium silicate opacifiers for ceramic glaze applications. Zirconium silicate products are still used today to produce heat-resistant refractory materials as lining for molten-metal ladles and for investment castings of metals. Many other new products were developed during this period. M&T produced its first organotin stabilizers for plastics such as polyvinyl chloride (PVC) in the late 1940s, thus making major inroads into the plastics industry. In 1942 M&T built a new central laboratory in Rahway, as continued research laid the foundation for the organotin business so important to the company today.

Rising costs and shrinking profits

M&T Chemicals is a leading producer of plastic additives that help protect vinyl siding, shutters, gutters, and downspouts against the elements.

led to the sale of the Thermit welding business in 1957, which was followed soon by the sale of the Thermit metals business. M&T strengthened its position in the ceramics industry with new products to provide opaqueness to pottery glazes and the acquisition of Orefraction Minerals, Inc., of Andrews, South Carolina.

In the early 1950s an export push began, and by 1959 exports topped $1.3 million. M&T Chemicals B.V., based in the Netherlands, began making organometallics in 1963 and marked the first significant presence of M&T in Europe.

Metal & Thermit Corporation was acquired by American Can Company in 1962 and was renamed M&T Chemicals Inc. The new name reflected the firm's diversification and the fact that it was no longer in the metals or Thermit business. Meanwhile there were new domestic acquisitions, and M&T's research and development staff had grown from about 40 people in 1941 to 145 by 1960. From 1954 to 1964 M&T

M&T applies its research expertise to develop products that enhance our lives everyday. For instance, specialty coatings produced by M&T are used to improve the strength and scratch resistance of glass packaging.

was granted 144 patents in the United States and some 480 abroad.

In 1977 M&T became a wholly owned subsidiary of Elf Aquitaine, the Paris, France-based oil, gas, and natural resource company. Elf Aquitaine's commitment to specialty chemicals has helped M&T expand and grow, through numerous overseas acquisitions and joint ventures.

Today's M&T comprises four operating divisions: Plastic Additives, Industrial Chemicals, Agricultural Chemicals, and Plating Chemicals. The Plastic Additives Division produces additives used in making plastic products, including packaging and bottles, vinyl siding and windows, as well as many other household products. The division recently established Metco America, Inc., a joint venture with Mitsubishi Rayon Company, Ltd., and built a new $25-million plant in Mobile, Alabama, that produces 30 million pounds annually of impact modifiers and process aids.

M&T's Industrial Chemicals Division produces specialty chemicals based on tin, antimony, and zirconium. These materials are used in paints, glass bottles and jars, ceramic products, and pharmaceuticals, to name just a few. The Agricultural Chemicals Division produces bioactive chemicals for agricultural and veterinary products such as fungicides, miticides, and other parasitic controls. M&T's Plating Division has been a leader since the 1920s, when it introduced the first commercial chromium-plating process, and today it supplies chemicals and systems for decorative, functional, and electronic plating applications.

At present the firm's headquarters is in Woodbridge, but M&T Chemicals Inc. is planning a move to a more centrally located New Jersey site by 1988.

M&T Chemicals was founded in 1908 to recycle tin can makers' scrap. Over the years the company has developed its expertise in tin chemistry to become the largest organotin and inorganic tin chemicals producer in the world.

FAITOUTE STEEL COMPANY, INC.

As New Jersey's second-oldest steel service center, Faitoute Steel Company, Inc., has supplied steel products for some of the state's most important structures. Roads, buildings, bridges, and many other projects in northern New Jersey have been completed with steel products from Faitoute.

Historically, Faitoute has been a supplier of steel for New Jersey's Standard Oil facilities, the Mutual Benefit Life Insurance building in Newark, and viaducts and bridges on the entire New Jersey Turnpike, to name just a few of its achievements in helping develop New Jersey's infrastructure.

As a steel service center, Faitoute is essentially a "lumber yard" for steel, cutting raw steel into various shapes and forms for construction and other uses. The firm cuts steel to suit customer specifications. Faitoute's products are hot-rolled and cold-finished bars, bar shapes and sheets, reinforcing bars, structural shapes, plates, strip, expanded metal, flexangle, and bar grating.

The company's history begins in 1904, when Moses Wilfred Faitoute and James A. Coe formed the Coe-Faitoute Company in Newark as a

Faitoute Steel Company, Inc., began in 1904 as the Coe-Faitoute Company in Newark, founded by Moses Wilfred Faitoute and James A. Coe. Here an early horse-drawn cart delivers steel to Newark.

steel warehouse, situated on Lawrence Street. By 1906 Coe had left the company, and Faitoute formed the Faitoute Iron and Steel Company. Subsequently, the firm moved to its present location on Frelinghuysen Avenue in Newark.

Faitoute started with about a half-dozen employees and some assets that help paint a picture of those early days. Company records from 1912 list a team of horses— "Bessie, Sam, Prince, Tom, Bill, and Fannie"— along with two mules, two motor trucks, and a trailer. Most of Faitoute's steel was sheared with hand tools, in stark contrast to today's computer-controlled cutting machinery.

By the early 1920s Faitoute was employing about 12 people in its warehouse, two in shipping, and several more in its offices. Roy Harrison, who joined Faitoute in 1920 and still works there, recalls that the company was then making deliveries with two motor trucks and wagons drawn by teams of horses. The larger wagon would carry about eight tons of steel.

During the mid-1920s Faitoute supplied concrete reinforcing bars and other steel products for highways, bridges, schools, municipal buildings, sewage- and water-treatment plants, churches, hospitals, banks, department stores, industrial plants, airplane hangars, and many other facilities.

Today Faitoute Steel Company, Inc., makes steel in large, irregular shapes such as this, cut to customer specifications and needs.

As Faitoute moved into the 1930s early development of New Jersey's suburban areas began. New roads were constructed, and bridges were built over streams and river branches. Faitoute supplied beams and reinforcing steel for a vast number of bridges that were built in Union, Morris, Middlesex, Bergen, and Somerset counties, as well as some bridges in Sussex and Monmouth counties.

During the 1940s, when milk bottles were being replaced by paraffined cardboard containers, Faitoute handled orders from American Can Co. for welded steel shapes that were formed and assembled to make the frames for the first paraffining machines.

In August 1941 Moses W. Faitoute died, and the following year, 1942, ownership of the company passed to William G. Carter and members of the Faitoute family. Carter, who had been with the firm for about 10 years, had served as right-hand man to Moses Faitoute.

The front entrance of the warehouse and offices of Faitoute Steel. The building is centrally located in Newark, just off New Jersey's Route 22 and close to both the Newark Airport and the New Jersey Turnpike.

During World War II the company became a valued supplier to the U.S. Army state arsenal, supplying parts for tanks and munitions. Faitoute was a key source of parts for production of the then-secret M7 Tank Killer and also fabricated steel for munitions elevators.

John W. White, Jr., Moses Faitoute's son-in-law, was representing the family in management of the business, essentially in partnership with Carter. In 1956 Carter died, and White became sole leader of the company.

By the 1960s Faitoute was not only supplying steel for buildings; it was also serving as a consultant in design in preliminary planning, preparation of structural framing plans, ordering of material to shop, and scheduling for delivery and erection of the steel. With this added expertise, the company began undertaking larger projects.

On October 1, 1969, Richard A. Mast and Ross H. Monks, Jr., purchased the business from the White family and reorganized as Faitoute Steel Company, Inc. In 1980 Mast sold his interest to Monks, who then became sole owner of the firm.

Monks' career with Faitoute has been something of a classic American success story. When he was in high school, the Junior Achievement Program of Essex-West Hudson counties recommended him for an entry-level job "for sales-minded young men" at Faitoute. "I know that you will meet their qualifications and that you will do well with them," his Junior Achievement adviser wrote to him. That prediction certainly came true—today Ross Monks is president and owner of the company.

Throughout its long history Faitoute Steel Company, Inc., has chosen to remain in Newark. As the state's transportation hub, Newark has afforded Faitoute a strong central location, just off New Jersey's Route 22 and close to Newark Airport and the New Jersey Turnpike. The firm expects to remain a part of that activity for a long time to come.

This rear addition to the warehouse was constructed in the 1950s. The inset is an exterior view of the warehouse addition.

CONNELL, FOLEY AND GEISER

Connell, Foley and Geiser, which recently celebrated its 50th anniversary, is one of New Jersey's most respected and influential law firms. It has long been recognized as one of New Jersey's premier litigation firms, one whose partners include some of the most respected trial lawyers in the state.

The firm's past partners include Richard J. Hughes, who was with Connell, Foley and Geiser during the years between his service as governor of New Jersey and his elevation as the state's chief justice. Robert Shaw, a founding partner, served as a Federal District Court judge until his death. Other firm members who later served the judiciary were William T. McElroy and Sonia Morgan, judges of the Superior Court, Appellate Division, and Jacques H. Gascoyne, judge of the Superior Court, Law Division. In addition, Peter D. Manahan left the firm to serve a five-year term as prosecutor for Morris County, returning after the expiration of his government service.

Adrian "Bud" Foley, Jr., former surrogate of Essex County, has been hailed as New Jersey's most powerful lawyer by the *New Jersey Monthly* magazine. Foley has acted as president of the 1966 New Jersey Constitutional Convention, president of the New Jersey State Bar Association, and chairman of the American Bar Association's Litigation Section. He was also a member of the board of governors of the American Bar Asso-

Ken Kunzman and John Murray (top, standing right to left), corporate law section chairman, are joined in a research project by Adrian Foley (top right), Kevin Gardner, Patrick McAuley, and Keith Krauss (seated).

ciation and has served many other public and private bodies.

Theodore Geiser, formerly general attorney for the New Jersey Highway Authority and one of the state's outstanding trial lawyers, is recognized as one of the premier legal specialists in engineering and construction law, as well as governmental and administrative law. Working with Geiser in construction litigation are firm partners Mark Fleder; Jerome Lynes, a former Essex County Bar president; and John Neary.

George W. Connell is one of New Jersey's foremost authorities in the

The senior and founding partners of Connell, Foley and Geiser are (from left) Theodore Geiser, Adrian M. Foley, Jr., and G. Walter Connell.

field of insurance law. In 1970 he was appointed by the governor to serve on the original No Fault Study Commission, which was responsible for the enactment of that law in 1973. He later served on executive and legislative task forces studying and recommending needed modifications in the auto insurance field. Insurance litgation, another of the firm's areas of activity, is handled by Connell and various partners, including Samuel Lord, one of three partners who are members of the International Association of Defense Counsel; Richard Badolato, one of three partners who are members of the American Board of Trial Advocates; and Linda Palazzolo, one of seven members of the firm who are certified by the Supreme Court as Certified Civil Trial Attorneys.

Connell, Foley and Geiser has become broadly diversified, with its members practicing in corporate, probate, and estate planning, insurance, real estate, banking, municipal, construction, public utility, public contract, and municipal bond law, as well as trial, chancery, and appellate litigation in numerous fields, including professional malpractice, environmental hazards, tort and intellectual property, and business litigation. Long involved in international legal matters, the firm has recently established a section designed to meet the needs of this rapidly expanding area of the law.

This expansion of expertise and

increase in major clients has resulted in its present growth to approximately 50 lawyers and its anticipation of further growth in the next few years. It was this rapid growth that necessitated its move to the new legal and corporate complex in Roseland, although it retains offices at Gateway Center in Newark to effectively serve its clients.

All of the members of Connell, Foley and Geiser are actively engaged in the representation of the firm's clients. The many legal specialties in which the firm engages are spearheaded by partners with years of education and experience: John LaVecchia in toxic tort and professional liability litigation; George Kenny in medical malpractice, products liability, and public entity litigation; Kenneth Kunzman in corporate and real estate matters; Kevin Coakley in the field of riparian rights; Richard Catenacci, a former assistant United States attorney who specializes in federal litigation; John Murray, who, with a master's degree in law, heads the firm's taxation section; and Peter Manahan, a certified criminal trial attorney, who handles its white-collar crime unit.

Some of the firm's major clients include Anheuser-Busch, Anchor Hocking, Westinghouse, Bethlehem Steel Corporation, Carter-Wallace, Centex Homes, CNA Insurance Group, Electro-Nucleonics, Fireman's Fund Insurance, Hilton Hotels, K mart, Miles Laboratories, New Jersey Bell Telephone Company, New Jersey Manufacturers Insurance Company, Princeton and Health Care Insurance companies, Rutgers University, The Roman Catholic Archdiocese of Newark, *The New York Times*, Associated General Contractors of New Jersey, Manufacturers Hanover, RKO General, The Borden Company, Englehard Industries, Zenith Laboratories, and Conrail, as well as numerous insurance carriers who have placed their trust in the firm's professional capability.

Connell, Foley and Geiser's pro-

John LaVecchia (center) and George Kenny (seated, left), co-chairmen of the litigation section, enjoy a brief respite from the courtroom with Michael Murphy, Peter Pizzi (standing), Kathleen Murphy, and George Connell (seated).

fessional excellence, commitment to involvement, and reputation for a close relationship among the members of the firm and with its associates act as a magnet for young attorneys. The human qualities of the firm are a legacy of the late John A. "Jack" Pindar, a legendary New Jersey trial lawyer, and other senior partners who have fostered a colle-

Partners in charge of the construction section, Mark Fleder (top, left) and Peter Manahan (top, right), leading a discussion of a serious problem with Joseph Amann (top, center), Tom Ryan, Theresa O'Gorman, Chris Paladino, and Peter Smith (seated).

gial spirit through the years.

Each new associate, selected from hundreds of applicants who are at the top of their law school class and are completing judicial clerkships, is viewed as having potential partnership quality. Connell, Foley and Geiser has never had a quota or ratio system in admitting to partnership, and because of its tradition of excellence and openness it is able to attract the finest young associates and move the best of them into partnership to continue its high quality of legal representation.

Professional competence, unquestioned integrity, public involvement, commitment to clients' interests, and emphasis on human qualities in its attorneys have been responsible for the respect with which Connell, Foley and Geiser is held by clients, courts, and other attorneys and which have made it one of the leading firms in the legal community, attracting national as well as statewide clients.

UNIVERSITY OF MEDICINE AND DENTISTRY OF NEW JERSEY

The University of Medicine and Dentistry of New Jersey (UMDNJ) is the state's public university of the health sciences. In addition to educating future physicians, dentists, and other health science professionals, the institution conducts vital medical research programs and provides health care to thousands of New Jersey residents. In its brief history UMDNJ has made major contributions to New Jersey health care. More than half of its nearly 7,000 alumni practice as health science professionals within the state, contributing to the quality of life in New Jersey. The university's numerous programs and facilities throughout the state have brought New Jersey into prominence in the health science field.

Created to consolidate all of the state's public programs in medical and dental education, UMDNJ was formed in 1970 by an act of the state legislature. First named the College of Medicine and Dentistry of New Jersey, in 1981 it was granted status as a freestanding university in recognition of its growth and development as a statewide health science institution.

The events that led to the creation of UMDNJ date back to the 1950s. After repeated attempts to establish a medical school in New Jersey over the years, Seton Hall College of Medicine and Dentistry was founded in Jersey City in 1954. A decade later that institution was acquired by the state and renamed the New Jersey College of Medicine and Dentistry. Meanwhile, the Rutgers Medical School—the state's first public program—had been founded in 1961 as a two-year basic science institution that enrolled its inaugural class of students in September 1966.

The Medical and Dental Education Act of 1970 united these two institutions under one board of trustees with one goal: to reverse the effects of New Jersey's long neglect of the health professions by increasing health manpower through education and by augmenting health care where needed. Since then UMDNJ has met that goal with remarkable growth and development. Its total enrollment now stands at 4,000.

Today UMDNJ has three major campuses: the Newark center, where a $200-million campus was opened in 1976; the Piscataway-New Brunswick campus, where the medical school opened in 1970 and a medical education building was dedicated in 1982; and the Camden-Stratford campus, where the Camden Education and Research Building, dedicated in 1984, is scheduled for expansion in 1987, and where a clinical education facility in Stratford will be completed in 1988.

In Newark, the university's schools and facilities include the UMDNJ-New Jersey Medical School, the UMDNJ-New Jersey Dental School, the UMDNJ-Graduate School of Biomedical Sciences, and the UMDNJ-School of Health Related Professions. University Hospital is also on the Newark campus, along with the UMDNJ-Community Mental Health Center.

The Piscataway-New Brunswick campus, opened in 1966, houses the Robert Wood Johnson Medical School in Piscataway and New Brunswick and the UMDNJ-Community Mental Health Center at Piscataway. On the South Jersey clinical campus facilities in Camden and Stratford, opened in 1976, are the UMDNJ-

The Newark Center, one of three University of Medicine and Dentistry of New Jersey campuses, was opened in 1976. Included on this $200-million campus are the UMDNJ-New Jersey Medical School, the UMDNJ-New Jersey Dental School, the UMDNJ-Graduate School of Biomedical Sciences, and the UMDNJ-School of Health Related Professions. University Hospital is also on the Newark campus, as is the UMDNJ-Community Mental Health Center.

Robert Wood Johnson Medical School at Camden and the UMDNJ-School of Osteopathic Medicine.

UMDNJ has affiliations with three core university teaching hospitals: the Robert Wood Johnson University Hospital in New Brunswick, the Cooper Hospital/University Medical Center in Camden, and the Kennedy Memorial Hospitals-University Medical Center in Stratford.

In a major development for the university, 1985 witnessed the dedication of the UMDNJ-University Hospital's New Jersey Cancer Center, now one of only six facilities in the United States offering sophisticated intraoperative radiation therapy to cancer patients. UMDNJ has many other noteworthy health science and research centers. Some of the most important are:

—*The Sammy Davis, Jr., National Liver Institute.* The nation's first medical resource devoted solely to patient care, education, and research for liver disease, this new center is on the Newark campus. The institute will expand and enhance the work of physicians and scientists at UMDNJ-New Jersey Medical School in the prevention, diagnosis, and treatment of liver disease. Popular entertainer Sammy Davis, Jr. launched a national fund-raising drive for the institute with a benefit dinner in the fall of 1985.

—*The Center for Molecular Medicine and Immunology.* A private research institute on the university's Newark Campus, it has developed a pioneering cancer diagnostic technique known as radioimmunodetection. This method for detecting and locating cancers by use of radioactive antibodies has proven particularly effectie in cases of colon and liver cancer.

—*The Center for Advanced Biotechnology and Medicine.* A joint project between UMDNJ and Rutgers University, the new center is being built at the Piscataway campus to conduct sophisticated research projects. The center will help place

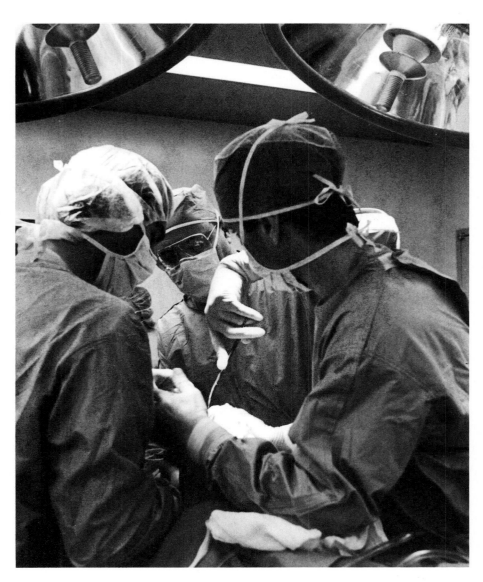

Here Andrew B. Weiss, M.D., and his surgical team perform knee surgery at the UMDNJ Hospital at Newark. With medical schools, research centers, and affiliated hospitals in New Jersey's three geographic regions, UMDNJ has built a network for health education and health care throughout the state.

New Jersey in the forefront of biotechnology.

—*The environmental Health Sciences Institute.* This new center, in its planning stages, is also a joint operation by UMDNJ and Rutgers University on the Piscataway campus. It will provide a comprehensive research and educational program in environmental health and toxicology, and occupational medicine and public health.

When UMDNJ was formed in 1970, one of its goals was to "fill the gaps" in New Jersey's health care system. The university has accomplished that goal, maintaining a particularly strong commitment to health care for New Jersey's urban poor, including the estimated 60 percent of Newark's residents living below the poverty level.

With medical schools, research centers, and affiliated hospitals in New Jersey's three geographic regions, UMDNJ has built a network for health education and health care throughout the state. For a university only 17 years old, that record of growth and development is truly impressive.

ARTHUR YOUNG

Arthur Young, one of the world's leading accounting firms, is a name recognized everywhere, and it is particularly familiar in the New Jersey business community.

The company opened its first New Jersey office in 1959 in Newark. The new office launched a successful effort to be responsive to New Jersey clients in providing accounting, auditing, tax, and management consulting services.

In 1972, to better serve its clients in the northern counties of New Jersey, Arthur Young opened a second office in Saddle Brook, at the junction of Route 80 and the Garden State Parkway. In 1984 a third Arthur Young office was established in Princeton, in order to provide easier access to clients in the southern portion of the state—particularly along the emerging Route 1 high-tech business corridor.

In 1987, after nearly four decades in Newark, Arthur Young moved its Newark office to MetroPark, the growing office complex at the junction of the Garden State Parkway, the New Jersey Turnpike, and routes

The MetroPark and Princeton partners of Arthur Young & Co. are (top row, left to right) Donald R. Richards, Peter M. Holloway, James E. Wheat, John F. Laezza, and Claude E. Fusco. In the bottom row (from left) are Edward M. Cupoli, Anthony J. Kolasa, John J. Reck, and Keith L. Brownlie. Not pictured are Michael C. Murphy and Albert J. Passanante.

1 and 9.

Today Arthur Young & Co.'s offices in MetroPark, Saddle Brook, and Princeton have a total of 17 partners and more than 200 additional personnel. Since its first New Jersey office opened in 1959, Arthur Young has significantly expanded its services. In addition to providing traditional accounting, auditing, and tax services, the New Jersey offices offer such specialized tax services as expatriate tax consulting for multinational companies with United States citizens working abroad and for foreign nationals living in the United States.

Other specialized tax services include compensation and benefits planning, and personal financial and tax planning. Arthur Young's New Jersey offices also have a valuation and appraisal services group that handles purchase price allocations associated with stock or asset acquisitions, valuation of closely held stock, and appraisal of real and personal property.

Arthur Young's management consulting services have expanded over the years as well. Today the New Jersey offices provide a full range of human resources consulting, such as executive search, outplacement, organization analysis, and executive compensation services. Other management services include strategic business planning, information systems consulting from microcomputers to mainframe computers, and manufacturing consulting. Arthur Young is also the leading consultant to New Jersey authorities and local governments, assisting them in obtaining debt financing and government grants.

Throughout their years of experience in the state, the New Jersey offices of Arthur Young have provided their clients with diversified and top-quality professional service.

The Saddle Brook partners of Arthur Young are (top row, left to right) Donald E. Danner, Bernard Leone, and Edward W. Flanagan. In the bottom row (from left) are Raymond J. Broek and Jeffrey P. Bolson.

UPSALA COLLEGE

On October 3, 1893, the Rev. Dr. Lars Herman Beck opened the doors of the Upsala Institute of Learning in Brooklyn with 16 enrolled students. Dr. Beck had come from Yale University to be Upsala's first president.

Upsala was founded by Lutherans of Swedish descent living in the eastern United States and took its name from the historic university of Uppsala in Sweden. In 1897 the institute was renamed Upsala College.

During its early years Upsala held classes in two Lutheran churches in downtown Brooklyn—Bethlehem and Saint Paul's. But the college clearly needed its own campus in order to prosper and grow. In 1889 Upsala moved to New Orange, New Jersey—now Kenilworth. Classes at New Orange were first conducted in a rented farmhouse until Old Main—the college's first permanent building—was completed in 1899.

Students relax and study on the lawn of the Upsala College library.

As enrollment rose, Upsala sought a campus closer to the metropolitan area. In 1924 the college moved to East Orange, settling into three elegant mansions on Prospect Street. Two of them are still in use—Kenbrook Hall and Old Main. In 1954 the College Chapel replaced Commons, the third mansion.

Today Upsala is a small, highly respected college with an excellent faculty. A 1985 *U.S. News & World Report* survey of "The Best Colleges in America" ranked Upsala in the top 10 of America's best colleges in the Smaller Comprehensive Institutions category for the eastern region. Upsala's graduates include executives in all areas of business, several hundred lawyers and physicians, many church officials and pastors, a Pulitzer Prize-winning historian, government officials, and almost 1,000 educators. Upsala is affiliated with the Lutheran Church in America but has a heterogeneous student body.

Upsala has remained deeply committed to providing quality liberal arts education. Today the coeduca-

More than 30 liberal arts programs in modern facilities are offered at Upsala's 45-acre East Orange campus.

tional liberal arts college has about 1,750 students, of whom about 1,300 are enrolled in programs at the 45-acre East Orange campus. About 450 students are enrolled in the two-year programs on the 271-acre Wirths campus in Sussex County, which opened in 1979.

The school's class sizes are small enough to provide the kind of exchange between professor and student that makes education a much more meaningful experience. Upsala offers a total of 31 majors, eight concentrations, six preprofessional programs, three cooperative programs, and two master's degree programs. About 650 of the school's 1,750 students are enrolled part time in continuing education programs.

Upsala College has about 600 full-time on-campus residents, and most of the other students commute from the area within a 30-mile radius of the campus. The college's East Orange location is only five minutes from the Garden State Parkway and Interstate 280.

WHIBCO, INC.

America's sand mining industry got its start in New Jersey in 1841. The state's first foundry sands were discovered on a Sayreville orchard by peach farmer Samuel Whitehead, who noticed that the sands on his farm were similar to the foundry sands being brought over by ship from England. The entire southern region of the state later found its acclaim as the greatest industrial sand source within the state's boundaries.

These sands today are called Classified Industrial Sands. They include coarse grains for cements, glass, and road construction. There are also filter gravels, dredged and used for filter media, landscaping, and paving. WHIBCO's mineral supplies are virtually endless, beneath more than 12,000 acres of prime sand mining land.

Whitehead's discovery of the sands in 1841 established what is today one of the nation's oldest producers and shippers of sand for the industry. His descendants incorporated the organization as Whitehead Brothers Company in 1892, continuing to operate under this name until 1987, when Walter Roland Sjogren, its owner, changed its name to WHIBCO, Inc.

Walter R. Sjogren, born in New York City and the son of a Swedish immigrant, is currently the owner of WHIBCO, Inc. The Sjogren family is actively involved with the business and its future. A daughter Loriann is vice-president and secretary, a son Walter is vice-president/sales, and Mrs. Sjogren is a director of the company.

Today WHIBCO, Inc., operates production facilities in New Jersey, Pennsylvania, Massachusetts, New York, and South Carolina, while maintaining various warehouse facilities in Ohio and other locations. With an abundance of natural resources and prime real estate, WHIBCO has actively been involved with leasing its property to a number of other sand producers in the industry.

In New Jersey, the company's

America's sand mining industry got its start in New Jersey in 1841, when peach farmer Samuel Whitehead discovered foundry sands on his Sayreville orchard. Whitehead's descendants incorporated the operation as Whitehead Brothers Company. Here the Whitehead Brothers Company excavates sand in the 1920s.

Dorchester facility handles mining, drying, screening, and blending of natural bonded sands. Its products are primarily for foundries, baseball infield mix, thermal sand markets, brick manufacturing, and construction. The firm's Port Elizabeth oper-

ation pumps and processes sands and gravels, which are sold in bags or bulk. Recently the plant expanded its production to include sandblast sands, filter sands and gravels, roofing sands, fiberglass sands, and construction sands.

In 1984 WHIBCO, Inc., relocated its headquarters from Florham Park to Leesburg. The company is situated within historic Leesburg, its office housed within a boat yard that was established in 1795 by the town's founders. The facility has been restored and now accommodates WHIBCO's corporate office and its research and development department. The company's research and development capabilities include technical advice and analysis of customer casting defects and customer recirculating sand systems, and also maintains an ongoing program for the development of new products.

With the Sjogren family and a new organization in the 1980s, WHIBCO, Inc., is a historic New Jersey company, geared for a new era of growth and development.

Today, under the name WHIBCO, Inc., the New Jersey company handles mining, drying, screening, and blending of natural bonded sands. Its products are used primarily for foundries, baseball infield mix, thermal sand markets, brick manufacturing, and construction.

THE LINPRO COMPANY

The Linpro Company is the owner, developer, and manager of more than seven million square feet of commercial real estate in major markets throughout the United States. Since its formation in 1978, Linpro's construction volume has exceeded one billion dollars, primarily in commercial and residential development.

One of the nation's largest development firms, Linpro has 18 regional offices. It is one of the few national real estate development companies with a broad spectrum of products, from shopping centers to office buildings, residential communities, and industrial facilities, as well as mixed-use developments. These projects are in such diverse markets as Van Nuys, California; East Hartford, Connecticut; Boca Raton, Florida; Boston, Massachusetts; Princeton and Marlton, New Jersey; Philadelphia, Pennsylvania; Reston, Virginia; Denver, Colorado; Raleigh, North Carolina; and Austin and Dallas, Texas.

The Linpro Company originated from a divestiture of interest in Lincoln Property Company in late 1977. Eric Eichler, who was Lincoln Property's regional partner for the Northeastern United States, joined with four Lincoln Property operating partners to form Linpro as a separate enterprise. Linpro operations officially began on January 1, 1978.

From its corporate headquarters in Berwyn, Pennsylvania, the company is led by Eichler, partner and chief executive officer, and the

managing partners: Jay G. Cranmer, Delaware Valley; John A. Berry, Metro Washington; William M. Swain, Jr., Metro New York; and George A. Higgins, New England. These five partners and the operating partners bring together diverse backgrounds, including engineering, construction, and finance.

The creation of living and working environments for New Jersey residents has been one of Linpro's hallmarks. In New Jersey, Linpro has been developing two major planned unit developments, in Plainsboro, Mercer County, and Marlton, Bur-

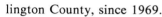

As a national real estate development firm, The Linpro Company has had major projects throughout the country but counts its creation of living and working environments for New Jersey residents as one of its hallmarks. Linpro constructs everything from office buildings such as this one (below) in Plainsboro to residential communities such as the Village Apartments (above) in Voorhees.

lington County, since 1969.

At Linpro's Greentree development in Marlton, the first buildings opened in 1977 and the final phase was completed in 1986. Considered one of the country's most successful mixed-use developments, Greentree consists of 450 acres with 600,000 square feet of mid-rise office space, 320,000 square feet of one-story office space, 220,000 square feet of flex space, 450,000 square feet of warehouse space, 110,000 square feet of retail space, and 1,000 varied residential units.

At Linpro's Princeton Meadows development in Plainsboro, the firm's property management skills can be readily seen. One of the East Coast's largest mixed-use developments, this project has achieved national recognition as the prototype of the complete community, combining housing, shopping, and leisure and sports activities. Since the development's inception in 1969, Linpro has overseen construction of 5,400 apartments, 350 single-family houses, 680 town houses, a 65,000-square-foot shopping center, and 140,000 square feet of one-story office space. Adjacent to the development Linpro is constructing Enterprise Business Center, an 83-acre, 15-building office complex.

The Linpro Company's objective is to develop, own, and manage real estate on a quality level, and evidence of its continued achievement of this goal is illustrated by its accomplishments in New Jersey.

NEW JERSEY DEPARTMENT OF COMMERCE AND ECONOMIC DEVELOPMENT

The New Jersey Department of Commerce and Economic Development was launched in 1982, and in its short history it has been a boon to the state's business environment. The department epitomizes a dynamic new style of government that other states have sought to adopt: It streamlines and speeds the path toward increased business growth—a heretofore almost unheard-of quality in a government agency.

The department was organized to promote job creation and job retention in New Jersey. Since the agency's inception, the state has achieved a net gain of more than 450,000 jobs. In 1979 the U.S. Department of Labor ranked New Jersey 43rd among states in job growth; it has since risen to eighth place, with almost 100,000 new jobs estimated in 1987 after three years of sizable increases.

The New Jersey Department of Commerce and Economic Development has helped promote New Jersey's favorable labor climate, tax structure, employment trends, and healthy economy to keep strong businesses in the state and attract new ones. The department is a tightly knit group of offices and affiliated agencies comprising just over 100 persons. Part of the department's function is to respond to calls from business leaders to help solve individual and general problems.

The department's main sectors are the Division of Economic Development, the Division of International Trade, Division of Devlopment for Small Businesses and Women and Minority Businesses, and the Division of Travel and Tourism. The Division of Economic Development works to bring new companies to New Jersey and help existing businesses expand. Its Office of Business Development provides extensive "site-search" assistance to companies considering moving to New Jersey, utilizing computerized listings of properties for sale and detailing such specifics as sprinkler systems, loading docks, and rail spurs.

Since its inception in 1982, the New Jersey Department of Commerce and Economic Development has been headed by Commissioner Borden R. Putnam.

Within the Division of Economic Development are several other offices. The Office of Business Advocacy helps solve regulatory problems and provides assistance on state permits, licensing, and certification.

The Business Retention Program meets with business and civic leaders throughout the state to hear their concerns and help develop solutions to their problems.

The Division for Small Businesses Assistance offers start-up and expansion counseling, financial advice, and other assistance to small-business owners.

The department's Division of International Trade works to bolster New Jersey exports and promote foreign investment in the state. Through a strong overseas trade show program, export seminars, and meetings with foreign trade officials and investors, this division has helped raise New Jersey exports and bring foreign-owned businesses to the state. New Jersey currently ranks fourth among U.S. states in foreign investment and eighth in exports.

The Division of Travel and Tourism carries out an aggressive advertising campaign and conducts statewide press familiarization tours. Its popular "New Jersey & You: Perfect

Together" campaign has greatly increased awareness of the state as a year-round tourist attraction. This division has led a much-heralded resurgence of New Jersey pride, which has produced some healthy results: New Jersey now ranks fifth nationally in tourism revenues but only 10th in advertising expenditures, a sign that New Jersey's tourism advertising expenditures are very effective.

Many new initiatives within the department are making headway. The newly formed Commission on Science and Technology fosters job creation in scientific fields and develops partnerships between New Jersey's academic and private sectors.

New Jersey Governor Thomas H. Kean works closely with the department in assisting and developing the state's business environment.

This commission has helped create a major high-technology presence in the state. It is being aided by a $90-million jobs, science, and technology bond issue, approved in 1984 to fund a network of technology centers at the state's public and private colleges.

In other areas the Office of Minority Business Enterprise assists minority entrepreneurs in financing and management training, and the Bureau for Hispanic Enterprise helps remove language and cultural barriers for Hispanic business owners by providing seminars and financial and managerial consultation.

The Office of Urban Programs spearheads the department's strong urban involvement, administering the Urban Enterprise Zone Program and other revitalization initiatives. There are urban enterprise zones (UEZs) in

10 New Jersey cities. To date more than one billion dollars in private investments have been committed, which will result in almost 16,000 new, permanent, full-time jobs. In a UEZ, businesses get tax exemptions and tax credits along with various job-training programs and opportunities to cut red tape to expedite job growth.

In 1985, for the second year in a row, New Jersey's manufacturing business climate ranked number one in the mideastern region (Delaware, Maryland, New Jersey, New York, Pennsylvania, and West Virginia) in the annual national business study by Grant Thornton, a nationwide accounting and consulting firm. New Jersey also outperformed all states in the Great Lakes region, the heartland of "Smokestack America." Nationally, New Jersey moved to 23rd place from 24th in the previous year after rising from 29th to 24th in 1984. A 1985 *Inc.* magazine survey found New Jersey had the eighth-best business climate in the nation for small-business growth, up from 20th in 1983.

This improvement in job growth and business environment has attracted major companies to the state. A recent arrival is Armco, the Ohio steelmaker, which has relocated its executive offices to Morristown. Several Korean firms, including Samsung Electronics and automaker Hyundai, have also moved into the state. New Jersey now has the third-highest concentration of corporate headquarters in the nation.

Since its inception the New Jersey Department of Commerce and Economic Development has been headed by Commissioner Borden R. Putnam, who had previously served as senior vice-president of American Cyanamid. His move from that distinguished private-sector post gave a big boost to the department's credibility. Under Putnam's leadership, the department has met its goals, opening the lines of communication with New Jersey businesses to aid in their growth.

PROVIDENT SAVINGS BANK

Provident Savings Bank, headquartered in Jersey City, was the first mutual savings bank in New Jersey's history, chartered in 1839 and opened for business in 1843. Today The Provident has banking offices throughout the state, in Hudson, Bergen, Essex, Ocean, Monmouth, Middlesex, Burlington, Camden, Somerset, and Mercer counties.

When The Provident opened in 1843—chartered as The Provident Institution for Savings in Jersey City—its president was Dudley S. Gregory, who would establish it as a vital force on the New Jersey banking scene. When Gregory became The Provident's president, the bank had only $250 in assets. When he retired in 1874 after a long and illustrious career, the bank's assets stood at $3.5 million. Gregory was also Jersey City's first mayor and a prime mover in developing the city's first streets, sidewalks, firehouses, and riverfront wharves.

The Provident had been located at Washington and Plymouth streets in Jersey City since 1853, but in 1890 it moved to a beautiful new headquarters building—still part of the bank today—at Washington and York streets. The site marks the Revolutionary War's famous Battle of Paulus Hook, which began on the night of August 18, 1779, when Major Henry "Light Horse Harry" Lee of the Continental Army attacked the British-held fort at Paulus Hook, taking 150 prisoners.

By the turn of the nineteenth century both The Provident and Jersey City were developing rapidly. By the time the bank celebrated its 100th anniversary in 1939, it was in its 86th year of uninterrupted dividends, a chain of dividend payments that remains unbroken to this day.

The Provident continued to grow after World War II, but it was during the late 1960s that it began its biggest expansion. In 1968 Kenneth F.X. Albers became the bank's chief executive officer, and he was to preside over the most dramatic growth period in the institution's history. At

Kenneth F.X. Albers, chairman of the board and chief executive officer.

the end of 1969 The Provident had a main office in Jersey City, five branches, and assets of $233.9 million. By 1985, under chairman of the board and chief executive officer Kenneth Albers, the bank would grow to 35 branches and assets of more than $1.25 billion.

In 1970 The Provident Institution for Savings—the bank's original name—was changed to Provident Savings Bank, and for the first time in its history the bank expanded beyond Jersey City by opening two branches in West New York. In 1972 came expansion outside of Hudson County, with branches in Dumont and Leonia in Bergen County. By 1974 Provident had 11 offices in Hudson and Bergen counties. Expansion continued through the decade as it established branches in Essex, Middlesex, Somerset, Monmouth, Ocean, Mercer, Camden, and Burlington counties.

In 1983 Bloomfield Savings Bank

of Bloomfield, New Jersey, merged into The Provident Savings Bank. Bloomfield Savings Bank, founded in 1871, had deep roots in Essex County, playing a vital role in Bloomfield's economic development. This very significant merger brought The Provident's assets to more than one billion dollars and added three new branches. The merger also expanded The Provident's capabilities, particularly with the addition of Bloomfield Savings Bank's highly regarded trust department. The Provident now provides a full range of trust services, including consultation on wills and administration of estates, trusts, and investment accounts.

The Bloomfield merger made The Provident a truly statewide bank, with more services than ever and an expanded staff. The merger brought The Provident some top management personnel, particularly James K. Feely, who was president of Bloomfield Savings and now is The Provident's president and member of its executive committee.

In 1983 The Provident also entered into business banking by establishing its Commerical Lending Division. The Provident today serves many business needs, acting as a major business financing source throughout New Jersey and offering business checking and related services. In addition, small business owners or start-up businesses can obtain low-interest U.S. Small Business Administration (SBA) loans through The Provident.

In 1984 the bank took a significant step by becoming a member of 1st Nationwide Network. The Network is an affiliation of independent banks located in various parts of the United States who cooperate with each other so that each may offer its customers the advantages of national financial services. Because the Network serves an important need, it is meeting rapid acceptance in the banking industry, and its combined assets have made it a national presence in the financial marketplace in just four years. Among its many services are national check-cashing capability and a national network of more than 2,500 ATMs. Membership in the 1st Nationwide Network brings no change in ownership or management of The Provident: The bank retains its independence.

The Provident has always been proud of its role in Jersey City's past and present. Jersey City was incorporated just one year before The Provident was chartered in 1839, and throughout its history the bank has developed with its home city. Despite The Provident's expansion, it has

An artist's rendering of The Provident's new headquarters building at 830 Bergen Avenue in Jersey City. The extensive redesign and construction work will be completed in 1987. The four-sided clock tower, a historical landmark in downtown Jersey City, will remain atop the building.

continually reaffirmed its commitment to its home city: In 1985 the bank acquired the Goodman Furniture buildings, a Jersey City landmark since 1921. Work began to convert the facility into a modern, 100,000-square-foot office facility, which became The Provident's new headquarters in 1987.

The Provident remains proud of its history of growth and innovation, and of its safety record. No depositor has ever lost a penny at The Provident, and the bank continues its record-breaking string of uninterrupted dividend payments.

Provident Savings Bank is a member of the New Jersey Council of Savings Institutions and the National Council of Savings Institutions, for both of which The Provident's chairman and chief executive officer, Kenneth F.X. Albers, has served as chairman.

SQUIBB CORPORATION

Squibb Corporation, a leading innovator, manufacturer, and marketer of pharmaceutical, medical, and personal care products, remains committed to the high standards established by the man who founded the company in Brooklyn, New York, 128 years ago.

The scope of that commitment has expanded considerably since 1858, the year Dr. Edward Robinson Squibb opened a laboratory on the Brooklyn waterfront. The firm he started now provides health care and personal care products to more than 140 countries. Squibb employs more than 17,000 people and maintains manufacturing, research, or distribution facilities in 47 nations.

From the worldwide headquarters of Squibb Corporation near Princeton, New Jersey, the company directs the research, production, and marketing activities of a broad range of pharmaceutical products (cardiovasculars, anti-infectives, anti-inflammatories, diagnostic agents, consumer health products, medical products, ostomy care, wound care and incontinence supplies, and medical/surgical instruments and supplies).

In the early 1970s Squibb initiated a concerted research program to alleviate cardiovascular disease, particularly in the areas of hypertension and heart failure. In 1979 the firm introduced Corgard® (nadolol), the first one-dose-a-day beta-blocking agent for high blood pressure and angina pectoris.

In 1981, following a decade of research, Squibb introduced Capoten® (captopril), the first oral angiotensin converting enzyme (ACE) inhibitor, which blocks the release of a hormone that causes a rise in blood pressure. The label of Capoten®, which has proven effective against both hypertension and heart failure, was broadened in 1985 to include first line therapy in all degrees of hypertension. During 1985 Capoten® became the world's fastest-growing cardiovascular product.

January 1986 marked the U.S. launch of Capozide® (captopril/hydrochlorothiazide), a new blood pressure-lowering treatment based on

---

The worldwide headquarters and research facilities of Squibb Corporation are located on a 273-acre campus in Lawrence Township. From here the company directs the research, production, and marketing activities of its pharmaceutical products.

the complementary action of two different types of medications in a single tablet.

In the field of anti-infectives, Squibb was prominent in the development of penicillin production during World War II. Later the firm was a pioneer in introducing antifungal medications such as nystatin and amphotericin B. Squibb's Velosef® (cephradine) capsule is an oral cephalosporin antibiotic for upper respiratory and urinary tract infections in twice-a-day dosage forms.

In 1981 Squibb discovered a new class of antibiotics with special properties, the monobactams. Azactam® (aztreonam), the first compound in this class, has shown remarkable activity against aerobic gram-negative organisms, which thrive in a hospital environment. Azactam® has been approved for use in many countries, including the United States, Italy, and Japan.

Princeton Pharmaceutical Products (PPP), a new ethical pharmaceutical marketing and sales organization, was formed in 1986. PPP is dedicated to using the latest technology to provide information about products and services to health care professionals in the most time-

A Squibb researcher tests a new generation counter-top gamma counter capable of simultaneously providing clinical information from 16 different patient samples.

effective way. The new organization has geared up a national sales force of 200.

Squibb Mark, a new consumer/multisource product organization, was formed in 1985 to market both Squibb's consumer health products

and its patent-expired, branded prescription products. Squibb and Marsam Pharmaceuticals Inc. formed a joint company, Squibb-Marsam, Inc., effective January 1, 1986, to develop and market multisource injectable products to hospitals and other institutions. In 1986 Squibb Mark introduced Proto-Chol® gelcaps, providing concentrated natural fish oil that is recommended for use in the context of a total cholesterol control program.

In the consumer health product area, the Theragran® line is one of the leading multivitamin product lines in the United States. The company's many consumer products include Squibb mineral oil, glycerin suppositories, and the Broxodent® electric toothbrush.

Squibb-Novo Inc., a joint company with Novo Industri S/A, Copenhagen, Denmark, markets insulin products in the United States from its headquarters in Princeton. Squibb-Novo now has a complete line of new human insulins for sale in the United States under the Novolin® brand name.

In the diagnostic area, Insovue® and Isovue-M® (iopamidol), nonionic contrast agents to enhance angiogram and myelogram pictures, were introduced for use in the United

States on January 1, 1986. The new compound has been found to provide better patient tolerance with less pain than previously used agents.

Squibb's ConvaTec Division is the worldwide leader with its Stomahesive® ostomy skin barrier product line, and in two-piece ostomy appliances. In early 1986 it launched its new Durahesive® urostomy skin barrier, with a much longer wearing time than products previously available. Also active in the field of wound care with its DuoDERM® Hydroactive® dressings, ConvaTec is well positioned to become a major force in targeted wound management with several new products in advanced stages of development.

Edward Weck & Company, Inc., develops and manufactures a wide variety of products for the physician and surgeon, including hand-held instruments, surgical closures, Argon® angiographic catheters and guide wires, and Surgicot® operating room supplies.

Research and development has always been the cornerstone on which the Squibb tradition rests, dating back to Dr. Edward R. Squibb's work in the nineteenth century. The Squibb Institute for Medical Research was established in 1938, the first industrial-based medical research organization of its kind and a forerunner of what has become a standard component of the pharmaceutical industry. Today the institute employs more than 1,000 scientists and technicians, with funding for research and development exceeding $163 million in 1986.

Squibb Corporation has grown immeasurably since Dr. Squibb opened his laboratory, but the philosophy behind it, as stated in its famous trademark, remains unchanged: "The Priceless Ingredient of every product is the honor and integrity of its maker."

The new Squibb state-of-the-art parenteral manufacturing building in New Brunswick.

THE VENET COMPANIES

Venet Advertising, founded in Irvington, New Jersey, in 1954, aimed to be something different right from the start. While most agencies specialized in product advertising, Venet specialized in advertising the place where products were sold.

The company quickly became the advertising leader in its area for supermarkets and other retail chains; the agency was able to get people into the supermarkets that moved the products. Those efforts have not gone unrewarded.

Venet has been New Jersey's top agency for the past several years, winning that honor for three consecutive years starting in 1983, when billings were at $36.5 million, and running through 1985, when billings reached $57.25 million. In 1986 billings rose to $71-plus million and once again made Venet number one.

Venet has helped emerging products and smaller companies market against huge competitors, using package design, point-of-sale, direct response, barter, and multimedia presentations, as well as superior consumer advertising. As a result, it has become more than an advertising agency; it is a total marketing communications complex, influencing decisions—as a marketing partner with its clients—at every stage in the selling process.

Many clients are content with traditional advertising agencies using traditional media to perform the agency's traditional role: reaching the consumer to generate and stimulate interest in a product. That's enough for some clients—but not Venet's.

Venet clients expect more for their product and more from their agency. High-impact consumer advertising with a selling message that sends shoppers to the store is a given, but only a beginning.

There's a lot more to the selling process. Many products need an extra dimension to establish a position in the marketplace. That requires selling to all the important publics: the broker, the chain buyer, the store

Zal Venet (center), founder, chairman, president, and chief executive officer of The Venet Companies.

manager, the retail employees, the client's employees, and, of course, the consumer.

A lot of products need extra leverage to cut through the clutter of the marketing environment. So, in addition to the established media—broadcast, print, outdoor—Venet employs the untraditional media: the package, the shelf, the store, the circular, the coupon. It's these media that help turn movement into tonnage.

New Jersey adman Zal Venet is chairman, president, founder, and chief executive officer of the agency that today is known as The Venet Companies, comprising Venet/New

Jersey, based in Union at 485 Chestnut Street; Venet/New York at 888 Seventh Avenue in Manhattan; and four subsidiary units, Mayer Visual Communications, LSF Media Services, Inc., VPS Productions Services, and Venet Direct Response. It is a subsidiary of the Graphic Media Corporation of Fairfield, New Jersey, a publicly held company.

Venet/New Jersey's explosive growth has made it the state's largest agency, with particular expertise in

Venet Advertising has been New Jersey's top agency for the past several years. Its hands-on approach and knowledge of the New Jersey marketplace has attracted clients ranging from health care to banking to packaged goods. Here Zal Venet (far right) and some of his staff critique the newspaper introduction of a new campaign.

retail and service industry marketing/advertising. Its hands-on approach and knowledge of the New Jersey marketplace has attracted clients ranging from health care to banking to packaged goods.

Venet's record of success in New Jersey speaks for itself. Clients include the state's top supermarket, Pathmark; the predominant audio, video, electronics, and appliance chain, Brick Church; and the chief retail automotive parts and service chain, R&S/Strauss. The firm has also helped the New Jersey Lottery achieve record revenues, and other clients include Ultra-Bank Corporation, *Business Journal of New Jersey,* Muhlenberg Regional Medical Center, Sony Video Communications Products, and WNET Channel 13.

Venet/New York is a full-service office, complementing the New Jersey facility and offering clients the best of both worlds. Venet's client billings are headed by the Pathmark chain. Taking over Pathmark's advertising in 1969, the company helped catapult it into the top position over a five-state area and make it number one nationwide in per-store volume.

Venet has scored many other successes, including its work for Prince Foods Company's expansion nationwide from its Boston base. Taking on Prince as a client in 1968, the agency used the company slogan "Wednesday is Prince Spaghetti Day" in radio jingles celebrating Wednesdays and Prince. TV spots featuring a boy named Anthony running home through North Boston's Italian section took Prince to major markets. Today Prince is number one in New England, Detroit, and Chicago, and solidly based in markets across the country.

Venet prides itself on its high number of long-term clients, some of whom date back more than 20 years. Agency clients over the years have included White Rock Beverages; Hillshire Farm; Fiat Cars; General Motors Cars, Trucks, and Parts; Shop-Rite Supermarkets; La Yogurt;

and Tuscan Farms. Current Venet clients include Pueblo and Xtra Stores in Puerto Rico, the Virgin Islands, and Florida; Rickel Home Centers; The Long Island Rail Road; To-Fitness Instant Goody Two Shakes Yogurt; and Jaques Borel Employee Dining Program.

Venet has won many industry awards, including the Clio Hall of Fame Award in 1977 for a Prince Spaghetti ad, numerous U.S. Television Commercial Festival awards for outstanding creativity, *Advertising Age's* annual 100 Best TV Commercials awards of 1978-1979 for Pathmark, and numerous others.

Aside from its New Jersey and New York offices, The Venet Companies has four subsidiary organizations:

—Venet Production Services is a totally integrated, state-of-the-art graphic arts facility in Cranford, New Jersey, operating 24 hours a day, six days a week, and providing complete service overnight.

—Mayer Visual Communications offers a full range of art/production/ communication services, including

promotion and collateral, package design, publication design, recruitment advertising, and audiovisual and multimedia presentations.

—LSF Media Services, Inc., provides complete media research, planning, and control. With LSF as its broadcast-media-buying unit, Venet offers its clients the negotiating expertise of a major broadcast-buying service without compromising the integrity of the advertising program.

—Venet Direct Response is a direct-response marketing division specializing in ad fulfillment, direct mail turnkey programs, list compilation, counseling management and maintenance, tracking, and analysis.

George Coscia, president Venet/New Jersey.

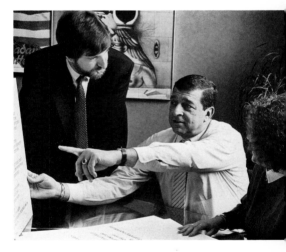

Venet Advertising has helped emerging products and smaller companies market against huge competitors. Covering all aspects of advertising, from package design to multimedia presentations, Venet is a total marketing communications complex.

SEA-LAND CORPORATION

In 1956 an enterprising young New Jersey company—a fledgling among the shipping giants of the world—pioneered an innovative "sea-land" concept in ocean transportation, with the shipment of the first containers from Port Newark, New Jersey, to Houston, Texas.

The concept, which was to change the way the world transported its goods, involved development of a large standard-size container compatible with ocean, truck, and rail transportation to speed cargo movement door-to-door.

In little more than three decades, containerization has become the world's primary form of ocean shipping for general cargo. And today Sea-Land is one of the world's largest containership carriers, operating a fleet of more than 50 vessels and over 100,000 containers on U.S. and foreign trade routes serving the transpacific, transatlantic, Alaska, Caribbean, Central America, Middle East, and India. In all, Sea-Land calls at 76 ports and serves 63 countries and territories around the globe.

Since its beginnings Sea-Land has been a leading force in New Jersey's emergence as a center for international trade. Sea-Land's home terminal at Port Elizabeth has served as an industry model. Nearly 1,900 of the firm's 8,000 employees live and work in the Garden State.

The story of Sea-Land Corporation and container shipping began quietly on a blustery day in April 1956, when the world's first containership, Sea-Land's *Ideal-X*, slipped out of Port Newark virtually unnoticed. In retrospect, the advent of container shipping passed unnoticed because the concept was such a simple one. But the popularity of container shipping caught on quickly, and by 1957 Sea-Land was providing regular sailings between New Jersey, Florida, and Texas.

Sea-Land had entered offshore trades by August 1958, when the SS *Fairland* sailed into San Juan Harbor, bringing Puerto Rico its first containership service. Since then

Sea-Land has continued its commitment to the Caribbean Basin, serving the Dominican Republic, Jamaica, Trinidad, Curacao, Aruba, and Haiti, as well as Central American countries, including Costa Rica, Guatemala, Honduras, and El Salvador.

With the expansion of services beyond the coastal waters of the United States came new technology for specialized containers. To serve citrus fruit shippers from Florida, refrigerated containers were developed. And to keep pace with its growing business, Sea-Land rapidly enlarged the size and capability of its containership fleet and improved its route structure.

In 1962 Sea-Land launched the first containership service between the East and West coasts of the United States when the *Elizabethport*, at that time one of the largest containerships built, made the inaugural voyage to the Port of Oakland, California.

That same year the Port Authority of New York and New Jersey, the first to recognize the promise of container shipping, began building a

In 1962 the Port Authority of New York and New Jersey, recognizing the promise of containerized shipping, began building a modern container terminal on reclaimed marshland in Elizabeth. Pictured here is the site of Sea-Land's container facility at Port Elizabeth before the facility was built.

Today Sea-Land's 217-acre Elizabeth facility is the world's largest privately operated container terminal.

modern container terminal on reclaimed marshland at Elizabeth, New Jersey. Today Sea-Land's 217-acre Elizabeth facility, its home port, is the largest and busiest privately operated container terminal in the world.

Two years later, in December 1964, Sea-Land's SS *Anchorage* broke through ice-clogged Cook Inlet, bringing the first year-round containership service to the state. Today Sea-Land serves as a major supply line for Alaska's military and private sector. Entrance into the Alaska trade led to development of insulated and special-purpose containers for transport of automobiles.

Then, in April 1966, Sea-Land brought its fleet of containerships into competition with major foreign and U.S. merchant carriers on international routes, entering the North Atlantic trade between New York and the European ports of Rotterdam, the Netherlands; Bremen, Germany; and Grangemouth in the United Kingdom.

That same year the U.S. government called on Sea-Land's expertise to recommend ways to eliminate port congestion and to expedite distribution of supplies in Vietnam. As a result, Sea-Land inaugurated military support service to Subic Bay in the Philippines, to Okinawa, and later to Saigon.

The following year Sea-Land set up and maintained container port facilities at Cam Rahn Bay, Da Nang, and Que Nhon. With the original containerships dedicated to Vietnam service, Sea-Land was able to transport 10 percent of Vietnam-destined supplies. To move the remaining 90 percent required the service of more than 250 other transport ships, proving the effectiveness of container shipping for military support.

To utilize the empty Vietnam spaces on the backhaul, the company inaugurated commercial container service in 1968 between Japan and the United States, expanding that service the following year to Hong Kong, Singapore, and Taiwan and in 1970 to Korea. That same year Sea-Land inaugurated service to Mediterranean ports in Spain, France, and Italy.

Six years later, in 1976, Sea-Land launched its Middle East service with a call at Dammam, Saudi Arabia. By the end of the decade, the company had inaugurated service to India, along with biweekly sailings between Dubai, United Arab Emirates, and Bombay and Cochin. And in 1980 Sea-Land signed an agreement to provide the first regularly scheduled containership service between Shanghai in the People's Republic of China and North America.

Since the start-up of its new con-

The Sea-Land Patriot, *the first of 12 new containerships commissioned in 1980, arrives in San Francisco Bay, signaling a new era of economical diesel propulsion for Sea-Land and for the U.S. Merchant Fleet.*

tainership service in 1956, Sea-Land has developed technology to attract new markets to containerization and to increase the efficiency of its equipment and operations. In 1978 Sea-Land led the American Liner Fleet in its shift to fuel-efficient diesel propulsion with the introduction of the first four U.S.-flag diesel containerships. Today more than two-thirds of the company's fleet is diesel powered.

A full "double-stack" train equals the capacity of a small containership. Comprised of 20 or more rail cars and between 200 and 300 containers, these trains represent the latest inland extension of Sea-Land's service.

Similarly, in 1985 Sea-Land opened complementary state-of-the-art port terminals on both sides of the Pacific: one at the Port of Kobe, Japan, and the other at the Port of Tacoma, Washington, gateway to the Pacific Northwest. At its Kwai Chung facility in Hong Kong, Sea-Land is a partner in Asia Terminals Ltd.—a unique, six-story structure, the largest of its kind in the world and Southeast Asia's major consolidation and warehousing center for containerized cargo. Together these landside developments position Sea-Land to capitalize on long-term Pacific Rim growth.

Today approximately 70 percent of the containers Sea-Land carries from Asia to Tacoma move further eastward by rail on advanced double-stack unit trains—the latest inland extension of containership operations first developed by Sea-Land and the Southern Pacific Railroad in 1979.

In 1986 Sea-Land Corporation's board of directors unanimously approved a merger proposal from the Richmond, Virginia-based CSX Corporation, whose transportation units operate rail, barge, and motor carrier services. The merger—which has created the world's first truly global transportation service company operating in all modes of surface transportation—further extends the concept of ship/rail/truck cargo transfer that Sea-Land pioneered in New Jersey in 1956.

CONSTELLATION BANCORP (THE NATIONAL STATE BANK)

Constellation Bancorp is a modern bank holding company geared to meet the challenges of the future. It has the benefit of a venerable history. When Constellation Bancorp was launched in March 1985, its subsidiary—The National State Bank— was in its 173rd year. Established in 1812, The National State Bank is the oldest bank in Union County and was the fourth institution to receive a banking charter from the state of New Jersey.

The National State Bank, now in its 175th year, still has many of the entrepreneurial characteristics of its early founders. It is similar in business style to the principal market it serves: the entrepreneurial company with annual sales of up to $20 million. The bank's primary marketing area is Essex, Hunterdon, Mercer, Middlesex, Monmouth, Somerset, and Union counties. National State is a strong community bank, serving New Jersey's citizens, businesses, and municipalities. Business financing, investment management, personal trust, and corporate trust complement traditional banking services. Full-service securities brokerage is available at National State, rounding out the bank's philosophy of deliver-

Colonel John Kean was the bank's leader in the crucial post-Civil War years. He served as the bank's president from 1873 until 1889, establishing a family tradition of civic and bank leadership.

ing all necessary financial services to the community.

The National State Bank was established as State Bank of Elizabethtown on January 28, 1812, and leased temporary offices in a house at the intersection of Caldwell Place and Broad Street. By 1814 the bank had built its own two-story headquarters at 68 Broad Street.

In colonial times Elizabethtown was New Jersey's transportation hub. Travelers to New York took the stage to Elizabethtown Point and crossed the Hudson River by boat. As the nineteenth century progressed, real estate and the railroads boomed. In 1840 rail service was established between New York and Philadelphia. An expanding Elizabethtown had its name shortened to Elizabeth in 1855, and, as the town grew, the bank's deposits grew with it. In 1865 State Bank of Elizabeth became The National State Bank of Elizabeth—the name would later be shortened to The National State Bank in 1957— as it came under a federal charter.

In the late nineteenth century and into the twentieth century, The National State Bank experienced strong continuity in leadership under New Jersey's Kean family. Among the bank's first shareholders, the Keans had been part of National State since its earliest days. Colonel John Kean, who served in the U.S. Senate and the House of Representatives, was the bank's president from 1873 to 1889. He founded a 113-year financial dynasty, guiding the bank through the ups and downs of the crucial post-Civil War years. John Kean, Jr., ran the bank from 1889 to 1914, and his brother Julian served as its president from 1914 to 1932. In 1933 John Kean III became president and continued the family tradition until a cousin, W. Emlen Roosevelt, succeeded him. Many descendants of Colonel John Kean have also served in public office, including one notable contemporary public servant—current New Jersey Governor Thomas Kean.

The institution's prudent banking practices enabled it to weather the difficult Depression years when many overextended banks had to apply for Reconstruction Finance Corporation loans to stay in business. It was not until the post-World War II era that National State began an aggressive expansion program under W. Emlen Roosevelt, who became president of the bank in 1950.

By 1914 The National State Bank of Elizabeth, as it was then called, had its own two-story headquarters at 68 Broad Street.

It was Roosevelt more than anyone else who led the bank through its major period of expansion. From 1950 to 1983 National State's assets rose from $33 million to more than $1.2 billion, and in that period expanded from three Elizabeth branches to 49 branches in seven counties.

With the same vision and business acumen of his predecessors, Roosevelt saw opportunities for entering the bank into unique busi-

It was not until the post-World War II era that National State began an aggressive expansion program under W. Emlen Roosevelt, who became bank president in 1950. It was Roosevelt more than anyone else who led the bank through its major period of expansion, most notably by entering unique business ventures and acquiring existing banks.

Even in 1920 The National State Bank offered its customers the best-possible services and conveniences, as this ad from the Elizabeth Daily Journal, *dated December 13, 1920, shows.*

---

nesses. One such business is the large-volume, cash-processing operation established in the early 1950s. Today it is still an important financial service provided by National State, whose money-processing unit rivals in volume the operations of several Federal Reserve banks. Toll authorities, major retailers, and other banks are among its customers.

Roosevelt's vision of the bank's future reflected a philosophy of growth. The acquisition of existing banks was a preferred course of action. From 1954 through 1958 National State acquired four Union County banks: Roselle Park Trust Company, First National Bank of Springfield, First National Bank and Trust Company of Summit, and Peoples Bank and Trust Company of Westfield.

In 1962, the bank's 150th anniversary year, it completed two acquisitions on the same day: the Hillside National and Rahway National banks. These important mergers increased National State's total assets from $110 million to $183 million. That trend of expansion has contin-

ued into the present.

The National State Bank of Plainfield became the 14th branch, and First Bank and Trust Company, N.A., of Perth Amboy, acquired in 1969, added nine more branches. The merger with First National Bank of Milford in 1971 brought three more locations, and that same year a new office was opened in Cranford.

The National State network of offices grew steadily over more than two decades. In 1972 it added 10 more offices through its merger with The Trenton Trust Company. This important union brought a major financial personality, Mary G. Roebling, into National State's management. She had been head of Trenton Trust since 1937. Upon the merger, Roebling became chairman of the board of The National State Bank and served until her retirement in 1984. Today she is chairman emeritus of the bank.

Roebling's intelligence, energy,

The National State Bank network of offices grew steadily over more than two decades and in 1972 added 10 more offices through its merger with the Trenton Trust Company. Upon the merger with Trenton Trust, Mary G. Roebling became chairman of the board of The National State Bank—a position she held until her retirement in 1984. Today she is chairman emeritus of the bank.

and creativity lend extraordinary dimensions to her careers in banking and public service. One of her early and notable accomplishments was her election as chairman of the board of Trenton Trust only four years after accepting its presidency. Roebling was the first woman in the country to serve in that twin banking capacity. Six U.S. presidents—from Roosevelt to Nixon—have named her to special assignments, and New Jersey governors have appointed her to a number of important state posts. She was also the first woman elected to the board of governors of the American Stock Exchange.

From the early 1970s through the early 1980s The National State Bank continued to expand into new markets under the direction of W. Emlen Roosevelt and Mary G. Roebling. Specialized banking facilities were opened at Newark International Airport and at several Exxon Corporation sites. In 1982 the bank obtained four Monmouth County branches with the purchase of the Jersey Shore Bank, and it opened an electronic banking center at Trenton State College. The following year it acquired Elizabeth Savings Bank and Essex Bank, with three offices in Essex County.

Upon Roosevelt's retirement in 1984, he became chairman of the board, and John J. Connolly was promoted into the presidency as chief executive officer of the bank. Later that same year shareholders voted approval of The National State Bank

Here, in a symbolic gesture of Constellation Bancorp's banking policies and services, commercial lending, international, and corporate trust bankers work together to "launch" Airship International's business. Constellation Bancorp is the bank holding company of The National State Bank.

to become a subsidiary of a new bank holding company, Constellation Bancorp. Connolly also serves as Constellation's president.

Today, Constellation Bancorp and The National State Bank continue to implement ideas designed to differentiate the bank from competitors. The bank's primary lending orientation is to businesses. It serves three primary markets: middle-market corporations, real estate developers, and automobile dealers. Specialization and segmentation mark its approach to each market. The Real Estate Group's single-source financing provides financing continuity from the inception of projects to their completion. For example, the bank lends for land acquisition, site development, construction financing, working capital, and, finally, for mortgages to residential owners. National State has financed many important commercial and residential real estate projects throughout the state and is proud of its relationships with most of the state's dynamic real estate developers.

It is as true today as in 1812 that National State is an important provider of banking services that foster entrepreneurial growth in New Jersey's economy. The Real Estate Group and two commercial lending regions are headquartered at the Wick Corporate Center in Woodbridge, the center of the bank's trade area. Additional lending personnel are strategically located throughout National State's seven primary counties. The Commercial Lending unit of the bank is a primary source of working capital, business expansion, and asset-based financing programs, which often involve collateral such as inventory, equipment, and real estate. The capability of providing customized financing through one banker brings confidence to those entrepreneurs who rely on a National State "Team Banker" for their financial support.

Consumer banking at National State is evolving rapidly into "the bank of the future." The Community Banking Division has taken a bold, new direction by introducing, to its extensive branch network, several types of offices, each one tailoring its service to the specific needs of the community in which it is located. At National State "private banking" levels of service are available to clients who have a qualifying minimum deposit relationship with the bank. They are served by account managers in Personal Financial Centers. The presence of Philips, Appel & Walden, New Jersey's largest securities firm, helps National State provide complete financial services under one roof.

In its newly opened offices, clients' demand for comfort and personal attention are met by a knowledgeable banking staff. At comfortable, sit-down teller stations clients receive more extensive services and information in a most congenial environment.

National State's corporate trust services have also grown as an extension of its long-standing business relationships with New Jersey companies. The first New Jersey trust operation to offer on-line account information services to its customers, National State has earned the confidence of a customer base that includes both *Fortune* 500 corporations and many of the state's dynamic and emerging public companies. A wide range of personal trust services for individuals, as well as employee benefit programs for businesses, complete the offerings of a Trust Division that is well on its way to becoming a recognized leader in its field.

National State's International Department serves New Jersey importers and exporters. It has expanded relationships with foreign banks that seek support for their clients who transact business in the United States. As a member of the Society for Worldwide Interbank Financial Telecommunications (SWIFT), National State is part of a telecommunications network of more than 2,000 banks worldwide.

Although its history has spanned 175 years, The National State Bank is still headquartered in its hometown

The National State Bank is an important provider of banking services that foster entrepreneurial growth in New Jersey's economy. The Real Estate Group and two commercial lending units are headquartered at the Wick Corporate Center in Woodbridge, the heart of the bank's trade area.

of Elizabeth. The bank is active in the Elizabeth Development Corp., which aids Elizabeth's economic growth, and it funds many community projects in the areas of health and human services, civic and community affairs education, and culture and the arts. During the 1950s National State began using the U.S. Frigate *Constellation* (named by George Washington) as its symbol. The bank's signature mark still includes a version of the "Sign of the Ship." The holding company's name, Constellation Bancorp, is appropriate—signifying modernization, it echos The National State Bank's heritage.

In Constellation Bancorp's newly opened offices, the client's demand for comfort and personal attention are met by a knowledgeable banking staff.

PITNEY, HARDIN, KIPP & SZUCH

Pitney, Hardin, Kipp & Szuch, founded in 1902 by John O.H. Pitney and John R. Hardin, is one of New Jersey's oldest and largest law firms. The two founders had practiced law since 1884 and had already established successful careers and distinguished reputations. The merger of their practices into the firm of Pitney & Hardin began the tradition of legal excellence that has continued to the present day.

John O.H. Pitney was the scion of a prominent New Jersey family that had contributed not only to the development of the state and Morris County since before the Revolution, but also to the legal profession. Pitney began his career with his father, Henry C. Pitney, who had been practicing in Morristown since 1851 and who later served as vice-chancellor of New Jersey from 1889 until 1907. John's brother, Mahlon Pitney, had been a New Jersey congressman, a justice of the Supreme Court of New Jersey, and chancellor of New Jersey, and later served as an Associate Justice of the United States Supreme Court from 1912 to 1922. This family tradition was passed down to Mahlon's sons, Shelton and Mahlon Jr., who became partners of the firm in 1922 and 1925, respectively, and is carried on today by Shelton's son, James C. Pitney, who became a partner in 1958.

John R. Hardin was considered one of the premier lawyers of his time. He had been a member of the New Jersey House of Representatives in 1891-1892 and a member of the New Jersey Constitutional Conven-

The principal office of Pitney, Hardin, Kipp & Szuch in Morristown. Courtesy, Dalia Photos, Morristown, New Jersey

tion in 1905 to study changes in the state's judicial structure. In his later years he became president of the Mutual Benefit Life Insurance Company and a director of several major banks and companies, including the Newark and Essex Banking Company, the Howard Savings Institution, and the New Jersey Bell Telephone Company.

The Hardin legacy in the firm has also been passed down through the generations to the present day. Both of John R. Hardin's sons, Charles R. and John R. Jr., became partners in 1923 and 1925, respectively, and Charles R. Jr. and William D., the grandsons of the founder, have been partners since 1958.

An early panorama scene of the Morristown Green, circa 1912. Courtesy, the Joint Free Public Library of Morristown and Morris Township

From its beginning and throughout its long history, Pitney, Hardin, Kipp & Szuch has had among its partners many of the state's outstanding attorneys. One of its most distinguished figures was Waldron M. Ward, who started with the firm in 1907 and became a partner in 1914, when it became Pitney, Hardin & Ward. Ward became a renowned expert in corporate and banking law and was considered one of the giants of New Jersey's legal profession until his retirement in 1960.

Another important early figure was Alfred F. Skinner, who joined the firm in 1907 after an impressive career in public service. He had been admitted to the New Jersey Bar in 1886 and served as a member of the Assembly in 1894-1895. In 1897 he was appointed register of Essex County and in 1899 he accepted the position of judge of the Common Pleas Court. Skinner served in that post until 1905, when he entered private practice.

In 1932 two other outstanding attorneys, William J. Brennan, Jr.,

and Donald B. Kipp, joined the firm. Each was destined to become preeminent in the legal profession. Brennan, son of a Newark police commissioner, became one of New Jersey's leading labor lawyers. Following Brennan's return from war service, the firm name was changed to Pitney, Hardin, Ward & Brennan. In 1949 Brennan became a judge of the new Superior Court of New Jersey and in 1952 he became an associate justice of the New Jersey Supreme Court. In 1956 he was appointed to the United States Supreme Court, where he now sits as the Senior Justice, after an illustrious career.

Kipp established himself as a major legal and business figure, following in Ward's footsteps as a premier corporate attorney and serving as a corporate director of American Can Company, Fireman's Fund, New Jersey Bell Telephone, and Midlantic National Bank. He subsequently gained wide acclaim in the trusts and estates field, in which he specialized until his retirement in 1980.

In 1958 Clyde A. Szuch joined the firm, quickly establishing an exemplary reputation as a trial attorney and litigation specialist. Szuch became a partner in 1962 and, under his leadership, the litigation practice of the firm increased dramatically. Indeed, the expansion of the litigation department was primarily responsible for the rapid growth of the firm to its present size of 110 lawyers. In 1981 the firm assumed its current name of Pitney, Hardin, Kipp & Szuch.

Today the practice of Pitney, Hardin, Kipp & Szuch includes securities, antitrust, corporate, and tax law; industrial, commercial, and residential real estate law; commercial law; banking law; labor law; trusts and estates law; constitutional law; and all types of civil litigation, including the relatively new areas of environmental and product liability litigation.

Pitney, Hardin, Kipp & Szuch's work has comprised such diverse un-

The Morristown Green. Courtesy, Dalia Photos

dertakings as the reorganization of Rutgers University, the organization, financing, and construction of the New Jersey Sports Authority Complex in the Meadowlands, the first test of New Jersey's "Takeover Bid Disclosure Law," participation in the drafting of the New Jersey Business Corporation Act and revising New Jersey's Nonprofit Corporation Act, and several leading cases establishing important principles of First Amendment litigation.

The firm serves as counsel to large and medium-size New Jersey-based companies, as well as to many national and multinational corporations organized under New Jersey law or with major facilities in the state. The firm also helps clients plan and organize start-up businesses or business acquisitions, as well as providing corporate and tax counsel on corporate reorganizations, recapitalizations, mergers, and acquisitions. In addition, the firm represents closely held companies, partnerships, and single-person enterprises as well as charitable organizations, educational institutions, and other nonprofit entities. For individuals, the firm performs a wide range of services, among them real estate, tax matters, estate planning, and litigation.

Pitney, Hardin, Kipp & Szuch's litigation department is now a national practice, handling matters spanning a broad spectrum of specialty areas. The firm is lead counsel

in the nationwide defense of asbestos litigation and represents national companies in environmental and products liability cases in the state. It also handles constitutional law and First Amendment cases on behalf of national and local print and television media clients; warranty, franchise, and dealer termination actions; and appears before the Casino Control Commission and other state agencies.

After spending the first 73 years of its existence in Newark, Pitney, Hardin, Kipp & Szuch made Morristown its permanent home in 1975, while maintaining a branch office in Newark. As with all successful institutions, time has brought growth and change to Pitney, Hardin, Kipp & Szuch but without compromise to those principles on which the firm was founded: a commitment to legal excellence and professional integrity with the understanding that lawyers serve their clients best when they also serve the ends of justice.

The Morris County Courthouse. Courtesy, Dalia Photos

COMPUTER POWER INC.

Computer Power Inc. began in 1967 in the Florham Park, New Jersey, home of Roger Love and his wife, Doris. Roger has served as president and chief executive officer since that time, and Doris served as comptroller until 1982, when she started the international operations phase of the business. Today Computer Power Inc. is an international firm with manufacturing facilities throughout the world.

The company, at first called Engineering Services, served as a consulting firm to the power conversion industry. In 1972 the name changed to Computer Power Inc., and the following year it began manufacturing UPS (uninterrupted power systems) and emergency-power products.

Today Computer Power makes products for the power-protection industry, primarily for computers. When the company started, the market for such products essentially did not exist because of the very small computer memory capacity of that era. Today utility/power failures or power-line noise can cause large memory loss to computers inasmuch as the microcomputer of the 1980s can easily contain a memory capacity of up to 20 million bytes. Such losses of data can be exceedingly costly. Thus, power-protection products such as those made by Computer Power Inc. became vital as the computer industry grew during the 1970s and 1980s.

By 1970 Roger Love had moved the firm out of his basement and had purchased a 3,000-square-foot facility in Madison. Love sold that building in 1973 and purchased an older 12,000-square-foot facility nearby.

In 1978 Computer Power moved to an 18,000-square-foot building in High Bridge, its present home. The following year Love was named New Jersey's Small Businessman of the Year for his accomplishments with Computer Power Inc. The High Bridge plant has been expanded twice in the 1980s, to a total of 60,000 square feet.

International in scope, Computer

Computer Power Inc.'s High Bridge, New Jersey, facility.

Power now operates three subsidiaries overseas: Computer Power of Haiti S.A., Computer Power of Venezuela S.A., and Computer GB (Great Britain) Ltd. Doris Love handles international operations from headquarters in High Bridge. Computer Power currently employs 200 people in the United States and 100 in its overseas affiliates.

Computer Power's other power-protection products are emergency backup power equipment to power emergency time-locks, lights, and telephone systems. These products power the emergency services of en-

Typical power-protection products made by Computer Power Inc.

tire buildings during power failures. Its third product line is trackside and rolling-stock rail-power equipment, providing emergency power for rail stations and passenger cars. The company's largest growth area is in computer peripheral products.

Computer Power's range of products runs from 200 VA (volt amperes) for powering microcomputers to 600 KVA (kilovolt amperes) for powering large mainframe computers. Computer Power has a unique 96-percent efficient patent for the UPS of tomorrow, which will be introduced by the early 1990s.

In July 1986 Computer Power Inc. went public. The company had a growth rate of 23 percent per year for the previous five years, and president Roger Love anticipates that growth should continue through the eighties and nineties.

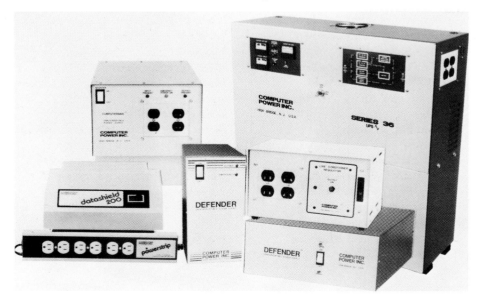